CLYMER®
MANUALS
YAMAHA
ROAD STAR • 1999-2007

WHAT'S IN YOUR TOOLBOX?

More information available at Clymer.com

Phone: 805-498-6703

Haynes Publishing Group
Sparkford Nr Yeovil
Somerset BA22 7JJ England

Haynes North America, Inc
859 Lawrence Drive
Newbury Park
California 91320 USA

ISBN-10: 1-59969-415-8
ISBN-13: 978-1-59969-415-3
Library of Congress: 2011927469

M282-2, 2Y3, 13-464   ABCDEFGHIJKLMNOP

Common spark plug conditions

NORMAL

Symptoms: Brown to grayish-tan color and slight electrode wear. Correct heat range for engine and operating conditions.
Recommendation: When new spark plugs are installed, replace with plugs of the same heat range.

WORN

Symptoms: Rounded electrodes with a small amount of deposits on the firing end. Normal color. Causes hard starting in damp or cold weather and poor fuel economy.
Recommendation: Plugs have been left in the engine too long. Replace with new plugs of the same heat range. Follow the recommended maintenance schedule.

TOO HOT

Symptoms: Blistered, white insulator, eroded electrode and absence of deposits. Results in shortened plug life.
Recommendation: Check for the correct plug heat range, over-advanced ignition timing, lean fuel mixture, intake manifold vacuum leaks, sticking valves and insufficient engine cooling.

CARBON DEPOSITS

Symptoms: Dry sooty deposits indicate a rich mixture or weak ignition. Causes misfiring, hard starting and hesitation.
Recommendation: Make sure the plug has the correct heat range. Check for a clogged air filter or problem in the fuel system or engine management system. Also check for ignition system problems.

PREIGNITION

Symptoms: Melted electrodes. Insulators are white, but may be dirty due to misfiring or flying debris in the combustion chamber. Can lead to engine damage.
Recommendation: Check for the correct plug heat range, over-advanced ignition timing, lean fuel mixture, insufficient engine cooling and lack of lubrication.

ASH DEPOSITS

Symptoms: Light brown deposits encrusted on the side or center electrodes or both. Derived from oil and/or fuel additives. Excessive amounts may mask the spark, causing misfiring and hesitation during acceleration.
Recommendation: If excessive deposits accumulate over a short time or low mileage, install new valve guide seals to prevent seepage of oil into the combustion chambers. Also try changing gasoline brands.

HIGH SPEED GLAZING

Symptoms: Insulator has yellowish, glazed appearance. Indicates that combustion chamber temperatures have risen suddenly during hard acceleration. Normal deposits melt to form a conductive coating. Causes misfiring at high speeds.
Recommendation: Install new plugs. Consider using a colder plug if driving habits warrant.

OIL DEPOSITS

Symptoms: Oily coating caused by poor oil control. Oil is leaking past worn valve guides or piston rings into the combustion chamber. Causes hard starting, misfiring and hesitation.
Recommendation: Correct the mechanical condition with necessary repairs and install new plugs.

DETONATION

Symptoms: Insulators may be cracked or chipped. Improper gap setting techniques can also result in a fractured insulator tip. Can lead to piston damage.
Recommendation: Make sure the fuel anti-knock values meet engine requirements. Use care when setting the gaps on new plugs. Avoid lugging the engine.

GAP BRIDGING

Symptoms: Combustion deposits lodge between the electrodes. Heavy deposits accumulate and bridge the electrode gap. The plug ceases to fire, resulting in a dead cylinder.
Recommendation: Locate the faulty plug and remove the deposits from between the electrodes.

MECHANICAL DAMAGE

Symptoms: May be caused by a foreign object in the combustion chamber or the piston striking an incorrect reach (too long) plug. Causes a dead cylinder and could result in piston damage.
Recommendation: Repair the mechanical damage. Remove the foreign object from the engine and/or install the correct reach plug.

CONTENTS

QUICK REFERENCE DATA

MODEL:_____YEAR:_____

VIN NUMBER:_____

ENGINE SERIAL NUMBER:_____

CARBURETOR SERIAL NUMBER OR I.D. MARK:_____

TIRE INFLATION PRESSURE[1]

1999-2003 Models	
0-90 kg (0-198 lb.)	
Front tire	250 kPa (36 psi)
Rear tire	250 kPa (36 psi)
90 kg (198 lb.)-maximum load[2]	
Front tire	250 kPa (36 psi)
Rear tire	280 kPa (40 psi)
2004-on models	
0-90 kg (0-198 lb.)	
Front tire	250 kPa (36 psi)
Rear tire	250 kPa (36 psi)
90 kg (198 lb.)-maximum load[2]	
Front tire	250 kPa (36 psi)
Rear tire	280 kPa (40 psi)

1. Tire inflation pressure is for original equipment tires. Aftermarket tires may require different inflation pressures; refer to the aftermarket manufacturer's specifications.
2. Maximum load equates to the total weight of the cargo, rider, passenger and accessories.

RECOMMENDED LUBRICANTS AND FLUIDS

Battery	Maintenance free
Brake fluid	DOT 4
Engine oil	
API classification	API SE, SF, SG (non-friction modified)
Viscosity	SAE 20W/40
Capacity	
Oil change only	3.7 L (3.9 qt.)
Oil and filter change	4.1 L (4.3 qt.)
When engine completely dry	5.0 L (5.3 qt.)
Fork oil	
Viscosity	Yamaha 5WT
Capacity per leg	554 ml (18.7 oz.)

(continued)

RECOMMENDED LUBRICANTS AND FLUIDS (continued)

Fork oil (continued)	
Oil level*	110 mm (4.33 in.)
Fuel	
Type	Regular unleaded
Octane	86 [(R + M)/method] or research octane 91 or higher
Capacity, including reserve	20 liter (5.3 US gal.)
Reserve	3.5 liter (0.9 US gal.)
Transfer gear oil	
API classification	SAE80 GL-4
Capacity	0.4 L (0.42 qt.)

*Measured from the top of the fully compressed fork tube with the fork spring removed

MAINTENANCE AND TUNE-UP SPECIFICATIONS

Item	Specification
Brake adjustment	
Front brake lever free play at handlebar	2-5 mm (0.08-0.20 in.)
Rear brake pedal height above footrest	100 mm (3.9 in.)
Brake pad wear limit	
Front	0.5 mm (0.02 in.)
Rear	0.5 mm (0.02 in.)
Clutch lever free play at handlebar	10-15 mm (0.39-0.59 in.)
Compression pressure @ at sea level	
Standard	1200 kPa (174 psi)
Minimum	1000 kPa (145 psi)
Maximum	1400 kPa (203 psi)
Drive belt free play	
Motorcycle on sidestand	7.5-13 mm (0.30-0.51 in.)
Motorcycle on swing arm stand	14-21 mm (0.55-0.83 in.)
Engine idle speed	850-950 rpm
Engine oil pressure at 60° C (140° F)	40-80 kPa (5.8-11.6 psi) @ 900 rpm
Idle speed	850-950 rpm
Ignition timing	
1999-2003	10° BTDC @ 1000 rpm
2004-2005	10° BTDC @ 900 rpm
2006-on	5° BTDC @ 900 rpm
Pilot screw	2 1/2 turns out
Shift rod length	374.4-378.4 mm (14.74-14.90 in.)
Shock absorber length adjustment	
Standard	42.5 mm (1.67 in.)
Minimum	42.5 mm (1.67 in.)
Maximum	51.5 mm (2.03 in.)
Spark plugs	
Recommended type	NGK DPR7EA-9, Denso X22EPR-U9
Spark plug gap	0.8-0.9 mm (0.031-0.035 in.)
Throttle cable free play at throttle grip	4-8 mm (0.16-0.31 in.)
Vacuum pressure (at idle)	52 kPa (15.4 in. Hg)
Valve clearance (cold)	
Intake	0-0.04 mm (0-0.0016 in.)
Exhaust	0-0.04 mm (0-0.0016 in.)
Wheels	
Maximum runout service limit (laced wheel)	
Axial	2 mm (0.08 in.)
Radial	2 mm (0.08 in.)
Maximum runout service limit (alloy wheel)	
Axial	1 mm (0.04 in.)
Radial	1 mm (0.04 in.)

MAINTENANCE AND TUNE UP TORQUE SPECIFICATIONS

Item	N•m	in.-lb.	ft.-lb.
Brake hose banjo bolt	34	–	25
Engine oil drain bolts			
Crankcase	43	–	32
Oil tank	43	–	32
Front axle			
Bolt	78	–	56
Pinch bolt	19	168	–
Fuel tank bolt and nut	7	62	–
Oil filter	17	150	–
Oil line gallery bolts (cylinder heads)	21	–	15.5
Oil pressure gallery hex bolt	20	–	15
Rear axle			
Nut	150	–	111
Adjuster locknut	32	–	24
Rear brake			
Caliper bracket bolt	40	–	30
Brake pedal adjuster locknut	18	159	–
Sidestand nut	48	–	35
Spark plug	18	159	–
Transfer gearcase			
Oil level check bolt	8	71	–
Oil drain bolt	18	159	–
Valve adjuster locknut	20	–	15

CHAPTER ONE

GENERAL INFORMATION

This detailed and comprehensive manual covers the Yamaha Road Star XV1600 and XV1700 models from 1999-on.

The text provides complete information on maintenance, tune-up, repair and overhaul. Hundreds of photographs and illustrations created during the complete disassembly of the motorcycle guide the reader through every job. All procedures are in step-by-step format and designed for the reader who may be working on the motorcycle for the first time.

MANUAL ORGANIZATION

A shop manual is a tool, and as in all Clymer manuals, the chapters are thumb-tabbed for easy reference. Main headings are listed in the table of contents and index. Frequently used specifications and capacities from the tables at the end of each chapter are listed in the Quick Reference Data section at the front of the manual. Specifications and capacities are provided in metric and U.S. Standard units of measure.

During some of the procedures there will be references to headings in other chapters or sections of the manual.

When a specific heading is called out in a step it is *italicized* as it appears in the manual. If a sub-heading is indicated as being "in this section," it is located within the same main heading. For example, the sub-heading *Handling Gasoline Safely* is located within the main heading *SAFETY*.

This chapter provides general information on shop safety, tools and their usage, service fundamentals and shop supplies. Refer to the end of the chapter, for the following tables:

Table 1 explains the vehicle identification number (VIN).
Table 2 lists the model name identifiers.
Table 3 lists vehicle dimensions and weights.
Table 4 lists decimal and metric equivalents.
Table 5 lists general torque specifications.
Table 6 lists conversion formulas.
Table 7 lists technical abbreviations.
Table 8 lists Metric tap and drill sizes.

Chapter Two provides methods for quick and accurate diagnosis of problems. Troubleshooting procedures present typical symptoms and logical methods to pinpoint and repair the problem.

Chapter Three explains all routine maintenance. Subsequent chapters describe specific systems such as engine, transmission, clutch, drive system, fuel system, suspension, brakes, exhaust system, and body.

WARNINGS, CAUTIONS AND NOTES

The terms WARNING, CAUTION and NOTE have specific meanings in this manual.

A WARNING emphasizes areas where injury or death could result from negligence. Mechanical damage may also occur. WARNINGS are to be taken seriously.

A CAUTION emphasizes areas where equipment damage could result. Disregarding a CAUTION could cause permanent mechanical damage, though injury is unlikely.

A NOTE provides additional information to make a step or procedure easier or clearer. Disregarding a NOTE could cause inconvenience, but would not cause equipment damage or injury.

SAFETY

Professional mechanics can work for years and never suffer a serious injury. Follow these guidelines and practice common sense to safely service the motorcycle.

1. Do not operate the motorcycle in an enclosed area. The exhaust gasses contain carbon monoxide, an odorless, colorless and tasteless poisonous gas. Carbon monoxide levels build quickly in small enclosed areas and can cause unconsciousness and death in a short time. Make sure to properly ventilate the work area or operate the motorcycle outside.

2. Never use gasoline or any extremely flammable liquid to clean parts. Refer to *Handling Gasoline Safely* and *Cleaning Parts* in this section.

3. Never smoke or use a torch in the vicinity of flammable liquids, such as gasoline or cleaning solvent.

4. If welding or brazing on the motorcycle, remove the fuel tank to a safe distance at least 15 m (50 ft.) away.

5. Use the correct type and size of tools to avoid damaging fasteners.

6. Keep tools clean and in good condition. Replace or repair worn or damaged equipment.

7. When loosening a tight fastener, be guided by what would happen if the tool slips.

8. When replacing fasteners, make sure the new fasteners are the same size and strength as the originals.

9. Keep the work area clean and organized.

10. Wear eye protection any time the safety of the eyes is in question. This includes procedures that involve drilling, grinding, hammering, compressed air and chemicals.

11. Wear the correct clothing for the job. Tie up or cover long hair so it does not get caught in moving equipment.

12. Do not carry sharp tools in clothing pockets.

13. Always have an approved fire extinguisher available. Make sure it is rated for gasoline (Class B) and electrical (Class C) fires.

14. Do not use compressed air to clean clothes, the motorcycle or the work area. Debris may be blown into the eyes or skin. Never direct compressed air at anyone. Do not allow children to use or play with any compressed air equipment.

15. When using compressed air to dry rotating parts, hold the part so it does not rotate. Do not allow the force of the air to spin the part. The air jet is capable of rotating parts at extreme speed. The part may disintegrate or become damaged, causing injury.

16. Do not inhale the dust created by brake pad and clutch wear. These particles may contain asbestos. In addition, some types of insulating materials and gaskets may contain asbestos. Inhaling asbestos particles is hazardous to health.

17. Never work on the motorcycle while someone is working under it.

18. When placing the motorcycle on a stand, make sure it is secure before walking away.

Handling Gasoline Safely

Gasoline is a volatile, flammable liquid and is one of the most dangerous items in the shop. Because gasoline is used so often, people often forget it is hazardous. Only use gasoline as fuel for gasoline internal combustion engines. When working on the machine, keep in mind that gasoline is always present in the fuel tank and fuel lines. To avoid accidents when working around the fuel system, observe the following:

1. Never use gasoline to clean parts. Refer to *Cleaning Parts* in this section.

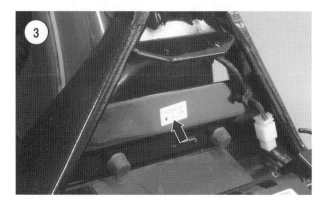

2. When working on the fuel system, work outside or in a well-ventilated area.

3. Do not add fuel to the fuel tank or service the fuel system while the motorcycle is near open flames, sparks or where someone is smoking. Gasoline vapor is heavier than air; it collects in low areas and is more easily ignited than liquid gasoline.

4. Allow the engine to cool completely before working on any fuel system component.

5. Do not store gasoline in glass containers. If the glass breaks, an explosion or fire may occur.

6. Immediately wipe up spilled gasoline with rags. Store the rags in a metal container with a lid until they can be properly disposed of, or place them outside in a safe place for the fuel to evaporate.

7. Do not pour water onto a gasoline fire. Water spreads the fire and makes it more difficult to put out. Use a class B, BC or ABC fire extinguisher to extinguish the fire.

8. Always turn off the engine before refueling. Do not spill fuel onto the engine or exhaust system. Do not overfill the fuel tank. Leave an air space at the top of the tank to allow room for the fuel to expand due to temperature fluctuations.

Cleaning Parts

Cleaning parts is one of the more difficult service jobs performed in the home garage. Many types of chemical cleaners and solvents are available for shop use. Most are poisonous and extremely flammable. To prevent chemical exposure, vapor buildup, fire and injury, observe each product warning label and note the following:

1. Read and observe the entire product label before using any chemical. Always know what type of chemical is being used and whether it is poisonous and/or flammable.

2. Do not use more than one type of cleaning solvent at a time. If mixing chemicals is required, measure the proper amounts according to the manufacturer.

3. Work in a well-ventilated area.

4. Wear chemical-resistant gloves.

5. Wear safety glasses.

6. Wear a vapor respirator if the instructions call for it.

7. Wash hands and arms thoroughly after cleaning parts.

8. Keep chemical products away from children and pets.

9. Thoroughly clean all oil, grease and cleaner residue from any part that must be heated.

10. Use a nylon brush when cleaning parts. Metal brushes may cause a spark.

11. When using a parts washer, only use the solvent recommended by the manufacturer. Make sure the parts washer is equipped with a metal lid that can lower in case of fire.

Warning Labels

Most manufacturers attach information and warning labels to the motorcycle. These labels contain instructions that are important to safety when operating, servicing, transporting and storing the motorcycle. Refer to the owner's manual for the description and location of labels. Order replacement labels from the manufacturer if they are missing or damaged.

SERIAL NUMBERS

Serial numbers are stamped on various locations on the motorcycle. Record these numbers in the *Quick Reference Data* section in the front of the book. Have these numbers available when ordering parts.

Refer to **Table 1** and **Table 2** for details on VIN and model identification.

The VIN number label (**Figure 1**) is located on the right side frame down tube. This number is also stamped on the right side of the steering head (**Figure 2**).

The model code (**Figure 3**) appears on the label on the frame cross member behind the battery.

The engine serial number is stamped on the upper rear left side of the crankcase (**Figure 4**).

FASTENERS

Proper fastener selection and installation is important to ensure the motorcycle operates as designed and can be serviced efficiently. The choice of original equipment fasteners is not arrived at by chance. Make sure replacement fasteners meet all the same requirements as the originals.

Threaded Fasteners

Threaded fasteners secure most of the components on the motorcycle. Most fasteners are tightened by turning them clockwise (right-hand threads). If the normal rotation of the component being tightened would loosen the fastener, it may have left-hand threads. If a left-hand threaded fastener is used, it is noted in the text.

Two dimensions are required to match the thread size of the fastener: the number of threads in a given distance and the outside diameter of the threads.

The two systems currently used to specify threaded fastener dimensions are the U.S. Standard system and the metric system (**Figure 5**). Pay particular attention when working with unidentified fasteners; mismatching thread types can damage threads.

> *NOTE*
> *To ensure that the fastener threads are not mismatched or cross-threaded, start all fasteners by hand. If a fastener is difficult to start or turn, determine the cause before tightening with a wrench.*

The length (L, **Figure 6**), diameter (D) and distance between thread crests (pitch [T]) classify metric screws and bolts. A typical bolt may be identified by the numbers, 8—1.25 × 130. This indicates the bolt has a diameter of 8 mm, the distance between thread crests is 1.25 mm and the length is 130 mm. Always measure bolt length as shown

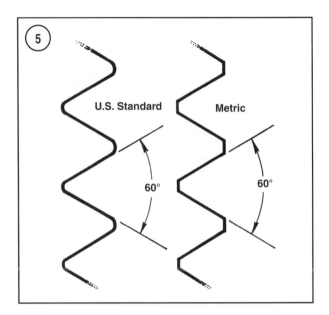

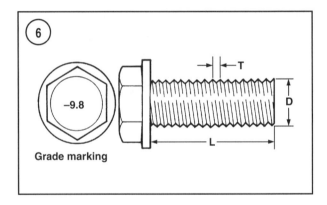

in L, **Figure 6** to avoid purchasing replacements of the wrong length.

> *WARNING*
> *Do not install fasteners with a strength classification lower than what was originally installed by the manufacturer. Doing so may cause equipment failure and/or damage.*

The numbers on the top of the fastener (**Figure 6**) indicate the strength of metric screws and bolts. The higher the number, the stronger the fastener. Typically, unnumbered fasteners are the weakest.

Many screws, bolts and studs are combined with nuts to secure particular components. To indicate the size of a nut, manufacturers specify the internal diameter and thread pitch.

The measurement across two flats on a nut or bolt indicates the wrench size.

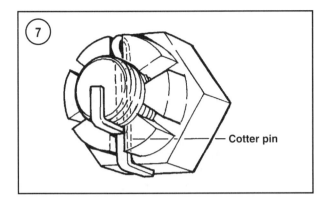

Cotter pin

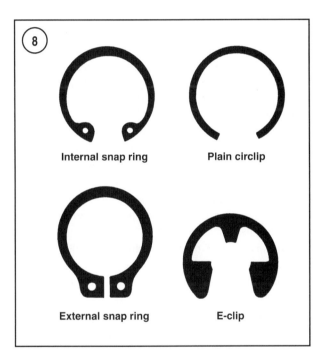

Internal snap ring

Plain circlip

External snap ring

E-clip

Torque Specifications

The materials used in the manufacturing of the motorcycle may be subjected to uneven stresses if the fasteners of the subassemblies are not installed and tightened correctly. Fasteners which are improperly installed or work loose can cause extensive damage. It is essential to use an accurate torque wrench as described in this chapter.

Specifications for torque are provided in Newton-meters (N•m), foot-pounds (ft.-lb.) and inch-pounds (in.-lb.). Refer to **Table 5** for general torque specifications. To determine the torque requirement, first determine the size of the fastener as described in *Threaded Fasteners* in this section. Torque specifications for specific components are at the end of the ap-

propriate chapters. Torque wrenches are covered in *Basic Tools* in this chapter.

Self-Locking Fasteners

Several types of bolts, screws and nuts are designed to create interference between the two fasteners. Interference is achieved in various ways, for instance with a nylon insert nut, or a dry adhesive coating on the threads of a bolt.

Self-locking fasteners offer greater holding strength than standard fasteners, which improves their resistance to vibration. Do not reuse self-locking fasteners. The materials used to form the lock become distorted after the initial installation and removal. Do not replace self-locking fasteners with standard fasteners.

Washers

The two basic types of washers are flat washers and lockwashers. Flat washers are simple discs with a hole to fit a screw or bolt. Lockwashers prevent a fastener from working loose. Washers can be used as spacers and seals, or can help distribute fastener load and prevent the fastener from damaging the component.

As with fasteners, when replacing washers, make sure the replacements are the same design and quality as the originals.

Cotter Pins

A cotter pin is a split metal pin inserted into a hole or slot to prevent a fastener from loosening. In certain applications, such as the rear axle on an ATV or motorcycle, the fastener must be secured in this way. For these applications, a cotter pin and castellated (slotted) nut is used.

To choose a cotter pin, make sure the diameter is correct for the hole in the fastener. After correctly tightening the fastener and aligning the holes, insert the cotter pin through the hole and bend the ends over the fastener (**Figure 7**). Unless instructed to do so, never loosen a tightened fastener to align the holes. If the holes do not align, tighten the fastener enough to achieve alignment.

Cotter pins are available in various diameters and lengths. Measure the length from the bottom of the head to the tip of the shortest pin.

Snap Rings and E-clips

Snap rings (**Figure 8**) are circular-shaped metal retaining clips. They are required to secure parts and gears on shafts, pins or rods. External snap rings are used to retain items on shafts. Internal snap rings secure parts within housing bores. In some applications, snap rings of varying thicknesses also determine endplay. These are usually called selective snap rings.

The two basic types of snap rings are machined and stamped snap rings. Machined snap rings (**Figure 9**) can be installed in either direction, because both faces have sharp edges. Stamped snap rings (**Figure 10**) have a sharp edge and a round edge. When installing a stamped snap ring in a thrust application, install the sharp edge facing away from the part producing the thrust.

E-clips are used when it is not practical to use a snap ring. Remove E-clips with a flat blade screwdriver by prying between the shaft and E-clip. To install an E-clip, center it over the shaft groove and push or tap it into place.

Observe the following when installing snap rings:

1. Remove and install snap rings with snap ring pliers. Refer to *Basic Tools* in this chapter.

2. In some applications, it may be necessary to replace snap rings after removing them.

3. Compress or expand snap rings only enough to install them. If overly expanded, they lose their retaining ability.

4. After installing a snap ring, make sure it seats completely.

5. Wear eye protection when removing and installing snap rings.

SHOP SUPPLIES

Lubricants and Fluids

Periodic lubrication helps ensure a long service life for any type of equipment. Using the correct type of lubricant is as important as performing the lubrication service, although in an emergency the wrong type is better than not using one. The following section describes the types of lubricants most often required. Make sure to follow the manufacturer's recommendations for lubricant types.

Engine oils

Engine oil for four-stroke motorcycle engine use is classified by three standards: the American Petroleum Institute (API) service classification, the Society of Automotive Engineers (SAE) viscosity rating and the Japanese Automobile Standards Organization (JASO) T 903 Standard rating.

The API and SAE information is on all oil container labels. The JASO information is found on oil containers sold by the oil manufacturer specifically for motorcycle

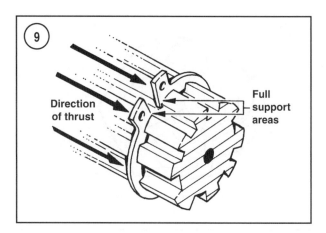

use. Two letters indicate the API service classification. The number or sequence of numbers and letter (10W-40 for example) is the oil's viscosity rating. The API service classification and the SAE viscosity index are not indications of oil quality.

The API service classification indicates that the oil meets specific lubrication standards. The first letter in the classification S indicates the oil is for gasoline engines. The second letter indicates the standard the oil satisfies.

Always use an oil with a classification recommended by the manufacturer. Using oil with a different classification can cause engine damage.

Viscosity is an indication of the oil's thickness. Thin oils have a lower number and thick oils have a higher number. Engine oils fall into the 5- to 50-weight range for single-grade oils.

Most manufacturers recommend multi-grade oil. These oils perform efficiently across a wide range of operating conditions. Multi-grade oils are identified by a W after the first number, which indicates the low-temperature viscosity.

Engine oils are most commonly mineral (petroleum) based, but synthetic and semi-synthetic types are used more frequently. When selecting engine oil, follow the manufacturer's recommendation for type, classification and viscosity.

Greases

Grease is lubricating oil with added thickening agents. The National Lubricating Grease Institute (NLGI) grades grease. Grades range from No. 000 to No. 6, with No. 6 being the thickest. Typical multipurpose grease is NLGI No. 2. For specific applications, manufacturers may recommend water-resistant type grease or one with an additive, such as molybdenum disulfide (MoS_2).

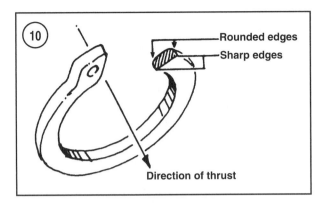

Rounded edges
Sharp edges
Direction of thrust

Brake fluid

> WARNING
> *Never put a mineral-based (petroleum) oil into the brake system. Mineral oil causes rubber parts in the system to swell and break apart, causing complete brake failure.*

Brake fluid is the hydraulic fluid used to transmit hydraulic pressure (force) to the wheel brakes. It is classified by the Department of Transportation (DOT). Current designations for brake fluid are DOT 3, DOT 4 and DOT 5. This classification appears on the fluid container.

Each type of brake fluid has its own definite characteristics. Do not intermix different types of brake fluid. DOT 5 fluid is silicone-based and is not compatible with other fluids or in a system not designed for it. Mixing DOT 5 fluid with other fluids may cause brake system failure. When adding brake fluid, *only* use the fluid recommended by the manufacturer.

Brake fluid damages plastic, painted or plated surfaces. Use extreme care when working with brake fluid and remove any spills immediately with soap and water.

Hydraulic brake systems require clean and moisture free brake fluid. Never reuse brake fluid. Keep containers and reservoirs properly sealed.

Cleaners, Degreasers and Solvents

Many chemicals are available to remove oil, grease and other residue from the motorcycle. Before using cleaning solvents, consider how they will be used and disposed of, particularly if they are not water-soluble. Local ordinances may require special procedures for the disposal of many types of cleaning chemicals. Refer to *Safety* in this chapter.

Use brake parts cleaner to clean brake system components. Brake parts cleaner leaves no residue. Use electri-

cal contact cleaner to clean electrical connections and components without leaving any residue. Carburetor cleaner is a powerful solvent used to remove fuel deposits and varnish from fuel system components. Use this cleaner carefully, as it may damage finishes.

Generally, degreasers are strong cleaners used to remove heavy accumulations of grease from engine and frame components.

Most solvents are designed to be used with a parts washing cabinet for individual component cleaning. For safety, use only nonflammable or high flash point solvents.

Gasket Sealant

Gasket sealant may be used in combination with a gasket or seal. In other applications, such as between crankcase halves, only a sealant is used. Follow the manufacturer's recommendation when using a sealant. Use extreme care when choosing a sealant different from the type originally recommended. Choose sealant based on its sealing capabilities, as well as resistance to heat and fluids.

A common sealant is room temperature vulcanization sealant, or RTV. This sealant cures at room temperature over a specific time period. This allows the repositioning of components without damaging gaskets.

Moisture in the air causes the RTV sealant to cure. Always install the tube cap as soon as possible after applying RTV sealant. RTV sealant has a limited shelf life and will not cure properly if the shelf life has expired. Keep partial tubes sealed, and discard them if they have passed the expiration date.

Applying RTV sealant

Clean all old gasket residue from the mating surfaces. Remove all gasket material from blind threaded holes to avoid inaccurate bolt torque. Spray the mating surfaces with aerosol parts cleaner, and wipe with a lint-free cloth. The area must be clean for the sealant to adhere.

Apply RTV sealant in a continuous bead 2-3 mm (0.08-0.12 in.) thick. Circle all the fastener holes unless otherwise specified. Do not allow any sealant to enter these holes. Assemble and tighten the fasteners to the specified torque within the time frame recommended by the sealant manufacturer.

Gasket Remover

Aerosol gasket remover can help remove stubborn gaskets. This product can speed up the removal process and prevent damage to the mating surface that may be caused by using a scraping tool. Most of these types of products are very caustic. Follow the gasket remover manufacturer's instructions for use.

Threadlocking Compound

A threadlocking compound is a fluid applied to the threads of fasteners. After tightening the fastener, the fluid dries and becomes a solid filler between the threads. This makes it difficult for the fastener to work loose from vibration or heat expansion and contraction. Some threadlocking compounds also provide a seal against fluid leaks.

Before applying a threadlocking compound, remove any old compound from both thread areas and clean them with aerosol parts cleaner. Use the compound sparingly. Excess fluid can run into adjoining parts.

CAUTION
Threadlocking compounds will stress, crack and damage most plastics. Use caution when using these products in areas where there are plastic components.

Threadlocking compounds are available in a wide range of compounds for various strength, temperature and repair applications. Follow the manufacturer's recommendations regarding compound selection.

BASIC TOOLS

Most of the procedures in this manual can be carried out with simple hand tools and test equipment familiar to the home mechanic. Always use the correct tools for the job at hand. Keep tools organized and clean. Store them in a tool chest with related tools organized together.

Quality tools are essential. The best are constructed of high-strength alloy steel. These tools are light, easy to use and resistant to wear. Their working surfaces are devoid of sharp edges and carefully polished. They have an easy-to-clean finish and are comfortable to use. Quality tools are a good investment.

Some of the procedures in this manual specify special tools. In many cases the tool is illustrated in use. In some cases it may be possible to use a substitute or fabricate a suitable replacement. However, the specialized equipment or expertise may make it impractical for the home mechanic to perform the procedure. It may be less expen-

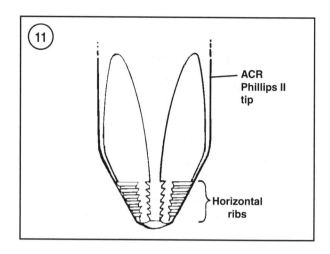

sive to have a professional perform these jobs, especially when considering the cost of equipment.

The manufacturer's part numbers are provided for many of the tools used in this manual. These part numbers are correct at the time of first-edition publication. The publisher cannot guarantee that the part numbers or tools listed in this manual will be available in the future.

When purchasing tools to perform the procedures covered in this manual, consider the tool's potential frequency of use and purchase accordingly. When starting a tool kit, consider purchasing a basic tool set from a quality tool supplier. These sets are available in many tool combinations and offer substantial savings when compared to individually purchased tools. As work experience grows and tasks become more complicated, specialized tools can be added.

Screwdrivers

Screwdrivers of various lengths and types are mandatory for the simplest tool kit. The two basic types are the slotted tip (flat blade) and the Phillips tip. These are available in sets that often include an assortment of tip sizes and shaft lengths.

As with all tools, use a screwdriver designed for the job. Make sure the size of the tip conforms to the size and shape of the fastener. Use them only for driving screws. Never use a screwdriver for prying or chiseling metal. Repair or replace worn or damaged screwdrivers. A worn tip may damage the fastener, making it difficult to remove.

Phillips-head screws are often damaged by incorrectly fitting screwdrivers. Quality Phillips screwdrivers are manufactured with their crosshead tip machined to Phillips Screw Company specifications. Poor quality or damaged Phillips screwdrivers can back out (camout) and

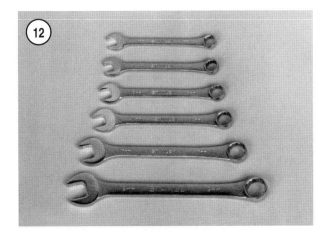

Wrenches

Open-end, box-end and combination wrenches (**Figure 12**) are available in a variety of types and sizes.

The number stamped on the wrench refers to the distance between the work areas. This size must match the size of the fastener head.

The box-end wrench grips the fastener on all sides, which reduces the chance of the tool slipping. The box-end wrench is designed with either a 6- or 12-point opening. For stubborn or damaged fasteners, the 6-point provides superior holding because it contacts the fastener across a wider area at all six edges. For general use, the 12-point works well. It allows the wrench to be removed and reinstalled without moving the handle over such a wide arc.

An open-end wrench is fast and works best in areas with limited overhead access. It contacts the fastener at only two points and may slip under heavy force, or if the tool or fastener is worn. A box-end wrench is preferred in most instances, especially when breaking loose and applying the final tightness to a fastener.

The combination wrench has a box-end on one end and an open-end on the other. This combination makes it a convenient tool.

Adjustable Wrenches

An adjustable wrench or Crescent wrench (**Figure 13**) can fit nearly any nut or bolt head that has clear access around its entire perimeter. An adjustable wrench is best used as a backup wrench to keep a large nut or bolt from turning while the other end is being loosened or tightened with a box-end or socket wrench.

Adjustable wrenches contact the fastener at only two points, which makes them more subject to slipping off the fastener. Because one jaw is adjustable and may become loose, this shortcoming is aggravated. Make sure the solid jaw is the one transmitting the force.

Socket Wrenches, Ratchets and Handles

Sockets that attach to a ratchet handle (**Figure 14**) are available with 6-point or 12-point openings (**Figure 15**) and different drive sizes. The drive size indicates the size of the square hole that accepts the ratchet handle. The number stamped on the socket is the size of the work area and must match the fastener head.

As with wrenches, a 6-point socket provides superior-holding ability, while a 12-point socket needs to be moved only half as far to reposition it on the fastener.

round over the screw head. In addition, weak or soft screw materials can make removal difficult.

The best type of screwdriver to use on Phillips screws is the ACR Phillips II screwdriver, patented by the Phillips Screw Company. ACR stands for the horizontal anti-camout ribs found on the driving faces or flutes of the screwdriver's tip (**Figure 11**). ACR Phillips II screwdrivers were designed as part of a manufacturing drive system to be used with ACR Phillips II screws, but they work well on all common Phillips screws. A number of tool companies offer ACR Phillips II screwdrivers in different tip sizes and interchangeable bits.

NOTE
Another way to prevent camout and to increase the grip of a Phillips screwdriver is to apply valve grinding compound or Permatex Screw & Socket Gripper onto the screwdriver tip. After loosening/tightening the screw, clean the screw recess to prevent engine oil contamination.

WARNING
Do not use hand sockets with air or impact tools because they may shatter and cause injury. Always wear eye protection when using impact or air tools.

Sockets are designated for either hand or impact use. Impact sockets are made of thicker material for more durability. Compare the size and wall thickness of a 19-mm hand socket (A, **Figure 16**) and the 19-mm impact socket (B). Use impact sockets when using an impact driver or air tools. Use hand sockets with hand-driven attachments.

Various handles are available for sockets. Use the speed handle for fast operation. Flexible ratchet heads in varying lengths allow the socket to be turned with varying force and at odd angles. Extension bars allow the socket setup to reach difficult areas. The ratchet is the most versatile. It allows the user to install or remove the nut without removing the socket.

Sockets combined with drivers make them the fastest, safest and most convenient tool for fastener removal and installation.

Impact Drivers

An impact driver provides extra force for removing fasteners by converting the impact of a hammer into a turning motion. This makes it possible to remove stubborn fasteners without damaging them. Impact drivers and interchangeable bits (**Figure 17**) are available from most tool suppliers. When using a socket with an impact driver, make sure the socket is designed for impact use. Refer to *Socket Wrenches, Ratchets and Handles* in this section.

WARNING
Do not use hand sockets with air or impact tools because they may shatter and cause injury. Always wear eye protection when using impact or air tools.

Allen Wrenches

Use Allen, or setscrew, wrenches (**Figure 18**) on fasteners with hexagonal recesses in the fastener head. These wrenches are available in L-shaped bar, socket and T-handle types. A metric set is required when working on Yamaha motorcycles. Allen bolts are sometimes called socket bolts.

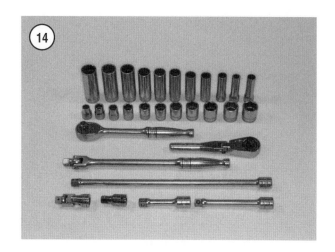

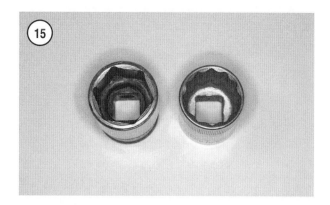

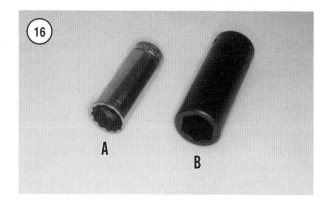

Torque Wrenches

Use a torque wrench with a socket, torque adapter or similar extension to tighten a fastener to a measured torque. Torque wrenches come in several drive sizes (1/4, 3/8, 1/2 and 3/4) and use various methods to indicate the torque value. The drive size indicates the size of the square drive that accepts the socket, adapter or extension. Common methods for indicating the torque value are the

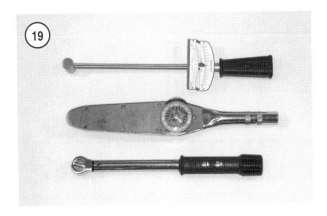

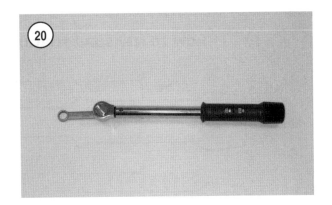

Torque Adapters

Torque adapters or extensions extend or reduce the reach of a torque wrench. The torque adapter shown in **Figure 20** is used to tighten a fastener that cannot be reached because of the size of the torque wrench head, drive, and socket. If a torque adapter changes the effective lever length (**Figure 21**), the torque reading on the wrench will not equal the actual torque applied to the fastener. It is necessary to recalibrate the torque setting on the wrench to compensate for the change of lever length. When using a torque adapter at a right angle to the drive head, calibration is not required, because the effective length has not changed.

To recalculate a torque reading when using a torque adapter, use the following formula and refer to **Figure 21**.

$$TW = \frac{TA \times L}{L + A}$$

TW is the torque setting or dial reading on the wrench.

TA is the torque specification and the actual amount of torque that is applied to the fastener.

A is the amount that the adapter increases (or in some cases reduces) the effective lever length as measured along the centerline of the torque wrench.

L is the lever length of the wrench as measured from the center of the drive to the center of the grip.

The effective length is the sum of L and A.

Example:

TA = 20 ft.-lb.
A = 3 in.
L = 14 in.
$$TW = \frac{20 \times 14}{14 + 3} = \frac{280}{17} = 16.5 \text{ ft.-lb.}$$

In this example, the torque wrench would be set to the recalculated torque value (TW = 16.5 ft.-lb.). When using

deflecting beam, the dial indicator and the audible click (**Figure 19**).

When choosing a torque wrench, consider the torque range, drive size and accuracy. The torque specifications in this manual provide an indication of the range required.

A torque wrench is a precision tool that must be properly cared for to remain accurate. Store torque wrenches in cases or separate padded drawers within a toolbox. Follow the manufacturer's instructions for their care and calibration.

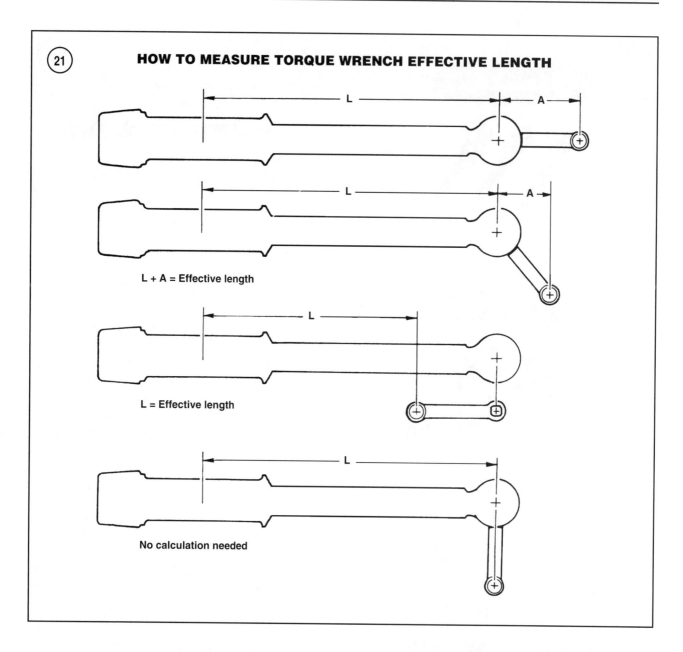

HOW TO MEASURE TORQUE WRENCH EFFECTIVE LENGTH

L + A = Effective length

L = Effective length

No calculation needed

a beam-type wrench, tighten the fastener until the pointer aligns with 16.5 ft.-lb. In this example, although the torque wrench is pre-set to 16.5 ft.-lb., the actual torque is 20 ft.-lb.

Pliers

Pliers come in a wide range of types and sizes. Pliers are useful for holding, cutting, bending, and crimping. Do not use them to turn fasteners. **Figure 22** and **Figure 23** show several types of useful pliers. Each design has a specialized function. Slip-joint pliers are general-purpose pliers used for gripping and bending. Diagonal-cutting pliers

are needed to cut wire and can be used to remove cotter pins. Use needlenose pliers to hold or bend small objects. Locking pliers (**Figure 23**), sometimes called Vise-Grips, are used to hold objects very tightly. They have many uses ranging from holding two parts together, to gripping the end of a broken stud. Use caution when using locking pliers, as the sharp jaws may damage the objects they hold.

Snap Ring Pliers

Snap ring pliers are specialized pliers with tips that fit into the ends of snap rings to remove and install them.

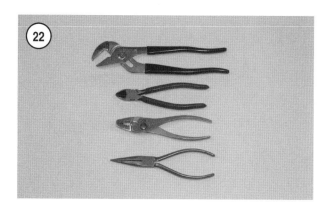

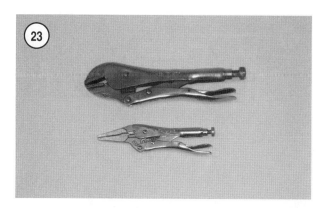

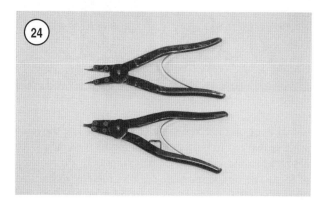

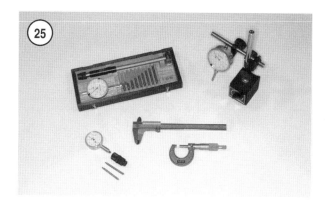

Hammers

Various types of hammers are available to fit a number of applications. Use a ball-peen hammer to strike another tool, such as a punch or chisel. Use soft-faced hammers when a metal object must be struck without damaging it. Never use a metal-faced hammer on engine or suspension components because damage occurs in most cases.

Always wear eye protection when using hammers. Make sure the hammer face is in good condition and the handle is not cracked. Select the correct hammer for the job and strike the object squarely. Do not use the handle or the side of the hammer to strike an object.

PRECISION MEASURING TOOLS

The ability to accurately measure components is essential to perform many of the procedures described in this manual. Equipment is manufactured to close tolerances, and obtaining consistently accurate measurements is essential to determine which components require replacement or further service.

Each type of measuring instrument (**Figure 25**) is designed to measure a dimension with a certain degree of accuracy and within a certain range. When selecting the measuring tool, make sure it is applicable to the task.

As with all tools, measuring tools provide the best results if cared for properly. Improper use can damage the tool and cause inaccurate results. If any measurement is questionable, verify the measurement using another tool. A standard gauge is usually provided with micrometers to check accuracy and calibrate the tool if necessary.

Precision measurements can vary according to the experience of the person performing the procedure. Accurate results are only possible if the mechanic possesses a feel for using the tool. Heavy-handed use of measuring tools produces less accurate results. Hold the tool gently by the fingertips to easily feel the point at which the tool contacts the object. This feel for the equipment produces

WARNING
Snap rings can slip and fly off during removal and installation. Also, the snap ring pliers' tips may break. Always wear eye protection when using snap ring pliers.

Snap ring pliers (**Figure 24**) are available with a fixed action (either internal or external) or convertible (one tool works on both internal and external snap rings). They may have fixed tips or interchangeable ones of various sizes and angles. For general use, select a convertible type pliers with interchangeable tips (**Figure 24**).

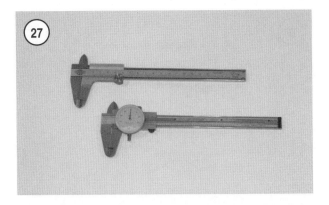

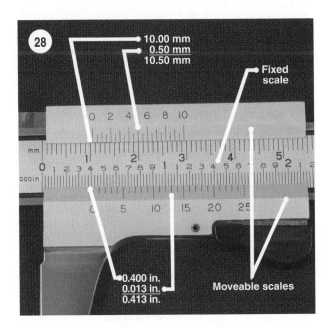

more accurate measurements and reduces the risk of damaging the tool or component. Refer to the following sections for specific measuring tools.

Feeler Gauge

Use feeler or thickness gauges (**Figure 26**) for measuring the distance between two surfaces.

A feeler gauge set consists of an assortment of steel blades of graduated thicknesses. Each blade is marked with its thickness. Blades can be of various lengths and angles for different procedures.

A common use for a feeler gauge is to measure valve clearance. Use wire (round) type gauges to measure spark plug gap.

Calipers

Calipers (**Figure 27**) are used to obtain inside, outside and depth measurements. Although not as precise as a micrometer, they allow reasonable precision, typically to within 0.05 mm (0.001 in.). Most calipers have a range up to 150 mm (6 in.).

Calipers are available in dial, vernier or digital versions. Dial calipers have a dial readout that provides convenient reading. Vernier calipers have marked scales that must be compared to determine the measurement. The digital caliper uses a liquid crystal display (LCD) to show the measurement.

Properly maintain the measuring surfaces of the caliper. There must not be any dirt or burrs between the tool and the object being measured. Never force the caliper to close around an object. Close the caliper around the highest point so it can be removed with a slight drag. Some calipers require calibration. Always refer to the manufacturer's instructions when using a new or unfamiliar caliper.

To learn how to read a vernier caliper see **Figure 28**. The fixed scale is marked in 1-mm increments. Ten indi-

vidual lines on the fixed scale equal 1 cm. The movable scale is marked in 0.05 mm (hundredth) increments. To obtain a reading, establish the first number by the location of the 0 line on the movable scale in relation to the first line to the left on the fixed scale. In this example, the number is 10 mm. To determine the next number, note which of the lines on the movable scale align with a mark on the fixed scale. A number of lines will seem close, but only one will align exactly. In this case, 0.50 mm is the reading to add to the first number. Adding 10 mm and 0.50 mm equals a measurement of 10.50 mm.

Micrometers

A micrometer is an instrument designed for linear measurement using the decimal divisions of the inch or meter (**Figure 29**). While there are many types and styles of micrometers, most of the procedures in this manual call for

	DECIMAL PLACE VALUES*	
0.1		Indicates 1/10 (one tenth of an inch or millimeter)
0.01		Indicates 1/100 (one one-hundreth of an inch or millimeter)
0.001		Indicates 1/1000 (one one-thousandth of an inch or millimeter)

*This chart represents the values of figures placed to the right of the decimal point. Use it when reading decimals from one-tenth to one one-thousandth of an inch or millimeter. It is not a conversion chart (for example: 0.001 in. is not equal to 0.001 mm).

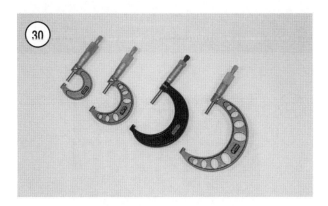

an outside micrometer. Use the outside micrometer to measure the outside diameter of cylindrical forms and the thickness of materials.

A micrometer's size indicates the minimum and maximum size of a part it can measure. The usual sizes are 0-25 mm (0-1 in.), 25-50 mm (1-2 in.), 50-75 mm (2-3 in.) and 75-100 mm (3-4 in.) (**Figure 30**).

Micrometers that cover a wider range of measurements are available. These use a large frame with interchangeable anvils of various lengths. This type of micrometer offers a cost savings, but its overall size may make it less convenient.

Adjustment

Before using a micrometer, check its adjustment as follows:

1. Clean the anvil and spindle faces.
2A. To check a 0-25 mm or 0-1 in. micrometer:
   a. Turn the thimble until the spindle contacts the anvil. If the micrometer has a ratchet stop, use it to ensure the proper amount of pressure is applied.

   b. If the adjustment is correct, the 0 mark on the thimble will align exactly with the 0 mark on the sleeve line. If the marks do not align, the micrometer is out of adjustment.
   c. Follow the manufacturer's instructions to adjust the micrometer.
2B. To check a micrometer larger than 25 mm or 1 in. use the standard gauge supplied by the manufacturer. A standard gauge is a steel block, disc or rod that is machined to an exact size.
   a. Place the standard gauge between the spindle and anvil, and measure its outside diameter or length. If the micrometer has a ratchet stop, use it to ensure the proper amount of pressure is applied.
   b. If the adjustment is correct, the 0 mark on the thimble will align exactly with the 0 mark on the sleeve line. If the marks do not align, the micrometer is out of adjustment.
   c. Follow the manufacturer's instructions to adjust the micrometer.

Care

Micrometers are precision instruments. They must be used and maintained with great care. Note the following:

1. Store micrometers in protective cases or separate padded drawers in a toolbox.

2. When in storage, make sure the spindle and anvil faces do not contact each other or another object. If they do, temperature changes and corrosion may damage the contact faces.

3. Do not clean a micrometer with compressed air. Dirt forced into the tool will cause wear.

4. Lubricate micrometers with WD-40 to prevent corrosion.

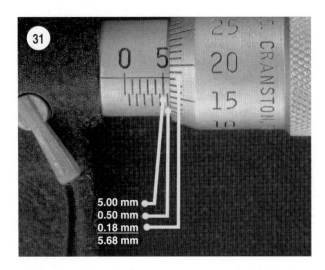

5.00 mm
0.50 mm
0.18 mm
5.68 mm

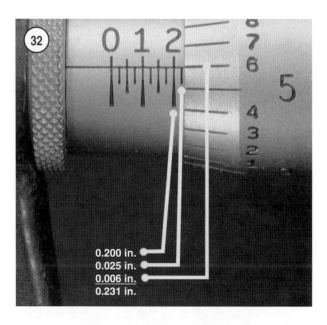

0.200 in.
0.025 in.
0.006 in.
0.231 in.

Reading

When reading a micrometer, numbers are taken from different scales and added together. The following sections describe how to read the measurements of outside micrometers.

For accurate results, properly maintain the measuring surfaces of the micrometer. There cannot be any dirt or burrs between the tool and the measured object. Never force the micrometer to close around an object. Close the micrometer around the highest point so it can be removed with a slight drag.

Metric micrometer

The standard metric micrometer (**Figure 31**) is accurate to one one-hundredth of a millimeter (0.01 mm). The sleeve line is graduated in millimeter and half millimeter increments. The marks on the upper half of the sleeve line equal 1.00 mm. Each fifth mark above the sleeve line is identified with a number. The number sequence depends on the size of the micrometer. A 0-25 mm micrometer, for example, has sleeve marks numbered 0 through 25 in 5 mm increments. This numbering sequence continues with larger micrometers. On metric micrometers, each mark on the lower half of the sleeve equals 0.50 mm.

The tapered end of the thimble has 50 lines marked around it. Each mark equals 0.01 mm. One complete turn of the thimble aligns its 0 mark with the first line on the lower half of the sleeve line or 0.50 mm.

When reading a metric micrometer, add the number of millimeters and half-millimeters on the sleeve line to the number of one one-hundredth millimeters on the thimble. Perform the following steps and refer to **Figure 31**.

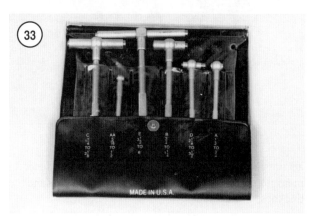

1. Read the upper half of the sleeve line and count the number of lines visible. Each upper line equals 1 mm.

2. If the half-millimeter line is visible on the lower sleeve line, add 0.50 mm to the reading in Step 1.

3. Read the thimble mark that aligns with the sleeve line. Each thimble mark equals 0.01 mm.

NOTE
If a thimble mark does not align exactly with the sleeve line, estimate the amount between the lines. For accurate readings in two-thousandths of a millimeter (0.002 mm), use a metric vernier micrometer.

4. Add the readings from Steps 1-3.

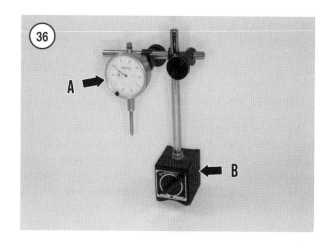

Standard inch micrometer

The standard inch micrometer (**Figure 32**) is accurate to one-thousandth of an inch or 0.001. The sleeve is marked in 0.025 in. increments. Every fourth sleeve mark is numbered 1, 2, 3, 4, 5, 6, 7, 8, 9. These numbers indicate 0.100, 0.200, 0.300 and so on.

The tapered end of the thimble has 25 lines marked around it. Each mark equals 0.001 in. One complete turn of the thimble aligns the zero mark with the first mark on the sleeve, or 0.025 in.

To read a standard inch micrometer, perform the following steps and refer to **Figure 32**.

1. Read the sleeve and find the largest number visible. Each sleeve number equals 0.100 in.

2. Count the number of lines between the numbered sleeve mark and the edge of the thimble. Each sleeve mark equals 0.025 in.

3. Read the thimble mark that aligns with the sleeve line. Each thimble mark equals 0.001 in.

NOTE
If a thimble mark does not align exactly with the sleeve line, estimate the amount between the lines. For accurate readings in ten-thou-

sandths of an inch (0.0001 in.), use a vernier inch micrometer.

4. Add the readings from Steps 1-3.

Telescoping and Small Bore Gauges

Use telescoping gauges (**Figure 33**) and small bore gauges (**Figure 34**) to measure bores. Neither gauge has a scale for direct readings. Use an outside micrometer to determine the reading.

To use a telescoping gauge, select the correct size gauge for the bore. Compress the movable post and carefully insert the gauge into the bore. Carefully move the gauge in the bore to make sure it is centered. Tighten the knurled end of the gauge to hold the movable post in position. Remove the gauge and measure the length of the posts. Telescoping gauges are typically used to measure cylinder bores.

To use a small bore gauge, select the correct size gauge for the bore. Carefully insert the gauge into the bore. Tighten the knurled end of the gauge to carefully expand the gauge fingers to the limit within the bore. Do not overtighten the gauge because there is no built-in release. Excessive tightening can damage the bore surface and damage the tool. Remove the gauge and measure the outside dimension (**Figure 35**). Small bore gauges are typically used to measure valve guides.

Dial Indicator

A dial indicator (A, **Figure 36**) is a gauge with a dial face and needle used to measure variations in dimensions and movements. Measuring brake rotor runout is a typical use for a dial indicator.

Dial indicators are available in various ranges and graduations and with three basic types of mounting bases:

magnetic (B, **Figure 36**), clamp, or screw-in stud. When purchasing a dial indicator, select one with a continuous dial (A, **Figure 36**).

Cylinder Bore Gauge

A cylinder bore gauge is similar to a dial indicator. The gauge set shown in **Figure 37** consists of a dial indicator, handle, and different length adapters (anvils) to fit the gauge to various bore sizes. The bore gauge is used to measure bore size, taper and out-of-round. When using a bore gauge, follow the manufacturer's instructions.

Compression Gauge

A compression gauge (**Figure 38**) measures combustion chamber (cylinder) pressure, usually in psi or kg/cm^2. The gauge adapter is either inserted or screwed into the spark plug hole to obtain the reading. Disable the engine so it will not start and hold the throttle in the wide-open position when performing a compression test. An engine that does not have adequate compression cannot be properly tuned. See Chapter Three.

Multimeter

A multimeter (**Figure 39**) is an essential tool for electrical system diagnosis. The voltage function indicates the voltage applied or available to electrical components. The ohmmeter function tests circuits for continuity, or lack of continuity, and measures the resistance of a circuit.

Some manufacturers' specifications for electrical components are based on results using a specific test meter. Results may vary if a meter not recommended by the manufacturer is used. Such requirements are noted when applicable.

If an analog ohmmeter is used, it must be calibrated. Refer to the manufacturer's instructions.

ELECTRICAL SYSTEM FUNDAMENTALS

A thorough study of the many types of electrical systems used in today's motorcycles is beyond the scope of this manual. However, an understanding of electrical basics is necessary to perform simple diagnostic tests.

Refer to *Electrical Testing* and *Electrical Troubleshooting* in Chapter Two for typical test procedures, equipment use, and general troubleshooting sequences. Refer to Chapter Nine for specific system test procedures.

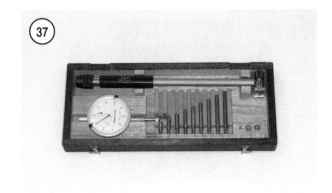

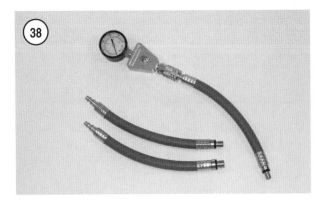

Voltage

Voltage is the electrical potential or pressure in an electrical circuit and is expressed in volts. The more pressure (voltage) in a circuit, the more work can be performed.

Direct current (DC) voltage means the electricity flows in one direction. All circuits powered by a battery are DC circuits.

Alternating current (AC) means the electricity flows in one direction momentarily and then switches to the opposite direction. Alternator output is an example of AC voltage. This voltage must be changed or rectified to direct current to operate in a battery powered system.

Resistance

Resistance is the opposition to the flow of electricity within a circuit or component and is measured in ohms. Resistance causes a reduction in available current and voltage.

Resistance is measured in an inactive circuit with an ohmmeter. The ohmmeter sends a small amount of current into the circuit and measures how difficult it is to push the current through the circuit.

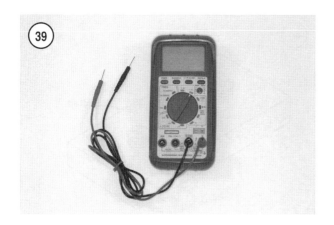

An ohmmeter, although useful, is not always a good indicator of a circuit's actual ability under operating conditions. This is because of the low voltage (6-9 volts) the meter uses to test the circuit. The voltage in an ignition coil secondary winding can be several thousand volts. Such high voltage can cause the coil to malfunction, even though it tests acceptable during a resistance test.

Resistance generally increases with temperature. Perform all testing with the component or circuit at room temperature. Resistance tests performed at high temperatures may indicate high resistance readings and cause unnecessary replacement of a component.

Amperage

Amperage is the unit of measurement for the amount of current within a circuit. Current is the actual flow of electricity. The higher the current, the more work can be performed up to a given point. If the current flow exceeds the circuit or component capacity, it will damage the system.

BASIC SERVICE METHODS

Most of the procedures in this manual are straightforward and can be performed by anyone reasonably competent with tools. However, consider personal capabilities carefully before attempting any operation involving major disassembly.

1. *Front*, in this manual, refers to the front of the motorcycle. The front of any component is the end closest to the front of the motorcycle. The left and right sides refer to the position of the parts as viewed by the rider sitting on the seat facing forward.

2. When servicing an engine or suspension component, secure the motorcycle in a safe manner.

3. Tag all similar parts for location and mark all mating parts for position. Record the number and thickness of any shims when removing them. Identify parts by placing them in sealed and labeled plastic sandwich bags.

4. Tag disconnected wires and connectors with masking tape and a marking pen. Do not rely on memory alone.

5. Protect finished surfaces from physical damage or corrosion. Keep gasoline and other chemicals off painted surfaces.

6. Use penetrating oil on frozen or tight bolts. Avoid using heat where possible. Heat can warp, melt or affect the temper of parts. Heat also damages the finish of paint and plastics.

7. When a part is a press fit or requires a special tool to remove, the information or type of tool is identified in the text. Otherwise, if a part is difficult to remove or install, determine the cause before proceeding.

8. To prevent objects or debris from falling into the engine, cover all openings.

9. Read each procedure thoroughly and compare the illustrations to the actual components before starting the procedure. Perform the procedure in sequence.

10. Recommendations are occasionally made to refer service to a dealership or specialist. In these cases, the work can be performed more economically by the specialist than by the home mechanic.

11. The term *replace* means to discard a defective part and replace it with a new part. *Overhaul* means to remove, disassemble, inspect, measure, repair and/or replace parts as required to recondition an assembly.

12. Some operations require using a hydraulic press. If a press is not available, have these operations performed by a shop equipped with the necessary equipment. Do not use makeshift equipment that may damage the motorcycle.

> *CAUTION*
> *Do not direct high-pressure water at steering bearings, fuel hoses, wheel bearings, suspension and electrical components. Water may force grease out of the bearings and possibly damage the seals.*

13. Repairs are much faster and easier if the motorcycle is clean before starting work. Degrease the motorcycle with a commercial degreaser; follow the directions on the container for best results. Clean all parts with cleaning solvent when removing them.

14. If special tools are required, have them available before starting the procedure. When special tools are required, they are described at the beginning of the procedure.

15. Make diagrams of similar-appearing parts. For instance, crankcase bolts are often not the same lengths. Do not rely on memory alone. Carefully laid out parts can be-

come disturbed, making it difficult to reassemble the components correctly.

16. Make sure all shims and washers are reinstalled in the same location and position.

17. Whenever rotating parts contact a stationary part, look for a shim or washer.

18. Use new gaskets if there is any doubt about the condition of old ones.

19. If self-locking fasteners are removed, replace them. Do not install standard fasteners in place of self-locking ones.

20. Use grease to hold small parts in place if they tend to fall out during assembly. Do not apply grease to electrical or brake components.

Removing Frozen Fasteners

If a fastener cannot be removed, several methods may be used to loosen it. First, apply penetrating oil liberally and let it penetrate for 10-15 minutes. Rap the fastener several times with a small hammer. Do not hit it hard enough to cause damage. Reapply the penetrating oil if necessary.

For frozen screws, apply penetrating oil as described, then insert a screwdriver in the slot and rap the top of the screwdriver with a hammer. This loosens the rust so the screw can be removed in the normal way. If the screw head is too damaged to use this method, grip the head with locking pliers and twist the screw out.

Avoid applying heat unless specifically instructed. Heat may melt, warp or remove the temper from parts.

Removing Broken Fasteners

If the head breaks off a screw or bolt, several methods are available for removing the remaining portion. If a large portion of the remainder projects out, try gripping it with locking pliers. If the projecting portion is too small, file it to fit a wrench or cut a slot in it to fit a screwdriver (**Figure 40**).

If the head breaks off flush, use a screw extractor. To do this, centerpunch the exact center of the remaining portion of the screw or bolt. Drill a small hole in the screw and tap the extractor into the hole. Back the screw out with a wrench on the extractor (**Figure 41**).

Repairing Damaged Threads

Occasionally, threads are stripped because of carelessness or impact damage. Often the threads can be repaired by running a tap (for internal threads on nuts) or die (for

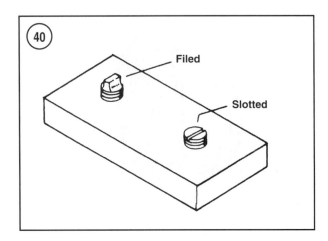

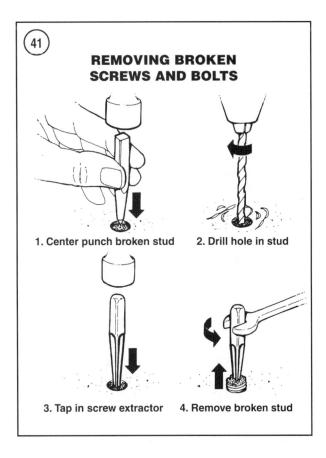

external threads on bolts) through the threads (**Figure 42**). To clean or repair spark plug threads, use a spark plug tap.

If an internal thread is damaged, it may be necessary to install a Helicoil or some other type of thread insert. Follow the manufacturer's instructions when installing their insert.

If it is necessary to drill and tap a hole, refer to **Table 8** for Metric tap and drill sizes.

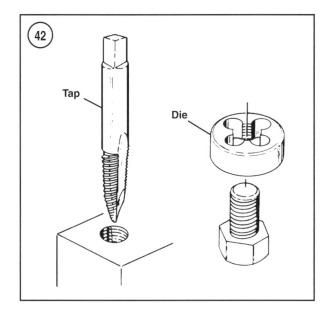

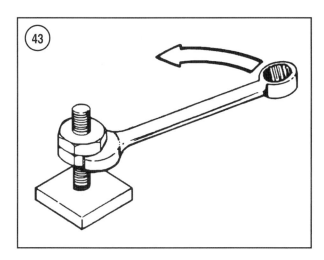

Stud Removal/Installation

A stud removal tool is available from most tool suppliers. This tool makes the removal and installation of studs easier. If one is not available, thread two nuts onto the stud and tighten them against each other (**Figure 43**). Remove the stud by turning the lower nut.

1. Measure the height of the stud above the surface.

2. Thread the stud removal tool onto the stud and tighten it, or thread two nuts onto the stud.

3. Remove the stud by turning the stud remover or the lower nut.

4. Remove any threadlocking compound from the threaded hole. Clean the threads with a aerosol parts cleaner.

5. Install the stud removal tool onto the new stud or thread two nuts onto the stud.

6. Apply threadlocking compound to the threads of the stud.

7. Install the stud and tighten with the stud removal tool or the top nut.

8. Install the stud to the height noted in Step 1 or its torque specification.

9. Remove the stud removal tool or the two nuts.

Removing Hoses

When removing stubborn hoses, do not exert excessive force on the hose or fitting. Remove the hose clamp and carefully insert a small screwdriver or pick tool between the fitting and hose. Apply a spray lubricant under the hose and carefully twist the hose off the fitting. Clean the fitting of any corrosion or rubber hose material with a wire brush. Clean the inside of the hose thoroughly. Do not use any lubricant when installing the hose (new or old). The lubricant may allow the hose to come off the fitting, even with the clamp secure.

Bearings

Bearings are used in the engine and transmission assembly to reduce power loss, heat and noise resulting from friction. Because bearings are precision parts, they must be maintained with proper lubrication and maintenance. If a bearing is damaged, replace it immediately. When installing a new bearing, take care to prevent damaging it. Bearing replacement procedures are included in the individual chapters where applicable; however, use the following sections as a guideline.

NOTE
Unless otherwise specified, install bearings with the manufacturer's mark or number facing outward.

Removal

While bearings are normally removed only when damaged, there may be times when it is necessary to remove a bearing that is in good condition. However, improper bearing removal damages the bearing and possibly the shaft or case. Note the following when removing bearings:

1. When using a puller to remove a bearing from a shaft, be careful not to damage the shaft. Always place a piece of metal between the end of the shaft and the puller screw. In

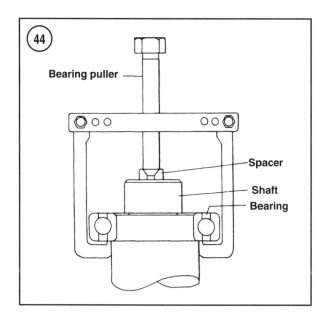

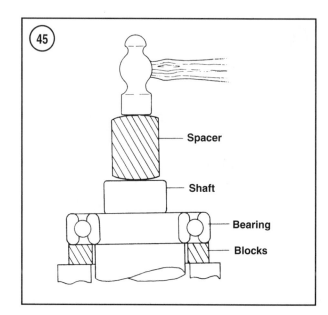

addition, place the puller arms next to the inner bearing race. Refer to **Figure 44**.

2. When using a hammer to remove a bearing from a shaft, do not strike the hammer directly against the shaft. Instead, use a brass or aluminum rod between the hammer and shaft (**Figure 45**) and make sure to support both bearing races with wooden blocks as shown.

3. The ideal method of bearing removal is with a hydraulic press. Note the following when using a press:

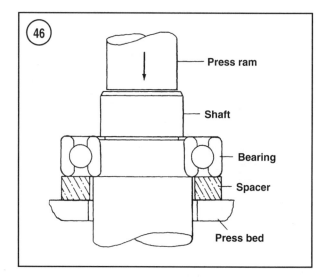

   a. Always support the inner and outer bearing races with a suitable size wooden or aluminum spacer (**Figure 46**). If only the outer race is supported, pressure applied against the balls and/or the inner race will damage them.

   b. Always make sure the press ram (**Figure 46**) aligns with the center of the shaft. If the ram is not centered, it may damage the bearing and/or shaft.

   c. The moment the shaft is free of the bearing, it drops to the floor. Secure or hold the shaft to prevent it from falling.

Installation

1. When installing a bearing in a housing, apply pressure to the outer bearing race (**Figure 47**). When installing a bearing on a shaft, apply pressure to the inner bearing race (**Figure 48**).

2. To install a bearing as described in Step 1, a driver is required. Never strike the bearing directly with a hammer or it will damage the bearing. When installing a bearing, use a piece of pipe or a driver with a diameter that matches the

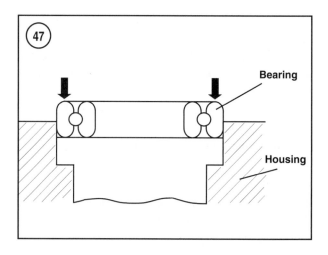

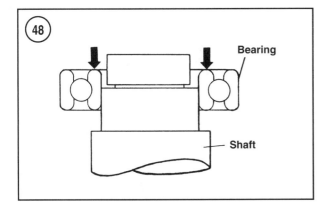

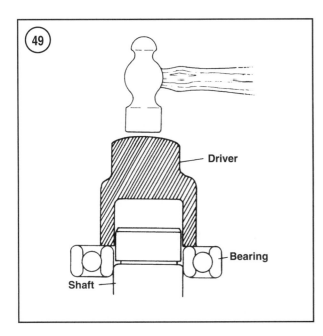

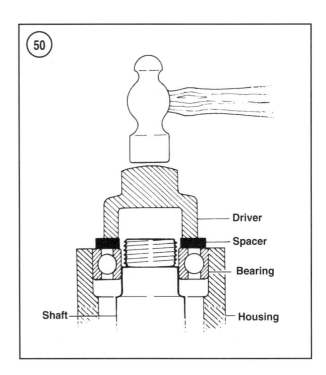

bearing inner race. **Figure 49** shows the correct way to use a driver and hammer to install a bearing.

3. Step 1 describes how to install a bearing in a case half or over a shaft. However, when installing a bearing over a shaft and into the housing at the same time, a tight fit is required for both outer and inner bearing races. In this situation, install a spacer underneath the driver tool so that pressure is applied evenly across both races. Refer to **Figure 50**. If the outer race is not supported as shown, the balls will push against the outer bearing race and damage it.

Interference fit

1. Follow this procedure when installing a bearing over a shaft. When a tight fit is required, the bearing inside diameter is smaller than the shaft. In this case, driving the bear-

ing on the shaft using normal methods may cause bearing damage. Instead, heat the bearing before installation:

a. Secure the shaft so it is ready for bearing installation.

b. Clean all residues from the bearing surface of the shaft. Remove burrs with a file or sandpaper.

c. Fill a suitable pot or beaker with clean mineral oil. Place a thermometer rated above 120° C (248° F) in the oil. Support the thermometer so it does not rest on the bottom or side of the pot.

d. Remove the bearing from its wrapper and secure it with a piece of heavy wire bent to hold it in the pot. Hang the bearing in the pot so it does not touch the bottom or sides of the pot.

e. Turn the heat on and monitor the thermometer. When the oil temperature rises to approximately 120° C (248° F), remove the bearing from the pot and quickly install it. If necessary, place a socket on the inner bearing race and tap the bearing into place. As the bearing chills, it will tighten on the shaft, so installation must be done quickly. Make sure the bearing is installed completely.

CAUTION
Before heating the housing in this procedure, wash the housing thoroughly with detergent and water. Rinse and rewash the cases as required to remove all traces of oil and other chemical deposits.

2. Follow this step when installing a bearing in a housing. Bearings are generally installed in a housing with a slight interference fit. Driving the bearing into the housing using normal methods may damage the housing or cause bearing damage. Instead, heat the housing before the bearing is installed:

CAUTION
Do not heat the housing with a propane or acetylene torch. Never bring a flame into contact with the bearing or housing. The direct heat will destroy the case hardening of the bearing and may warp the housing.

a. Heat the housing to approximately 100° C (212° F) in an oven or on a hot plate. An easy way to check that it is the proper temperature is to place tiny drops of water on the housing; if they sizzle and evaporate immediately, the temperature is correct. Heat only one housing at a time.

b. Remove the housing from the oven or hot plate, and hold onto the housing with welding gloves. It is hot!

NOTE
Remove and install the bearings with a suitable size socket and extension.

c. Hold the housing with the bearing side down and tap the bearing out. Repeat for all bearings in the housing.

d. Before heating the bearing housing, place the new bearing in a freezer if possible. Chilling a bearing slightly reduces its outside diameter while the heated bearing housing assembly is slightly larger due to heat expansion. This makes bearing installation easier.

NOTE
Unless instructed otherwise, install bearings with the manufacturer's mark or number facing out.

e. While the housing is still hot, install the new bearing(s) into the housing. Install the bearings by hand, if possible. If necessary, lightly tap the bearing(s) into the housing with a driver placed on the outer bearing race (**Figure 47**). Do not install new bearings by driving on the inner-bearing race. Install the bearing(s) until it seats completely.

Seal Replacement

Seals (**Figure 51**) contain oil, water, grease or combustion gasses in a housing or shaft. Improperly removing a

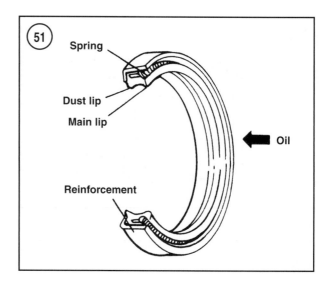

seal can damage the housing or shaft. Improperly installing the seal can damage the seal.

1. Prying is generally the easiest and most effective method of removing a seal from the housing. However, always place a rag underneath the pry tool (**Figure 52**) to prevent damage to the housing. Note the seal's installed depth or if it is installed flush.

2. Pack waterproof grease in the seal lips before the seal is installed.

3. In most cases, install seals with the manufacturer's numbers or marks facing out.

4. Install seals with a socket or driver placed on the outside of the seal as shown in **Figure 53**. Drive the seal squarely into the housing until it is to the correct depth or flush as noted during removal. Never install a seal by hitting against the top of it with a hammer.

STORAGE

Several months of non-use can cause a general deterioration of the motorcycle. This is especially true in areas of extreme temperature variations. This deterioration can be minimized with careful preparation for storage. A properly stored motorcycle is much easier to return to service.

Storage Area Selection

When selecting a storage area, consider the following:

1. The storage area must be dry. A heated area is best, but not necessary. It should be insulated to minimize extreme temperature variations.

2. If the building has large window areas, mask them to keep sunlight off the motorcycle.

non-use, storage area conditions and personal preference. Consider the following list the minimum requirement:

1. Wash the motorcycle thoroughly. Make sure all dirt, mud and road debris are removed.

2. Fill the fuel tank with a mixture of fuel and fuel stabilizer. Mix the fuel and stabilizer in the ratio recommended by the stabilizer manufacturer. Run the engine for a few minutes so the stabilized fuel can enter the fuel system. If the motorcycle will be stored for a long period, consider draining the fuel system.

3. Start the engine and allow it to reach operating temperature. Drain the engine oil regardless of the riding time since the last service. Fill the engine with the recommended type of oil.

4. Remove the spark plugs and pour a teaspoon (15-20 ml) of engine oil into the cylinders. Place a rag over the openings and slowly turn the engine over to distribute the oil. Reinstall the spark plugs.

5. Remove the battery. Store the battery in a cool and dry location. Charge the battery once a month.

6. Cover the exhaust and intake openings.

7. Apply a protective substance to the plastic and rubber components. Make sure to follow the manufacturer's instructions for each type of product being used.

8. Place the motorcycle on its centerstand. Rotate the front tire periodically to prevent flat spots from developing.

9. Cover the motorcycle with old bed sheets or something similar. Do not cover it with any plastic material that will trap moisture.

3. Avoid buildings in industrial areas where corrosive emissions may be present. Avoid areas close to saltwater.

4. Consider the area's risk of fire, theft or vandalism. Check with an insurer regarding motorcycle coverage while in storage.

Preparing the Motorcycle for Storage

The amount of preparation a motorcycle should undergo before storage depends on the expected length of

Returning the Motorcycle to Service

The amount of service required when returning a motorcycle to service after storage depends on the length of non-use and storage conditions. In addition to performing the reverse of the above procedure, make sure the brakes, clutch, throttle and engine stop switch work properly before operating the motorcycle. Refer to Chapter Three and evaluate the service intervals to determine which areas require service.

Table 1 VEHICLE IDENTIFICATION NUMBER (VIN)[1,2]

Characters 1-3	Characters 4-8	Character 9	Character 10	Character 11	Characters 12-17
XXX	XXXXX	X	X	X	XXXXXX

Characters 1-3: World Manufacturing Identifier (WMI). These characters represent the manufacturer and the type of vehicle.

Characters 4-8: Vehicle attributes. These characters represent make, model and engine type.

(continued)

Table 1 VEHICLE IDENTIFICATION NUMBER (VIN)[1,2] (continued)

Character 9: Check digit. This digit verifies the accuracy of the VIN transcription. The digit is mathematically determined using values assigned to the other characters in the VIN.

Character 10: Model year. The year is assigned to the model by the manufacturer and does not represent the year of manufacture. The letters I, O, Q, U, Z and the numeral 0 are not used in the model year code.
The letter X= 1999, Y=2000.
The number 1= 2001, 2= 2002, and so on until 2010.
The letter A= 2010, B=2011, and so on.

Character 11: Manufacturing plant location.

Characters 12-17: Sequential production number, as assigned by the manufacturer.

1. The VIN consists of 17 characters, with character groups representing the manufacturer and unique information about the motorcycle model.
2. VIN standards are periodically revised by the National Highway Traffic Safety Administration (NHTSA). Refer to their documentation for additional information.

Table 2 MODEL NAME IDENTIFIERS[1]

Base model/engine	Type/Feature	Year	California Model	Other
XV1600A (1999-2003) (XV16A) XV1700A (2004-on) (XV17A)	LE= Limited Edition M= Midnight (2004-on) S= MM Limited (2000) S= Midnight (2002, 2003) T= Silverado W[2]= Cast wheels	L= 1999 M= 2000 N= 2001 P= 2002 R= 2003 S= 204 T= 2005 V= 2006 W= 2007	C	-F=Flames
Example: XV17ATMVC= Road Star with 1700 cc engine, Silverado, Midnight, 2006, California model				

1. The following codes represent basic model identification. They do not represent all the options that may have been available at the time of production. This list may not represent all codes that may have been available at the time of model release.
2. Applies to 2005-2007 base-model Road Stars with cast wheel, or cast wheels and flames. The letter does not appear in codes for other 2005-2007 models with cast wheels.

Table 3 VEHICLE DIMENSIONS AND WEIGHTS

Overall length	2500 mm (98.4 in.)
Overall width	980 mm (38.6 in.)
Overall height	
Road Star models	1140 mm (44.9 in.)
Road Star Silverado models	1500 mm (59.1 in)
Seat height	710 mm (28.0 in.)
Wheelbase	
1995-2005	1685 mm (66.3 in.)
2006-on	1688 mm (66.5 in.)
Minimum ground clearance	145 mm (5.71 in.)
Minimum turning radius	3200 mm (126 in.)
(continued)	

Table 3 VEHICLE DIMENSIONS AND WEIGHTS (continued)

Curb mass (with oil and full tank)	
1999-2003	
Road Star models	332 kg (732 lbs.)
Road Star Silverado models	347 kg (765 lbs.)
2004-on	
Road Star models	334 kg (736 lbs.)
Road Star Silverado models	349 kg (769 lbs.)
Maximum load	
1999-2003	
Road Star models	196 kg (432 lbs.)
Road Star Silverado models	181 kg (399 lbs.)
2004-on	
Road Star models	194 kg (428 lbs.)
Road Star Silverado models	179 kg (395 lbs.)

Table 4 METRIC, INCH AND FRACTIONAL EQUIVALENTS

mm	in.	Nearest fraction	mm	in.	Nearest fraction
1	0.0394	1/32	26	1.0236	1 1/32
2	0.0787	3/32	27	1.0630	1 1/16
3	0.1181	1/8	28	1.1024	1 3/32
4	0.1575	5/32	29	1.1417	1 5/32
5	0.1969	3/16	30	1.1811	1 3/16
6	0.2362	1/4	31	1.2205	1 7/32
7	0.2756	9/32	32	1.2598	1 1/4
8	0.3150	5/16	33	1.2992	1 5/16
9	0.3543	11/32	34	1.3386	1 11/32
10	0.3937	13/32	35	1.3780	1 3/8
11	0.4331	7/16	36	1.4173	1 13/32
12	0.4724	15/32	37	1.4567	1 15/32
13	0.5118	1/2	38	1.4961	1 1/2
14	0.5512	9/16	39	1.5354	1 17/32
15	0.5906	19/32	40	1.5748	1 9/16
16	0.6299	5/8	41	1.6142	1 5/8
17	0.6693	21/32	42	1.6535	1 21/32
18	0.7087	23/32	43	1.6929	1 11/16
19	0.7480	3/4	44	1.7323	1 23/32
20	0.7874	25/32	45	1.7717	1 25/32
21	0.8268	13/16	46	1.8110	1 13/16
22	0.8661	7/8	47	1.8504	1 27/32
23	0.9055	29/32	48	1.8898	1 7/8
24	0.9449	15/16	49	1.9291	1 15/16
25	0.9843	31/32	50	1.9685	1 31/32

Table 5 GENERAL TORQUE SPECIFICATIONS

Fastener size or type	N•m	in.-lb.	ft.-lb.
5 mm screw	4	35	–
5 mm bolt and nut	5	44	–
(continued)			

Table 5 GENERAL TORQUE SPECIFICATIONS (continued)

Fastener size or type	N•m	in.-lb.	ft.-lb.
6 mm screw	9	80	–
6 mm bolt and nut	10	88	–
6 mm flange bolt			
(8 mm head, small flange)	9	80	–
6 mm flange bolt			
(10 mm head) and nut	12	106	–
8 mm bolt and nut	22	–	16
8 mm flange bolt and nut	27	–	20
10 mm bolt and nut	35	–	26
10 mm flange bolt and nut	40	–	30
12 mm bolt and nut	55	–	41

Table 6 CONVERSION FORMULAS

Multiply:	By:	To get the equivalent of:
Length		
Inches	25.4	Millimeter
Inches	2.54	Centimeter
Miles	1.609	Kilometer
Feet	0.3048	Meter
Millimeter	0.03937	Inches
Centimeter	0.3937	Inches
Kilometer	0.6214	Mile
Meter	0.0006214	Mile
Fluid volume		
U.S. quarts	0.9463	Liters
U.S. gallons	3.785	Liters
U.S. ounces	29.573529	Milliliters
Imperial gallons	4.54609	Liters
Imperial quarts	1.1365	Liters
Liters	0.2641721	U.S. gallons
Liters	1.0566882	U.S. quarts
Liters	33.814023	U.S. ounces
Liters	0.22	Imperial gallons
Liters	0.8799	Imperial quarts
Milliliters	0.033814	U.S. ounces
Milliliters	1.0	Cubic centimeters
Milliliters	0.001	Liters
Torque		
Foot-pounds	1.3558	Newton-meters
Foot-pounds	0.138255	Meters-kilograms
Inch-pounds	0.11299	Newton-meters
Newton-meters	0.7375622	Foot-pounds
Newton-meters	8.8507	Inch-pounds
Meters-kilograms	7.2330139	Foot-pounds
Volume		
Cubic inches	16.387064	Cubic centimeters
Cubic centimeters	0.0610237	Cubic inches
Temperature		
Fahrenheit	$(°F - 32) \times 0.556$	Centigrade
Centigrade	$(°C \times 1.8) + 32$	Fahrenheit

(continued)

Table 6 CONVERSION FORMULAS (continued)

Multiply:	By:	To get the equivalent of:
Weight		
Ounces	28.3495	Grams
Pounds	0.4535924	Kilograms
Grams	0.035274	Ounces
Kilograms	2.2046224	Pounds
Pressure		
Pounds per square inch	0.070307	Kilograms per square centimeter
Kilograms per square centimeter	14.223343	Pounds per square inch
Kilopascals	0.1450	Pounds per square inch
Pounds per square inch	6.895	Kilopascals
Speed		
Miles per hour	1.609344	Kilometers per hour
Kilometers per hour	0.6213712	Miles per hour

Table 7 TECHNICAL ABBREVIATIONS

A	Ampere
AIS	Air induction system
ABDC	After bottom dead center
AC	Alternating current
A•h	Ampere hour
ATDC	After top dead center
BBDC	Before bottom dead center
BDC	Bottom dead center
BTDC	Before top dead center
C	Celsius
cc	Cubic centimeter
CDI	Capacitor discharge ignition
cm	Centimeter
cu. in.	Cubic inch and cubic inches
cyl.	Cylinder
DC	Direct current
EVAP	Evaporative emission control system
F	Fahrenheit
fl. oz.	Fluid ounces
ft.	Foot
ft.-lb.	Foot pounds
gal.	Gallon and gallons
hp	Horsepower
Hz	Hertz
in.	Inch and inches
in.-lb.	Inch-pounds
in. Hg	Inches of mercury
kg	Kilogram
kg/cm^2	Kilogram per square centimeter
kgm	Kilogram meter
km	Kilometer
km/h	Kilometer per hour
kPa	Kilopascals
kW	Kilowatt
L	Liter and liters
L/m	Liters per minute
lb.	Pound and pounds
m	Meter
mL	Milliliter
	(continued)

Table 7 TECHNICAL ABBREVIATIONS (continued)

mm	Millimeter
MPa	Megapascal
N	Newton
N• m	Newton meter
oz.	Ounce and ounces
p	Pascal
psi	Pounds per square inch
pt.	Pint and pints
qt.	Quart and quarts
rpm	Revolution per minute
SCCR	Starting Circuit Cutoff Relay
TPS	Throttle Position Sensor
V	Volt
VAC	Alternating current voltage
VDC	Direct current voltage
W	Watt

Table 8 METRIC TAP AND DRILL SIZES

Metric size	Drill equivalent	Decimal fraction	Nearest fraction
3 × 0.50	No. 39	0.0995	3/32
3 × 0.60	3/32	0.0937	3/32
4 × 0.70	No. 30	0.1285	1/8
4 × 0.75	1/8	0.125	1/8
5 × 0.80	No. 19	0.166	11/64
5 × 0.90	No. 20	0.161	5/32
6 × 1.00	No. 9	0.196	13/64
7 × 1.00	16/64	0.234	15/64
8 × 1.00	J	0.277	9/32
8 × 1.25	17/64	0.265	17/64
9 × 1.00	5/16	0.3125	5/16
9 × 1.25	5/16	0.3125	5/16
10 × 1.25	11/32	0.3437	11/32
10 × 1.50	R	0.339	11/32
11 × 1.50	3/8	0.375	3/8
12 × 1.50	13/32	0.406	13/32
12 × 1.75	13/32	0.406	13/32

CHAPTER TWO

TROUBLESHOOTING

Begin any troubleshooting procedure by defining the symptoms as precisely as possible. Gather as much information as possible to aid diagnosis. Never assume anything and do not overlook the obvious. Make sure there is fuel in the tank, and the fuel valve is in the on position. Make sure the engine stop switch is in the run position and the spark plug wires are attached to the spark plugs.

If a quick check does not reveal the problem, turn to the troubleshooting procedures described in this chapter. Identify the procedure that most closely describes the symptoms, and perform the indicated tests.

In most cases, expensive and complicated test equipment is not needed to determine whether repairs can be performed at home. A few simple checks could prevent an unnecessary repair charge. On the other hand, be realistic and do not attempt repairs beyond your capabilities. Many service departments will not take work that involves the reassembly of damaged or abused equipment. If they do, expect the cost to be high.

ENGINE OPERATING REQUIREMENTS

An engine needs three basic requirements to run properly: correct air/fuel mixture, compression and a spark at the proper time. If any element is missing, the engine will not run. Four-stroke engine operating principles are described in **Figure 1**.

If the machine has been sitting for any length of time and refuses to start, check and clean the spark plugs and then look to the fuel delivery system. This includes the fuel tank, fuel valve, fuel pump and fuel lines to the carburetor. Gasoline deposits may have gummed up the carburetor jets and air passages.

Gasoline tends to lose its potency after standing for long periods. Condensation may contaminate the fuel with water. Drain the old fuel (fuel tank, fuel lines and carburetor) and try starting with a tank of fresh gasoline.

STARTING THE ENGINE

Starting System Operation

1. A sidestand ignition cutoff system is used on these models. The position of the sidestand affects engine starting. For instance:

   a. The engine cannot start when the sidestand is down and the transmission is in gear.

   b. The engine can start when the sidestand is down and the transmission is in neutral. The engine will stop,

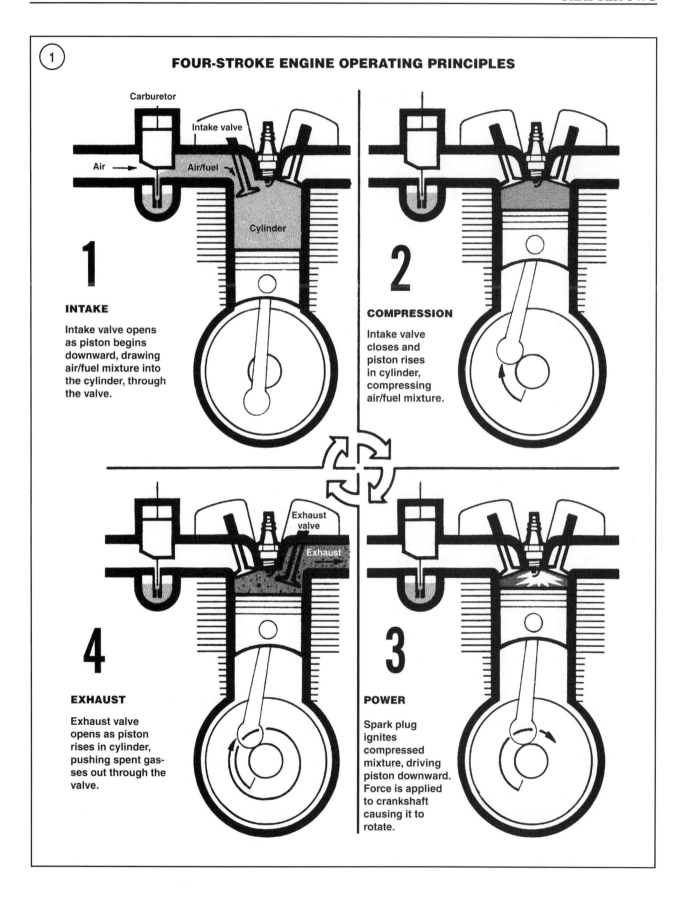

① **FOUR-STROKE ENGINE OPERATING PRINCIPLES**

1

INTAKE

Intake valve opens as piston begins downward, drawing air/fuel mixture into the cylinder, through the valve.

2

COMPRESSION

Intake valve closes and piston rises in cylinder, compressing air/fuel mixture.

4

EXHAUST

Exhaust valve opens as piston rises in cylinder, pushing spent gasses out through the valve.

3

POWER

Spark plug ignites compressed mixture, driving piston downward. Force is applied to crankshaft causing it to rotate.

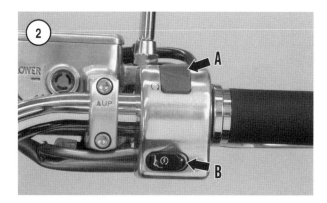

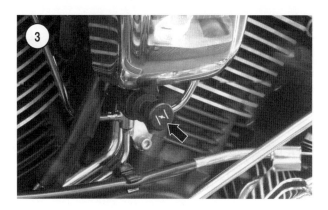

7. Excessive choke use can cause an excessively rich fuel mixture. This condition can wash oil off the piston and cylinder walls causing piston and cylinder scuffing.

Cold Engine

1. Shift the transmission into neutral.
2. Pull the choke knob (**Figure 3**) out to the fully on position.
3. Turn the ignition switch to on.
4. Make sure the engine stop switch (A, **Figure 2**) is set to run.

NOTE
When a cold engine is started with the throttle open and the starter (choke) on, a lean mixture will result and cause hard starting.

5. Press the starter button (B, **Figure 2**) and start the engine. Do not open the throttle when pressing the starter button.
6. Once the engine is running, keep the starter (choke) knob (**Figure 3**) out to the warm up position to help warm the engine. Continue warming the engine until the starter (choke) can be pushed to the fully off position and the engine responds to the throttle cleanly.

Warm or Hot Engine

1. Shift the transmission into neutral.
2. Turn the ignition switch to on.
3. Make sure the starter (choke) knob (**Figure 3**) is pushed all the way into the fully off position.
4. Make sure the engine stop switch is set to run.
5. Open the throttle slightly and press the starter button (B, **Figure 2**).

Flooded Engine

NOTE
If the engine refuses to start, check the carburetor overflow hose attached to the bottom of the float bowl. If fuel runs out the end of the hose, the fuel inlet valve is stuck open, allowing the carburetor to overfill. Remove the carburetor and correct the problem. Refer to Chapter Nine.

If you smell gasoline after attempting to start the engine, the engine is probably flooded. To start a flooded engine:

1. Push the choke knob (**Figure 3**) all the way in to the fully off position.

however, if the transmission is put in gear while the sidestand is down.
   c. The engine can start when the sidestand is up and the transmission is in neutral.
   d. If the sidestand is up, the engine will also start if the transmission is in gear and the clutch lever is pulled in.
2. Before starting the engine, shift the transmission into neutral and make sure the engine stop switch (A, **Figure 2**) is set to run.
3. Turn the ignition switch to on. The neutral indicator light should be on (when transmission is in neutral).
4. Turn the fuel shutoff valve to on.
5. The engine is now ready to start. Refer to the starting procedure in this section that best describes the air temperature and engine conditions.

CAUTION
Do not operate the starter motor for more than five seconds at a time. Wait approximately ten seconds between starting attempts.

6. If the engine idles at a fast speed for more than 5 minutes or if the throttle is repeatedly snapped on and off at normal air temperatures, the exhaust pipes may discolor.

2. Turn the engine stop switch to the run position (A, **Figure 2**).

3. Open the throttle completely and press the starter button (B, **Figure 2**). If the engine starts, close the throttle quickly. If necessary, operate the throttle to keep the engine running until it smoothes out. If the engine does not start, wait 10 seconds and then try to restart the engine by following normal starting procedures. If the engine will not start, refer to *Starting Difficulties* in this chapter.

ENGINE WILL NOT START

Perform each step while remembering the engine operating requirements described in this chapter. If the engine still will not start, refer to the appropriate troubleshooting procedures in this chapter.

1. Make sure the fuel shutoff valve is in the on position.

2. Make sure the start (choke) knob (**Figure 3**) is in the correct position.

> *WARNING*
> *Do not use an open flame to check fuel in the tank. A serious explosion is certain to result.*

3. Make sure the engine stop switch (A, **Figure 2**) moves freely and works properly. Also confirm that the switch wire is not broken or shorting out. If necessary, test the switch as described in Chapter Ten.

4. Make sure the sidestand is up and the sidestand switch operates properly. If necessary, test the switch as described in Chapter Ten.

5. Make sure all four spark plug wires are on tight. Push each spark plug cap and slightly rotate it to clean the electrical connection between the plug and the connector.

6. Test the integrity of the ignition system by performing the *Spark Test* described in this section.

7. If the test produces a good spark, proceed with Step 8. If the spark is weak or if there is no spark, troubleshoot the ignition system as described in this chapter.

8. Check engine compression as described in Chapter Three. If the compression is good, perform Step 9. If the compression is low, check for one or more of the following:

   a. Leaking cylinder head gasket(s).

   b. Cracked or warped cylinder head(s).

   c. Worn piston rings, pistons and cylinder(s).

   d. Valve stuck open.

   e. Worn or damaged valve seat(s).

   f. Incorrect valve timing.

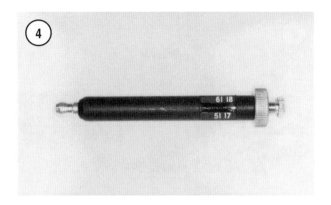

9. Perform the fuel pump operational test described in Chapter Nine. If the fuel flow is good, check for one or more of the following:

   a. Clogged fuel filter or fuel line.

   b. Stuck or clogged carburetor float valve.

Spark Test

The ignition spark test checks the integrity of the ignition system. The greater the air gap that a spark will jump, the stronger the ignition system. Use the Yamaha Ignition Checker (part No. YM-34487 [U.S] or 90890-06754 [U.K.]), the Motion Pro Ignition System Tester (part No. 08-122) (**Figure 4**), or a similar tool to perform this test. Connect the tester and perform the test as described by the tool manufacturer's instructions. The ignition system is working properly if a spark jumps a gap equal to or greater than the ignition minimum spark gap of 6 mm (0.24 in.).

If the above equipment is not available, perform the test with a new spark plug.

1. Remove one of the spark plugs from the cylinder as described in Chapter Three.

2. Insert the spark plug (**Figure 5**), or spark tester (**Figure 6**) into the plug cap. Touch the plug base to a good en-

gine ground. Position the plug so you can see the electrode.

> *WARNING*
> *Make sure the spark plug is away from the spark plug hole in the cylinder so the spark cannot ignite the mixture in that cylinder. If the engine is flooded, do not perform this test. The firing of the spark plug can ignite fuel ejected from the opened spark plug hole.*

> *WARNING*
> *During the next step, do not hold the spark plug, plug wire or connector by hand. Serious electrical shock may result.*

3. Turn the ignition switch to on, and turn the engine over with the starter. A fat blue spark should be evident across the plug terminals. Repeat this test for the other cylinder.

4. Repeat Steps 1-3 for the remaining spark plugs.

5. If the spark is good at each spark plug, the ignition system is functioning properly. Check for one or more of the following possible malfunctions:
   a. Obstructed fuel line or fuel filter.
   b. Damaged fuel pump system.
   c. Low compression or engine damage.
   d. Flooded engine.

6A. If there is no spark at both plugs, there may be a problem in the input side of the ignition system, ignitor unit, sidestand switch or neutral switch. Troubleshoot the ignition system as described this chapter.

6B. If there is no spark at only one spark plug, the spark plug is probably faulty or there is a problem with that spark plug's wire, plug cap or ignition coil. Retest it with a spark tester or use a new spark plug. If there is still no spark at that plug, make sure the spark plug cap is installed correctly. Check the spark plug wiring and cap, and test the related ignition coil as described in Chapter Ten.

Engine is Difficult to Start

1. Check for fuel flow to the carburetors. If fuel is reaching the carburetors, go to Step 2. If not, check for one or more of the following possible malfunctions:
   a. Clogged fuel hose and/or fuel filter.
   b. Clogged fuel tank breather hose.
   c. Damaged fuel pump.
   d. Damaged starting circuit cutoff relay.
   e. Loose or disconnected starting circuit cutoff relay connector.

2. Perform the *Spark Test* described in this section. Note the following:
   a. If the spark plugs are wet, go to Step 3.
   b. If the spark is weak or if there is no spark, go to Step 4.
   c. If the spark is good, go to Step 5.

3. If the plugs are wet, the engine may be flooded. Check the following:
   a. Flooded carburetor.
   b. Dirty air filter.
   c. Throttle valve(s) binding or stuck open.
   d. Incorrect choke operation.
   e. Needle valve in carburetor stuck open.

4. If the spark is weak or if there is no spark, check the following:
   a. Fouled spark plug(s).
   b. Damaged spark plug(s).
   c. Loose or damaged spark plug wire(s).
   d. Loose or damaged spark plug cap(s).
   e. Damaged ignitor unit.
   f. Damaged ignition coil(s).
   g. Damaged engine stop switch.
   h. Damaged ignition switch.
   i. Damaged sidestand switch.
   j. Dirty or loose terminals.

5. If the spark is good, proceed as follows:
   a. Try starting the engine as described in this chapter. If the engine does not start, go to Step 6.
   b. If the engine starts but then stops, check for an inoperative starter (choke), incorrect carburetor adjustment, leaking intake manifolds, improper ignition timing or contaminated fuel.

6. If the engine turns over but does not start, the engine compression is probably low. Check for the following possible malfunctions:
   a. Leaking cylinder head gasket(s).
   b. Valve clearance too tight.
   c. Bent or stuck valve(s).
   d. Incorrect valve timing.
   e. Improper valve-to-seat contact.
   f. Worn cylinders and/or piston rings.

Engine Does Not Crank

If the engine will not turn over, check for one or more of the following:
1. Blown main fuse.
2. Discharged battery.
3. Defective starter, starter relay, starting circuit cutoff switch, or starter switch.
4. Faulty starter clutch.
5. Seized pistons(s).
6. Seized crankshaft bearing(s).
7. Broken connecting rod(s).
8. Locked-up transmission or clutch assembly.
9. Defective starter clutch.

ENGINE PERFORMANCE

In the following checklists, it is assumed that the engine runs, but is not operating at peak performance. This section serves as a starting point from which to isolate a performance problem. Where ignition timing is mentioned as a problem, remember that the ignition timing cannot be adjusted. If the ignition timing is incorrect, a part within the ignition system is faulty. Check the individual ignition system components, and replace any faulty part.

Engine Will Not Idle

1. Incorrect idle speed adjustment.
2. Fouled or improperly gapped spark plug(s).
3. Leaking head gasket(s) or vacuum leak.
4. Incorrect valve clearance or camshaft timing.
5. Obstructed fuel line or fuel valve.
6. Low engine compression.
7. Starter (choke) valve stuck in the open position.
8. Incorrect pilot screw adjustment.
9. Clogged pilot jet or pilot air jet.
10. Clogged air filter element.
11. Faulty fuel pump.
12. Incorrect throttle cable free play.
13. Faulty ignition system component.

Low or Poor Engine Power

1. Securely support the motorcycle with the rear wheel off the ground, and spin the rear wheel by hand. If the wheel spins freely, perform Step 2. If the wheel does not spin freely, check for the following conditions:
    a. Dragging rear brake.
    b. Excessive rear axle torque.
    c. Worn or damaged rear wheel bearings.
    d. Incorrect drive belt tension.
2. Check the tire pressure. If pressure is normal, perform Step 3. If pressure is low, the tire valve is faulty.
3. Ride the motorcycle, and accelerate rapidly from first to second gear. If the engine speed reduces when the clutch is released, perform Step 4. If the engine speed does not change when the clutch is released, check for the following:
    a. Slipping clutch.
    b. Worn or warped clutch plates or friction discs.
    c. Weak clutch spring.
    d. Incorrect clutch cable free play.
    e. Check the engine oil for additives.
4. Ride the motorcycle and accelerate lightly. If the engine speed increases relative to throttle operation, perform Step 5. If engine speed does not increase, check for the following:
    a. Choke valve opened.
    b. Clogged air cleaner.
    c. Fuel flow restricted.
    d. Clogged muffler.
    e. Faulty fuel pump.
    f. Faulty starting circuit cutoff relay.
5. Check for one of the following:
    a. Incorrect ignition timing due to a malfunctioning ignition component.
    b. Improperly adjusted valves or worn valve seats.
    c. Low engine compression.
    d. Clogged carburetor jet(s).
    e. Fouled spark plug(s).
    f. Incorrect spark plug heat range.
    g. Oil level too low or too high.
    h. Contaminated oil.
    i. Worn or damaged valve train assembly.
    j. Engine overheating. See *Engine Overheating* in this section.
6. If the engine knocks when accelerating or when running at high speed, check for the following:
    a. Incorrect type of fuel.
    b. Lean carburetor jetting.
    c. Advanced ignition timing caused by malfunctioning ignition component.
    d. Excessive carbon buildup in the combustion chamber.
    e. Worn pistons and/or cylinder bores.

Poor Idle Speed or Low Speed Performance

1. Check the valve clearance. Adjust the valves as necessary.

2. Check for damaged intake manifold, or loose carburetor, air filter housing, or surge tank clamps.

3. Perform the spark test described in this chapter. Note the following:

    a. If the spark is good, perform to Step 4.

    b. If the spark is weak, test the ignition system as described in this chapter.

4. Check the ignition timing as described in Chapter Three. If the ignition timing is incorrect, troubleshoot the ignition system as described in this chapter. If the ignition timing is correct, check the carburetor and fuel system.

Poor High Speed Performance

1. Check the ignition timing as described in Chapter Three. If the ignition timing is correct, perform Step 2. If the timing is incorrect, test the following ignition system components as described in Chapter Ten:

    a. Pickup coil.

    b. Ignition coils.

    c. Ignitor unit.

2. Perform the fuel pump operational test described in Chapter Nine. If the fuel flow is acceptable, check for one or more of the following:

    a. Clogged fuel line.

    b. Stuck or clogged carburetor float valve.

3. Remove the carburetor assembly as described in Chapter Nine. Then remove the float bowl and check for contamination and plugged jets. If there is any contamination, disassemble and clean the carburetor. Also pour out and discard the remaining fuel in the fuel tank and flush the tank thoroughly. If there was no contamination and the jets were not plugged, perform Step 4.

4. Incorrect valve timing and worn or damaged valve springs can cause poor high-speed performance. If the valve timing was set just before the onset of this type of problem, the valve timing may be incorrect. If the valve timing was not recently set or changed, remove the cylinder head and inspect the valve train assembly.

5. Check the carburetor and fuel system. Pay particular attention to the following:

    a. A faulty diaphragm in the carburetor.

    b. Improperly set fuel level.

    c. Clogged or loose main jet.

    d. Faulty fuel pump.

    e. Clogged air filter.

Engine Overheating

1. Incorrect spark plug gap.

2. Improper spark plug heat range.

3. Faulty ignitor unit.

4. Incorrect carburetor adjustment or jet selection.

5. Incorrect fuel level.

6. Clogged air filter.

7. Heavy engine carbon deposits in combustion chamber.

8. Low oil level.

9. Incorrect oil viscosity.

10. Oil not circulating properly.

11. Valves leaking.

12. Dragging brake(s).

13. Clutch slipping.

Engine Runs Roughly

1. Clogged air filter element.

2. Carburetor adjustment incorrect; mixture too rich.

3. Choke not operating correctly.

4. Contaminants in the fuel.

5. Clogged fuel line.

6. Spark plug(s) fouled.

7. Ignition coil defective.

8. Ignitor unit or pickup coil defective.

9. Loose or defective ignition circuit wire.

10. Short circuit from damaged wire insulation.

11. Loose battery cable connection(s).

12. Valve timing incorrect.

Engine Lacks Acceleration

1. Carburetor mixture too lean.

2. Clogged fuel line.

3. Improper ignition timing.

4. Dragging brake(s).

5. Slipping clutch.

Engine Backfires

1. Improper ignition timing.

2. Carburetor improperly adjusted.

3. Lean fuel mixture.

Engine Misfires During Acceleration

1. Improper ignition timing.

2. Lean fuel mixture.

3. Excessively worn or defective spark plug(s).

4. Ignition system malfunction.

5. Incorrect carburetor adjustment.

ENGINE NOISES

Often the first evidence of an internal engine problem is a strange noise. A new knocking, clicking or tapping sound may be an early sign of trouble. While engine noises can indicate problems, they are difficult to interpret correctly.

Professional mechanics often use a special stethoscope to isolate engine noises. A home mechanic can do nearly as well with a length of dowel or a section of small hose. Place one end in contact with the area in question and the other end to the front of your ear (not directly in your ear) to hear the sounds emanating from that area. Distinguishing a normal noise from an abnormal one can be difficult. If necessary, have an experienced mechanic help you sort out the noises.

Consider the following when troubleshooting engine noises:

1. A knocking or pinging during acceleration is usually caused by the use of a low octane fuel. It may also be caused by poor fuel, a spark plug of the wrong heat range or carbon buildup in the combustion chamber. Refer to *Spark Plugs* and *Compression Test* in Chapter Three.

2. Slapping or rattling noises at low speed or during acceleration may be caused by excessive piston-to-cylinder wall clearance (piston slap).

NOTE
Piston slap is easier to detect when the engine is cold and before the pistons have expanded. Once the engine has warmed up, piston expansion reduces piston-to-cylinder clearance.

3. A knocking or rapping during deceleration is usually caused by excessive connecting rod bearing clearance.

4. A persistent knocking and vibration that occurs every crankshaft rotation is usually caused by worn connecting rod or main bearing(s). It can also be caused by broken piston rings or damaged piston pins.

5. A rapid on-off squeal may indicate a compression leak around a cylinder head gasket or spark plug(s).

6. If valve train noise is evident, check for the following:
   a. Excessive valve clearance.
   b. Excessively worn or damaged camshaft.
   c. Worn or damaged valve lifters and/or pushrods.
   d. Damaged valve bore(s) in the cylinder head.
   e. Valve sticking in guide.
   f. Broken valve spring.
   g. Low oil pressure.
   h. Clogged cylinder oil hole or oil passage.
   i. Excessively worn or damaged timing chain.

ENGINE LUBRICATION

An improperly operating engine lubrication system will quickly lead to engine seizure. Check the engine oil level before each ride, and top off the oil as described in Chapter Three. Oil pump service is described in Chapter Five.

Oil Consumption High or Engine Smokes Excessively

1. Worn valve guides.
2. Worn or damaged piston rings.

Excessive Engine Oil Leaks

1. Clogged air filter breather hose.
2. Loose engine parts.
3. Damaged gasket sealing surfaces.

Black Smoke

1. Clogged air filter.
2. Incorrect carburetor fuel level (too high).
3. Starter (choke) stuck open.
4. Incorrect main jet (too large).

White Smoke

1. Worn valve guide.
2. Worn valve oil seal.
3. Worn piston ring oil ring.
4. Excessive cylinder and/or piston wear.

Low Oil Pressure

1. Low oil level.
2. Damaged oil pump.
3. Clogged oil strainer screen.
4. Clogged oil filter.
5. Internal oil leak.
6. Incorrect type of engine oil being used.
7. Oil pressure relief valve stuck open.

High Oil Pressure

1. Incorrect type of engine oil being used.
2. Plugged oil filter, oil gallery or metering orifices.
3. Oil pressure relief valve stuck closed.

No Oil Pressure

1. Damaged oil pump.
2. Excessively low oil level.
3. Damaged oil pump drive shaft.
4. Damaged oil pump drive sprocket.
5. Incorrect oil pump installation.

Low Oil Level

1. Oil level not maintained at correct level.
2. Worn piston rings.
3. Worn cylinder.
4. Worn valve guides.
5. Worn valve stem seals.
6. Piston rings incorrectly installed during engine overhaul.
7. External oil leak.
8. Oil leaking into the cooling system.

Oil Contamination

1. Blown head gasket allowing coolant to leak into the engine.
2. Water contamination.
3. Oil and filter not changed at specified intervals or when operating conditions demand more frequent changes.

ENGINE LEAKDOWN TEST

Perform an engine leakdown test to pinpoint engine problems caused by compression leaks. While a compression test (Chapter Three) can identify a weak cylinder, a leakdown test can determine where the leak occurs. A cylinder leakdown test is made by applying compressed air through the cylinder head (with the valves closed), then measuring the leak rate as a percentage. Under pressure, air leaks past worn or damaged parts. You will need a cylinder leakdown tester and an air compressor to perform this test.

1. Start and run the engine until it is warm. Then turn the engine off.
2. Remove the air filter housing and surge tank as described in Chapter Nine. Open and secure the throttle at its wide-open position.
3. Set the No. 1 cylinder (rear) to top dead center on its compression stroke as described in *Valve Clearance* in Chapter Three.
4. Remove one of the spark plugs from the No. 1 cylinder.

5. Thread the tester adapter into the No. 1 cylinder spark plug hole following the manufacturer's instructions. Then connect the leakdown tester onto the adapter. Connect an air compressor hose onto the tester's fitting.

WARNING
To prevent the engine from turning over as compressed air is applied to the cylinder, shift the transmission into fifth gear and have an assistant apply the rear brake. Remove any tools attached to the end of the crankshaft.

6. Apply compressed air to the leak tester and perform a cylinder leakdown test following the manufacturer's instructions. Read the percent of leak on the gauge. Note the following:
   a. For a new or rebuilt engine, a leak rate difference of 0 to 5 percent per cylinder is desirable. A leak rate of 6 to 14 percent is acceptable and means the engine is in good condition.
   b. For a used engine, the critical rate is not the leak percent for each cylinder but the difference between the cylinders. On a used engine, a leak rate difference of 10 percent or less between cylinders is satisfactory.
   c. A leak rate difference exceeding 10 percent between cylinders points to an engine that is in very poor condition and requires further inspection and possible engine repair.

7. After measuring the percent of leak, and with air pressure still applied to the combustion chamber, listen for air escaping from the following areas:

NOTE
Use a mechanic's stethoscope to help listen for air leaks in the following areas.

   a. Air leaking through the exhaust pipe indicates a leaking exhaust valve.
   b. Air leaking through the carburetor indicates a leaking intake valve.
   c. Air leaking through the crankcase breather suggests worn piston rings or a worn cylinder bore.

8. Remove the leakdown tester, and repeat these steps for each cylinder.

CLUTCH

Basic clutch troubles and their causes are listed in this section. Clutch service procedures are in Chapter Seven.

Clutch Lever Hard to Pull In

If the clutch lever has become hard to pull in, look for the following:
1. Clutch cable requires lubrication.
2. Clutch cable improperly routed or bent.
3. Damaged clutch lifter bearing.

Rough Clutch Operation

1. Excessively worn, grooved or damaged clutch hub and clutch housing slots.
2. Worn friction disc tangs.

Clutch Slips

If the engine speed increases without an increase in motorcycle speed, the clutch is probably slipping. Some main causes of clutch slipping are:
1. Incorrect clutch cable adjustment.
2. Weak clutch diaphragm spring.
3. Worn clutch or friction plates.
4. Damaged pressure plate.
5. Clutch release mechanism.
6. Incorrectly assembled clutch.
7. Loose clutch nut.
8. Improper oil level.
9. Improper oil viscosity.
10. Engine oil additive being used (clutch plates contaminated).

Clutch Drag

If the clutch will not disengage or if the bike creeps with the transmission in gear and the clutch disengaged, the clutch is dragging. Some main causes of clutch drag are:
1. Incorrectly assembled clutch.
2. Uneven clutch diaphragm spring tension.
3. Warped clutch plates or pressure plate.
4. Damaged clutch boss.
5. Damaged primary driven gear bushing.
6. Swollen friction discs.
7. Clutch marks not properly aligned.
8. Engine oil level too high.
9. Incorrect oil viscosity.
10. Engine oil additive being used.
11. Incorrect clutch cable adjustment.
12. Damaged clutch release mechanism.

GEARSHIFT LINKAGE

The gearshift linkage assembly connects the shift pedal to the shift drum (internal shift mechanism). The external shift mechanism can be examined after the clutch has been removed. The internal shift mechanism can only be examined once the engine has been removed and the crankcase disassembled.

Common gearshift linkage troubles and their checks are listed below.

Transmission Jumps Out of Gear

1. Incorrect shift pedal position.
2. Bent or worn shift fork.
3. Bent shift fork shaft.
4. Gear groove worn.
5. Damaged stopper bolt.
6. Weak or damaged stopper arm spring.
7. Loose or damaged shift cam.
8. Worn gear dogs or slots.
9. Damaged shift drum grooves.
10. Weak or damaged gearshift linkage springs.

Difficult Shifting

1. Improperly assembled clutch.
2. Incorrect oil viscosity.
3. Bent shift fork shaft(s).
4. Bent or damaged shift fork(s).
5. Worn gear dogs or slots.
6. Damaged shift drum grooves.
7. Weak or damaged gearshift linkage springs.

Shift Pedal Does Not Return

1. Bent shift shaft.
2. Weak or damaged shift shaft spindle return spring.
3. Shift shaft incorrectly installed.
4. Improper shift pedal linkage adjustment.
5. Bent shift fork shaft.
6. Damaged shift fork.
7. Seized transmission gear.
8. Improperly assembled transmission.

TRANSMISSION

Transmission symptoms are sometimes hard to distinguish from clutch symptoms. Common transmission troubles and their checks are listed below. Refer to Chapter Eight for transmission service procedures. Before working on the transmission, make sure the clutch and gearshift linkage assemblies are working properly.

Difficult Shifting

1. Incorrect clutch adjustment.
2. Incorrect clutch operation.
3. Bent shift fork shaft.
4. Damaged shift fork guide pin(s).
5. Bent or damaged shift fork(s).
6. Worn gear dogs or slots.
7. Damaged shift drum grooves.

Jumps Out of Gear

1. Loose or damaged shift drum stopper arm.
2. Bent or damaged shift fork(s).
3. Bent shift fork shaft(s).
4. Damaged shift drum grooves.
5. Worn gear dogs or slots.
6. Broken shift linkage return spring.
7. Improperly adjusted shift lever position.

Incorrect Shift Lever Operation

1. Bent shift lever.
2. Stripped shift lever splines.
3. Damaged shift lever linkage.
4. Improperly adjusted shift pedal rod.

Excessive Gear Noise

1. Worn bearings.
2. Worn or damaged gears.
3. Excessive gear backlash.

CARBURETOR

Test the indicated items when experiencing a particular symptom.

Engine Will Not Start

Check the following items if the engine will not start and the electrical and mechanical systems are working correctly.
1. If there is no fuel going to the carburetors, check for the following:
   a. Clogged fuel tank breather.
   b. Clogged fuel tank-to-carburetor line.
   c. Clogged fuel filter.
   d. Faulty fuel pump.
   e. Faulty starting circuit cutoff relay.
   f. Incorrect float adjustment.

g. Stuck or clogged float valve in carburetor.
2. If the engine is flooded (too much fuel), check the following:
   a. Flooded carburetor.
   b. Float valve in carburetor stuck open.
   c. Clogged air filter element.
3. A faulty emission control system (if equipped) can cause fuel problems. Check for a loose, disconnected or plugged emission control system hoses.
4. If the problem has not been located in Steps 1-3, check for the following:
   a. Contaminated or deteriorated fuel.
   b. Intake manifold air leak.
   c. Clogged pilot or starter (choke) circuit.

Engine Starts but Idles and Runs Poorly or Stalls Frequently

An engine that idles roughly or stalls may have one or more of the following problems:
1. Clogged air cleaner.
2. Contaminated fuel.
3. Incorrect pilot screw adjustment.
4. Incorrect idle speed.
5. Loose, disconnected or damaged fuel and emission control vacuum hoses.
6. Intake air leak.
7. Incorrect air/fuel mixture.
8. Plugged carburetor jets.
9. Partially plugged fuel tank breather hose.
10. Faulty fuel pump.
11. Faulty starting circuit cutoff relay.

Incorrect Fast Idle Speed

A fast idle speed can be due to one of the following problems:
1. Idle adjust screw incorrectly set.
2. Stuck starter (choke) valve.
3. Intake leak.

Poor Fuel Mileage and Engine Performance

Poor fuel mileage and engine performance can be caused by infrequent engine tune-ups. Check the service records against the recommended tune-up intervals in Chapter Three. If the last tune-up was within the specified service intervals, check for one or more of the following problems:
1. Clogged air filter.

2. Clogged fuel system.

3. Loose, disconnected or damaged fuel and emission control vacuum hoses.

4. Ignition system malfunction.

Rich Fuel Mixture

A rich carburetor fuel mixture can be caused by one or more of the following conditions:

1. Clogged or dirty air filter.

2. Worn or damaged fuel valve and seat.

3. Clogged air jets.

4. Incorrect float level (too high).

5. Flooded carburetor.

6. Damaged vacuum piston.

Lean Fuel Mixture

A lean carburetor fuel mixture can be caused by one or more of the following conditions:

1. Clogged carburetor jet(s).

2. Clogged fuel filter.

3. Restricted fuel line.

4. Intake air leak.

5. Incorrect float level (too low).

6. Worn or damaged float valve.

7. Faulty throttle valve.

8. Faulty vacuum piston.

Engine Backfires

1. Lean fuel mixture.

2. Incorrect carburetor adjustment.

Engine Misfires During Acceleration

When there is a pause before the engine responds to the throttle, the engine is misfiring. An engine misfire can occur when starting from a dead stop or at any speed. An engine misfire may be due to one of the following:

1. Lean fuel mixture.

2. Faulty ignition coil secondary wires. Check for cracking, hardening or bad connections.

3. Faulty vacuum hoses. Check for kinks, splits or bad connections.

4. Vacuum leaks at the carburetor and/or intake manifold.

5. Fouled spark plug(s).

6. Low engine compression, especially at one cylinder only. Check engine compression as described in Chapter Three. Low compression can be caused by worn engine components.

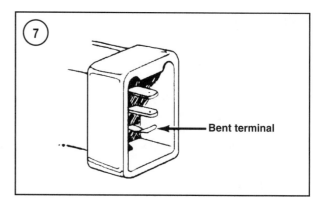

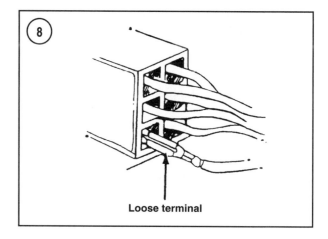

7. Faulty fuel pump.

CARBURETOR HEATER

Whenever there is a problem with the carburetor heater system, follow these carburetor heater troubleshooting procedures. Refer to the wiring diagram at the end of this manual.

Perform the troubleshooting test procedures in the listed sequence. Each test presumes the components tested in the earlier steps are working properly. The tests can yield invalid results if they are performed out of sequence. If a test indicates that a component is working properly, reconnect the electrical connections and proceed to the next step.

1. Inspect the main fuse and the carburetor fuse as described in Chapter Ten.

2. Check the battery as described in Chapter Three.

3. Check the continuity of the ignition switch (Chapter Ten).

4. Check the continuity of the neutral switch (Chapter Ten).

5. Test the carburetor heater relay (Chapter Ten).

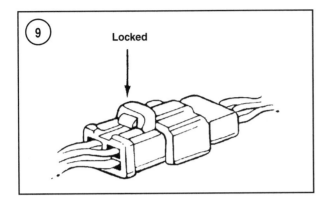

6. Test the carburetor heater (Chapter Ten).

FUEL PUMP

When troubleshooting a fuel pump problem, first perform the fuel pump operational test described in Chapter Nine. If the fuel pump is operational, the problem is in the fuel pump system circuit. Troubleshoot the circuit as described in the following troubleshooting procedures. Refer to the wiring diagram at the end of this manual.

Fuel Pump Circuit Troubleshooting

Perform these test procedures in the listed sequence. Each test presumes the components tested in the earlier steps are working properly. The tests can yield invalid results if they are performed out of sequence. If a test indicates that a component is working properly, reconnect the electrical connections and proceed to the next step.
1. Inspect the main fuse and the ignition fuse as described Chapter Ten.
2. Check the battery (Chapter Three).
3. Check the continuity of the ignition switch (Chapter Ten).
4. Check the continuity of the engine stop switch (Chapter Ten).
5. Check the fuel pump relay in the starting circuit cutoff relay (Chapter Nine).
6. Check the resistance of the fuel pump (Chapter Nine).
7. Check the fuel system wiring and all connectors. Repair as necessary.

ELECTRICAL TESTING

This section describes the basics of electrical testing and the use of test equipment.

Preliminary Checks and Precautions

Prior to starting any electrical troubleshooting perform the following:
1. Check the main fuse (Chapter Ten). If the fuse is blown, replace it.
2. Check the individual fuses mounted in the fuse box (Chapter Ten). Inspect the suspected fuse, and replace it if it is blown.
3. Inspect the battery (Chapter Three). Make sure it is fully charged, and the battery leads are clean and securely attached to the battery terminals.
4. Disconnect each electrical connector in the suspect circuit and make sure there are no bent metal terminals inside the electrical connector (**Figure 7**). A bent terminal will not connect to its mate in the other connector, causing an open circuit.
5. Make sure the terminals on the end of each wire (**Figure 8**) are pushed all the way into the connector. If not, carefully push them in with a narrow blade screwdriver.
6. Check all electrical wires where they join with the individual metal terminals in both the male and female connectors.

NOTE
Dielectric grease is a special grease used on electrical components such as connectors and battery connections. Dielectric grease can be purchased at automotive part stores.

7. Make sure all electrical terminals within the connectors are clean and free of corrosion. Clean them, if necessary, and pack the connectors with dielectric grease.
8. Push the connector halves together. Make sure they are fully engaged and locked together (**Figure 9**).
9. Never pull the electrical wires when disconnecting an electrical connector. Pull only on the connector plastic housing.

NOTE
Always consider electrical connectors the weak link in the electrical system. Dirty, loose-fitting and corroded connectors cause numerous electrical problems, especially on high-mileage motorcycles. When troubleshooting an electrical problem, carefully inspect the connectors and wiring harness.

Test Light or Voltmeter

A test light can be constructed from a 12-volt light bulb with a pair of test leads carefully soldered to the bulb. To check for battery voltage in a circuit, attach one lead to ground and the other lead to various points along the circuit. The bulb lights when battery voltage is present.

A voltmeter is used in the same manner as the test light to find out if battery voltage is present in any given circuit. The voltmeter, unlike the test light, also indicates how much voltage is present at each test point. When using a voltmeter, attach the positive test lead to the component or wire to be checked and the negative test lead to a good ground (**Figure 10**).

Ammeter

An ammeter measures the flow of current (amps) in a circuit (**Figure 11**). When connected in series in a circuit, the ammeter determines if current is flowing through the circuit and if that current flow is excessive because of a short in the circuit. Current flow is often referred to as current draw. Comparing actual current draw in the circuit or component to the manufacturer's specified current draw provides useful diagnostic information.

Self-powered Test Light

CAUTION
Never use a self-powered test light on circuits that contain solid-state devices. The solid-state device may be damaged.

A self-powered test light can be constructed from a 12-volt light bulb, a pair of test leads and a 12-volt battery. When the test leads are touched together the light bulb should go on.

Use a self-powered test light as follows:
1. Touch the test leads together to make sure the light bulb turns on. If it does not, correct the problem before using the test light in a test procedure.
2. Disconnect the motorcycle's battery or remove the fuse(s) that protects the circuit to be tested.
3. Select two points within the circuit where there should be continuity.
4. Attach one lead of the self-powered test light to each point.
5. If there is continuity, the self-powered test light bulb will turn on.
6. If there is no continuity, the self-powered test light bulb will not come on indicating an open circuit.

Ohmmeter

An ohmmeter measures the resistance in ohms to current flow in a circuit or component. Like the self-powered

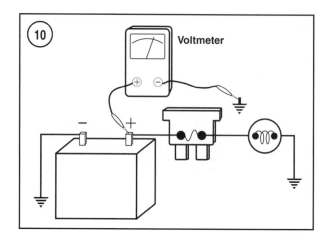

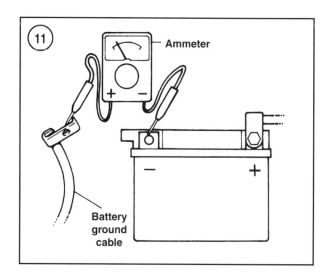

test light, an ohmmeter contains its own power source and should not be connected to a live circuit.

Ohmmeters may be analog (needle scale) or digital (LCD or LED readout). Both types of ohmmeters have different ranges of resistance for accurate readings. The analog ohmmeter also has a set-adjust control which is used to zero or calibrate the meter; digital ohmmeters do not require calibration.

Connect an ohmmeter to the terminals or leads of the circuit or component to be tested (**Figure 12**). When using an analog meter, calibrate it by touching the test leads together and turning the set-adjust knob until the meter needle reads zero. When the leads are uncrossed, the needle should move to the other end of the scale indicating infinite resistance.

During a continuity test, a reading of infinity indicates that there is an open in the circuit or component. A reading of zero indicates continuity, which means there is no measurable resistance in the circuit or component being

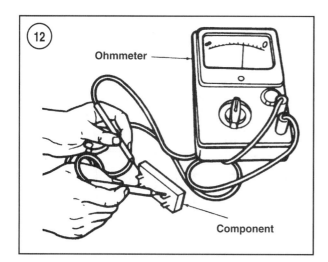

Ohmmeter

Component

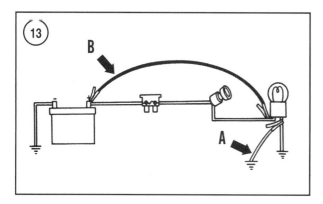

side of a device. In the example shown in **Figure 13**, test the ground (A) by connecting a jumper between the lamp and a good ground. If the lamp comes on, the problem is the connection between the lamp and ground. If the lamp does not come on with the jumper installed, the lamp's connection to ground is good so the problem is between the lamp and the power source.

To isolate the problem, connect the jumper between the battery and the lamp (B, **Figure 13**). If it comes on, the problem is between these two points. Next, connect the jumper between the battery and the fuse side of the switch. If the lamp comes on, the switch is good. By moving the jumper from one point to another, the problem can be isolated to a particular place in the circuit.

Note the following when using a jumper wire:

1. Make sure the jumper wire gauge (thickness) is the same as that used in the circuit being tested. Smaller gauge wire will rapidly overhead and could melt.

2. Install insulated boots over alligator clips. This prevents accidental grounding, sparks or possible shock when working in cramped quarters.

3. Jumper wires are temporary test measures only. Do not leave a jumper wire installed as a permanent solution. This creates a severe fire hazard that could easily lead to complete loss of the motorcycle.

4. When using a jumper wire, always install an inline fuse/fuse holder (available at most automotive supply stores or electronic supply stores) to the jumper wire.

5. Never use a jumper wire across any load (a component that is connected and turned on). This will result in a direct short and blow the fuse(s).

tested. If the meter needle falls between the two ends of the scale, this indicates the actual resistance to current flow that is present. To determine the resistance, multiply the meter reading by the ohmmeter scale. For example, a meter reading of 5 multiplied by the R × 1000 scale is 5000 ohms of resistance.

CAUTION
Never connect an ohmmeter to a circuit which has power applied to it. Always disconnect the battery negative lead before using an ohmmeter.

Jumper Wire

A jumper wire is a simple way to bypass a potential problem and isolate it to a particular point in a circuit. If a faulty circuit works properly with a jumper wire installed, an open exists between the two jumper points in the circuit.

To troubleshoot with a jumper wire, first use the wire to determine if the problem is on the ground side or the load

Voltage Testing

Make all voltage tests with the electrical connectors still connected unless otherwise specified. Insert the test leads into the backside of the connector and make sure the test lead touches the electrical wire or metal terminal within the connector housing. Touching the wire insulation will yield a false reading.

Always check both sides of the connector as one side may be loose or corroded thus preventing electrical flow through the connector. This type of test can be performed with a test light or a voltmeter. A voltmeter gives the best results.

NOTE
When using a test light, either lead can be attached to ground.

1. Attach the voltmeter negative test lead to a good ground. Make sure the part used for ground is not insulated with a rubber gasket or rubber grommet.

2. Attach the voltmeter positive test lead to the point (electrical connector, etc.) to be checked (**Figure 13**).

3. Turn the ignition switch on. When using a test light, the test light will come on if voltage is present. When using a voltmeter, note the voltage reading. The reading should be within 1 volt of battery voltage. If the voltage is significantly less than battery voltage, there is a problem in the circuit.

Voltage Drop Test

Since resistance causes voltage to drop, a voltmeter can be used to determine resistance in an active circuit. This is called a voltage drop test. A voltage drop test measures the difference between the voltage at the beginning of the circuit and the available voltage at the end of the circuit while the circuit is operating. If the circuit has no resistance, there is no voltage drop so the voltmeter indicates 0 volts. The greater resistance present in a circuit, the greater the voltage drop reading. A voltage drop of 1 or more volts indicates that a circuit has excessive resistance.

Remember a 0 reading on a voltage drop test is good. Battery voltage, on the other hand, indicates an open circuit. For example, consider a starting problem where the battery is fully charged but the starter turns over slowly. Voltage drop would be the difference in the voltage at the battery and the voltage at the starter as the engine is being started. A corroded battery cable would cause a high voltage drop (high resistance) and slow engine cranking.

Common sources of voltage drop are loose, damaged, or corroded connectors and poor ground connections. A voltage drop test is an excellent way to check the condition of solenoids, relays, battery cables and other high-current electrical components.

1. Connect the voltmeter positive test lead to the end of the wire or device closest to the battery.

2. Connect the voltmeter negative test lead to the ground side of the wire or device (**Figure 14**).

3. Turn on the components in the circuit.

4. The voltmeter should indicate 0 volts. If there is a drop of 1 volt or more, there is a problem within the circuit. A voltage drop reading of 12 volts indicates an open in the circuit.

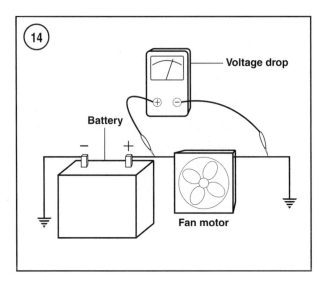

Continuity Test

A continuity test is used to determine the integrity of a circuit, wire or component. A circuit has continuity if it forms a complete circuit; if there are no opens in either the electrical wires or components within the circuit. A circuit with an open has no continuity.

This type of test can be performed with a self-powered test light or an ohmmeter. An ohmmeter gives the best results. When using an analog ohmmeter, calibrate the meter by touching the leads together and turning the calibration knob until the meter reads zero.

1. Disconnect the negative battery cable.

2. Attach one test lead (test light or ohmmeter) to one end of the part of the circuit to be tested.

3. Attach the other test lead to the other end of the part or the circuit to be tested.

4. The self-powered test light comes on if there is continuity. An ohmmeter reads 0 or very low resistance if there is continuity. A reading of infinite resistance indicates no continuity; the circuit has an open.

Testing for a Short with a Self-powered Test Light or Ohmmeter

1. Disconnect the negative battery cable.

2. Remove the blown fuse from the fuse panel.

3. Connect one lead of the test light or ohmmeter to the load side (battery side) of the fuse terminal in the fuse panel.

4. Connect the other test lead to a good ground. Make sure the part used for a ground is not insulated with a rubber gasket or rubber grommet.

5. With the self-powered test light or ohmmeter attached to the fuse terminal and ground, wiggle the wiring harness of the suspect circuit at 15.2 cm (6 in.) increments. Start next to the fuse panel and work away from the fuse panel.

6. Watch the self-powered test light or ohmmeter. If the test light blinks or the needle on the ohmmeter moves when the harness is wiggled, there is a short-to-ground at that point in the harness.

**Testing For a Short with a
Test Light or Voltmeter**

1. Remove the blown fuse from the fuse panel.

2. Connect the test light or voltmeter across the fuse terminals in the fuse panel. Turn the ignition switch on and check for battery voltage.

3. With the test light or voltmeter attached to the fuse terminals, wiggle the wiring harness of the suspect circuit at 15.2 cm (6 in.) intervals. Start next to the fuse panel and work away from the panel.

4. Watch the test light or voltmeter. If the test light blinks or if the needle on the voltmeter moves when the harness is wiggled, there is a short-to-ground at that point in the harness.

ELECTRICAL
TROUBLESHOOTING

Before troubleshooting an electrical component/circuit, refer to the wiring diagrams at the end of the manual for component and connector identification. Use the wiring diagrams to trace the current paths from the power source through the circuit components to ground. Also check any circuits that share the same fuse, ground or switch. If the other circuits work properly and the shared wiring is good, the cause must be in the wiring used only by the suspect circuit. If all related circuits are faulty at the same time, the probable cause is a poor ground connection or a blown fuse(s).

As with all troubleshooting, analyze typical symptoms in a systematic manner. Never assume anything, and do not overlook the obvious, like a blown fuse or an electrical connector that has separated. Test the simplest and most obvious items first and try to make tests at easily accessible points on the motorcycle.

The troubleshooting procedures for various electrical systems are listed below. Whenever there is a problem with the electrical system, perform the troubleshooting procedures for the affected system. Start with the first inspection in the list and perform the indicated check(s). If a test indicates that a component is working properly, re-connect the electrical connections and proceed to the next step. Systematically work through the troubleshooting checklist until the problem is found. Repair or replace faulty parts as described in the appropriate section of the manual.

Perform these procedures in the listed sequence. Each test presumes that the components tested in the earlier steps are working properly. The tests can yield invalid results if they are performed out of sequence.

Electrical Component Replacement

Most motorcycle dealerships and parts suppliers will not accept the return of any electrical part. If the exact cause of any electrical system malfunction cannot be determined, have a Yamaha dealership retest that specific system to verify the test results. If a new electrical component(s) is purchased and installed, but the system still does not work correctly, it will probably be impossible to return the unit for a refund.

Consider any test results carefully before replacing a component that tests only slightly out of specification, especially resistance. A number of variables can affect test results dramatically. These include: the testing meter's internal circuitry, ambient temperature, and conditions under which the machine has been operated. All instructions and specifications have been checked for accuracy; however, successful test results depend to a great degree upon individual accuracy.

Charging System

1. Check the main fuse.
2. Check the battery as described in Chapter Three.
3. Perform the current draw test (Chapter Ten).
4. Perform the charging voltage test (Chapter Ten).
5. Test the alternator stator resistance (Chapter Ten).
6. Check the wiring and connections in the entire charging system.
7. Replace the voltage regulator/rectifier.

Ignition System

1. Inspect the main fuse and the ignition fuse as described in Chapter Ten.
2. Check the battery (Chapter Three).
3. Check the condition of each spark plug (Chapter Three).
4. Perform the ignition spark test in this chapter.
5. Check the resistance of each spark plug cap (Chapter Ten).

6. Check the ignition coil resistance (Chapter Ten).

7. Check the pickup coil resistance (Chapter Ten).

8. Check the continuity of the ignition switch (Chapter Ten).

9. Check the continuity of the engine stop switch (Chapter Ten).

10. Check the continuity of the neutral switch (Chapter Ten).

11. Check the continuity of the sidestand switch (Chapter Ten).

12. Check the ignition system diode as described under *Diode* in Chapter Ten.

13. Check the connections in the entire ignition system.

14. Have a dealership or qualified shop check the ignitor unit.

Starting System

1. Check the main fuse and the ignition fuse.

2. Check the battery as described in Chapter Three.

3. Perform the starter operational test (Chapter Ten).

4. Test the starting circuit cutoff relay (SCCR) as described under *SCCR Diode Test* in Chapter Ten.

5. Test the starting system diode as described under *Diode* in Chapter Ten.

6. Test the continuity of the starter relay (Chapter Ten).

7. Check the continuity of the main switch (Chapter Ten).

8. Check the continuity of the engine stop switch (Chapter Ten).

9. Check the continuity of the neutral switch (Chapter Ten).

10. Check the continuity of the sidestand switch (Chapter Ten).

11. Check the continuity of the clutch switch (Chapter Ten).

12. Check the continuity of the start switch (Chapter Ten).

13. Check the wiring and each connector in the starting circuit.

Lighting System

The lighting system consists of the headlight, taillight, high beam indicator light, meter illumination lights and front turn signal/position light.

1. Check the affected bulb.

2. Check the main fuse and the headlight fuse.

3. Check the battery as described in Chapter Three.

4. Check the continuity of the ignition switch (Chapter Ten).

5. Check the continuity of the dimmer switch (Chapter Ten).

6. Check the continuity of the pass switch (Chapter Ten).

7. Locate the symptom among the following descriptions and perform the indicated tests.

The headlight and high beam indicator do not turn on

1. Check the continuity of the headlight bulb and socket.

2. Perform the headlight voltage test in Chapter Ten.

A meter light does not turn on

1. Check the continuity of the affected meter bulb and socket.

2. Perform the meter indicator light test in Chapter Ten.

The taillight does not turn on

NOTE
Refer to Signal System if the brake light does not turn on.

1. Check the continuity of the taillight bulb and socket.

2. Perform the taillight/brake light test in Chapter Ten.

Signal System

The signal system includes the horn, turn signal lights, brake light and indicator lights (except the high beam indicator, which is part of the lighting system).

1. Check the main fuse and the signal system fuse.

2. Check the battery as described in Chapter Three.

3. Check the continuity of the ignition switch (Chapter Ten).

4. Check the wiring and each connector in the signal system circuit.

5. Locate the symptom among the following descriptions and perform the indicated tests.

The horn does not sound

Perform the horn circuit test in Chapter Ten.

The brake light does not turn on

1. Check the continuity of the brake light bulb and socket.

2. Check the continuity of the affected brake light switch (Chapter Ten).

3. Perform the brake light test in *Taillight/Brake Light* in Chapter Ten.

A turn signal light and/or turn signal indicator fails to flash

1. Check the continuity of the affected turn signal bulb and socket.
2. Check the continuity of the bulb and socket for the turn signal indicator light.
3. Check the continuity of the turn signal switch (Chapter Ten).
4. Perform the turn signal flash test (Chapter Ten).

The neutral indicator light does not turn on

1. Check the continuity of the bulb and socket for the neutral indicator light.
2. Check the continuity of the neutral switch (Chapter Ten).
3. Perform the neutral indicator circuit test in Chapter Ten.

The oil level light does not turn on

1. Check the continuity of the bulb and socket for the oil level indicator light.
2. Check the continuity of the oil level switch (Chapter Ten).
3. Perform the oil level indicator test (Chapter Ten).

SUSPENSION AND STEERING

Poor handling may be caused by improper tire pressure, a damaged/bent frame or front steering components, a worn front fork assembly, worn wheel bearings or dragging brakes.

Steering is Sluggish

1. Incorrect steering stem adjustment (too tight).
2. Improperly installed upper or lower fork bridge.
3. Damaged steering head bearings.
4. Tire pressure too low.
5. Worn or damaged tire.

Steering to One Side

1. Bent front or rear axle.
2. Bent frame or fork.

3. Worn or damaged wheel bearings.
4. Worn or damaged swing arm pivot bearings.
5. Damaged steering head bearings.
6. Bent swing arm.
7. Incorrectly installed wheels.
8. Front and rear wheels are not aligned.
9. Uneven front fork adjustment.
10. Fork legs positioned unevenly in the fork bridges.

Front Suspension Noise

1. Loose mounting fasteners.
2. Damaged fork or rear shock absorber.
3. Low fork oil capacity.

Wheel Wobble/Vibration

1. Loose front or rear axle.
2. Loose or damaged wheel bearing(s).
3. Damaged wheel rim(s).
4. Damaged tire(s).
5. Loose swing arm pivot bolt.
6. Unbalanced tire and wheel.
7. Loose spokes (models so equipped).

Hard Suspension (Front)

1. Insufficient tire pressure.
2. Damaged steering head bearings.
3. Incorrect steering head bearing adjustment.
4. Bent fork tubes.
5. Binding slider.
6. Incorrect weight fork oil.
7. Plugged fork oil passage.
8. Worn or damaged fork tube bushing or slider bushing.
9. Damaged damper rod.

Hard Suspension (Rear)

1. Excessive rear tire pressure.
2. Bent or damaged shock absorber.
3. Incorrect shock adjustment.
4. Damaged shock absorber bushing(s).
5. Damaged swing arm pivot bearings.
6. Poorly lubricated suspension components.

Soft Suspension (Front)

1. Insufficient tire pressure.
2. Insufficient fork oil level or fluid capacity.
3. Incorrect oil viscosity.

4. Weak or damaged fork springs.

Soft Suspension (Rear)

1. Insufficient rear tire pressure.
2. Weak or damaged shock absorber spring.
3. Damaged shock absorber.
4. Incorrect shock absorber adjustment.
5. Leaking damper unit.

BRAKE SYSTEM

The front and rear brake units are critical to riding performance and safety. Inspect the front and rear brakes frequently, and repair any problem immediately. When adding or changing the brake fluid, use only DOT 4 brake fluid from a closed container. See Chapter Fourteen for additional information on brake fluid selection and disc brake service.

When checking brake pad wear, make sure the brake pads in each caliper contact the disc squarely. If one of the brake pads is wearing unevenly, suspect a warped or bent brake disc or damaged caliper.

Brake Drag

1. Clogged brake hydraulic system.
2. Sticking caliper pistons.
3. Sticking master cylinder piston.
4. Incorrectly installed brake caliper.
5. Warped brake disc.
6. Incorrect wheel alignment.
7. Contaminated brake pad and disc.
8. Excessively worn brake disc or pad.
9. Caliper not sliding correctly.

Brake Grab

1. Contaminated brake pads and disc.

2. Incorrect wheel alignment.
3. Warped brake disc.
4. Caliper not sliding correctly.

Brake Squeal or Chatter

1. Contaminated brake pads and disc.
2. Incorrectly installed brake caliper.
3. Warped brake disc.
4. Incorrect wheel alignment.

Soft or Spongy Brake Lever or Pedal

1. Low brake fluid level.
2. Air in brake hydraulic system.
3. Leaking brake hydraulic system.
4. Clogged brake hydraulic system.
5. Worn brake caliper seals.
6. Worn master cylinder seals.
7. Sticking caliper piston.
8. Sticking master cylinder piston.
9. Damaged front brake lever.
10. Damaged rear brake pedal.
11. Contaminated brake pads and disc.
12. Excessively worn brake disc or pad.
13. Warped brake disc.

Hard Brake Lever or Pedal Operation

1. Clogged brake hydraulic system.
2. Sticking caliper piston.
3. Sticking master cylinder piston.
4. Worn caliper piston seal.
5. Glazed or worn brake pads.
6. Damaged front brake lever.
7. Damaged rear brake pedal.
8. Caliper not sliding correctly.

CHAPTER THREE

LUBRICATION, MAINTENANCE AND TUNE-UP

This chapter describes lubrication, maintenance and tune-up procedures.

Minor problems found during periodic inspections are generally simple and inexpensive to correct. However, they could lead to major problems if not corrected promptly.

Before servicing the motorcycle, become acquainted with the tools and parts available at motorcycle dealerships and parts supply houses. Also pay attention to the various service and maintenance products such as engine oil, brake fluid, threadlocking compounds and greases. Refer to Chapter One.

If this is the first experience with motorcycle maintenance, start by doing simple tune-up, lubrication and maintenance procedures. Attempt more complicated jobs as you gain experience.

When inspecting the components mentioned in this chapter, compare any measurements to the maintenance and tune-up specifications at the end of this chapter. Replace any part that is damaged, worn or out of specification. During assembly, tighten fasteners as specified.

FUEL TYPE

The engine is designed to use gasoline with a pump octane rating of 86 or higher (or a research octane of 91 or higher). Gasoline with a lower octane rating can cause pinging or spark knock. Either condition can lead to engine damage.

MAINTENANCE INTERVALS

Refer to **Table 1** for maintenance intervals. Strict adherence to these recommendations helps ensure a long service life from the motorcycle. If the motorcycle is operated in an area of high humidity, the lubrication services must be performed more frequently to prevent rust and corrosion.

Most of the procedures listed in **Table 1** are described in this chapter. Procedures that require more than minor disassembly or adjustment are covered in the appropriate chapter in the manual. Refer to the Table of Contents or Index to locate a particular procedure.

CYLINDER NUMBERING

The rear cylinder is the No. 1 cylinder; the front cylinder is No. 2.

ENGINE ROTATION

Engine rotation is *counterclockwise* when viewed from the left side. Use the primary drive gear bolt on the left end of the crankshaft to rotate the crankshaft manually, and always turn the crankshaft *counterclockwise*.

TUNE-UP

A complete tune-up restores performance that is lost due to normal wear and deterioration. Because engine wear occurs over a combined period of time and mileage, perform the engine tune-up procedures at the intervals specified in **Table 1**. More frequent tune-ups may be required if the motorcycle is primarily operated in stop-and-go traffic.

The specification label is located on the inside surface of the left side cover (**Figure 1**). Always refer to the specifications on this label when servicing the motorcycle. If the specifications on the label differ from those in this manual, use the specifications from the label.

When performing a tune-up, service the following items as described in this chapter:

1. Air filter.
2. Spark plugs.
3. Engine compression.
4. Engine oil and filter.
5. Ignition timing.
6. Valve clearance.
7. Carburetor adjustment.
8. Brake system.
9. Suspension components.
10. Tires and wheels.
11. Fasteners.

Air Filter Replacement

The dry-element air filter removes dust and abrasive particles from the incoming air before it enters the carburetor and the engine. Without an air filter, very fine particles could enter the engine and rapidly wear the piston rings, cylinders and bearings. These particles could also clog small passages in the carburetor. Never run the motorcycle without the air filter element installed. Proper air filter servicing can do more to ensure long service from the engine than almost any other single item.

Remove and clean the air filter element at the interval listed in **Table 1**. Replace the air filter if it is soiled, severely clogged or broken in any area.

1. Turn the ignition switch off.
2. Securely support the motorcycle on level ground. Block the rear wheel so the motorcycle will not roll in either direction.

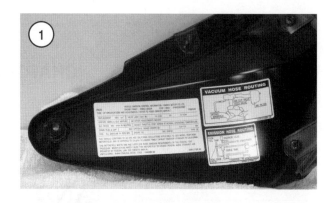

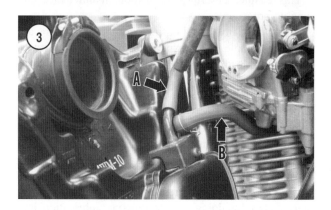

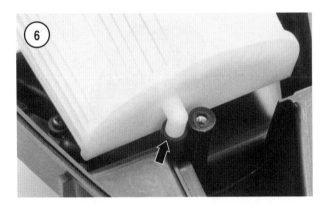

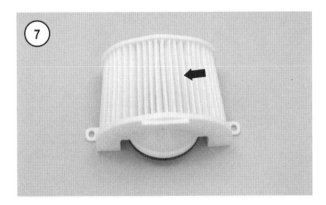

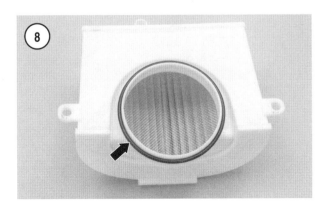

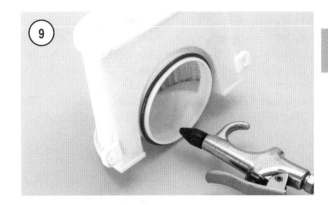

CAUTION
Avoid scratching the fuel tank when loosening the clamping screw in the following step. The fuel tank is shown removed to better illustrate the step.

3. Loosen the clamping screw (A, **Figure 2**) securing the air filter assembly to the carburetor.

4. Remove the screws and washers (B, **Figure 2**) securing the air filter case assembly to the engine.

5. Pull the air filter case assembly partially away from the carburetor.

6. Disconnect the carburetor vacuum chamber breather hose (A, **Figure 3**) and cylinder head breather hose (B) from the backside of the air filter case. Remove the air filter case assembly.

7. Remove the mounting screw (**Figure 4**) and remove the cover from the case.

8. Remove the screws (**Figure 5**) securing the air filter to the case.

9. Disconnect the air filter elbow fitting from the case receptacle (**Figure 6**) and remove the air filter from the case.

10. Inspect the air filter element (**Figure 7**) for tears or other damage that would allow unfiltered air to pass into the engine. Also check the element O-ring gasket (**Figure 8**) for hardness or deterioration. Replace the element and/or O-ring gasket if necessary.

11. Gently tap the air filter element to loosen the dust.

CAUTION
In the next step, do not direct compressed air directly toward the outside surface of the element. This will force the dirt and dust into the pores of the element, thus restricting air flow.

12. Apply compressed air toward the *inside* surface of the element (**Figure 9**) to remove all loosened dirt and dust from the element.

13. Wipe the interior of the air filter housing with a shop
rag dampened with cleaning solvent. Refer to **Figure 10**
(1999-2003 models) or **Figure 11** (2004-on models). Remove any debris that may have passed through a broken
element.

14. Inspect the air filter case-to-carburetor boot and
clamp (**Figure 12**) for deterioration and/or damage. Replace if necessary.

15. Installation is the reverse of removal. Note the following:

  a. Make sure the air filter elbow fitting is inserted correctly into the case receptacle (**Figure 6**). Push it on
until it bottoms.

  b. Securely tighten the screws (**Figure 5**) securing the
air filter to the case.

  c. Connect the carburetor vacuum chamber breather
hose (A, **Figure 3**) and cylinder head breather hose
(B) onto the backside of the air filter case. Push both
on until they seat.

  d. Securely tighten the screws and washers (B, **Figure
2**) securing the air filter case assembly to the engine.

  e. Securely tighten the clamping screw (A, **Figure 2**)
securing the air filter assembly to the carburetor.

Compression Test

An engine compression test is a quick way to check the
condition of the rings, head gaskets, pistons and cylinder
blocks. During each tune-up, record the compression
reading in the maintenance log at the end of the manual.
Compare the current reading with those taken during earlier tune-ups to help identify any developing problems.

Use a screw-in type compression gauge with a flexible
adapter (**Figure 13**) when performing this test. Check the
rubber gasket on the end of the adapter before each use.
This gasket seals the cylinder to ensure accurate compression readings.

Before starting this test, confirm that the cylinder head
bolts are tightened to the specified torque specification
(Chapter Four), the valves are properly adjusted as described in this chapter, and the battery is fully charged to
ensure proper cranking speed.

1. Warm the engine to normal operating temperature, and
turn the engine off.

2. Remove all four spark plugs as described in this chapter.

> *WARNING*
> *Make sure the spark plugs are away from
> the spark plug holes in the cylinder so the
> spark cannot ignite the mixture in that cylin-
> der. If the engine is flooded, do not perform*

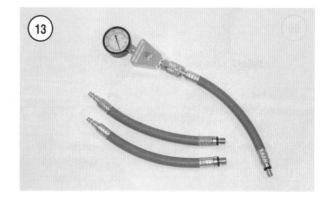

this test. The firing of the spark plug can ig-
nite fuel ejected from the opened spark plug
hole.

WARNING
*During the next step, do not hold the spark
plugs, plug wires or connector by hand. Serious electrical shock may result.*

3. Insert each spark plug into its spark plug cap, and
ground the spark plug against the cylinder head.

4. Screw the compression gauge into one cylinder (**Figure 14**) following the manufacturer's instructions. Make
sure the gauge is properly seated in the cylinder head.
5. Completely open the throttle, and crank the engine until there is no further rise in pressure. Remove the gauge
and record the reading.
6. Repeat Steps 3-5 for the other cylinder.
7. Standard compression pressure is specified in **Table 5**.
When interpreting the results, note the difference between
the cylinders. Large differences indicate worn or broken
rings, leaky or sticky valves, a blown head gasket or a
combination of these problems.
   a. If the compression reading between cylinders does
     not differ by more than 10%, the rings and valves
     are in good condition.
   b. If the reading is low (10% or more) on one of the
     cylinders, it indicates valve or ring trouble. To de-
     termine which, pour about a teaspoon of engine oil
     through the spark plug hole onto the top of the pis-
     ton. Turn the engine over once to distribute the oil,
     then take another compression test and record the
     reading. If the compression returns to normal, the
     rings are worn or defective. If compression does not
     increase, the valves are leaking.

NOTE
*If the compression is low, the engine cannot
be tuned to maximum performance. The
worn parts must be replaced.*

Ignition Timing Inspection

Ignition timing is not adjustable. However, the timing
can be checked to make sure all ignition components are
operating correctly.
1. Support the motorcycle on level ground. Block the rear
wheel so the motorcycle will not roll in either direction.
2. Start the engine and let it reach normal operating temperature. Shut the engine off.
3. Remove the rider seat as described in Chapter Fifteen.
4. Remove the left side footrest assembly as described in
Chapter Fifteen.

NOTE
*On some models, it may not be possible to
remove the front lower side cover bolt due to
interference with the side stand switch.
Leave it in place on the cover.*

5. Remove the bolts securing the left side cover (**Figure
15**) and remove the cover.
6. Remove the timing inspection cover (A, **Figure 16**)
from the clutch cover.

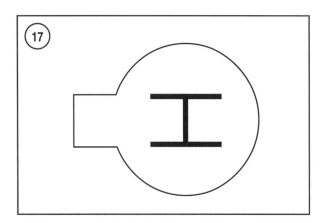

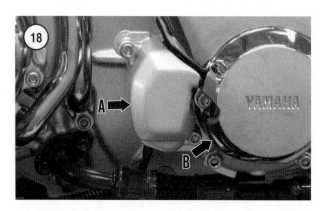

7. Connect a portable tachometer according to the manufacturer's instructions.

8. Remove the bolt securing the rear of the fuel tank. Raise the fuel tank enough to gain access to the rear cylinder spark plug lead. Prop the fuel tank in the raised position.

9. Connect a timing light to the either No. 1 spark plug wire (rear cylinder) following the manufacturer instructions.

10. Start the engine and let it idle at the speed in **Table 5**.

11. Aim the timing light at the timing window. The timing is correct if the timing mark on the flywheel aligns with the cutout in the timing window (**Figure 17**).

12. If the timing is incorrect, there is a problem in the ignition system. Follow the ignition system troubleshooting procedures listed in Chapter Two. The ignition timing cannot be adjusted.

13. Shut off the engine, and disconnect the timing light and portable tachometer.

14. Install the timing inspection cover (A, **Figure 16**) onto the clutch cover.

15. Install the left side cover (**Figure 15**) and tighten the screws securely.

16. Install the left side footrest assembly as described in Chapter Fifteen.

17. Install the rider seat as described in Chapter Fifteen.

Valve Clearance Inspection/Adjustment

Valve clearance measurement and adjustment must be performed with the engine at room temperature (below 35° C [95° F]).

The exhaust valves are located on the rear side of the rear cylinder and on the front side of the front cylinder.

1. Remove the rider seat as described in Chapter Fifteen.

2. Remove the fuel tank as described in Chapter Nine.

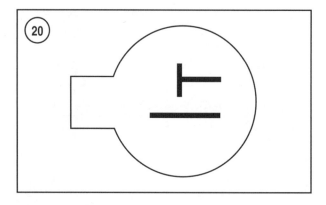

3. Remove the cylinder head covers as described in Chapter Four.

4. Remove the shift rod assembly as described in Chapter Eight.

5. Remove the left side footrest assembly as described in Chapter Fifteen.

6. Remove the decompression solenoid cover (A, **Figure 18**) and camshaft cover (B) as described in Chapter Five.

NOTE
On some models, it may not be possible to remove the front lower side cover bolt due to

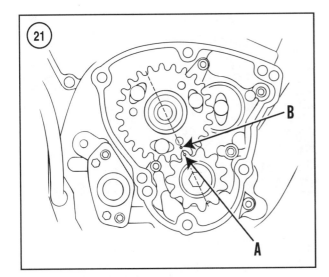

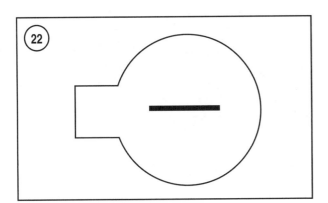

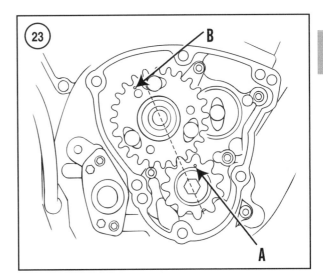

c. If the timing mark and the camshaft marks do not align, rotate the engine an additional 360° until alignment is correct.

NOTE
*A cylinder at TDC on the compression stroke has a **minimal amount** of free play in both rocker arms, indicating that all four valves are closed. The valve lifters take up most of the slack in the free play.*

d. Make sure the rear cylinder is at TDC by pressing each rocker arm. The intake and exhaust rocker arms should have minimal free play.

11. Check the clearance of both the intake and exhaust valves as follows:

a. Insert a feeler gauge between the valve stem and the adjuster end.

b. The clearance (**Table 5**) is correct if there is a slight drag on the feeler gauge when it is inserted and withdrawn.

c. If necessary, adjust the valve(s) as described in Step 12.

12. Position the front cylinder (No. 2) at TDC on the compression stroke as follows:

a. From the crankshaft position achieved in Step 10, use the flywheel nut (**Figure 19**) and turn the crankshaft *counterclockwise* 405° until the front cylinder is at top dead center on the compression stroke.

b. The front cylinder is at TDC on the compression stroke when the mark on the ignition timing rotor aligns with the cutout in the clutch cover (**Figure 22**), and the timing marks appear as shown in **Figure 23**.

interference with the side stand switch. Leave it in place on the cover.

7. Remove the bolts securing the left side cover (**Figure 15**) and remove the cover.

8. Remove the timing inspection cover (A, **Figure 16**) and flywheel nut cover (B) from the clutch cover.

9. Remove all four spark plugs. This makes it easier to rotate the engine.

10. Position the rear cylinder (No. 1) at TDC on the compression stroke as follows:

a. Use the primary drive gear bolt (**Figure 19**) and turn the crankshaft *counterclockwise* until the rear cylinder is at top dead center on the compression stroke.

b. The rear cylinder is at TDC on the compression stroke when the horizontal T-mark on the ignition timing rotor aligns with the cutout in the clutch cover (**Figure 20**), and when the timing mark on the camshaft drive gear (A, **Figure 21**) aligns with camshaft driven gear (B).

NOTE
*A cylinder at TDC on the compression stroke has a **minimal** amount of free play in both rocker arms, indicating all four valves are closed. The valve lifters take up most of the slack in the free play.*

c. Make sure the front cylinder is at TDC by pressing each rocker arm. The intake and exhaust rocker arms should have minimal free play.

13. If necessary, adjust the valve clearance as follows:

a. Loosen the locknut (A, **Figure 24**) on the valve adjuster.

b. With the feeler gauge between the valve stem and the adjuster end, turn the valve adjuster (B, **Figure 24**) to obtain the specified clearance.

c. Hold the adjuster to prevent it from turning, and tighten the valve adjuster locknut to 20 N•m (15 ft.-lb.).

d. Repeat this step until all valves are adjusted to specification.

14. When the clearance of each valve is within specification, reinstall the removed parts by reversing the removal procedure.

SPARK PLUGS

Removal

A spark plug can be used to help determine the operating condition of its cylinder when it is properly read. As each spark plug is removed, label it with its cylinder number and right and left side.

1. Securely support the motorcycle on level ground. Block the rear wheel so the motorcycle will not roll in either direction.

2. Remove the rider seat as described in Chapter Fifteen.

3. Remove the fuel tank as described in Chapter Nine.

4. Grasp the spark plug lead (**Figure 25**) as near to the plug as possible and pull the lead off the plug.

CAUTION
Whenever a spark plug is removed, dirt around it can fall into the plug hole. This can cause serious engine damage.

5. Blow away any dirt that has accumulated in the spark plug well.

NOTE
If a plug is difficult to remove, apply penetrating oil around the base of the plug and let it soak in for about 10-20 minutes.

6. Remove the spark plug (**Figure 26**) with a spark plug wrench with a rubber insert to hold the plug. Label the spark plug by cylinder number and left or right side.

7. Repeat for the remaining spark plugs.

CAUTION
Do not clean the spark plugs with a sand-blasting device. This type of cleaning may leave abrasive material on the plug, which can enter the cylinder and cause damage.

8. Inspect the spark plug carefully. Look for a plug with broken center porcelain, excessively eroded electrodes, and excessive carbon or oil fouling. Replace a damaged plug. If deposits are light, the plug may be cleaned in solvent with a wire brush. Re-gap the plug as described in this section.

9. Inspect the spark plug cap and wires for cracks, hardness or other damage. If necessary, test the spark plug cap resistance as described in Chapter Ten.

Gap and Installation

1. Remove the new spark plugs from the boxes. If the terminal nut is installed, unscrew it from the end of the plug. This nut is not used.

2. Insert a wire feeler gauge between the center and side electrodes of the plug (**Figure 27**). The gap (**Table 5**) is correct if there is a slight drag as the wire is pulled through. If there is no drag or if the gauge will not pass through, bend the side electrode with a gaping tool (**Figure 28**) and set the gap to specification.

3. Apply a light coat of anti-seize compound onto the threads of the spark plug before installing it. Do not use engine oil on the plug threads.

> *CAUTION*
> *The cylinder head is aluminum. Cross-threading the spark plug can easily damage the spark plug hole threads.*

4. Screw the spark plug in by hand until it seats. Very little effort is required. If force is necessary, the plug is cross-threaded. Unscrew it and try again.

> *CAUTION*
> *Do not over tighten the spark plug. This will distort the plug gasket and may strip the threads in the cylinder head.*

5. Tighten the spark plugs to 18 N•m (159 in.-lb.). If a torque wrench is not available, turn the plug until the gasket makes contact with the head, then tighten the plug an additional quarter to one-half turn. If reinstalling old, re-gapped spark plugs with the old gasket, tighten the spark plug an additional quarter turn.

> *CAUTION*
> *Do not use a plastic hammer or any type of tool to tap the plug cap assembly onto the spark plug. The cap assembly will be damaged.*

> *NOTE*
> *Be sure to push the plug cap all the way down to make full contact with the spark plug post. If the cap does not completely contact the plug, the engine may falter.*

6. Install each plug cap onto the correct spark plug. Press the cap onto the spark plug and rotate the assembly slightly in both directions. Make sure it is attached to the spark plug.

7. Install the fuel tank as described in Chapter Nine.

8. Install the rider seat as described in Chapter Fifteen.

Heat Range

Spark plugs are available in various heat ranges that are hotter or colder than the plugs originally installed by the manufacturer.

Select a spark plug with a heat range designed for the loads and conditions under which the motorcycle will be operated. A spark plug with an incorrect heat range can foul, overheat and cause piston damage.

In general, use a hot spark plug for low speeds and low temperatures. Use a cold spark plug for high speeds, high engine loads and high temperatures. The plug should operate hot enough to burn off unwanted deposits, but not so hot that it is damaged or causes preignition. To determine if plug heat range is correct, remove each spark plug and examine the insulator.

Do not change the spark plug heat range to compensate for adverse engine or carburetor conditions.

When replacing plugs, make sure the reach (**Figure 29**) is correct. A longer than standard plug could interfere with the piston resulting in engine damage.

Refer to **Table 5** for the recommended spark plugs.

Reading

Reading the spark plugs can provide information about spark plug operation, air/fuel mixture composition and engine conditions (such as oil consumption or pistons). Before checking new spark plugs, operate the motorcycle under a medium load for approximately 6 miles (10 km). Avoid prolonged idling before shutting off the engine.

Remove the spark plugs as described in this section. Examine each plug and compare it to those in **Figure 30**, typical. Refer to the following sections to determine the operating conditions.

If the spark plugs are being inspected to determine if carburetor jetting is correct, start with new spark plugs and operate the motorcycle at the load that corresponds to the jetting information desired. For example, if the main jet is in question, operate the motorcycle at full throttle, shut the engine off and coast to a stop.

Normal condition

A light tan- or gray-colored deposit on the firing tip, and no abnormal gap wear or erosion indicate good engine, ignition and air/fuel mixture conditions. A plug with the proper heat range is being used. It may be serviced and returned to use.

Carbon fouled

Soft, dry, sooty deposits covering the entire firing end of the plug are evidence of incomplete combustion. Even though the firing end of the plug is dry, the deposits decrease the plug's insulation. The carbon forms an electrical path that bypasses the electrodes resulting in a misfire. One or more of the following conditions can cause carbon fouling:
1. Air/fuel mixture too rich.
2. Spark plug heat range too cold.
3. Clogged air filter.
4. Improperly operating ignition component.
5. Ignition component failure.
6. Low engine compression.

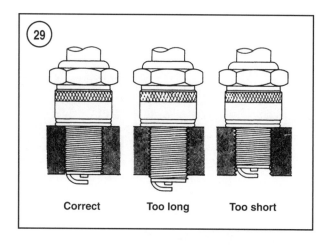

Correct   Too long   Too short

7. Prolonged idling.

Oil fouled

An oil fouled plug has a black insulator tip, a damp oily film over the firing end and a carbon layer over the entire nose. The electrodes are not worn. Common causes for this condition are:
1. Incorrect air/fuel mixture.
2. Low idle speed or prolonged idling.
3. Ignition component failure.
4. Spark plug heat range too cold.
5. Engine still being broken in.
6. Valve guides worn.
7. Piston rings worn or broken.

Oil fouled spark plugs may be cleaned in an emergency, but it is better to replace them. It is important to correct the cause of fouling before the engine is returned to service.

Gap bridging

Plugs with this condition have deposits building up between the electrodes. The deposits reduce the gap and eventually close it entirely. If this condition is encountered, check for excessive carbon or oil in the combustion chamber. Be sure to locate and correct the cause of this condition.

Overheating

Badly worn electrodes and premature gap wear are signs of overheating, along with a gray or white blistered porcelain insulator surface. This condition is commonly caused by a spark plug with a heat range that is too hot. If the spark plug heat range is correct, consider the following causes:

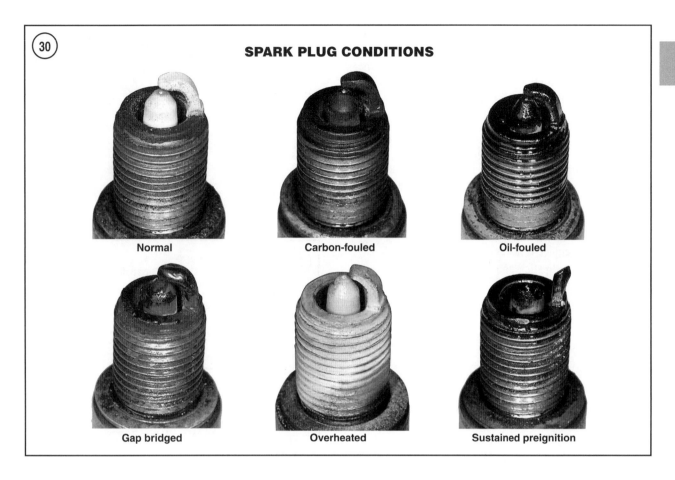

SPARK PLUG CONDITIONS

Normal   Carbon-fouled   Oil-fouled

Gap bridged   Overheated   Sustained preignition

1. Lean air/fuel mixture.
2. Improperly operating ignition component.
3. Engine lubrication system malfunction.
4. Cooling system malfunction.
5. Engine air leak.
6. Improper spark plug installation (over-tightening).
7. No spark plug gasket.

Worn out

Corrosive gases formed by combustion and high voltage sparks have eroded the electrodes. A spark plug in this condition requires more voltage to fire under hard acceleration. Install a new spark plug.

Preignition

If the electrodes are melted, preignition is probably the cause. Check for carburetor mounting or intake manifold leaks and advanced ignition timing. The plug heat range may also be too hot. Find the cause of the preignition before returning the engine to service. For additional information on preignition, refer to Chapter Two.

ENGINE OIL

The engine is a *dry sump* type with no oil pan. The engine oil is stored in the oil tank portion of the transfer case and is pumped back and forth between the transfer case and the engine. The transfer case has its own supply and type of oil and is not compatible with the engine oil. Do not intermix the two different lubricants.

Engine Oil Level Check

1. Securely support the motorcycle on level ground. Block the rear wheel so the motorcycle will not roll in either direction.
2. Start the engine and let it reach normal operating temperature.
3. Stop the engine and let the oil settle.
4. Remove the rider seat as described in Chapter Fifteen.

CAUTION
If the motorcycle is not parked correctly on level ground, the oil level reading will be incorrect.

5. Have an assistant hold the motorcycle so it stands straight and level.

6. Remove the engine oil dipstick (**Figure 31**) from the oil tank filler neck on the transfer case cover.

7. Wipe off the dipstick with a clean shop cloth.

8. Reinsert and then remove the dipstick.

9. The oil level should be between the maximum and minimum lines on the dipstick (**Figure 32**).

10. If necessary, insert a funnel into the oil tank filler neck and add enough of the recommended oil (see **Table 4**) to raise the oil to the proper level. Do not overfill the oil tank.

11. Inspect the O-ring seal on the dipstick for hardness or deterioration. Replace if necessary.

12. Reinstall the dipstick and push it down until it bottoms.

13. Install the rider seat as described in Chapter Fifteen.

Engine Oil and Filter Change

The recommended oil and filter change interval is specified in **Table 1**. If a motorcycle is operated under dusty or other extreme conditions, change the oil more frequently than recommended.

Select engine oil with a API service classification of SE. The classification is on the container label. Try to use the same brand of oil at each oil change and avoid the use of oil additives as they may cause clutch slip. Refer to **Table 4** for oil capacity. Select a viscosity for the anticipated ambient air temperatures, not the engine oil temperature.

> *CAUTION*
> *Do not use engine oil classified as **Energy Conserving**. These types of oils are designed specifically for automotive applications. The additives added to these oils may cause engine and/or clutch damage in motorcycle applications.*

> *NOTE*
> *Never dispose of engine oil in the trash, on the ground or down a storm drain. Many service stations and oil retailers accept used oil for recycling. Do not combine other fluids with engine oil for recycling. To locate a recycler, contact the American Petroleum Institute (API) at **www.recycleoil.org**.*

1. Start the engine and run it until it reaches normal operating temperature, then turn the engine off.

2. Remove the rider seat as described in Chapter Fifteen.

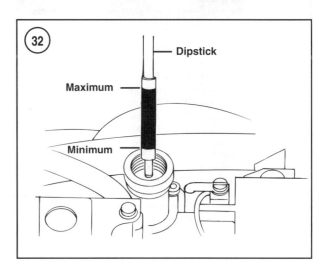

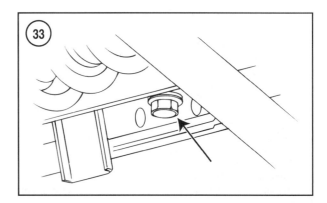

3. Securely support the motorcycle on a level surface. Block the front wheel so the motorcycle will not roll in either direction.

> *CAUTION*
> *There are two different drain bolts, one on the crankcase and one on the oil tank portion of the transfer case. Both bolts must be removed to change the engine oil.*

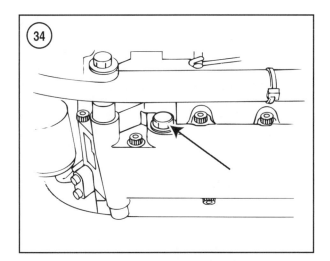

8. Remove the oil filter (**Figure 35**) from the oil filter mount.

9. Apply fresh oil to the O-ring seal of a *new* oil filter and install the filter. Tighten the filter to 17 N•m (150 in.-lb.).

10. Pull straight up and remove the engine oil dipstick (**Figure 31**) from the oil tank filler neck on the transfer case cover.

11A. If the engine has *not* been disassembled, perform the following:

    a. Insert a funnel into the oil tank filler neck.

    b. Add approximately 2.5 L (2.6 qt.) of oil to the tank (**Table 4**).

CAUTION
Remove the funnel, install the oil dipstick and push it down until it bottoms.

    c. Start the engine and rev it 3 to 5 times, then shut the engine off.

    d. Remove the dipstick and add the remaining oil quantity.

    e. Remove the funnel, install the oil dipstick and push it down until it bottoms.

CAUTION
If the engine has been disassembled, oil must be added to the crankcase prior to the initial startup of the non-lubricated engine. Failure to do so will cause internal engine damage.

11B. If the engine *has been disassembled*, perform the following:

    a. Remove the crankcase oil fill cap (**Figure 36**) from the top right side of the crankcase.

    b. Insert a funnel into the crankcase fill cap opening.

    c. Add approximately 2.5 L (2.6 qt.) of oil to the crankcase.

    d. Install the crankcase oil fill cap and tighten securely.

CAUTION
Remove the funnel, install the oil dipstick and push it down until it bottoms.

    e. Start the engine and rev it 3 to 5 times, then shut the engine off.

    f. Insert a funnel into the oil tank filler neck and add the remaining quantity of oil.

    g. Remove the funnel, install the oil dipstick and push it down until it bottoms.

12. Check the oil flow as follows:

4. Place a drain pan under the crankcase, and remove the transfer case oil tank drain bolt (**Figure 33**) and the crankcase drain bolt (**Figure 34**).

5. Let the oil drain for at least 15-20 minutes.

6. Inspect the sealing washer on both drain bolts. Replace the washer(s) if its condition is in doubt.

7. Install both oil drain bolts and washers and tighten to 43 N•m (32 ft.-lb.).

a. Place a clean shop cloth under the external oil line oil gallery bolt on the front cylinder (**Figure 37**) and loosen the bolt.

b. Start the engine and let it idle. Oil should seep from the loosened oil gallery bolt. If it does not do so within one minute, turn the engine off and inspect the oil lines, oil filter and oil pump for damage.

c. Turn the engine off.

d. Secure the oil line with an open end wrench and tighten the oil line gallery bolt to 21 N•m (15.5 ft.-lb.).

e. Even though the oil flows correctly; check the oil pressure as described in the following procedure.

13. Check for oil leaks. Once the oil has settled, check the oil level on the dipstick (**Figure 32**). Adjust the oil level if necessary.

14. Install the rider seat as described in Chapter Fifteen.

Oil Pressure Check

Tools

The following Yamaha special tools, or their equivalent, are required for this procedure:

1. Oil pressure gauge (part No. 90890-03153).
2. Oil pressure gauge adapter E (part No. 90890-03129).

Procedure

1. Securely support the motorcycle on level ground. Block the rear wheel so the motorcycle will not roll in either direction.

2. Connect a portable tachometer following the manufacturer's instructions.

3. Place a layer of heat protective material over the front cylinder exhaust pipe to protect the oil pressure gauge hose.

4. Perform *Engine Oil Level Check* as described in this section. The engine oil must be at 90° C (140° F) to achieve accurate test results.

5. Place a drain pan under the oil gallery bolt on the right side.

> *WARNING*
> *The exhaust system and engine oil are extremely hot. Protect hands and arms during this procedure.*

> *NOTE*
> ***Figure 38*** *is shown with the exhaust system removed for clarity.*

6. Remove the oil gallery hex head bolt and washer. Refer to **Figure 38** and **Figure 39**. Keep hands out of the

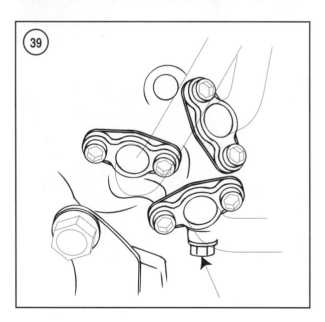

way as some *hot* oil will drain out of the crankcase dry sump.

7. Install the adapter and the oil pressure gauge onto the oil gallery threaded hole (**Figure 40**). Tighten securely.

8. Start the engine and run at approximately 900 rpm.

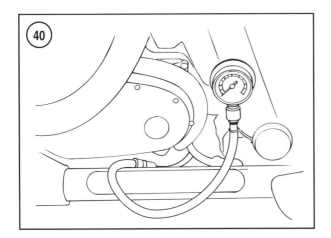

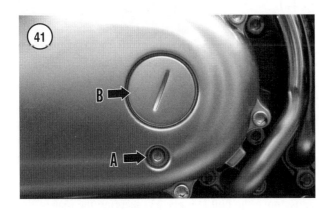

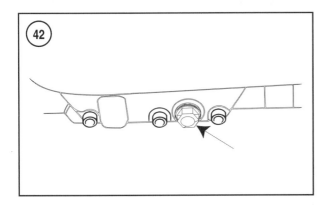

9. The specified oil pressure is 40-80 kPa (5.8-11.6 psi) at 900 rpm.

10. If the oil pressure is below specification, the probable causes are as follows:

a. Faulty oil pump.

b. Clogged oil filter and/or pickup screen on oil pump.

c. Leaking oil passage(s) within engine.

d. Oil viscosity too low.

11. If the oil pressure is above specification, the probable causes are the following:

a. Faulty oil pump.

b. Faulty oil filter.

c. Oil viscosity too high.

12. Disconnect the oil pressure gauge and adapter.

13. Install a *new* washer and the oil gallery hex head bolt. Tighten to 20 N•m (15 ft.-lb.).

14. Check oil level and adjust if necessary.

TRANSFER GEARCASE

Transfer Gearcase Oil Level Check

1. Securely support the motorcycle on level ground. Block the rear wheel so the motorcycle will not roll in either direction.

CAUTION
If the motorcycle is not parked correctly, the oil level reading will be incorrect.

2. Have an assistant hold the motorcycle so it stands straight and level.

3. Remove the oil level check bolt and gasket (A, **Figure 41**) on the transfer gearcase outer cover.

4. The oil level should be up to the brim on the threaded hole.

5. If necessary, remove the oil filler cap (B, **Figure 41**), insert a funnel into the oil filler neck and add enough of the recommended oil (**Table 4**) to raise the oil to the proper level. Do not overfill the transfer gearcase.

6. Inspect the O-ring seal on the oil filler cap for hardness or deterioration. Replace if necessary.

7. Install the oil filler cap and tighten to 8 N•m (71 in.-lb.).

8. Install the oil level check bolt and gasket and tighten to 8 N•m (71 in.-lb.).

Transfer Gearcase Oil Change

1. Ride the motorcycle several miles until the oil has reached normal operating temperature.

2. Securely support the motorcycle on a level surface. Block the front wheel so the motorcycle will not roll in either direction.

3. Remove the oil filler cap (B, **Figure 41**) to help speed up the flow of oil.

4. Place a drain pan under the transfer gearcase, and remove the drain bolt and washer (**Figure 42**) on the base of the gearcase.

5. Let the oil drain for at least 15-20 minutes.

6. Inspect the sealing washer on the drain bolt. Replace the washer if its condition is in doubt.

7. Install the oil drain bolt and washer and tighten to 18 N•m (159 in.-lb.).

8. Remove the oil filler cap (B, **Figure 41**) and insert a funnel into the oil filler neck and add 0.4 L (0.42 qt.) of the recommended oil (**Table 4**). Do not overfill the transfer gearcase.

9. Inspect the O-ring seal on the oil filler cap for hardness or deterioration. Replace if necessary. Install the oil filler cap and tighten to 8 N•m (71 in.-lb.)

10. Ride the motorcycle several miles until the transfer gearcase oil has reached normal operating temperature.

11. Check for oil leaks. Once the oil has settled, check the oil level as described in this section. Adjust the oil level if necessary.

FUEL AND EXHAUST SYSTEMS

Fuel Line Inspection

Inspect the condition of all fuel lines for cracks or deterioration; replace them if necessary. Make sure the hose clamps are in place and holding securely.

Fuel Filter Replacement

Replace the fuel filter when it is dirty or at the interval specified in **Table 1**. Refer to Chapter Nine.

Exhaust System Inspection

Check for leaks at all fittings. Tighten all bolts and nuts; replace any gaskets as necessary. Refer to Chapter Nine.

Emission Control System Inspection
(California Models)

At the service intervals in **Table 1**, check all of the emission control lines and the EVAP canister for loose connections or damage. Refer to Chapter Nine.

Idle Speed Adjustment

Before adjusting the idle speed, clean or replace the air filter, and test the engine compression. Also make sure the throttle cables are adjusted correctly. Idle speed cannot be properly adjusted if these items are not within specification. Refer to the procedures in this chapter.

1. Securely support the motorcycle on level ground. Block the rear wheel so the motorcycle will not roll in either direction.

2. Remove the rider seat as described in Chapter Fifteen.

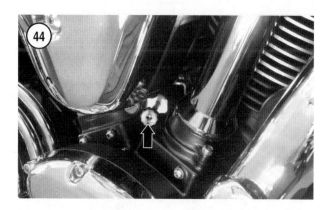

3. Remove the bolt (**Figure 43**) securing the rear of the fuel tank. Raise the fuel tank sufficiently to gain access to the rear cylinder spark plug lead. Secure the fuel tank in the raised position.

4. Attach a portable tachometer to the No. 1 cylinder (the rear cylinder) spark plug lead following the manufacturer's instructions.

5. Start the engine and warm it to normal operating temperature.

6. Turn the throttle stop screw (**Figure 44**) to set the idle speed to the specification in **Table 5**.

7. Rev the engine a couple of times and make sure the speed remains as set. Readjust as necessary.

8. Shut off the engine and disconnect the portable tachometer.

9. Lower the fuel tank, and install the mounting bolt. Tighten the bolt to 7 N•m (62 in.-lb.).

10. Install the rider seat as described in Chapter Fifteen.

Throttle Cable Adjustment

Always check the throttle cables before making any carburetor adjustments. Too much free play causes delayed throttle response; too little free play causes unstable idling.

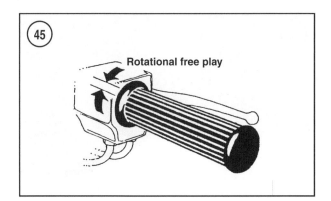

Rotational free play

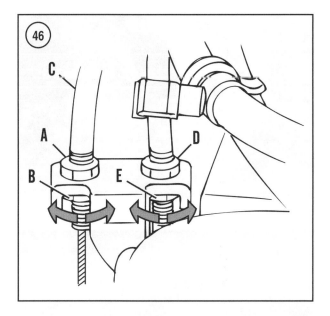

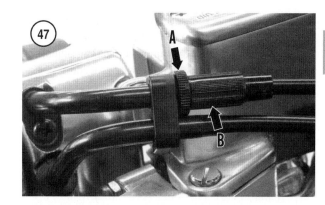

Inspect the throttle cables from the throttle grip to the carburetor. Make sure they are not kinked or chafed. Replace the cables if necessary.

Make sure the throttle grip rotates smoothly from fully closed to fully open. Check free play with the handlebars at the center, full-left and full-right steering positions.

Check free play at the throttle grip flange (**Figure 45**). Free play should be within the range specified in **Table 5**. If adjustment is necessary, proceed as follows:

1. Securely support the motorcycle on level ground. Block the rear wheel so the motorcycle will not roll in either direction.

2. Remove the rider seat as described in Chapter Fifteen.

3. Remove the fuel tank and air filter housing as described in Chapter Nine.

4. At the handlebar, make sure the throttle cable locknut and adjuster are tight.

5. At the carburetor assembly, loosen the decelerator (push) cable locknut (A, **Figure 46**).

6. Rotate the decelerator cable adjuster (B, **Figure 46**) and take up all slack in the decelerator cable (C).

7. Loosen the accelerator (pull) cable locknut (D, **Figure 46**).

8. Rotate the accelerator cable adjuster (E, **Figure 46**) in either direction until the specified amount of throttle cable free play is achieved.

9. Tighten both locknuts securely.

NOTE
If the correct amount of free play cannot be achieved at the carburetor, additional adjustment can be obtained at the adjuster on the handlebar.

10. At the handlebar, loosen the throttle cable adjuster locknut (A, **Figure 47**).

11. Rotate the adjuster (B, **Figure 47**) in either direction until the correct amount of free play is achieved. Tighten the adjuster locknut.

WARNING
If idle speed increases when the handlebar is turned to right or left, check the throttle cable routing. Do not ride the motorcycle in this unsafe condition.

12. Start the engine and let it idle in neutral. Listen to the engine speed while turning the handlebar from steering lock to steering lock. If idle speed changes as the handlebar is turned, the throttle cable is routed incorrectly or there is insufficient cable free play. Make the necessary corrections.

CONTROL CABLE LUBRICATION (NON-NYLON LINED CABLES ONLY)

Lubricate the non-nylon lined control cables with a cable lubricant and cable lubricator (**Figure 48**) during cable adjustment or if they become stiff or sluggish. The main cause of cable breakage or stiffness is improper lubrication. Periodic lubrication ensures a long service life. Inspect the cables for fraying, and check the sheath for chafing. Replace any defective cables.

> *CAUTION*
> *If servicing nylon-lined and other aftermarket cables, follow the cable manufacturer's lubrication instructions.*

> *NOTE*
> *If lubricant does not flow out the end of the cable, check the entire cable for fraying, bending or other damage.*

Lubricate and adjust the control cables at the intervals specified in **Table 1**. When lubricating a cable, also inspect it for fraying and check the cable sheath for chafing.

Throttle Cable

1. Remove the two mounting screws and separate the halves of the right handlebar switch assembly (**Figure 49**) as described in Chapter Ten.
2. Disengage the ends (**Figure 50**) of both the pull and push cables from the throttle drum.
3. Attach a cable lubricator to the cable following the manufacturer's instructions.

> *NOTE*
> *Place a shop cloth at the carburetor end of the cable to catch all excess lubricant that flows out.*

4. Insert the nozzle of the lubricant can into the lubricator (**Figure 48**), press the button on the can and hold it down until the lubricant begins to flow out of the other end of the cable. If lubricant does not flow out the end of the cable, check the entire cable for fraying, bending or other damage.
5. Remove the lubricator, reconnect the cables and adjust the throttle cable as described in this chapter. When installing the right handlebar assembly, make sure the pin on the switch assembly aligns with the hole in the handlebar.

Clutch Cable

1. At the handlebar, slide the clutch lever boot (**Figure 51**) away from the adjuster.
2. Loosen the clutch cable locknut (A, **Figure 52**) and rotate the adjuster (B) to provide maximum slack in the cable.
3. Disconnect the cable end from the clutch hand lever.

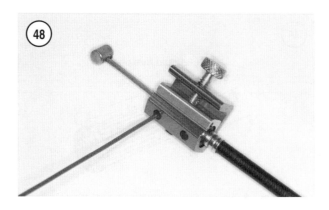

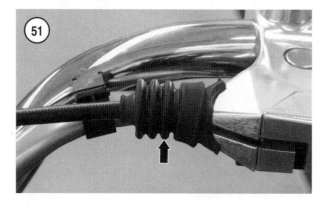

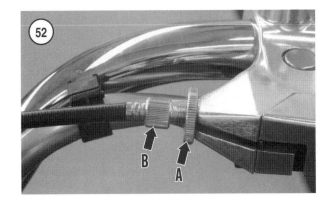

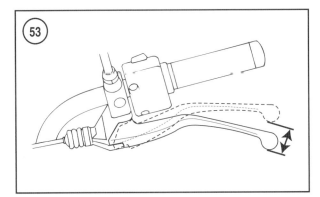

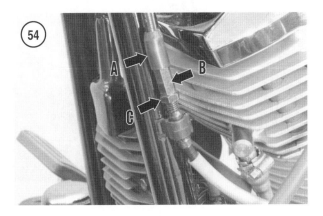

4. Attach a cable lubricator to the cable following the manufacturer's instructions.

NOTE
Place a shop cloth at the clutch lever end of the cable to catch any excess lubricant that flows out.

5. Insert the nozzle of the lubricant can into the lubricator (**Figure 48**), press the button on the can and hold it down until the lubricant begins to flow out of the other end of the cable.

NOTE
If lubricant does not flow out the end of the cable, check the entire cable for fraying, bending or other damage.

6. Remove the lubricator, and reconnect and adjust the clutch cable as described in this chapter.

CLUTCH CABLE ADJUSTMENT

Adjust the clutch cable free play at the interval in **Table 1**. The clutch will not engage or disengage properly if the free play is not maintained within the range specified in **Table 5**. Note that this clutch release mechanism loosens as the engine warms up. Therefore, set the free play to the minimum setting.

Measure the clutch lever free play at the end of the hand lever (**Figure 53**). If the clutch lever free play is outside the specification in **Table 5**, adjust as follows:

1. At the clutch hand lever, pull the rubber boot (**Figure 51**) back from the adjuster.
2. Loosen the clutch cable locknut (A, **Figure 52**).
3. Turn the adjuster (B, **Figure 52**) in or out to set the free play.
4. Tighten the locknut and reinstall the rubber boot.
5. If the proper free play cannot be achieved at the hand lever adjuster, adjust the clutch cable at the mid-point adjuster as follows:

   a. Slide the rubber boot (A, **Figure 54**) up off the clutch cable adjuster.

   b. Loosen the locknut (B, **Figure 54**) on the clutch cable adjuster.

   c. Turn the adjuster (C, **Figure 54**) in either direction to set the free play.

   d. Tighten the locknut securely.

6. Recheck the amount of free play at the hand lever and perform any minor adjustments at the lever if necessary.

TRANSMISSION

Shift Pedal Adjustment

Measure the length of the shift rod on the shift pedal assembly. The shift rod length equals the distance from the center of the shift pedal pivot to the center of the shift lever pivot points (**Figure 55**). If the length does not equal the value specified in **Table 5**, adjust the length as follows:

1. Loosen the locknut (A, **Figure 55**) at each end of the shift rod.
2. Turn the shift rod (B, **Figure 55**) to attain the desired length.

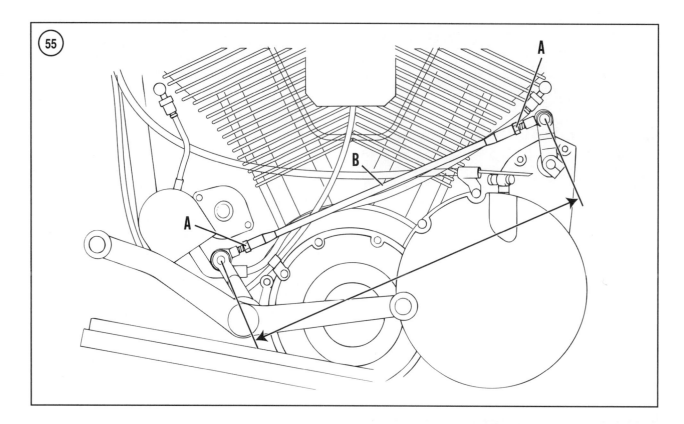

3. Tighten each locknut (**Figure 56**) securely.

SIDESTAND

Inspection

Check the operation of the sidestand and the sidestand switch at the interval in **Table 1**.

1. Securely support the motorcycle on level ground. Block the rear wheel so the motorcycle will not roll in either direction.

2. Operate the sidestand, and check its movement and spring tension. Replace the spring if it is weak or damaged.

3. Lubricate the sidestand pivot surfaces with lithium soap grease.

4. Check the sidestand switch operation as follows:

    a. Park the motorcycle on a level surface. Both wheels must be on the ground.

    b. Sit on the motorcycle and raise the sidestand.

    c. Shift the transmission to neutral.

    d. Start the engine and let it idle.

    e. Pull in and hold the clutch lever. Shift the transmission into gear.

    f. While holding the clutch lever in, move the sidestand down. The engine should stop.

    g. If the engine does not stop when the sidestand is lowered, inspect the sidestand switch as described in Chapter Ten.

5. If the sidestand nut was loosened, tighten it to 48 N•m (35 ft.-lb.).

GENERAL LUBRICATION

Swing Arm Bearings

Clean the swing arm bearings in solvent and pack them with medium weight wheel bearing grease at the intervals

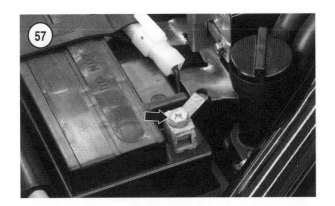

BATTERY

All the models covered in this manual are equipped with a maintenance free, sealed battery. The electrolyte level cannot be checked. Never attempt to remove the sealing bar cap from the top of the battery.

The negative side of the battery is ground. When removing the battery, always disconnect the negative cable first (**Figure 57**), then the positive cable. This minimizes the chance of a tool shorting to ground when the positive cable is disconnected.

Battery specifications are listed in **Table 3**.

specified in **Table 1**. The swing arm must be removed to service the bearings. Refer to Chapter Thirteen.

Steering Stem Bearings

Remove, clean and lubricate the steering stem bearings with lithium grease at the interval specified in **Table 1**. Refer to the procedure in Chapter Twelve.

Wheel Bearings

Worn wheel bearings cause excessive wheel play that will result in vibration and other steering troubles. Inspect the wheel bearings at the intervals specified in **Table 1**. Refer to the procedures in Chapter Eleven.

Miscellaneous

Unless otherwise indicated, lubricate the following items with lithium soap grease: O-rings, oil seal lips, shift pedal shaft, brake pedal shaft, footrest pivots, clutch lever, front brake lever, control cable ends, and the sidestand bolt and sliding surfaces.

Removal/Installation

1. Securely support the motorcycle on level ground. Block the rear wheel so the motorcycle will not roll in either direction.

2. Remove the rider seat as described in Chapter Fifteen.

3. Disconnect the negative cable (A, **Figure 58**) and the secondary negative connector (B) from the battery.

4. Pull back the boot (A, **Figure 59**) and disconnect the positive cable.

5. Remove the battery hold-down strap (B, **Figure 59**), and lift the battery from the battery box.

6. Set the battery on some newspapers or shop cloths to protect the workbench surface.

7. After the battery has been recharged or replaced, install it by reversing these removal steps. Note the following:

   a. Apply dielectric grease to each battery terminal.

   b. Connect the positive battery cable. Then connect the negative cable and the secondary negative connector.

   c. Tighten each screw securely.

Inspection

Check the state of charge in a maintenance free battery by measuring the voltage with the battery disconnected.

If the battery case is damaged and electrolyte spills onto clothing or skin, immediately neutralize the electrolyte with a solution of baking soda and water.

> *WARNING*
> *A damaged battery case could leak electrolyte. Electrolyte splashed into the eyes is extremely harmful. Always wear safety glasses when servicing a battery. If electrolyte gets into the eyes, call a physician immediately. Force the eyes open and flush them with cool, clean water for approximately 15 minutes or until medical help arrives.*

1. Remove the battery as described in this section. Do not clean the battery while it is mounted in the frame.

2. Inspect the battery pads in the battery box (**Figure 60**) for contamination or damage. Clean the pads and compartment with a solution of baking soda and water.

3. Set the battery on a stack of newspapers or shop cloths to protect the workbench surface.

4. Check the entire battery case (A, **Figure 61**) for cracks or other damage. If the battery case is warped, discolored or has a raised top, the battery has been overcharged or overheated. Replace the battery.

5. Check the battery terminals and bolts (B, **Figure 61**) for corrosion or damage. Clean parts thoroughly with a solution of baking soda and water. Replace severely corroded or damaged parts.

6. If the top of the battery is corroded, clean it with a stiff bristle brush using the baking soda and water solution.

7. Check the battery cable terminals for corrosion and damage. If corrosion is minor, clean the battery cable terminals with a stiff wire brush. Replace severely worn or damaged cables.

8. Check the state of charge by connecting a digital voltmeter across the battery terminals. Make sure the battery temperature is approximately 20° C (68° F). Connect the voltmeter negative test lead to the negative battery terminal and the positive test lead to the positive terminal (**Figure 62**).

   a. If the battery voltage is 12.8 volts or higher, the battery is fully charged.

   b. If the battery voltage is 12.0-12.8 volts, the battery is undercharged and requires charging.

   c. If battery voltage is less than 12.0 volts, replace the battery.

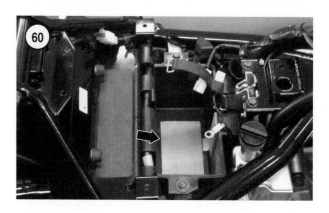

Charging

A digital voltmeter and a charger with an adjustable amperage output are required when charging a maintenance free battery. If this equipment is not available, have the battery charged by a shop with the proper equipment. Excessive voltage and amperage from an unregulated charger can damage the battery and shorten service life. Refer to the label (**Figure 63**) on top of the battery.

A battery self-discharges approximately one percent of its capacity each day. If the battery is not in use (without any loads connected), and loses its charge within a week after charging, the battery is defective. If the motorcycle is not used for long periods of time, an automatic battery charger with variable voltage and amperage outputs is recommended for optimum battery service life.

> *WARNING*
> *During charging, highly explosive hydrogen gas is released from the battery. Only charge the battery in a well-ventilated area away from open flames, including appliance pilot lights. Do not allow smoking in the area. Never check the charge of the battery by arcing across the terminals; the resulting spark can ignite the hydrogen gas.*

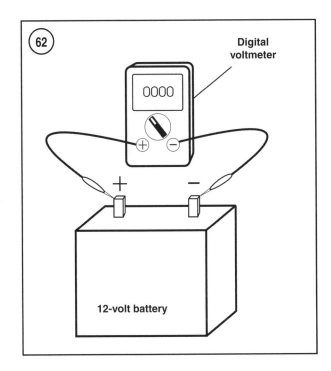

Digital voltmeter

0000

+ −

12-volt battery

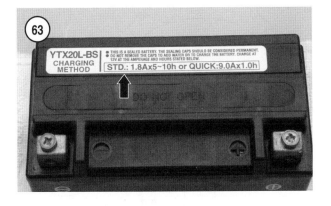

YTX20L-BS
CHARGING
METHOD
STD.: 1.8Ax5~10h or QUICK:9.0Ax1.0h

CAUTION
Always disconnect the battery cables from the battery. If the cables are left connected during the charging procedure, the charger may damage the diodes within the voltage regulator/rectifier.

NOTE
Some maintenance chargers can be used while the battery is connected to the motorcycle. These types of chargers are specifically designed for motorcycle batteries and will not damage the diodes in the regulator/rectifier.

1. Remove the battery from the motorcycle as described in this section.

2. Set the battery on a stack of newspapers or shop cloths to protect the surface of the workbench.

3. Connect the positive charger lead to the positive battery terminal and the negative charger lead to the negative battery terminal.

4. Set the charger to 12 volts and select a low amperage setting.

CAUTION
Never set the battery charger to more than 4 amps. The battery will be damaged if the charge rate exceeds 4 amps.

5. The charging time depends on the discharged condition of the battery. Use the charging amperage and length of time suggested on the battery label. Normally, a battery should be charged at a slow rate of 1/10 its rated capacity.

6. Turn the charger on.

7. After the battery has been charged for the pre-determined time, turn the charger off and disconnect the leads.

8. Wait 30 minutes, and then measure the battery voltage. Refer to the following:

   a. If the battery voltage is greater than 12.8 volts, the battery is fully charged.

   b. If the battery voltage is less than 12.8 volts, the battery is undercharged and requires charging.

9. If the battery remains stable for one hour, the battery is charged.

10. Install the battery into the motorcycle as described in this chapter.

New Battery Initialization

Always replace a maintenance free battery with another maintenance free battery. Also make sure the battery is charged completely before installing it. Failure to do so will reduce the life of the battery. Check with the dealership on the type of pre-service that the battery received.

NOTE
Recycle the old battery. Most motorcycle dealerships will accept an old battery in trade with the purchase of a new one. Never place an old battery in the household trash. It is illegal in most states to place any acid or lead (heavy metal) contents in landfills.

TIRES

Tire Pressure

Check and adjust tire pressure to accommodate the rider and cargo weight. The tire pressure specifications are shown in **Table 2**.

Tire Inspection

The likelihood of tire failure increases with tread wear. Check tire tread for excessive wear, cuts and embedded objects. Also check for high spots that indicate internal tire damage. Replace tires that show high spots or swelling. If the tire is punctured, mark its location with a light crayon before pulling the object out. This will help locate the hole for repair. Refer to Chapter Eleven for tire changing procedures.

Measure tread wear (**Figure 64**) at the center of the tire tread with a tread depth gauge or small ruler. Because tires sometimes wear unevenly, measure the wear at several points. Replace the original equipment tires if any tread depth measurement is less than the value specified in **Table 2**.

Wheel Inspection

Frequently inspect the wheels for cracks, warping or dents. A damaged bead surface may cause an air leak.

Wheel runout is the amount of wobble a wheel shows as it rotates. To quickly check runout, support the bike with the wheel off the ground. Slowly turn the wheel while holding a pointer solidly against a fork leg or the swing arm with the other end against the rim (**Figure 65**). If either axial runout (side-to-side movement) or radial runout (up-and-down movement) exceeds the specification in **Table 5**, remeasure both axial and radial runout as described in Chapter Eleven.

FRONT SUSPENSION

Fork Oil Change

Yamaha does not provide an oil change interval for the front fork. It is a good practice to change the fork oil once a year. If the fork oil becomes contaminated with dirt or water, change it immediately.

When changing the fork oil, refer to *Front Fork* in Chapter Twelve.

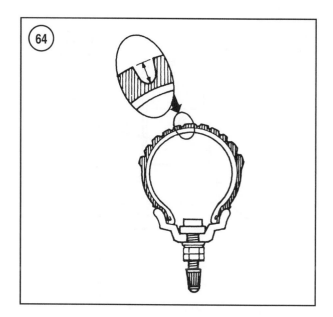

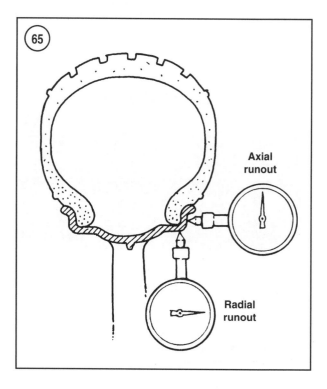

Inspection

1. Securely support the motorcycle on level ground. Block the rear wheel so the motorcycle will not roll in either direction.

2. Apply the front brake and pump the fork up and down as vigorously as possible. Check for smooth fork operation and check for any oil leaks.

NOTE
*The upper fork cover must be partially removed to gain access to the lower fork bridge clamp bolts shown in **Figure 66**. Refer to Chapter Twelve.*

NOTE
If any of the fasteners mentioned below are loose, refer to Chapter Eleven for tightening procedures.

3. Make sure the upper (**Figure 67**) and lower (**Figure 66**) fork bridge clamp bolts are tight.

4A. On 1999-2003 models, make sure the handlebar holder bolts (**Figure 68**) are tight, and the handlebar is securely held in place.

4B. On 2004-on models, make sure the handlebar holder bolts (**Figure 69**) are tight, and the handlebar is securely held in place.

5. Make sure the front axle clamp bolt (A, **Figure 70**) and axle (B) are tight. If necessary, tighten the front axle to 78 N•m (56 ft.-lb.) and the axle clamp bolt to 19 N•m (168 in.-lb.).

STEERING HEAD

Check the steering head for looseness at the intervals in **Table 1** or whenever the following conditions exist:

1. Handlebar vibrates more than normal.

2. The front fork makes a clicking or clunking noise when the front brake is applied.

3. The steering feels tight or slow.

4. The motorcycle does not want to steer straight on level road surfaces.

Inspection

1. Securely support the motorcycle so that the front tire clears the ground.

2. Check the bearing preload as follows:

   a. Center the front wheel. Push lightly against the left handlebar grip to start the wheel turning to the right, then let go. The wheel should continue turning under its own momentum until the fork legs hit their stop.

   b. Center the wheel and push lightly against the right handlebar grip.

   c. If the front wheel does not turn all the way to the stop when you lightly push a handlebar grip, the steering is too tight. Adjust the steering head bearings as described under *Steering Head Installation* in Chapter Twelve.

3. Check the bearing free play as follows:

   a. Center the front wheel. Grasp the bottom of the two fork sliders, and try to rock the fork legs back and forth. There should be little or no rocking in the steering head.

   b. If there is any play, the steering head is too loose. Adjust the steering head bearings as described in *Steering Head Installation* in Chapter Twelve.

REAR SUSPENSION

Inspection

1. Securely support the motorcycle on a level surface with the rear wheel off the ground.

2. Have an assistant secure the motorcycle, then push the rear wheel sideways hard to check for side play in the swing arm bearings.

3. Remove the rider and passenger seats as described in Chapter Fifteen.

NOTE
The following photographs are shown with the engine removed to better illustrate the steps.

NOTE
If any of the nuts or bolts mentioned below are loose, refer to Chapter Thirteen for tightening procedures.

4. Check the tightness of the following hardware:

   a. The swing arm pivot bolt nut (**Figure 71**).

   b. The shock absorber front (A, **Figure 72**) and rear (**Figure 73**) mounts.

   c. The relay arm and the connecting arm mounts (**Figure 74**).

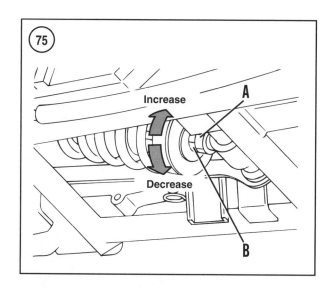

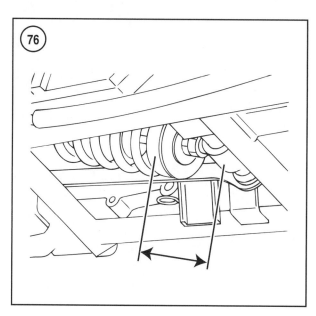

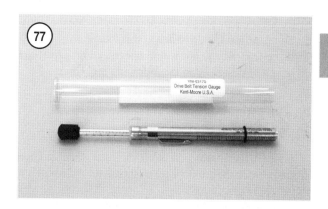

DRIVE BELT

Free Play Inspection

A Yamaha special tool (YM-03170) is required to correctly adjust the drive belt (**Figure 77**).

The drive belt can be adjusted with the motorcycle on the side stand or on a swing arm stand. The drive belt free play specification is in **Table 5**.

1. Securely support the motorcycle on level ground. Block the front wheel so the motorcycle will not roll in either direction.

NOTE
The level marks on the drive belt guard are in 0.20 in. (5 mm) increments.

2. Note the position of the drive belt within the level window on the drive belt guard (**Figure 78**).

3. Place the special tool up against the lower run of the drive belt (**Figure 79**). Apply 4.5 kg (10 lbs) of pressure against the drive belt.

4. With the specified pressure applied, note the position of the drive belt in the level window on the drive belt guard.

5. The difference between the two marks is the drive belt free play.

Shock Absorber Spring Preload Adjustment

CAUTION
*Never turn the adjusting ring (B, **Figure 72**) beyond the maximum or minimum length positions in **Table 5**.*

1. Securely support the motorcycle on a level surface with the rear wheel off the ground.

2. Loosen the locknut (A, **Figure 75**) and turn the adjusting ring (B) to achieve the desired spring preload.

3. Refer to the standard, minimum and maximum length (**Figure 76**) specifications in **Table 5**.

4. Tighten the locknut securely.

6. Rotate the rear wheel several times to locate the tightest point. Adjust the drive belt at this location.

7. If the free play is not within specification, adjust the drive belt as described in the following procedure.

Free Play Adjustment

1. Loosen the rear axle nut (**Figure 80**).

2. Support the motorcycle with the rear wheel off the ground. Block the front wheel so the motorcycle will not roll in either direction.

3. Loosen the rear brake caliper mounting bracket bolt (**Figure 81**).

4. Loosen the rear axle adjuster locknut (A, **Figure 82**) on both sides.

5. Turn the axle adjusting bolts (B, **Figure 82**) in equal amounts on both sides to achieve the correct amount of drive belt free play.

6. Make sure both axle adjusters are set to the same mark position on the swing arm (**Figure 83**). If not, readjust as necessary.

7. Recheck drive belt free play as previously described in this section. If drive belt free play is correct, tighten the following fasteners:

    a. Rear axle adjuster locknut (A, **Figure 82**) to 32 N•m (24 ft.-lb.).

    b. Rear axle nut (**Figure 80**) to 150 N•m (111 ft.-lb.).

    c. Rear brake caliper mounting bracket bolt (**Figure 81**) to 40 N•m (30 ft.-lb.).

BRAKES

Brake Hoses and Seals

Yamaha recommends replacing the brake hoses every four years and the seals in the master cylinder and calipers every two years.

Check the brake hoses between the master cylinder and each brake caliper. If there is any leak, tighten the connections and bleed the brakes as described in Chapter Fourteen. If this does not stop the leak or if a line is obviously damaged, cracked, or chafed, replace the hose(s) and/or seals, then bleed the brake as described in Chapter Fourteen.

Brake Fluid Change

A small amount of dirt and moisture enters the brake fluid each time the reservoir cap is removed, if a leak occurs or when any part of the hydraulic system is loosened or disconnected. Dirt can clog the system and cause unnecessary wear. Water in the fluid vaporizes at high tem-

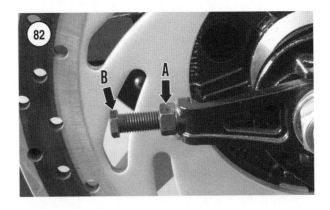

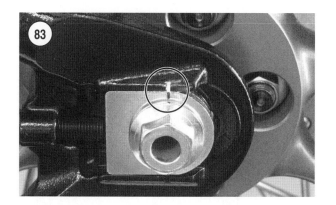

peratures, impairing the hydraulic action and reducing brake performance.

Change the brake fluid at the intervals specified in **Table 1**. To do so, drain the fluid from the brakes as described in Chapter Fourteen. Add new fluid to the master cylinder, and bleed the brake at the caliper(s) until the fluid leaving the caliper is clean and free of contaminants and air bubbles. Refer to the brake bleeding procedure in Chapter Fourteen.

Brake Fluid Level Inspection

If the brake fluid level reaches the lower level mark in the master cylinder, or reservoir, correct the fluid level by adding fresh brake fluid. Refer to A, **Figure 84** for the front or **Figure 85** for the rear.

1. Securely support the motorcycle on level ground. Block the rear wheel so the motorcycle will not roll in either direction.

2A. When checking and adding fluid to the front master cylinder, position the handlebar so the master cylinder reservoir is level.

2B. On the rear master cylinder, make sure the top of the reservoir is level.

3. Clean any dirt from the area around the top cover before removing the cover.

4A. On the front master cylinder, perform the following:

  a. Remove the screws and remove the top cover (B, **Figure 84**).

  b. Remove the diaphragm plate and the diaphragm.

4B. On the rear master cylinder, perform the following:

  a. Remove the screw (A, **Figure 86**) securing the reservoir and cover to the frame.

  b. Remove the cover (B, **Figure 86**) from the cap.

  c. Unscrew the top cap, (**Figure 87**), diaphragm plate and the diaphragm.

5. Add brake fluid from a sealed brake fluid container.

6. Reinstall the diaphragm, diaphragm plate and the top cover. Tighten the screws (front) or cap (rear) securely.

7. On the rear master cylinder, install the cover on the cap. Install the screw securing the reservoir and cover to the frame. Tighten the screw securely.

Brake Pad Inspection

Inspect the brake pads for excessive or uneven wear, scoring and oil or grease on the friction surface.

1. Securely support the motorcycle on level ground.

2. Look into the caliper assembly and inspect the wear indicators. Compare to **Figure 88** or **Figure 89** as appropriate.

3. Replace both pads in the caliper if either pad is worn to the wear limit. On the front brakes, replace both pads in both front calipers if any pad is worn to the wear limit. Refer to Chapter Fourteen for brake pad replacement.

Brake Lever Adjustment

The front brake lever free play is the distance the brake lever moves before the master cylinder piston starts moving. Brake lever free play is measured at the end of the hand lever.

1. Push the brake lever forward, away from the handle grip.

2. Pull the lever, and measure free play.

3. If the free play is outside the range specified in **Table 5**, perform the following:

    a. Loosen the brake adjuster locknut (A, **Figure 90**).

    b. Turn the adjuster (B, **Figure 90**) in or out until the free play is within the specification. Turning the adjuster in (clockwise) decreases free play; turning it out (counterclockwise) increases free play.

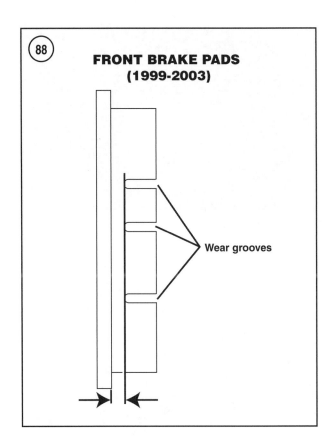

88

**FRONT BRAKE PADS
(1999-2003)**

Wear grooves

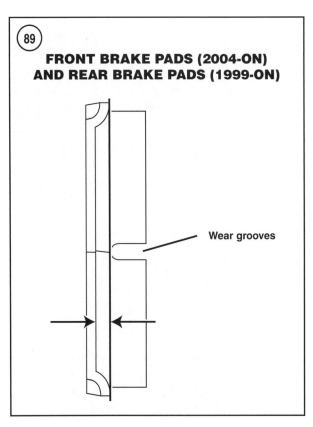

89

**FRONT BRAKE PADS (2004-ON)
AND REAR BRAKE PADS (1999-ON)**

Wear grooves

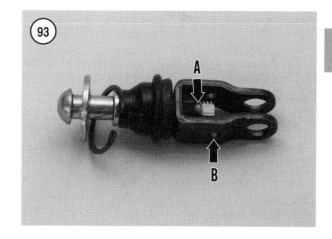

4. After adjusting the free play, spin the wheel and check for brake drag. Readjust the free play as necessary.

5. Tighten the lock nut securely.

Brake Pedal Adjustment

Rear brake pedal height is the distance from the top of the brake pedal to the top of the footrest (**Figure 91**).

1. Support the motorcycle so it is straight and level. Block the front wheel so the motorcycle will not roll in either direction.

2. Make sure the brake pedal is in the at-rest position.

3. Measure the distance from the top of the brake pedal to the top of the footrest. If the pedal height is not within the specification in **Table 5**, adjust the pedal height as follows:

    a. Loosen the adjuster locknut (A, **Figure 92**) on the rear master cylinder clevis. Turn the adjuster (B, **Figure 92**) until the pedal height is within the specification. Turn the adjuster clockwise to raise the brake pedal and counterclockwise to lower it.

    b. Tighten the locknut to 18 N•m (159 in.-lb.).

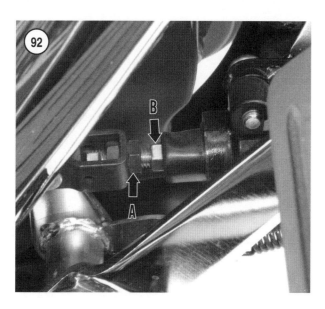

NOTE
***Figure 93** is shown with the pushrod and clevis removed to better illustrate the step.*

    c. Check the end of the brake pushrod threads (A, **Figure 93**). The threads must be visible through the bracket hole (B, **Figure 93**) in the clevis.

4. After adjusting the brake pedal height, make sure the rear brake does not drag. Readjust the brake pedal height as necessary.

5. Adjust the rear brake light switch as described in this section.

Rear Brake Light Switch Adjustment

1. Turn the ignition switch on.

2. Depress the brake pedal. The brake light should come on when the brake pedal is depressed, and just before the rear brake is applied. If necessary, adjust as follows.

3. Hold the rear brake light switch body (A, **Figure 94**) and turn the adjuster nut (B) until the brake light operates properly. Turn the nut clockwise and the brake light comes on sooner; turn it counterclockwise and the light comes on later.

WARNING
Do not ride the motorcycle until the rear brake light operates properly.

FASTENERS

Constant vibration can loosen many fasteners on a motorcycle. Check the tightness of all fasteners, especially:

1. Engine mounting hardware.
2. Engine crankcase covers.
3. Handlebar and front fork.

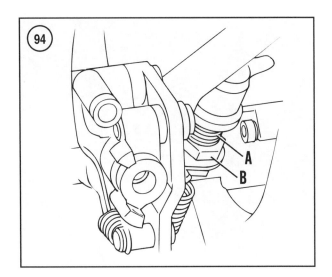

4. Gearshift lever.
5. Brake pedal and lever.
6. Exhaust system.
7. Lighting equipment.

Table 1 MAINTENANCE SCHEDULE*

Initial 600 miles (1000 km) or 1 month
Change engine oil and replace oil filter
Replace transfer case oil
Lubricate all control cables
Lightly lubricate all pivot and contact surfaces
with lithium grease
Check idle speed; adjust as necessary
Check the operation of the front and rear brakes
Check brake fluid level in master cylinders;
adjust as necessary
Check the operation of the clutch; adjust if necessary
Check operation of the sidestand switch
Check the drive belt tension; adjust if necessary
Check steering play
Check all fasteners; tighten as necessary
Every 2500 miles (4000 km)
Check the drive belt tension; adjust if necessary
Every 4000 miles (6500 km) or 6 months
Check the condition of the spark plugs; clean and adjust the gap as necessary
Check the fuel lines for cracks or damage; replace as necessary
Check the exhaust system for leaks; tighten all fasteners
(continued)

Table 1 MAINTENANCE SCHEDULE (continued)*

Every 4000 miles (6500 km) or 6 months (continued)
  Check engine idle speed and throttle free play;
    adjust either as necessary
  Change engine oil
  Clean air filter with compressed air; replace if necessary
  Check the operation of the front and rear brakes;
    replace brake pads if necessary
  Check brake fluid level in master cylinders;
    adjust as necessary
  Check the operation of the clutch; adjust the cable free play
    or replace the cable as necessary
  Lubricate all control cables
  Lubricate the brake and clutch lever pivot shafts
    with lithium grease
  Lubricate the brake pedal and shift pedal pivot shafts
    with lithium grease
  Check the operation of sidestand
  Lubricate the sidestand pivot and contact surfaces
    with lithium grease
  Check the operation of the front fork and check for leaks
  Check the steering head bearings for smoothness
    or excessive play; adjust if necessary
  Check the operation of the shock absorber
    and check for damage and leaks
  Check the wheel bearings for wear or damage;
    replace as necessary
  Check the wheels for runout and balance; adjust if necessary
  Check the spoke tightness (laced wheels); adjust if necessary
  Check the tire tread for wear or damage; replace as necessary
  Check all fasteners; tighten as necessary
Every 8000 miles (13,000 km) checks
  Perform the 4000 mile (6000 km) checks
  Replace the spark plugs
  Change engine oil and filter
  Check the transfer case oil level and for leakage; adjust the level if necessary
  Check rear swing arm operation for looseness; tighten if necessary
Every 12000 miles (19,000 km) checks or 19 months
  Perform the 4000 mile (6000 km) checks
  On California models, check the evaporation emission
    control system for damage; replace as necessary
Every 15000 miles (24,000 km)
  Check the valve clearance; adjust if necessary
Every 16000 miles (25,000 km) checks or 24 months
  Perform the 4000 mile (6000 km) checks
  Replace the spark plugs
  Replace front and rear brake systems brake fluid
  Replace the transfer case oil
  Repack swing arm pivot bearings with
    medium weight wheel bearing grease
  Repack steering head bearings with lithium based grease
  Replace brake master cylinders and calipers copper washers
Every 20000 miles (32,000 km) checks or 30 months
  Perform the 4000 mile (6000 km) checks
  Replace the fuel filters
Every 2 years
  Replace master cylinder and caliper piston seals
Every 4 years, or if cracked or damaged
  Replace all brake hoses

* Consider this maintenance schedule as a guide to general maintenance and lubrication intervals. Service these items more frequently if the motorcycle is exposed to mud, sand or high humidity, or it is run harder than normal (stop-and-go traffic for example).

Table 2 TIRE SPECIFICATIONS

Tire sizes	
Front	130/90-16 67H
Rear	150/80 B16 71H
Tire series	
1999-2003	
Front	G703 Bridgestone
	D404 Dunlop
Rear	G702 Bridgestone
	D404 Dunlop
2004-2005	
Front	G703 Bridgestone (U.S. and Canada)
	D404 Dunlop (Canada)
Rear	G702 Bridgestone (U.S.)
	D404 Dunlop (Canada)
2006-on	
Front	G703 Bridgestone
	D404 Dunlop
Rear	G702 Brigestone
	D404 Dunlop
Tire inflation pressure[1]	
0-90 kg (0-198 lb.)	
Front tire	250 kPa (36 psi)
Rear tire	250 kPa (36 psi)
90 kg (198 lb.)-maximum load[2]	
Front tire	250 kPa (36 psi)
Rear tire	280 kPa (40 psi)
Minimum tread depth	
1999-2003 models	1.6 mm (0.06 in.)
2004-on models	1.0 mm (0.04 in.)

1. Tire inflation pressure is for original equipment tires. Aftermarket tires may require different inflation pressures; refer to the aftermarket manufacturer's specifications.
2. Maximum load equates to the total weight of the cargo, rider, passenger and accessories.

Table 3 BATTERY SPECIFICATIONS

Type	Maintenance free (sealed) YTX20L-BS
Capacity	12 V 18 AH
Open circuit voltage @ 20° C (68° F)	
Fully charged	12.8 volts or higher
Requires charging	12.0-12.8 volts
Replace the battery	Less than 12.0 volts

Table 4 RECOMMENDED LUBRICANTS AND FLUIDS

Battery	Maintenance free
Brake fluid	DOT 4
Engine oil	
API classification	API SE, SF, SG (non-friction modified)
Viscosity	SAE 20W/40
Capacity	
Oil change only	3.7 L (3.9 qt.)
Oil and filter change	4.1 L (4.3 qt.)
When engine completely dry	5.0 L (5.3 qt.)
(continued)	

Table 4 RECOMMENDED LUBRICANTS AND FLUIDS (continued)

Fork oil	
Viscosity	Yamaha 5WT
Capacity per leg	554 ml (18.7 oz.)
Oil level*	110 mm (4.33 in.)
Fuel	
Type	Regular unleaded
Octane	86 [(R + M)/method] or research octane 91 or higher
Capacity, including reserve	20 liter (5.3 U.S. gal.)
Reserve	3.5 liter (0.9 U.S. gal.)
Transfer gearcase oil	
API classification	SAE80 GL-4
Capacity	0.4 L (0.42 qt.)

*Measured from the top of the fully compressed fork tube with the fork spring removed.

Table 5 MAINTENANCE AND TUNE-UP SPECIFICATIONS

Item	Specification
Brake adjustment	
Front brake lever free play at handlebar	2-5 mm (0.08-0.20 in.)
Rear brake pedal height above footrest	100 mm (3.9 in.)
Brake pad wear limit	
Front	0.5 mm (0.02 in.)
Rear	0.5 mm (0.02 in.)
Clutch lever free play at handlebar	10-15 mm (0.39-0.59 in.)
Compression pressure @ at sea level	
Standard	1200 kPa (174 psi)
Minimum	1000 kPa (145 psi)
Maximum	1400 kPa (203 psi)
Drive belt free play	
Motorcycle on sidestand	7.5-13 mm (0.30-0.51 in.)
Motorcycle on swing arm stand	14-21 mm (0.55-0.83 in.)
Engine idle speed	850-950 rpm
Engine oil pressure (at oil pressure switch)	
at 60° C (140° F)	40-80 kPa (5.8-11.6 psi) @ 900 rpm
Idle speed	850-950 rpm
Ignition timing	10° BTDC @ 1000 rpm
Pilot screw	2 1/2 turns out
Shift rod length	374.4-378.4 mm (14.74-14.90 in.)
Shock absorber length adjustment	
Standard	42.5 mm (1.67 in.)
Minimum	42.5 mm (1.67 in.)
Maximum	51.5 mm (2.03 in.)
Spark plugs	
Recommended type	NGK DPR7EA-9, Denso X22EPR-U9
Spark plug gap	0.8-0.9 mm (0.031-0.035 in.)
Throttle cable free play at throttle grip	4-8 mm (0.16-0.31 in.)
Vacuum pressure (at idle)	52 kPa (15.4 in. Hg)
Valve clearance (cold)	
Intake	0-0.04 mm (0-0.0016 in.)
Exhaust	0-0.04 mm (0-0.0016 in.)
Wheels	
Maximum runout service limit (laced wheel)	
Axial	2 mm (0.08 in.)
Radial	2 mm (0.08 in.)
Maximum runout service limit (alloy wheel)	
Axial	1 mm (0.04 in.)
Radial	1 mm (0.04 in.)

Table 6 MAINTENANCE AND TUNE UP TORQUE SPECIFICATIONS

Item	N•m	in.-lb.	ft.-lb.
Brake hose banjo bolt	34	–	25
Engine oil drain bolts			
Crankcase	43	–	32
Oil tank	43	–	32
Front axle			
Bolt	78	–	56
Pinch bolt	19	168	–
Fuel tank bolt and nut	7	62	–
Oil filter	17	150	–
Oil line gallery bolts (cylinder heads)	21	–	15.5
Oil pressure gallery hex bolt	20	–	15
Rear axle			
Nut	150	–	111
Adjuster locknut	32	–	24
Rear brake			
Caliper bracket bolt	40	–	30
Brake pedal adjuster locknut	18	159	–
Sidestand nut	48	–	35
Spark plug	18	159	–
Transfer gearcase			
Oil filler cap	8	71	–
Oil level check bolt	8	71	–
Oil drain bolt	18	159	–
Valve adjuster locknut	20	–	15

CHAPTER FOUR

ENGINE TOP END

This chapter provides complete service and overhaul procedures for the engine top end components. This includes the rocker arms, pushrods, valves, cylinder heads, pistons, piston rings and cylinders. The two camshafts are located in the crankcase and they are covered in Chapter Five. Refer to Chapter Three for valve adjustment procedures.

When inspecting components, compare the measurements to the specifications in **Table 2** at the end of this chapter. Replace any part that is damaged, worn or out of specification. During assembly, tighten fasteners as specified.

The Road Star engine is an air-cooled, four-stroke V-twin.

Tables 1-3 are at the end of the chapter.

SERVICING ENGINE IN THE FRAME

The following components can be serviced while the engine is in the frame:
1. External shift mechanism.
2. Clutch.
3. Carburetor.
4. Starter.
5. Alternator.

CYLINDER HEAD COVERS

The cylinder head cover design varies between 1999-2003 models and 2004-on models. Where differences occur they are noted in the following procedures.

This procedure covers both the front and rear cylinder head covers.

Refer to **Figure 1** and **Figure 2**.

Removal

1. Securely support the motorcycle on level ground. Block the front wheel so the motorcycle will not roll in either direction.
2. Remove the seats as described in Chapter Fifteen.
3. Disconnect the negative battery cable as described in Chapter Three.
4. Remove the fuel tank as described in Chapter Nine.

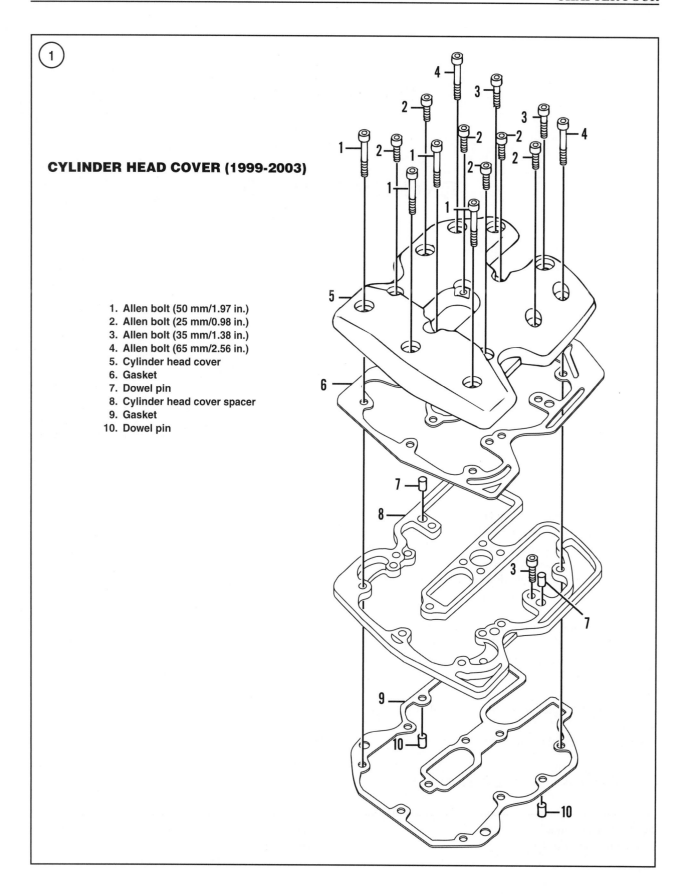

1

CYLINDER HEAD COVER (1999-2003)

1. Allen bolt (50 mm/1.97 in.)
2. Allen bolt (25 mm/0.98 in.)
3. Allen bolt (35 mm/1.38 in.)
4. Allen bolt (65 mm/2.56 in.)
5. Cylinder head cover
6. Gasket
7. Dowel pin
8. Cylinder head cover spacer
9. Gasket
10. Dowel pin

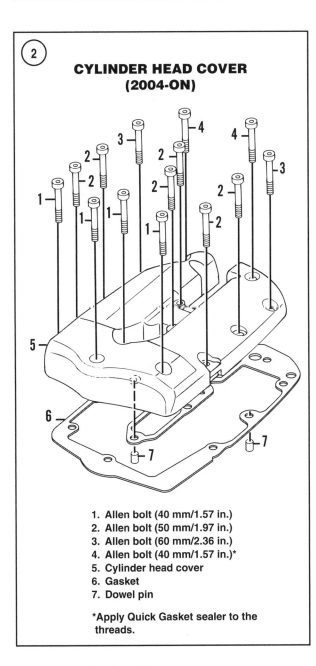

② CYLINDER HEAD COVER
(2004-ON)

1. Allen bolt (40 mm/1.57 in.)
2. Allen bolt (50 mm/1.97 in.)
3. Allen bolt (60 mm/2.36 in.)
4. Allen bolt (40 mm/1.57 in.)*
5. Cylinder head cover
6. Gasket
7. Dowel pin

*Apply Quick Gasket sealer to the
  threads.

5. Disconnect the spark plug leads from both spark plugs. Move the leads out of the way.

6. Disconnect the breather hoses from the fittings (**Figure 3**, typical) on the rear cylinder head cover.

7. Remove the bolts securing the cylinder head cover. Refer to **Figure 4** and **Figure 5**.

8. Carefully pull the cylinder head cover straight up and off the cylinder head. Do not scratch the chrome finish.

9. Remove the cylinder head cover gasket. Remove the dowel pins if loose.

10. On 1999-2003 models, use a crisscross pattern, and remove the bolts securing the cylinder head spacer (**Figure 6**). Remove the spacer and gasket, and the dowel pins if loose.

11. Inspect the parts as described in this section.

Installation

1. Make sure the cylinder head mating surface is clean.

2. On 1999-2003 models, install the cylinder head spacer as follows:

    a. Install the dowel pins (A, **Figure 7**), if removed.

    b. Install a *new* gasket (B, **Figure 7**).

    c. Install the cylinder head spacer (**Figure 6**).

    d. Apply a medium strength threadlocking compound to the bolt threads.

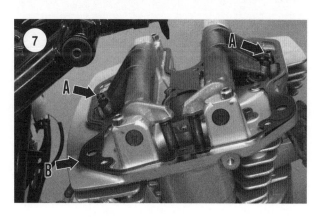

e. Install the bolts and tighten in a crisscross pattern to 10 N•m (88 in.-lb.).

3A. On 1999-2003 models, install the dowel pins (if removed) (A, **Figure 8**) and a *new* gasket (B).

3B. On 2004-on models, install the dowel pins (if removed) (A, **Figure 9**) and a *new* gasket (B).

4. Install the cylinder head cover. Refer to **Figure 4** and **Figure 5**.

5. Apply a medium strength threadlocking compound to the bolt threads.

6. The cylinder head bolts are different lengths and must be installed in the correct location in the cylinder head cover. Refer to **Figure 10** for 1999-2003 models. Refer to **Figure 11** for 2004-on models. On the 2004-on models, apply a light coat of Quick Gasket to the threads of the two left side bolts (40 mm [1.57 in.] long).

7. Install the bolts securing the cylinder head cover. Tighten the bolts in a crisscross pattern to 10 N•m (88 in.-lb.).

8. Connect the breather hoses onto the fittings (**Figure 3**, typical) on the rear cylinder head cover.

9. Connect the spark plug leads onto both spark plugs and push them on until they bottom.

10. Install the fuel tank as described in Chapter Nine.

11. Connect the negative battery cable.

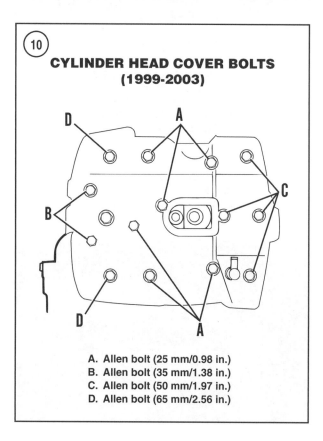

CYLINDER HEAD COVER BOLTS (1999-2003)

A. Allen bolt (25 mm/0.98 in.)
B. Allen bolt (35 mm/1.38 in.)
C. Allen bolt (50 mm/1.97 in.)
D. Allen bolt (65 mm/2.56 in.)

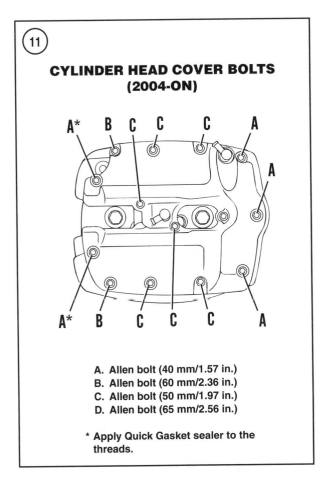

CYLINDER HEAD COVER BOLTS
(2004-ON)

A. Allen bolt (40 mm/1.57 in.)
B. Allen bolt (60 mm/2.36 in.)
C. Allen bolt (50 mm/1.97 in.)
D. Allen bolt (65 mm/2.56 in.)

* Apply Quick Gasket sealer to the
threads.

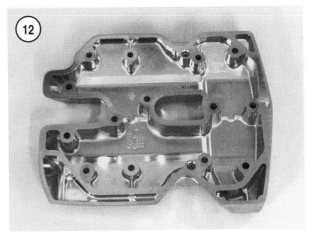

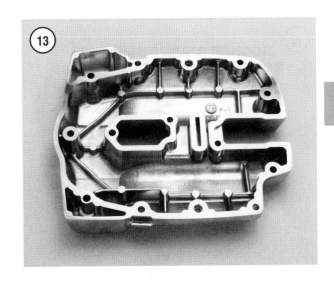

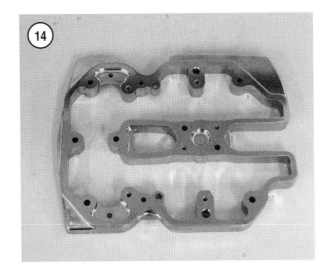

Inspection

1. Clean all parts in solvent and dry with compressed air.

2. Inspect the cylinder head covers for damage. Make sure the sealing surfaces are free of corrosion and nicks. Refer to **Figure 12** and **Figure 13**.

3. On 1999-2003 models, inspect the cylinder head spacer for damage. Make sure the sealing surfaces are free of corrosion and nicks (**Figure 14**).

ROCKER ARMS AND PUSHRODS

The rocker arm and pushrod design varies between the 1999-2003 model and 2004-on models. Where differences occur they are noted in the following procedures.

This procedure covers both the front and rear cylinders.

Refer to **Figure 15** and **Figure 16**.

Removal

1. Remove the cylinder head cover and the cylinder head spacer (1999-2003 models) as described in this chapter.

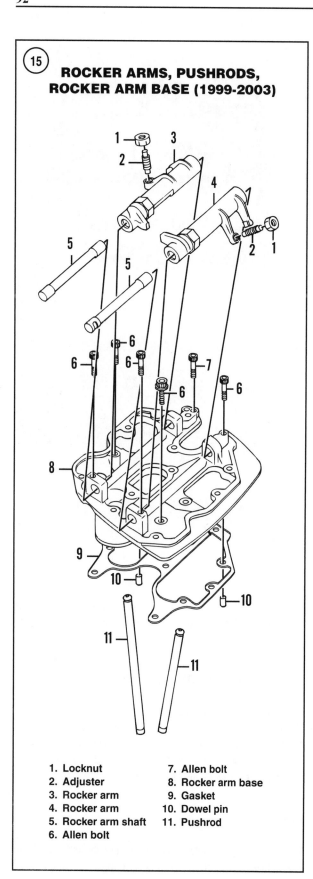

⑮ ROCKER ARMS, PUSHRODS, ROCKER ARM BASE (1999-2003)

1. Locknut
2. Adjuster
3. Rocker arm
4. Rocker arm
5. Rocker arm shaft
6. Allen bolt
7. Allen bolt
8. Rocker arm base
9. Gasket
10. Dowel pin
11. Pushrod

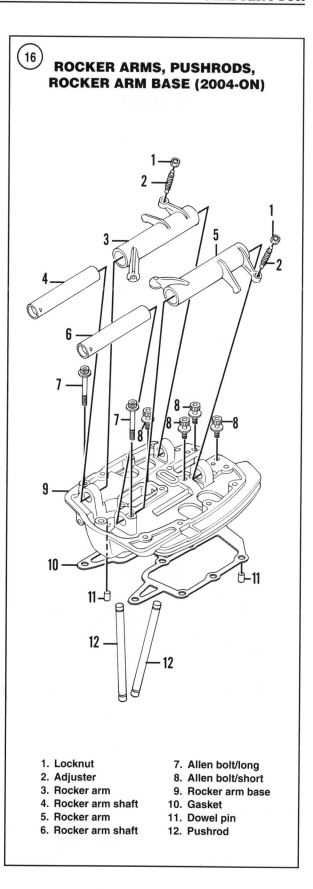

⑯ ROCKER ARMS, PUSHRODS, ROCKER ARM BASE (2004-ON)

1. Locknut
2. Adjuster
3. Rocker arm
4. Rocker arm shaft
5. Rocker arm
6. Rocker arm shaft
7. Allen bolt/long
8. Allen bolt/short
9. Rocker arm base
10. Gasket
11. Dowel pin
12. Pushrod

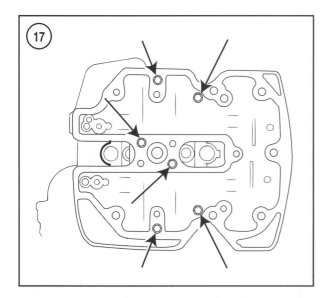

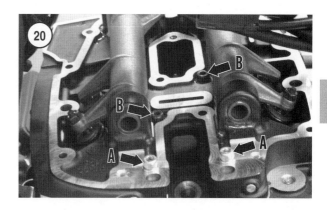

is at TDC there is less strain on the rocker arms and pushrods.

4. Use a crisscross pattern and loosen the bolts securing the rocker arm base.

5A. On 1999-2003 models, refer to **Figure 17**, and perform the following:

    a. On the left side, remove the two bolts (**Figure 18**).

    b. On the right side, remove the two short bolts and washers (A, **Figure 19**) and the two long bolts (B).

5B. On 2004-on models, perform the following:

    a. On the left side, remove the two bolts (A, **Figure 20**).

    b. Remove the two center bolts (B, **Figure 20**).

    c. On the right side, remove the two long bolts (**Figure 21**).

6. Work the cylinder head base off the cylinder head sufficiently to release the rocker arm pressure on the pushrods.

7. Remove both pushrods (**Figure 22**) from the pushrod cover.

CAUTION
When the rocker arm base is removed from the cylinder head, it may pull the small left side dowel pins along with it. If the dowel pin works loose and comes off at this time it may

2. Remove the air filter assembly and the carburetor as described in Chapter Nine.

3. Correctly position the cylinder being worked on at TDC on the compression stroke. Refer to *Valve Clearance Inspection/Adjustment* in Chapter Three. When the cylinder

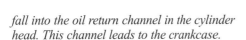

fall into the oil return channel in the cylinder head. This channel leads to the crankcase.

8. Lift the rocker arm base straight part way up and remove the dowel pins from the left side.

9. Remove the rocker arm base from the cylinder head. Refer to **Figure 23** or **Figure 24**.

10. Remove the gasket and dowel pins, if still in place.

11. Pull the pushrod cover straight up and out of the valve lifter case. Refer to **Figure 25** or **Figure 26**.

12. If necessary, remove valve lifters as described in this chapter.

13. Inspect the parts as described in this section.

Installation

1. If removed, install valve lifters as described in this chapter.

2A. On 1999-2003 models, install *new* O-rings (A, **Figure 27**) and lower oil seal (B) onto the pushrod covers. Apply engine oil to the O-rings.

2B. On 2004-on models, install *new* O-rings (**Figure 28**) onto the pushrod covers. Apply engine oil to the O-rings.

3A. On 1999-2003 models, perform the following:

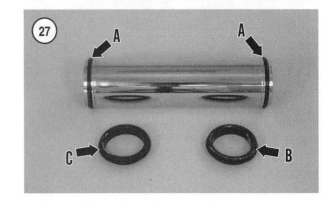

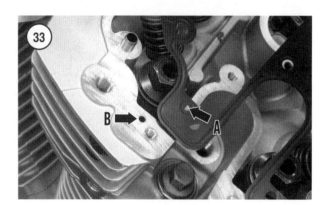

a. Install the pushrod cover into the valve lifter case (**Figure 29**). Either end can be installed into the case. Push it down until it bottoms in the case.

b. Install the oil seal (**Figure 30**) onto the top of the pushrod cover, if removed. Apply engine oil to the oil seal.

3B. On 2004-on models, position the pushrod cover with the flared end, with two O-rings, facing down and install it into the valve lifter case (**Figure 26**). Push it down until it bottoms in the case.

4. Place a clean shop cloth (A, **Figure 31**, typical) into the cylinder head oil return channel on the left side to prevent the loss of the dowel pin(s) in the following steps.

5. Install the dowel pins. Refer to A, **Figure 32** and B, **Figure 31**.

6. On 1999-2003 models, align the cylinder head gasket oil control hole (A, **Figure 33**) with the oil control hole in the cylinder head (B).

7. Install a *new* cylinder head gasket. Refer to B, **Figure 32** or **Figure 34**.

8. Install the rocker arm base part way onto the cylinder head and carefully remove the shop rag. Do not dislodge the dowel pins at this time.

9. Guide the pushrod cover into the rocker arm base, and pull the rocker arm base straight down onto the cylinder

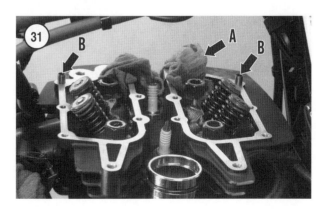

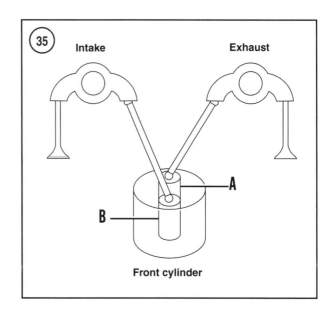

head. Refer to **Figure 23** or **Figure 24**. Do not completely seat it at this time.

10. Make sure the cylinder being worked on is still at TDC on the compression stroke.

CAUTION
On 2004 models, the pushrod for the intake rocker arm on the rear cylinder is longer (290.5 mm [11.437 in.]) than the remaining three (288.5 mm [11.358 in.]) pushrods. The longer pushrod must be installed in the correct location to avoid engine damage.

11. The pushrods must be installed in the correct location in the valve lifters as well as the rocker arms. Refer to **Figure 35** for the front cylinder and **Figure 36** for the rear cylinder.

12. Install the pushrods (**Figure 22**) into the pushrod covers and into the correct location in the valve lifters. Use a flashlight and look down into the pushrod cover to ensure correct pushrod installation within the valve lifters. Relocate if necessary.

13. Correctly position the upper end of the pushrods into the rocker arm sockets. Refer to **Figure 37** or **Figure 38**.

14. Make sure the pushrods are correctly seated, then pull the rocker arm base down until it bottoms on the cylinder head.

15A. On 1999-2003 models, install the following bolts and tighten finger-tight:

   a. The two bolts and washers (A, **Figure 19**) on the right side, and the two long bolts (B).

   b. The two bolts (**Figure 18**) on the left side.

15B. On 2004-on models, install the following bolts (**Figure 39**) and tighten finger-tight:

   a. The two long bolts (**Figure 21**) on the right side.

   b. The two center bolts (B, **Figure 20**).

   b. The two bolts (A, **Figure 20**) on the left side.

16A. On 1999-2003 models, use a crisscross pattern and tighten all bolts to 10 N•m (88 in.-lb.).

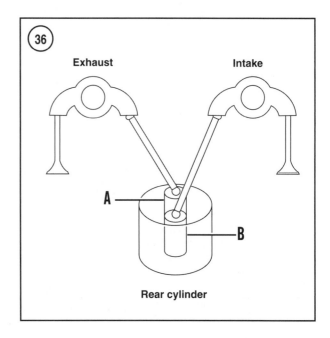

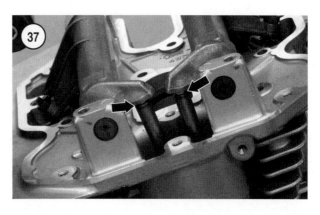

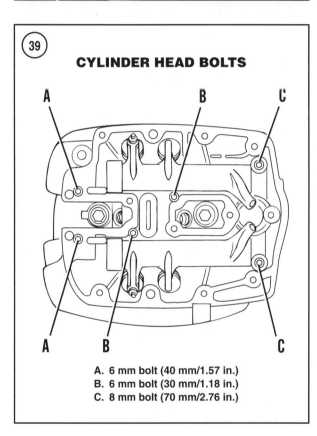

CYLINDER HEAD BOLTS

A. 6 mm bolt (40 mm/1.57 in.)
B. 6 mm bolt (30 mm/1.18 in.)
C. 8 mm bolt (70 mm/2.76 in.)

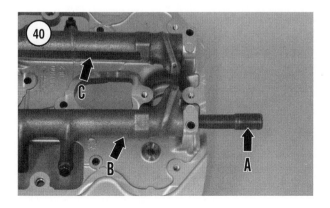

16B. On 2004-on models, use a crisscross pattern and tighten the bolts as follows:

   a. On the right side, tighten the two 8 mm long bolts (**Figure 21**) to 24 N•m (18 ft.-lb.).

   b. Tighten the remaining four 6 mm bolts (B, **Figure 20**) and (A) to 10 N•m (88 in.-lb.).

17. Install the carburetor and the air filter assembly as described in Chapter Nine.

18. Install the cylinder head spacer (1999-2003 models), and the cover as described in this chapter.

**Rocker Arm Disassembly/Assembly
(1999-2003 Models)**

This procedure covers both the front and rear cylinders. Disassemble one set of rockers and shafts at a time. Keep the sets separate to avoid intermixing identical parts.

Refer to **Figure 15**.

1. Remove the rocker arm base as described in this section.

2. Completely withdraw the rocker arm shaft (A, **Figure 40**) from the rocker arm and base.

3. Remove the rocker arm (B, **Figure 40**) from the rocker arm base.

4. Repeat Steps 2 and 3 for the remaining rocker arm (C, **Figure 40**) and shaft.

5. Clean all parts in solvent. Blow compressed air through all oil passages.

6. Inspect the parts as described in this section.

7. Apply engine oil to the inner surface of the rocker arms and the exterior of the rocker arm shafts.

8. Install the rocker arm (B, **Figure 40**) into the rocker arm base.

9. Align the rocker arm with the rocker arm support.

10. Position the rocker arm shaft with the notch end (A, **Figure 40**) going in last and install the shaft into the rocker arm.

11. Push the rocker arm shaft almost all the way in, align the notch (A, **Figure 41**) with the mating bolt hole (B), then

push it in all the way. Check the alignment of the notch to the hole and readjust if necessary with a screwdriver in the notches (**Figure 42**, typical).

12. Repeat Steps 8-11 for the remaining rocker arm and shaft.

Rocker Arm Disassembly/Assembly (2004-on Models)

This procedure covers both the front and rear cylinders. Disassemble one set of rockers and shafts at a time. Keep the sets separate to avoid intermixing identical parts.

Refer to **Figure 16**.

1. Remove the rocker arm base as described in this section.

2. Completely withdraw the rocker arm shaft (A, **Figure 43**) from the rocker arm and base.

3. Remove the rocker arm (B, **Figure 43**) from the rocker arm base.

4. Repeat Steps 2 and 3 for the remaining rocker arm (C, **Figure 43**) and shaft.

5. Clean all parts in solvent. Blow compressed air through all oil passages.

6. Inspect the parts as described in this section.

7. Apply engine oil to the inner surface of the rocker arms and the exterior of the rocker arm shafts.

8. Install the rocker arm (B, **Figure 43**) into the rocker arm base.

9. Align the rocker arm with the rocker arm support.

10. Position the rocker arm shaft with the notch end (A, **Figure 43**) going in last and install the shaft into the rocker arm.

11. Push the rocker arm shaft almost all the way in, align the notch (A, **Figure 44**) with the mating bolt hole (B), then push it in all the way. Check the alignment of the notch to the hole and readjust if necessary with a screwdriver in the notches (**Figure 42**, typical).

12. Repeat Steps 8-11 for the remaining rocker arm and shaft.

Rocker Arm Component Inspection (All Models)

When measuring the rocker arm components compare the actual measurements to the specifications listed in **Table 2**. Replace any part that is damaged or out of specification as described in this section.

1. Inspect the rocker arm pads (A, **Figure 45**) and adjuster tip (B) for pitting and excessive wear.

2. Examine the push rod socket (**Figure 46**) for scoring or excessive wear.

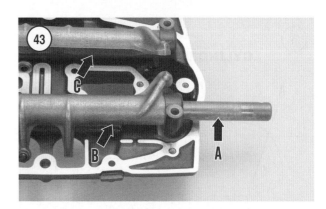

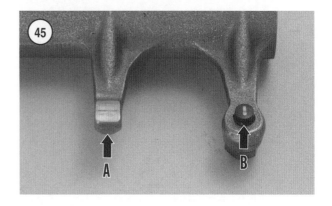

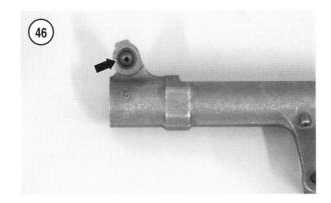

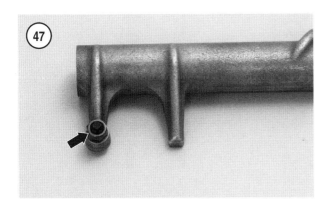

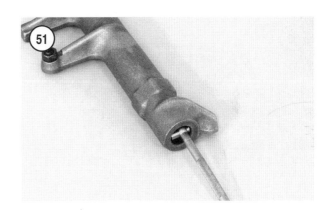

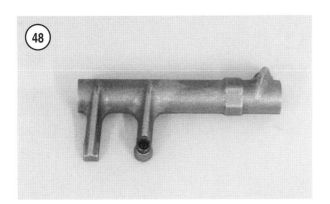

3. Make sure the adjuster and locknut (**Figure 47**) both turn smoothly.

4. Check the rocker arm (**Figure 48**) for cracks and damage.

5. Examine the rocker arm shaft for scoring, ridge wear or other damage. If these conditions are present, replace the rocker arm shaft. If the shaft does not show any wear or damage, continue with Step 7.

6. Insert the rocker arm shaft into the rocker arm (**Figure 49**) and rotate it slowly. It must rotate smoothly with no binding.

7. Measure the rocker arm shaft outside diameter (**Figure 50**) where it rides in the rocker arm and in the rocker arm housing. Record both sets of measurements at both ends of the shaft.

8. Measure the rocker arm inside diameter (**Figure 51**) where the rocker arm shaft rides. Record both sets of measurements at each end of the rocker arm.

9. Subtract the measurements taken in Step 7 from those taken in Step 8 to obtain the oil clearance. If worn to the service limit, replace both parts as a set.

10. Check the rocker arm base bore where the shaft locates (A, **Figure 52**, typical) for wear or corrosion.

11. Inspect the rocker arm base for damage (**Figure 53**, typical). Make sure the sealing surfaces (B, **Figure 52**, typical) are free of corrosion and nicks.

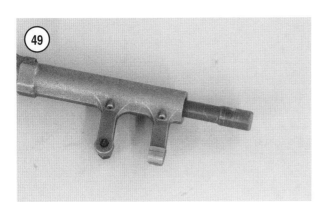

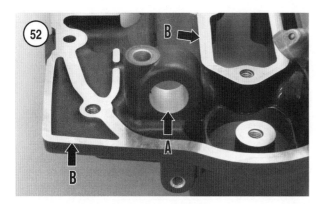

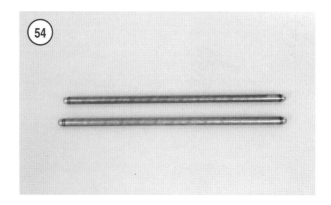

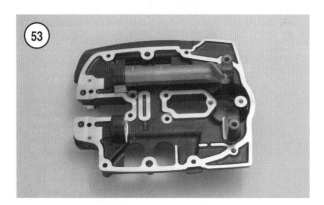

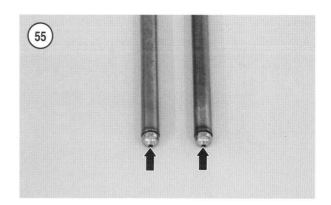

Pushrod and Pushrod Covers Inspection

1. Clean the pushrods and covers in solvent and dry with compressed air.

2. Check the pushrods (**Figure 54**) for bending, cracks and worn or damaged ball heads (**Figure 55**).

3. Replace any damaged pushrod.

4. On 1999-2003 models, inspect the pushrod cover, O-rings (A, **Figure 27**), oil seal (B), and oil seat (C) for hardness or deterioration. Replace as necessary.

5. On 2004-on models, inspect the pushrod cover, the upper O-ring (**Figure 56**), the lower oil seal (A, **Figure 57**) and O-ring (B).

6. Replace O-rings and seals as a set if they are starting to harden or deteriorate.

VALVE LIFTERS

Figure 58 and **Figure 59** shows the valve lifter in relation to the valve lifter case and cover. The valve lifters and covers are installed on the right side of the engine. During engine operation, the lifters are pumped full of engine oil, thus taking up the play in the valve train. When the engine is turned off, the lifters will leak down after a period of time as some of the oil drains out. When the engine is started, the lifters

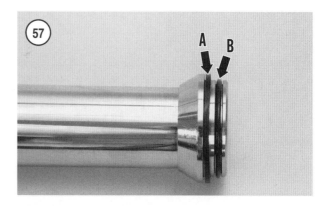

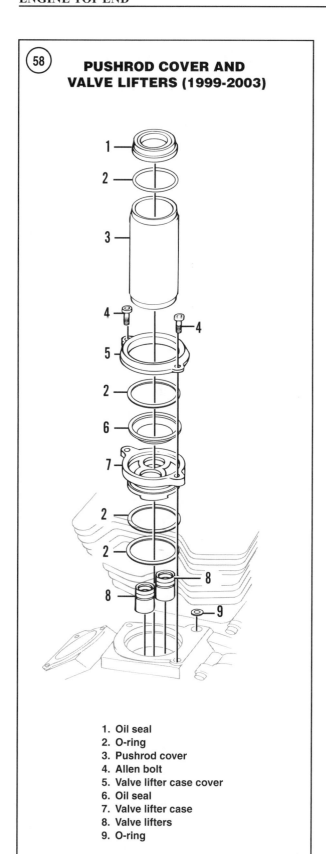

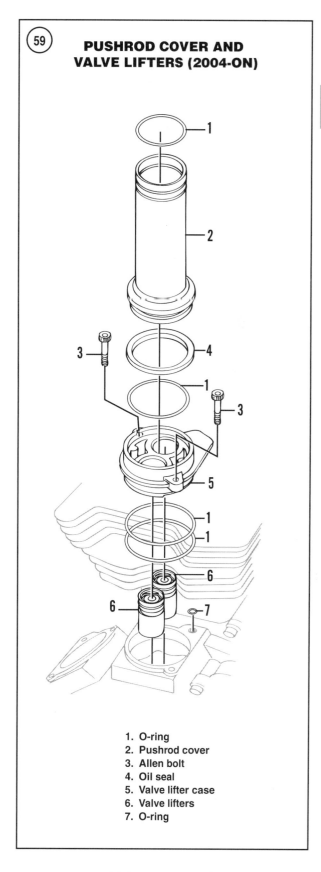

58

**PUSHROD COVER AND
VALVE LIFTERS (1999-2003)**

1. Oil seal
2. O-ring
3. Pushrod cover
4. Allen bolt
5. Valve lifter case cover
6. Oil seal
7. Valve lifter case
8. Valve lifters
9. O-ring

59

**PUSHROD COVER AND
VALVE LIFTERS (2004-ON)**

1. O-ring
2. Pushrod cover
3. Allen bolt
4. Oil seal
5. Valve lifter case
6. Valve lifters
7. O-ring

4

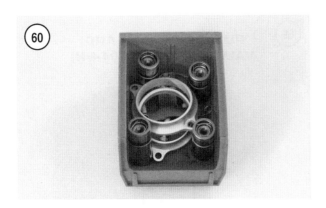

will click until they completely refill with oil. The lifters are working properly when they stop clicking after the engine is run for a few minutes.

Removal

After removal, store lifters in proper sequence, in a vertical position (**Figure 60**) and in their original position in the valve lifter case.

1. Remove the pushrods as described under *Rocker Arms And Pushrods* in this chapter.

2. Remove the valve lifters (A, **Figure 61**) from the valve lifter case and keep them vertical to avoid the loss of the internal engine oil.

NOTE
Figure 62 is shown with the crankcase disassembled to better illustrate the step.

3. To remove the valve lifter case, proceed as follows:
   a. Remove the pushrod covers (A, **Figure 63**) as described in this chapter.
   b. Disconnect the idle control knob and cable from the bracket.
   c. Remove the screws securing the cable bracket (B, **Figure 63**).
   d. Remove the screws securing the valve lifter case (B, **Figure 61**) to the crankcase and remove it (**Figure 62**, typical).

4. Cover the crankcase opening with duct tape to prevent the entry of small parts.

5. If the lifters are not going to be inspected, as described in the following section, store them upright in a container filled with new engine oil until installation.

Installation

1. If removed, install the valve lifter case as follows:

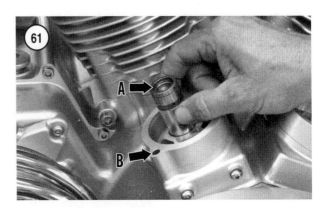

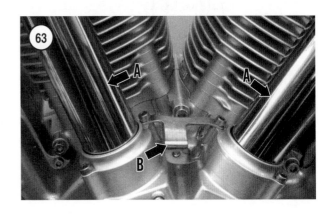

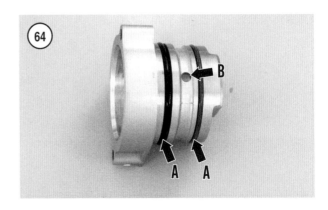

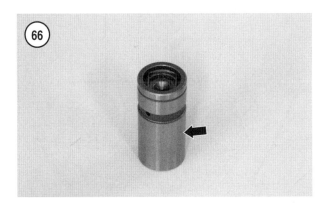

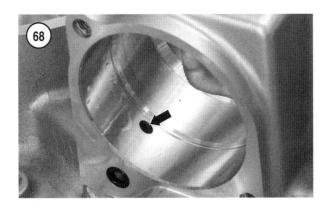

a. Apply engine oil to the valve lifter case O-rings (A, **Figure 64**).

b. Install the valve lifter case into the crankcase (**Figure 62**) and push in until it bottoms.

c. Align the screw holes in the case with the crankcase screw holes (B, **Figure 61**).

d. Install the idle control knob bracket (B, **Figure 63**).

e. Install the screws and tighten securely.

2. Remove two of the lifters from the oil filled container and keep them vertical.

3. Install both valve lifters (A, **Figure 61**) into the case receptacles.

4. Add engine oil to both valve lifters until the oil runs out.

5. Repeat Steps 1-4 to install the other set of lifters.

6. Install the pushrods as described under *Rocker Arms And Pushrods* in this chapter.

Inspection

> *CAUTION*
> *Place the lifters on a clean, lint-free cloth when handling and inspecting them in the following steps. When finished inspecting the lifters, store them in oil as previously described.*

1. Check the pushrod socket (**Figure 65**) in the top of the valve lifter for wear or damage.

2. Check the sides of the valve lifter (**Figure 66**) for wear or damage.

3. Inspect the valve lifter case bore (**Figure 67**) for scratches or damage.

4. Make sure the oil control hole (B, **Figure 64**) is clear. Also check the oil control hole in the crankcase (**Figure 68**). Clean out with compressed air if necessary.

5. Determine the lifter-to-guide clearance as follows:

a. Measure the lifter bore receptacle inside diameter in the valve lifter case (**Figure 69**) and record the measurement.

b. Measure the lifter outside diameter (**Figure 70**) and record the measurement.

c. Subtract sub-step b from sub-step a to determine the lifter-to-lifter case bore clearance, then compare the clearance to the service limit in **Table 2**. Replace the lifter or lifter case if the clearance is worn to the service limit.

6. If a valve lifter does not show visual damage, but it may be contaminated with dirt or has internal damage, replace it. The lifters are not serviceable and must be replaced as a unit.

7. After inspecting the lifters, store them in a container filled with engine oil until installation.

8. If most of the oil has drained out of the lifter, refill it with a pump-type oil can through the oil hole in the side of the lifter.

CYLINDER HEAD

Refer to **Figure 71**.

The cylinder head procedures are shown on the front cylinder. The procedures are the same for the rear cylinder head.

Removal

NOTE
*The cylinder heads are **not** identical. Mark them with a FRONT or REAR mark on the top surface of the cylinder head.*

1. Remove the fuel pump/fuel filter module as described in Chapter Nine.

2. Remove the bolts (**Figure 72**) securing the cylinder heads-to-frame bracket and remove the bracket.

3. Remove the external oil pipe assembly as follows:

a. Secure the oil pipe fitting with an open-end wrench (A, **Figure 73**), then loosen and remove the Allen head banjo bolt (B). Remove the copper washer from each side of the fitting.

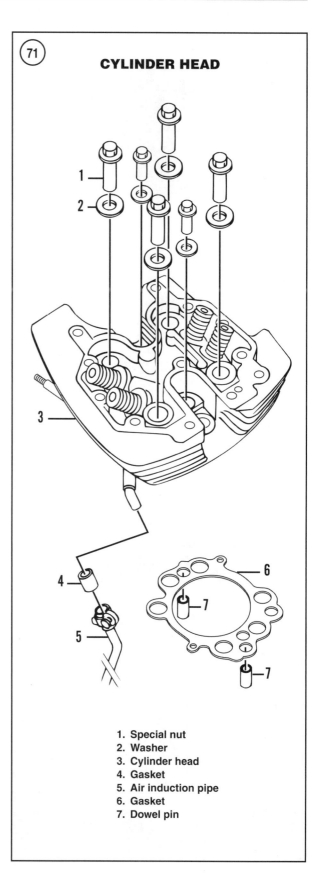

CYLINDER HEAD

1. Special nut
2. Washer
3. Cylinder head
4. Gasket
5. Air induction pipe
6. Gasket
7. Dowel pin

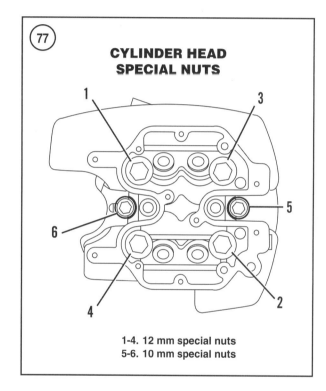

**CYLINDER HEAD
SPECIAL NUTS**

1-4. 12 mm special nuts
5-6. 10 mm special nuts

b. Repeat for the fitting (**Figure 74**) on the other cylinder head.

c. Loosen and remove the hex heat banjo bolt (**Figure 75**) securing the oil pipe to the crankcase. Remove the copper washer from each side of the fitting.

d. Remove the oil pipe assembly and drain out the oil.

4. Disconnect the air induction pipe (**Figure 76**, typical) from the cylinder head. Refer to Chapter Nine.

5. Remove the rocker arm assemblies and pushrods as described in this chapter.

6. Using a crisscross pattern, loosen the six cylinder head special nuts 1/8 turn at a time in the reverse order shown in **Figure 77**. Refer to **Figure 78** and **Figure 79**. Remove the washers under each special nut.

7. Tap the cylinder head with a rubber mallet to free it, and lift it off the cylinder block (**Figure 80**).

8. Remove and discard the cylinder head gasket.

9. Remove the two dowel pins, if loose.

10. Repeat these steps to remove the opposite cylinder head.

Installation

1. If removed, install the piston and cylinder as described in this chapter.

2. Lubricate the cylinder head special nuts as follows:
   a. Clean the cylinder head special nuts in solvent and dry with compressed air.
   b. Apply engine oil to the cylinder head nut threads and to the under side of the shoulder. Wipe off any excess oil from the special nuts. Leave only an oil film on the threads and shoulders.

3. Install the two dowel pins (A, **Figure 81**) into the top of the cylinder block, if removed.

4. Install a *new* cylinder head gasket (B, **Figure 81**) onto the cylinder block.

> *CAUTION*
> *Do not use sealer on the original equipment cylinder head gasket. If using an aftermarket head gasket, follow the manufacturer's instructions for gasket installation.*

> *NOTE*
> *The cylinder heads are **not** identical. Refer to the FRONT or REAR marks made prior to removal.*

5. Install the cylinder head (**Figure 80**) onto the cylinder block and the dowel pins. Position the head carefully to avoid moving the head gasket out of alignment.

> *NOTE*
> *There are two different size and length special nuts. The center two special nuts are 10 mm and the remaining four nuts are 12 mm. Install the special nuts in the correct locations.*

6. Install the center special 10 mm nuts and washers in the outer crankcase studs next to the spark plug holes. Tighten the cylinder head center special nuts only finger-tight at this time.

7. Install the remaining 12 mm special nuts and washers and tighten only finger-tight at this time.

> *CAUTION*
> *Failure to follow the torque stages and sequence in Step 8 may cause cylinder head distortion and gasket leakage.*

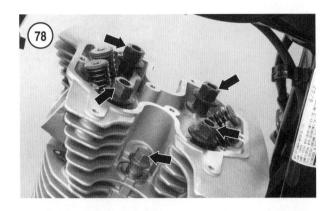

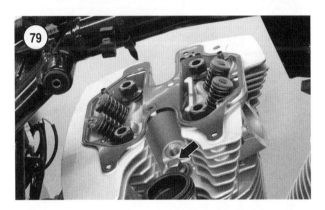

8. Tighten the cylinder head special nuts in two stages in the torque sequence shown in **Figure 77**. Refer to **Table 3** for torque specifications.

9. Install the rocker arm assemblies and pushrods as described in this chapter.

10. Connect the air induction pipe (**Figure 76**) onto the cylinder head. Refer to Chapter Nine.

11. Install the external oil pipe assembly as follows:
   a. Install a *new* copper washer on each side of all fittings.

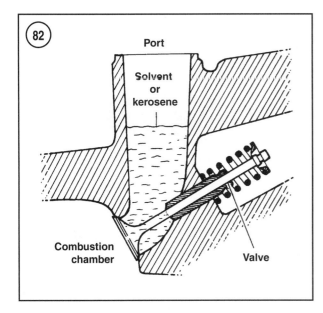

b. Install the oil pipe assembly onto the cylinder heads and crankcase.

c. Install the 10 mm Allen head banjo bolts and *new* copper washers at both cylinder heads (**Figure 74**, typical). Tighten the banjo bolts finger-tight.

d. Install the 8 mm hex heat banjo bolt (**Figure 75**) and *new* copper washers securing the oil pipe to the crankcase. Tighten the banjo bolt finger-tight.

e. Tighten the 8 mm hex head banjo bolt (**Figure 75**) to 18 N•m (159 in.-lb.).

f. Secure the oil pipe fitting with an open-end wrench (A, **Figure 73**), then tighten and remove the 10 mm Allen head banjo bolt (B) to 21 N•m (15 ft.-lb.).

g. Repeat for the fitting on the other cylinder head.

12. Install the cylinder heads-to-frame bracket and the bolts (**Figure 72**) and tighten securely.

13. Install the fuel pump/fuel filter module as described in Chapter Nine.

Inspection

1. Before removing the valves or cleaning the cylinder head, perform the following leak test:

a. Position the cylinder head so the exhaust port faces up. Pour solvent or kerosene into the exhaust port (**Figure 82**).

b. Turn the head over slightly and check the exhaust valve area on the combustion chamber side. If the valve and seats are in good condition, there will be no leaks past the valve seats. If any area is wet, the valve seat is not sealing correctly. This can be caused by a damaged valve seat and/or valve face, or by a bent or damaged valve. Remove the valve, and inspect the valve and seat for wear or damage.

c. Repeat Step 1b and pour solvent into the intake port and check the intake valves.

2. Remove all traces of gasket material from the mating surfaces on the cylinder head and cylinder.

CAUTION
Cleaning the combustion chamber with the valves removed can damage the valve seat surfaces. A damaged or even slightly scratched valve seat will cause poor valve seating.

3. Thoroughly clean the outside of the cylinder head. Use a stiff brush, soap and water and clean out all road dirt from the cooling fins (**Figure 83**). If necessary, use a piece of wood and scrape away any lodged dirt. Clogged cooling fins can cause overheating leading to possible engine damage.

4. *Without removing the valves*, use a wire brush to remove all carbon deposits from the combustion chamber (A, **Figure 84**). Use a fine wire brush and solvent or make a scraper from hardwood. Do not damage the cylinder head, valves or spark plug threads.

5. Examine both spark plug threads (B, **Figure 84**) in the cylinder head for damage. If damage is minor or if the

threads are dirty or clogged with carbon, use a spark plug thread tap (**Figure 85**) and clean the threads following the manufacturer instructions. If thread damage is severe, the threads can be restored by installing a steel thread insert. Thread insert kits can be purchased at automotive supply stores or the inserts can be installed by a Yamaha dealership or machine shop.

CAUTION
Coat the thread tap with aluminum tap cutting fluid or kerosene.

CAUTION
Aluminum spark plug threads are commonly damaged due to galling, cross-threading and over-tightening. To prevent galling, apply an anti-seize compound on the plug threads before installation and do not over-tighten.

6. After all carbon is removed from combustion chambers and valve ports, and the spark plug thread holes have been repaired, clean the entire head in solvent. Blow dry with compressed air.

7. Examine the crown on the piston. The crown should show no signs of wear or damage. If the crown appears pecked or spongy-looking, also check the spark plug, valves and combustion chamber for aluminum deposits. If these deposits are found, the cylinder is suffering from excessive heat caused by a lean fuel mixture or preignition.

8. Check for cracks in the combustion chamber, the intake port (**Figure 86**), the exhaust port (A, **Figure 87**). A cracked head must be replaced if it cannot be repaired by welding.

9. Inspect the mounting stud threads (B, **Figure 87**) for the exhaust pipe mounting nuts for damage. Clean up with an appropriate size metric tap if damaged.

CAUTION
If the cylinder head was bead-blasted, clean the head thoroughly with solvent and then with hot soapy water. Residual grit seats in small crevices and other areas and can be hard to get out. Also chase each exposed thread with a tap to remove grit between the threads or the threads may be damaged later. Grit left in the engine will contaminate the oil and cause premature piston, ring and bearing wear.

10. After the head has been thoroughly cleaned, place a straightedge across the gasket sealing surface at several points. Measure warp by attempting to insert a feeler gauge between the straightedge and cylinder head at several locations (**Figure 88**). Maximum allowable warp is in

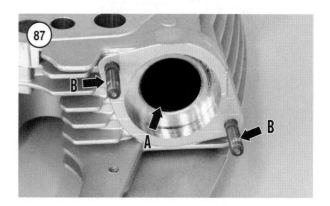

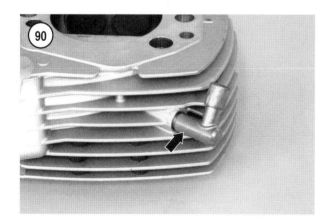

Table 2. Warp or nicks in the cylinder head surface could cause an air leak and result in overheating. If warp exceeds the limit, the cylinder head must be resurfaced or replaced. Consult a Yamaha dealership or machine shop experienced in this type of work.

11. Check the rocker arm base mating surface (**Figure 89**, typical) for warp at several locations. Warp or nicks in the cylinder head surface could cause an oil leak.

12. Check the secondary air intake fittings (**Figure 90**, typical) for damage.

13. Check the valves and valve guides as described under *Valves and Valve Components* in this chapter.

VALVES AND VALVE COMPONENTS

Complete valve service requires a number of special tools. The following procedures describe how to check valve components and determine the needed service.

A valve spring compressor (Yamaha part No. YM-04019 [U.S.] or 90890-04019 [U.K.]), or equivalent, is required to remove and install the valves.

Valve Removal

Refer to **Figure 91**.

> *CAUTION*
> *Keep the components of each particular valve assembly together. Do not mix components from different valve assemblies or excessive wear may occur.*

1. Remove the cylinder head as described in this chapter.
2. Perform the cylinder head leak test described in *Cylinder Head* in this chapter.
3. Install a valve spring compressor squarely over the valve retainer (**Figure 92**). Make sure the opposite end of the compressor rests against the valve head.

> *CAUTION*
> *To avoid loss of spring tension, do not compress the valve spring any more than necessary to remove the valve keepers.*

4. Tighten the compressor until the valve keepers separate from the valve stem. Remove both valve keepers with a magnet, tweezers (**Figure 93**) or needle nose pliers.
5. Release the pressure and carefully remove the valve spring compressor.
6. Remove the spring retainer (**Figure 94**).
7. Remove the outer valve spring (**Figure 95**) and inner valve spring (**Figure 96**).
8. Remove the oil seal (A, **Figure 97**) from the valve guide. Discard the oil seal.
9. Remove the spring seat (B, **Figure 97**).

> *CAUTION*
> *Remove any burrs from the valve stem grooves before removing the valve. Burrs on the valve stem will damage the valve guide when the stem passes through it.*

10. Inspect the valve stem grooves for burrs (**Figure 98**) and remove if necessary.

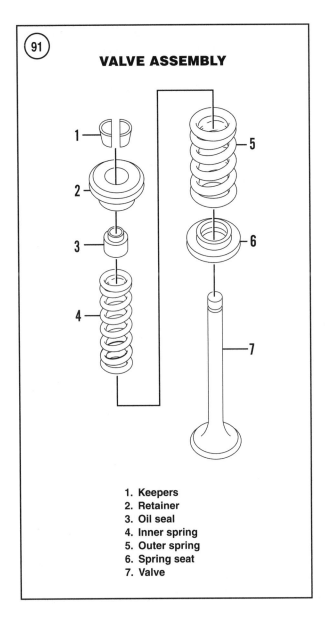

VALVE ASSEMBLY

1. Keepers
2. Retainer
3. Oil seal
4. Inner spring
5. Outer spring
6. Spring seat
7. Valve

11. Remove the valve (C, **Figure 97**) from the cylinder head while rotating it slightly.

> *CAUTION*
> *All the components of each valve assembly must be kept together (**Figure 99**). Place each set in a divided carton or into separate small boxes. Label the set as to which cylinder it came from and whether it is an intake or an exhaust valve. Do not mix components from different valve assemblies or excessive wear may occur.*

12. Repeat Steps 3-11 for the remaining valve assemblies. Keep the parts from each valve assembly separate.

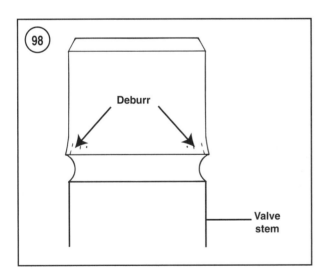

seal straight down onto the valve guide until the seal bottoms (**Figure 101**).

4. Apply molybdenum disulfide oil to the valve stem. Install the valve partway into the guide (**Figure 102**). Slowly turn the valve as it enters the oil seal, and continue turning the valve until it is completely installed.

5. Position the inner valve spring (**Figure 96**) with the closer wound coils going on first facing toward the combustion chamber. Install the spring.

Valve Installation

1. Clean the end of the valve guide.

2. Install the spring seat and seat it on the cylinder head (**Figure 100**).

3. Apply molybdenum disulfide oil to a new oil seal and install the seal over the end of the valve guide. Push the

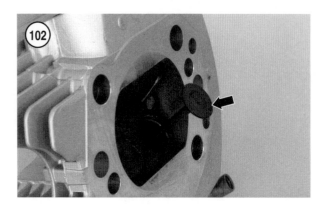

6. Position the outer valve spring (**Figure 95**) with the closer wound coils going on first facing toward the combustion chamber. Install the spring.

7. Install the spring retainer (**Figure 103**) and seat it on top of both springs (**Figure 94**). Make sure it is centered on the valve springs.

8. Install a valve spring compressor squarely over the spring retainer (**Figure 104**). Make sure the opposite end of the compressor sits against the valve head.

CAUTION
To avoid loss of spring tension, do not compress the springs any more than necessary to install the valve keepers.

9. Compress the valve springs with a valve spring compressor (**Figure 92**) and install both valve keepers (**Figure 105**).

10. When both valve keepers are correctly seated around the valve stem, slowly release the compressor. Remove the compressor and inspect the keepers (**Figure 106**). Tap the end of the valve stem with a soft-faced mallet to ensure the keepers are properly seated.

11. Repeat Steps 1-10 for the remaining valves.

12. Install the cylinder head as described in this chapter.

13. Adjust the valve clearance as described in Chapter Three.

Valve Inspection

CAUTION
When a valve needs to be replaced also replace its valve guide. Do not install a new valve into an old guide or excessive wear will occur.

1. Clean the valve in solvent. Do not gouge or damage the valve seating surface.

2. Inspect the contact surface of each valve (**Figure 107**) for burning. Minor roughness or pitting can be removed

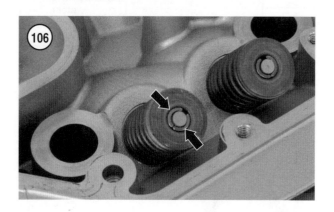

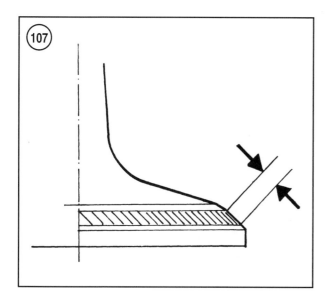

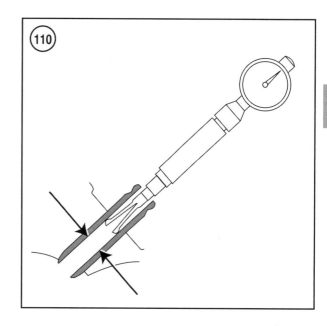

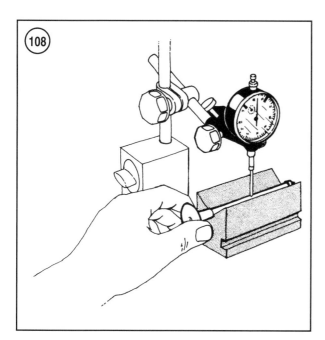

by lapping the valve as described in this chapter. Excessive unevenness indicates that the valve is not serviceable. Replace the valve and the valve guide.

3. Inspect the valve stem for wear and roughness. Measure the runout with V-blocks and a dial indicator, as shown in **Figure 108**. Replace the valve and valve guide if runout is outside the specified range.

4. Measure the diameter of the valve stem with a micrometer (**Figure 109**). Replace the valve and valve guide if the diameter of the valve stem is outside the specified range.

5. Remove all carbon and varnish from the valve guides with a stiff spiral wire brush.

6. Measure the inside diameter of the valve guide with a small bore gauge (**Figure 110**), then measure the bore gauge with a micrometer. Take a measurement at the top, middle and bottom of the guide. Replace the valve guide if any measurement is outside the specified range.

7. Subtract the valve stem outside diameter (Step 4) from the valve guide inside diameter (Step 6). The difference is the valve stem-to-guide clearance. If the clearance exceeds the service limit, replace the valve and valve guide as a set.

8. Check the valve spring as follows:

a. Visually inspect the valve spring for bends, cracks or other signs of distortion.

b. Measure each valve spring free length with a vernier caliper (**Figure 111**). Replace the spring if its free length is less than the service limit.

c. Use a square to measure the tilt of each spring (**Figure 112**). Tilt should be within the specification in **Table 2**.

d. Replace any defective or worn spring.

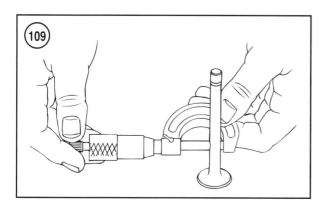

9. Measure the valve margin thickness (**Figure 113**) with a vernier caliper. Replace the valve and valve guide if the margin thickness is worn to the wear limit.

10. Check the spring seat, spring retainer and valve keepers for cracks or other damage.

11. Inspect each valve seat (**Figure 114**) in the cylinder head. If a seat is burned or worn, it must be reconditioned. This should be performed by a dealership or local machine shop. Seats and valves in near perfect condition can be reconditioned by lapping with fine carborendum paste.

Valve Guide Replacement

Special tools

When valve stem-to-guide clearance is excessive, the valve guides must be replaced. If a valve guide is replaced, also replace its respective valve. This procedure requires the following special tools and should be entrusted to a Yamaha dealership or other qualified specialist.

1. 6 mm (0.24 in.) valve guide remover (YM- 4064-A [U.S.] or 90890-04094 [U.K.]).

2. 6 mm (0.24 in.) valve guide installer (YM- 4065-A [U.S.] or 90890-04065 [U.K.]).

3. 6 mm (0.24 in.) valve guide reamer (YM-4066 [U.S.] or 90890-04066 [U.K.]).

Procedure

1. Install *new* circlips onto the new valve guides.

2. Place the *new* valve guides in a freezer for several hours to reduce their overall size for ease of installation. Do not remove until they are ready to be installed.

CAUTION
Do not heat the cylinder head with a torch. Never bring a flame into contact with the cylinder head. The direct heat will destroy

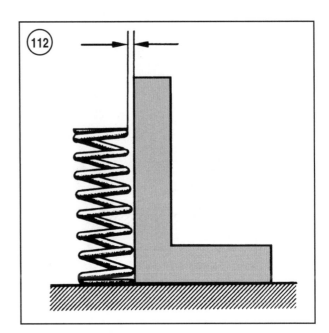

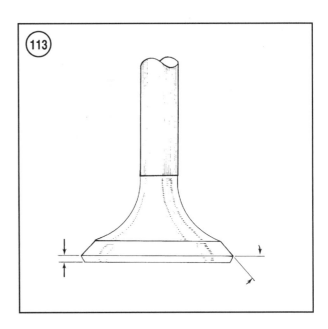

the case hardening of the valve guide and may warp the cylinder head.

3. Place the cylinder head on a hot plate or in a shop oven and warm it to 100° C (212° F). Monitor the temperature with heat sticks, available at welding supply stores.

WARNING
Wear welding gloves or similar insulated gloves when handling the cylinder head. The cylinder head will be very hot.

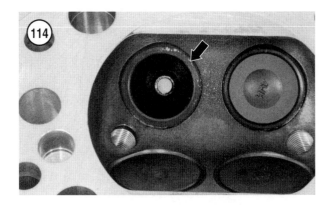

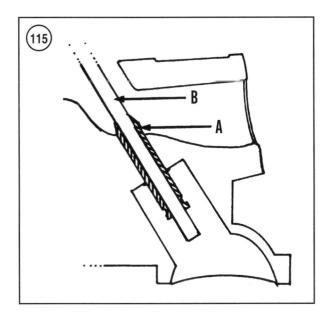

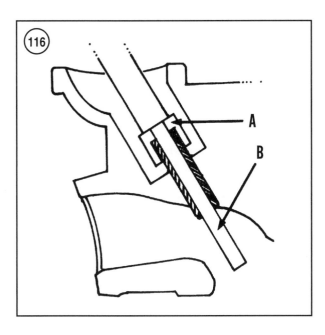

4. Remove the cylinder head from the hot plate or oven and place it on wooden blocks with the combustion chamber facing *up*.

5. From the combustion side of the head, drive the old valve guide (A, **Figure 115**) out of the cylinder head with the valve guide remover (B) and a hammer. Quickly repeat this step for each guide to be replaced. Reheat the cylinder head if necessary. Discard the valve guides and circlips after removing them.

CAUTION
Do not remove the valve guides if the cylinder head is not hot enough. Doing so may damage the valve guide bore in the cylinder head.

6. Allow the cylinder head to cool.

7. Clean and inspect the valve guide bores. Check for cracks along the bore wall.

8. Reheat the cylinder head as described in Step 3, then remove it from the hot plate and place it on wooden blocks with the valve spring side facing *up*.

9. Remove one *new* valve guide from the freezer. Make sure the *new* circlip is in place on the valve guide.

CAUTION
Failure to lubricate the new valve guide and guide bore will result in damage to the cylinder head and/or valve guide.

10. Apply engine oil to the new valve guide and to the valve guide bore in the cylinder head.

11. Align the valve guide in the bore. From the top side of the cylinder head (valve spring side), drive the new valve guide into the cylinder head with a hammer, the valve guide installer (A, **Figure 116**) and the valve guide remover (B). Drive the valve guide into the bore until the circlip is completely seated against the cylinder head. Quickly repeat this step for each guide to be installed.

12. Allow the cylinder head to cool to room temperature.

13. Ream the new valve guides (**Figure 117**) as follows:

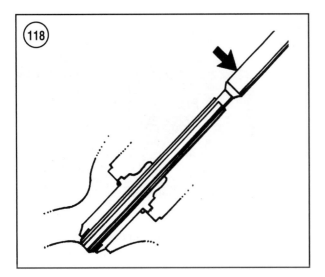

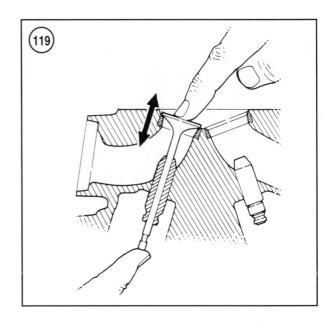

a. Place the cylinder head on wooden blocks with the valve spring side facing *up*. The valve guides must be reamed from this side.

b. Coat the *new* valve guide and the valve guide reamer with cutting oil.

CAUTION
*Always rotate the valve guide reamer **clockwise** through the entire length of the valve guide, both when reaming the guide and when removing the reamer. Rotating the reamer **counterclockwise** will reverse cut and damage (enlarge) the valve guide bore.*

CAUTION
Do not allow the reamer to tilt. Keep the tool square to the hole and apply even pressure and twisting motion during the entire operation.

c. Insert the 6 mm (0.24 in.) valve guide reamer from the valve spring side (**Figure 118**) and rotate the reamer through the guide, while periodically adding cutting oil

d. As the reamer has passed through the guide, maintain the *clockwise* rotation and work the reamer back out of the guide while continuing to add cutting oil.

e. Clean the reamer of all chips and re-lubricate with cutting oil prior to start on another guide. Repeat for each additional guide as required.

14. Thoroughly clean the cylinder head and valve components in solvent, then in detergent and hot water to remove all cutting particles. Rinse in cold water. Dry with compressed air. Then apply a light coat of engine oil to all non-aluminum surfaces to prevent rust.

15. Lightly oil the valve guides to prevent rust.

16. Measure the valve guides inside diameter with a small bore gauge. The measurement must be within the specifications in **Table 2**.

17. Recondition the valve seats as described in this section.

Valve Seat Inspection

1. Remove all carbon residue from each valve seat (**Figure 114**). Then clean the cylinder head as described under *Valve Inspection* in this section.

NOTE
The most accurate method of checking the valve seat width and position is with machinist's dye.

2. Inspect the valves and valve seats in their original locations with machinist's dye as follows:

a. Thoroughly clean the valve face and valve seat with contact cleaner.

b. Spread a thin layer of Prussian blue or machinist's dye evenly on the valve face.

c. Insert the valve into its guide.

d. Support the valve by hand (**Figure 119**) and tap the valve up and down in the cylinder head. Do not rotate the valve or a false reading will result.

e. Remove the valve and examine the impression left by the machinist's dye. The impressions on the valve and the seat must be even around their circumferences and the width (**Figure 120**) must be within the specifications in **Table 2**. If the width is beyond

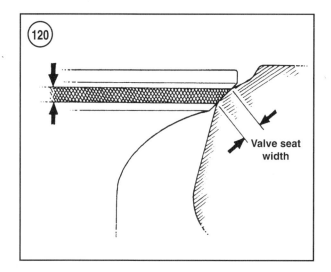

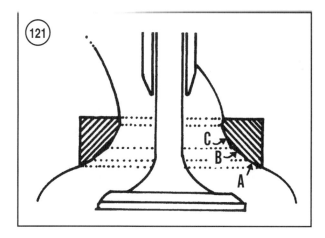

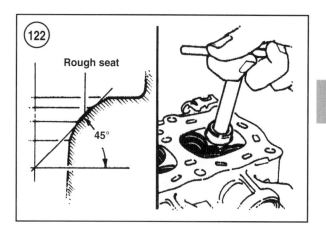

the specification or if the impression is uneven, re-condition the valve seats.

3. Closely examine the valve seat in the cylinder head (**Figure 114**). It must be smooth and even with a polished seating surface.

4. If the valve seat is in good condition, install the valve as described in this chapter.

5. If the valve seat is not correct, recondition the valve seat as described in this section.

Valve Seat Reconditioning

Special valve cutters and considerable expertise are required to properly recondition the valve seats in the cylinder head.

In most cases it is more economical and practical to have these procedures performed by a Yamaha dealership or machine shop.

A valve seat cutter set (consisting of 30°, 45° and 60° cutters and the appropriate handle) is required. These tool sets are available from a Yamaha dealership or from machine shop supply outlets. Follow the manufacturer instructions.

The valve seats for both the intake valves and exhaust valves are machined to the same angles. The area below the contact surface (closest to the combustion chamber) is cut to a 30° angle (A, **Figure 121**). The valve contact surface is cut to a 45° angle (B, **Figure 121**). The area above the contact surface (closest to the valve guide) is cut to a 60° angle (C, **Figure 121**).

1. Using the 45° cutter, descale and clean the valve seat with one or two turns (**Figure 122**).

CAUTION
Measure the valve seat contact area in the cylinder head with a vernier caliper after each cut to make sure the contact area is correct and to prevent removing too much material. If too much material is removed, the cylinder head must be replaced.

2. If the seat is still pitted or burned, turn the 45° cutter additional turns until the surface is clean. Avoid removing too much material from the cylinder head.

3. Remove the valve cutter and T-handle from the cylinder head.

4. Use marking compound to inspect the valve seat as described in *Valve Seat Inspection* in this section.

5. If the contact area is centered on the valve face but is too wide (**Figure 123**), use either the 30° or the 60° cutter and remove a portion of the valve seat material to narrow the contact area.

6. If the contact area is centered on the valve face but is too narrow (**Figure 124**), use the 45° cutter and remove a portion of the valve seat material to increase the contact area.

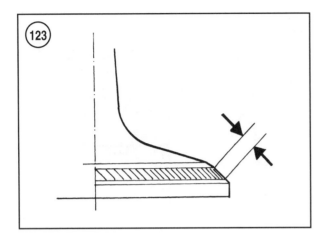

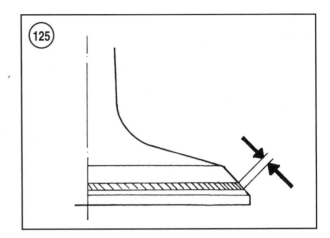

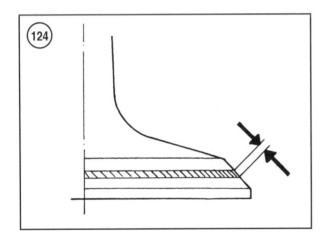

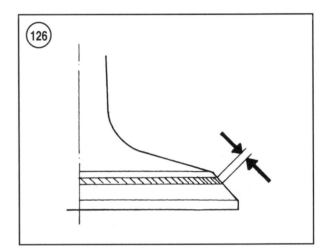

7. If the contact area is too narrow and close to the valve head (**Figure 125**), first use the 30° cutter and then use the 45° cutter to center the contact area.

8. If the contact area is too narrow and down away from the valve head (**Figure 126**), first use the 60° cutter and then use the 45° cutter to center the contact area.

9. After the desired valve seat position and width is obtained, use the 45° cutter and T-handle and very lightly clean away any burrs that may have been caused by the previous cuts; remove only enough material as necessary.

10. Make sure the finish has a smooth and velvety surface, it should not be shiny or highly polished. The final seating will take place when the engine is first run.

11. Repeat Steps 1-10 for all remaining valve seats.

12. Thoroughly clean the cylinder head and valve components in solvent, then in detergent and hot water. Rinse in cold water. Dry with compressed air. Then apply a light coat of engine oil to all non-aluminum surfaces to prevent rust.

13. After the valve seat has been reconditioned, lap the seat and valve as described in this section.

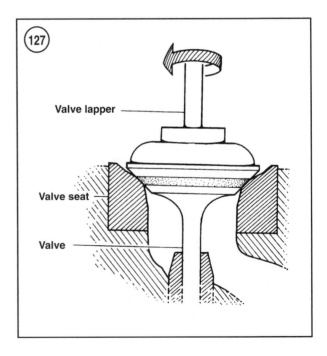

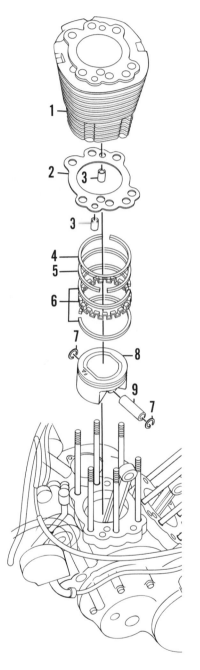

CYLINDER AND PISTON

1. Cylinder
2. Gasket
3. Dowel pin
4. Compression ring
5. Compression ring
6. Oil ring set
7. Circlip
8. Piston
9. Piston pin

Valve Lapping

Valve lapping is an operation that can restore the valve seal without machining if wear or distortion is not excessive.

Perform this procedure after determining that the valve seat width and outside diameter are within specifications. Use a valve lapping tool and compound for this procedure.

1. Smear a light coating of fine grade valve lapping compound on the seating surface of the valve.
2. Insert the valve into the head.
3. Wet the suction cup of the lapping tool and stick it onto the head of the valve. Spin the tool in both directions, while pressing it against the valve seat, and lap the valve to the seat (**Figure 127**). Every 5 to10 seconds, lift the valve and rotate the valve 180° in the valve seat. Continue until the gasket surfaces on the valve and valve seat are smooth and equal in size.
4. Closely examine the valve seat in the cylinder head. The seat must be smooth and even with a polished seating ring.
5. Repeat steps 1-4 for the remaining valves.
6. Thoroughly clean the cylinder head and valve components in solvent, then in detergent and hot water. Rinse in cold water. Dry with compressed air. Then apply a light coat of engine oil to all non-aluminum surfaces to prevent rust.
7. After installing the valves into the cylinder head, test each valve for proper seating. Check by pouring solvent into the intake and exhaust ports. Solvent must not leak past the valve seats. If solvent leaks past any of the seats, disassemble that valve assembly and repeat the lapping procedure until there is no leakage.
8. After the lapping has been completed and the valve assemblies have been reinstalled into the cylinder head, the valve seat should be tested. Check the seat by performing the leakage test described under *Cylinder Head* in this chapter. If fluid leaks past any of the seats, disassemble that valve assembly and repeat the lapping procedure until there are no leaks.

CYLINDER

Refer to **Figure 128**.

The cylinder procedures are shown on the front cylinder, with the rear cylinder removed to better illustrate the steps. The procedures are the same for the rear cylinder.

Removal

1. Remove the cylinder head as described in this chapter.
2. Remove all debris from the top of the cylinder.
3. If still in place, remove the two dowel pins (A, **Figure 129**) and gasket (B) from the top of the cylinder.

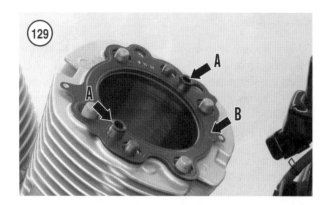

4. Turn the crankshaft until the piston is at bottom dead center (BDC).

5. Tap around the perimeter with a rubber or plastic mallet to loosen the cylinder.

NOTE
The front and rear cylinders are identical (same part number). Mark each cylinder so it will be reinstalled in its original position.

6. Pull the cylinder straight up until it clears the piston and the crankcase studs (**Figure 130**).

7. Pivot the cylinder to the right side and remove the cylinder (**Figure 131**).

8. Place clean shop rags (A, **Figure 132**) into the crankcase opening to keep foreign objects out of the crankcase.

9. Install a vinyl or rubber hose over the front or rear two studs (B, **Figure 132**). This will protect the piston and rings.

NOTE
***Figure 133** is shown with the piston removed to illustrate both dowel pins.*

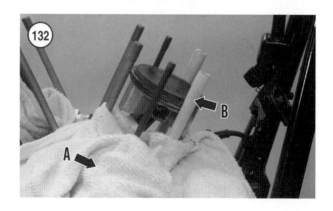

10. Remove the base gasket (A, **Figure 133**) from the crankcase. Remove the dowel pins (B, **Figure 133**), if loose.

CAUTION
After removing the cylinder, take care when working around the cylinder studs to avoid bending or damaging them. The slightest bend could cause a stud failure during operation.

11. Repeat these steps to remove the opposite cylinder.

Installation

1. Remove all gasket residue and clean the cylinder as described under *Inspection* in this section.

2. Install the dowel pins (B, **Figure 133**), if removed.

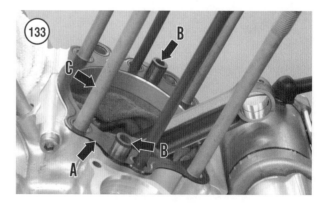

6. Remove the shop cloths from the crankcase (A, **Figure 132**).

7. Turn the crankshaft until the piston is at top dead center (TDC).

8. Lubricate the cylinder bore, piston and piston rings with engine oil.

9. Make sure the rings seat completely in their grooves all the way around the piston and that the end gaps are distributed around the piston as shown in **Figure 134**. The ring gaps must not align with each other during installation to prevent compression pressure from escaping past them during initial start up.

NOTE
Install the cylinder in its original position as noted during removal.

10. Install the cylinder from the right side (**Figure 131**) and over the crankcase studs.

11. Align the cylinder with the crankcase studs (**Figure 130**), and slowly lower it down toward the piston (**Figure 135**).

12. Slowly lower the cylinder until the piston starts to enter the cylinder bore.

13. Use your fingers to compress the piston rings, on both sides of the piston, and slowly lower the cylinder over the piston and its rings (**Figure 136**). Use both hands and square the piston within the cylinder bore (**Figure 137**).

14. Continue to slide the cylinder down until it bottoms on the crankcase base gasket (**Figure 138**).

15. Repeat to install the other cylinder.

16. Install the cylinder heads as described in this chapter.

Inspection

CAUTION
The cylinder bore must be cleaned thoroughly before attempting any measurements, if not

3. Install a *new* base gasket (A, **Figure 133**) on the crankcase.

4. Install the pistons and rings as described in this chapter, if removed.

5. Remove the vinyl or rubber hose from the crankcase studs (B, **Figure 132**).

thoroughly cleaned, incorrect readings will be obtained.

CAUTION
The cylinder must be at room temperature to obtain accurate measurements. Do not measure the cylinder directly after it has been honed as it will still be warm. Measurements can vary by 0.051 mm (0.002 in.) if the cylinder is warmer than room temperature.

1. Thoroughly clean the outside of the cylinder. Use a stiff brush, soap and water and clean out all road dirt from the cooling fins (**Figure 139**). If necessary, use a piece of wood and scrape away any lodged dirt. Clogged cooling fins can cause overheating, leading to possible engine damage.

2. Carefully remove all gasket residue from the top (A, **Figure 140**) and bottom (**Figure 141**) cylinder gasket surfaces.

3. Thoroughly clean the cylinder with solvent and dry with compressed air. Lightly oil the cylinder bore to prevent rust after performing Step 4.

4. Check the top cylinder gasket surfaces with a straightedge and feeler gauge (**Figure 142**). Replace the cylinder if the warp exceeds the service limit in **Table 2**.

5. Measure the cylinder bore, with a bore gauge or inside micrometer (**Figure 143**) at the positions indicated in **Figure 144**.

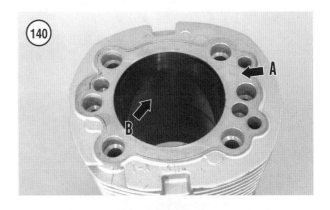

6. Measure the bore in two axes: in-line with the piston pin and 90° to the piston pin. If the taper or out-of-round measurements exceeds the service limits in **Table 2**, replace the cylinder, piston and rings as a set.

7. Check the cylinder walls (B, **Figure 140**) for scuffing, scratches or other damage.

8. Confirm all cylinder measurements with a Yamaha dealership before ordering replacement parts.

9. After servicing the cylinders, wash each cylinder in hot, soapy water. This is the only way to clean the cylinder walls of the fine grit material left from a honing process. After washing the cylinder bore, run a clean white cloth through it. If the cloth shows traces of grit or oil, wash again until the cloth comes out clean. Dry with compressed air, then lubricate with engine oil. Repeat for the other cylinder.

CAUTION
Solvent and kerosene cannot wash fine grit out of the cylinder crevices. Grit left in the cylinder will cause premature wear to the engine components.

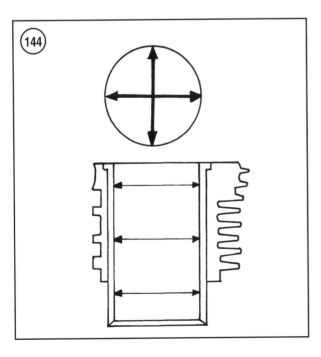

Cylinder Studs and Cylinder Head Special Nuts Inspection and Cleaning

The cylinder studs and cylinder head special nuts must be in good condition and properly cleaned prior to installing the cylinder and the cylinder heads. Damaged or dirty studs may cause cylinder head distortion and gasket leakage.

CAUTION
The original equipment cylinder studs, cylinder head special nuts and washers are specifically designed for this application. Do not replace these components with generic parts.

1. Inspect the cylinder head special nuts. Replace any that are damaged.
2. Examine the cylinder studs (C, **Figure 133**) for bending, looseness or damage. Have the damaged studs replaced by a Yamaha dealership or machine shop. If the studs are in good condition, perform Step 3.
3. Cover both crankcase openings with shop rags to prevent debris from falling into the engine.
4. Remove all carbon residue from the cylinder studs and cylinder head special nuts as follows:
    a. Apply solvent to the cylinder stud and mating cylinder head special nut threads and thread the special nut onto the stud.
    b. Turn the cylinder head bolt back and forth to loosen and remove the carbon residue from the threads. Remove the nut from the stud. Wipe off the residue with a shop rag moistened in cleaning solvent.
    c. Repeat until both thread sets are free of all carbon residues.
    d. Spray the cylinder stud and cylinder head bolt with an aerosol parts cleaner and allow them to dry.
    e. Set the cleaned bolt aside and install it on the same stud when installing the cylinder head.
5. Repeat Step 4 for each cylinder stud and cylinder head bolt set.

PISTONS AND PISTON RINGS

The pistons are made of an aluminum alloy. The piston pins are made of steel and are a precision fit. The piston pin is held in place by a snap ring at each end.
Refer to **Figure 128**.

Piston Removal

1. Remove the cylinder head and cylinder as described in this chapter.

2. Lightly mark the top of the piston (front or rear) so it can be installed in the correct cylinder during installation.

WARNING
The edges of all piston rings are very sharp. Be careful when handling them to avoid cut fingers.

3. Before removing the piston, hold the connecting rod tightly and rock the piston (**Figure 145**). Any rocking motion (do not confuse with the normal sliding motion) indicates wear on the piston pin, piston pin bore or connecting rod small-end bore (more likely a combination of these). If necessary, replace the piston and piston pin as a set.

4. Block off the crankcase below the piston with a clean shop cloth to prevent the circlip from falling into the crankcase.

5. Remove a circlip (**Figure 146**) from one side of the piston pin bore with a small screwdriver or scribe. Hold a thumb over one edge of the circlip when removing it to prevent the snap ring from flying out. Deburr the piston pin and the circlip groove as necessary.

6. Support the piston and from the other side, push the piston pin out of the piston by hand. If the piston pin is tight, remove it with the homemade tool shown in **Figure 147**. Do not drive out the piston pin as this could damage the piston pin, connecting rod and/or piston.

7. Remove the piston from the connecting rod and remove the remaining circlip from the piston. Discard both piston pin circlip.

8. Mark the piston pin and piston so they can be reassembled as a set.

9. If the piston is going to be left off for some time, place a piece of foam insulation tube over the end of the connecting rod to protect it.

10. If necessary, remove the piston rings as described in this section.

Piston Installation

1. Apply engine oil to the inside surface of the connecting rods.

CAUTION
Install new piston pin snap rings during assembly.

2. Install a *new* piston pin circlip into one side of the piston. Make sure the circlip end gap does not align with the notch in the piston (**Figure 148**).

3. Apply engine oil to the piston pin, and install the pin into the piston until it is flush with the inside of the piston pin boss (**Figure 149**).

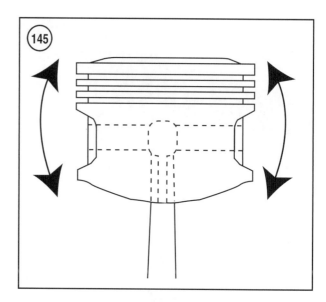

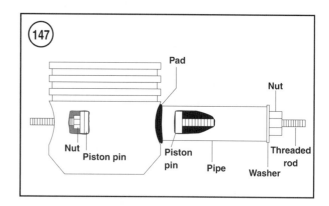

4. Place the piston over the connecting rod. Make sure the ▲ mark and F mark on the piston crown (**Figure 150**) face toward the front of the engine.

CAUTION
When installing the piston pin in Step 5, do not push the pin in too far. The piston pin

*snap ring installed in Step 2 will be forced
into the piston material, destroying the snap
ring groove and loosening the snap ring.*

5. Line up the piston pin with the hole in the connecting
rod. Push the piston pin through the connecting rod and
into the boss on the other side of the piston (**Figure 151**).
It may be necessary to slightly move the piston until the
piston pin enters the connecting rod. Do not force the
pivot pin during installation or damage may occur. Push
the piston pin in until it bottoms against the circlip on the
other side of the piston.

6. If the piston pin does not slide easily, use the homemade tool (**Figure 147**) used during removal but eliminate the piece of pipe. Pull the piston pin in until it stops.

7. After the piston is installed, recheck and make sure the
▲ mark and F mark (**Figure 150**) on the piston crown face
toward the front of the engine.

8. Install the second piston pin circlip (**Figure 152**) into
the groove in the piston. Make sure the snap ring's end
gap does not align with the notch in the piston (**Figure
148**). Also, make sure both piston pin circlips are seated in
their grooves in the piston.

9. Check the installation by rocking the piston back and
forth around the pin axis and from side to side along the
axis. It should rotate freely back and forth, but not from
side to side.

10. If removed, install the piston rings as described in this
section.

11. Install the cylinder and cylinder head as described in
this chapter.

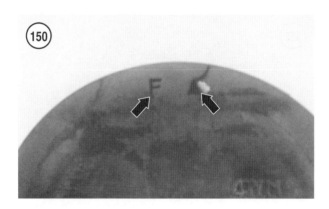

Piston Inspection

1. Carefully clean the carbon from the piston crown (**Figure 153**) with a chemical remover or with a soft scraper.
Re-mark the piston (front or rear) as soon as it has been
cleaned. Do not remove or damage the carbon ring around
the circumference of the piston above the top ring. If the

piston, rings and cylinder are dimensionally correct and can be reused, removal of the carbon ring from the top of the piston and/or removal of the carbon ridge from the top of the cylinder block wall will promote excessive oil consumption in that cylinder.

CAUTION
Do not use a wire brush on the piston skirts.

2. After cleaning the piston, examine the crown. It should show no signs of wear or damage.

3. Examine each ring groove for burrs, dented edges and wide wear (A, **Figure 154**). Pay particular attention to the top compression ring groove. It usually wears more than the other grooves. Since the oil rings are constantly bathed in oil, these rings and grooves wear little compared to compression rings and their grooves. If the oil ring groove shows signs of wear, or if the oil ring assembly is tight and difficult to remove, the piston skirt may have collapsed. If so, replace the piston.

4. Check the oil control holes (**Figure 155**) in the piston for carbon or oil sludge build-up. If necessary, clean the holes and blow them out with compressed air.

5. Check the piston skirt (B, **Figure 154**) for galling and abrasion, which may have been caused by piston seizure. If a piston shows signs of partial seizure (bits of aluminum build-up on the piston skirt), replace the piston to reduce the possibility of engine noise and further piston seizure. When replacing the piston, lightly hone the cylinder with a bottle brush hone.

NOTE
If the piston skirt is worn or scuffed un-evenly from side to side, the connecting rod may be bent or twisted.

6. Check the circlip groove (**Figure 156**) on each side of the piston for wear or other damage. Install a new circlip into each piston circlip groove and try to move the circlip from side to side. If the circlip has any side play, the groove is worn and the piston must be replaced.

7. Measure the outside diameter of the piston across the skirt at right angles to the piston pin (**Figure 157**). Refer to **Table 2** for the measurement point from the bottom of the piston skirt. If the piston diameter is out of specification, replace the piston and rings as a set. When installing the new piston, lightly hone the cylinder with a bottle brush hone.

8. Measure the piston-to-cylinder clearance as described in *Piston Clearance* in this section. If clearance is out of specification (**Table 2**), replace the cylinder, piston and rings as a set. Oversized pistons are not available.

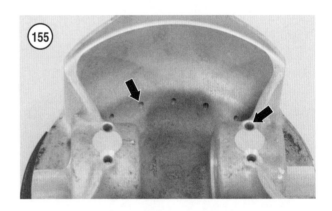

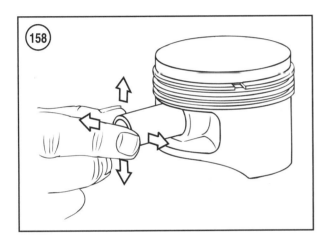

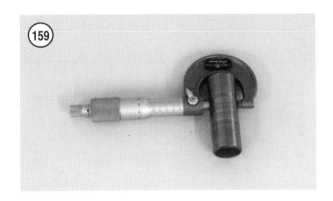

3. Measure the outside diameter of the piston across the skirt at right angles to the piston pin. Measure the piston at a point 5 mm (0.20 in.) from the bottom of the piston skirt (**Figure 157**).

4. Piston-to-cylinder clearance is the difference between the piston outside diameter and the cylinder bore diameter. Subtract the outside diameter of the piston from the cylinder bore diameter calculated in Step 2. If the piston-to-cylinder clearance is out of specification (**Table 2**), replace the cylinder, piston and rings as a set. Oversized pistons are not available.

Piston Pin Inspection

When measuring the piston pin, compare the actual measurements to the specifications in **Table 2**. Replace the piston pin if out of specification or if it shows signs of damage as described in this section. If the piston pin is replaced, also replace the piston as a set.

1. Clean the piston pin in solvent and dry it thoroughly.

2. Inspect the piston pin for chrome flaking or cracks. Replace the pin if necessary.

3. Oil the piston pin and install it in the connecting rod. Slowly rotate the piston pin, and check for radial and lateral play (**Figure 158**). If there is play, the connecting rod should be replaced (if the piston pin outside diameter is within specification). Inspect the connecting rod as described in Chapter Five.

4. Measure the outside diameter of the piston pin with a micrometer (**Figure 159**).

5. Measure the inside diameter of the piston pin bore in the piston with a small bore gauge.

6. Subtract the measurements made in Step 5 from the measurements made in Step 6. The difference is the piston-to-pin clearance.

Piston Ring Removal and Inspection

A three-ring assembly is used with each piston. The top and second rings are compression rings. The lower ring is an oil control ring assembly (consisting of two ring rails and an expander spacer).

When measuring the piston rings in this section, compare the actual measurements to the specifications in **Table 2**. Replace the piston rings as a set if out of specification or if they show signs of damage as described in this section.

1. Measure the side clearance of each ring in its groove with a flat feeler gauge (**Figure 160**):

   a. If the clearance is greater than specified, replace the rings as a set. If the clearance is still excessive with the new rings, replace the piston.

Piston Clearance

1. Make sure the pistons and cylinder walls are clean and dry.

2. Measure the cylinder bore with a cylinder bore gauge (**Figure 143**) at a point 40 mm (1.57 in.) below the top of the cylinder block. Measure the cylinder bore in two axes: in-line with the piston pin and 90° to the pin. Calculate the average of the two measurements. This average is the cylinder bore diameter.

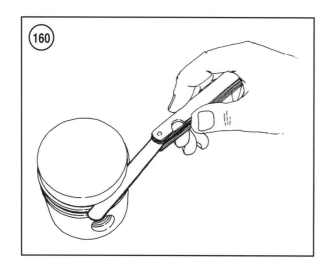

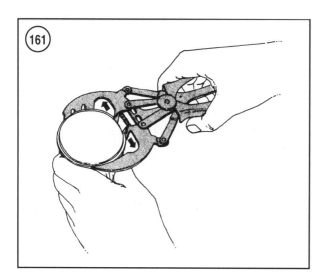

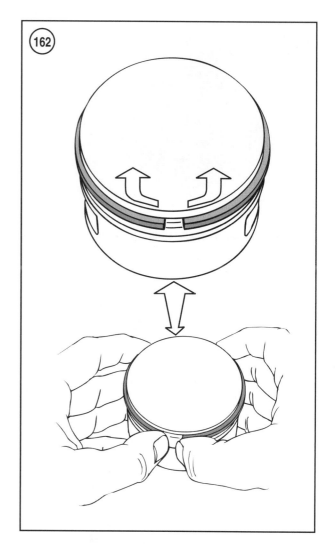

b. If the clearance is too small, check the ring and ring grove for carbon and oil residue. Carefully clean the ring without removing any metal from its surface. Clean the piston ring groove as described in this section.

WARNING
The edges of all piston rings are very sharp. Be careful when handling them to avoid cut fingers.

CAUTION
Store the piston rings in order of removal.

2. Remove the compression rings with a ring expander tool (**Figure 161**) or by spreading the rings by hand (**Figure 162**).

3. Remove the oil ring assembly by first removing the upper then the lower ring rails. Remove the spacer.

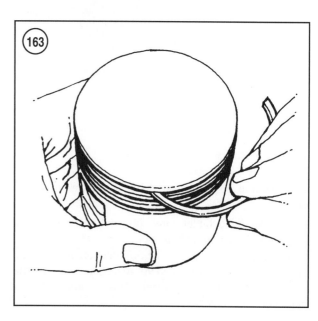

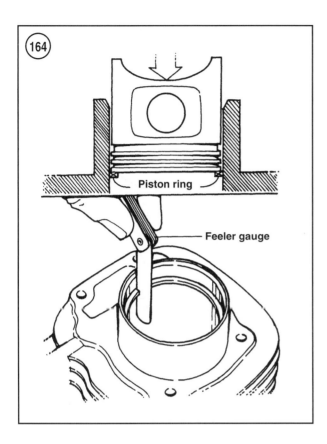

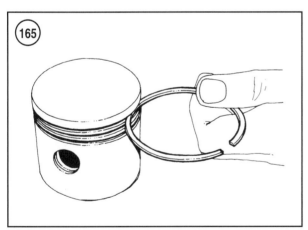

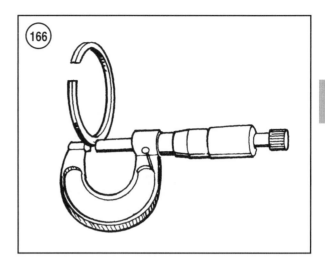

place the rings if the gap is too large. If the gap on the new rings is smaller than specified, hold a small file in a vise. Grasp the ends of the ring with fingers and slowly enlarge the gap.

NOTE
When checking the oil control ring assembly, measure the upper and lower ring rail end gaps only. Do not measure the spacer.

7. Roll each compression ring around its piston groove (**Figure 165**) to measure ring-to-ring groove clearance and to check for binding. Minor binding may be cleaned up with a fine-cut file.

8. Measure the thickness of each ring with a micrometer (**Figure 166**). If the thickness is less than specified, replace the ring(s).

Piston Ring Installation

1. When installing new piston rings, hone or deglaze the cylinder wall. This helps the new rings to seat in the cylinder. If necessary, refer this service to a Yamaha dealership. After honing, measure the end gap of each ring and compare to the dimensions in **Table 2**.

NOTE
*If the cylinder was honed or deglazed, clean the cylinder as described under **Cylinder Inspection** in this chapter.*

2. Lubricate the ring and piston groove with engine oil.

3. Install the oil control ring assembly into the bottom ring groove. Install the oil ring expander spacer first (A, **Figure 167**), then install each ring rail (B). Make sure the ends of the expander spacer butt together (**Figure 168**).

4. Remove carbon and oil residue from the piston grooves (**Figure 163**) with a broken piston ring (if available). Do not remove aluminum material from the ring grooves as this increases side clearance.

5. Inspect the grooves for burrs, nicks or broken and cracked lands. Replace the piston if necessary.

6. Check the end gap of each ring. Insert the ring into the bottom of the cylinder bore and square it with the cylinder wall by pushing it with the piston (**Figure 164**). Measure the ring end gap with a flat feeler gauge (**Figure 164**). Re-

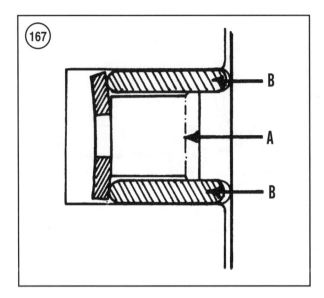

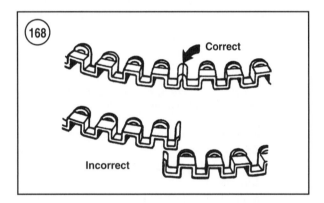

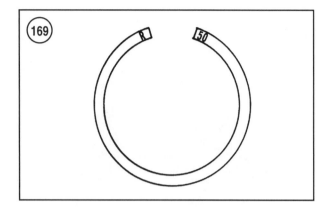

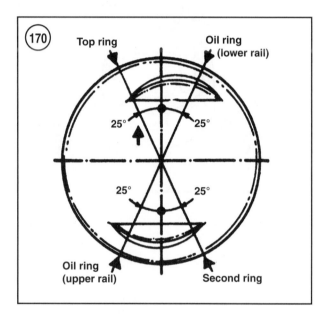

They should not overlap. When reassembling the existing parts, install the ring rails in their original location.

4. Install the second compression ring, and then install the top ring. Carefully spread the ends of each ring by hand and slip the ring over the top of the piston (**Figure 162**). Install each compression ring with its manufacturing marks (**Figure 169**) facing up.

5. Make sure the rings are seated completely in their grooves all the way around the piston and the ends are distributed around the piston.

6. Check the side clearance of each ring as shown in **Figure 160**. If the side clearance is not within the specification in **Table 2**, reexamine the piston and rings.

7. Distribute the ring gaps around the piston as shown in **Figure 170**.

8. Follow the break-in procedure in Chapter Five if a new piston or new piston rings have been installed, or if the cylinder was honed.

Table 1 GENERAL ENGINE SPECIFICATIONS

Item	Specification
Engine type	Four-stroke, air cooled, OHV 4-valve head
Bore x stroke	
1999-2003	95 × 113 mm (3.74 × 4.45 in.)
2004-on	97 × 113 mm (3.82 × 4.45 in.)
Displacement	
1999-2003	1602 cc (97.75 cu. in.)
2004-on	1670 cc (102 cu. in.)
Compression ratio	
1999-2003	8.3:1
2004-on	8.36:1
Compression pressure @ at sea level	
Standard	1200 kPa (174 psi)
Minimum	1000 kPa (145 psi)
Maximum	1400 kPa (203 psi)
Ignition type	Electronic (fully transistorized)

Table 2 ENGINE TOP END SPECIFICATIONS

Item	New mm (in.)	Service limit mm (in.)
Cylinder head warp		
1999-2005	–	0.10 (0.004)
2006-on	–	0.03 (0.0012)
Rocker arms and shafts (1999-2003)		
Rocker arm inside diameter	15.000-15.018 (0.5906-0.5913)	15.036 (0.5920)
Rocker arm shaft outside diameter	14.981-14.991 (0.5898-0.5902)	14.970 (0.5894)
Oil clearance	0.009-0.037 (0.0004-0.0015)	0.080 (0.003)
Rocker arms and shafts (2004-on)		
Rocker arm inside diameter	18.000-18.018 (0.7087-0.7094)	18.036 (0.0360)
Rocker arm shaft outside diameter	17.976-17.991 (0.7077-0.7083)	–
Oil clearance	0.009-0.042 (0.0004-0.0017)	0.080 (0.003)
Valve lifters (1999-2003)		
Valve lifter outside diameter	22.9680-22.9744 (0.9043-0.9045)	–
Valve lifter case inside diameter	22.9900-23.0100 (0.9051-0.9059)	–
Valve lifter-to-case oil clearance	0.0156 0.0420 (0.0006-0.0017)	–
Valve lifters (2004-on)		
Valve lifter outside diameter	22.962-22.974 (0.9040-0.9045)	–
Valve lifter case inside diameter	23.000-23.021 (0.9055-0.9063)	–
Valve lifter-to-case oil clearance	0.026 0.059 (0.0010-0.0023)	–
Valve push rods (1999-2003)		
Length	293.45-293.95 (11.553-11.573)	–
Runout	0.3 (0.012)	–
Valve push rods (2004-on)		
Length (No. 1)	288.25-288.75 (11.348-11.368)	–
Length (No. 2)	290.25-290.75 (11.427-11.447)	–
Runout	0.3 (0.012)	–
Valves and valve springs		
Valve clearance (cold)		
Intake	0.0-0.04 (0.0-0.0016)	–
Exhaust	0.0-0.04 (0.0-0.0016)	–
Valve stem outside diameter		
Intake	5.975-5.990 (0.2352-0.2358)	5.945 (0.2341)
Exhaust	5.960-5.975 (0.2346-0.2352)	5.920 (0.2331)

(continued)

Table 2 ENGINE TOP END SPECIFICATIONS (continued)

Item	New mm (in.)	Service limit mm (in.)
Valve guide		
Inside diameter	6.000-6.012 (0.2362-0.2367)	6.05 (0.2382)
Valve stem-to-guide clearance		
Intake	0.010-0.037 (0.0004-0.0015)	0.08 (0.0031)
Exhaust	0.025-0.052 (0.0010-0.0020)	0.10 (0.004)
Valve stem runout	–	0.01 (0.0004)
Valve seat width	0.90-1.10 (0.035-0.043)	
Valve face width		
Intake	1.3-2.3 (0.0512-0.906)	–
Exhaust	1.2-2.4 (0.0472-0.945)	–
Valve seat width	0.90-1.10 (0.035-0.043)	–
Valve margin thickness	0.7-1.3 (0.028-0.051)	–
Valve spring free length		
Outer springs	43.25 (1.70)	41.26 (1.62)
Inner springs	38.26 (1.51)	36.26 (1.43)
Valve spring tilt		
1999-2005, all springs	–	2.5°/2.4 (2.5°/0.094)
2006-2007		
Inner spring	–	2.5°/1.9 (2.5°/0.067)
Outer spring	–	2.5°/1.9 (2.5°/0.075)
Cylinder (1999-2003)		
Bore	95.000-95.010 (3.7402-3.7406)	–
Maximum taper	–	0.05 (0.0019)
Maximum out of round	–	0.05 (0.0019)
Cylinder (2004-on)		
Bore	97.000-97.010 (3.8189-3.8193)	–
Maximum taper	–	0.05 (0.0019)
Maximum out of round	–	0.05 (0.0019)
Pistons (1999-2003)		
Outside diameter*	94.960-94.975 (3.7386-3.7392)	–
Piston-to-cylinder clearance	0.025-0.050 (0.001-0.002)	0.15 (0.006)
Pistons (2004-on)		
Outside diameter*	96.960-96.975 (3.8173-3.8179)	–
Piston-to-cylinder clearance	0.025-0.050 (0.001-0.002)	0.15 (0.006)
Piston pin bore inside diameter	22.004-22.015 (0.8663-0.8667)	22.045 (0.8679)
Piston offset	1.0 (0.04)	–
Piston pins		
Outside diameter	21.991-22.000 (0.8658-0.8661)	21.971 (0.8650)
Piston pin-to-piston clearance	0.004-0.024 (0.00016-0.00094)	0.074 (0.0029)
Piston rings		
Side clearance (ring-to-groove clearance)		
Top ring	0.03-0.08 (0.0012-0.0031)	0.12 (0.0047)
Second ring	0.03-0.07 (0.0012-0.0028)	0.12 (0.0047)
Ring thickness		
Top ring	1.2 (0.047)	–
Second ring	1.2 (0.047)	–
Oil ring	2.5 (0.098)	–
Ring end gap (installed)		
Top ring	0.30-0.45 (0.012-0.018)	0.65 (0.026)
Second ring	0.30-0.45 (0.012-0.018)	0.65 (0.026)
Oil ring	0.2-0.7 (0.008-0.028)	–

* For 1999-2005 models, measure 5 mm (0.20 in.) from the bottom of the piston skirt. For 2006-on models, measure 10 mm (0.40 in.) from bottom of piston skirt.

Table 3 ENGINE TOP END TORQUE SPECIFICATIONS

Item	N•m	in.-lb.	ft.-lb.
Camshaft			
Drive gear bolt	30	–	22
Driven gear bolt	52	–	38
End cover bolt (front cylinder)	10	88	–
Cover bolts	7	62	–
Cylinder head cover bolt	10	88	–
Cylinder head spacer bolt (1999-2003)	10	88	–
Cylinder head nuts[1]			
10 mm	39	–	29
12 mm			
1999-2003	50	–	37
2004-on	60	–	44
Decompression solenoid bolt	7	62	–
Exhaust pipe			
To cylinder head nuts	20	–	15
To muffler clamp bolts	25	–	18
Oil delivery banjo bolts[2]			
8 mm	18	159	–
10 mm	21	–	15
Rocker arm base bolts (1999-2003)	10	88	–
Rocker arm base bolts (2004-on)			
6 mm	10	88	–
8 mm	24	–	18
Spark plug	18	159	–

1. Apply engine oil to bolt threads, underside of bolt flange and washer.
2. Install new washers under the banjo bolts.

CHAPTER FIVE

ENGINE LOWER END

This chapter provides service procedures for lower end components. These include the crankcase, crankshaft, connecting rods, oil pump and camshafts. This chapter also includes removal and installation procedures for the transmission and internal shift mechanism assemblies. However, service procedures for these components are covered in Chapter Eight.

Refer to **Tables 1-3** at the end of the chapter for specifications.

ENGINE

Service Precautions

Before servicing the engine, note the following:

1. Clean the engine and frame with a degreaser. The disassembly job is easier and there is less chance of dirt entering the assemblies. Keep the work environment as clean as possible.
2. Read *Basic Service Methods* in Chapter One.
3. The text mentions the left and right side of the engine. This refers to the engine position in the frame, not as it sits on the workbench.
4. Always replace a worn or damaged fastener with one of the same size, type and torque requirements. Identify each bolt before replacing it. Lubricate bolt threads with engine oil, unless otherwise specified, before tightening. If **Table 3** does not list a torque specification, refer to the torque and fastener information in Chapter One.
5. Use special tools where noted in the procedures.
6. Store parts in boxes, plastic bags and containers. Use masking tape and a permanent, waterproof marking pen to label parts.
7. Use a box of assorted size and color vacuum hose identifiers (**Figure 1**) for identifying hoses and fittings during engine removal and disassembly.
8. Use a vise with protective jaws to hold parts.
9. Use a press or special tools when force is required to remove and install parts. Do not pry, hammer or otherwise force them on or off.
10. Replace all O-rings and oil seals during assembly. Apply a small amount of grease to the inner lips of each new oil seal to prevent damage.
11. Keep a record of all shims and where they were located.
12. The engine is heavy. A minimum of two people are required to safely remove the engine from the frame.

Service in Frame

The frame is an excellent holding fixture, especially for loosening tight fasteners.

The following components can be serviced while the engine is in the frame:

1. Cylinder head cover, rocker arms and pushrods.
2. Cylinder heads.
3. Cylinders and pistons.
4. Camshafts.
5. External gearshift mechanism.

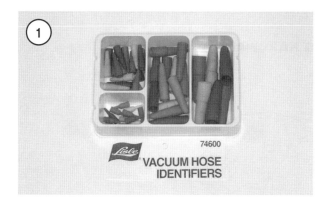

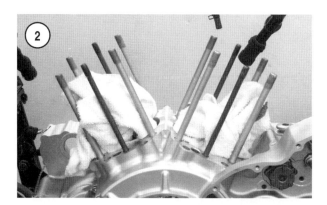

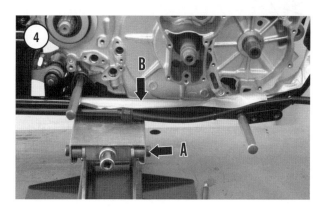

6. Clutch.

7. Carburetor.

8. Starter and gears.

9. Alternator and electrical systems.

Removal

1. Remove both seats as described in Chapter Fifteen.

2. Remove the frame side covers as described in Chapter Fifteen.

3. Disconnect the negative battery cable as described Chapter Three.

4. Drain the engine oil and transfer gearcase oil as described in Chapter Three.

5. Remove the fuel tank as described in Chapter Nine.

6. Remove the air filter assembly and carburetor as described in Chapter Nine.

7. Remove the fuel pump/filter assembly as described in Chapter Nine.

8. Remove the exhaust system as described in Chapter Nine.

9. Remove the oil filter mount as described in this chapter.

CAUTION
Examine the position of the cam timing marks for each cylinder before removing the cylinder heads. Refer to the valve clearance procedure in Chapter Three.

10. Remove both cylinder head assemblies and both cylinders as described in Chapter Four. Place clean shop cloths into the crankcase openings (**Figure 2**) to keep out debris.

11. Remove both footrest assemblies as described in Chapter Fifteen.

12. Remove both horns as described in Chapter Ten.

13. Remove the starter as described in Chapter Ten.

14. Remove the clutch assembly as described in Chapter Seven.

15. Remove the alternator stator and flywheel as described in Chapter Ten.

16. Remove the voltage regulator as described in Chapter Ten.

17. Remove the decompression solenoid as described in Chapter Ten.

18. Remove the speed sensor as described in Chapter Ten.

19. Remove the neutral switch as described in Chapter Ten.

20. Remove the transfer gearcase assembly (A, **Figure 3**) as described in Chapter Six.

21. Block the front wheel so the motorcycle will not roll in either direction.

22. Wrap the frame tubes (B, **Figure 4**) with protective tape to prevent surface damage in the following steps.

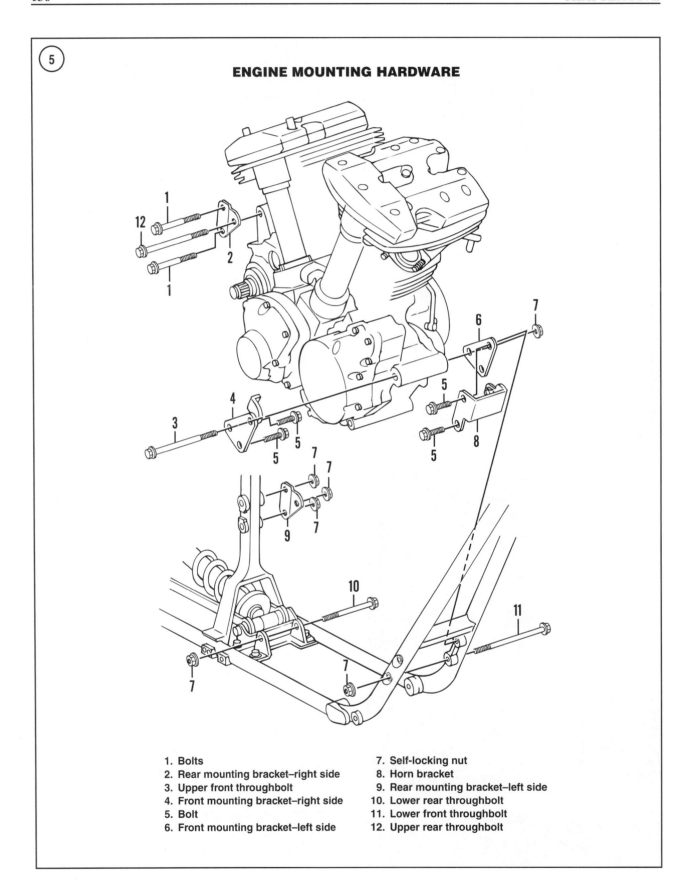

⑤

ENGINE MOUNTING HARDWARE

1. Bolts
2. Rear mounting bracket–right side
3. Upper front throughbolt
4. Front mounting bracket–right side
5. Bolt
6. Front mounting bracket–left side
7. Self-locking nut
8. Horn bracket
9. Rear mounting bracket–left side
10. Lower rear throughbolt
11. Lower front throughbolt
12. Upper rear throughbolt

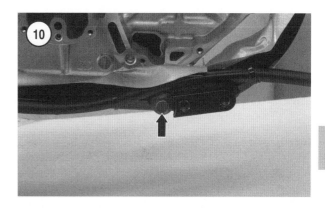

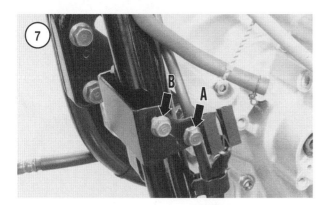

23. Place a floor jack, or the K&L MC450 Center Jack (A, **Figure 4**) with a piece of wood across the jack, underneath the frame under the engine.

24. Check the engine to make sure all electrical wiring, hoses and other related components have been disconnected from the engine. Make sure nothing will interfere with the removal of the engine from the right side of the frame.

25. Refer to **Figure 5** and perform the following:

   a. Remove the self-locking nut (**Figure 6**) securing the lower rear throughbolt.

   b. Remove the self-locking nut securing the lower front throughbolt.

   c. Remove the self-locking nut securing the upper front throughbolt.

   d. Withdraw the upper front throughbolt (A, **Figure 7**).

   e. Remove the bolts securing the left side mounting bracket and horn bracket to the frame (**Figure 8** and B, **Figure 7**). Remove both brackets.

   f. Remove the bolts (**Figure 9**) securing the front right side mounting bracket. Remove the bracket.

NOTE
Figure 3 shows only two of the bolts and nuts. Remove all three.

   g. Remove the bolts and self-locking nuts (B, **Figure 3**) securing the rear mounting brackets to the frame and the crankcase. Withdraw the upper rear throughbolt and remove the mounting brackets on both sides.

   h. Withdraw the lower front throughbolt (**Figure 10**).

   i. Withdraw the lower rear throughbolt.

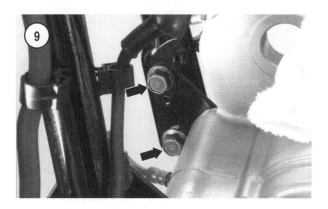

CAUTION
Do not use the transfer gearcase alignment post (Figure 11) as a handle during engine removal and installation as it may be bent out of alignment.

26. Lift up and remove the engine from the right side of the frame.

27. Clean the front and rear engine mounting bolts with solvent and dry thoroughly.

28. Clean and inspect the frame. Check for cracks and damage, particularly at welded joints.

Installation

1. Spray the engine mounting bolts with a rust inhibitor. Do not spray the threads.

2. Make sure all electrical wiring, hoses and other related components will not interfere with engine installation.

3. Block the front wheel so the motorcycle will not roll in either direction.

4. Correctly position a floor jack and piece of wood under the frame to support the engine when it is installed into the frame.

5. Install the engine from the right side of the frame and place it on the floor jack. Raise the jack to support the crankcase before installing the engine mounting bolts.

6. Insert a long drift into the lower throughbolt holes (**Figure 12**) to align the engine with the frame mounting bosses.

7. Do not tighten any of the engine mounting bolts and nuts until all brackets and fasteners have been installed and finger-tightened. Install *new* self-locking nuts.

8. Refer to **Figure 5** and perform the following:

   a. Install the lower rear throughbolt.

   b. Install the lower front throughbolt (**Figure 10**).

   NOTE
   Figure 3 shows only two of the bolts and nuts. Install all three.

   c. Install the rear mounting brackets onto the frame and the crankcase. Install the upper rear throughbolt and bracket bolts and *new* self-locking nuts (B, **Figure 3**).

   d. Install the front right side mounting bracket and the bolts (**Figure 9**).

   e. Install the left side mounting bracket and horn bracket to the frame and the bolts. Refer to **Figure 8** and B, **Figure 7**.

   f. Install the upper front throughbolt (A, **Figure 7**).

   g. Install a *new* self-locking nut on the upper front throughbolt.

   h. Install a *new* self-locking nut on the lower front throughbolt.

   i. Install a *new* self-locking nut (**Figure 6**) on the lower rear throughbolt.

9. Tighten the engine mounting bolts and nuts as follows:

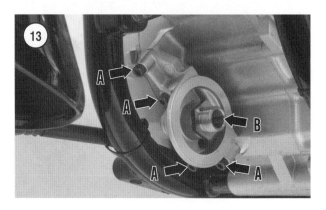

   a. The front mounting bracket and horn bracket bolts to 48 N•m (35 ft.-lb.).

   b. The rear mounting brackets self-locking nuts to 48 N•m (35 ft.-lb.).

   c. The three throughbolts self-locking nuts. Refer to **Table 3** for torque specifications.

10. Install the transfer gearcase assembly (A, **Figure 3**) as described in Chapter Six.

11. Install the neutral switch as described in Chapter Ten.

12. Install the speed sensor as described in Chapter Ten.

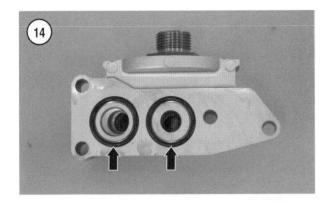

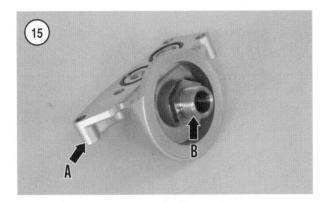

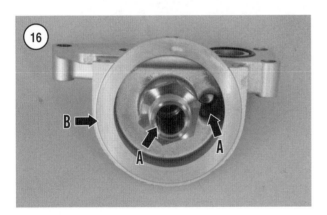

13. Install the decompression solenoid as described in Chapter Ten.

14. Install the voltage regulator as described in Chapter Ten.

15. Install the alternator stator and flywheel as described in Chapter Ten.

16. Install the clutch assembly as described in Chapter Seven.

17. Install the starter as described in Chapter Ten.

18. Install both horns as described in Chapter Ten.

19. Install both footrest assemblies as described in Chapter Fifteen.

20. Install both cylinders and cylinder head assemblies as described in Chapter Four.

21. Install the oil filter mount as described in this chapter.

22. Install the exhaust system as described in Chapter Nine.

23. Install the fuel pump/filter assembly as described in Chapter Nine.

24. Install the carburetor and air filter assembly as described in Chapter Nine.

25. Install the fuel tank as described in Chapter Nine.

26. Refill the engine oil and transfer gearcase oil as described in Chapter Three.

27. Connect the negative battery cable as described Chapter Three.

28. Install the frame side covers as described in Chapter Fifteen.

29. Install both seats as described in Chapter Fifteen.

OIL FILTER MOUNT

Removal/Installation

1. Securely support the motorcycle on a level surface. Block the front wheel so the motorcycle will not roll in either direction.

2. Drain the engine oil and remove the oil filter as described in Chapter Three.

3. Place several shop cloths under the oil filter mount as some residual oil will drain out in the next step.

4. Remove the bolts (A, **Figure 13**) securing the oil filter mount to the crankcase.

5. Remove the oil filter mount and O-rings from the crankcase.

6. Thoroughly clean the crankcase mating surface.

7. Install *new* O-ring seals (**Figure 14**) onto the mount and apply engine oil to them.

8. Install the oil filter mount onto the crankcase and tighten the bolts (A, **Figure 13**) to 10 N•m (88 in.-lb.).

9. If loose, tighten the oil filter bolt (B, **Figure 13**) to 70 N•m (52 ft.-lb.).

10. Install a new oil filter and refill the engine oil as described in Chapter Three.

11. Start the engine and check for leaks.

Inspection

1. Clean the oil filter mount in solvent and dry with compressed air.

2. Inspect the oil filter mount (A, **Figure 15**) for damage that could cause an oil leak.

3. Make sure the oil passageways (A, **Figure 16**) are clear. Clean out if necessary.

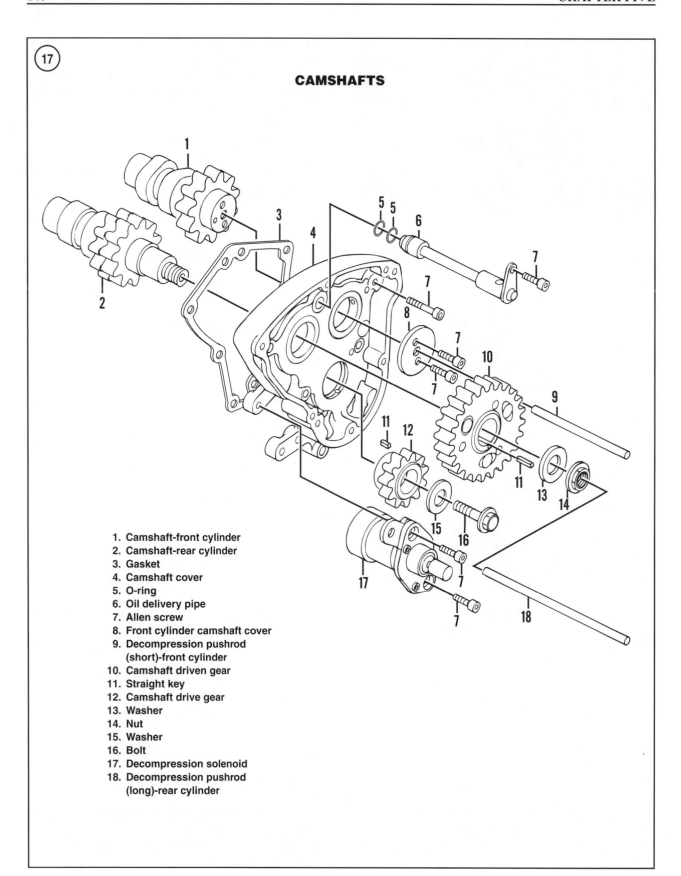

CAMSHAFTS

1. Camshaft-front cylinder
2. Camshaft-rear cylinder
3. Gasket
4. Camshaft cover
5. O-ring
6. Oil delivery pipe
7. Allen screw
8. Front cylinder camshaft cover
9. Decompression pushrod
   (short)-front cylinder
10. Camshaft driven gear
11. Straight key
12. Camshaft drive gear
13. Washer
14. Nut
15. Washer
16. Bolt
17. Decompression solenoid
18. Decompression pushrod
   (long)-rear cylinder

4. Check the oil filter mounting surface (B, **Figure 16**) and oil filter mounting threads (B, **Figure 15**) for wear or damage.

CAMSHAFTS

Removal

The camshafts can be removed with the engine installed in the frame. Refer to **Figure 17**.

1. Drain the engine oil as described in Chapter Three.

2. Remove the exhaust system as described in Chapter Nine.

3. Remove the right side foot rest assembly as described in Chapter Fifteen.

4. Remove the rocker arms and pushrods as described in Chapter Four.

5. Remove the valve lifters as described in Chapter Four.

6. Remove the bolts securing the decompression solenoid cover (**Figure 18**) and remove the cover.

7. Disconnect the decompression solenoid from the actuator (A, **Figure 19**) in the camshaft cover.

8. Remove the Allen bolts (B, **Figure 19**) securing the decompression solenoid. Remove the solenoid and the washers behind it. Move the solenoid out of the way, but do not disconnect the electrical connector from the harness.

9. Remove the bolts securing the camshaft sprocket cover (**Figure 20**) and gasket. Do not lose the dowel pins.

10. Remove the short front (A, **Figure 21**) and the long rear (B) decompression pushrods from the camshafts.

11. Place a clean shop rag (A, **Figure 22**) into the crankcase opening to keep out small parts.

12. Place a soft brass washer (B, **Figure 22**) in front and between the camshaft drive and driven gears.

13. Loosen the camshaft drive gear bolt and washer (C, **Figure 22**). Remove the brass washer.

14. Place a soft brass washer (A, **Figure 23**) behind and between the camshaft drive and driven gears.

15. Loosen the camshaft driven gear nut and washer (B, **Figure 23**). Remove the brass washer.

16. Remove the bolts and nuts loosened in Steps 14 and 15 along with the washers.

17. Remove the camshaft drive and driven gears. Remove the straight key from the crankshaft and rear cylinder camshaft.

18. Remove the Allen bolts (A, **Figure 24**) from the front cylinder camshaft cover (B) and remove the cover.

19. Remove the Allen bolts (**Figure 25**) securing the camshaft cover and the oil delivery pipe.

20. Remove the oil delivery pipe (A, **Figure 26**) and the camshaft cover (B).

21. Remove the gasket and the dowel pins, if loose.

22. Remove the front cylinder camshaft (A, **Figure 27**) and rear cylinder camshaft (B) from the crankcase.

23. Inspect the camshafts as described in this section.

Installation

1. Rotate the crankshaft until the No. 1 rear cylinder piston is at top dead center (TDC). Observe the location of piston at TDC through one of the spark plug holes.

2. Apply molybdenum disulfide grease to the camshaft bearing receptacles in the crankcase.

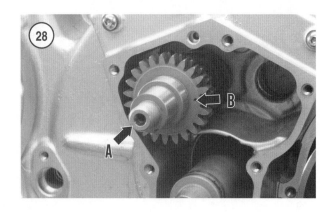

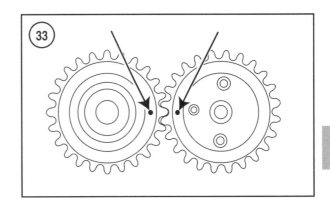

3. Apply molybdenum disulfide grease to the camshaft lobes and bearing journals.

4. Install the rear cylinder camshaft (A, **Figure 28**) into the crankcase. Slowly push it in until it bottoms and position the gear so the index mark is at the 3 o'clock position (B, **Figure 28**).

5. The rear cylinder camshaft has a spring loaded split-tooth gear (**Figure 29**). The teeth on the split gears must be aligned in order to accept the front cylinder camshaft gear in Step 6.

6. Use a narrow flat blade screwdriver to align and hold the split gears (**Figure 30**) in this alignment.

7. Position the rear cylinder camshaft gear so the index mark is at the 9 o'clock position (**Figure 31**) and install the front cylinder camshaft. Remove the screwdriver and slowly push the camshaft in until it bottoms. The face of both gears must be flush with each other.

CAUTION
*The camshaft gear index marks must be correctly aligned as shown in (**Figure 32**). Incorrect alignment will result in engine damage.*

8. At this time, both index marks must be aligned and face directly at each other (**Figure 33**). If not, correct the problem.

9. Install a *new* gasket (**Figure 34**) onto the crankcase.

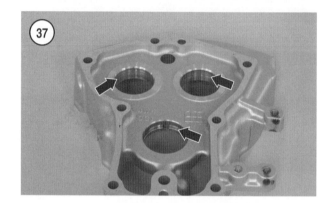

10. Install the upper dowel pin (**Figure 35**) and lower dowel pin (**Figure 36**), if removed.

11. Apply molybdenum disulfide grease to the camshaft cover bearing journals (**Figure 37**).

12. Install the camshaft cover (B, **Figure 26**) onto the camshafts and crankshaft, and press it against the crankcase gasket. Push it on until it bottoms.

13. Install the oil delivery pipe (A, **Figure 26**). Align the flange with the raised pad on the camshaft cover (**Figure 38**) to lock it in place. Push it in until it bottoms.

14. Install the camshaft cover Allen bolts (**Figure 25**) and tighten in a crisscross pattern to 7 N•m (62 in.-lb.).

15. Install the front cylinder camshaft cover (B, **Figure 24**) and Allen bolts (A). Tighten the bolts 10 N•m (88 in.-lb.).

16. The rear cylinder camshaft driven gear has a spring loaded split-tooth gear (**Figure 39**). The teeth on the split gears must be aligned in order to accept the drive gear. Align the driven gear split gears as follows:

   a. Cut off the threaded end of a 6 mm bolt.

   b. Align the gears and insert the 6 mm bolt through the holes (A, **Figure 40**) in both gears.

17. Place a clean shop rag (A, **Figure 41**) into the crankcase opening to keep out small parts.

18. Install the straight key on the rear cylinder camshaft and install the driven gear and 6 mm bolt (B, **Figure 41**). Push it on until it bottoms.

19. Rotate the driven gear until the timing mark is pointing directly at the crankshaft (B, **Figure 40**).

20. Install the straight key on the crankshaft and install the drive gear (**Figure 42**) while aligning the index mark (A, **Figure 43**) with that on the driven gear (B). Push the drive gear on until it bottoms.

CAUTION
*The camshaft drive and driven gear index marks must be correctly aligned as shown in (**Figure 43**). Incorrect alignment will result in internal engine damage.*

5

21. At this time, both camshaft index marks must be aligned and face directly at each other (**Figure 33**). If not, correct the problem.

22. Remove the 6 mm bolt from the driven gear.

23. Install the washer and nut securing the driven gear to the camshaft.

24. Install the washer and bolt securing the drive gear to the crankshaft.

25. Place as soft brass washer (A, **Figure 44**) in front and between the camshaft drive and driven gears.

26. Tighten the camshaft driven gear nut (B, **Figure 44**) to 52 N•m (38 ft.-lb.).

27. Place a soft brass washer (A, **Figure 45**) behind and between the camshaft drive and driven gears.

28. Tighten the camshaft drive gear bolt (B, **Figure 45**) to 30 N•m (22 ft.-lb.).

29. Remove the shop rag from the crankcase opening.

30. Install the short front pushrod (A, **Figure 46**) and the long rear pushrod (B) into the camshafts. Push them until they bottom (**Figure 47**).

31. Install a *new* camshaft sprocket cover gasket (A, **Figure 48**) and dowel pins (B), if removed.

32. Install the camshaft sprocket cover (**Figure 49**) and bolts. Tighten the bolts securely in a crisscross pattern.

33. Install the decompression solenoid, Allen bolts and washers (A, **Figure 50**). Tighten the bolts to 7 N•m (62 in.-lb.).

34. Connect the solenoid onto the actuator (B, **Figure 50**) in the camshaft cover.

35. Install the solenoid cover and tighten the screws securely.

36. Install the valve lifters as described in Chapter Four.

37. Install the rocker arms and pushrods as described in Chapter Four.

38. Install the right side foot rest assembly as described in Chapter Fifteen.

39. Install the exhaust system as described in Chapter Nine.

40. Refill the engine oil as described in Chapter Three.

Inspection

When measuring the camshaft components, compare the measurements to the specifications in **Table 2**. Replace worn or damaged parts as described in this section.

1. Clean the camshafts, gears and cover in solvent and dry thoroughly before inspecting and measuring them.

2. Check the camshaft lobes (A, **Figure 51**) for wear. The lobes should not be scored and the edges should be

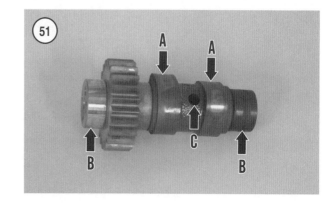

square. Replace the camshaft(s) if the lobes are scored, worn or damaged.

3. Check the camshaft bearing journals (B, **Figure 51**) for wear or scoring. Replace the camshaft if the journals are scored, worn or damaged. If the camshaft lobes exhibit wear, also check the valve lifters for wear at the contact surfaces.

4. Measure each camshaft lobe height and width with a micrometer. Refer to **Figure 52** and **Figure 53**.

5A. On the front cylinder camshaft, measure each camshaft journal outer diameter with a micrometer as follows:

    a. Measure the crankcase side bearing journal outer journal (**Figure 54**).

    b. Measure the camshaft cover side bearing outer journal (**Figure 55**).

5B. On the rear cylinder camshaft, measure each camshaft journal outer diameter with a micrometer as follows:

    a. Measure the crankcase side bearing outer journal (**Figure 56**).

    b. Measure the camshaft cover side bearing outer journal (**Figure 57**).

6. Make sure all oil holes (C, **Figure 51**) are clear. Clean out with solvent and compressed air if necessary.

7. Inspect rear cylinder camshaft spring loaded split-tooth gear as follows:

a. Check the gears (**Figure 58**) for chipped or missing teeth.

b. Make sure the large snap ring (**Figure 59**) is secure in the camshaft groove. Do not disassemble the gear assembly as replacement parts are not available.

8. Check the rear cylinder camshaft as follows:

a. Inspect the straight key slot (**Figure 60**) for wear or damage.

b. Install the straight key onto the camshaft, and install the driven gear (A, **Figure 61**) onto the camshaft (B). This must be a tight fit with no radial play. If play exists, first replace the straight key, and if there is still play; replace the driven gear and/or camshaft.

9. Inspect the decompression release system in both camshafts as follows:

a. Make sure the decompression pushrods are not bent or damaged. Roll them on a piece of plate glass and check for a clicking sound indicating a bent pushrod.

b. Insert the decompression pushrod (A, **Figure 62**) into the camshaft.

c. Push the pushrod in and make sure the decompression pin (B, **Figure 62**) moves out and then back in when the pushrod is withdrawn.

d. Make sure the pushrod moves back and forth smoothly within the camshaft channel.

10. Inspect the rear cylinder camshaft spring loaded split-tooth driven gear as follows:

a. Check the gears (A, **Figure 63**) for chipped or missing teeth.

b. Inspect the key way (**Figure 64**) for wear or damage.

c. Check the fasteners (B, **Figure 63**) securing the two gears together. If loose, or missing, replace the driven gear as it can not be serviced.

11. Inspect camshaft drive gear as follows:

a. Check the gear (**Figure 65**) for chipped or missing teeth.

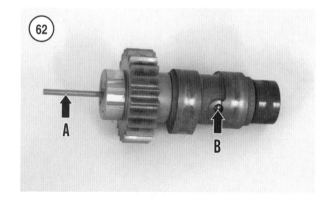

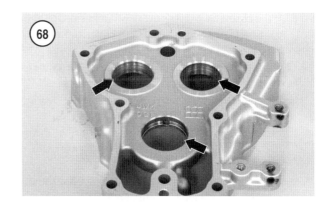

b. Inspect the key way (**Figure 66**) for wear or damage.

12. Inspect the camshaft cover as follows:

a. Check the cover for warp or damage.

b. Check the inner gasket sealing surface (**Figure 67**) for nicks or damage.

c. Inspect the bearing surfaces (**Figure 68**) for wear or damage.

d. Make sure crankshaft bearing surface oil control hole (**Figure 69**) is open.

13. Determine the camshaft-to-cover oil clearance as follows:

   a. Measure each camshaft cover journal outside diameter with a micrometer (**Figure 55**, typical).

   b. Measure the inside diameter bearing surface of the camshaft cover with a small bore gauge (**Figure 70**).

   c. Subtract the dimension in Substep a, from the dimension in Substep b. Compare to the oil clearance dimension in **Table 2**.

   d. If the clearance exceeds the new dimension for one camshaft, replace the camshaft and recheck the oil clearance.

   e. If the clearance exceeds the new dimension for both camshafts, replace the camshaft cover and recheck the oil clearance.

14. Determine the camshaft-to-crankcase oil clearance as follows:

   a. Measure the camshaft's crankcase side bearing journal outer journal (**Figure 54**, typical).

   b. Measure the inside diameter of the camshaft bearing surface (**Figure 71**) in the crankcase with a small bore gauge.

   c. Subtract the dimension in Substep a, from the dimension in Substep b. Compare to the oil clearance dimension in **Table 2**.

   d. If the clearance exceeds the new dimension for the camshaft, replace the camshaft and recheck the oil clearance.

NOTE
Have the dimensions confirmed by a Yamaha dealership before replacing the crankcase assembly.

   e. If the clearance exceeds the new dimension for both camshafts, replace the crankcase and recheck the oil clearance.

15. Inspect the oil delivery pipe for damage. Make sure the oil hole (A, **Figure 72**) is clear. Clean out with solvent and compressed air. Inspect the O-rings (B, **Figure 72**) for hardness or deterioration; replace as necessary.

OIL PUMP

The oil pump (**Figure 73**) is mounted in the right side of the crankcase half. The oil pump consists of two sections: a feed pump (narrow rotors) which supplies oil under pressure to the engine components, and a scavenger pump (wide rotors) which returns the oil from the engine to the oil tank. The oil travels from the engine to the oil tank through two external oil lines on the right side of the engine.

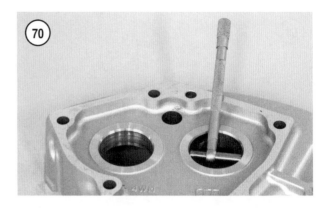

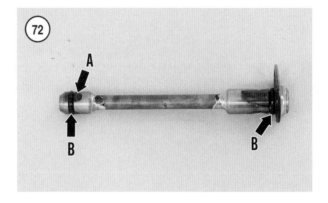

Removal/Installation

1. Remove the engine and disassemble the crankcase as described in this chapter.

2. Remove the crankshaft assembly from the right side crankcase half.

3. Remove the Allen bolts (A, **Figure 74**), then remove the oil strainer (B) from the oil pump.

4. Remove the Allen bolts (A, **Figure 75**), then remove the oil pump (B) from the crankcase.

5. Disassemble and inspect the components as described in this section.

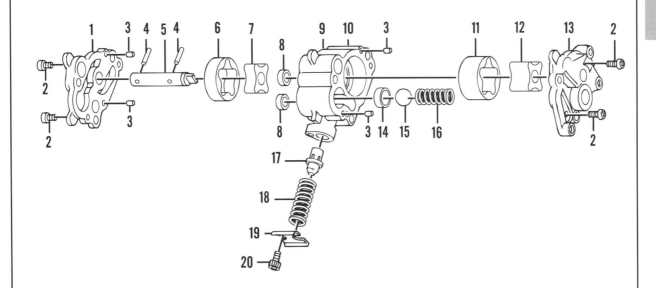

OIL PUMP

1. Feed pump cover
2. Screw*
3. Dowel pin
4. Drive pin
5. Shaft
6. Outer rotor-feed pump
7. Inner rotor-feed pump
8. Oil seal
9. Housing
10. Bar
11. Outer rotor-scavenge pump
12. Inner rotor-scavenge pump
13. Scavenge pump cover
14. Collar
15. Ball
16. Spring
17. Relief valve
18. Spring
19. Retainer
20. Screw

* Apply medium strength threadlocking compound.

5

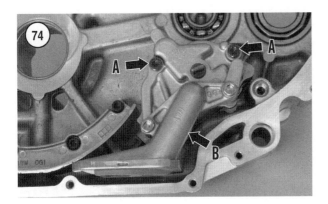

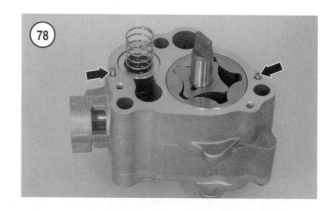

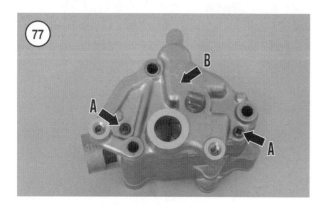

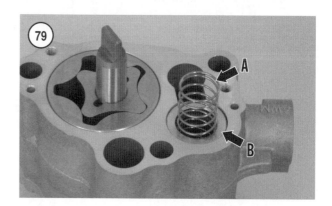

6. Install the oil pump onto the crankcase and tighten the Allen bolts to 10 N•m (88 in.-lb.).

7. If removed, make sure the strainer cover is installed with the arrow (**Figure 76**) facing toward the front of the engine.

8. Install the oil strainer and tighten the Allen bolts (A, **Figure 74**) to 10 N•m (88 in.-lb.).

9. Install the crankshaft assembly into the right side crankcase half.

10. Assemble the crankcase and install the engine as described in this chapter.

Disassembly

1. Remove the two small Phillips screws (A, **Figure 77**) and remove the scavenge pump cover (B).

2. Remove the two small dowel pins (**Figure 78**).

3. Remove the spring (A, **Figure 79**) and collar (B). Remove the ball in the receptacle below the spring.

4. Remove the scavenge pump inner and outer rotors (**Figure 80**) from the housing.

5. Remove the drive pin (**Figure 81**) from the shaft.

6. Turn the oil pump over and remove the two small Phillips screws (A, **Figure 82**) and remove the feed pump cover (B).

7. Remove the two small dowel pins (**Figure 83**).

8. Remove the drive pin (A, **Figure 84**) from the shaft.

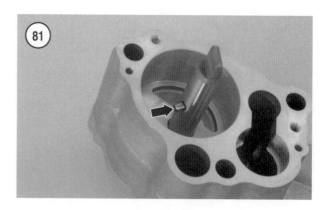

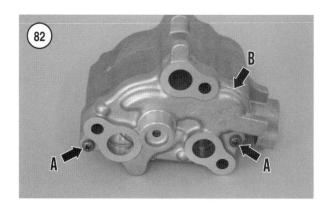

5

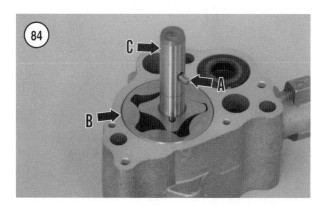

9. Remove the feed pump inner and outer rotors (B, **Figure 84**) from the housing.

10. Remove the shaft (C, **Figure 84**) from the housing.

11. Disassemble the check valve as follows:

   a. Remove the screw (A, **Figure 85**) and remove the retainer (B).

   b. Remove the spring (**Figure 86**) and the relief valve (**Figure 87**) from the housing.

12. Inspect all components as described in this section.

Assembly

1. Apply engine oil to all rotating parts prior to installation.

2. Assemble the check valve as follows:

   a. Position the relief valve as shown in **Figure 88** and install the relief valve (**Figure 87**) into the housing.

   b. Install the spring (**Figure 86**) onto the relief valve.

   c. Install the retainer (B, **Figure 85**) and screw (A). Tighten the screw to 10 N•m (88 in.-lb.).

3. Position the housing with the feed pump side facing up.

4. Position the shaft with the drive tab (**Figure 89**) end going in first and install the shaft.

5. Install the feed pump outer rotor (A, **Figure 90**) and inner rotor (B) into the housing.

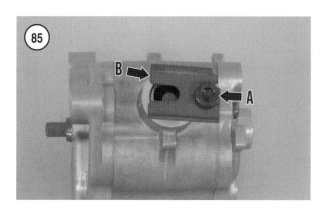

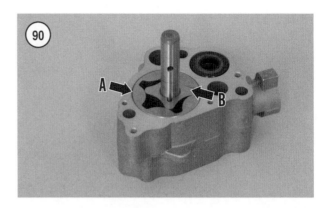

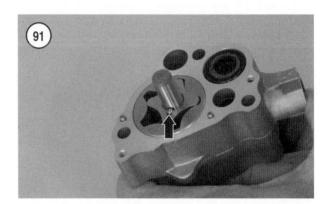

6. Install the drive pin (A, **Figure 84**) into the shaft and center it.

7. Install the two small dowel pins (**Figure 83**) into the housing.

8. Lift the housing up and allow the shaft to move down onto the inner rotor. Align the drive pin so it engages the inner rotor (**Figure 91**).

9. Hold onto the exposed end of the shaft and install the feed pump cover (B, **Figure 82**). Hold the cover in place and slowly rotate the shaft to ensure the shaft drive pin is correctly meshed with the inner rotor.

10. Apply a medium strength threadlocking compound to the two small Phillips screws and install them (A, **Figure 82**). Tighten the screws securely. Check the shaft rotation for binding.

11. Turn the oil pump housing over with the scavenge pump side facing up.

12. Install the drive pin (**Figure 81**) into the shaft and center it.

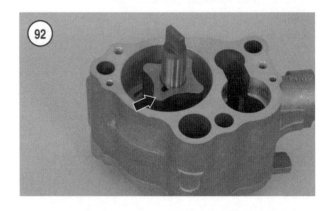

13. Install in the inner rotor onto the shaft so it engages the drive pin (**Figure 92**).

14. Install the outer rotor (**Figure 80**) into the housing.

15. Install the steel ball (**Figure 93**) into the receptacle.

16. Install the spring (A, **Figure 94**) onto the steel ball, and the collar (B) over the spring.

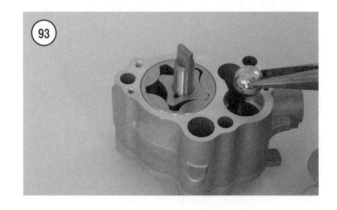

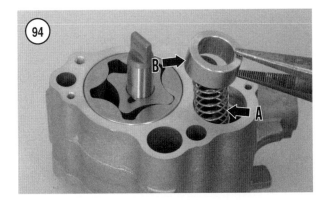

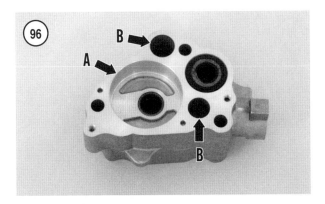

17. Install the two small dowel pins (**Figure 78**).

18. Install the scavenge pump cover (B, **Figure 77**).

19. Apply a medium strength threadlocking compound to the two small Phillips screws and install them (A, **Figure 77**). Tighten the screws securely. Once again check the shaft rotation for binding. If there is binding; correct the problem at this time.

Inspection

1. Clean all parts thoroughly in solvent and place on a clean, lint-free cloth.

2. Inspect both sets of inner and rotors (**Figure 95**) for scratches and abrasion.

3. Inspect both sides of the oil pump housing for scratches caused by the rotors. Refer to A, **Figure 96** and **Figure 97**.

4. Inspect the interior passageways of the oil pump housing. Make sure all oil sludge and foreign matter is removed. Blow low-pressure compressed air through all oil pump housing passages.

5. Inspect both the feed pump and scavenge pump covers for wear and scratches caused by the rotors.

6. Install *new* oil seals (B, **Figure 96**) in the housing.

7A. On the feed pump, perform the following:

    a. Install the inner and the outer rotors into the housing.

    b. Check the clearance between the inner tip and outer rotor (**Figure 98**) with a flat feeler gauge.

    c. Check the clearance between the outer rotor and the housing (**Figure 99**) with a flat feeler gauge.

    d. Replace the rotors as a set if the clearance exceeds the dimension listed in **Table 2**.

7B. On the scavenge pump, perform the following:

    a. Install the inner and the outer rotors into the housing.

    b. Check the clearance between the inner tip and outer rotor (**Figure 100**) with a flat feeler gauge.

    c. Check the clearance between the outer rotor and the housing (**Figure 101**) with a flat feeler gauge.

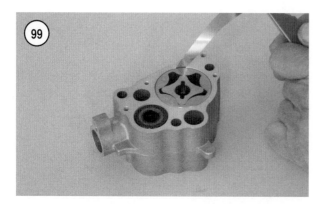

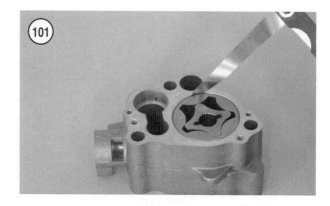

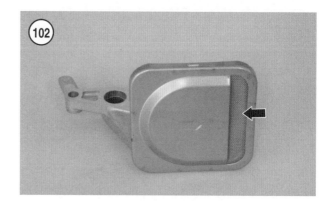

d. Replace the rotors as a set if the clearance exceeds the dimension listed in **Table 2**.

8. Inspect the oil strainer as follows:

a. Inspect the screen (**Figure 102**) for tears or other damage that could allow contaminates into the oil system.

b. Make sure the outlet hole (**Figure 103**) is clear. Clean out with compressed air if necessary.

CRANKCASE

The following procedures detail the disassembly and assembly of the crankcase. When the two halves of the crankcase are disassembled or split, the crankshaft, transmission and oil pump can be removed for inspection and repair.

The crankcase is made of two halves of precession die cast aluminum alloy. To avoid damage, do not hammer or pry on any of the interior or exterior projected walls. These areas are easily damaged. The crankcase is split vertically down the centerline of the connecting rods. The crankcase is assembled without a gasket; only gasket sealer is used. Dowel pins align the crankcase halves where they are bolted together. The crankcase halves are sold as an assembly and fitted to the crankshaft.

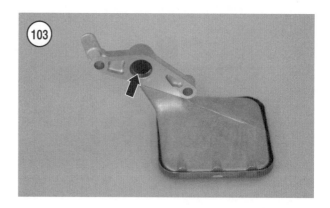

To protect the crankcase halves during the service procedures, support them on wooden blocks and thick pieces of rubber (old car floor mats) placed across the workbench.

Disassembly

As components are removed, keep each part/assembly separated from the other components. Keep seals and O-rings oriented with their respective parts to help with inspection, parts identification and reassembly.

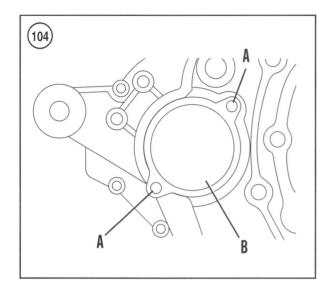

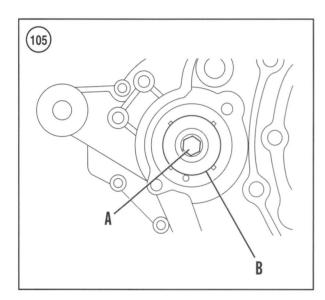

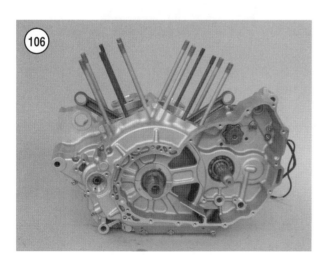

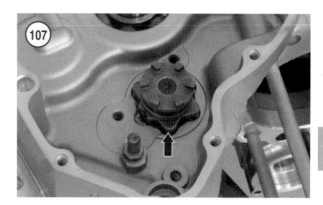

Remember that the right and left side of the engine relates to the engine as it sits in the frame, not as it may sit on the workbench.

1. Remove the engine from the frame as described in this chapter.

2. If still attached to the crankcase, remove the following exterior assemblies from the crankcase as described in the respective chapters:

   a. Oil filter mount (this chapter).
   b. Cylinder heads (Chapter Four).
   c. Rocker arms and pushrods (Chapter Four).
   d. Cylinders and pistons (Chapter Four).
   e. Camshafts (this chapter).
   f. Clutch (Chapter Seven).
   g. Primary drive gear (Chapter Seven).
   h. Oil pump driven gear (Chapter Seven).
   i. Flywheel (Chapter Ten).
   j. External shift mechanism (Chapter Eight).

3. Remove the Allen bolts (A, **Figure 104**) and the alternator shaft cover and O-ring (B). Remove the bolt (A, **Figure 105**) and washer (B) securing the alternator shaft to the left crankcase half.

4. Place the engine on wooden blocks high enough to allow crankshaft clearance to the workbench surface. Place the engine with the left side (**Figure 106**) facing up.

5. Rotate the shift drum until the shift cam segments align with the openings in the crankcase surface (**Figure 107**). If not properly aligned, there will be interference and the left crankcase will not separate.

NOTE
To ensure the crankcase bolts are correctly located during assembly, draw an outline of the left and right crankcase shapes on a piece of cardboard. Punch holes in the cardboard at the same location as the bolts. When each bolt is removed from the crankcase, place the bolt it its respective hole.

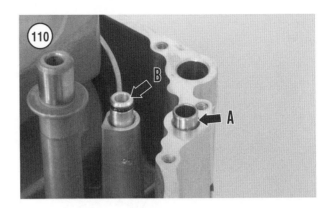

6. On the left side of the crankcase (**Figure 106**), working in a crisscross pattern, loosen the crankcase bolts in several steps. Remove all of the bolts.

7. Hold the crankcase halves together and turn the engine over and place it on wooden blocks.

8. On the right side of the crankcase (**Figure 108**), working in a crisscross pattern, loosen the crankcase bolts in several steps. Remove all of the bolts.

CAUTION
*During crankcase separation, make sure the shift drum cam segments are still aligned with the openings in the crankcase surface (**Figure 107**). Readjust if necessary.*

CAUTION
Do not hammer or pry on areas of the crankcase that are not reinforced. Never pry between the case halves. Doing so may cause an oil leak, requiring replacement of the crankcase.

9. Use a soft mallet, alternately tap on the ends of the transmission shafts, shift drum and crankshaft, while separating the case halves. Do not allow the case halves to bind. If binding occurs, reseat the halves and start again.

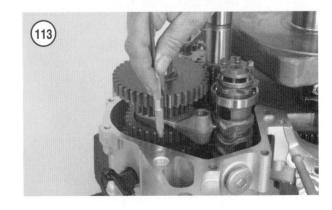

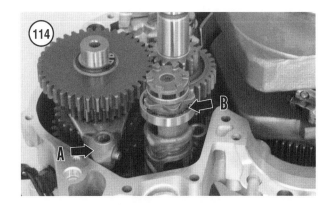

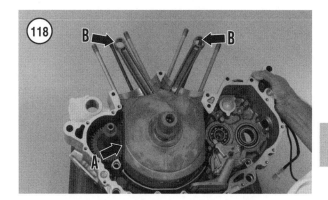

10. Slowly lift the left case half off the right case half. The transmission and crankshaft assemblies should remain in the right case half.

11. Remove the two dowels from the right case mating surface. Refer to **Figure 109** and A, **Figure 110**.

12. Remove the joint pipe and O-rings (B, **Figure 110**).

13. Remove the shift fork shaft (**Figure 111**) for the center shift fork.

14. Remove the shift fork shaft (**Figure 112**) for the right and left shift forks.

15. Use a narrow screwdriver or scribe (**Figure 113**) and move the left shift fork away from the shift drum.

16. Move the right shift fork away from the shift drum (A, **Figure 114**).

17. Pull straight up and remove the shift drum (B, **Figure 114**) from the crankcase.

18. Remove the right shift fork (**Figure 115**), and the center shift fork (**Figure 116**).

19. Withdraw the transmission shaft assemblies and the left shift fork as an assembly (**Figure 117**) from the crankcase. Store each individual shaft assembly in a sealed and labeled plastic bag.

WARNING
The crankshaft is very heavy. Do not damage the main bearing insert in the right case half or drop it while removing it in the next step.

20. Have an assistant hold onto and steady the right case half and remove the crankshaft assembly (A, **Figure 118**).

21. Pull straight up and remove the alternator drive shaft (**Figure 119**) from the crankcase.

22. Remove the oil pump assembly as described in this chapter, if necessary.

23. Inspect the components as described in this section.

Assembly

> *CAUTION*
> *Coat all parts with engine oil prior to assembly.*

1. Install the oil pump assembly as described in this chapter, if removed.

2. Place the right case half on wooden blocks (**Figure 120**) high enough to allow crankshaft clearance to the workbench surface.

3. Install the alternator drive shaft (**Figure 119**) into the crankcase. Make sure it is properly seated.

> *WARNING*
> *The crankshaft is very heavy. Do not drop it while installing it in the next step. Do not scrape and damage the main bearing inserts in the crankcase half during installation.*

4. Have an assistant hold onto and steady the right case half.

5. Correctly position the connecting rods within the crankcase openings as shown in B, **Figure 118**. Slowly and carefully install the crankshaft assembly (A, **Figure 118**) into the right case half and mesh it with the alternator drive shaft gears.

6. Slowly rotate the crankshaft back and forth and make sure it is correctly seated in the main bearing.

7. Mesh the mainshaft (A, **Figure 121**) and countershaft (B) assemblies together.

> *NOTE*
> *Each shift fork is identified by a letter embossed on its face (**Figure 122**). Install each shift fork with the letter facing down toward the right side of the engine.*

8. Install the right shift fork (C, **Figure 121**) onto the countershaft.

9. Install the transmission shaft assemblies and right shift fork (**Figure 117**) into the bearings in the right case half.

10. Slightly rotate the transmission shaft assemblies back and forth and make sure they are correctly seated in the bearings.

11. Install the center shift fork into the mainshaft second/third combination gear (**Figure 116**).

12. Install the left shift fork into the countershaft forth gear shift fork groove (**Figure 115**).

13. Move the shift forks away from the area where the shift drum will occupy.

14. Position the shift drum so the neutral indicator post is located as shown in **Figure 123** and install the shift drum

(B, **Figure 114**). Push the shift drum down until it bottoms.

15. Rotate each shift fork so its guide pin engages its groove in the shift drum (**Figure 124**).

16. Install the shift fork shaft (**Figure 112**) for the left and right shift forks. Push it into the case receptacle until it bottoms.

17. Install the shift fork shaft (**Figure 111**) for the center shift fork. Push it into the case receptacle until it bottoms.

18. Spin the transmission shafts and turn the shift drum by hand to check transmission operation. Make sure each fork travels through its operating groove in the shift drum and bottoms against both ends. Observe the shift forks as the transmission is shifted into the different gears.

19. Once it is confirmed that the transmission shifts correctly, shift it into neutral.

20. Correctly position the connecting rods within the crankcase openings as shown in (**Figure 125**).

21. Install *new* O-rings onto the joint pipe. Apply lithium grease to the O-rings and install the joint pipe. Push it down until it bottoms (B, **Figure 110**).

22. Install the two dowels into the right crankcase mating surface (**Figure 109** and A, **Figure 110**).

23. Check the left and right crankcase mating surfaces for old sealant material or other residue. Clean them as necessary.

24. Apply engine oil to the transmission shafts and journals in the left case half. Also lubricate the bearings, including the inner races, in the right crankcase half.

25. Apply a light coat of Yamaha Quick Gasket or an equivalent sealant to the mating surface of the left crankcase half. Make the coating as thin as possible while completely covering the mating surface.

NOTE
*Make sure the shift drum is still in the correct position so the shift cam segments align with the openings in the left crankcase surface (**Figure 107**) during installation. If not properly aligned, there will be interference and the left crankcase will not assemble.*

26. Carefully lower the left case half onto the right case half (**Figure 126**) until it is completely seated. If the left case will not seat on the right, remove the left case and determine the source of the obstruction. Do not use the crankcase bolts to pull the case halves together. Note the following:

    a. Align the bearings in the left case half with their respective assemblies in the right case half.

    b. Make sure the shift cam segments correctly entered the cutouts in the left crankcase half (**Figure 107**).

27. Lubricate the crankcase bolt threads with engine oil.

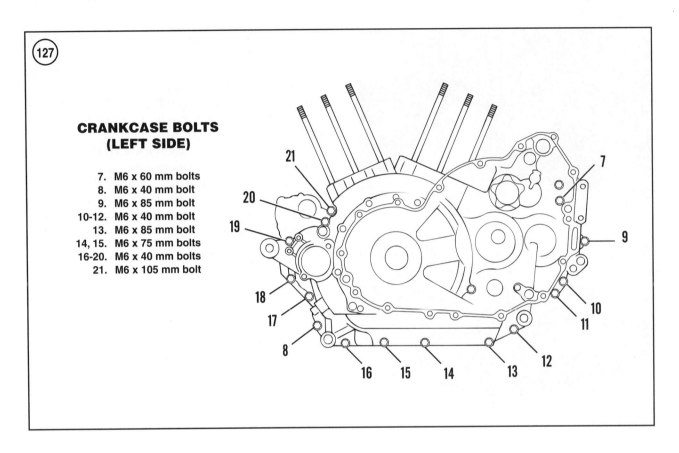

**CRANKCASE BOLTS
(LEFT SIDE)**

  7. M6 x 60 mm bolts
  8. M6 x 40 mm bolt
  9. M6 x 85 mm bolt
10-12. M6 x 40 mm bolt
 13. M6 x 85 mm bolt
14, 15. M6 x 75 mm bolts
16-20. M6 x 40 mm bolts
 21. M6 x 105 mm bolt

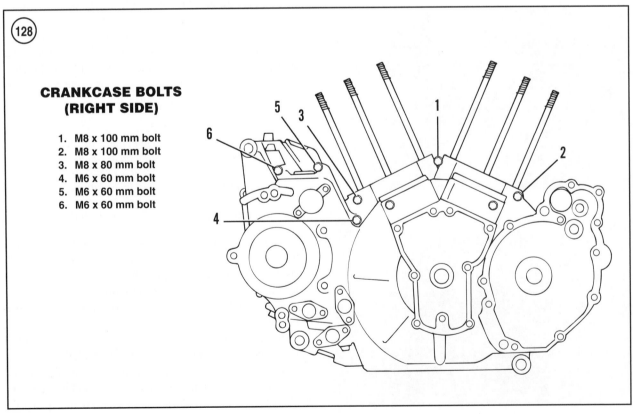

**CRANKCASE BOLTS
(RIGHT SIDE)**

  1. M8 x 100 mm bolt
  2. M8 x 100 mm bolt
  3. M8 x 80 mm bolt
  4. M6 x 60 mm bolt
  5. M6 x 60 mm bolt
  6. M6 x 60 mm bolt

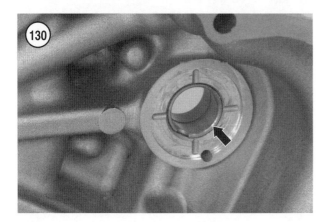

34. Install the alternator shaft cover and O-ring (B) and the Allen bolts (A, **Figure 104**). Tighten the bolts securely.

35. Install the following exterior assemblies onto the crankcase:
   a. External shift mechanism (Chapter Eight).
   b. Flywheel (Chapter Ten).
   c. Oil pump driven gear (Chapter Seven).
   d. Primary drive gear (Chapter Seven).
   e. Clutch (Chapter Seven).
   f. Camshafts (this chapter).
   g. Cylinders and pistons (Chapter Four).
   i. Rocker arms and pushrods (Chapter Four).
   j. Cylinder heads (Chapter Four).
   k. Oil filter mount (this chapter).

36. Install the engine into the frame as described in this chapter.

Inspection

1. Remove all residual sealer from the gasket surfaces.
2. Remove the oil seal as described in this chapter.
3. Clean the case halves in solvent.
4. Using clean solvent, flush out each bearing (**Figure 129**, typical).
5. Dry the bearings with compressed air.

WARNING
When drying a bearing with compressed air, do not allow the inner bearing race to rotate. The air can spin the bearing at excessive speed, possibly causing the bearing to destruct.

6. Blow out the oil passages with compressed air.
7. Lightly oil the crankcase bearings with engine oil before inspecting their conditions. A dry bearing exhibits more noise and play than a properly lubricated bearing.
8. Inspect the bearings for roughness, pitting, galling and play. Replace any bearing that is not in good condition. Always replace the opposite bearing at the same time.
9. Inspect the alternator shaft bushing (**Figure 130**) and the shift drum bushing (**Figure 131**) for wear.
10. Inspect the crankcase for fractures around all mounting and bearing bosses, stiffening ribs and threaded holes. If repair is required, have a Yamaha dealership or machine shop that is experienced in the repair of precision aluminum casting inspect the crankcase.
11. Check the threaded holes for thread damage, dirt or oil buildup. Clean or repair the threads with a suitable size metric tap. Coat the tap threads with kerosene or an aluminum tap fluid before use.

28. Refer to **Figure 127** and install the left crankcase bolts into the correct locations. Tighten the bolts enough to hold the crankcase together at this time. These bolts will be tightened after the right crankcase bolts are tightened.

29. Turn the crankcase over.

CAUTION
Rotate the crankshaft frequently during the tightening process. If there is any binding, stop and correct the cause before proceeding.

30. Refer to **Figure 128** and install the right crankcase bolts into the correct locations. Tighten the bolts in a crisscross pattern as follows:
   a. Tighten the 6 mm bolts to 10 N•m (88 in.-lb.).
   b. Tighten the 8 mm bolts to 24 N•m (18 ft.-lb.).

31. Turn the crankcase back over to the left side.

32. Tighten the 6 mm left crankcase bolts (**Figure 127**) in a crisscross pattern to 10 N•m (88 in.-lb.).

33. Install the washer and bolt (A, **Figure 105**) securing the alternator shaft and tighten to 28 N•m (21 ft.-lb.).

5

12. Check the tightness of the shift shaft assembly stopper arm (**Figure 132**).

13. Check the tightness of the bolts (A, **Figure 133**) securing the oil baffle plate (B). Tighten to 10 N•m (88 in.-lb.).

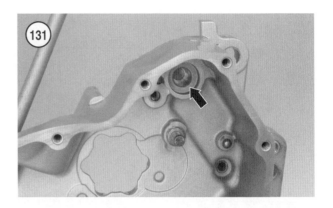

CRANKCASE SEAL AND BEARING REPLACEMENT

Refer to Chapter One for general bearing removal and installation.

Refer to this section for removal and installation of the transmission bearings. The crankshaft main bearings are not replaceable. If the main bearing oil clearance is greater than specified, as described in this chapter, replace the crankshaft or the crankcase assembly.

Seal Replacement

When servicing the crankcase, replace the countershaft oil seal (**Figure 134**).

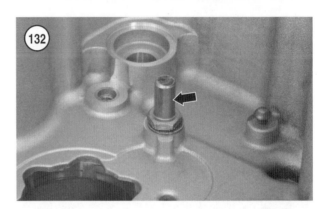

CAUTION
Do not allow the pry tool to contact the seal bore when removing the seal. It may gouge the bore and cause the new seal to leak.

1. Pry out the old seal with a seal puller, wide-blade screwdriver or tire iron. Place a folded shop cloth under the tool to prevent damage to the case.

2. If a new bearing is going to be installed, replace the bearing before installing the new seal.

3. Clean the seal bore in the case. Sand or file any raised grooves in the bore surface and clean thoroughly.

4. Pack grease into the lip of the new seal.

5. Place the *new* seal in the bore, with the closed side of the seal facing out. The seal must be square to the bore.

6. Install the *new* seal with a seal driver until its outer edge is even with the top of the bore.

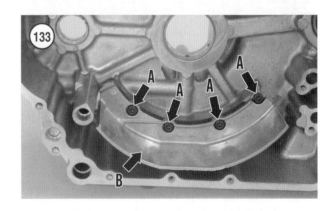

CAUTION
When driving seals, the driver must fit at the perimeter of the seal. If the driver presses toward the center of the seal, the seal can distort and the internal garter spring can become dislodged, causing the seal to leak.

Bearing Replacement

This section covers the transmission bearings installed in the crankcase.

1. When replacing the crankcase bearings, note the following:

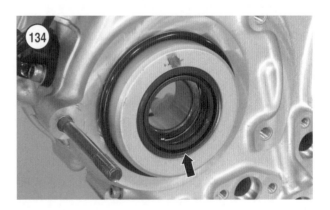

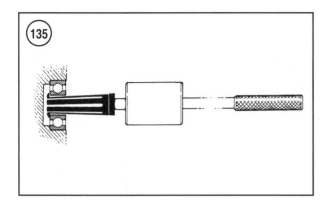

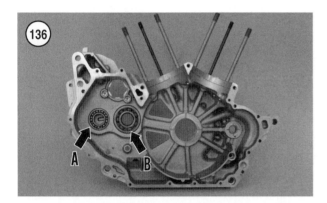

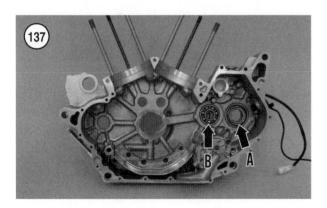

a. Identify and record the size code of each bearing before it is removed from the crankcase.

b. Record the orientation of each bearing in its bore. Note whether the size code faces toward the inside or outside of the case.

c. Use a hydraulic press or set of bearing drivers to remove and install the bearings.

d. Bearings that are only accessible from one side of the case are removed with a blind bearing puller. The puller is fitted through the bearing, then expanded to grip the back-side of the bearing (**Figure 135**).

e. For later models that have a bearing retainer, remove the retainer before driving out the damaged bearing. During assembly, position the retainer so the word OUT faces up. Use threadlocking compound on the retainer fasteners and tighten them to the specification shown in **Table 3**.

2. Refer to the following to identify the *left* crankcase bearings:

a. Countershaft bearing (A, **Figure 136**).

b. Mainshaft bearing (B, **Figure 136**).

3. Refer to the following to identify the *right* crankcase bearings:

a. Countershaft bearing (A, **Figure 137**).

b. Mainshaft bearing (B, **Figure 137**).

CRANKSHAFT

Removal/Installation

Remove and install the crankshaft as described under *Crankcase* in this chapter.

Inspection

Carefully handle the crankshaft assembly during inspection.

1. Clean the crankshaft and connecting rods thoroughly with solvent. Clean the crankshaft oil passageways with compressed air. Dry the crankshaft with compressed air, and lubricate all journal surfaces with a light coat of engine oil.

2. Inspect each crankshaft main journal (**Figure 138**) for scratches, ridges, scoring, nicks or heat discoloration. Very small nicks and scratches can be removed with crocus cloth. Anything more serious must be referred to a Yamaha dealership or machine shop.

3. To determine main journal wear, perform *Main Bearing Inspection* in this section.

4. Inspect the crankshaft taper, keyways and alternator drive shaft gear (**Figure 139**) for chipped or missing teeth.

5. Measure the crankshaft runout with the crankshaft mounted in a set of V-blocks (A, **Figure 140**, typical). Rotate the crankshaft two full turns with a dial gauge mounted

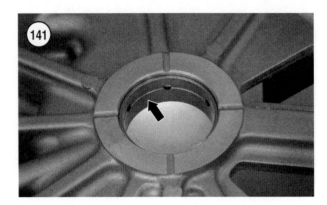

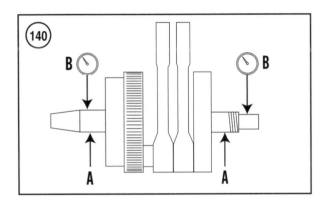

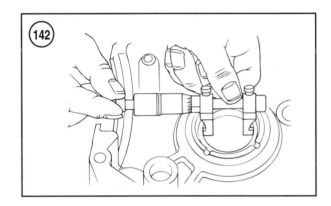

at the locations shown in B, **Figure 140**. If the runout exceeds the service limit in **Table 1**, replace the crankshaft.

Main Bearing Inspection

The crankcase is equipped with insert-type main bearings (**Figure 141**). The main bearing inserts cannot be replaced. If excessively worn or damaged, the crankcase must be replaced. Do not remove the inserts when inspecting them in the following steps.

1. Inspect the inside surface of each bearing insert (**Figure 141**) for excessive wear, a bluish or burned appearance or flaking and scoring. If the insert is questionable, replace the crankcase assembly.
2. Clean the crankshaft main journal (**Figure 138**) and the crankcase bearing insert (**Figure 141**).
3. Measure the main bearing oil clearance as follows:
    a. Measure the inside diameter of the bearing insert with a bore gauge or inside micrometer (**Figure 142**).
    b. Measure the crankshaft bearing journal outside diameter with a micrometer. Refer to **Figure 143** and **Figure 144**.
    c. Subtract the main journal outside diameter from the bearing insert inside diameter to determine the main journal oil clearance. If the main journal oil clear-

ance exceeds the service limit in **Table 1**, replace the crankshaft.
4. Repeat the procedure with the new crankshaft.

CONNECTING RODS

Removal/Installation

Refer to **Figure 145**.

1. Separate the crankcase and remove the crankshaft assembly as described under *Crankcase* in this chapter.

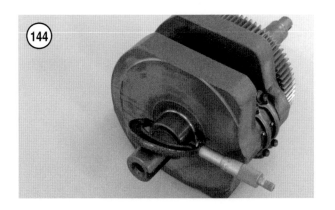

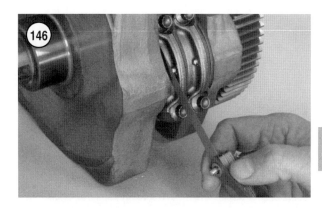

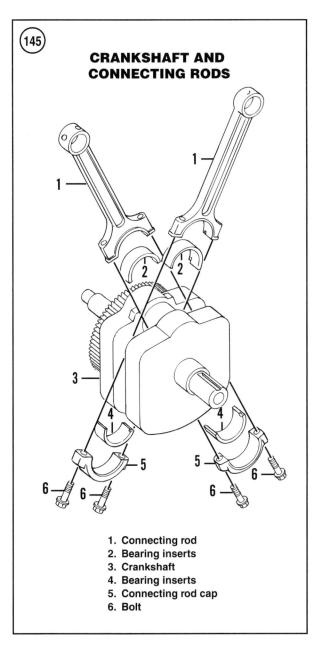

CRANKSHAFT AND
CONNECTING RODS

1. Connecting rod
2. Bearing inserts
3. Crankshaft
4. Bearing inserts
5. Connecting rod cap
6. Bolt

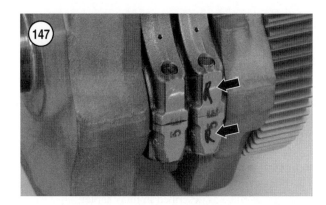

2. Measure the connecting rod side clearance with a feeler gauge between the connecting rod and crankshaft machined surface (**Figure 146**). Compare to the connecting rod side clearance service limit in **Table 1**. Measure each connecting rod. If the measurement is out of specification, replace the connecting rod as described in this section. Recheck the clearance with the new connecting rod(s).

3. Prior to disassembly, mark each connecting rod and cap with an F or R (**Figure 147**) so the rods can be installed in their original locations.

4. Remove the bolts (A, **Figure 148**) securing the connecting rod caps and remove the cap (B).

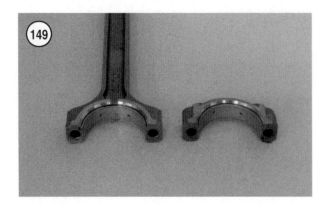

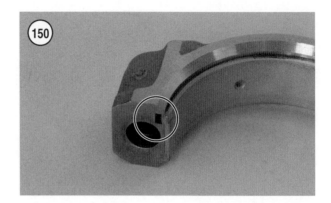

5. Carefully remove the connecting rod from the crankshaft.

6. Mark the rod, bearing and cap to show the correct cylinder and crankpin position for reassembly.

7. Remove and identify each bearing insert (**Figure 149**) as to its upper and lower position.

8. Clean all parts and the crankshaft in solvent and dry with compressed air.

9. Inspect the connecting rods and bearings as described in this section.

10. If new bearing inserts will be installed, check the bearing clearance as described in this chapter.

11. Wipe off any oil from the bearing inserts, connecting rod and cap contact surfaces. No lint or debris can be on the contact surfaces when installing the inserts.

12. Install the bearing inserts into each connecting rod and cap (**Figure 149**). Make sure they are locked in place correctly (**Figure 150**).

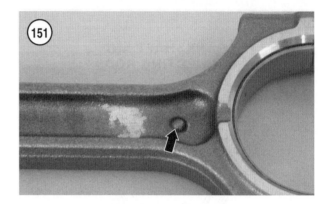

CAUTION
If the old bearing inserts are reused, they must be installed in their original positions (Step 3 and 4); otherwise, engine damage will occur.

13. Apply molybdenum disulfide grease to the bearing inserts and crank pin bearing thrust surfaces.

14. Install the connecting rod and cap (B, **Figure 148**) onto the crankshaft in their original position. The projection must face toward the left side of the crankshaft (**Figure 151** and A, **Figure 152**). Make sure the characters on both the connecting rod and cap are aligned (B, **Figure 152**).

CAUTION
The fine threads used on the connecting rod bolts can be easily damaged. Start the bolts carefully by hand.

15A. On 1999-2003 models, proceed as follows:

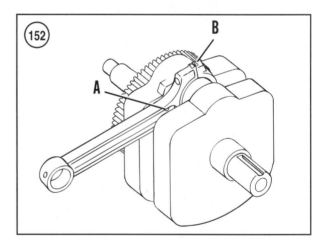

a. Apply molydenum disulfide grease to the threads and seating surface of *new* connecting rod bolts (A, **Figure 148**). Finger-tighten the bolts.

CAUTION
When tightening a connecting rod bolt to specification, once 33 N•m (24 ft.-lb.) of torque is applied, tightening cannot be stopped until the final torque value is achieved. If tightening is interrupted between 33-40 N•m (24-29 ft.-lb.), loosen the

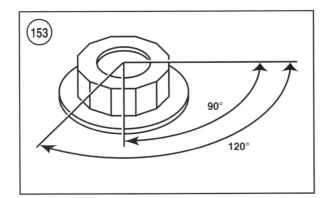

bolt to less than 33 N•m (24 ft.-lb.), then tighten it to 40 N•m (29 ft.-lb.) in one continuous motion.

    b. Tighten each connecting rod bolt to 40 N•m (30 ft.-lb.). Apply continuous torque when tightening the bolt from 33 N•m (24 ft-lb.) to 40 N•m (30 ft.-lb.).

15B. On 2004-on models, proceed as follows:

    a. Apply molydenum disulfide grease to the threads and seating surface of *new* connecting rod bolts (A, **Figure 148**). Finger-tighten the bolts.

    b. Tighten the connecting rod bolts to 15 N•m (133 in.-lb.).

NOTE
Do not use a torque wrench when tightening the bolts to the specified angle in the following sub-step.

    c. Tighten the bolts an additional 90° to 120° as shown in **Figure 153**.

CAUTION
If the bolt is tightened past the specified 120°, do not loosen and re-tighten it. The bolt has stretched and will not properly secure the connecting rod cap. Remove and discard the bolt; install a new bolt.

16. Rotate the connecting rod several times to make sure there is no binding or roughness.

17. Repeat for the other connecting rod.

Connecting Rod Inspection

    When inspecting the connecting rods, compare any measurements to the specifications in **Table 1**. Replace any connecting rods that are damaged or out of specification.

1. Remove and identify the connecting rods from the crankshaft as described in this section.

2. Clean the connecting rods and inserts in solvent and dry with compressed air.

3. Carefully inspect each rod journal (A, **Figure 154**) on the crankshaft for scratches, ridges, scoring and other damage. Make sure the oil hole (B, **Figure 154**) is clear. Clean out with compressed air if necessary.

4. Inspect each insert (**Figure 155**) for evidence of wear, abrasion and scoring. They are usable if in good condition.

5. Measure the rod journal with a micrometer (**Figure 156**) and check for out-of-round and taper.

6. Check each connecting rod big end for signs of seizure, bearing or connecting rod damage.

7. Check each connecting rod small end for signs of excessive heat (blue coloration) or other damage.

8. Check the small end bore for wear or scoring.

9. If all parts are within specification and do not show any type of visible damage, check the connecting rod bearing clearance as described in this section.

Connecting Rod Bearing

Clearance measurement

1. Clean any oil from the bearing insert and crankpins clean.

> *CAUTION*
> *Make sure the bearing inserts are installed in their original mounting positions.*

2. Install the inserts (**Figure 149**) into their original connecting rod or rod cap. Make sure they are locked in place correctly (**Figure 150**).

3. Place a strip of Plastigage (**Figure 157**) over each rod journal parallel to the crankshaft. Do not place the Plastigage material over an oil hole in the crankshaft.

> *CAUTION*
> *Do not rotate the connecting rod or crankshaft while Plastigage is in place.*

4. Install the connecting rod and cap (B, **Figure 148**) onto the crankshaft in it original position. The projection must face the left side of the crankshaft. Refer to **Figure 151** and A, **Figure 152**. Make sure the characters on both the connecting rod and cap are aligned (B, **Figure 152**).

> *CAUTION*
> *The fine threads used on the connecting rod bolts are easily damaged. Start the bolts carefully by hand.*

> *NOTE*
> *Do not use new bolts for this procedure since they will be stretched and cannot be reused. Use the old bolts removed in the prior procedures.*

5A. On 1999-2003 models, proceed as follows:
   a. Install the *old* connecting rod bolts (A, **Figure 148**) and tighten finger-tight.

> *CAUTION*
> *When tightening a connecting rod bolt to specification, once 33 N•m (24 ft.-lb.) of torque is applied, tightening cannot be*

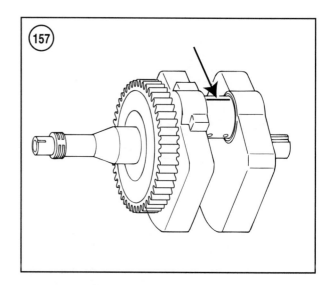

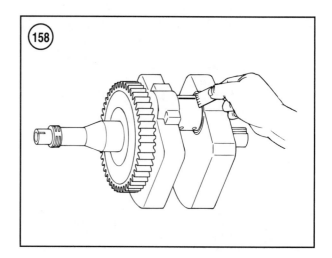

stopped until the final torque value is achieved. If tightening is interrupted between 33 and 40 N•m (24 and 30 ft.-lb.), loosen the bolt to less than 33 N•m (24 ft.-lb.), then tighten it to 40 N•m (30 ft.-lb.) in one continuous motion.

   b. Tighten each connecting rod bolt to 40 N•m (30 ft.-lb.). Apply continuous torque when tightening the bolt from 33 N•m (24 ft-lb.) to 40 N•m (30 ft.-lb.).

5B. On 2004-on models, proceed as follows:

   a. Install the *old* connecting rod bolts (A, **Figure 148**) and tighten finger-tight.

   b. Tighten the connecting rod bolts to 15 N•m (133 in.-lb.).

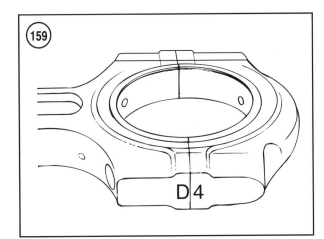

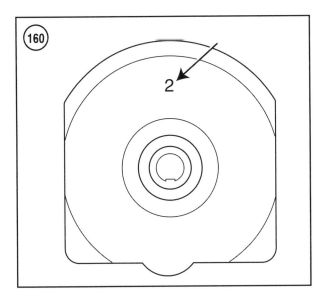

NOTE
Do not use a torque wrench when tightening the bolts to the specified angle in the following sub-step.

c. Tighten the bolts an additional 90° to 120° as shown in **Figure 153**.

6. Remove the bolts and carefully remove the caps from the connecting rods. Discard the bolts.

7. Measure the width of the flattened Plastigage strip (**Figure 158**) following the manufacturer's instructions. Measure both ends of the Plastigage strip.

a. A difference of 0.025 mm (0.001 in.) or more indicates a tapered journal. Confirm the measurement with a micrometer.

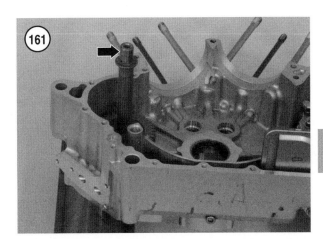

b. If the connecting rod bearing clearance exceeds the service limit in **Table 1**, select new bearing inserts as described in this section.

8. Remove all Plastigage material from the crankshaft journals and connecting rods and caps.

Selection

Bearing inserts are identified by color. To determine the proper bearing inserts, calculate the bearing number as follows.

1. The connecting rods and caps are marked with a No. 4 or No. 5 (**Figure 159**).

2. The crankshaft web is marked with a number (**Figure 160**) that relates to the connecting rod crankpin.

3. To select the proper bearing insert number, subtract the crankpin number from the number on the connecting rod and cap. For example, if the connecting rod is marked with a 4 and the matching crankpin number is a 2, then 4 - 2 = 2. The new bearing insert is a No. 2.

4. Refer to **Table 2** and use the bearing insert number to determine the color code for the bearing insert.

5. Repeat Steps 1-4 for the other connecting rod.

6. After new bearings have been selected, recheck the oil clearance as described in this section. If clearance is still out of specification, take the crankshaft and connecting rods to a Yamaha dealership for further service. Yamaha does not provide connecting rod or crankpin wear specifications.

ALTERNATOR DRIVE SHAFT

Removal/Installation

Remove and install the alternator drive shaft (**Figure 161**) as described under *Crankcase* in this chapter.

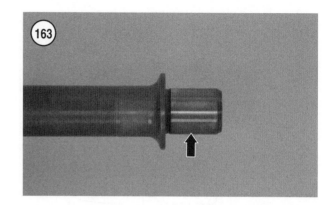

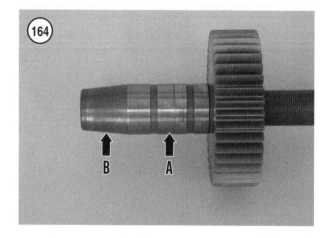

Inspection

1. Clean the alternator drive shaft thoroughly with solvent and dry with compressed air.

2. Inspect the alternator drive shaft gear (**Figure 162**) for chipped or missing teeth.

3. Inspect each shaft surface that rides in the crankcase bushings for scratches, scoring, nicks or heat discoloration. Refer to **Figure 163** and A, **Figure 164**.

4. Inspect the alternator drive shaft taper (B, **Figure 164**) for scratches, scoring and nicks.

ENGINE BREAK-IN

Following cylinder service (honing, new rings) and major lower end work, the engine must be broken in as if it were new. The service and performance life of the engine depends on a careful and sensible break-in.

1. For the first 50 mi. (80 km), maintain engine speed below 2500 rpm in any gear. However, do not lug the engine. Do not exceed 50 mph during this period.

2. From 50-500 mi. (80-804 km) vary the engine speed. Avoid prolonged steady running at one engine speed. During this period, increase engine speed to 3000 rpm. Do not exceed 55 mph during this period.

3. After the first 500 mi. (804 km), the engine break-in is complete.

Table 1 ENGINE LOWER END SPECIFICATIONS

Item	New mm (in.)	Service limit mm (in.)
Camshaft		
Crankcase hole inside		
diameter	25.000-25.021 (0.9843-0.9851)	–
Cover hole inside diameter	28.000-28.021 (1.1024-1.1032)	–
Bearing journal outside diameter		
Crankcase side	24.937-24.950 (0.9818-0.9823)	–
Cover side	27.967-27.980 (1.1011-1.1016)	–
Oil clearance		
Camshaft-to-crankcase	0.050-0.84 (0.0020-0.0033)	–
Camshaft-to-cover	0.020-0.054 (0.0008-0.0021)	–
	(continued)	

Table 1 ENGINE LOWER END SPECIFICATIONS (continued)

Item	New mm (in.)	Service limit mm (in.)
Camshaft lobe height (1999-2003)		
Intake	36.594-36.649 (1.4407-1.4429)	36.494 (1.4368)
Exhaust	36.554-36.654 (1.4391-1.4431)	36.454 (1.4352)
Camshaft lobe width (1999-2003)		
Intake	31.950-32.050 (1.2579-1.2618)	31.850 (1.2539)
Exhaust	31.950-32.050 (1.2579-1.2618)	31.850 (1.2539)
Camshaft lobe height (2004-on)		
Intake (front cylinder)	38.242-38.342 (1.5056-1.5095)	38.142 (1.5017)
Intake (rear cylinder)	38.241-38.341 (1.5055-1.5095)	38.141 (1.5016)
Exhaust	38.236-38.336 (1.5054-1.5093)	38.136 (1.5014)
Camshaft lobe width (2004-on)		
Intake	31.977-32.077 (1.2589-1.2629)	31.877 (1.2550)
Exhaust	32.013-32.113 (1.2604-1.2643)	31.913 (1.2564)
Connecting rods		
Oil clearance	0.037-0.074 (0.0015-0.0029)	–
Big end side clearance	0.320-0.474 (0.013-0.019)	–
Crankshaft		
Main bearing oil clearance	0.030-0.062 (0.0012-0.0024)	0.05 (0.002)
Runout	–	0.04 (0.0016)
Crank web-to-web width		
1999-2005	132.8-133.2 (5.228-5.244)	–
2006-on	105.8-106.2 (4.165-4.181)	–
Oil pump		
Inner rotor-to-outer rotor tip clearance	0.00-0.12 (0.000-0.005)	0.17 (0.007)
Outer rotor-to-housing clearance (feed pump)	0.00-0.12 (0.000-0.005)	0.17 (0.007)
Outer rotor-to-housing clearance (scavenger pump)	0.06-0.11 (0.002-0.004)	0.16 (0.006)

Table 2 CONNECTING ROD BEARING INSERT SELECTION

Connecting rod bearing number	Bearing insert color
1	Blue
2	Black
3	Brown
4	Green
5	Yellow

Table 3 ENGINE LOWER END TORQUE SPECIFICATIONS

Item	N•m	in.-lb.	ft.-lb.
Alternator			
Cover bolt	10	88	–
Rotor bolt	80	–	59
Shaft bolt	28	–	21
Stator coil bolts	7	62	–
Bearing retainers (2006-on)			
Left crankcase bolts	10	88	–
Right crankcase screws	12	106	–
Camshaft			
Cover Allen bolts	7	62	–
Drive gear bolt	30	–	22
Driven gear nut	52	–	38

(continued)

Table 3 ENGINE LOWER END TORQUE SPECIFICATIONS (continued)

Item	N•m	in.-lb.	ft.-lb.
Connecting rod cap bolt			
1999-2003	40	–	30
2004-on			
Initial	15	133	–
Final	additional 90°-120°		
Crankcase bolts			
6 mm	10	88	–
8 mm	24	–	18
Crankcase baffle bolt	10	88	–
Decompression solenoid bolt	7	62	–
Engine mounting hardware			
Front mounting bracket			
and horn bracket bolt	48	–	35
Rear mounting bracket bolt	48	–	35
Throughbolts nuts			
1999-2003	88	–	65
2004-on			
Lower front	103	–	76
All other throughbolts	88	–	65
Transfer gearcase stay			
and frame bolt	30	–	22
Neutral switch	7	62	–
Oil baffle plate bolts	10	88	–
Oil delivery pipe (alternator			
cover-to-crankcase) bolts	10	88	–
Oil drain plug (crankcase)	43	–	32
Oil filter mount			
Bolts	10	88	–
Filter mount bolt	70	–	52
Oil pump			
Mounting bolt	10	88	–
Driven gear bracket bolt	10	88	–
Check valve retainer bolt	10	88	–
Oil strainer bolts	10	88	–

CHAPTER SIX

TRANSFER GEARCASE

This chapter provides service procedures for the drive sprocket and the components within the transfer gearcase.

Specifications are in **Table 1**. During assembly, tighten fasteners to the specification in **Table 2**.

DRIVE SPROCKET

Removal

1. Securely support the motorcycle on level ground. Block the front wheel so the motorcycle will not roll in either direction.
2. Remove both seats as described in Chapter Fifteen.
3. On models so equipped, remove both saddlebags as described in Chapter Fifteen.
4. Remove the muffler assembly as described in Chapter Nine.
5. Remove the screws securing the drive belt upper cover and remove the cover.
6. Loosen the rear axle nut (**Figure 1**).
7. Place a floor jack underneath the engine and frame. Place a thick piece of wood on the jack to protect the frame. Adjust the jack and raise the motorcycle until the rear wheel just clears the ground.

8. Loosen the rear brake caliper mounting bracket bolt (**Figure 2**).
9. Loosen the rear axle adjuster locknut (A, **Figure 3**) on both sides.
10. Loosen the adjusting bolts (B, **Figure 3**) in equal amounts on both sides to achieve the maximum amount of drive belt slack.
11. Remove the mounting bracket (**Figure 4**).
12. Remove the bolts (A, **Figure 5**) securing the drive sprocket cover and remove the cover. Note the location of the cable clamp (B, **Figure 5**). The clamp must be reinstalled in the same location.
13. Remove both sliders and pins (**Figure 6**) from the transfer gearcase.
14. Shift the transmission into fifth gear.
15. Straighten the tabs on the lockwasher (**Figure 7**). For 2006-on models, straighten the staked nut.
16. Loosen and remove the drive sprocket nut (**Figure 8**) and lockwasher (**Figure 9**).
17. Disengage the drive belt and remove the drive sprocket (**Figure 10**) from the transmission countershaft. Mark the outer face of the sprocket to ensure it is oriented properly during installation.
18. Remove the collar (A, **Figure 11**) and O-ring (**Figure 12**) from the transmission countershaft.

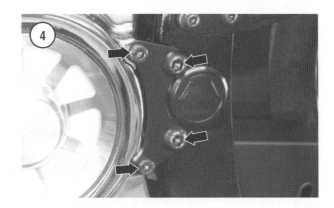

19. Inspect the parts as described in this section.

Installation

1. Install a *new* O-ring (**Figure 12**) on the transmission countershaft. Make sure it seats correctly in the counter-shaft groove.

2. Position the collar with the chamfered end going on last (B, **Figure 11**) and install the collar onto the transmission countershaft.

3. Push the collar in until it bottoms on the shaft and against the O-ring (**Figure 13**).

4. Install the drive sprocket (**Figure 10**), checking that the marked side is facing out. For 2006-on models, the side with the flat mounting boss must face out.

5. Install a *new* lockwasher (**Figure 9**). For 2006-on models, lubricate and install a *new* spring washer with the word OUT facing out.

6. Install the drive sprocket nut (**Figure 8**). For 2006-on models, lubricate and install a *new* nut.

7. Check that the transmission is in fifth gear, then tighten the sprocket nut. Refer to **Table 2** for torque specifications.

8. Bend the lockwasher tabs against the nut (**Figure 7**). For 2006-on models, stake the nut into the notches at the end of the shaft.

9. Install both sliders and pins (**Figure 6**) into the transfer gearcase.

10. Engage the drive belt and install it on the drive sprocket.

11. Install the drive sprocket cover and the bolts (A, **Figure 5**). Install the cable clamp (B, **Figure 5**) on the front lower bolt. Tighten the bolts to 10 N•m (88 in.-lb.).

12. Install the mounting bracket (**Figure 4**) and bolts. Refer to **Table 2** for torque specifications.

13. Adjust the drive belt as described in Chapter Three.

14. Install the drive belt upper cover and tighten the screws securely.

15. Install the muffler assembly as described in Chapter Nine.

16. On models so equipped, install both saddlebags as described in Chapter Fifteen.

17. Install both seats as described in Chapter Fifteen.

Inspection

1. Inspect the drive sprocket teeth. If the teeth are visibly worn, replace the drive belt and both sprockets as a set.

2. Inspect the drive sprocket inner splines (**Figure 14**) for wear. If damaged, inspect the transmission countershaft splines for damage.

3. Inspect the drive sprocket cover for damage; replace if necessary.

TRANSFER GEARCASE

Removal/Disassembly

Refer to **Figure 15**.

1. Securely support the motorcycle on level ground. Block the front wheel so the motorcycle will not roll in either direction.

2. Remove both seats as described in Chapter Fifteen.

3. On models so equipped, remove both saddlebags as described in Chapter Fifteen.

4. Remove the muffler assembly as described in Chapter Nine.

5. Drain the engine and transfer gearcase oil as described in Chapter Three.

6. Remove the drive sprocket as described in this chapter.

7. On the left side, remove the bolts securing the drive sprocket case to the transfer gearcase (A, **Figure 16**), and crankcase (B). Remove the drive sprocket case.

TRANSFER GEARCASE

1. Allen bolt	49. Drive sprocket
2. Hex head bolt	case
3. Cap	50. Allen bolt
4. O-ring	51. Bearing
5. Oil level check bolt	52. Oil seal
6. Gasket	53. O-ring
7. Dowel pin	54. Collar
8. O-ring	55. Drive sprocket
9. Outer cover	56. Lockwasher*
10. Oil pump assembly	57. Nut*
11. O-ring	58. Bolt
12. Dowel pin	59. Special washer
13. Screw	60. Grommet
14. Gasket	61. Pin
15. Flange bolt	62. Slider
16. Washer	63. Drive sprocket
17. Special nut	cover
18. Inner cover	64. Allen bolt
19. Dowel pin	65. Allen bolt
20. Washer	66. Clamp
21. Primary chain	67. Allen bolt
22. Nut*	68. Trim plate
23. Lockwasher*	69. Cap
24. Middle drive gear	
25. Transmission	* For 2006-on
countershaft	models, a spring
26. Middle driven gear	washer and
27. Bearing	stake-type nut are
28. Filter	used.
29. Gasket	
30. Allen bolt	
31. Oil level dipstick	
32. O-ring	
33. Dipstick joint	
34. Allen bolt	
35. O-ring	
36. Cover	
37. Gasket	
38. Allen bolt	
39. Cap plate	
40. Oil strainer	
41. Dowel pin	
42. Allen bolt	
43. Case	
44. Gasket	
45. Drain bolt	
46. Dowel pin	
47. Dowel pin	
48. Hex head bolt	

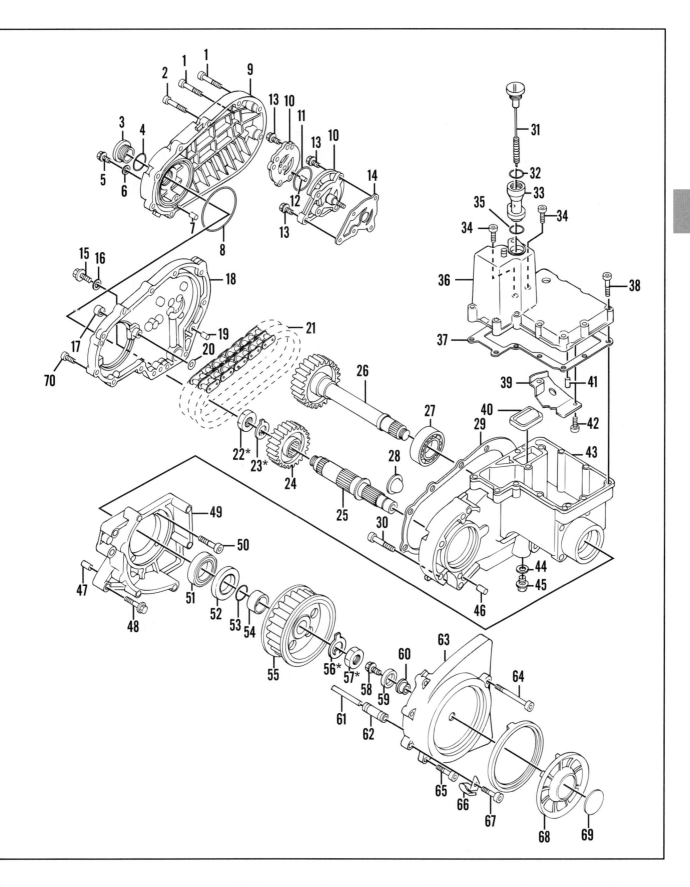

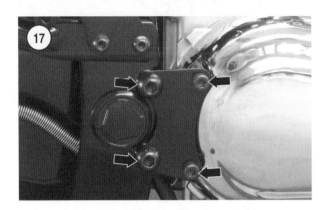

8. Remove the bolts (**Figure 17**) securing the right side mounting bracket and remove the mounting bracket. On 2004-on models, remove the washers located between the mounting bracket and the transfer gearcase, and the crankcase.

9. Remove the bolts securing the outer cover (**Figure 18**) and remove the outer cover. Do not lose the two dowel pins (**Figure 19**).

10. Remove the Allen bolts securing the short oil delivery pipe to the engine (A, **Figure 20**) and transfer gearcase (B). Remove the oil delivery pipe (C, **Figure 20**) and drain out any residual oil.

11. Remove the Allen bolts securing the long oil pipes (**Figure 21**) to the engine and transfer gearcase. Remove both oil pipes and drain out the residual oil.

12. Remove the Allen bolt and ground strap (**Figure 22**) securing the dipstick joint to the transfer gearcase cover. Remove the dipstick joint (**Figure 23**).

13. Remove the special nut (**Figure 24**) securing the inner cover (**Figure 25**) to the threaded stud. Remove the inner cover and remove the washer (**Figure 26**) from the threaded stud.

14. Remove the gasket (A, **Figure 27**) and the dowel pins (B), if loose.

15. Straighten the tab on the middle drive gear lockwasher. For 2006-on models, straighten the staked nut.

16. Loosen and remove the middle drive gear nut (**Figure 28**). Remove and discard the lockwasher/spring washer.

17. Pull straight out and remove the middle driven shaft (A, **Figure 29**), middle drive gear (B), and primary chain (C) as an assembly from the transfer gearcase.

NOTE
The middle drive gear is not symmetrical. Before removing the gear from the primary chain, note the slight concave bevel

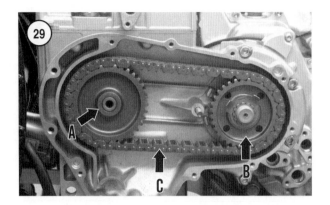

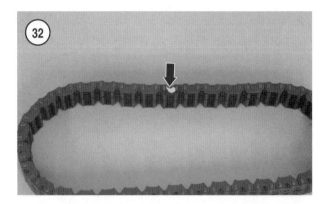

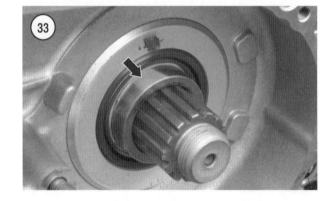

(Figure 30) adjacent to the inner splines. The middle drive gear must be installed with this bevel facing toward the case. On some models, there may be a white paint mark on the inside surface of the middle drive gear (Figure 31) and the primary chain (Figure 32). These marks indicate that the two components must be installed with the white marks facing toward the case.

18. Separate the middle drive gear and primary chain from the middle driven shaft.

19. Remove the collar (**Figure 33**) and the O-ring from the transmission countershaft. Discard the O-ring.

20. Remove the bolts (**Figure 34**) securing the transfer gearcase to the crankcase.

21. Carefully pull the transfer gearcase assembly (**Figure 35**) straight off to the right, and off the long threaded stud (A, **Figure 36**) on the crankcase. Remove the case from the frame. Do not lose the dowel pins and the large O-ring seal.

22. Remove the O-ring from the transmission countershaft.

23. Inspect the components as described in this section.

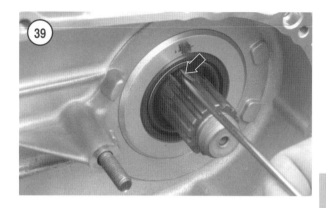

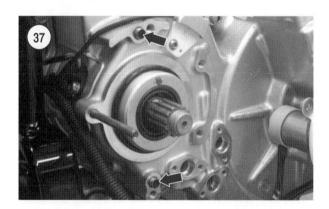

Assembly/Installation

1. Install a *new* O-ring seal (B, **Figure 36**) onto the crankcase, and apply engine oil to it.

2. If removed, install the dowel pins (**Figure 37**) onto the crankcase.

3. Position the transfer gearcase (**Figure 35**) straight onto the long threaded stud (A, **Figure 36**) on the crankcase. Install the case into the frame and against the crankcase. Push it on until it bottoms on the crankcase.

4. Install the bolts (**Figure 34**) securing the transfer gearcase to the crankcase. Tighten the bolts to 30 N•m (22 ft.-lb.).

5. Install a *new* O-ring (**Figure 38**) onto the transmission countershaft. Carefully push the O-ring into place with a flat tip screwdriver (**Figure 39**). Make sure it is correctly seated on the shaft.

6. Position the collar with the bevel side (**Figure 40**) going in first. Slowly push the collar into place (**Figure 33**) against the O-ring on the shaft. Push the collar in until it bottoms.

NOTE
The middle drive gear is not symmetrical and must be positioned correctly in Step 7. Also refer to the white paint marks on the

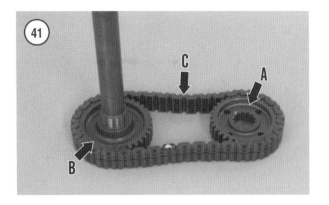

gear and primary chain, on models so marked.

7. Assemble the middle drive gear (A, **Figure 41**), the middle driven shaft (B), and the primary chain (C) as follows:
    a. Position the middle drive gear with the slight bevel side (**Figure 30**), noted during removal, facing toward the crankcase.
    b. Position the primary chain with the white paint mark facing toward the case on models so marked.

8. Slowly guide the middle driven shaft (A, **Figure 29**) assembly into the case and through the bearing on the left side.

9. Align the middle drive gear splines (B, **Figure 29**) with the transmission countershaft and push the assembly onto the case until it bottoms.

10. Install a *new* lockwasher onto the countershaft splines (**Figure 42**). For 2006-on models, lubricate and install a *new* spring washer with the word OUT facing out.

11. Install the middle drive gear nut with the recessed side toward the engine (**Figure 43**). For 2006-on models, lubricate and install a *new* nut. Refer to **Table 2** for torque specifications.

12. Bend the lockwasher tabs against the nut. For 2006-on models, stake the nut into the notches at the end of the shaft.

13. Install a *new* gasket (A, **Figure 27**) and the dowel pins (B), if removed.

14. If removed, install the oil strainer (**Figure 44**) into the case receptacle. Push it in until it bottoms.

15. Install the washer (**Figure 26**) onto the threaded stud.

NOTE
If necessary, slightly rotate the left side end of the middle drive shaft to align the splines in Step 16.

16. Align the oil pump drive shaft splines (A, **Figure 45**) with the splines within the middle drive shaft (B), and install the inner cover onto the case (**Figure 25**), and the threaded stud. Push the inner cover on until it bottoms on the case.

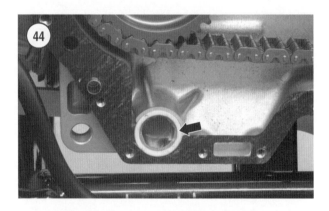

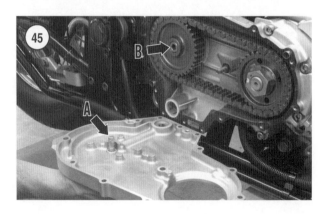

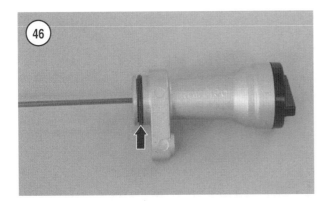

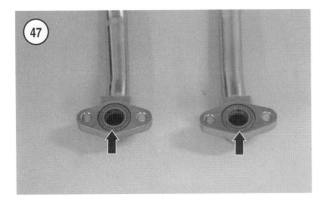

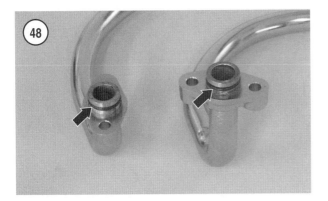

17. Install the special nut (**Figure 24**) onto the threaded stud and tighten to 30 N•m (22 ft.-lb.).

18. Install a *new* O-ring (**Figure 46**) onto the dipstick joint.

19. Install the dipstick joint and secure with the Allen bolt and ground strap (**Figure 22**). Tighten the bolt securely.

20. Install *new* O-rings on both ends of both oil pipes. Refer to **Figure 47** and **Figure 48**.

21. Install the long oil pipes (**Figure 21**) onto the engine and transfer gearcase.

22. Install the Allen bolts securing the oil pipes to the crankcase (**Figure 49**) and transfer gearcase (**Figure 50**). Tighten all bolts finger tight to make sure the oil pipes are correctly seated. Tighten all bolts to 10 N•m (88 in.-lb.).

23. Install a *new* O-ring on both ends of the securing the short oil delivery pipe.

24. Install the short oil delivery pipe onto the engine (A, **Figure 51**) and transfer gearcase (B). Install the Allen bolts and tighten to 10 N•m (88 in.-lb.).

25. If removed, install the dowel pins onto the inner cover. Refer to **Figure 52** and **Figure 53**.

26. Install the outer cover and bolts and tighten in a criss-cross pattern to the following:

    a. 6 mm bolts: 10 N•m (88 in.-lb.).

b. 8 mm bolts: 24 N•m (18 ft.-lb.).

NOTE
On 2004-on models, install the washers be-
tween the mounting bracket and the transfer
gearcase, and the crankcase.

27. Install the right side mounting bracket and bolts (**Figure 54**). Tighten the bolts to the following:
   a. 6 mm bolts: 30 N•m (22 ft.-lb.).
   b. 8 mm bolts: 53 N•m (39 ft.-lb.).
28. On the left side, install the drive sprocket case onto the transfer gearcase (A, **Figure 55**) and crankcase (B). Tighten all bolts to 30 N•m (22 ft.-lb.).
29. Install the drive sprocket as described in this chapter.
30. Refill the engine and transfer gearcase oil as described in Chapter Three.
31. Install the muffler as described in Chapter Nine.
32. On models so equipped, install both saddlebags as described in Chapter Fifteen.
33. Install both seats as described in Chapter Fifteen.

Inspection

1. Thoroughly clean all parts in solvent and dry with compressed air.

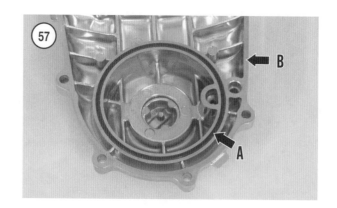

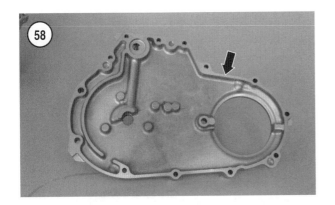

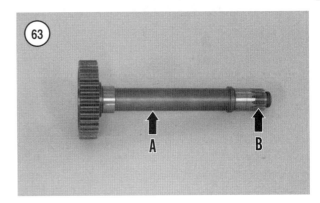

2. Inspect the outer cover (**Figure 56**) for crack or damage.

3. Replace the outer cover O-ring seal (A, **Figure 57**) if starting to deteriorate or harden.

4. Inspect the outer cover-to-inner cover sealing surface (B, **Figure 57**) for nicks or damage that would cause an oil leak.

5. Inspect the inner cover (**Figure 58**) for cracks or damage.

6. Inspect both sides of the inner cover sealing surfaces for nicks or damage that would cause an oil leak.

7. Inspect the primary chain (**Figure 59**) for wear or damage; replace as necessary. Make sure both gears mesh correctly with the primary chain.

8. Inspect the gears for broken or chipped teeth. Refer to **Figure 60** and **Figure 61**.

9. Inspect the middle drive gear inner splines (**Figure 62**) for wear or damage. If damaged, inspect the outer splines on the transmission counter shaft for damage. Refer to Chapter Eight.

10. Inspect the middle driven shaft (A, **Figure 63**) for damage. Inspect the left side outer splines (B, **Figure 63**) for damage. If damaged, inspect the drive sprocket inner splines for damage.

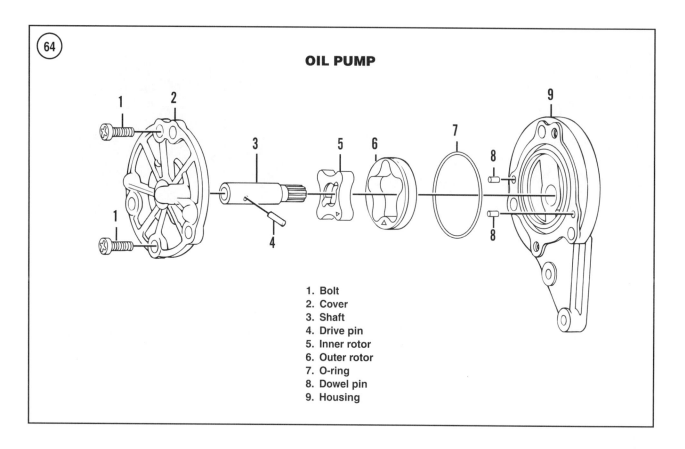

OIL PUMP

1. Bolt
2. Cover
3. Shaft
4. Drive pin
5. Inner rotor
6. Outer rotor
7. O-ring
8. Dowel pin
9. Housing

OIL PUMP

Disassembly/Assembly

Refer to **Figure 64**.

1. Perform Steps 1-13 of *Transfer Gearcase, Removal/ Disassembly* in this chapter and remove the inner cover.

2. Remove the Allen bolts (**Figure 65**) securing the oil pump cover and remove the inner cover. Do not lose the dowel pins.

3. Remove the drive shaft and drive pin (A, **Figure 66**).

4. Remove the inner (B, **Figure 66**) and outer (C) rotors and the large O-ring (D) from the inner housing.

5. Remove the bolts (**Figure 67**) securing the oil pump housing and remove the housing and gasket.

6. Inspect the parts and inner cover as described in this section.

7. Install a *new* oil pump housing gasket (**Figure 68**) onto the inner cover.

8. Install the oil pump housing and the Allen bolts (**Figure 67**) and finger-tighten.

9. Position both rotors with the arrow mark facing out. Install the outer rotor (A, **Figure 69**) and inner rotor (B) into the housing.

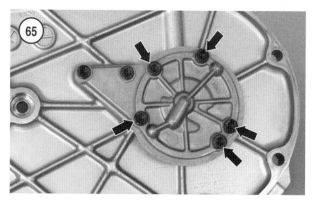

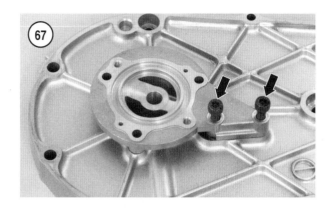

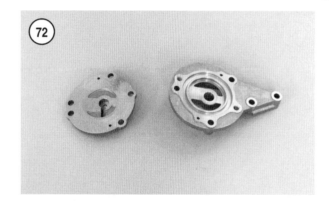

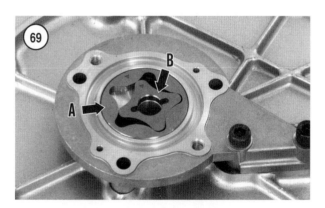

10. Install the *new* the large O-ring (D, **Figure 66**) into the housing. Apply a light coat of oil to the O-ring.

11. Install the drive shaft (A, **Figure 70**) and the drive pin. Engage the drive pin with the inner rotor groove (B, **Figure 70**). Push the drive shaft down until it bottoms.

12. If removed, install the dowel pins (C, **Figure 70**) into the housing. Push them down until they bottom.

13. Install the cover and the remaining Allen bolts (**Figure 65**). Tighten all Allen bolts to 10 N•m (88 in.-lb.).

14. Perform Steps 16-35 of *Transfer Gearcase, Removal/Disassembly* in this chapter.

Inspection

When measuring the oil pump components, compare the actual measurements to the specifications in **Table 1**. If any part is damaged or out of specification, replace the oil pump. The large O-ring and dowel pins are the only parts that are available for replacement.

1. Wash all parts in solvent and dry with compressed air.

2. Make sure the oil gallery opening (**Figure 71**) in the inner cover is clear. Clean with compressed air if necessary.

3. Inspect the housing and cover (**Figure 72**), and the inner and outer rotors (**Figure 73**) for wear, cracks or other damage.

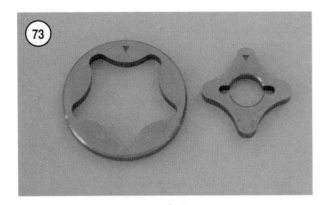

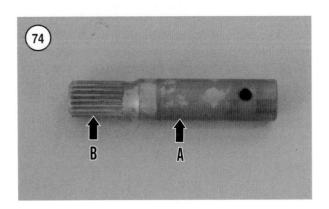

4. Roll the drive shaft (A, **Figure 74**) on a piece of glass and check for flatness. Check the drive pin hole in the shaft for cracks or other damage.

5. Check the drive shaft outer splines (B, **Figure 74**) for wear or damage. If damaged, inspect the middle drive shaft inner splines (**Figure 75**) for damage.

6. Install the outer and inner rotors into the housing and inspect the clearance as follows:

  a. Measure the tip clearance between the inner rotor tip and the outer rotor with a flat feeler gauge (**Figure 76**).

  b. Measure the body clearance between the outer rotor and the housing with a flat feeler gauge (**Figure 77**).

7. Remove the rotors from the housing.

CASE AND COVER

Disassembly/Assembly

1. Remove and disassemble the transfer gearcase as described in this chapter.

2. Remove the bolts securing the cover (**Figure 78**) to the case and remove the cover. Do not forget the two bolts (**Figure 79**) adjacent to the breather.

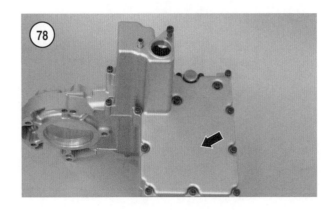

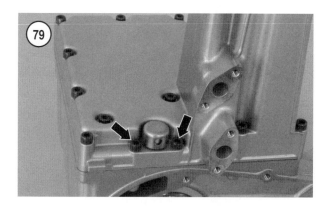

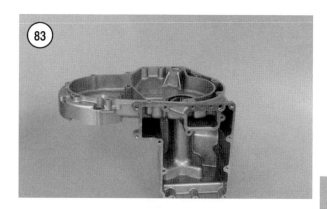

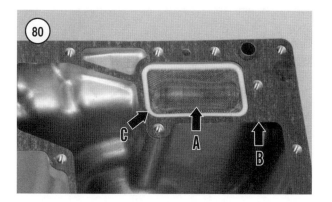

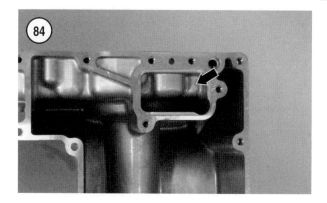

3. Remove the oil strainer (A, **Figure 80**) and gasket (B) from the case. Do not lose the dowel pins.

4. Inspect the case and cover as described in this section.

5. Install the dowel pins (A, **Figure 81**), if removed.

6. Install a *new* gasket (B, **Figure 81**).

7. Install the oil strainer (A, **Figure 80**) and make sure it seats correctly within the gasket (C).

8. Install the cover (**Figure 78**) onto the case and install the bolts. Tighten the bolts in a crisscross pattern to 10 N•m (88 in.-lb.).

9. Assemble and install the transfer gearcase as described in this chapter.

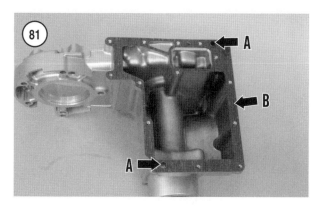

Inspection

1. Thoroughly clean the case and cover in solvent and dry with compressed air.

2. Inspect the cover (A, **Figure 82**) for damage. Inspect the oil pipe sealing surfaces (B, **Figure 82**) for scratches or damage.

3. Inspect the case (**Figure 83**) for damage. Make sure the oil strainer opening (**Figure 84**) is clean and that the opening in the base is clear.

4. Check the case-to-inner cover sealing surface for nicks or damage that would cause an oil leak.

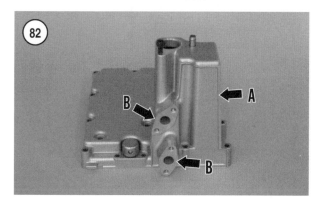

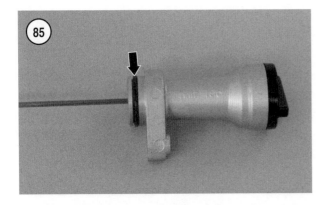

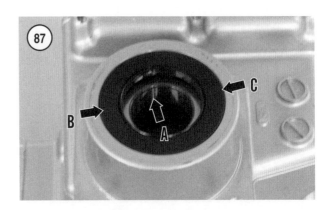

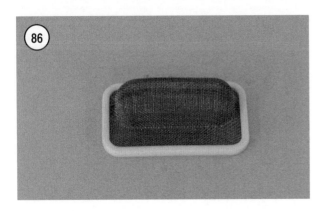

5. Inspect the bearings as described in this section.

6. Inspect the dipstick joint for damage. Install a *new* O-ring (**Figure 85**).

7. Check the oil strainer (**Figure 86**) for damage; replace as necessary.

Bearing and Oil Seal Inspection and Replacement

1. Inspect the bearings as follows:

   a. Turn each bearing inner race by hand. Refer to A, **Figure 87** and **Figure 88**. Each bearing must turn smoothly with no trace of roughness, binding or excessive noise. Some axial play (side-to-side) is normal, but radial play (up and down) must be negligible. See **Figure 89**. If either case bearing is damaged, replace them.

   b. Check the bearing fit in the case by trying to move the bearing laterally by hand. The bearing should be tight in the bore. Loose bearings allow the middle driven shaft to wobble. If a bearing(s) is loose, the bearing bore in the case is probably worn or damaged and the case must be replaced.

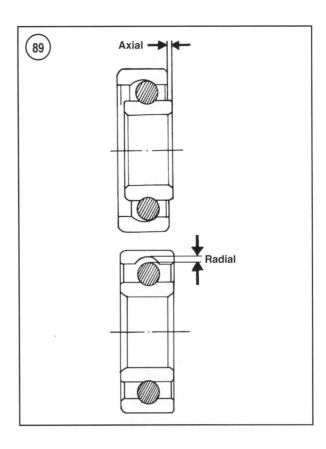

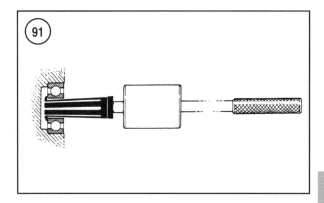

6

2. Check the left side bearing oil seal (B, **Figure 87**) for buckling or other damage that would allow dirt to enter the bearing and case.

3. Pry the oil seal out of the case (**Figure 90**). Support the tool with a rag to avoid damage to the case. Discard the oil seal.

4. A blind bearing remover (**Figure 91**) is required to remove the bearings from the case as follows:

    a. Insert the puller into the bearing and expand the puller behind the bearing inner race.

    b. Use quick in and out strokes on the slide hammer and remove the bearing from the case.

    c. Repeat for the other bearing if necessary.

5. Place the new bearings in a freezer for an hour. This will ease installation.

6. Remove any dirt or debris from the bearing bore in the case before installing the bearing.

7. Place the bearing squarely on the bore opening with the manufacturer marks facing out.

8. Select a bearing driver or socket with an outside diameter that matches (or is slightly smaller than) the outside diameter of the bearing. Drive the bearing into the bore until it bottoms.

9. On the left side bearing install a *new* oil seal. Place the oil seal squarely against the case bore opening with the closed side facing out. Drive the seal into the case bore until it is flush with the outside surface of the case boss (C, **Figure 87**).

Table 1 TRANSFER GEARCASE SPECIFICATIONS

Item	New mm (in.)	Service limit mm (in.)
Oil pump		
Inner rotor-to-outer rotor tip clearance	0.07-0.12 (0.003-0.005)	0.17 (0.007)
Outer rotor-to-housing clearance	0.03-0.08 (0.001-0.003)	0.16 (0.006)

Table 2 TRANSFER GEARCASE TORQUE SPECIFICATIONS

Item	N·m	in.-lb.	ft.-lb.
Drive sprocket case bolts	30	–	22
Drive sprocket nut			
1999-2003	85	–	63
2004-2005	100	–	74
2006-2007	120	–	89
Driven sprocket case bolts	30	–	22
Driven sprocket			
Case nut	85	–	63
Cover bolts	10	88	–
Inner cover			
Bolts	30	–	22
Special nut	30	–	22
Middle drive gear nut			
1999-2003	85	–	63
2004-on	100	–	74
Mounting bracket bolts			
1999-2003			
Long 6 mm	30	–	22
Short 8 mm	53	–	39
2004-on			
Long 6 mm	30	–	22
Short 8 mm	72	–	53
Oil pipe Allen bolts	10	88	–
Oil pump mounting Allen bolts	10	88	–
Outer cover bolts			
6 mm	10	88	–
8 mm	24	–	18
Transfer gearcase			
Case-to-cover bolts	10	88	–
Case-to-crankcase bolts	30	–	22

CHAPTER SEVEN

CLUTCH AND PRIMARY DRIVE GEAR

This chapter contains service procedures for the clutch, release mechanism and primary drive gear. When inspecting the components, compare any measurement to the specifications in **Table 1** at the end of the chapter. Replace any part that is damaged, worn or out of specification. During assembly, tighten fasteners to the specification in **Table 2**.

The wet, multi-plate clutch is mounted on the left side of the transmission mainshaft.

The clutch release mechanism is mounted in the clutch cover on the right side of the crankcase. It is cable operated by the clutch lever on the left side handlebar.

CLUTCH COVER

Removal/Installation

Refer to **Figure 1**.
1. Securely support the motorcycle on level ground. Block the front wheel so the motorcycle will not roll in either direction.

2. Remove the seats and side covers as described in Chapter Fifteen.
3. Disconnect the negative battery cable as described in Chapter Three.
4. Drain the engine oil as described in Chapter Three.
5. Slide back the clutch cable rubber boot (**Figure 2**). Loosen the locknut (A, **Figure 3**) and turn the adjuster (B) to allow maximum slack in the clutch cable.
6. Remove the left side rider footrest and gearshift assembly as described in Chapter Fifteen.
7. Remove the bolts and remove the lower horn from the frame. Refer to Chapter Ten.
8. Follow the pickup coil gray and black electrical wires from the base of the clutch cover (A, **Figure 4**) to the electrical connectors behind the fuse box. Disconnect the 2-pin electrical connector (**Figure 5**).

NOTE
*On some models, it may not be possible to remove the cover with the lower bolt in place (**Figure 6**) due to interference with the*

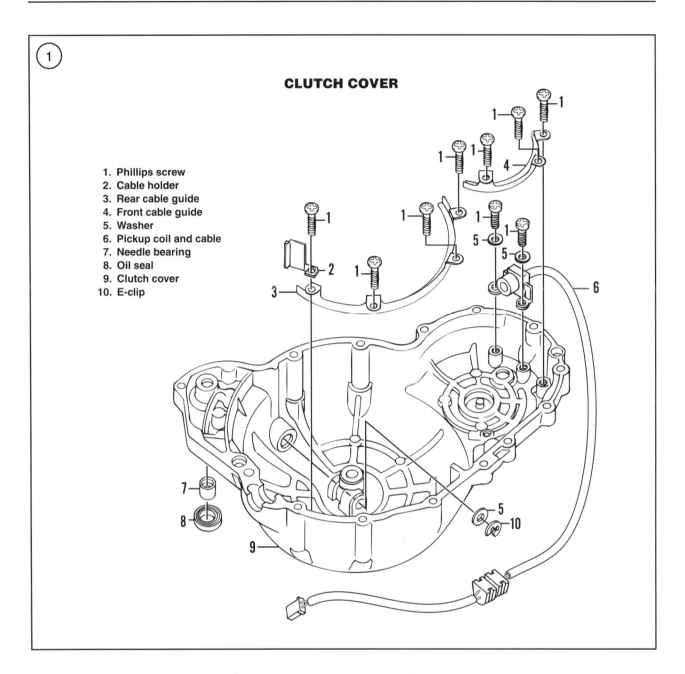

CLUTCH COVER

1. Phillips screw
2. Cable holder
3. Rear cable guide
4. Front cable guide
5. Washer
6. Pickup coil and cable
7. Needle bearing
8. Oil seal
9. Clutch cover
10. E-clip

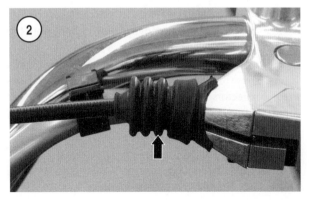

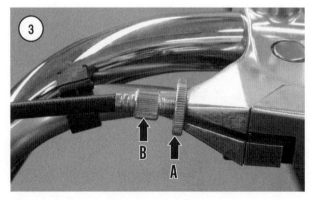

side stand switch. Leave it in place on the cover.

9. Remove the bolts securing the timing inspection cover (**Figure 7**) and remove the cover. Do not lose the dowel pin (**Figure 8**).

10. Remove the clamp bolt (A, **Figure 9**) and remove the clutch lifter lever (B).

11. Remove the clutch lifter lever return spring (**Figure 10**) from the clutch cover.

12. Remove the bolts and the clutch cable bracket (C, **Figure 9**) on the clutch coil cover.

13. Using a crisscross pattern, loosen and then remove the bolts securing the clutch cover (B, **Figure 4**).

14. Remove the clutch cover and the gasket.

15. If loose, remove the two dowel pins. Refer to **Figure 11** and **Figure 12**.

16. Remove all gasket residue from the crankcase and the cover mating surfaces.

17. Install the two dowel pins, if removed. Refer to **Figure 11** and **Figure 12**.

18. Make sure the teeth on the lifter piece is positioned correctly toward the rear (**Figure 13**) to ensure correct engagement with the clutch lifter arm gear.

19. Install the *new* gasket (**Figure 14**).

20. Install the clutch cover while turning the clutch lifter arm *clockwise* to engage the lifter arm teeth with the lifter piece teeth.

21. Push the clutch cover (B, **Figure 4**) up against the crankcase until it bottoms.

22. Install all bolts securing the clutch cover and tighten securely.

23. Tighten the clutch cover bolts to 10 N•m (88 in.-lb.).

24. Move the clutch cable and bracket (C, **Figure 9**) into position. Install the bolts and tighten securely.

25. Install the clutch lifter lever return spring (**Figure 10**) onto the locating hole in the clutch cover.

26. Align the split on the lever with the index mark on the shaft. Install the clutch lifter lever (B, **Figure 9**) and tighten the clamp bolt securely (A).

27. Install the return spring onto the lever. Measure the free play distance between the clutch lifter lever and the cable holder (**Figure 15**). The specified distance is 31.8 mm (1.25 in.). If necessary, reposition the lever on the shaft and tighten the clamp bolt securely.

28. Make sure the rubber damper (**Figure 16**) is installed on the inside of the timing inspection cover.

29. Install the dowel pin (**Figure 8**), if removed.

30. Install the timing inspection cover (**Figure 7**) onto the clutch cover. Tighten the bolts to 10 N•m (88 in.-lb.).

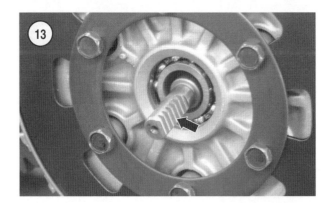

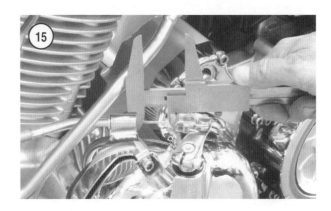

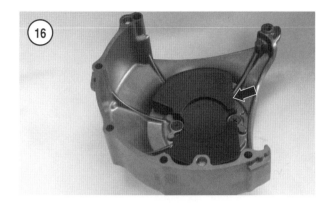

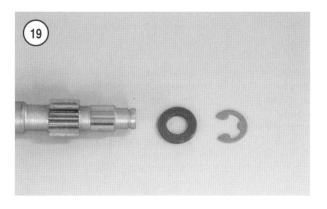

31. Correctly position the pickup coil electrical wires and connect the pickup coil 2-pin electrical connector (**Figure 5**) located behind the fuse box.

32. Install the lower horn and the bolts. Tighten the bolts securely.

33. Install the left side rider footrest assembly as described in Chapter Fifteen.

34. Install the side covers and seats as described in Chapter Fifteen.

> *CAUTION*
> *Debris generated by burnt clutch plates contaminates the engine oil. If the clutch plates are burnt or damaged, replace them and change the engine oil and filter. This step is important, even though the engine may be between oil changes, to remove contaminants from the lubrication system.*

35. Refill the engine with oil as described in Chapter Three.

36. Adjust the clutch cable as described in Chapter Three.

Release Mechanism
Removal/Inspection/Installation

The clutch release mechanism is located within the clutch cover.

1. Remove the E-clip and washer (**Figure 17**) from the end of the release shaft.

2. Withdraw the release shaft (**Figure 18**) from the clutch cover.

3. Inspect all parts (**Figure 19**) for wear or damage. Check the splines in the shaft for damage.

4. Install the release shaft (**Figure 18**) into the clutch cover.

5. At the inner end of the release shaft, install the washer and a *new* E-clip (**Figure 17**). Make sure the E-clip is completely seated in the shaft groove.

Oil Seal Replacement

1. Inspect the clutch cover for cracks or damage.

2. Inspect the clutch release lever oil seal (**Figure 20**) and shift shaft oil seal (**Figure 21**) for damage or signs of leakage. If necessary, replace the oil seal(s) as follows:

    a. Carefully pry the oil seal out of the cover with a flat blade screwdriver.

    b. Lubricate the *new* oil seal with lithium grease.

    c. Install the oil seal with the manufacturer's marks facing out.

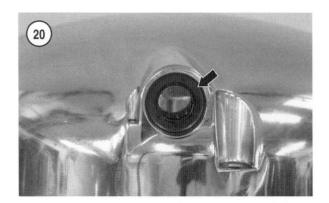

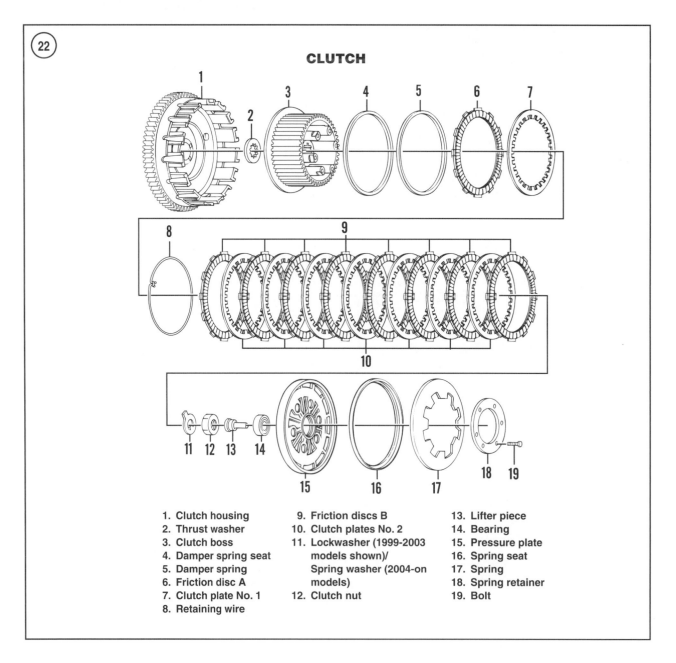

CLUTCH

1. Clutch housing
2. Thrust washer
3. Clutch boss
4. Damper spring seat
5. Damper spring
6. Friction disc A
7. Clutch plate No. 1
8. Retaining wire
9. Friction discs B
10. Clutch plates No. 2
11. Lockwasher (1999-2003 models shown)/ Spring washer (2004-on models)
12. Clutch nut
13. Lifter piece
14. Bearing
15. Pressure plate
16. Spring seat
17. Spring
18. Spring retainer
19. Bolt

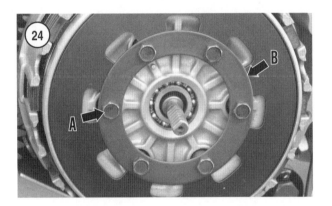

d. Drive the oil seal(s) into the cover with a driver with the outside diameter slightly smaller than the seals outside diameter. Then drive the oil seal into the bore until it bottoms.

CLUTCH

Removal

Refer to **Figure 22**.

1. Remove the clutch cover as described in this chapter.

2. Place an aluminum or brass washer (**Figure 23**) between the gears to keep the clutch housing from rotating in Step 3.

3. Remove the bolts (A, **Figure 24**) securing the clutch spring retainer (B) and remove the retainer. Remove the washer installed in Step 2.

4. Remove the clutch spring (**Figure 25**).

5. Remove the spring seat (**Figure 26**).

6. Remove the pressure plate (A, **Figure 27**) and clutch lifter piece (B). Remove the lifter piece (**Figure 28**) from the backside of the pressure plate.

7. Remove the clutch plates and friction discs B (**Figure 29**) from the clutch hub. Keep them in order.

8. Straighten the tabs on the clutch nut lockwasher (A, **Figure 30**). For 2004-on models, straighten the staked nut.

9A. If the engine is installed in the frame, shift the transmission into fifth gear. Have an assistant apply the rear brake.

CAUTION
When using the clutch holder in Step 9B, make sure to secure it squarely onto the clutch hub splines. If the clutch holder slips, release the pressure from the clutch locknut and reposition the clutch holder. If the clutch holder slips, it may damage the clutch hub splines.

9B. If the engine is removed from the frame, secure the clutch hub with a clutch holder (**Figure 31**).

10A. On 1999-2003 models, proceed as follows:
  a. Loosen and remove the clutch locknut (B, **Figure 30**).
  b. Remove the lockwasher (A, **Figure 30**).

10B. On 2004-on models, proceed as follows:
  a. Straighten the staked nut. Remove and discard the nut.
  b. Remove and discard the spring washer.

11. Remove the clutch boss assembly (**Figure 32**).

12. Remove the thrust washer (**Figure 33**) from the clutch housing.

13. Pull straight out and remove the clutch housing assembly (**Figure 34**).

14. If necessary, disassemble the clutch boss as follows:

    a. Carefully remove the ends of the wire retainer (A, **Figure 35**) and remove the wire retainer from the clutch boss.

    b. Remove the clutch plate No. 1 (B, **Figure 35**).

    c. Remove the friction disc A, the damper spring, and the spring seat from the clutch hub (**Figure 36**).

15. If necessary, remove the oil pump drive gear as follows:

    a. Remove the snap ring (A, **Figure 37**) and the washer (B).

    b. Remove the oil pump drive gear (C, **Figure 37**) from the clutch housing.

16. Inspect the clutch assembly as described in this section.

Installation

1. Coat all clutch parts with engine oil before assembly.

2. If the oil pump drive gear was removed, proceed as follows:

    a. Align the notch (A, **Figure 38**) in the oil pump drive gear with the locating pin (B) on the clutch housing.

    b. Install the oil pump drive gear (A, **Figure 39**) onto the clutch housing.

    c. Install the washer (B, **Figure 39**) and the *new* snap ring (**Figure 40**). Make sure the snap ring is correctly seated in the clutch housing groove (A, **Figure 37**).

3. If the clutch boss was disassembled, proceed as follows:

    a. Install the spring seat (**Figure 41**) onto the clutch boss.

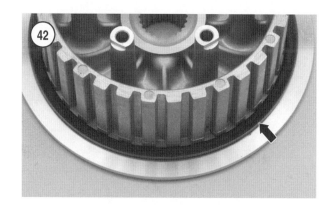

b. Position the damper spring with the OUTSIDE mark facing out and install the damper spring (**Figure 42**).

c. Install the narrow friction disc A (A, **Figure 43**). Make sure it is correctly seated within the damper spring and spring seat (**Figure 36**).

d. Install the clutch plate No. 1 (**Figure 44**).

e. Insert one end of the wire retainer (**Figure 45**) into the hole in the clutch boss.

f. Wrap the wire retainer around the clutch boss and install the other end (A, **Figure 35**) into the same hole in the clutch boss. Make sure both ends are correctly seated.

4. Install the clutch housing as follows:

a. Install the clutch housing onto the transmission shaft and push it on until it contacts the oil pump drive sprocket.

b. Insert a scribe or narrow screwdriver under the clutch housing (**Figure 46**) and slowly rotate the oil pump drive sprocket until the two gears mesh.

c. Push the clutch housing on until it bottoms. Remove the scribe or screwdriver.

d. At this point the outer surface of the clutch outer housing gear should be flush with the outer surface of the primary drive gear.

5. Install the thrust washer (**Figure 33**) onto the transmission shaft.

6. Install the clutch boss (**Figure 32**).

NOTE
*The mainshaft splines must be visible (A, **Figure 47**) in order to accept the lockwasher. If the splines are not visible, the clutch housing is not completely seated.*

7A. On 1999-2003 models, proceed as follows:

a. Install the *new* lockwasher (B, **Figure 47**) onto the mainshaft splines. Push it on until it is engaged with the mainshaft splines (A, **Figure 47**).

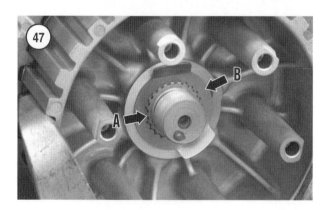

b. Position the clutch nut with the recessed side going on first and install the clutch nut. Tighten finger-tight.

7B. On 2004-on models, proceed as follows:

a. Install a new spring washer onto the mainshaft with the word OUT facing out.

b. Install a new nut.

8A. If the engine is mounted in the frame, make sure the transmission is still in gear. Have an assistant apply the rear brake.

CAUTION
When using the clutch holder in Step 8B, make sure to secure it squarely onto the clutch hub splines. If the clutch holder starts to slip, stop tightening the clutch locknut and reposition the clutch holder. If the clutch holder slips, it may damage the clutch hub splines.

8B. If the engine is removed from the frame, hold the clutch hub with the same clutch holder tool (**Figure 31**) used during disassembly.

9. Tighten the clutch nut (B, **Figure 30**).

a. 1999-2003 models: 70 N•m (52 ft.-lb.).

b. 2004-on models: 105 N•m (77 ft.-lb.).

10. Remove the clutch holder tool.

NOTE
Check the clutch hub splines for any burrs caused by the clutch holder. Remove burrs with a file, and then clean the area of all aluminum debris.

11A. On 1999-2003 models, bend down one of the lockwasher tabs against the flat on the clutch locknut (A, **Figure 30**).

11B. For 2004-on models, stake the nut into the notch at the end of the shaft.

12. The friction discs must be orientated into the correct clutch housing groove (**Figure 48**) as follows:

a. On 1999-2003 models: the two friction disc notches must align with the clutch housing groove marked with two index marks (**Figure 49**).

b. On 2004-on models: the friction disc single notch must align with the clutch housing groove marked with two index marks (**Figure 50**).

13. Install a friction disc B (**Figure 51**), then a clutch plate No. 2 (**Figure 52**).

14. Continue to alternately install a friction disc B and a No. 2 clutch plate.

15. A friction disc B (**Figure 53**) must be installed last.

16. If removed, install the bearing into the pressure plate.

17. Install the clutch lifter piece (**Figure 28**) through the backside of the pressure plate.

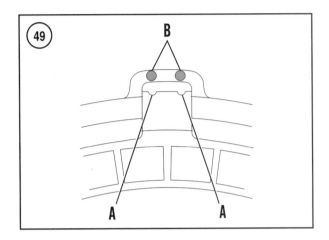

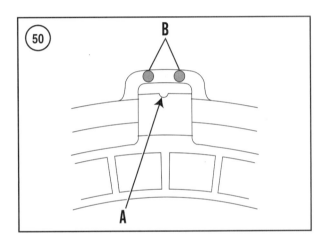

18. Align the index mark on the clutch pressure plate (A, **Figure 54**) with the index mark on the clutch boss (B) and install the clutch pressure plate (**Figure 55**). Make sure the pressure plate seats flush against the outer friction disc B.

19. Install the spring seat and make sure it is correctly seated in the pressure plate (**Figure 56**).

20. Install the spring (**Figure 57**) onto the spring seat. Make sure it is correctly seated.

21. Install the spring retainer (A, **Figure 58**) and install the bolts (B).

22. Place an aluminum or brass washer (**Figure 59**) between the gears to keep the clutch housing from rotating.

23. Using a crisscross pattern, tighten the clutch spring bolts to 8 N•m (71 in.-lb.). Remove the washer.

24. Install the clutch cover as described in this chapter.

25. Refill the engine with the correct type and quantity of oil as described in Chapter Three.

26. Adjust the clutch lever free play as described in Chapter Three.

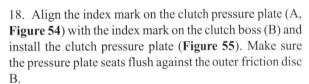

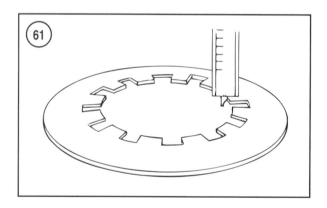

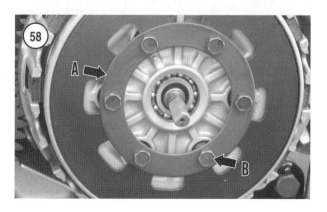

Inspection

When measuring the clutch components, compare the actual measurements to the specifications in **Table 1**. Replace worn or damaged parts as described in this section.

1. Clean and dry all parts and thoroughly dry.

2. Inspect the spring (**Figure 60**) for cracks or damaged fingers.

3. Measure the spring height at the tip of the fingers (**Figure 61**) with a vernier caliper.

4. Inspect the spring retainer for cracks or damage.

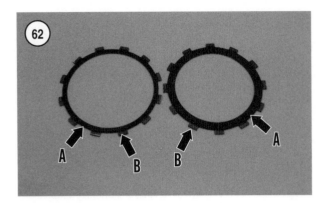

5. Inspect the friction discs as follows:

> *NOTE*
> *If any friction disc is damaged or out of specification as described in the following steps, replace all of the friction discs as a set.*

a. The friction material used on the friction discs (A, **Figure 62**) is bonded onto an aluminum plate. Inspect the friction material for excessive or uneven wear, cracks and other damage. Check the disc tangs (B, **Figure 62**) for surface damage. The sides of the disc tangs must be smooth where they contact the clutch housing fingers; otherwise, the discs cannot engage and disengage correctly.

> *NOTE*
> *If the disc tangs are damaged, inspect the clutch housing fingers carefully as described in this section.*

b. Measure the thickness of each friction disc with a vernier caliper (**Figure 63**). Measure the discs at several places around the disc.

6. Inspect the steel clutch plates as follows:

a. Inspect the clutch plates for cracks, damage or color change. Overheated clutch plates will have a blue discoloration.

b. Check the clutch plates for an oil glaze buildup. Remove buildup by lightly sanding both sides of each plate with 400 grit sandpaper placed on a surface plate or piece of glass.

c. Measure the thickness of each clutch plate with a vernier caliper. Measure the plates at several places around the plate.

d. Place each clutch plate on a surface plate or piece of glass and check for warp with a feeler gauge (**Figure 64**). If the clutch plates are warped, compare the measurement to the service limit in **Table 1**. If any

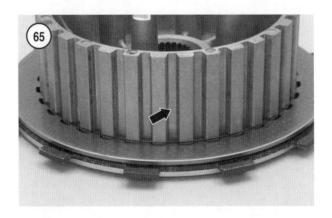

are warped beyond specification, replace the entire set.

e. The clutch plate inner teeth mesh with the clutch hub splines. Check the clutch plate teeth for any roughness or damage. The teeth contact surfaces

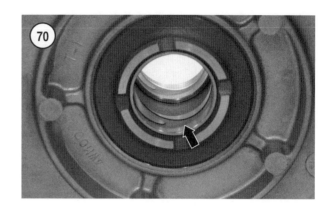

must be smooth; otherwise, the plates cannot engage and disengage correctly.

NOTE
If the clutch plate teeth are damaged, inspect the clutch hub splines carefully as described in this section.

7. Inspect the clutch boss for the following conditions:
   a. The clutch plate teeth slide in the clutch hub splines (**Figure 65**). Inspect the splines for rough spots, grooves or other damage. Repair minor damage with a file or oil stone. If the damage is excessive, replace the clutch hub.
   b. Damaged spring towers and threads (**Figure 66**).
   c. Inspect the inner splines (**Figure 67**) for damage.

8. Check the clutch housing for the following conditions:
   a. The friction disc tangs slide in the clutch housing grooves. Inspect the grooves (**Figure 68**) for cracks or galling. Repair minor damage with a file. If the damage is excessive, replace the clutch housing.
   b. Check the clutch housing gear (**Figure 69**) for excessive wear, pitting, chipped gear teeth or other damage.

NOTE
If the clutch housing gear is excessively worn or damaged, check the primary drive gear assembly for the same wear conditions.

   c. Inspect the bearing surface (**Figure 70**) for wear or heat damage.
   d. Make sure the oil pump drive gear locating pin (**Figure 71**) is secure.

9. Inspect the pressure plate for the following conditions:
   a. Inspect for cracks or other damage.
   b. Slowly turn the ball bearing (**Figure 72**) by hand. If it turns roughly or binds, replace the bearing.
   c. Check the fingers (**Figure 73**) for damage.

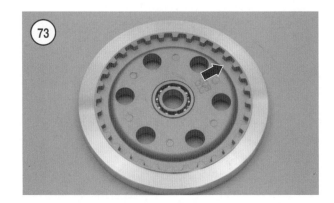

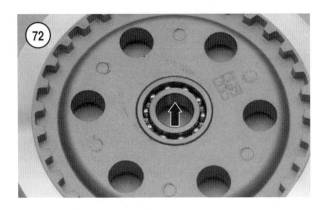

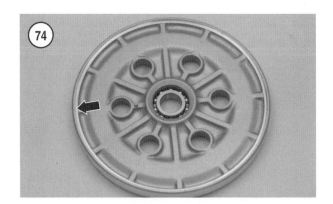

d. Inspect the diaphragm spring seat and the pressure plate surface (**Figure 74**) where the seat rides for excessive wear or damage.

10. Inspect the diaphragm spring and the seat (**Figure 75**) for cracks, warp or other damage. Replace as a set even if only one requires replacement.

11. Check the lifter piece for straightness and damage. Inspect the teeth and the end where it contacts the lifter lever for abnormal wear.

12. Inspect the thrust washer for wear or damage.

13. Check the oil pump drive gear (**Figure 76**) for excessive wear, pitting, chipped gear teeth or other damage.

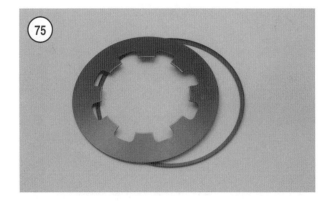

PRIMARY DRIVE GEAR

Removal/Installation

1. Remove the clutch outer cover as described in this chapter.

2. Place an aluminum or brass washer (A, **Figure 77**) between the gears to keep the primary drive gear from rotating.

3. Loosen the bolt (B, **Figure 77**) securing the primary drive gear to the crankshaft. Remove the washer.

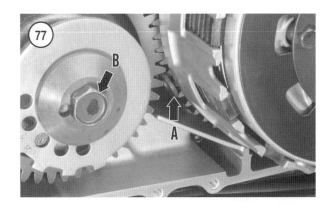

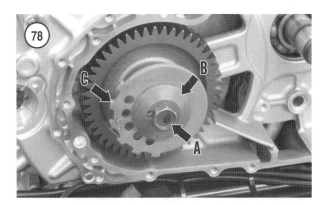

7

NOTE
The following steps are shown with the clutch assembly removed. It is not necessary to remove the clutch for primary drive gear removal and installation.

4. Remove the bolt (A, **Figure 78**), spacer (B) and pick up coil timing rotor (C).

5. Remove the primary drive gear (**Figure 79**) and straight key (**Figure 80**) from the crankshaft.

6. Inspect the primary drive gear as described in this section.

7. Install the straight key (**Figure 80**) into the crankshaft. Make sure it is seated correctly in the crankshaft groove.

8. Install the primary drive gear (**Figure 79**) onto the straight key and crankshaft.

9. Position the pick up coil timing rotor with the timing marks facing out and install the rotor (C, **Figure 78**). Make sure the pickup coil timing rotor tab (**Figure 81**) is seated correctly in the crank shaft groove.

10. Install the spacer (B, **Figure 78**) onto the bolt.

11. Apply a medium strength thread locking compound on the bolt threads and install the bolt (A, **Figure 78**).

12. Place an aluminum or brass washer (A, **Figure 77**) between the gears to keep the primary drive gear from rotating.

13. Tighten the bolt to the specification in **Table 2**. Remove the washer.

14. Install the clutch outer cover as described in this chapter.

Inspection

Replace worn or damaged parts as described in this section.

NOTE
If the primary drive gear is excessively worn or damaged, check the clutch housing gear assembly for the same wear conditions.

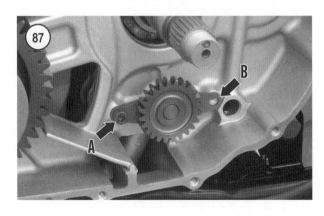

1. Check the primary drive gear (**Figure 82**) for excessive wear, pitting, chipped gear teeth, or other damage.

2. Check the straight gear groove (**Figure 83**) for wear or damage.

3. Check the pick up coil timing rotor (**Figure 84**) for damage or distortion.

OIL PUMP DRIVEN GEAR

Removal/Installation

1. Remove the clutch as described in this chapter.

2. Remove the Allen bolt (**Figure 85**) securing the oil pump driven gear stopper and oil delivery pipe.

3. Withdraw the oil delivery pipe (**Figure 86**) from the crankcase.

4. Remove the remaining Allen bolt (A, **Figure 87**) and stopper (B).

5. Remove the oil pump driven gear (**Figure 88**).

6. Inspect the oil pump driven gear and oil delivery pipe as described in this section.

7. Install the oil pump driven gear (**Figure 88**). Slowly rotate the gear and mesh it with the oil pump. Push the gear in until it bottoms and check for correct engagement with the oil pump.

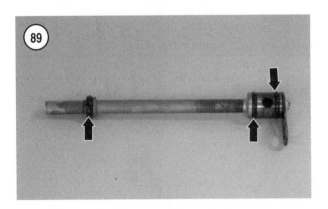

7

10. Install the front Allen bolt (A, **Figure 87**) and tighten finger tight.

11. Install *new* O-rings (**Figure 89**) and make sure they are in place on the oil delivery pipe.

12. Install the oil delivery pipe (**Figure 86**) into the crankcase and push it in until it bottoms (A, **Figure 90**). Align the bolt holes (B, **Figure 90**).

13. Install the Allen bolt (**Figure 85**) securing the oil pump driven gear stopper, the oil delivery gear, and the oil pipe.

14. Tighten the bolt to 10 N•m (88 in.-lb.).

15. Install the clutch as described in this chapter.

Inspection

Replace worn or damaged parts as described in this section.

1. Check the oil pump driven gear (A, **Figure 91**) for excessive wear, pitting, chipped gear teeth or other damage.

NOTE
If the oil pump driven gear is excessively worn or damaged, check the oil pump drive gear on the clutch housing gear assembly for the same wear conditions.

8. Install the stopper with the open slot facing down and place it on the oil pump drive gear (B, **Figure 87**).

9. Apply a medium strength thread locking compound on the Allen bolt threads.

2. Check the engagement slot (B, **Figure 91**) where it meshes with the oil pump for damage.

3. Make sure the oil delivery pipe openings are open. Apply low air pressure and clean out if necessary.

Table 1 and Table 2 are on the following page.

Table 1 CLUTCH SPECIFICATIONS

Item	New mm (in.)	Service limit mm (in.)
Friction disc		
Quantity	9	
Thickness	2.9-3.1 (0.114-0.122)	2.8 (0.110)
Clutch lifter lever-to-cable		
holder distance	31.8 (1.25)	–
Clutch plate		
Quantity	8	
Thickness	2.2-2.4 (0.087-0.094)	–
Warp	–	0.30 (0.012)
Clutch spring free height	7.0 (0.276)	6.5 (0.256)

Table 2 CLUTCH AND PRIMARY DRIVE GEAR TORQUE SPECIFICATIONS

Item	N•m	in.-lb.	ft.-lb.
Cover bolts	10	88	–
Clutch nut			
1999-2003	70	–	52
2004-on	105	–	77
Clutch diaphragm spring retainer bolts	8	71	–
Gearshift stopper arm bolt	22	–	16
Oil delivery gear and pipe bolt	10	88	–
Oil pump driven gear stopper bolt	10	88	–
Primary drive gear bolt			
1999-2003	115	–	85
2004-on	100	–	74
Timing inspection cover bolts	10	88	–

CHAPTER EIGHT

TRANSMISSION AND SHIFT MECHANISM

This chapter describes service procedures for the transmission, internal shift mechanism and external shift mechanism.

When inspecting these components, compare any measurement to the specifications in **Table 1** at the end of the chapter. Replace any components that are worn, damaged or out of specification. During assembly, tighten fasteners to the specified torque.

SHIFT PEDAL/FOOTREST ASSEMBLY

Removal/Installation

Refer to **Figure 1** for the original shift mechanism components and the parts that were revised in 2006. The removal procedure is identical for both assemblies.

1. Place the motorcycle securely on level ground. Block the front wheel so the motorcycle will not roll in either direction.
2. Note that the index mark on the shift shaft aligns with the slot in the shift lever. If the mark is worn or missing, make a new one so the shift lever can be properly installed on the shift shaft during assembly.
3. Loosen the clamp bolt (A, **Figure 2**) and remove the shift shaft lever (B) from the shift shaft.
4. On California models, disconnect the hoses (**Figure 3**) from the charcoal canister.

5. Remove the bolts securing the footrest/gearshift assembly (A, **Figure 4**) to the frame.
6. Remove the footrest/gearshift assembly (B, **Figure 4**).
7. If the shift pedal assembly must be removed from the footrest bracket, note the following:
   a. Before removing a clamp bolt (A, **Figure 5**), note the alignment index mark(s) on the end of the shaft (B, **Figure 5**). The pedal assembly must be assembled with these marks properly positioned.
   b. Clean all parts and lubricate with pivot points with grease.
   c. Assemble the parts and install a *new* snap ring/E-clip.
8. Reverse the procedure to install the shift pedal and footrest assembly. Note the following:
   a. Check that all alignment marks are correct.
   b. Tighten the bolts to the specifications in **Table 2**.
   c. Adjust the shift pedal as described in Chapter Three.

EXTERNAL SHIFT MECHANISM

Removal

Refer to **Figure 6**.

1. Securely support the motorcycle on level ground. Block the rear wheel so the motorcycle will not roll in either direction.

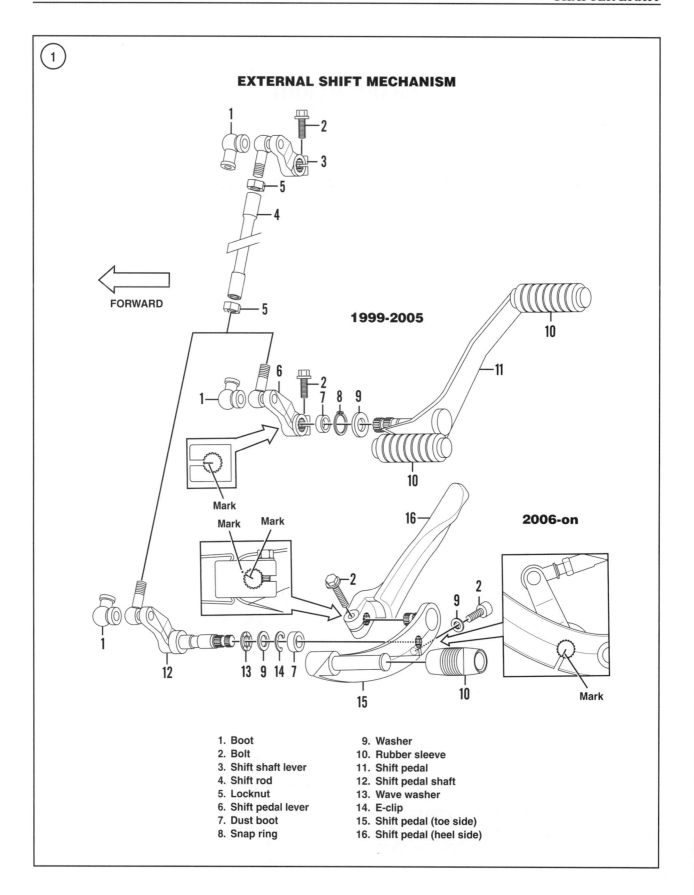

①

EXTERNAL SHIFT MECHANISM

FORWARD

1999-2005

Mark

Mark   Mark

2006-on

Mark

1. Boot
2. Bolt
3. Shift shaft lever
4. Shift rod
5. Locknut
6. Shift pedal lever
7. Dust boot
8. Snap ring
9. Washer
10. Rubber sleeve
11. Shift pedal
12. Shift pedal shaft
13. Wave washer
14. E-clip
15. Shift pedal (toe side)
16. Shift pedal (heel side)

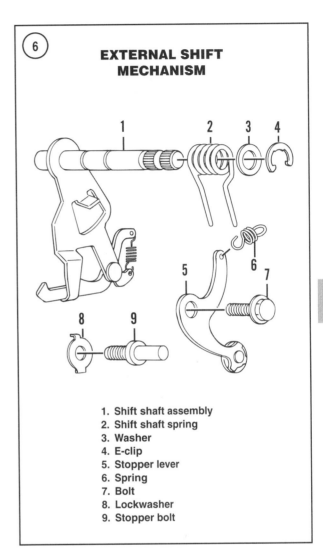

EXTERNAL SHIFT MECHANISM

1. Shift shaft assembly
2. Shift shaft spring
3. Washer
4. E-clip
5. Stopper lever
6. Spring
7. Bolt
8. Lockwasher
9. Stopper bolt

8

2. Shift the transmission into neutral.

3. Remove the clutch assembly as described in Chapter Seven.

4. Press the shift arm away (A, **Figure 7**) away from the shift cam until it clears the shift pins.

5. Withdraw the shift shaft (B, **Figure 7**) and pull the assembly from the crankcase.

6. Unhook the stopper lever spring from the crankcase pin (**Figure 8**).

7. Remove the bolt (A, **Figure 9**) securing the stopper lever to the crankcase.

8. Remove the stopper lever (B, **Figure 7**).

9. Inspect the components as described in this section.

Installation

1. Install the spring onto the stopper lever.

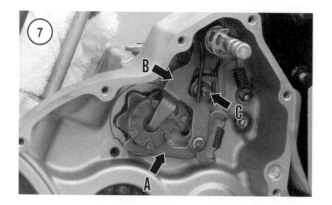

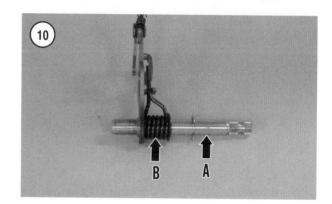

2. Apply a medium strength thread locking compound to the stopper lever bolt.

3. Install the stopper lever (B, **Figure 9**) onto the crankcase and install the bolt (A). Tighten the bolt securely.

4. Move the roller into position on the stopper plate (C, **Figure 9**), then hook the spring onto the crankcase pin (**Figure 8**).

5. Move the shift arm (A, **Figure 7**) down so the pawl will clear the pins in the shift cam.

6. Install the end of the shift shaft into the crankcase boss until the assembly bottoms.

7. Center the shift shaft return spring over the stopper pin (C, **Figure 7**) on the crankcase.

8. When the shift arm is released, the shift pawl must engage the pins on the shift cam (A, **Figure 7**).

9. Install the clutch assembly as described in Chapter Seven.

Inspection

> *NOTE*
> *There are no replacement parts for the shift shaft assembly other than the stopper lever small return spring. Replace the assembly if any of the parts are worn or damaged.*

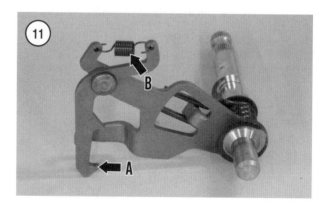

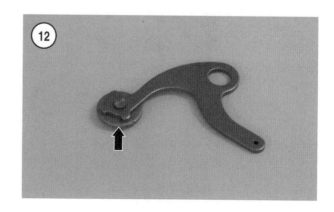

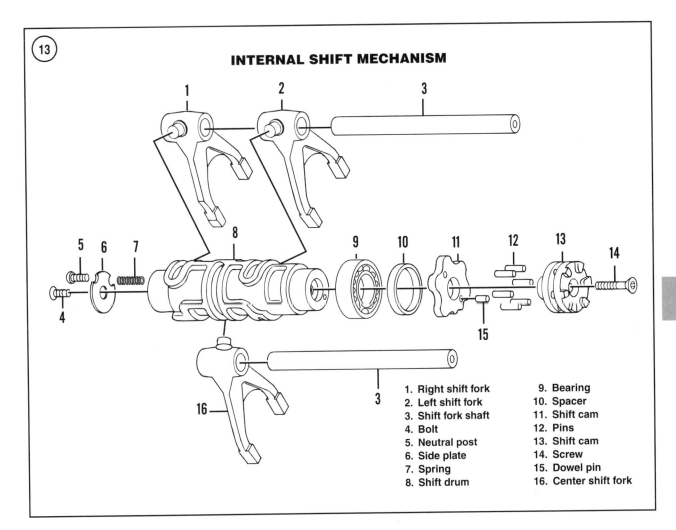

INTERNAL SHIFT MECHANISM

8

1. Right shift fork
2. Left shift fork
3. Shift fork shaft
4. Bolt
5. Neutral post
6. Side plate
7. Spring
8. Shift drum

9. Bearing
10. Spacer
11. Shift cam
12. Pins
13. Shift cam
14. Screw
15. Dowel pin
16. Center shift fork

1. Inspect the shift shaft (A, **Figure 10**) for bends or damage.

2. Inspect the shift arm (A, **Figure 11**) for bends or damage. Pay particular attention to the shift pawls.

3. Check the shift arm spring (B, **Figure 11**) and the shift shaft return springs (B, **Figure 10**) for cracks or signs of fatigue.

4. Check the operation of the roller (**Figure 12**) on the stopper lever. It should move smoothly.

5. Inspect the stopper lever for bends or other damage.

INTERNAL SHIFT MECHANISM

Removal/Installation

Remove and install the internal shift mechanism as described in *Crankcase Disassembly* and *Crankcase Assembly* in Chapter Five.

Inspection

Refer to **Figure 13**.

1. Inspect each shift fork for signs of wear or cracking. Examine each fork at the points where the fingers (**Figure 14**) contact the gears and where the guide post (**Figure 15**) contacts the shift drum. These surfaces should be smooth with no signs of wear or damage.

2. Make sure each fork slides smoothly on the shaft (**Figure 16**). If there is any binding, check for a bent shift fork shaft, see Step 3.

3. Roll the shift fork shaft along a surface plate or piece of glass. Any clicking sounds indicate that the shaft is bent and must be replaced.

4. Use a micrometer and measure the width of the shift fork fingers (**Figure 17**). Replace if worn to less than 6.26 mm (0.246 in.).

5. Inspect the grooves in the shift drum (A, **Figure 18**) for wear or roughness. Replace the shift drum if any groove is worn.

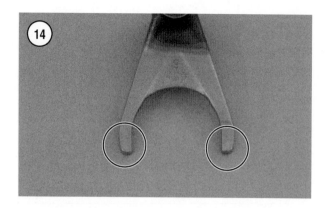

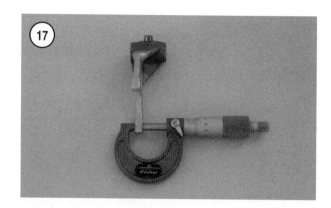

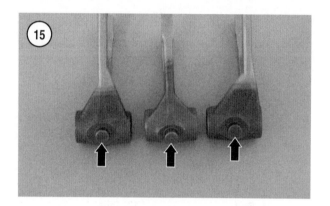

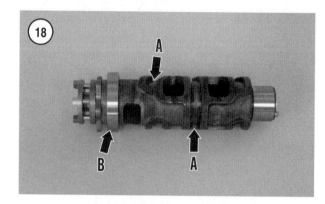

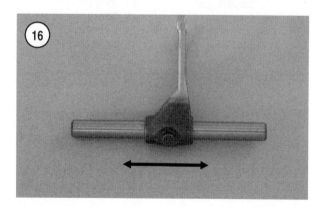

6. Spin the drum bearing (B, **Figure 18**), and check for excessive play or roughness.

7. Inspect the neutral post (**Figure 19**) for wear or damage.

8. Check the pins (A, **Figure 20**) and shift cam ramps (B) for wear.

   a. If necessary, remove the shift drum screw (C, **Figure 20**) and replace the shift cam, pins or bearing.

   b. Apply a medium strength thread locking compound to the shift drum screw. Install the screw and tighten securely.

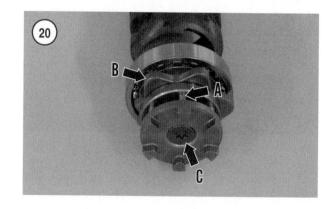

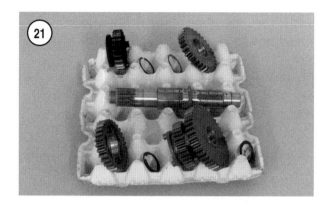

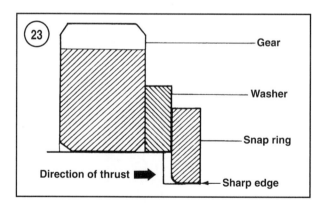

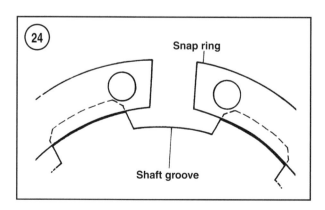

8

TRANSMISSION

Removal/Installation

Remove and install the transmission shaft assemblies as described in *Crankcase Disassembly* and *Crankcase Assembly* in Chapter Five.

Service Notes

1. A large egg flat can be used to help maintain correct alignment and positioning of the parts. As each part is removed, set it into one of the depressions in the egg flat with the same orientation it had when on the transmission shaft (**Figure 21**). This is an easy way to retain the correct relationship of all parts.

2. The snap rings fit tightly on the transmission shafts. They usually become distorted during removal. All snap rings must be replaced during assembly.

3. Snap rings will turn and fold over, making removal and installation difficult. To ease replacement, open a snap ring with a pair of snap ring pliers while at the same time holding the back of the ring with pliers (**Figure 22**).

4. Install a snap ring so its flat side faces away from the direction of thrust (**Figure 23**).

5. Position each snap ring so its end gap sits above a groove in the transmission shaft as shown in **Figure 24**.

6. Apply molybdenum disulfide oil to each gear during assembly.

> *NOTE*
> *Yamaha determined a possible problem with some transmission components. Owners of certain 2001-2003 models were notified by mail that the transmission required modification by a Yamaha dealership. If the transmission modification was performed, a punch mark was placed above the frame serial number on the steering head (**Figure 25**). If this punch mark is not visible, it is*

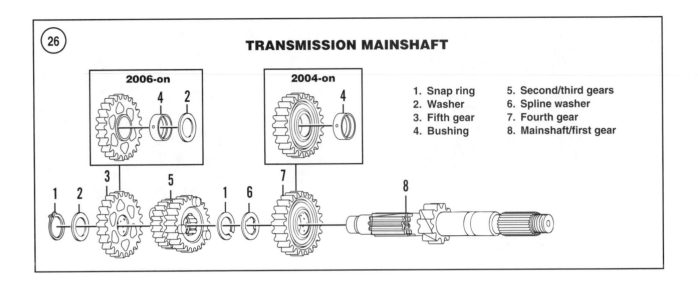

TRANSMISSION MAINSHAFT

1. Snap ring
2. Washer
3. Fifth gear
4. Bushing
5. Second/third gears
6. Spline washer
7. Fourth gear
8. Mainshaft/first gear

possible that the necessary modifications were not performed. Refer further service to a Yamaha dealership.

Mainshaft Disassembly

The following photos and procedure show the mainshaft parts for 2004 and 2005 models. On 2006-on models fifth gear was revised. Refer to **Figure 26** for all model years.

1. Clean the assembled shaft in solvent. Dry all components with compressed air or let the assembly sit on rags to drip dry.
2. Remove the snap ring and washer from the mainshaft.
3. Slide off the fifth gear, then slide off the second-third combination gear.
4. Remove the snap ring and the spline washer.
5. Slide off the fourth gear and fourth gear bushing from the mainshaft.
6. Inspect the mainshaft and gears as described in this section.

Mainshaft Assembly

The following photos and procedure show the mainshaft parts for 2004 and 2005 models. On 2006-on models fifth gear was revised. Refer to **Figure 26** for all model years.

NOTE
Before installing any component, coat all surfaces with molybdenum disulfide oil.

1. Install the fourth gear bushing (**Figure 27**) onto the mainshaft, and slide it up against first gear.

2. Position the fourth gear with the shift dog side going on last and install the fourth gear (**Figure 28**) onto the bushing. Slide it up against first gear.
3. Install the spline washer (A, **Figure 29**) and *new* snap ring (B). The flat side of the snap ring must face away from the spline washer, and the snap ring must be completely seated in the shaft groove (**Figure 30**). Position the snap ring so its end gap sits within a groove in the mainshaft (**Figure 24**).

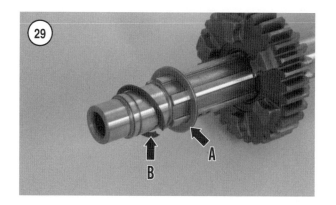

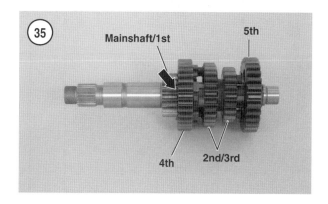

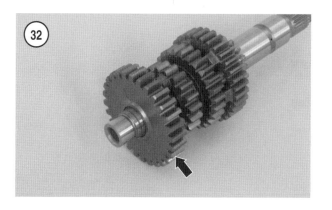

4. Position the second-third combination gear with the third gear side (**Figure 31**) going on first. Slide on the second-third gear.

5. Position the fifth gear with the shift dog receptacle side going on first and install the fifth gear (**Figure 32**).

6. Install the washer (**Figure 33**) and *new* snap ring (**Figure 34**). The flat side of the snap ring should face out away from the washer. The snap ring must be completely seated in the shaft groove.

7. Refer to **Figure 35** for correct placement of the mainshaft gears. Make sure each gear engages properly to the adjoining gear where applicable.

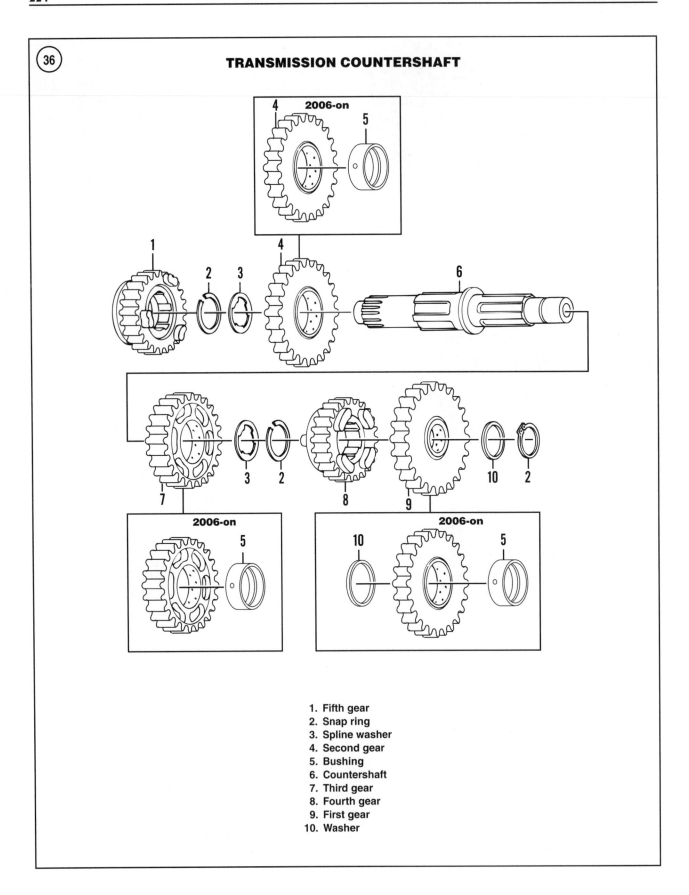

36

TRANSMISSION COUNTERSHAFT

1. Fifth gear
2. Snap ring
3. Spline washer
4. Second gear
5. Bushing
6. Countershaft
7. Third gear
8. Fourth gear
9. First gear
10. Washer

Countershaft Disassembly

The following photos show the countershaft parts for 2004 and 2005 models. Refer to **Figure 36** for 2006-on model differences.

1. Clean the assembled shaft in solvent. Dry all components with compressed air or let the assembly sit on rags to drip dry.

2. Remove the snap ring and the spline washer.

3. Slide off the first gear and the fourth gear.

4. Remove the snap ring and the spline washer.

5. Slide off the third gear.

6. At the opposite end of the countershaft (the short end), slide off the fifth gear.

7. Remove the snap ring and spline washer.

8. Slide off the second gear.

9. Inspect the countershaft and gears as described in this chapter.

Countershaft Assembly

The following photos show the countershaft parts for 2004 and 2005 models. Refer to **Figure 36** for 2006-on model differences.

NOTE
Before installing any component, coat all surfaces with molybdenum disulfide oil.

1. Position the second gear with the shift dog receptacle side going on last and install the gear onto the short end of the countershaft (**Figure 37**). Slide the gear up against the stop.

2. Install a spline washer (**Figure 38**) and a *new* snap ring (**Figure 39**). The flat side of the snap ring must face away from the spline washer and the snap ring must be completely seated in its groove (**Figure 40**). Position the end gap (**Figure 24**) so it sits above a groove in the countershaft.

3. Position the fifth gear with the shift fork groove side going on last and install the fifth gear (**Figure 41**).

8

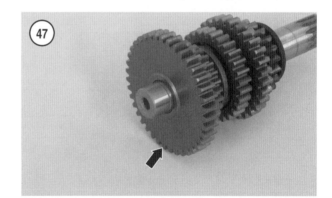

4. Position the third gear with the shift dog receptacle side going on last and install the gear onto the opposite end of the shaft (**Figure 42**).

5. Install the spline washer (A, **Figure 43**) and a *new* snap ring (B). The flat side of the ring must face away from the spline washer and the snap ring must be completely seated in its groove (**Figure 44**).

6. Position the fourth gear with the shift fork groove (**Figure 45**) side going on first and install the fourth gear (**Figure 46**).

7. Position the first gear with the flush side going on last and install the first gear (**Figure 47**).

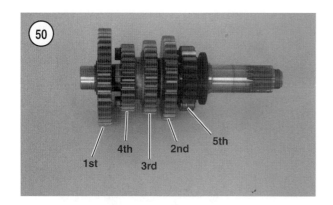

1st   4th   3rd   2nd   5th

8. Install the spline washer (A, **Figure 48**) and a *new* snap ring (B). The flat side of the ring must face away from the spline washer and the snap ring must be completely seated in its groove (**Figure 49**).

9. Refer to **Figure 50** for correct placement of the mainshaft gears. Make sure each gear engages properly to the adjoining gear where applicable.

10. Mesh both assembled transmission shafts together (**Figure 51**). Make sure all gears mate properly.

Transmission Inspection

1. Clean all parts in cleaning solvent and dry thoroughly.

> *NOTE*
> *Any defective gear should be replaced. It is also a good idea to replace the gear's mate on the opposite shaft, even though the mate may not show as much wear or damage. Worn parts usually cause accelerated wear on new parts. Replace gears in sets to ensure proper mating and wear.*

2. Visually inspect the gears for cracks, chips or broken or burnt teeth (**Figure 52**).

3. Check the engagement dogs (**Figure 53**) and engagement receptacles (**Figure 54**). Replace any gear(s) with

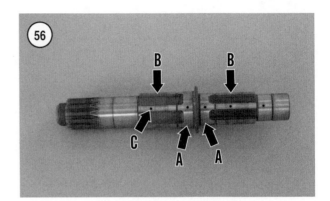

rounded or damaged edges on the dogs or within the receptacles.

4. Inspect all free-wheeling gear bearing surfaces (**Figure 55**) for wear, discoloration and galling. Also inspect the respective shaft's bearing surfaces (A, **Figure 56**). If there is any metal flaking or visual damage, replace both parts.

5. Inspect the splines (B, **Figure 56**) on each shaft for wear or discoloration.

6. Make sure any oil hole (A, **Figure 57**) in a gear or shaft (C, **Figure 56**) is clear.

7. Inspect each shift fork groove (B, **Figure 57**) for wear or damage. Replace the gear(s) if necessary.

8. Replace any washers that are worn.

9. Discard all snap rings and replace them during assembly.

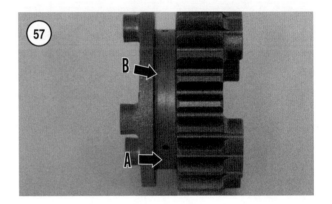

10. If any transmission parts are worn or damaged, inspect the shift drum and shift forks as described in this chapter.

Table 1 TRANSMISSION AND GEARSHIFT SPECIFICATIONS

Transmission	Constant mesh, 5-speed
Mainshaft runout	0.08 mm (0.003 in.) maximum
Countershaft runout	0.08 mm (0.003 in.) maximum
Transmission gear ratios	
First gear	39/16 (2.438)
Second gear	30/19 (1.579)
Third gear	29/25 (1.160)
Fourth gear	29/32 (0.906)
Fifth gear	21/28 (0.750)
Primary reduction ratio	72/47 (1.532)
Secondary reduction ratio	35/32 x 70/33 (2.320)
Shift fork finger width minimum service limit	6.26 mm (0.246 in.)

Table 2 SHIFT MECHANISM TORQUE SPECIFICATIONS

Item	N•m	in.-lb.	ft.-lb.
Footrest mounting bolts	48	–	35
Shift pedal lever clamp bolt (1999-2005)	10	88	–
Shift shaft lever clamp bolt (1999-2005)	10	88	–
Shift pedal clamp bolt (heel side) (2006-on)	8	71	–
Shift pedal clamp bolt (toe side) (2006-on)	18	–	13

CHAPTER NINE

FUEL, EXHAUST AND EMISSION CONTROL SYSTEMS

This chapter describes service procedures for the carburetor, exhaust and emission control systems. During inspection, compare measurements to the specifications in the tables at the end of this chapter. Replace any components that are worn, damaged or out of specification. Tighten fasteners to the specified torque during assembly.

FUEL SYSTEM SAFETY

The fuel system consists of a fuel tank, shutoff valve, fuel pump, fuel filter, single Mikuni constant velocity carburetor, and air filter.

When working around gasoline, always observe the following warnings:

1. Disconnect the negative battery cable before working on the fuel system. Refer to Chapter Three.
2. Gasoline dripping on a hot engine component may cause a fire. Always allow the engine to cool completely before working on any fuel system component.
3. Some fuel may spill and fuel vapors may be present when removing fuel system components. Wipe up spilled gasoline immediately with dry rags. Store the rags in a suitable metal container until they can be disposed of or cleaned.

4. Do not service any fuel system component in the vicinity of open flames, sparks or while anyone is smoking adjacent to the motorcycle.
5. Store gasoline in a sealed gasoline storage container and kept away from heat, sparks or flames.
6. Always have a fire extinguisher nearby.

FUEL HOSE IDENTIFICATION

The fuel system uses a number of fuel and vacuum hoses. To allow easier reassembly, develop a system to identify the hoses before disconnecting them. Make tags with strips of masking tape and pen. There are also a number of aftermarket hose identification kits, such as the Lisle vacuum hose Identifiers (part No. 74600). This kit consists of 48 color-coded hose fittings in 1/8-to-1/2 inch sizes. Automotive and aftermarket part supplies carry this kit or similar equivalents.

FUEL TANK

Removal/Installation

Refer to **Figure 1**.

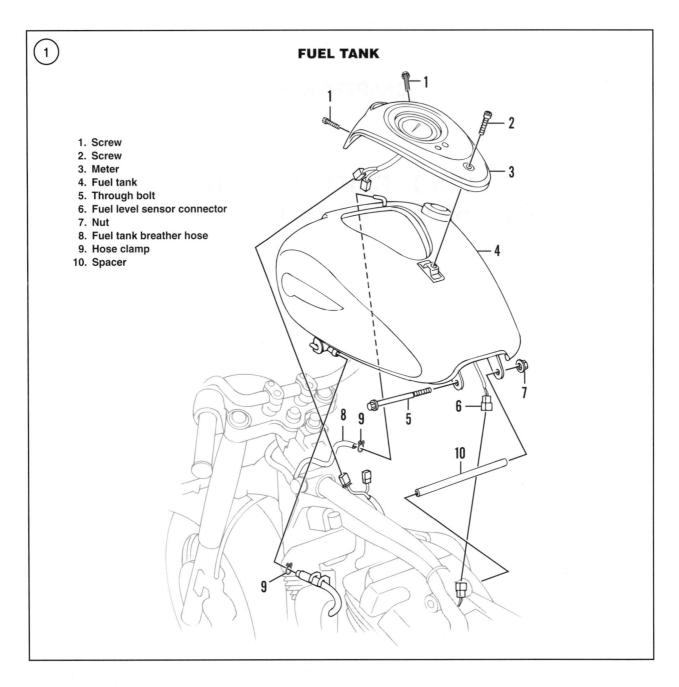

FUEL TANK

1. Screw
2. Screw
3. Meter
4. Fuel tank
5. Through bolt
6. Fuel level sensor connector
7. Nut
8. Fuel tank breather hose
9. Hose clamp
10. Spacer

Read this procedure through before starting work. Make sure all of the necessary equipment is on hand to keep from damaging the fuel tank.

1. Securely support the motorcycle on level ground. Block the front wheel so the motorcycle will not roll in either direction.

2. Remove the rider seat as described in Chapter Fifteen.

3. Disconnect the negative battery cable as described in Chapter Three.

4. If the fuel tank is more than one-quarter full, siphon the fuel into a container approved for gasoline storage as follows:

a. Open the fuel filler cap (A, **Figure 2**).

b. Place a siphon hose into the fuel tank. Place the other end of the siphon hose into the container.

c. Operate the siphon to drain as much fuel from the tank as possible.

d. When the siphon stops, remove it from the fuel tank and storage can. Close the fuel filler cap and place the storage can in a safe place, away from all flames

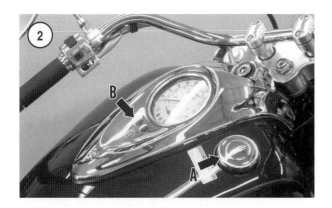

and sparks. Drain the siphon of all gasoline before putting it away.

5. Remove the meter assembly (B, **Figure 2**) as described in Chapter Ten.

6. Disconnect the electrical connector from the fuel level sensor (**Figure 3**).

7. Remove the bolt and nut (A, **Figure 4**) securing the rear of the fuel tank. Remove the spacer between the tank mounting bosses.

8. Disconnect the breather hose (**Figure 5**), or EVAP hose (California models), from the fitting at the front of the fuel tank.

9. Pull the fuel tank toward the rear and release it from the frame mounting posts.

10. Raise the rear of the fuel tank and block it in this position with a piece of wood.

11. Turn the fuel shutoff valve off. Place several shop cloths under the fuel hose to catch any fuel remaining in the hose. Disconnect the fuel hose from the valve.

12. Remove the piece of wood and remove the fuel tank.

13. Install the fuel tank by reversing these removal steps while noting the following:

    a. Correctly position the electrical harness (B, **Figure 4**) between the mounting bolt spacer and the fuel tank.

    b. Turn the fuel shutoff valve on.

    c. Ensure the hose is securely in place and that the clamps are tight.

    d. Turn the ignition switch on and allow the fuel pump to pressurize the system. Check the fuel tank hose for leaks.

Inspection

1. Inspect all of the hoses for cracks, deterioration and other damage. Replace damaged hoses with the same Yamaha type and size materials. The hoses must be flexible and strong enough to withstand fuel pressure, engine heat and vibration.

2. Inspect the front rubber dampers on the frame for deterioration or other damage. Replace if necessary.

3. Check the meter assembly mounting brackets (**Figure 6**) for damage. Make sure the mounting nuts (**Figure 7**) are tight.

4. Check the fuel tank rear mounting brackets for damage. Make sure the mounting screws (**Figure 8**) are tight.

5. Open the fuel filler cap. Inspect the fuel filler cap gasket. If the gasket is damaged or starting to deteriorate, replace the filler cap assembly.

6. On California models, make sure the EVAP hose fitting is clear (**Figure 9**). Clean out with compressed air if necessary.

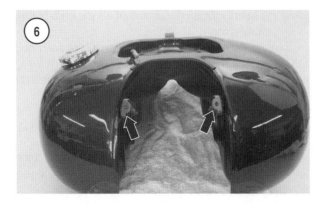

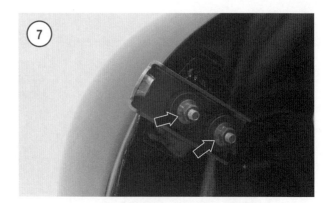

Fuel Shutoff Valve Removal/Installation

1. Remove the fuel tank as described in this section.
2. Place several heavy towels on the workbench to protect the fuel tank finish.
3. Turn the fuel tank on its side on the workbench.
4. Remove the mounting screws (A, **Figure 10**) and remove the shutoff valve (B) from the fuel tank.
5. Clean the filter of all dirt and debris. Replace the fuel shutoff valve filter and O-ring if worn or damaged.
6. Installation is the reverse of removal, plus the following:
   a. After installing the fuel valve, pour a small amount of fuel into the tank and check for leaks. If there is a leak, solve the problem before installing the fuel tank.
   b. Check for fuel leakage after the fuel tank is installed and the fuel pump has been turned on.

Fuel Level Sender Removal/Installation

1. Remove the fuel tank as described in this section.
2. Place several heavy towels on the workbench to protect the fuel tank finish.
3. Turn the fuel tank on its side on the workbench.
4. Remove the mounting screws and washers (A, **Figure 11**) securing the fuel level sender to the fuel tank.
5. Carefully withdraw the sender (B, **Figure 11**) from the fuel tank. Do not bend the float arm during removal and installation.
6. Install by reversing these removal steps. Check for fuel leakage after the fuel tank is installed and the fuel pump has been turned on.

AIR FILTER HOUSING

Removal/Installation

Refer to Chapter Three for air filter service.

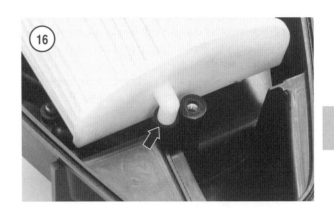

9

1. Remove the fuel tank as described in this chapter.

2. Loosen the clamping screw (A, **Figure 12**) securing the air filter assembly to the carburetor.

3. Remove the screws and washers (B, **Figure 12**) securing the air filter case assembly to the engine.

4. Pull the air filter case assembly partially away from the carburetor.

5. Disconnect the carburetor vacuum chamber breather hose (A, **Figure 13**) and cylinder head breather hose (B) from the backside of the air filter case. Remove the air filter case assembly.

6. Remove the mounting screw (**Figure 14**) and remove the cover from the case.

7. Remove the screws (**Figure 15**) securing the air filter to the case.

8. Disconnect the air filter elbow fitting from the case receptacle (**Figure 16**) and remove the air filter from the case.

9. Installation is the reverse of removal. Note the following:

    a. Make sure that the air filter elbow fitting is inserted correctly into the case receptacle (**Figure 16**). Push it on until it bottoms.

    b. Securely tighten the screws (**Figure 15**) securing the air filter to the case.

c. Connect the carburetor vacuum chamber breather hose (A, **Figure 13**) and cylinder head breather hose (B) onto the backside of the air filter case. Push both on until they seat.

d. Securely tighten the screws and washers (B, **Figure 12**) securing the air filter case assembly to the engine.

e. Securely tighten the clamping screw (A, **Figure 12**) securing the air filter assembly to the carburetor.

Inspection

1. Inspect all components of the air filter housing assembly for cracks or other damage that would allow unfiltered air into the engine. Replace any part that is damaged or starting to deteriorate.

2. Inspect the air filter case-to-carburetor boot and clamp (**Figure 17**) for deterioration and/or damage. Replace if necessary.

3. Wipe the interior of the air filter housing with a shop rag dampened with cleaning solvent. Refer to **Figure 18** (1999-2003 models) or **Figure 19** (2004-on models). Remove any debris that may have passed through a broken element.

SURGE TANK SOLENOID VALVE (CALIFORNIA MODELS)

Removal/Installation

Refer to **Figure 20**.

> *NOTE*
> *There are numerous vacuum hoses connected to the following components. During removal, mark each hose and its fitting so the hoses can be installed on the correct fittings during assembly. Also note how each hose is routed along the engine and frame. Hoses must be rerouted along their original paths.*

> *NOTE*
> *The hoses can be removed from either component and/or can remain attached to either component.*

1. Remove the fuel tank as described in this chapter.

2. To remove the solenoid valve, proceed as follows:

   a. Disconnect the 2-pin electrical connector (A, **Figure 21**) from the valve.

   b. Remove the upper hose (B, **Figure 21**) going to the purge tank.

c. Remove the lower hose (C, **Figure 21**) going to the carburetor.

d. Remove the valve (D, **Figure 21**) from the frame mounting tab.

3. To remove the surge tank, proceed as follows:

   a. Remove the fuel pump and fuel filter assembly as described in this chapter.

   b. Disconnect the bottom hose (A, **Figure 22**) going to the EVAP charcoal canister.

   c. Disconnect the upper hose (B, **Figure 22**) going to the solenoid valve.

⑳ **SURGE TANK SOLENOID VALVE (CALIFORNIA MODELS)**

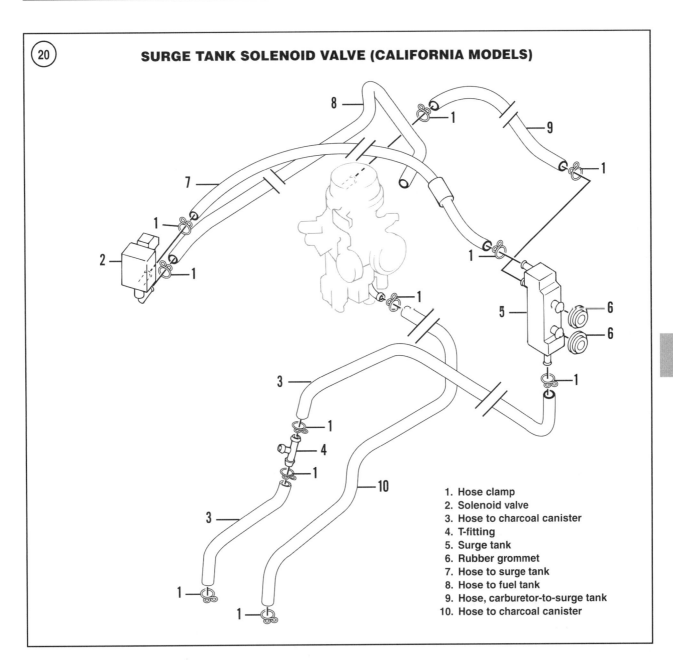

1. Hose clamp
2. Solenoid valve
3. Hose to charcoal canister
4. T-fitting
5. Surge tank
6. Rubber grommet
7. Hose to surge tank
8. Hose to fuel tank
9. Hose, carburetor-to-surge tank
10. Hose to charcoal canister

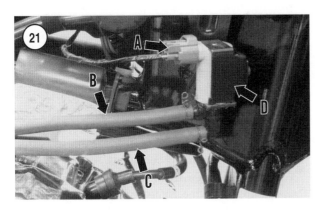

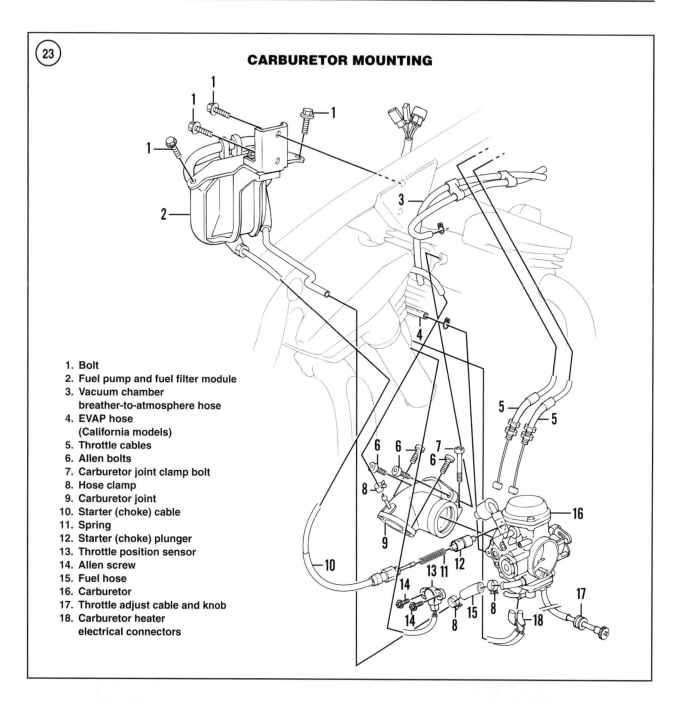

CARBURETOR MOUNTING ②

1. Bolt
2. Fuel pump and fuel filter module
3. Vacuum chamber
   breather-to-atmosphere hose
4. EVAP hose
   (California models)
5. Throttle cables
6. Allen bolts
7. Carburetor joint clamp bolt
8. Hose clamp
9. Carburetor joint
10. Starter (choke) cable
11. Spring
12. Starter (choke) plunger
13. Throttle position sensor
14. Allen screw
15. Fuel hose
16. Carburetor
17. Throttle adjust cable and knob
18. Carburetor heater
    electrical connectors

d. Disconnect the middle hose (C, **Figure 22**) going to the carburetor.

e. Remove the surge tank.

4. Installation is the reverse of removal. Note the following:

  a. Replace the hose(s) that are damaged or starting to deteriorate.

  b. Connect the hoses to the correct fittings on both components.

  c. Make sure all hose clamps are tight.

CARBURETOR

Operation

For proper operation, a gasoline engine must be supplied with air and fuel mixed in proper proportions. A properly adjusted carburetor supplies the proper air/fuel mixture under all operating conditions.

The carburetor consists of several major systems. A float and float valve mechanism maintain a constant fuel

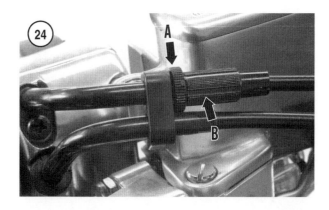

level in the float bowl. The pilot system supplies fuel at low speeds. The main fuel system supplies fuel at medium and high speeds.

A starter (choke) system supplies the very rich mixture needed to start a cold engine. The choke lever in this system opens a starter valve rather than closing the butterfly in the venturi.

Service

If poor engine performance, hesitation and little or no response to mixture adjustment are observed, and if all other factors that could affect performance are correct, perform major carburetor service (removal and cleaning) as described in this chapter. Alterations in jet size, throttle slide cutaway and jet needle position should only be attempted by those experienced in this type of tuning work. Do not adjust or modify the carburetors in an attempt to fix a driveability problem caused by another system.

Removal/Installation

NOTE
There are numerous vacuum hoses connected to various fittings on the carburetor. During removal, mark each hose and its fitting so the hoses can be installed on the correct fittings during assembly. Also note how each hose and cable is routed along the engine and frame. Hoses and cables must be rerouted along their original paths.

Refer to **Figure 23**.
1. Remove the fuel tank as described in this chapter.
2. Remove the air filter housing as described in this chapter.
3. At the throttle grip, loosen the throttle cable locknut (A, **Figure 24**) and turn the adjuster (B) to achieve the maximum amount of throttle cable free play.
4. Loosen the clamp (**Figure 25**) securing the carburetor to the carburetor joint.
5. Disconnect the idle adjust knob and cable (**Figure 26**) from the bracket on the right side of the crankcase.
6. Disconnect the vacuum chamber breather hose (A, **Figure 27**) from the carburetor going to the surge tank.
7. On California models, disconnect the EVAP charcoal canister hose (**Figure 28**) from the carburetor.
8. Remove the carburetor part way from the carburetor joint.

NOTE
All models are equipped with two throttle cables. The accelerator (or pull) cable is lo-

*cated at the outboard location on the throttle cable bracket (A, **Figure 29**) and in the outboard notch on the throttle wheel (B). The decelerator (or push) cable is located at the inboard location on the throttle cable bracket (C, **Figure 29**) and in the inboard notch on the throttle wheel (D).*

9. Loosen the locknuts (**Figure 30**) on both throttle cables and disconnect them from the throttle wheel and the cable bracket.

NOTE
*Do not remove the throttle position sensor from the carburetor body. Refer to **Throttle Position Sensor** in this chapter for TPS inspection and adjustment procedures.*

10. On the left side of the frame, disconnect the following electrical connectors:
    a. Throttle position connector: triangle, 3-pin (blue, yellow, and black/blue wires).
    b. Carburetor heater connector: 1999-2003 models (brown/yellow and black/yellow wires), 2004-on models (brown/black and brown/yellow wires).
11. Remove the mounting screw and remove the fuel pump/fuel filter module cover (**Figure 31**).
12. Disconnect the starter (choke) knob and cable (**Figure 32**) from the bracket.
13. Disconnect the fuel line (B, **Figure 27**) from the carburetor fitting.

NOTE
Note the path of the starter (choke) cable and electrical harness between the cylinders.

14. Slowly pull the carburetor away from the cylinder heads. Pull the starter (choke) cable, the electrical harness and connectors from the engine and frame.
15. While the carburetor assembly is removed, examine the carburetor joint. Look for cracks or other damage that would allow unfiltered air into the engine. Replace if damaged.
16. To remove the carburetor joint, proceed as follows:
    a. Disconnect the vacuum hose from the fitting (A, **Figure 33**).
    b. Remove the screws (B, **Figure 33**) securing the carburetor joint to both cylinder heads and remove the joint.
17. Cover the carburetor joint openings with clean shop cloths to keep foreign matter out of the cylinder heads.
18. Install the carburetor assembly by reversing these removal steps and note the following:

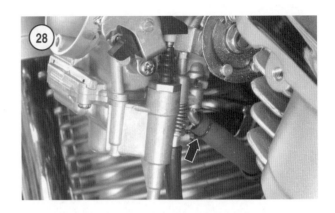

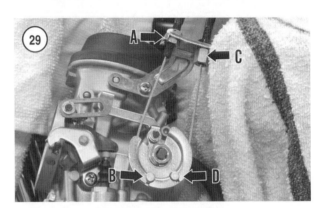

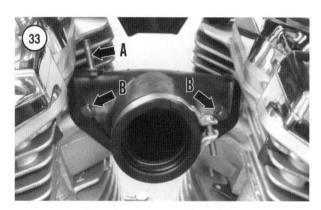

CAUTION
The carburetor forms an airtight seal with the carburetor joint. Air leaks can cause engine damage due to a lean air/fuel mixture or dirt entering with the incoming air.

a. Install *new* O-ring seals (**Figure 34**) on the carburetor joint. Apply a light coat of grease to the O-rings to ensure an air-tight seal.

b. Route the starter (choke) cable and electrical harness along their original paths. The cable must not

be twisted, kinked or pinched. Secure the cable in the holder (**Figure 32**).

c. Install the carburetor assembly and fully seat it in the carburetor joint. Push it in until it bottoms and tighten the carburetor clamp (**Figure 25**) securely.

d. Connect each hose to its fitting as noted during removal and route the hose along its original path.

e. Adjust the throttle cable as described in Chapter Three.

CARBURETOR OVERHAUL

Alterations in jet size, throttle slide cutaway and jet needle position should only be attempted by those experienced in this type of tuning work. Do not adjust or modify the carburetor in an attempt to fix a drivability problem caused by another system.

Disassembly

CAUTION
The throttle position sensor is pre-set by the manufacturer. Do not remove the throttle position sensor from the carburetor unless it requires replacement. Removal of the sensor may cause the sensor to move out of position, resulting in improper ignition timing.

Refer to **Figure 35**.

CAUTION
*When cleaning a carburetor, do not adjust the pilot screw. Refer to **Pilot Screw** in this chapter.*

1. Unscrew and remove the starter (choke) assembly (**Figure 36**) and cable.

2. Remove the screws (A, **Figure 37**) securing the top cover and remove the top cover (B).

3. Remove the spring (A, **Figure 38**) and diaphragm/piston valve (B).

4. Disassemble the diaphragm/piston valve as follows:
   a. Use needle nose pliers and withdraw the needle jet holder.
   b. Withdraw the spring, jet needle and washers (**Figure 39**).

5. Disassemble the coasting enricher valve as follows:
   a. Remove the mounting screws (A, **Figure 40**) and remove the cover (B).
   b. Remove the spring (A, **Figure 41**) and diaphragm (B).

6. Unscrew and remove the pilot jet (**Figure 42**).

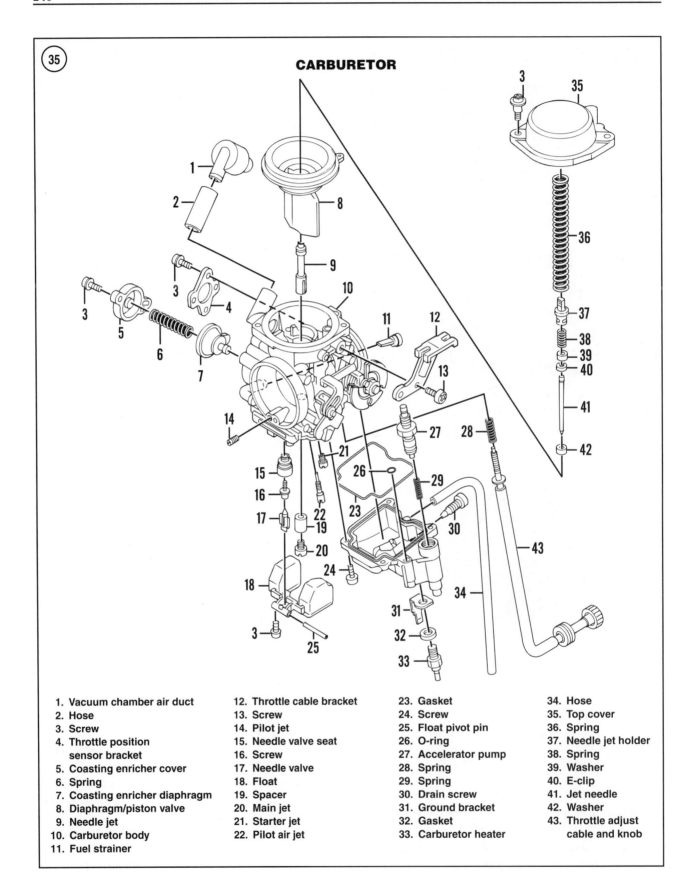

CARBURETOR

1. Vacuum chamber air duct
2. Hose
3. Screw
4. Throttle position
   sensor bracket
5. Coasting enricher cover
6. Spring
7. Coasting enricher diaphragm
8. Diaphragm/piston valve
9. Needle jet
10. Carburetor body
11. Fuel strainer
12. Throttle cable bracket
13. Screw
14. Pilot jet
15. Needle valve seat
16. Screw
17. Needle valve
18. Float
19. Spacer
20. Main jet
21. Starter jet
22. Pilot air jet
23. Gasket
24. Screw
25. Float pivot pin
26. O-ring
27. Accelerator pump
28. Spring
29. Spring
30. Drain screw
31. Ground bracket
32. Gasket
33. Carburetor heater
34. Hose
35. Top cover
36. Spring
37. Needle jet holder
38. Spring
39. Washer
40. E-clip
41. Jet needle
42. Washer
43. Throttle adjust
    cable and knob

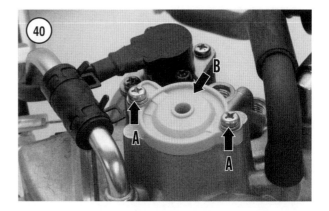

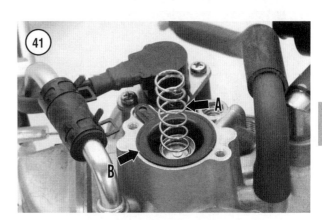

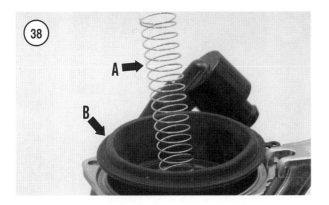

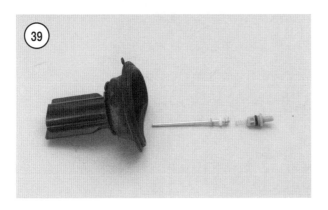

9

7. Disconnect the electrical connectors (**Figure 43**) from the carburetor heater.

8. Unscrew and remove the carburetor heater (A, **Figure 44**), gasket and ground bracket (B).

9. Remove the screws securing the float bowl and remove the float bowl (**Figure 45**).

10. Remove the screw (A, **Figure 46**) securing the float pivot pin.

11. Remove the float (B, **Figure 46**), pivot pin and needle valve.

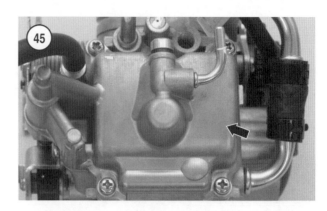

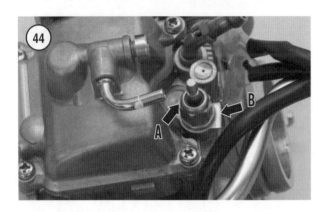

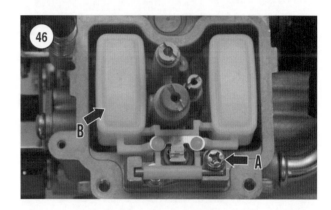

12. Remove the screw (A, **Figure 47**) securing the needle valve seat and remove the seat (B).

13. Unscrew and remove the pilot air jet (**Figure 48**).

14. Unscrew and remove the starter jet (**Figure 49**).

15. Unscrew and remove the main jet (A, **Figure 50**) and spacer (B).

16. Insert your finger into the carburetor venturi, press the needle jet (**Figure 51**) toward the float bowl and remove it.

17. Do not remove the fixed starter jet No. 2 (**Figure 52**).

> *CAUTION*
> *When cleaning a carburetor, do not adjust the pilot screw setting. Changing this setting will decrease engine performance.*

18. If necessary, remove the pilot screw (**Figure 53**) as described under *Pilot Screw* in this chapter.

> *NOTE*
> *Further disassembly is neither necessary nor recommended. Do not remove the throttle shaft and butterfly assemblies (**Figure 54**). If these parts are damaged, the carburetor must be replaced, as these items are not available separately.*

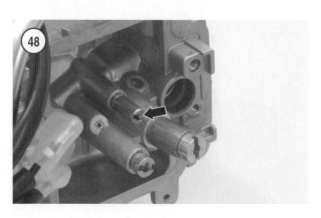

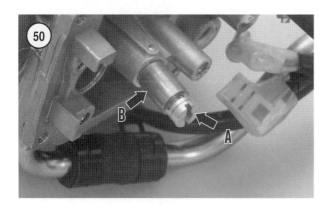

19. Clean and inspect the components as described in this section.

Assembly

1. If the pilot screw was removed, install it as described under *Pilot Screw* in this chapter.

2. Install the needle jet part way into the post (A, **Figure 55**). Align the groove (B, **Figure 55**) with the location pin (C) and push it in until it bottoms.

3. Install the main jet spacer (B, **Figure 50**) onto the needle jet and push it on until it bottoms.

4. Install the main jet (A, **Figure 50**) and tighten securely.

5. Install the starter jet (**Figure 49**) and tighten securely.

6. Install the pilot air jet (**Figure 48**) and tighten securely.

7. Install a *new* O-ring on the needle valve seat (**Figure 56**). Push it in until it seats (B, **Figure 47**) and install the screw (A). Tighten the screw securely.

8. Hook the needle valve (**Figure 57**) onto the float tang and install the float.

9. Install the float pivot pin (**Figure 58**) and index it into the locating groove.

10. Install the screw (A, **Figure 46**) securing the float pivot pin and tighten securely.

11. Install a *new* gasket (**Figure 59**) onto the float bowl.

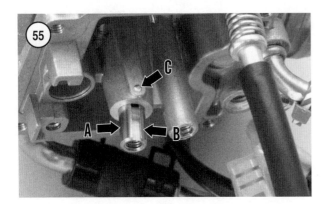

12. Install the float bowl (**Figure 45**) and tighten the screws securely.

13. Install a *new* gasket, the carburetor heater (A, **Figure 44**) and ground bracket (B). Tighten the heater securely.

14. Attach both electrical connectors (**Figure 43**) onto the heater and ground bracket.

15. Install the pilot jet (**Figure 42**) and tighten securely.

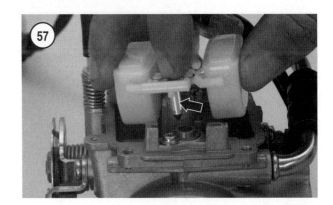

16. Assemble the coasting enricher valve as follows:

    a. Install the diaphragm and align the tab with the opening in the carburetor body (**Figure 60**).

    b. Install the spring (A, **Figure 41**) into the diaphragm (B).

    c. Make sure the diaphragm is seated correctly, then install the cover (B, **Figure 40**). Install the screws (A) and tighten securely.

17. Assemble the diaphragm/piston valve as follows:

    a. Insert the spring, needle jet and washers (**Figure 39**) into the diaphragm/piston valve.

    b. Install the needle jet holder and press it down until it bottoms.

18. Install the diaphragm/piston valve assembly as follows:

    a. Install the diaphragm/piston valve assembly into the slide bore (**Figure 61**).

    b. The diaphragm will not seat against the carburetor body at this point (**Figure 62**).

    c. Apply a light coat of grease to the perimeter of the diaphragm (A, **Figure 63**) and press it into place in the carburetor body groove. This will ensure that the diaphragm will seat correctly when the top cover is installed.

    d. Align the tab with the opening in the carburetor body (B, **Figure 63**).

    e. Install the spring (C, **Figure 63**) into the diaphragm.

19. Align the opening in the top cover (A, **Figure 64**) with the diaphragm opening (B) and install the top cover (B, **Figure 37**).

20. Install the screws (A, **Figure 37**) and tighten finger tight.

21. Insert your finger into the venturi area and move the piston valve up in the carburetor body (**Figure 65**). The piston valve should rise all the way up into the bore and slide back down immediately with no binding. If it binds or if the movement is sluggish, chances are the diaphragm did not seat correctly, or the spring is misaligned to one side or not centered within the top cover. If necessary, remove the top cover and reposition the spring.

22. If the spring is installed correctly, tighten the top cover screws securely.

23. Install the starter (choke) assembly (**Figure 36**) and cable and tighten securely.

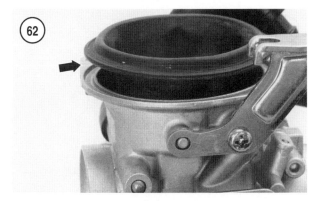

Cleaning and Inspection

> *CAUTION*
> *The carburetor body is equipped with plastic parts that cannot be removed. Do not dip the carburetor body, O-rings, float assembly, needle valve or diaphragm/piston valve into carburetor cleaner or other harsh solutions that can damage these parts. Yamaha does not recommend the use of a caustic carburetor cleaning solvent. Instead, clean*

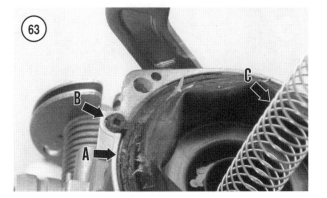

the carburetors and related parts in a petro-
leum- based solvent.

1. Clean all parts in a mild petroleum-based cleaning solution. Wash the parts in hot soap and water and rinse
them with cold water. Blow-dry the parts with compressed air.

> *CAUTION*
> *If compressed air is not available, allow the
> parts to air-dry or use a clean lint-free cloth.
> Do not use a paper towel to dry carburetor
> parts. The small paper particles could plug
> openings in the carburetor housing or jets.*

2. Allow the carburetor body and components to dry
thoroughly before assembly. Blow out the jets and the
needle jet holder with compressed air.

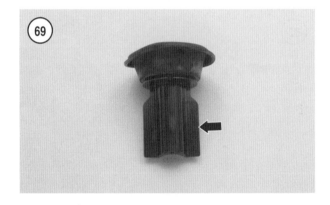

> *CAUTION*
> *Do not use wire or drill bits to clean jets.
> Even minor gouges in a jet can alter the
> air/fuel mixture.*

3. Make sure the float bowl drain screw (**Figure 66**) is in
good condition and does not leak. Replace the drain screw
if necessary.

4. Inspect the float bowl O-ring seal (**Figure 59**) for
hardness or deterioration. Replace as necessary.

5. Unscrew the accelerator pump plunger (**Figure 67**)
and remove it and the spring from the float bowl. Check
the plunger and spring for wear or damage.

6. Inspect the piston valve diaphragm (**Figure 68**) for
cracks, deterioration or other damage. Check the sides of
the piston valve (**Figure 69**) for excessive wear. Install the
piston valve into the carburetor body and move it up and
down in the bore. The piston valve should move smoothly
with no binding or excessive play. Replace the piston
valve and/or carburetor if necessary.

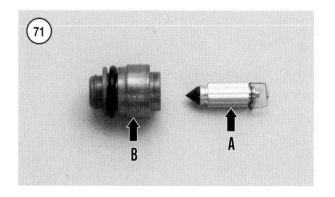

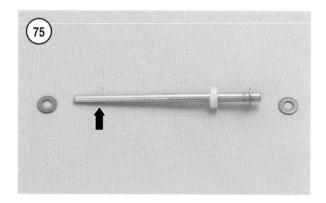

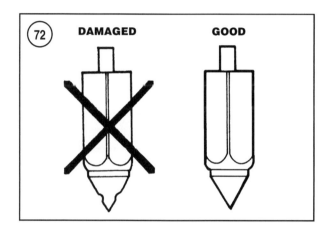

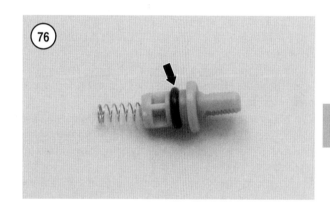

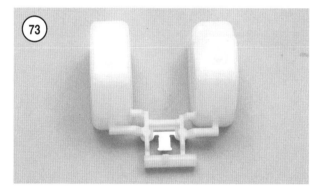

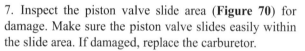

9

7. Inspect the piston valve slide area (**Figure 70**) for damage. Make sure the piston valve slides easily within the slide area. If damaged, replace the carburetor.

8. Inspect the tapered end of the needle valve (A, **Figure 71**) for steps, uneven wear or damage (**Figure 72**).

9. Inspect the needle valve seat (B, **Figure 71**) for steps, uneven wear or other damage. Insert the needle valve into the valve seat, and slowly move it back and forth and check for smooth operation. If either part is worn or damaged, replace both parts as a set.

10. Inspect the float (**Figure 73**) for deterioration or damage. Place the float in a container of water and push it down. If the float sinks or if bubbles appear (indicating a leak), replace the float.

11. Inspect all of the jets (**Figure 74**). Make sure all holes are open and no part is worn or damaged. Replace the worn or unserviceable parts.

12. Inspect the needle jet taper (**Figure 75**) for steps, uneven wear or other damage. Install a *new* O-ring (**Figure 76**) on the holder.

13. If removed, inspect the pilot screw O-ring. Replace the O-ring if it has become hard or is starting to deteriorate.

14. Inspect the choke (starter) valve (**Figure 77**) for wear and make sure the spring has not sagged.

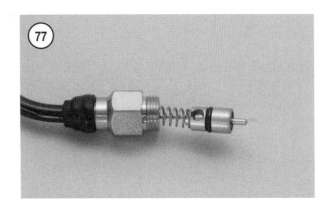

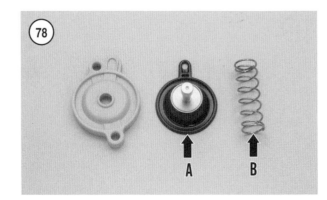

15. Inspect the coasting enrichner diaphragm (A, **Figure 78**) for hardness or deterioration. Check that the spring (B, **Figure 78**) has not sagged or is damaged.

16. Inspect the carburetor heater (A, **Figure 79**) for damage. Check the ground bracket (B, **Figure 79**) for rust or corrosion; clean off if necessary.

17. Make sure all openings in the carburetor housing are clear. Refer to **Figures 80-82**. Clean them out if they are plugged in any way, and then apply compressed air to all openings.

18. Check the top cover for cracks or damage, and replace if necessary.

19. Make sure the throttle plate screws (**Figure 54**) are tight.

20. Inspect the carburetor body for internal or external damage. If damaged, replace the carburetor assembly. The body cannot be replaced separately.

21. Move the throttle wheel back and forth from stop to stop. The throttle lever should move smoothly and return under spring tension. Replace the carburetor if the throttle wheel does not move freely or if it sticks in any position.

22. Make sure the screw (**Figure 83**) securing the throttle stop plate is secure; tighten if necessary.

PILOT SCREW

Removal/Installation

The pilot screw is sealed. A plug is installed at the top of the pilot screw bore. A pilot screw does not require adjustment unless the carburetor is overhauled, the pilot screw has been incorrectly adjusted, or the pilot screw was replaced.

NOTE
An exhaust gas analyzer is required to precisely set the air/fuel mixture with the pilot screw. If a pilot screw must be removed, perform the procedure as described, and have a

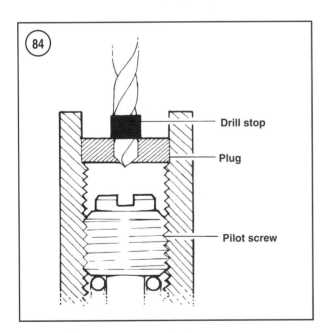

Yamaha dealership perform the final adjustment for proper carburetor operation.

1. Install a drill stop 3 mm (1/8 in.) from the end of a 5/32 in. drill bit. See **Figure 84**.

CAUTION
If tape is used as a stop, use it as a visual guide only. The tape will not stop the drill bit from drilling deeper into the plug.

2. Carefully drill a hole in the plug (**Figure 53**) at the top of the pilot screw bore on the carburetor body as shown in **Figure 84**. Do not drill too deeply. The pilot screw will be difficult to remove if the head is damaged.
3. Thread a sheet metal screw into the drilled hole. Continue to turn the screw until the plug starts to turn with the screw.
4. Remove the plug and screw with pliers and blow away all metal shavings from the area.

CAUTION
The pointed end of the pilot screw can break off if the screw is tightened against the carburetor seat. Seat the screw as described in Step 5.

5. Screw the pilot screw in until it *lightly* seats in the bore while counting and recording the number of turns. The pilot screw must be reinstalled to this same position during assembly.
6. Remove the pilot screw, spring, washer and O-ring from the carburetor body.
7. Inspect the O-ring and the end of the pilot screw. Replace the screw and/or O-ring if damaged or worn (grooved).
8. Install the pilot screw assembly and turn the pilot screw until it *lightly* seats in the bore. Turn the pilot screw back out the number of turns noted during removal Step 4.
9. Drive in a *new* pilot screw plug until the outer surface is recessed about 1 mm (0.004 in.) into the pilot screw bore.

FUEL LEVEL

The fuel level in the carburetor float bowl is critical to proper performance. The fuel flow rate from the bowl up to the carburetor bore depends not only on the vacuum in the throttle bore and the size of the jets, but also on the fuel level in the float bowl. **Tables 1-3** provide the specification for fuel level, measured from the upper edge of the float bowl (**Figure 85**) with the carburetor mounted on the motorcycle. Fuel level inspection requires a Yamaha fuel level gauge (part No. YM-01312-A [U.S.] or 90890-01312 [U.K.]).

NOTE
A piece of clear plastic of the appropriate size can be substituted for the Yamaha tool.

Inspection/Adjustment

1. Remove the fuel tank, air filter housing and surge tank as described in this chapter.

2. Level the motorcycle to ensure the carburetor is level.

3. Connect the fuel level gauge (A, **Figure 85**) to the drain on the carburetor. Secure the gauge so it sits vertically against the float bowl.

4. Loosen the carburetor drain screw (B, **Figure 85**).

5. Wait until the fuel in the gauge settles.

6. Fuel level (C, **Figure 85**) equals the distance between the fuel level in the gauge and the upper edge of the float bowl. Record the fuel level and compare the reading to the specification in **Tables 1-3**.

> *NOTE*
> *If the float bowl empties during this proce-*
> *dure, temporarily install the fuel tank and*
> *refill the float bowl. Remove the fuel tank,*
> *then proceed to the next step.*

7. If the fuel level requires adjustment, adjust the float height as follows:

   a. Remove the carburetor assembly as described in this chapter.

   b. Remove the screws securing the float bowl and remove the float bowl (**Figure 45**).

   c. Remove the screw (A, **Figure 46**) securing the float pivot pin.

   d. Remove the float (B, **Figure 46**), pivot pin and needle valve.

   e. Remove the needle valve from the float tang.

   f. Bend the float tang (**Figure 86**) to achieve the correct fuel level.

   g. Install the float and the float bowl as described in this chapter.

   h. Reinstall the carburetor assembly and recheck the fuel level. Readjust if necessary.

IDLE SPEED ADJUSTMENT

Refer to Chapter Three.

THROTTLE CABLE ADJUSTMENT

Refer to Chapter Three.

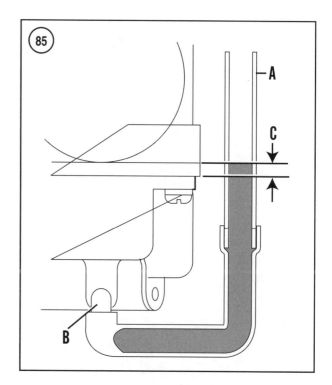

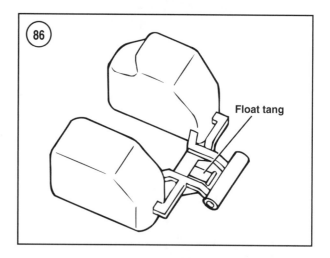

Float tang

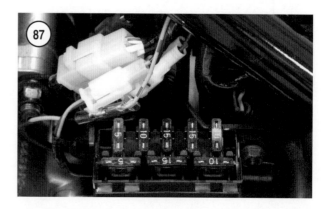

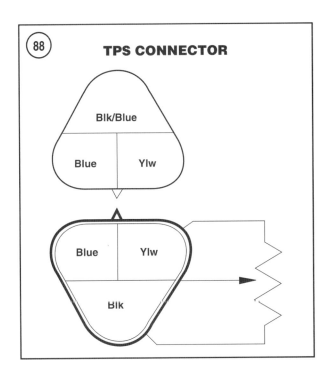

THROTTLE POSITION SENSOR

Testing

Perform the following test procedure whenever the self-diagnostic system (Chapter Ten) flashes a TPS error (code 3). Perform the test in the following sequence. Each step presumes that the components tested in the earlier steps are working properly. The tests can yield invalid results if they are performed out of sequence. If a test indicates that a component is working properly, reconnect the electrical connections and proceed to the next step.

1. Remove the left side frame cover as described in Chapter Fifteen.

2. Refer to the wiring diagram at the end of the manual and check the continuity of the throttle position sensor wiring as follows:

NOTE
*Multiple electrical connectors are located behind the fuse panel (**Figure 87**). Locate the connector by matching the wire colors.*

  a. Disconnect the triangular, 3-pin throttle position sensor connector (**Figure 87**) from the main harness.

  b. Disconnect the 8-pin connector from the ignitor unit.

  c. Check the continuity on the blue, yellow and black/blue wires between the ignitor connector and throttle position sensor connector.

  d. If necessary, make any necessary repairs to the wiring.

3. Refer to **Figure 88** and check the R1 resistance as follows:

  a. Connect the ohmmeter positive test lead to the blue terminal in the sensor side of the connector and connect the negative test lead to the black terminal.

  b. Replace the sensor if the R1 resistance is outside the range specified in **Table 4**.

4. Refer to **Figure 88** and check the R2 resistance as follows:

  a. Connect the ohmmeter positive test lead to the yellow terminal in the sensor side of the connector and connect the negative test lead to the black terminal.

  b. Note the resistance while slowly opening the throttle.

  c. Replace the sensor if the R2 resistance is outside the range specified in **Table 4**.

Adjustment

Adjust the throttle position sensor by turning the sensor until its resistance is within the specified range.

NOTE
The throttle position sensor is mounted on the side of the carburetor.

1. Properly adjust the idle speed as described in Chapter Nine.

2. Remove the carburetor assembly sufficiently to gain access to the throttle position sensor as described in this chapter.

3. Disconnect the throttle position sensor from the main harness.

4. Loosen the throttle position sensor mounting screws (**Figure 89**).

5. Connect the positive lead of an ohmmeter to the yellow terminal on the sensor side of the connector and connect the negative lead to the black terminal.

6. With the throttle fully closed, rotate the sensor body (**Figure 90**) until the resistance is within the fully closed range specified in **Table 4**.

7. Tighten the throttle position sensor screws securely.

8. Install the carburetor assembly.

CARBURETOR HEATER

Thermoswitch Test

1. Remove the left side frame cover as described in Chapter Fifteen.

2. Remove the thermoswitch (**Figure 91**) from the rubber mount on the frame.

> *NOTE*
> *Multiple electrical connectors are located behind the fuse panel (**Figure 92**) Locate the connector by matching the wire colors.*

3. Disconnect the thermoswitch 2-pin connector from the main harness.

4. Fill a beaker or pan with water and place it on a stove or hot plate.

5. Suspend the thermoswitch so it is immersed in the water as shown in **Figure 93**.

> *NOTE*
> *The thermometer and the thermoswitch must not touch the side or bottom of the container during this test. If either does, test results will be inaccurate.*

5. Suspend a thermometer in the water. Use a cooking or candy thermometer that is rated higher than the test temperatures.

6. Connect the ohmmeter positive test lead to the black terminal on the thermoswitch connector. Connect the negative test lead to the other black terminal (**Figure 93**).

7. Gradually heat the water and watch the continuity as the temperature rises.

   a. While the temperature is less than $23 \pm 3°$ C ($73 \pm 5°$ F), there should be continuity between the switch terminals.

   b. When the temperature exceeds $23 \pm 3°$ C ($73 \pm 5°$ F), there should be no continuity between the switch terminals.

8. Turn the heat off and watch the continuity as the temperature decreases.

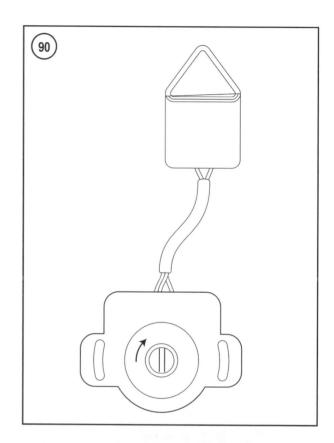

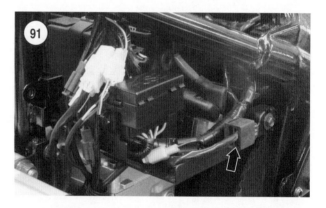

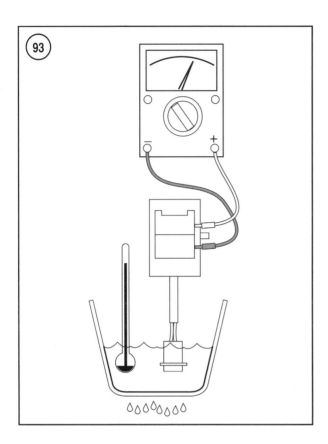

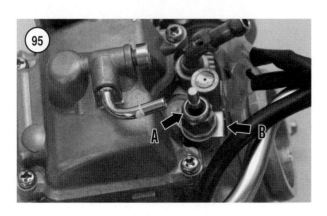

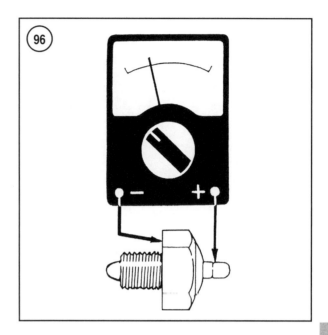

a. While the temperature is above $12 \pm 4°$ C ($53 \pm 7°$ F), there should be no continuity between the switch terminals.

b. When the temperature drops below $12 \pm 4°$ C ($53 \pm 7°$ F), there should be continuity between the switch terminals.

9. Replace the thermoswitch if the test results are not within the above specifications.

10. Connect the thermoswitch 2-pin connector to its harness mate.

11. Install the thermoswitch (**Figure 91**) into the rubber mount on the frame.

12. Install the left side frame cover.

Carburetor Heater Test

1. Remove the carburetor as described in this chapter.

2. Disconnect the electrical connectors (**Figure 94**) from the carburetor heater.

3. Unscrew and remove the carburetor heater (A, **Figure 95**), gasket and ground bracket (B).

4. Connect an ohmmeter to the carburetor heater as shown in **Figure 96** and check the heater's resistance.

5. Replace the carburetor heater if the resistance is not within the range specified in **Table 4**.

6. Install a *new* gasket, the carburetor heater (A, **Figure 95**) and ground bracket (B). Tighten the heater securely.

7. Attach both electrical connectors (**Figure 94**) onto the heater and ground bracket.

8. Install the carburetor as described in this chapter.

THROTTLE CABLE REPLACEMENT

Always replace both throttle cables as a set.

1. Securely support the motorcycle on level ground. Block the front wheel so the motorcycle will not roll in either direction.

2. Remove the fuel tank as described in this chapter.

3. Remove the air filter housing as described in this chapter.

4. At the throttle grip, loosen the throttle cable locknut (**Figure 97**) and turn the adjuster (B) to achieve the maximum amount of throttle cable free play.

5. Loosen the clamp (**Figure 98**) securing the carburetor to the carburetor joint.

6. Disconnect the idle adjust knob and cable (**Figure 99**) from the bracket on the right side of the crankcase.

7. Disconnect the vacuum chamber breather hose (A, **Figure 100**) and fuel hose (B) from the carburetor.

8. On California models, disconnect the EVAP purge hose (**Figure 101**) from the carburetor.

9. Remove the carburetor part way from the carburetor joint.

NOTE
All models are equipped with two throttle cables. Use masking tape and label the old cables before removing them. The accelera-

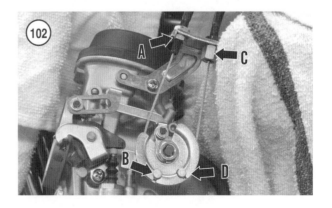

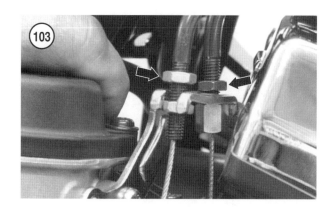

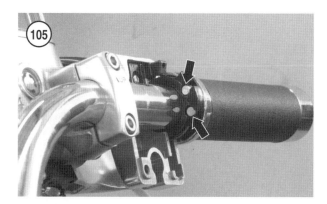

tor (or pull) cable is located at the outboard location on the throttle cable bracket (A, Figure 102) and in the outboard notch on the throttle wheel (B). The decelerator (or push) cable is located at the inboard location on the throttle cable bracket (C) and in the inboard notch on the throttle wheel (D).

10. Loosen the locknuts (**Figure 103**) on both throttle cables and disconnect them from the throttle wheel and the cable bracket.

11. Remove the two mounting screws and separate the halves of the right handlebar switch assembly (**Figure 104**).

12. Disengage the ends (**Figure 105**) of both the pull and push cables from the throttle grip drum.

13. Remove the screw (**Figure 106**) and clamp on the backside of the switch assembly.

14. Make a drawing of the cable routing from the right hand throttle housing to the carburetor assembly. Record this information for proper cable routing and installation.

15. Remove the cables from around the front of the right side fork tube and front upper brake hose (**Figure 107**), then around the steering head (**Figure 108**). Note the position of any cable clamps for installation.

16. Compare the new and old cables.

17. If cables *without* nylon liners are used, lubricate them as described in Chapter Three.

18. Route the new cables through the same path as the old cables.

19. On models equipped with a windshield, route the throttle cables (and front brake hose) (**Figure 109**) through both guides.

> *WARNING*
> *The throttle cables are the push/pull type and must not be interchanged. Attach the cables following the identification labels made on the old cables.*

20. Lightly grease the throttle cable ends and connect them to the throttle grip in the correct location as follows:

   a. Install the push cable (A, **Figure 110**) onto the receptacle in throttle grip, then slowly rotate the throttle grip.

   b. Slightly rotate the throttle grip, then install the pull cable (B, **Figure 110**) onto the receptacle in the throttle grip.

   c. Install the screw (**Figure 106**) and clamp on the backside of the switch assembly. Tighten the screw securely.

   d. Install the front portion of the right handlebar switch assembly (**Figure 104**) and tighten the screws securely.

21. Install the throttle cables onto the throttle cable bracket and throttle wheel as follows:

   a. Install the accelerator (or pull) cable onto the outboard groove on the throttle cable bracket (A, **Figure 102**) and in the outboard notch on the throttle wheel (B).

   b. Install the decelerator (or push) cable onto the inboard groove on the throttle cable bracket (C, **Figure 102**) and in the inboard notch on the throttle wheel (D).

22. Tighten the locknuts (**Figure 103**) on both throttle cables to hold them in place.

23. Install the carburetor into the carburetor joint. Push it on until it bottoms.

24. On California models, connect the EVAP purge hose (**Figure 101**) onto the carburetor.

25. Connect the vacuum chamber breather hose (A, **Figure 100**) and fuel hose (B) onto the carburetor.

26. Connect the idle adjust knob and cable (**Figure 99**) onto the bracket on the right side of the crankcase.

27. Securely tighten the clamp (**Figure 98**) securing the carburetor to the carburetor joint.

28. Open the throttle and release it. The throttle should snap back smoothly. If operation is incorrect, make sure the cables are attached correctly and there are no tight

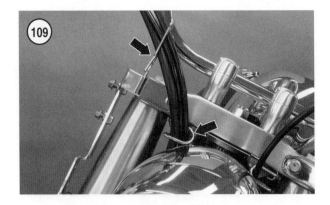

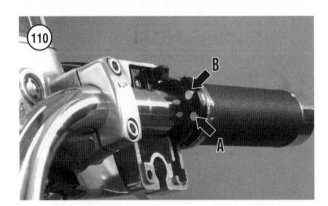

bends in the cables. Repeat with the front wheel pointing straight ahead and then with the wheel turned full left and full right.

29. Adjust the throttle cables as described in Chapter Three.

30. Install the air filter housing as described in this chapter.

31. Install the fuel tank as described in this chapter.

32. When the throttle is operating correctly, start the engine and run it at idle speed with the transmission in neutral. Turn the handlebar from side to side, making sure the

idle speed does not increase. If it does, the throttle cables are improperly installed. If the idle speed did not increase, test ride the motorcycle slowly at first. If there is any problem with the throttle, stop the motorcycle and make the necessary repairs.

WARNING
An improperly adjusted or incorrectly routed throttle cable can cause the throttle to stick in the open position. This could cause a loss of control. Do not ride the motorcycle until the throttle cable operation is correct.

STARTER (CHOKE) CABLE REPLACEMENT

1. Securely support the motorcycle on level ground. Block the front wheel so the motorcycle will not roll in either direction.
2. Remove the fuel tank as described in this chapter.
3. Remove the air filter housing as described in this chapter.
4. Loosen the clamp (**Figure 98**) securing the carburetor to the carburetor joint.
5. Disconnect the idle adjust knob and cable (**Figure 99**) from the bracket on the right side of the crankcase.
6. Disconnect the vacuum chamber breather hose (A, **Figure 100**) and fuel hose (B) from the carburetor.
7. On California models, disconnect the EVAP purge hose (**Figure 101**) from the carburetor.
8. Remove the carburetor part way from the carburetor joint.
9. Remove the mounting screw and remove the fuel pump/fuel filter assembly cover (**Figure 111**).
10. Disconnect the starter (choke) knob and cable (**Figure 112**) from the bracket.
11. Carefully pull the starter (choke) cable from between the cylinders (**Figure 113**).

NOTE
Figure 114 is shown with the carburetor removed to better illustrate the step.

12. Unscrew the starter (choke) cable (**Figure 114**) from the carburetor.
13. Compare the new and old cable.
14. If the cable is *without* a nylon liner, lubricate it as described in Chapter Three.
15. Screw the starter (choke) cable (**Figure 114**) into the carburetor and tighten securely.
16. Route the new cable through the same path as the old cable.
17. Connect the starter (choke) knob and cable (**Figure 112**) onto the bracket.
18. Install the cover (**Figure 111**) onto the fuel pump/fuel filter assembly and tighten the screw securely.
19. Install the carburetor into the carburetor joint. Push it on until it bottoms.
20. On California models, connect the EVAP purge hose (**Figure 101**) onto the carburetor.
21. Connect the vacuum chamber breather hose (A, **Figure 100**) onto the carburetor.
22. Tighten the clamp (**Figure 98**) securing the carburetor to the carburetor joint.
23. Operate the choke knob and make sure the carburetor linkage operates correctly with no binding. If the cable

9

operation is incorrect, make sure the cable is attached correctly and there are no tight bends in the cable.

24. Install the air filter housing as described in this chapter.

25. Install the fuel tank as described in this chapter.

FUEL FILTERS

All models are equipped with two fuel filters adjacent to the fuel pump on the left side of the engine.

NOTE
*The fuel filter cannot be cleaned and must be replaced when it is dirty or at the interval specified in **Table 1** in Chapter Three.*

Fuel Filter Removal/Installation

1. Support the motorcycle on level ground. Block the front wheel so the motorcycle will not roll in either direction.

2. Disconnect the negative battery cable as described in Chapter Three.

3. Remove the mounting screw and remove the fuel pump/fuel filter assembly cover (**Figure 111**).

4. Turn the fuel shutoff valve to the off position.

5. Disconnect the inlet (A, **Figure 115**) and outlet hoses (B) from the fuel filter.

6. Remove the filter (C, **Figure 115**) from the rubber grommet.

7. Installation is the reverse of removal. Note the following:

    a. Position the filter so its arrow points toward the fuel pump. Also the flange (D, **Figure 115**) will face forward.

    b. Securely seat the filter in its rubber grommet.

    c. Check the hose clamps for damage; replace them if necessary.

    d. After installation is complete, thoroughly check for leaks.

Inline Fuel Filter Removal/Installation

1. Remove the carburetor as described in this chapter.

2. Move the hose clamp back from the inlet fitting.

3. Slide the hose off the inlet fitting and move the hose and inlet pipe to one side (A, **Figure 116**).

4. Remove the inline fuel filter (B, **Figure 116**) from the inlet fitting.

5. Inspect the fuel filter for damage; replace as necessary.

6. Install the *new* fuel filter into the inlet fitting and push it in until it bottoms.

7. Push the hose and inlet pipe onto the inlet fitting.

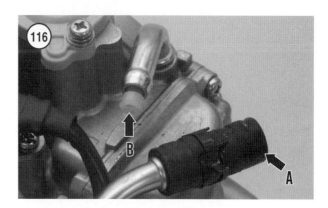

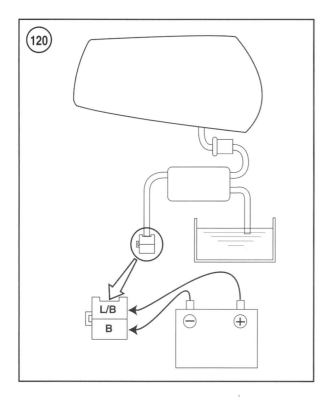

8. Install the hose clamp into position on the inlet fitting.

9. Install the carburetor as described in this chapter.

FUEL PUMP

Removal/Installation

1. Securely support the motorcycle on level ground. Block the front wheel so the motorcycle will not roll in either direction.

2. Disconnect the negative battery cable as described in Chapter Three.

3. Remove the mounting screw and remove the fuel pump/fuel filter module cover (**Figure 111**).

4. Remove the fuel tank as described in this chapter.

5. Disconnect the fuel pump 2-pin electrical connector (**Figure 117**) from the main harness.

6. Disconnect the outlet fuel hose (**Figure 118**) going to the carburetor.

7. Disconnect the fuel hose (A, **Figure 119**) going to the fuel filter.

8. Remove the fuel pump (B, **Figure 119**) from the rubber grommet. Note the path of the electrical harness.

9. Installation is the reverse of removal. Note the following:

    a. Position the fuel pump with the inlet fitting facing forward.

    b. Securely seat the fuel pump in its rubber grommet.

    c. Check the hose clamps for damage; replace them if necessary.

    d. After installation is complete, thoroughly check for leaks.

Operational Test

To check the fuel pump operation, apply battery power directly to the fuel pump bypassing the fuel pump relay.

1. Securely support the motorcycle on level ground. Block the front wheel so the motorcycle will not roll in either direction.

2. Disconnect the negative battery cable as described in Chapter Three.

3. Remove the mounting screw and remove the fuel pump/fuel filter module cover (**Figure 111**).

4. Remove the fuel tank as described in this chapter.

5. Disconnect the fuel pump 2-pin electrical connector (**Figure 117**).

6. Disconnect the outlet fuel hose (**Figure 118**) going to the carburetor. Connect a test hose to the outlet fitting on the pump and feed the other end of the hose into a container.

7. Use jumpers to connect the battery to the fuel pump side of the connector as shown in **Figure 120**. Fuel should flow from the fuel pump outlet hose. There are no specifications relating to flow rate or volume.

8. The fuel pump is faulty if fuel does not flow from the fuel pump outlet hose. Replace the fuel pump.

9. Disconnect the test hose from the fuel pump and reconnect the outlet fuel hose (**Figure 118**) onto the fuel pump.

10. Connect the fuel pump 2-pin electrical connector (**Figure 117**).

11. Install the fuel tank as described in this chapter.

12. Install the fuel pump/fuel filter module cover (**Figure 111**) and tighten the screw securely.

13. Connect the negative battery cable as described in Chapter Three.

Resistance Test

1. Securely support the motorcycle on level ground. Block the front wheel so the motorcycle will not roll in either direction.
2. Disconnect the negative battery cable as described in Chapter Three.
3. Remove the mounting screw and remove the fuel pump/fuel filter module cover (**Figure 111**).
4. Remove the fuel tank as described in this chapter.
5. Disconnect the fuel pump 2-pin electrical connector (**Figure 117**).
6. Connect the ohmmeter positive test lead to the blue/black terminal (A, **Figure 121**) in the pump side of the connector. Connect the negative test lead to the black terminal (B, **Figure 121**) and measure the fuel pump resistance.
7. The specified resistance is 1.6-2.2 ohms. Replace the fuel pump if it fails this test.
8. Connect the fuel pump 2-pin electrical connector (**Figure 117**) from its harness mate.
9. Install the fuel tank as described in this chapter.
10. Install the fuel pump/fuel filter module cover (**Figure 111**) and tighten it securely.
11. Connect the negative battery cable as described in Chapter Three.

Relay Resistance Test

1. Remove both seats as described in Chapter Fifteen.
2. Remove both side covers as described in Chapter Fifteen.
3. Remove the relay unit (**Figure 122**) from the mounting tang and disconnect the connector from the relay.
4. Check the continuity of the fuel pump relay as follows:
   a. Use a jumper wire to connect the positive battery terminal to the red/black terminal (A, **Figure 123**) on the relay and connect the negative battery terminal to the blue/red terminal (B).
   b. Connect the ohmmeter positive test lead to the red/black terminal (A, **Figure 123**) on the relay and connect the negative test lead to the blue/black terminal (C).
   c. The fuel pump relay should have continuity during this test. Replace the starting circuit cutoff relay if there is no continuity.
5. Reconnect the connector to the relay unit and install the relay unit (**Figure 122**) onto the mounting tang.
6. Install both side covers as described in Chapter Fifteen.
7. Install both seats as described in Chapter Fifteen.

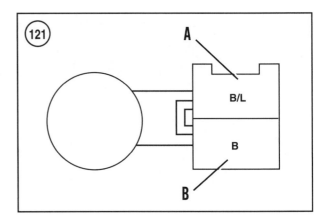

FUEL PUMP/FUEL FILTER MODULE

Removal/ Installation

1. Securely support the motorcycle on level ground. Block the front wheel so the motorcycle will not roll in either direction.
2. Remove the mounting screw and remove the fuel pump/fuel filter module cover (**Figure 111**).
3. Remove the fuel tank as described in this chapter.
4. Disconnect the outlet fuel hose (**Figure 118**) going to the carburetor.
5. Disconnect the starter (choke) knob and cable (**Figure 112**) from the bracket.
6. Disconnect the fuel pump 2-pin electrical connector (A, **Figure 124**).
7. Remove the bolts (B, **Figure 124**) securing the mounting bracket to the cylinder head-to-frame bracket.
8. Remove the fuel pump/fuel filter module.
9. Installation is the reverse of removal. Note the following:
   a. Tighten the mounting bolts securely.
   b. Check the hose clamps for damage; replace them if necessary.

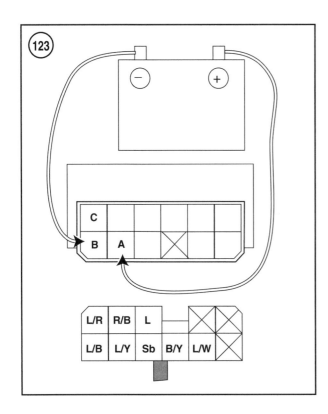

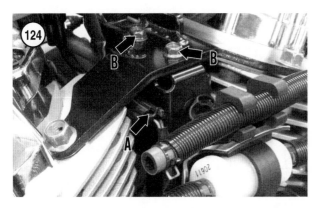

c. After installation is complete, thoroughly check for leaks.

AIR INDUCTION SYSTEM

The air induction system (AIS) reduces hydrocarbon emissions by promoting more complete combustion. Refer to **Figure 125** and **Figure 126**. The system injects fresh air into each exhaust port so any unburned fuel in the exhaust gasses are burned instead of being released into the atmosphere.

The system consists of an air cut valve, AIS filter, a reed valve, and air and vacuum lines. During normal operation,

the air cut valve is open so secondary air flows from the AIS filter, through the air cut valve, to the reed valve, then into the AIS fitting at the exhaust port in each cylinder.

The air cut valve closes during deceleration to prevent backfiring. When the throttle is closed, vacuum from the intake port closes the air cut valve so secondary air cannot flow to the reed valve.

Preliminary Inspection

There are no test procedures for the AIS system. If the engine valve clearance is adjusted properly and the engine will not idle correctly, then there may be a problem within the AIS system.

1. Securely support the motorcycle on level ground. Block the front wheel so the motorcycle will not roll in either direction.
2. Inspect the hoses for hardness or deterioration. Replace as necessary.
3. Check the tightness of the fitting clamps at the cylinder heads. Tighten if necessary.
4. If these preliminary inspections do not reveal any problems, remove the assembly for further inspection as described in the following procedure.

Removal/Installation

Refer to **Figure 127** and **Figure 128**.
1. Remove the voltage regulator/rectifier as described in Chapter Ten.
2. Release the hose clamp and disconnect the AIS pipe from its fitting on each cylinder head as follows.
   a. Front cylinder: 1999-2003 models **Figure 129**; 2004-on models **Figure 130**.
   b. Rear cylinder: 1999-2003 models **Figure 131**; 2004-on models **Figure 132**.
3. On 1999-2003 models, remove the Allen bolt (**Figure 133**) securing the rear cylinder line to the cover. Reinstall the bolt onto the cover and tighten securely.
4. Remove the screws securing the air filter assembly (**Figure 134**) to the frame. Disconnect the hoses from the backside of the assembly and remove the air filter assembly.
5. Disconnect the vacuum hose from the air cut valve.
6. Remove the mounting screws and remove the AIS assembly (**Figure 135**) from the frame.
7. On 2004-on models, remove the Allen bolts securing the fittings to the cylinder head. Refer to **Figure 136** and **Figure 137**. Remove the fitting and the gasket from the cylinder heads.
8. Remove the assembly from the engine and frame.

9

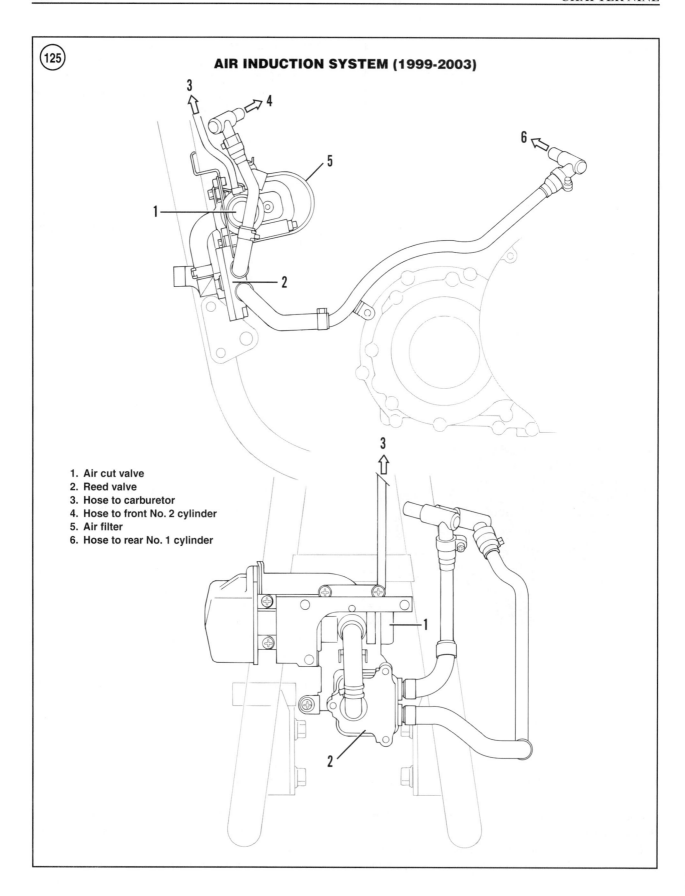

AIR INDUCTION SYSTEM (1999-2003)

1. Air cut valve
2. Reed valve
3. Hose to carburetor
4. Hose to front No. 2 cylinder
5. Air filter
6. Hose to rear No. 1 cylinder

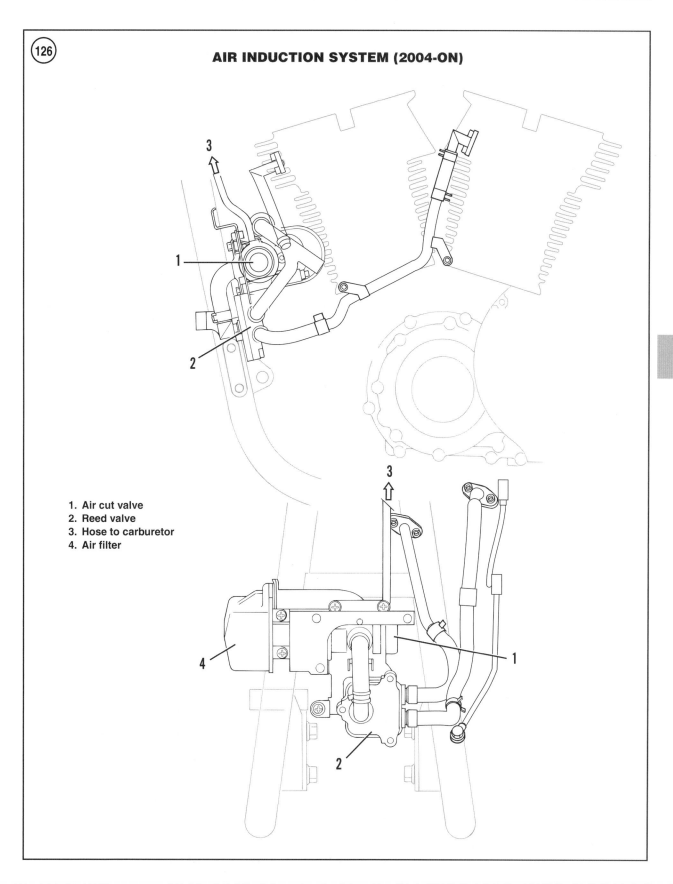

(126)

AIR INDUCTION SYSTEM (2004-ON)

1. Air cut valve
2. Reed valve
3. Hose to carburetor
4. Air filter

9

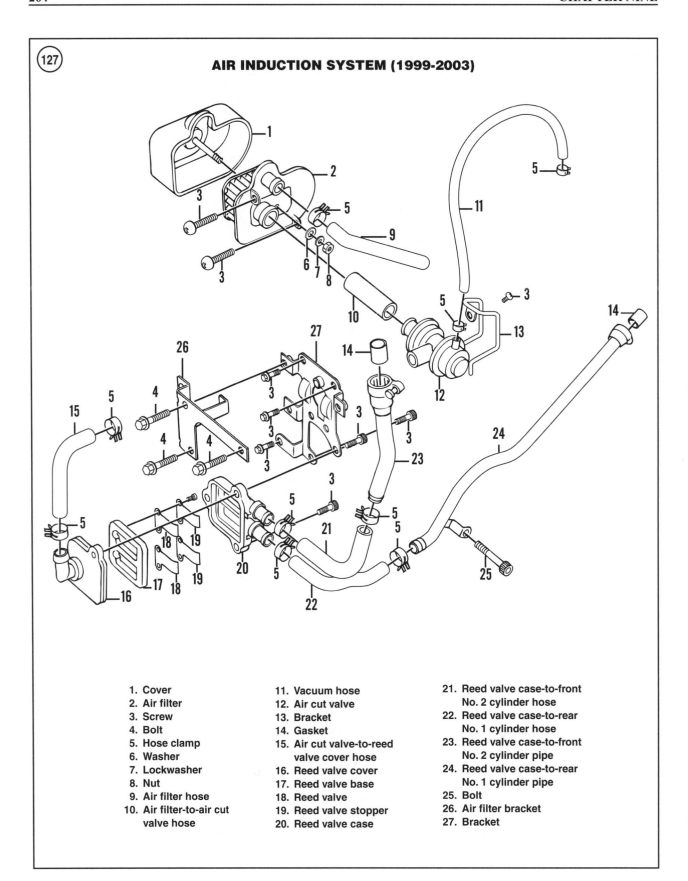

AIR INDUCTION SYSTEM (1999-2003)

1. Cover
2. Air filter
3. Screw
4. Bolt
5. Hose clamp
6. Washer
7. Lockwasher
8. Nut
9. Air filter hose
10. Air filter-to-air cut valve hose
11. Vacuum hose
12. Air cut valve
13. Bracket
14. Gasket
15. Air cut valve-to-reed valve cover hose
16. Reed valve cover
17. Reed valve base
18. Reed valve
19. Reed valve stopper
20. Reed valve case
21. Reed valve case-to-front No. 2 cylinder hose
22. Reed valve case-to-rear No. 1 cylinder hose
23. Reed valve case-to-front No. 2 cylinder pipe
24. Reed valve case-to-rear No. 1 cylinder pipe
25. Bolt
26. Air filter bracket
27. Bracket

(128)

AIR INDUCTION SYSTEM (2004-ON)

1. Bolt
2. Cover
3. Bolt
4. Air filter
5. Hose clamp
6. Washer
7. Lockwasher
8. Nut
9. Air filter hose
10. Air filter-to-air
    cut valve hose
11. Vacuum hose
12. Tie wrap
13. Bracket
14. Air cut valve
15. Screw
16. Bolt
17. Air filter bracket
18. Bracket
19. Air cut valve-to-reed
    valve cover hose
20. Reed valve cover
21. Reed valve base
22. Reed valve
23. Reed valve stopper
24. Reed valve case
25. Screw
26. Screw
27. Gasket
28. Reed valve case-to-rear
    No. 1 cylinder hose
29. Bolt
30. Reed valve
    case-to-rear
    No. 1 cylinder
    pipe No. 1
31. Reed valve
    case-to-front
    No. 2 cylinder pipe No. 2
32. Reed valve case-to-front
    No. 2 cylinder hose
33. Hose
34. Reed valve case-to-rear
    No. 1 cylinder pipe No. 2

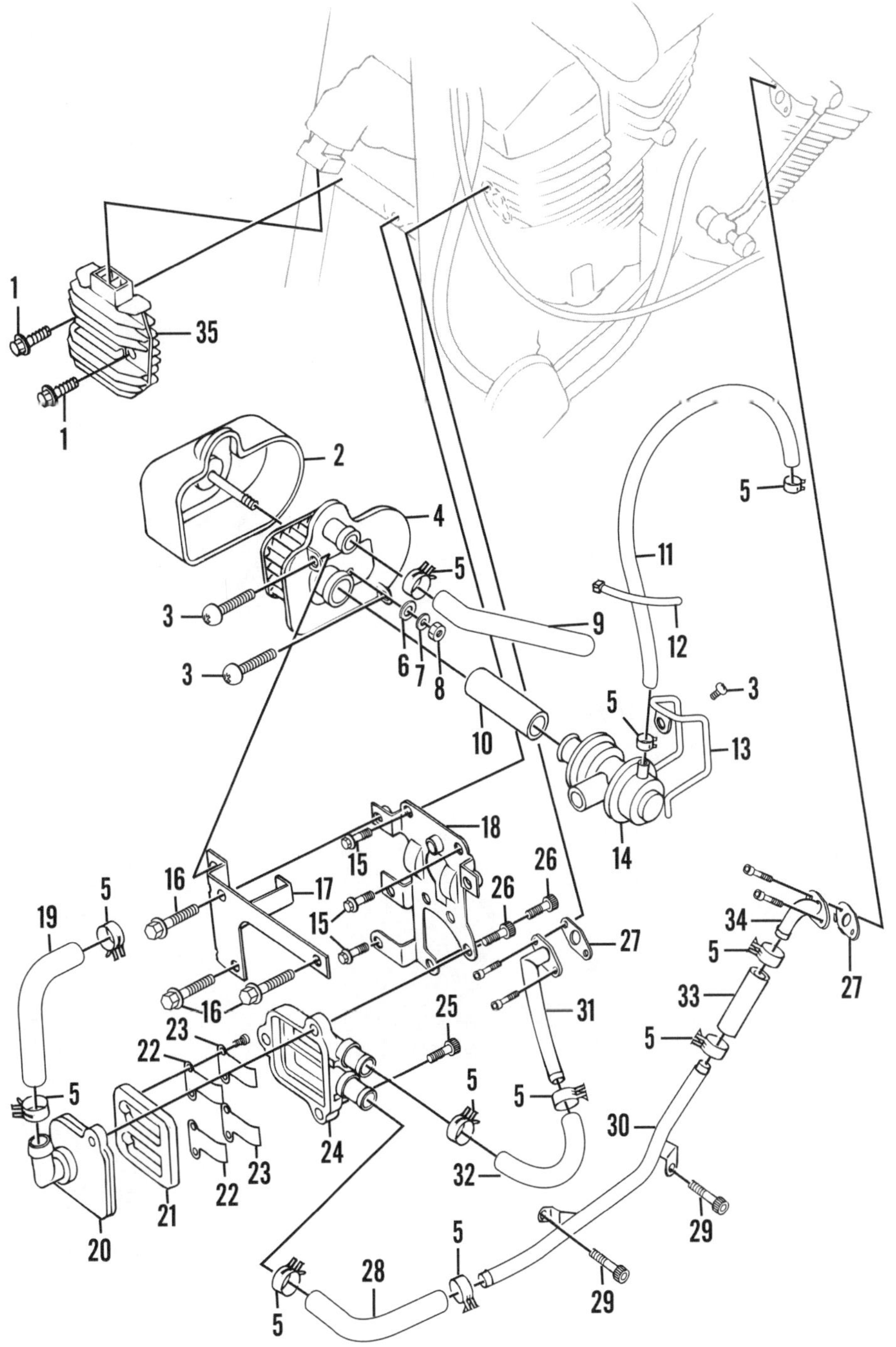

9

9. Installation is the reverse of removal. Note the following:

    a. Make sure the lines and hoses are correctly routed as shown in **Figure 125** and **Figure 126**.

    b. Properly secure each hose to its respective fitting.

Inspection

1. Inspect the air filter and housing (**Figure 138**) for cracks or damage.

2. Inspect the reed valve and the air cut valve. Replace any component that is damaged.

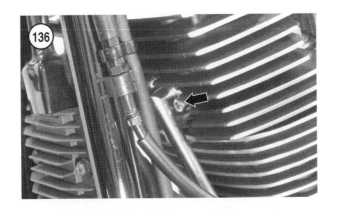

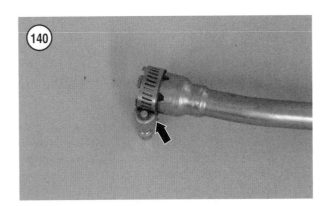

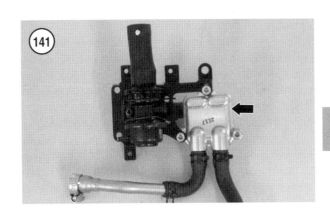

9

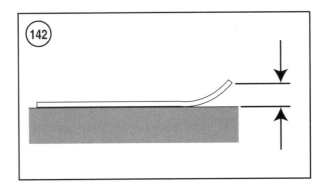

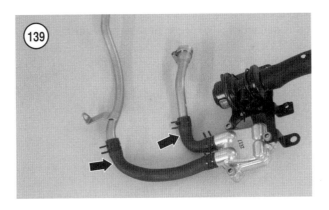

3. Make sure the ports in the reed valve, air cut valve and AIS filter are unobstructed. Clean them if possible or replace the clogged component.

4. Inspect the air and vacuum lines and hoses (**Figure 139**, typical) for cracks or signs of leaks. Replace any hose or pipe as necessary.

5. Inspect the hose connections for signs of leaks (**Figure 140**, typical).

6. Remove the mounting screws and lift the cover from the reed valve case (**Figure 141**).

7. Measure the reed valve height as shown in **Figure 142**. Replace the reed valve if its height exceeds the specification in **Table 5**.

8. Replace any component that is worn, damaged or out of specification.

EVAPORATIVE EMISSION CONTROL (CALIFORNIA MODELS)

All models sold in California are equipped with an evaporative emission control (EVAP) system, which reduces the amount of fuel vapors released into the atmosphere. The system consists of a charcoal canister, rollover valve, solenoid valve, assorted hoses, and modified carburetor and fuel tank. A schematic of the emission control system (**Figure 143**) is on a label on the inside of the frame left side cover.

The EVAP system captures fuel tank fumes and stores them in a charcoal canister. See **Figure 144**. While the motorcycle is parked or when it is operated at low engine speeds, the fuel vapors remain in the charcoal canister. When the motorcycle is ridden at high speed, the vapors pass through a hose to the carburetor and are burned.

The rollover valve, which is installed in line between the fuel tank and charcoal canister, assures that the fumes remain in the canister until they can be safely burned. The gravity-operated rollover valve is opened and closed by an internal weight. During normal riding (when the motorcycle is upright), the weight keeps the valve open so fuel vapors can flow from the tank to the charcoal canister. When the motorcycle is tilted (as when it is parked on the sidestand), the weight closes the valve so vapors cannot flow back into the fuel tank and escape into the atmosphere.

Inspection

Maintenance to the evaporative emission control system consists of inspecting the condition and routing of the hoses, making sure the canister is securely mounted to the engine mounting bracket, and testing the EVAP solenoid valve. Do not modify or remove the emission control system.

> *WARNING*
> *Because the evaporative emission control system stores fuel vapors, make sure the work area is free of flames or sparks before working on the EVAP system.*

1. When servicing the evaporative system, make sure the ignition switch is off.
2. Make sure all hoses are attached and are not damaged or pinched.
3. Replace any worn or damaged parts immediately. Replacement parts must be specific to California models.

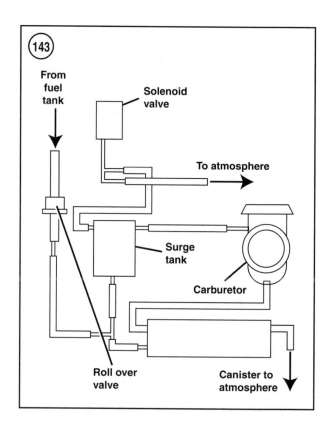

4. The canister is capable of working through the motorcycle's life without maintenance, unless it is damaged or contaminated.

Rollover Valve Removal/Installation

1. Remove the fuel tank as described in this chapter.
2. The rollover valve is in-line with the hose that connects the fuel tank to the EVAP canister.
3. Remove the screw (A, **Figure 145**) and release the rollover valve from the clamp that secures it to the toolbox panel.
4. Release the hose clamps (B, **Figure 145**), pull the hoses from the valve fittings, and remove the rollover valve.
5. Installation is the reverse of removal. Note the following:
   a. Install the rollover valve with the long neck (C, **Figure 145**) facing up.
   b. Make sure the hose clamps are tight.

Canister Removal/Installation

> *NOTE*
> *The two ports on the top of the EVAP canister are identified as TANK and CARB. Label*

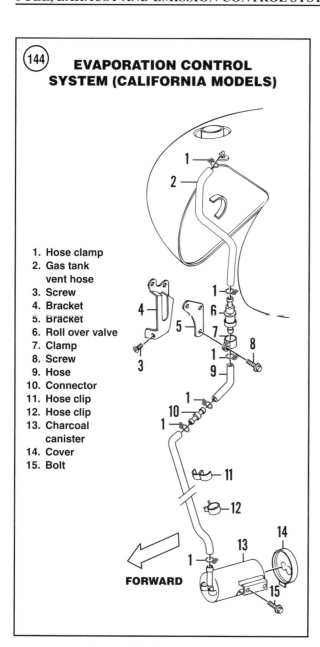

144 **EVAPORATION CONTROL SYSTEM (CALIFORNIA MODELS)**

1. Hose clamp
2. Gas tank vent hose
3. Screw
4. Bracket
5. Bracket
6. Roll over valve
7. Clamp
8. Screw
9. Hose
10. Connector
11. Hose clip
12. Hose clip
13. Charcoal canister
14. Cover
15. Bolt

FORWARD

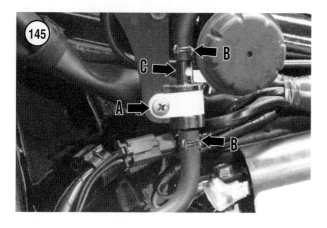

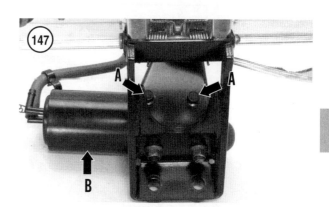

each hose before removal so they can be easily identified during assembly.

1. Label each hose on top of the canister.

2. Release the hose clamp and disconnect the hoses (**Figure 146**) from the canister.

NOTE
***Figure 147** is shown with the right side footboard removed to better illustrate the step.*

3. Remove the bolts (A, **Figure 147**) securing the canister to the footboard and remove the canister (B).

4. Installation is the reverse of removal while noting the following:

    a. Each hose must be connected to the correct port on the canister (**Figure 146**).

    b. Make sure the hose clamps and bolts are tight.

EXHAUST SYSTEM

Removal/Installation

Refer to **Figure 148**.

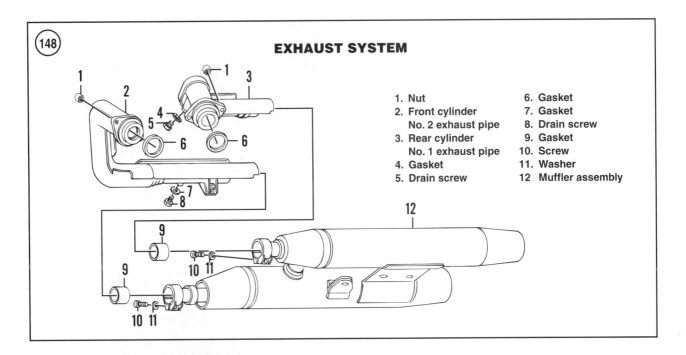

EXHAUST SYSTEM

1. Nut
2. Front cylinder
   No. 2 exhaust pipe
3. Rear cylinder
   No. 1 exhaust pipe
4. Gasket
5. Drain screw
6. Gasket
7. Gasket
8. Drain screw
9. Gasket
10. Screw
11. Washer
12 Muffler assembly

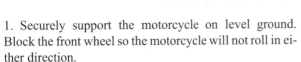

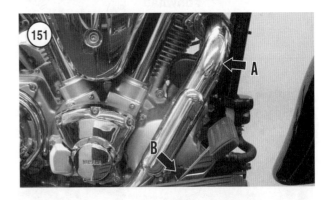

1. Securely support the motorcycle on level ground. Block the front wheel so the motorcycle will not roll in either direction.

2. On models so equipped, remove the right side saddlebag as described in Chapter Fifteen.

3. Remove the bolts securing the muffler assembly to the frame bracket.

> *WARNING*
> *The exhaust pipe heat shields have very sharp edges. Protect your hands while loosening the muffler clamp screws adjacent to the heat shields.*

4. Loosen the muffler clamp screw on each muffler.

5. Pull the muffler assembly rearward (**Figure 149**). Separate the mufflers from its respective exhaust pipe and remove the muffler assembly. Discard each muffler gasket.

6. Remove the front exhaust pipe as follows:
   a. Remove the nuts (**Figure 150**) securing the exhaust pipe to the exhaust port.
   b. Move the exhaust pipe away from the studs on the cylinder head.

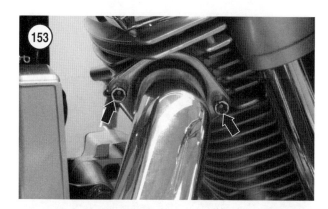

c. Carefully remove the exhaust pipe (A, **Figure 151**) from behind the footrest and the rear brake pedal assembly (B).

d. Remove and discard the exhaust gasket (**Figure 152**) from the cylinder head exhaust port.

7. Remove the rear exhaust pipe as follows:

   a. Remove the nuts (**Figure 153**) securing the exhaust pipe to the exhaust port.

   b. Move the exhaust pipe away from the studs on the cylinder head and remove it (**Figure 154**).

   c. Remove and discard the exhaust gasket (**Figure 155**) from the cylinder head exhaust port.

8. Inspect the system as described in this section.

9. Install a *new* exhaust gasket into both exhaust ports on the cylinder head.

10. Install a *new* muffler gasket (**Figure 156**) into each muffler.

11. Make sure each exhaust pipe is correctly seated in the exhaust port or exhaust manifold.

12. Loosely install the entire exhaust system and finger-tighten the hardware.

13. Tighten the exhaust pipe-to-cylinder head nuts to 20 N•m (15 ft-lb.). Refer to **Figure 150** and **Figure 153**.

14. Tighten the muffler clamp screws to 25 N•m (18 ft.-lb.).

15. Tighten the muffler assembly mounting bolts to 30 N•m (33 ft.-lb.).

16. After installation is complete, start the engine and make sure there are no exhaust leaks. Correct any leak prior to riding the motorcycle.

17. Install the right side saddlebag as described in Chapter Fifteen, on models so equipped.

Inspection

The exhaust system is vital to the motorcycle's operation and performance. Periodically inspect the exhaust system.

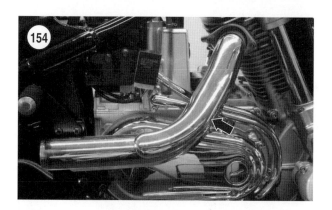

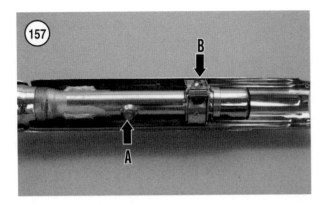

Replace parts that have excessive dents, which can restrict flow.

1. Periodically remove the drain bolt and washer (A, **Figure 157**) from each exhaust pipe.

2. Check for leaks where each muffler joins an exhaust pipe.

3. Inspect the drain bolts (A, **Figure 157**) for corrosion or exhaust leaks. Replace the bolts and washers if necessary.

4. Inspect the exhaust pipe heat shields and mounting clamps (B, **Figure 157**) for corrosion and looseness. Tighten if necessary. The heat shields are not replaceable.

5. Check the muffler clamps and bolts (**Figure 158**) for wear or damage. Replace as necessary.

6. Inspect the muffler mounting bracket (**Figure 159**) for wear or damage. Replace the muffler as necessary.

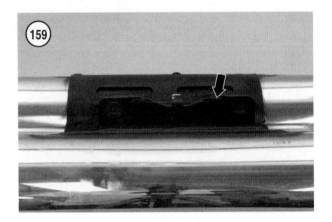

Table 1 CARBURETOR SPECIFICATIONS (1999-2003 U.S. AND CANADA MODELS)

Item	Specification
Model type	Mikuni BSR40
Carburetor identification number	
49-state and Canada	4WM1 00
California	4WM2 10
Main jet	No. 165
Main air jet	No. 60
Jet needle	6HDC26
Needle jet	X-2
Pilot air jet	No. 100
Pilot outlet	1.0 (XV16A), 1.1 (XV16AT)
Pilot jet	No. 35
Bypass No. 1	0.9
Bypass No. 2	1.0
Bypass No. 3	0.9
Pilot screw	2 1/2 turns out
Valve seat size	2.0
Starter jet No. 1	No. 57.5
Starter jet No. 2	1.0 (fixed, not removable)
Butterfly valve size	No. 110
Fuel level (above float chamber mating surface)	4.0-5.0 mm (0.16-0.20 in.)
Idle speed	850-950 rpm
Throttle cable free play at throttle grip	4-8 mm (0.16-0.31 in.)

Table 2 CARBURETOR SPECIFICATIONS (2004-ON U.S. AND CANADA MODELS)

Item	Specification
Model type	Mikuni BSR40
Carburetor identification number	
49-state and Canada	5VN1 00
California	5VN2 10
Main jet	No. 182.5
Main air jet	No. 60
Jet needle	6HDC26-1
Needle jet	X-2M
Pilot air jet 1	No. 100
Pilot air jet 2	2.0
Pilot outlet	1.1
Pilot jet	No. 35
Bypass No. 1	0.9
Bypass No. 2	1.0
Bypass No. 3	0.9
Pilot screw	2 1/2 turns out
Valve seat size	2.0
Starter jet No. 1	0.65
Starter jet No. 2	0.7 (fixed, not removable)
Butterfly valve size	No. 110
Fuel level (above float chamber mating surface)	4.0-5.0 mm (0.16-0.20 in.)
Idle speed	850-950 rpm
Throttle cable free play at throttle grip	4-6 mm (0.16-0.24 in.)

9

Table 3 CARBURETOR SPECIFICATIONS (OTHER THAN U.S. AND CANADA MODELS)

Item	Specification
Model type	Mikuni BSR40
Carburetor identification number	5JA100
Main jet	No. 165
Main air jet	No. 60
Jet needle	6HDC27-3
Needle jet	X-2
Pilot air jet	No. 100
Pilot outlet	1.1
Pilot jet	No. 35
Bypass No. 1	0.9
Bypass No. 2	1.0
Bypass No. 3	0.9
Pilot screw	2 1/2 turns out
Valve seat size	2.0
Starter jet No. 1	No. 57.5
Starter jet No. 2	1.0 (fixed, not removable)
Butterfly valve size	No. 110
Fuel level (above float chamber mating surface)	2.0-3.0 mm (0.08-0.12 in.)
Idle speed	850-950 rpm
Throttle cable free play at throttle grip	4-8 mm (0.16-0.31 in.)

Table 4 FUEL AND EMISSION SYSTEMS ELECTRICAL SPECIFICATIONS*

Item	Specification
Carburetor heater	
Resistance	10 ohms
Voltage, wattage	12 volts, 30 watts

(continued)

Table 4 FUEL AND EMISSION SYSTEMS ELECTRICAL SPECIFICATIONS* (continued)

Item	Specification
Fuel pump	
Amperage	1.0 amps
Resistance	1.6-2.2 ohms
Throttle position sensor	
R1 resistance	4.0-6.0k ohms
R2 resistance	0.56-0.84k ohms
Fully closed resistance	0.56-0.84k ohms
* Resistance specifications @ 20° C (68° F)	

Table 5 FUEL AND EXHAUST SYSTEM SPECIFICATIONS

Item	Specification
AIS reed valve height	0.4 mm (0.016 in.)
Fuel pump	
Model	
1999-2003	4WM (Mitsubishi)
2004-2005	UC-A10C (Mitsubishi)
2006-on	UC-Z10C (Mitsubishi)
Output pressure	15-20 kPa (2.2-2.9 psi)
Fuel tank capacity	
Capacity, including reserve	20 liter (5.3 U.S. gal.)
Reserve	3.5 liter (0.9 U.S. gal.)
Fuel	
Type	Regular unleaded
Octane	86 [(R + M)/method] or research octane 91 or higher

Table 6 FUEL AND EXHAUST SYSTEM TORQUE SPECIFICATIONS

Item	N•m	in.-lb.	ft.-lb.
Air filter case bolts	7	62	–
Alternator cover bolts	10	88	–
Exhaust pipe-to-cylinder head nuts	20	–	15
Exhaust pipe-to-muffler clamp bolts	25	–	18
Fuel tank rear bolt	7	62	–
Fuel shut off valve-to-tank	7	62	–
Fuel sender-to-fuel tank bolt	7	62	–
Meter cover-to-fuel tank	7	62	–
Muffler			
Mounting bolts	30	–	22
Clamp bolts	25	–	18

CHAPTER TEN

ELECTRICAL SYSTEM

This chapter describes service and test procedures for the following electrical sub-systems and components:
1. Charging system.
2. Ignition system.
3. Lighting system.
4. Signal system.
5. Switches.
6. Self-diagnostic system.

Refer to **Tables 1-4** at the end of the chapter for specifications.

ELECTRICAL COMPONENT REPLACEMENT

Most motorcycle dealerships and parts suppliers will not accept the return of any electrical part. If the exact cause of any electrical system malfunction cannot be determined, have a Yamaha dealership retest that specific system to verify the test results. If a *new* electrical component is purchased and installed, and the system still does not work properly, it will probably not be possible to return the unit for a refund.

Consider any test results carefully before replacing a component that tests only slightly out of specification, especially resistance. A number of variables can affect test results dramatically. These include the testing meter's internal circuitry, ambient temperature, and conditions under which the machine has been operated. All instructions and specifications have been checked for accuracy; however, test results depend to a great extent upon individual accuracy.

ELECTRICAL CONNECTORS

All models are equipped with numerous electrical components, connectors and wires. Corrosion-causing moisture can enter these electrical connectors and cause poor electrical connections, leading to component failure. Troubleshooting an electrical circuit with one or more corroded electrical connectors can be time-consuming and frustrating.

Prior to reconnecting electrical connectors, pack them with a dielectric grease compound. Dielectric grease is specially formulated for sealing and waterproofing electrical connections without interfering with current flow. Use only this compound or an equivalent designed for this specific purpose. Do not use a substitute that may interfere with the current flow within the electrical connector. Do not use silicone sealant.

CHARGING SYSTEM

The charging system consists of the battery, ignition fuse, ignition switch, alternator, and the regulator/rectifier assembly.

Alternating current generated by the alternator is rectified to direct current. The voltage regulator maintains the voltage to the battery and electrical loads at a constant voltage regardless of variations in engine speed and load.

Troubleshooting

Refer to Chapter Two.

Current Draw Test

1. Turn the ignition switch to off.
2. Remove the rider seat as described in Chapter Fifteen.
3. Disconnect the negative battery cable as described in Chapter Three.
4. Connect an ammeter between the battery negative lead and the negative terminal of the battery (**Figure 1**).
5. The ammeter should read less than 0.1 mA. A current draw that exceeds 0.1 mA must be found and repaired.
6. If the current draw is excessive, consider the following probable causes:
    a. Damaged battery.
    b. Faulty voltage regulator/rectifier.
    c. Short circuit in the system.
    d. Loose, dirty or faulty electrical connectors.
    e. Aftermarket electrical accessories added to the electrical system.
7. To find the short circuit that is causing the current draw, refer to the wiring diagrams at the end of this manual. Disconnect different electrical connectors one by one while monitoring the ammeter. When the current draw returns to an acceptable level, the faulty circuit is indicated. Test the circuit further to find the problem.
8. Disconnect the ammeter.
9. Reconnect the negative battery cable.

Charging Voltage Test

1. Connect an engine tachometer to the spark plug lead on the No. 1 (rear) cylinder.
2. Connect a 0-20 DC voltmeter to the battery terminals as shown in **Figure 2**.
3. Start the engine and increase engine speed to approximately 5000 rpm. The measured voltage should equal the charging voltage specified in **Table 1**.

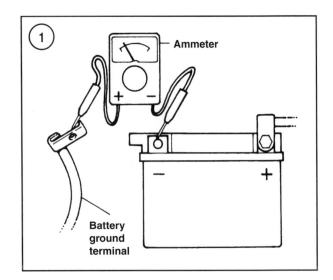

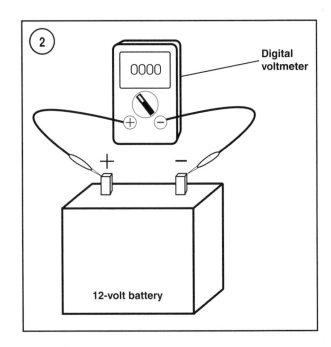

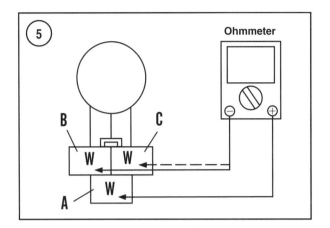

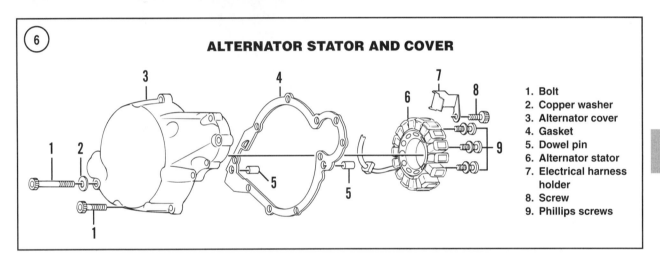

ALTERNATOR STATOR AND COVER

1. Bolt
2. Copper washer
3. Alternator cover
4. Gasket
5. Dowel pin
6. Alternator stator
7. Electrical harness holder
8. Screw
9. Phillips screws

4. If the charging voltage is out of specification, check the stator coil resistance as described in this chapter.

ALTERNATOR STATOR

Resistance Test

Test the stator assembly at a minimum temperature of 20° C (68° F).

1. Remove both side covers as described in Chapter Fifteen.
2. Follow the electrical harness from the alternator and decompression solenoid (**Figure 3**) behind the transfer gearcase assembly and up behind the fuse panel.
3. Disconnect the 3-pin white stator connector (**Figure 4**) from the wiring harness.
4. Measure the stator coil resistance.

NOTE
In each of the following tests, connect the ohmmeter's positive lead to the connector's

center terminal (A, Figure 5) and the ohmmeter's negative lead to the other terminal (B or C).

5. Measure the resistance between the center terminal (A, **Figure 5**) and the left terminal (B) in the stator side of the connector.
6. Measure the resistance between the center terminal (A, **Figure 5**) and the right terminal (C) in the stator side of the connector.
7. Replace the stator assembly if either resistance is not within the range specified in **Table 1**.
8. Check the continuity between each terminal and ground. There should be no continuity (infinite resistance). Continuity between any stator wire and ground indicates that either the stator or one of the stator wires is shorted to ground. Replace the stator coil assembly.

Removal/Installation

Refer to **Figure 6**.

10

1. Securely support the motorcycle on level ground. Block the front wheel so the motorcycle will not roll in either direction.

2. Remove both side covers as described in Chapter Fifteen.

3. Remove the front cylinder exhaust pipe as described in Chapter Nine.

4. Remove the bolts (A, **Figure 7**) securing the footrest assembly to the frame. Remove the footrest assembly (B, **Figure 7**) and rest it on a box to allow access to the stator cover bolts. It is not necessary to completely remove the footrest assembly.

5. Follow the electrical harness from the alternator (**Figure 3**) and decompression solenoid behind the transfer gearcase assembly and up behind the fuse panel. Note the routing of the harness.

6. Disconnect the 3-pin white stator connector (**Figure 4**) from the wiring harness.

7. Disconnect the two decompression solenoid electrical connectors as follows:
   a. 2-pin brown connector (green/red and black/ blue wires).
   b. 2-pin brown connector (red/white and yellow/ black wires).

NOTE
Figure 8 *is shown with the transfer gearcase removed to better illustrate the step.*

8. Carefully remove the two sets of wires, contained within the plastic conduit (**Figure 8**) from behind the transfer gearcase assembly and up behind the fuse panel.

9. Withdraw the alternator stator wire and connector from the plastic conduit.

10. Remove the bolts securing the alternator stator cover (A, **Figure 9**). Note the location of the copper washer (B, **Figure 9**) under the lower rear bolt. This washer must be installed in the same location during installation.

11. Pull the stator cover straight off the rotor and remove the cover.

12. Remove the gasket and the dowel pins if loose. Discard the gasket.

13. If necessary, remove the stator coil as follows:
   a. Remove the screw securing the wire clamp to the cover.
   b. Pry the grommet from the cover.
   c. Remove the screws securing the stator coil assembly to the cover and remove the coil assembly.
   d. Do not clean the stator coils (A, **Figure 10**) in solvent. Wipe off with a clean rag.

14. If removed, install the stator coil as follows:
   a. Apply a medium-strength threadlocking compound to the threads of the stator mounting screws and

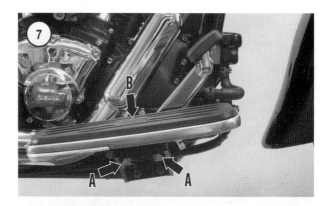

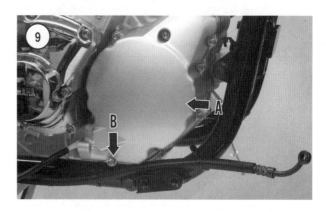

wire clamp screw. Tighten the stator screws to 7 N•m (62 in.-lb.).
   b. Apply a light coat of Yamaha Quick Gasket, or an equivalent, to the grommet (B, **Figure 10**) prior to installation.
   c. Securely seat the grommet in the cover.

15. Install a *new* gasket (A, **Figure 11**).

16. Install the dowel pins (B, **Figure 11** and **Figure 12**), if removed.

17. Install the stator cover straight onto the rotor and push it on until it bottoms on the crankcase.

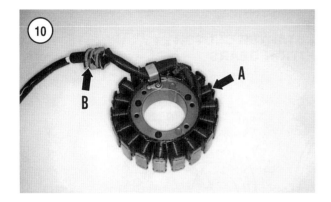

18. Install the alternator stator wire and connector into the plastic conduit.

19. Route the two sets of wires, contained within the plastic conduit (**Figure 8**) behind the transfer gearcase assembly and behind the fuse panel, along the same path noted during removal.

20. Make sure the electrical connectors are free of corrosion and apply a dielectric compound to the electrical terminals.

21. Connect the connectors and make sure both sides are completely coupled to each other.

22. Move the right side footrest into position and install the bolts (A, **Figure 7**). Tighten the bolts to 48 N•m (35 ft.-lb.).

23. Install the front cylinder exhaust pipe as described in Chapter Nine.

24. Install both side covers as described in Chapter Fifteen.

FLYWHEEL, STARTER CLUTCH AND STARTER REDUCTION GEARS

The following Yamaha special tools, or their equivalents, are needed to remove or install the flywheel and starter clutch:

1. Sheave holder: part No. YS-01880 (U.S.) or 90890-1701 (U.K.).

2. Flywheel puller: part No. YM-01080 (U.S.) or 90890-01080 (U.K.).

Flywheel Removal

Refer to **Figure 13**.

1. Securely support the motorcycle on level ground. Block the front wheel so the motorcycle will not roll in either direction.

2. Remove the alternator stator assembly as described in this chapter.

3. Remove the No. 2 starter reduction idle gear set shaft (A, **Figure 14**) and the gears (B).

4. Remove the No. 1 starter reduction idle gear set shaft (A, **Figure 15**) and gears (B).

5. Hold the flywheel with the holder and loosen the flywheel bolt (**Figure 16**). Then remove the bolt and washer.

> *CAUTION*
> *Do not try to remove the flywheel without the correct puller. Any attempt to do so may damage the flywheel and crankshaft.*

6. Screw the puller into the flywheel.

7. Hold the flywheel with the flywheel holder and gradually tighten the flywheel puller until the flywheel pops off the crankshaft taper.

8. Hold the backside of the assembly to prevent the starter clutch from falling off the rotor.

9. Remove the rotor and starter clutch from the crankshaft taper.

10. Remove the rotor puller from the rotor.

10

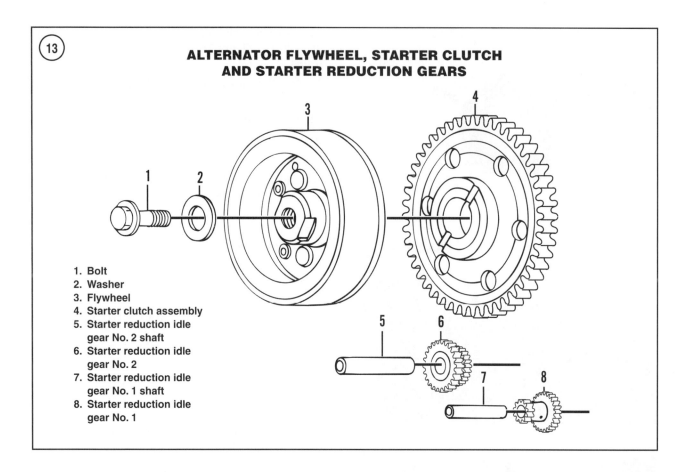

ALTERNATOR FLYWHEEL, STARTER CLUTCH AND STARTER REDUCTION GEARS

1. Bolt
2. Washer
3. Flywheel
4. Starter clutch assembly
5. Starter reduction idle gear No. 2 shaft
6. Starter reduction idle gear No. 2
7. Starter reduction idle gear No. 1 shaft
8. Starter reduction idle gear No. 1

Flywheel Installation

1. Degrease both the crankshaft taper and the flywheel inner taper with contact cleaner. Allow both tapers to dry before installing the flywheel.

2. Install the flywheel and starter clutch onto the crankshaft taper.

3. Install the washer and bolt (**Figure 16**) and tighten securely.

4. Hold the flywheel with the flywheel holder (A, **Figure 17**) and tighten the flywheel bolt (B). Refer to **Table 4** for the torque specification.

5. Install the No. 1 starter reduction idle gear set shaft (A, **Figure 15**) and gears (B). Push the shaft in until it bottoms.

6. Position the No. 2 starter reduction idle gear set with the smaller diameter gear side (**Figure 18**) going on first.

7. Install the No. 2 starter reduction idle gear set shaft (A, **Figure 14**) and gears (B). Push the shaft in until it bottoms.

8. Install the alternator stator assembly as described in this chapter.

Flywheel Inspection

1. Clean the flywheel in solvent and dry with compressed air.

2. Check the flywheel for cracks or breaks.

WARNING
Replace a cracked or chipped flywheel. A damaged flywheel can fly apart at high engine speeds, throwing metal fragments into

10

the engine. Do not attempt to repair a damaged flywheel.

3. Check the flywheel tapered bore and the crankshaft taper for damage.

4. Inspect the inside of the flywheel (**Figure 19**) for metal debris picked up by the magnet. Remove all debris to avoid damage to the stator assembly.

5. Inspect the threads (**Figure 20**) of the flywheel puller for damage. Clean with a metric thread tap if necessary.

Starter Reduction Gears Inspection

1. Inspect the No. 2 starter reduction idle gear set (**Figure 21**) for chipped or missing teeth.

2. Rotate the No. 2 starter reduction idle gear set on the shaft (B, **Figure 21**) and make sure it rotates smoothly with no binding.

3. Inspect the No. 1 starter reduction idle gear set (**Figure 22**) for chipped or missing teeth.

4. Rotate the No. 1 starter reduction idle gear set on the shaft (B, **Figure 22**) and make sure it rotates smoothly with no binding.

Starter Clutch Removal/Installation

The starter clutch assembly is removed during flywheel removal as described in this section.

Starter Clutch Operational Test

1. Set the flywheel on the bench so the starter clutch faces up.
2. Hold the flywheel and turn the starter wheel gear *counterclockwise* (**Figure 23**). The starter clutch gear should turn freely within the starter clutch.
3. Hold the flywheel and try to turn the starter wheel gear *clockwise*. The starter clutch gear should not turn in this direction.
4. The one-way clutch is faulty if it fails either test. Replace the starter clutch assembly as described in this section.

Starter Clutch Disassembly/ Inspection/Assembly

1. Hold the flywheel with one hand, then turn the starter driven gear *counterclockwise* (**Figure 23**) and pull up at the same time to remove it.
2. Inspect the starter driven gear teeth (A, **Figure 24**) for damage.
3. Inspect the inner bushing (B, **Figure 24**) for wear or damage where it rides on the crankshaft.
4. Inspect the outer bushing (C, **Figure 24**) for wear or damage where it rides on the one-way sprag clutch.
5. Inspect the rollers (**Figure 25**) in the one-way sprag clutch for wear or looseness. Replace if necessary.
6. To remove the starter clutch assembly, perform the following:
   a. Install an adjustable holding tool onto the flywheel.
   b. Use an impact driver and loosen the Allen bolts (A, **Figure 26**).
   c. Remove the bolts and remove the one-way sprag clutch (B, **Figure 26**) from the flywheel.
7. Clean the one-way sprag clutch and driven gear in solvent and dry with compressed air.
8. Remove all threadlocking compound from the Allen bolts.
9. Install the starter clutch as follows:
   a. Lubricate the one-way sprag clutch with engine oil.
   b. Install the one-way sprag clutch (B, **Figure 26**) into the flywheel.
   d. Apply a medium strength threadlocking compound to the Allen bolts and install them.
   e. Secure the flywheel with the holding tool and tighten the Allen bolts (A, **Figure 26**) to 24 N•m (17 ft.-lb.).

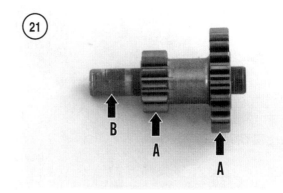

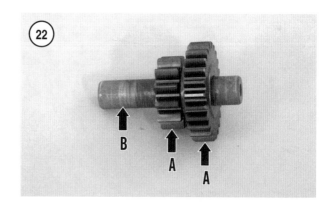

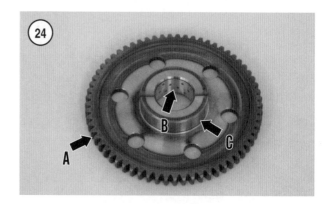

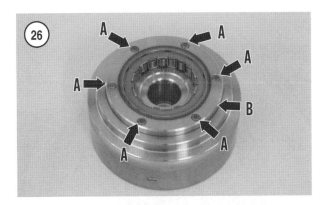

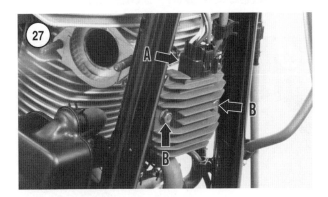

f. Recheck the one-way sprag clutch operation. Hold the flywheel with one hand and turn the starter driven gear. The gear should turn *counterclockwise* (**Figure 23**) but not clockwise.

VOLTAGE REGULATOR/RECTIFIER

Removal/Installation

1. Securely support the motorcycle on level ground. Block the front wheel so the motorcycle will not roll in either direction.

2. Remove the rider seat as described in Chapter Fifteen.

3. Disconnect the negative battery cable as described in Chapter Three.

4. Slide the boot off the electrical connector and disconnect the electrical connector (A, **Figure 27**) from the regulator/rectifier.

5. Remove the regulator/rectifier bolts (B, **Figure 27**) and remove the regulator/rectifier from the frame bracket.

6. Install the regulator/rectifier onto the frame bracket and tighten the bolts securely.

7. Make sure the electrical connector is free of corrosion.

8. Apply a dielectric compound to the electrical connector before reconnecting it.

9. Attach the electrical connector and make sure it is completely coupled to the voltage regulator.

10. Slide the boot back over the connector.

11. Connect the battery negative cable.

12. Install the rider seat as described in Chapter Fifteen.

IGNITION SYSTEM

Ignition timing and advance are not adjustable. Use the ignition timing procedures in Chapter Three to determine whether the ignition system is operating properly.

When the pickup coil rotor on the primary drive gear passes the pickup coil, an electrical pulse is generated within the pickup coil. This pulse flows to the switching and distribution circuits in the ignitor unit. The ignitor unit interrupts current flow through the ignition coil and the magnetic field within the coil collapses. This induces a very high voltage in the secondary windings of the ignition coil. This voltage is sufficient to jump the gap at the spark plugs.

Troubleshooting

The ignition system is designed to operate only when the sidestand is up or when the transmission is in neutral. If there is a no-spark condition, check the neutral switch and sidestand switch as described in this chapter.

For additional troubleshooting procedures, refer to Chapter Two.

Precautions

Damage to the semiconductors in the system may occur if the following precautions are not observed.

1. Never connect the battery backwards. If the battery polarity is incorrect, the voltage regulator, alternator and ignitor unit will be damaged.

10

2. Do not disconnect the battery while the engine is running.

3. Keep all connections between the various units clean and tight. Make sure the wiring connectors are firmly pushed together.

4. Do not substitute another type of ignition coil or battery.

5. Each solid-state unit is mounted on a rubber vibration isolator. Make sure the isolators are in place when replacing any units.

SPARK PLUG CAP

Resistance Test

1. Disconnect the spark plug cap from the spark plug.

2. Measure the resistance between each end of the cap as shown in **Figure 28**.

3. Replace the spark plug cap if the resistance is not within the specification in **Table 1**.

4. Repeat this test for the other spark plug caps

IGNITION COIL

The front cylinder ignition coil is mounted on the right side of the frame; the rear cylinder ignition coil is attached to the left side. Make sure the coils are mounted securely.

Resistance Test

Test the ignition coils at a minimum temperature of 20° C (68° F).

1. Securely support the motorcycle on level ground. Block the front wheel so the motorcycle will not roll in either direction.

2. Remove the rider seat as described in Chapter Fifteen.

3. Disconnect the negative battery cable as described in Chapter Three.

4. Remove the fuel tank as described in Chapter Nine.

5. Disconnect the spark plug caps (**Figure 29**) from the respective set of spark plugs.

6. Disconnect the two primary coil spade connectors (A, **Figure 30**) from the terminals on the ignition coil.

7. Measure the primary coil resistance as follows:
   a. Connect the ohmmeter positive test probe to the red/black terminal on the ignition coil; connect the negative test probe to the orange (or gray) terminal (**Figure 31**).
   b. Replace the ignition coil(s) if the primary resistance is not within the specification in **Table 1**.

8. Measure the secondary coil resistance as follows:

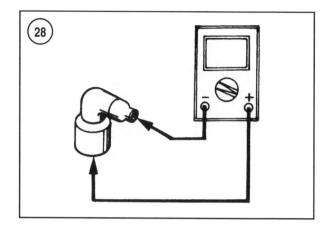

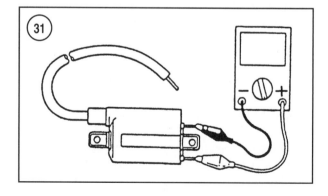

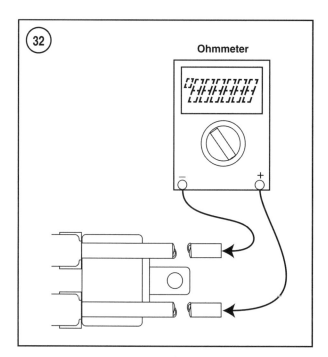

Ohmmeter

a. With both spark plug caps removed, measure secondary coil resistance between both spark plug leads (**Figure 32**).

b. Replace the ignition coil(s) if the secondary coil resistance is not within the specification in **Table 1**.

9. Repeat this test for the other ignition coil.

10. Reconnect the spark plug secondary wires.

11. Apply a dielectric compound to the primary coil spade connectors (A, **Figure 30**) prior to reconnecting them. This will help seal out moisture.

12. Make sure the electrical connectors are free of corrosion and are completely coupled to each other.

13. Install all removed items.

Removal/Installation

1. Securely support the motorcycle on level ground. Block the front wheel so the motorcycle will not roll in either direction.
2. Remove the rider seat as described in Chapter Fifteen.
3. Disconnect the negative battery cable as described in Chapter Three.
4. Remove the fuel tank as described in Chapter Nine.
5. Disconnect the spark plug cap (**Figure 29**) from the respective set of spark plugs.
6. Disconnect the two primary coil spade connectors (A, **Figure 30**) from the terminals on the ignition coil.

> *CAUTION*
> *Note how the ignition coil secondary leads are routed along the frame rail (**Figure 33**, typical). Make sure to reroute them along the same path during installation using the same clips and clamps.*

7. Remove the ignition coil mounting bolts and remove the coil (B, **Figure 30**). Repeat for the remaining coil, if necessary.
8. Installation is the reverse of removal. Note the following:

    a. Tighten the ignition coil bolts to 7 N•m (62 in.-lb.).

    b. Apply a dielectric compound to the primary coil spade connectors (A, **Figure 30**) before reconnecting them. This will help seal out moisture.

    c. Make sure all connections are free of corrosion and are tight; pack the connector with dielectric grease.

    d. Install all removed items.

PICKUP COIL AND TIMING ROTOR

Pickup Coil Resistance Test

Test the pickup coil at a minimum temperature of 20° C (68° F).

1. Securely support the motorcycle on level ground. Block the front wheel so the motorcycle will not roll in either direction.
2. Remove the rider seat as described in Chapter Fifteen.
3. Remove the frame side covers as described in Chapter Fifteen.
4. Disconnect the 2-pin white pickup coil connector (**Figure 34**) (gray and black/blue wires) from the wiring harness.
5. Connect the ohmmeter positive test probe to the gray terminal (A, **Figure 35**) in the pickup coil side of the connector; connect the negative test probe to the black/blue terminal (B).

10

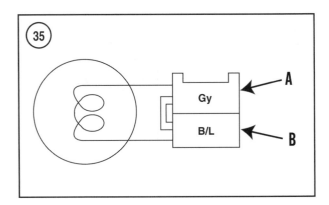

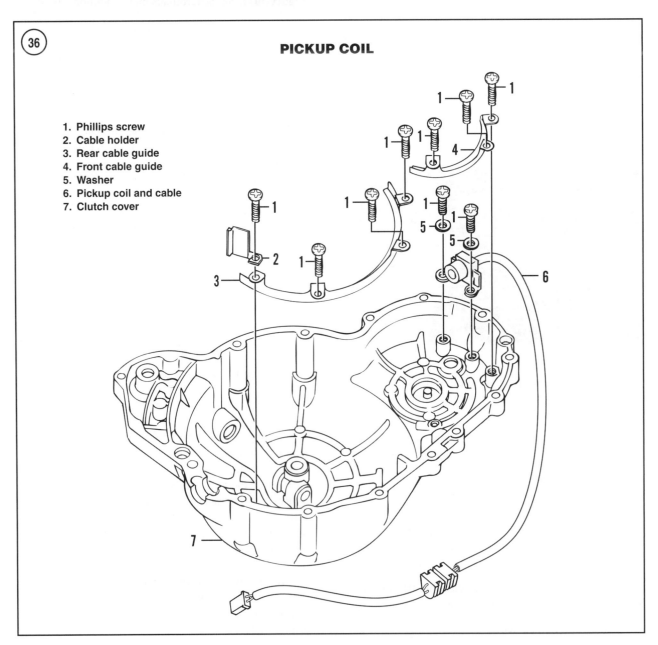

PICKUP COIL

1. Phillips screw
2. Cable holder
3. Rear cable guide
4. Front cable guide
5. Washer
6. Pickup coil and cable
7. Clutch cover

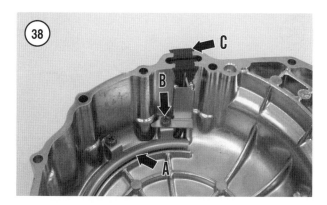

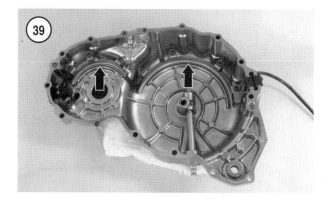

6. If the pickup coil resistance is outside the range specified in **Table 1**, replace the coil assembly as described in this section.

Pickup Coil Removal/Installation

Refer to **Figure 36**.

1. Remove the clutch outer cover as described in Chapter Seven.

2. Clean the inner and outer surfaces of the clutch outer cover with solvent and dry with compressed air.

3. Turn the cover upside down on several shop cloths on the workbench.

4. Remove the screws securing the front cable guide to the cover (A, **Figure 37**). Remove the front cable guide.

5. Remove the screws (B, **Figure 37**) securing the pickup coil to the cover.

6. Pull the pickup coil (C, **Figure 37**) up and out of the cover.

7. Remove the screws securing the rear cable guide (A, **Figure 38**) to the cover. Remove the rear cable guide.

8. Remove the screw (B, **Figure 38**) securing the cable grommet to the cover.

9. Carefully pull the grommet (C, **Figure 38**) out of the cover groove.

10. Remove the assembly from the clutch outer cover.

11. Installation is the reverse of removal. Note the following:

    a. Push the pickup coil (C, **Figure 37**) down into the cover until it bottoms.

    b. Install the cable guides as shown in **Figure 39** to securely hold the cables in place away from the clutch components.

    c. Apply a low-strength threadlocking compound to all screw threads of both cable guides and pickup coil and tighten to 7 N•m (62 in.-lb.).

    d. Apply a light coat of Yamaha Quick Gasket, or an equivalent, to the grommet prior to installation.

    e. Securely seat the grommet in the cover.

Timing Rotor Removal/Installation

1. Remove the clutch outer cover as described in Chapter Seven.

2. Place an aluminum or brass washer (A, **Figure 40**) between the gears to keep the primary drive gear from rotating in Step 3.

3. Loosen the bolt (B, **Figure 40**) securing the primary drive gear and timing rotor to the crankshaft.

10

NOTE
The following steps are shown with the clutch assembly removed. It is not necessary to remove the clutch for pick up coil timing rotor removal and installation.

4. Remove the bolt (A, **Figure 41**), spacer (B) and pick up coil timing rotor (C).

5. Check the pick up coil timing rotor (**Figure 42**) for damage or distortion.

6. Position the pick up coil timing rotor with the timing marks facing out.

7. Align the locating tab on the rotor with the keyway slot in the crankshaft and install the rotor (C, **Figure 41**).

8. Apply a medium-strength threadlocking compound on the bolt threads and install the bolt (A, **Figure 41**).

9. Place an aluminum or brass washer (**Figure 43**) between the gears to keep the primary drive gear from rotating in Step 10.

11. Tighten the bolt to 115 N•m (85 ft.-lb.). Remove the washer.

12. Install the clutch outer cover as described in Chapter Seven.

DIODE (1999-2003)

The diode is part of the clutch switch/sidestand switch circuit. This procedure tests for continuity.

1. Remove the rider seat as described in Chapter Fifteen.

NOTE
Figure 44 indicates the location of the diodes; it is not shown in the photograph.

2. Disconnect the 2-pin diode connector from the diode (**Figure 44**).

3. Connect the ohmmeter positive test probe to the blue/yellow terminal (A, **Figure 45**) in the diode; connect the negative test probe to the blue/white terminal (B). The diode should have continuity in this direction.

4. Reverse the ohmmeter leads and check the continuity. The diode should not have continuity in this direction.

5. Replace the diode if it fails either portion of the test.

6. Install the rider seat as described in Chapter Fifteen.

IGNITOR UNIT

Testing

The ignitor unit cannot be tested. If all other ignition system components perform within test specifications, consider the ignitor unit defective by a process of elimination.

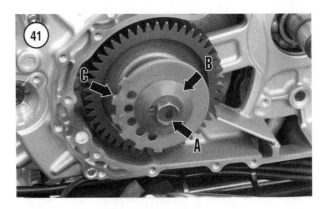

Before purchasing a new ignitor unit, have the system checked by a Yamaha dealership or qualified shop. Most motorcycle dealerships will *not* accept the return of an electrical component.

Removal/Installation

1. Securely support the motorcycle on level ground. Block the front wheel so the motorcycle will not roll in either direction.

2. Remove the rider seat as described in Chapter Fifteen.

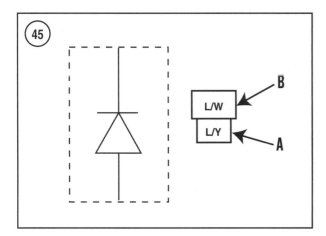

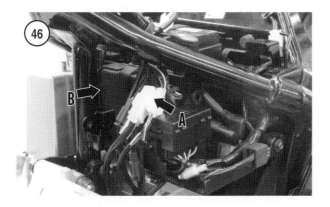

NOTE
Figure 46 *is shown with the rear cylinder and cylinder head removed to better illustrate the steps.*

3. Remove or disconnect all electrical harness clamps and tie wraps securing the electrical connectors (A, **Figure 46**) to the frame.

4. Carefully disconnect the three electrical connectors from the ignitor unit.

5. Unhook the ignition unit strap and remove the ignitor unit (B, **Figure 46**) from the battery box.

6. Installation is the reverse of removal. Note the following:

   a. Apply a dielectric compound to the electrical connectors before reconnecting them.

   b. Make sure all connections are free of corrosion and are tight; pack the connector with dielectric grease.

   c. Install all removed items.

STARTING SYSTEM

When the starter button is pressed under the correct conditions, current flows through the starter relay coil, which energizes the relay. The starter relay contacts close and load current flows directly from the battery to the starter.

The starter will only operate when the transmission is in neutral or when the clutch lever is pulled in while the sidestand is up. The starting circuit cutoff relay (SCCR) prevents the flow of control current to the starter relay unless one of these conditions has been met. The starting circuit cutoff relay is energized and the contacts close only when the neutral switch is closed (the transmission is in neutral) or when both the clutch switch and sidestand switch are closed (when the clutch lever is pulled in and the sidestand is up).

CAUTION
Do not operate the starter for more than five seconds at a time. Let it cool approximately ten seconds, then use it again.

Troubleshooting

Refer to Chapter Two.

STARTER

Operational Test

1. Securely support the motorcycle on level ground. Block the front wheel so the motorcycle will not roll in either direction.

2. Shift the transmission into neutral.

3. Turn the ignition switch off.

4. Disconnect the negative battery cable.

5. Pull back the rubber boot (A, **Figure 47**) and disconnect the electrical cable from the starter terminal (B). Disconnect the positive battery cable from the battery. Secure the cable so it will not make contact with the frame or surrounding components.

6. Reconnect the negative battery cable.

> *WARNING*
> *The jumper cable used in the next step must be large enough to handle the current flow from the battery. If the wire is too small, it could melt.*

> *WARNING*
> *The following test may produce sparks. Make sure no flammable gas or fluid is in the vicinity.*

7. Connect the jumper cable from the battery positive terminal to the starter terminal. The starter should operate.
8. If the starter does not operate when battery voltage is applied, repair or replace the starter. Reverse these steps when the test is complete.

Removal/Installation

1. Securely support the motorcycle on level ground. Block the front wheel so the motorcycle will not roll in either direction.
2. Turn the ignition switch off.
3. Disconnect the negative battery cable as described in Chapter Three.
4. Remove the front horn as described in this chapter.
5. Pull back the rubber boot (A, **Figure 47**) and disconnect the electrical cable from the starter terminal (B).
6. Remove the two starter mounting bolts (**Figure 48**). Pull the starter toward the left and remove it.
7. Installation is the reverse of removal. Note the following:
   a. Install a *new* O-ring (**Figure 49**). Lubricate the O-ring with lithium grease or engine oil.
   b. Tighten the starter mounting bolts (**Figure 48**) to 7 N•m (62 in.-lb.).
   c. Make sure the electrical connector is free of corrosion and the nut is tight.
   d. Pack the connector with dielectric grease.

Disassembly

Refer to **Figure 50**.

> *CAUTION*
> *The number of washers used in each starter varies. Record the number, type and thickness of the shims and washer used on both ends of the armature shaft. Store each part in order and in a divided container (**Figure 51**).*

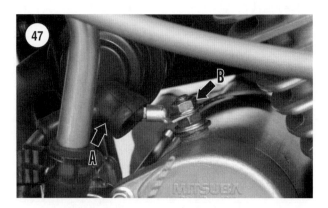

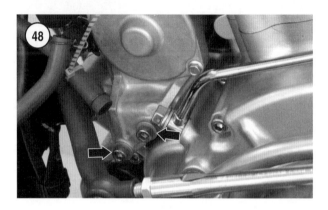

These shims and washer must be installed in their original order and positions.

1. Locate the alignment marks on the starter housing and both end covers (**Figure 52**). If the marks are not evident, make alignment marks with a permanent marking pen.
2. Loosen and remove the starter case throughbolts (**Figure 53**).
3. Remove the snap ring (**Figure 54**) securing the gear and slide the gear (**Figure 55**) off the armature shaft.
4. Slide the front cover (**Figure 56**) off of the armature shaft.

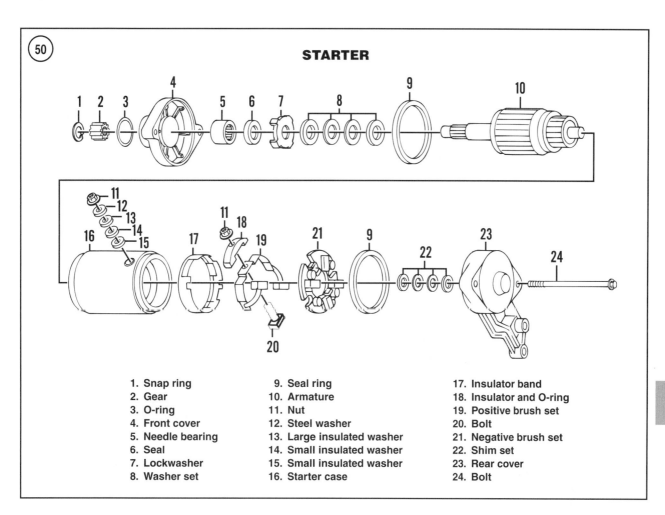

STARTER

1. Snap ring
2. Gear
3. O-ring
4. Front cover
5. Needle bearing
6. Seal
7. Lockwasher
8. Washer set

9. Seal ring
10. Armature
11. Nut
12. Steel washer
13. Large insulated washer
14. Small insulated washer
15. Small insulated washer
16. Starter case

17. Insulator band
18. Insulator and O-ring
19. Positive brush set
20. Bolt
21. Negative brush set
22. Shim set
23. Rear cover
24. Bolt

10

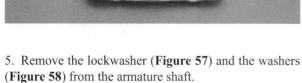

5. Remove the lockwasher (**Figure 57**) and the washers (**Figure 58**) from the armature shaft.

6. Slide the rear cover (**Figure 59**) off the armature shaft and remove the shims (A, **Figure 60**).

7. Slide the starter case off the armature.

8. Disconnect the positive brush set (A, **Figure 61**) from the negative brush holder assembly.

9. Remove the negative brush holder assembly (B, **Figure 61**).

CAUTION
*Before removing the nut and washers (**Figure 62**) in Step 10, record their description and their order. They must be reinstalled in*

the same order to insulate the positive brush set from the case.

10. Remove the nut and washers (A, **Figure 63**) securing the positive terminal bolt to the starter case.

11. Remove the terminal bolt, positive brush set (B, **Figure 63**), terminal bolt, insulator and O-ring.

> *CAUTION*
> *Do not immerse the armature coil or starter case in solvent, as the insulation may be damaged. Wipe the windings with a cloth lightly moistened in solvent and dry with compressed air.*

12. Clean all lubrication, dirt and carbon from the components.

13. Inspect the starter as described in this section.

Assembly

1. Install the positive brush set (B, **Figure 63**) as follows:
   a. Install the insulator on top of the positive brush set, then install the O-ring.

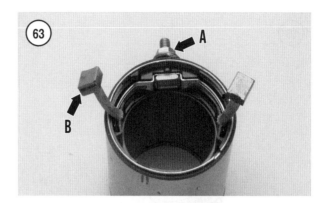

10

b. Insert the positive brush set into the starter case with the tab on the insulator facing toward the brush plate.

c. Install the terminal bolt through the brush set, the insulator and starter case.

CAUTION
Reinstall all parts in the same order as noted during disassembly. This is essential in order to insulate this set of brushes from the starter case.

d. Install the two small insulated washers over the terminal bolt.

e. Install the large insulated washer.

f. Install the steel washer.

g. Install the nut finger tight.

2. Install the negative brush plate onto the starter case, inserting the two positive brush wires through the plate as shown in A, **Figure 61**. Align the brush plate locating tab with the notch in the starter case (C, **Figure 61**).

3. Install the brushes into their receptacles. Install a small shim between each spring and brush (**Figure 64**) to eliminate spring pressure on the brushes.

4. Position the commutator end of the armature toward the negative brush plate and slowly insert the armature

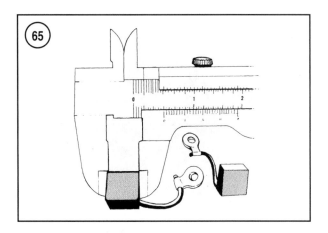

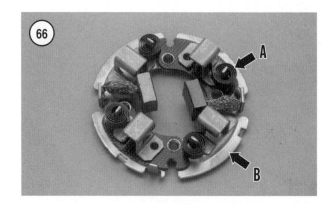

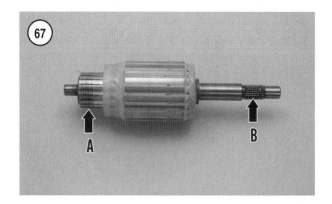

into the front of the starter case. Do not damage the brushes during this step.

5. Remove the shims (**Figure 64**) installed in Step 3.

6. Make sure that each brush seats squarely against the commutator (B, **Figure 60**).

7. Install the shims (A, **Figure 60**) onto the commutator end of the shaft.

8. Install the seal ring onto each end of the case groove and apply a light coat of oil to the seal.

9. Make sure the brush plate locating tab is still aligned with the notch in the starter case (C, **Figure 61**).

10. Install the rear cover (**Figure 59**) and push it on until it bottoms.

11. Install the washers (B, **Figure 58**) onto the front of the armature shaft.

12. Position the lockwasher with the tabs facing out (**Figure 57**) and install it onto the shaft.

13. Install the front cover (**Figure 56**) onto the shaft and correctly index the lockwasher.

14. Align the index marks (**Figure 52**) on all three components.

15. Install the throughbolts (**Figure 53**) and tighten securely.

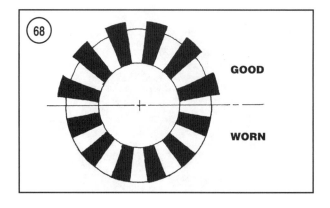

> *NOTE*
> *If the throughbolt does not extend past the starter case and through the end covers, the components are installed incorrectly.*

16. Install the gear (**Figure 55**) onto the shaft.

17. Install a *new* snap ring onto the shaft and make sure it is correctly seated in the shaft groove (**Figure 54**).

Inspection

Check with a Yamaha dealership regarding what replacement components are available for the starter.

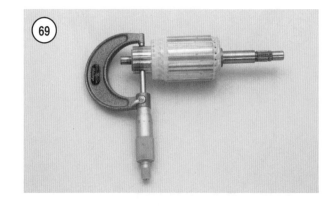

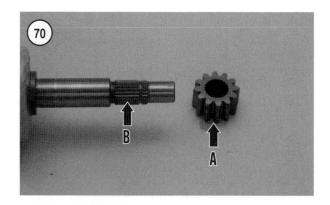

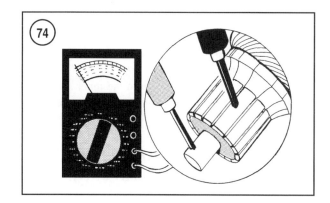

1. Measure the length of each brush (**Figure 65**) with a vernier caliper. If any brush is too short, replace both brush sets as part of the brush replacement parts set.

2. Inspect the brush springs (A, **Figure 66**) for fatigue, cracks or other damage. Replace the negative brush plate (B, **Figure 66**) if the springs (A) are severely worn or damaged. The positive brush plate is part of the brush replacement parts set.

3. Inspect the commutator (A, **Figure 67**) for abnormal wear or discoloration; neither condition can be repaired and requires replacement of the armature.

4. The mica in a good commutator is below the surface of the copper bars. On a worn commutator the mica and copper bars may be worn to the same level (**Figure 68**). If necessary, undercut the mica between each pair of bars.

5. Measure the outside diameter of the commutator (**Figure 69**) and compare to the dimension in **Table 1**.

6. Check the armature shaft splines (B, **Figure 67**) for the gear for wear or damage. Slide the gear (A, **Figure 70**) onto the shaft splines (B) and check for positive engagement.

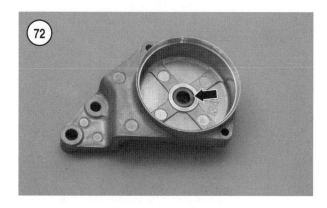

7. Inspect the gear (A, **Figure 70**) for chipped or missing teeth. If worn or damaged, also inspect the starter reduction gear for damage.

8. Inspect the front cover seal and needle bearing (**Figure 71**) for wear or damage.

9. Inspect the rear cover bushing (**Figure 72**) for severe wear or damage.

10. Use an ohmmeter to make the following tests:
   a. Check for continuity between the commutator bars (**Figure 73**); there should be continuity between pairs of bars.
   b. Check for continuity between the commutator bars and the shaft (**Figure 74**); there should be no continuity.
   c. If the commutator fails either of these tests, replace the starter assembly. The armature is not available separately.

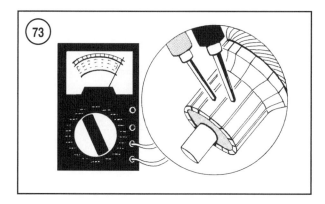

10

11. Check for continuity between the positive terminal and rear cover; there should be no continuity.

12. Install *new* seal rings (**Figure 75**) if they are starting to deteriorate or harden.

13. Check the magnets bonded into the inner surface of the starter case. If damaged or loose, replace the starter assembly.

STARTING CIRCUIT
CUTOFF RELAY (RELAY UNIT)

The starting circuit cutoff relay (SCCR), part of the relay unit, interrupts the flow of current to the starter relay unless the transmission is in neutral or unless the clutch lever is pulled in and the sidestand is in the up position.

SCCR Removal/Installation

1. Securely support the motorcycle on level ground. Block the front wheel so the motorcycle will not roll in either direction.

2. Turn the ignition switch off.

3. Disconnect the negative battery cable as described in Chapter Three.

4. Remove both seats as described in Chapter Fifteen.

5. Remove both frame side covers as described in Chapter Fifteen.

6. Remove the relay unit (**Figure 76**) from the frame mount and disconnect the 12-pin electrical connector from the relay.

7. Installation is the reverse of removal. Make sure all connections are free of corrosion and are tight; pack the connector with dielectric grease.

SCCR Continuity Test

1. Remove the starting circuit cutoff relay as described in this section.

2. Disconnect the 12-pin electrical connector from the relay unit.

3. Check the continuity of the starting circuit cutoff relay as follows:

    a. Use jumpers to connect the positive battery terminal to the red/black terminal in the relay (A, **Figure 77**); connect the negative battery terminal to the black/yellow terminal (B).

    b. Connect the ohmmeter positive test lead to the blue terminal (C, **Figure 77**) in the relay and connect the negative test lead to the blue/white terminal (D).

    c. The unit should have continuity during this test.

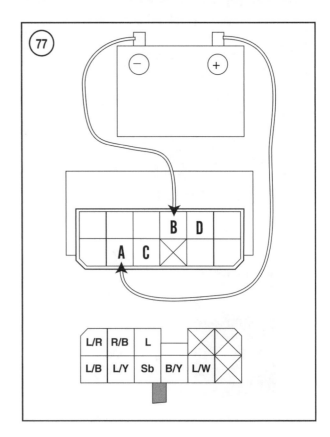

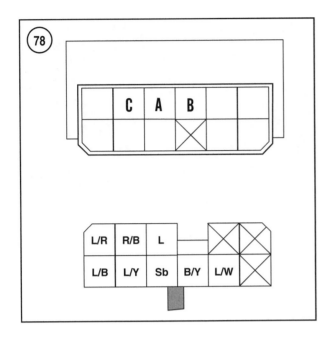

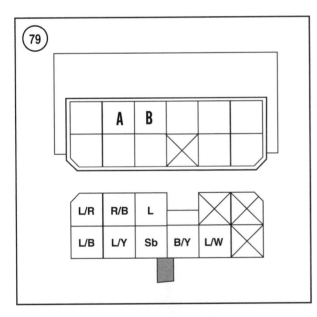

4. Replace the relay unit if there is no continuity at any one location.

SCCR Diode Test (Starting Circuit)

1. Remove the starting circuit cutoff relay as described in this chapter.
2. Disconnect the 12-pin electrical connector from the relay unit.
3. Check the continuity of the starting system diode portion of the relay as follows:

a. Connect the ohmmeter positive test lead to the sky blue terminal (A, **Figure 78**) in the relay; connect the negative test lead to the black/yellow terminal (B). The diode should have continuity.
b. Connect the ohmmeter positive test lead to the sky blue terminal (A, **Figure 78**) in the relay; connect the negative test lead to the blue/yellow terminal (C). The diode should have continuity.
c. Connect the ohmmeter negative test lead to the sky blue terminal (A, **Figure 78**) in the relay; connect the positive test lead to the black/yellow terminal (B). The diode should have no continuity.
d. Connect the ohmmeter negative test lead to the sky blue terminal (A, **Figure 78**) in the relay; connect the positive test lead to the blue/yellow terminal (C). The diode should have no continuity.

4. Replace the relay unit if the starting system diode fails any part of the test.

SCCR Diode Test (Ignition Circuit)

1. Remove the starting circuit cutoff relay as described in this chapter.
2. Disconnect the 12-pin electrical connector from the relay unit.
3. Check the continuity of the ignition system diode portion of the relay as follows:

a. Connect the ohmmeter positive test lead to the blue/yellow terminal (A, **Figure 79**) in the relay; connect the negative test lead to the sky blue terminal (B). The diode should have continuity.
b. Reverse the connectors and check the continuity. The diode should have no continuity when the positive test lead is connected to the sky blue terminal in the relay unit (B, **Figure 79**) and the negative test lead is connected to the blue/yellow terminal (A).

4. Replace the relay unit if the ignition system diode fails either portion of the test.

STARTER RELAY

Removal/Installation

1. Securely support the motorcycle on level ground. Block the front wheel so the motorcycle will not roll in either direction.
2. Turn the ignition switch off.
3. Disconnect the negative battery cable as described in Chapter Three.
4. Remove the rider seat as described in Chapter Fifteen.
5. Remove the left side frame side cover as described in Chapter Fifteen.

6. Pull back the boot on each starter relay cable connector and remove the terminal nuts.

7. Disconnect the red battery lead (A, **Figure 80**) from the positive relay terminal and disconnect the black (B) starter lead.

8. Remove the relay from the rubber mount.

9. Press the release tab on the 4-pin connector (C, **Figure 80**) and disconnect the connector from the starter relay and remove the relay.

10. Installation is the reverse of removal. Note the following:

    a. Install the relay in the rubber mount.

    b. Make sure all connections are free of corrosion and are tight; pack the connector with dielectric grease.

    c. Tighten the relay terminal nuts to 7 N•m (62 in.-lb.).

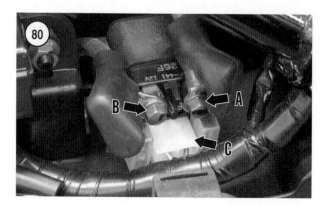

Continuity Test

1. Remove the starter relay as described in this section.

2. Use jumper wires to connect the positive battery terminal to the red/white terminal (A, **Figure 81**) in the relay connector; connect the negative battery terminal to the blue terminal (B) in the relay connector.

3. Connect the ohmmeter positive test lead to the large red (C, **Figure 81**) terminal in the relay; connect the negative test lead to the large black terminal (D). The relay should have continuity.

4. Replace the starter relay if it fails this test.

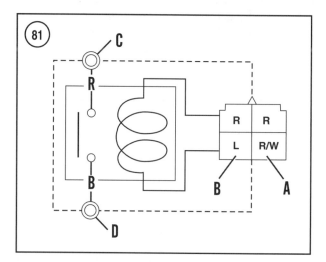

LIGHTING SYSTEM

The lighting system consists of the headlight, taillight, high beam indicator light, meter illumination lights, front turn signal/position light and rear turn signal light. If there is trouble with any of these lights, check the affected bulb first. Bulb specifications are in **Table 2**. If the bulb is good, follow the lighting system troubleshooting procedures in Chapter Two.

HEADLIGHT

Headlight Bulb and Lens Replacement

WARNING
If the headlight has just burned out or just has just been turned off, the bulb will be hot. Do not touch the bulb until it cools.

CAUTION
All models are equipped with a quartz-halogen bulb. Do not touch the bulb glass with your fingers, because traces of oil on the

bulb will drastically reduce the life of the bulb. Clean the bulb with a cloth moistened in alcohol or lacquer thinner.

1. Remove the mounting screw (**Figure 82**) on each side of the headlight housing and lower the lens assembly from the housing.

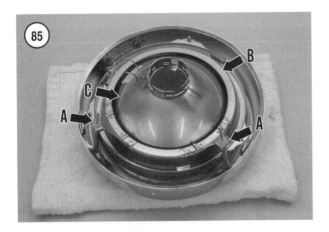

2. Disconnect the headlight connector (**Figure 83**) from the bulb and remove the lens assembly.

3. Remove the boot from the lens assembly.

4. Release the securing clip (A, **Figure 84**), and remove the bulb (B) from the lens assembly.

5. To remove the lens, proceed as follows:

    a. Completely unscrew and remove both adjuster nuts and springs (A, **Figure 85**).

    b. Unhook the mounting ring (B, **Figure 85**) from the headlight rim.

    c. Remove the mounting ring and lens assembly from the headlight rim.

    d. Remove the screws and washers securing the retaining ring and lens to the mounting ring.

    e. Separate the lens (C, **Figure 85**) from the retaining ring.

6. Installation is the reverse of removal. Note the following:

    a. Install the bulb and make sure the projections on the bulb engage the slots (C, **Figure 84**) in the lens assembly.

    b. Make sure all electrical connectors are free of corrosion; pack the connector with dielectric grease.

Headlight Housing Removal/Installation

Refer to **Figure 86**.

1. Pull straight out and remove the trim cap (**Figure 87**) from the turn signal mounting bracket.

2. Remove the mounting screw (**Figure 82**) on both sides of the headlight housing and lower the lens assembly from the housing.

3. Disconnect the headlight connector (**Figure 83**) from the bulb and remove the lens assembly.

4. Remove the screws and washers (A, **Figure 88**) securing the headlight housing to the mounting brackets.

5. Feed the wiring harness lead and the turn signal leads through the opening in the headlight housing (B, **Figure 88**).

6. Remove the housing from the headlight bracket.

7. Installation is the reverse of removal. Note the following:

    a. Make sure the electrical connectors are free of corrosion; pack the connectors with dielectric grease.

    b. Adjust the headlight as described in this section.

    c. Tighten the headlight housing screws securely.

Headlight Adjustment

Adjust the headlight horizontally and vertically according to the local Department of Motor Vehicles regulations.

1. To adjust the beam to the right, turn the horizontal adjuster (**Figure 89**) counterclockwise. To adjust the beam to the left, turn the adjuster clockwise.

2. To raise the beam, turn the vertical adjuster (**Figure 90**) clockwise. To lower the beam, turn the adjuster counterclockwise.

10

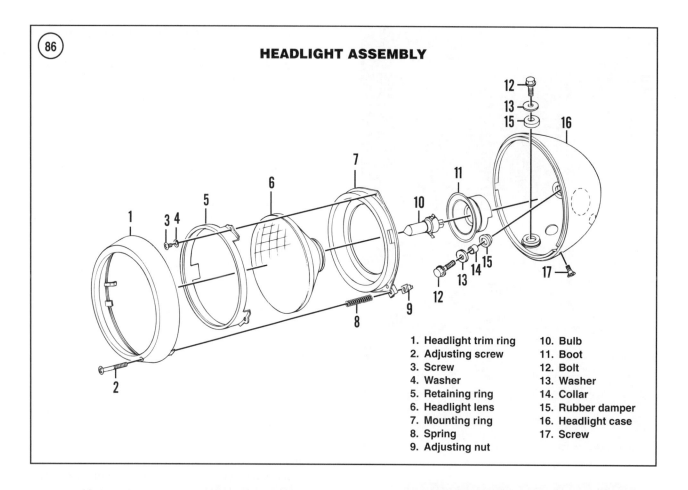

86 **HEADLIGHT ASSEMBLY**

1. Headlight trim ring
2. Adjusting screw
3. Screw
4. Washer
5. Retaining ring
6. Headlight lens
7. Mounting ring
8. Spring
9. Adjusting nut
10. Bulb
11. Boot
12. Bolt
13. Washer
14. Collar
15. Rubber damper
16. Headlight case
17. Screw

Headlight Voltage Test

If the headlight does not turn on but its bulb is in good working order, test the headlight circuit voltage as follows.

1. Remove the mounting screw (**Figure 82**) on both sides of the headlight housing and lower the lens assembly from the housing.

2. Disconnect the headlight connector (**Figure 83**) from the bulb and remove the lens assembly.

3. Set a voltmeter to the DC 20 volt range.

4. Turn the dimmer switch to LO, and check the voltage as follows:

   a. Connect the voltmeter negative test lead to the black terminal (A, **Figure 91**) in the headlight connector; connect the voltmeter positive test lead to the green terminal (B).

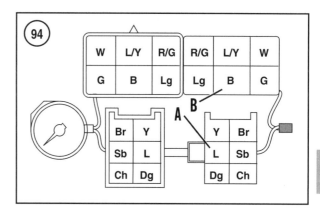

10

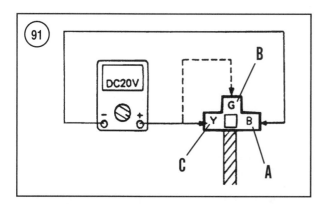

b. Turn the ignition switch on and check the voltmeter. It should read battery voltage.

5. Turn the dimmer switch to HI, and check the voltage as follows:

   a. Connect the voltmeter negative test lead to the black terminal (A, **Figure 91**) in the headlight connector; connect the voltmeter positive lead to the yellow terminal (C).

   b. Turn the ignition switch on, and check the voltmeter. It should read battery voltage.

6. Cover the fuel tank with a towel (A, **Figure 92**) to protect the finish.

7. Remove the front screw (A, **Figure 93**) on each side and the rear screw and washer (B) securing the meter assembly to the fuel tank.

8. Partially remove the meter assembly and disconnect the two meter assembly 6-pin electrical connectors (B, **Figure 92**).

9. Connect the voltmeter positive test lead to the yellow terminal (A, **Figure 94**) in the harness side of the connector; connect the voltmeter negative test probe to the black terminal (B).

10. Turn the ignition switch on and turn the dimmer switch to HI. The meter should read battery voltage.

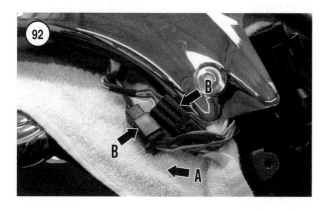

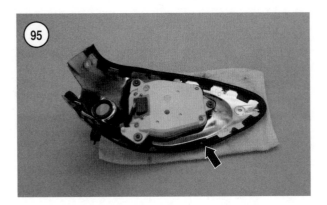

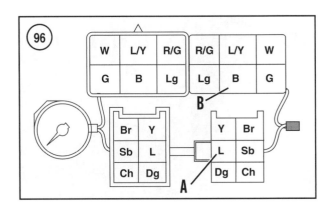

11. If any voltage reading does not equal battery voltage, the wiring between the ignition switch and the headlight connector is faulty.

METER ASSEMBLY

Removal/Installation

1. Remove the front screw (A, **Figure 93**) on each side and the rear screw and washer (B) securing the meter assembly to the fuel tank.

2. Cover the fuel tank with a towel (A, **Figure 92**) to protect the finish.

3. Partially remove the meter assembly and disconnect the two meter assembly 6-pin electrical connectors (B, **Figure 92**).

4. Remove the meter assembly from the fuel tank.

5. Installation is the reverse of removal. Note the following:

    a. Make sure the trim gasket (**Figure 95**) is in place around the perimeter of the meter assembly.

    b. Make sure all connections are free of corrosion.

    c. Apply a dielectric compound to the electrical connectors before reconnecting them.

    d. Make sure the connectors are tight.

    e. Tighten the screw securely.

Meter Indicator Light Test

If the meter illumination lights do not operate, perform the following test.

1. Remove the front screw (A, **Figure 93**) on each side and the rear screw and washer (B) securing the meter assembly to the fuel tank.

2. Cover the fuel tank with a towel (A, **Figure 92**) to protect the finish.

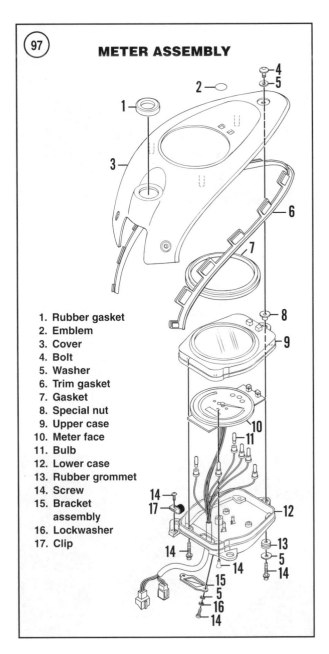

METER ASSEMBLY

1. Rubber gasket
2. Emblem
3. Cover
4. Bolt
5. Washer
6. Trim gasket
7. Gasket
8. Special nut
9. Upper case
10. Meter face
11. Bulb
12. Lower case
13. Rubber grommet
14. Screw
15. Bracket assembly
16. Lockwasher
17. Clip

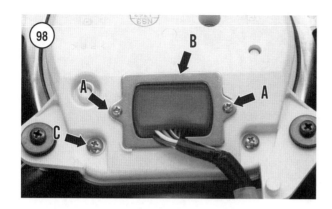

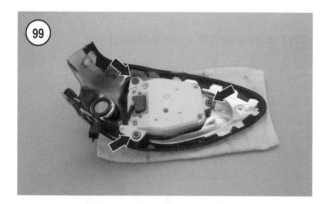

3. Partially remove the meter assembly and disconnect the two meter assembly 6-pin electrical connectors (B, **Figure 92**).

4. Check the voltage in the illumination light circuit as follows:

   a. Set a voltmeter to the 20 DC volt range.

   b. Connect the voltmeter positive test lead to the blue terminal (A, **Figure 96**) in the harness side of one of the meter connectors; connect the voltmeter negative test lead to the black terminal (B) in the other connector.

   c. Turn the ignition switch on.

   d. If the voltmeter does not read battery voltage, the wiring between the ignition switch and the meter connector is faulty. Make the necessary repairs.

5. Make sure all connections are free of corrosion and are tight; pack the connector with dielectric grease.

6. Tighten the meter assembly screws securely.

Meter Indicator Light Replacement

Refer to **Figure 97**.

1. Remove the meter assembly as described in this section.

2. Turn the meter assembly upside down on shop cloths.

3. Remove the screws, spring washer and washer (A, **Figure 98**) securing the bracket (B) and remove the bracket assembly.

4. Remove the screws and washers (**Figure 99**) securing the meter assembly to the case. Remove the meter assembly.

5. Remove the screw (C, **Figure 98**) at each corner of the lower case. Carefully separate the upper and lower case.

6. Replace the faulty bulb(s).

7. Assemble the upper and lower case and secure with the screws (C, **Figure 98**). Tighten the screws securely.

8. Make sure the gasket is in place on the cover.

9. Install the meter assembly onto the gasket and install the screws and washers (**Figure 99**). Tighten the screws securely.

10. Install the bracket assembly (B, **Figure 98**), the washer, spring washer and screws (A, **Figure 98**). Tighten the screws securely.

11. Install a new rubber grommet (**Figure 100**) if starting to harden or deteriorate.

TAILLIGHT/BRAKE LIGHT (1999-2003 MODELS)

Taillight/Brake Light Replacement

1. Remove the mounting screws (A, **Figure 101**) and carefully remove the taillight lens (B) from the taillight assembly.

2. Turn the bulb (A, **Figure 102**) counterclockwise and remove it.

3. Push the new bulb into the socket and turn it clockwise to lock it in position.

4. Make sure the gasket (B, **Figure 102**) is in place and reinstall the lens.

5. Install the screws and tighten securely.

10

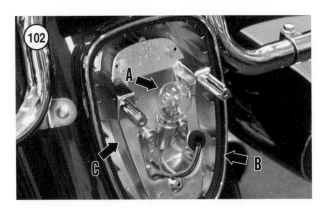

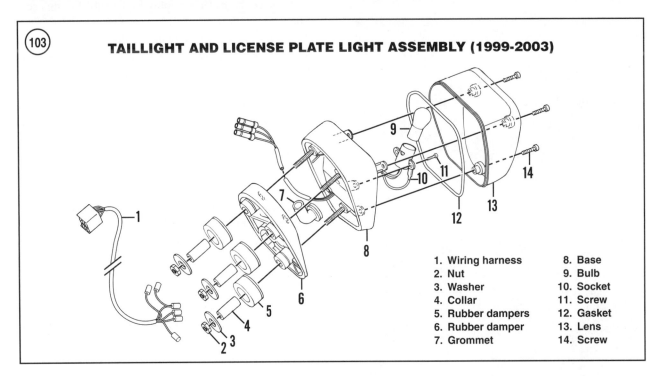

TAILLIGHT AND LICENSE PLATE LIGHT ASSEMBLY (1999-2003)

1. Wiring harness   8. Base
2. Nut   9. Bulb
3. Washer   10. Socket
4. Collar   11. Screw
5. Rubber dampers   12. Gasket
6. Rubber damper   13. Lens
7. Grommet   14. Screw

Taillight/Brake Light Assembly Removal/Installation

Refer to **Figure 103**.

1. Securely support the motorcycle on level ground. Block the front wheel so the motorcycle will not roll in either direction.

2. Remove the mounting screws (A, **Figure 101**) and carefully remove the taillight lens (B) from the taillight assembly.

3. Remove the cover from the license plate bracket.

4. Disconnect the black, blue and yellow taillight bullet connectors inside the housing on the license plate bracket (**Figure 104**).

5. Working under the rear fender, remove the nuts and washers securing the taillight base (C, **Figure 102**) to the rear fender.

6. Remove the base, rubber dampers and wiring harness from the rear fender. Do not lose the collars within the round rubber dampers.

7. Installation is the reverse of removal. Note the following:
    a. Make sure all connections are free of corrosion.
    b. Apply a dielectric compound to the electrical connectors before reconnecting them.
    c. Make sure the connectors are tight.

Taillight and Brake Light Test

If a taillight does not operate, test the circuit as follows:

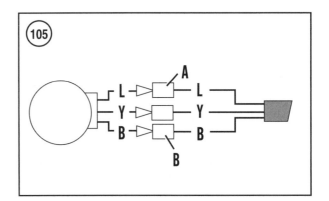

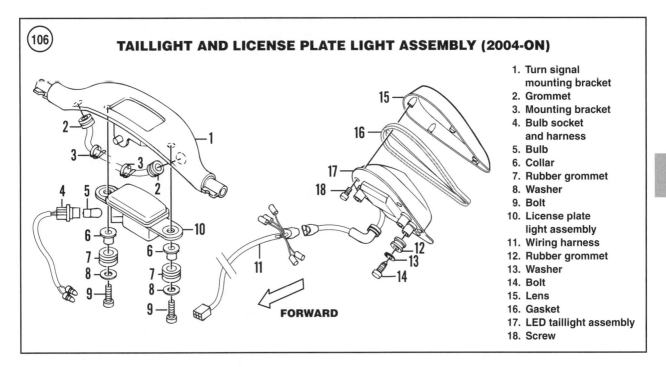

TAILLIGHT AND LICENSE PLATE LIGHT ASSEMBLY (2004-ON)

1. Turn signal mounting bracket
2. Grommet
3. Mounting bracket
4. Bulb socket and harness
5. Bulb
6. Collar
7. Rubber grommet
8. Washer
9. Bolt
10. License plate light assembly
11. Wiring harness
12. Rubber grommet
13. Washer
14. Bolt
15. Lens
16. Gasket
17. LED taillight assembly
18. Screw

FORWARD

10

1. Set a voltmeter to the 20 DC volt range.

2. Remove the license plate from the bracket.

3. Disconnect the black and blue taillight bullet connectors inside the housing on the license plate bracket (**Figure 104**).

4. Connect the voltmeter positive test lead to the harness side of the blue bullet connector (A, **Figure 105**).

5. Connect the voltmeter negative test lead to the harness side of the black bullet connector (B, **Figure 105**).

6. Turn the ignition switch on.

7. If the voltmeter does not read battery voltage, the wiring between the ignition switch and the taillight/brake light connector is faulty. Make the necessary repairs.

8. Make sure all connections are free of corrosion and are tight; pack the connector with dielectric grease.

**TAILLIGHT/BRAKE LIGHT
(2004-ON MODELS)**

Taillight/Brake Light Replacement

The taillight/brake light portion of the assembly is a sealed LED unit and must be replaced as an assembly. Only the lens and gasket are available as replacement parts.

**Taillight/Brake Light Assembly
Removal/Installation**

Refer to **Figure 106**.

1. Securely support the motorcycle on level ground. Block the front wheel so the motorcycle will not roll in either direction.

2. Remove the rear bolt (**Figure 107**) on each side of the fender stay or backrest mounting bracket.

3. Working under the rear fender, perform the following:
   a. Remove the screws securing the rear fender under shield and remove the under shield.
   b. Remove the screws and washers securing the taillight/brake light assembly to the rear fender.

4. Disconnect the black, blue and yellow taillight bullet connectors under the rear fender.

5. Remove the taillight/brake light assembly (**Figure 108**) from the rear fender. Do not lose the collars within the round rubber dampers.

6. Remove the screw securing the lens to the LED assembly and remove the lens and gasket. Install the gasket and lens and tighten the screws securely.

7. Installation is the reverse of removal. Note the following:
   a. Make sure all connections are free of corrosion.
   b. Apply a dielectric compound to the electrical connectors before reconnecting them.
   c. Make sure the connectors are tight.

Taillight/Brake Light Test

The manufacturer does not provide any test procedures for the taillight and brake light assembly.

LICENSE PLATE LIGHT
(2004-ON MODELS)

Removal/Installation

Refer to **Figure 106**.

1. Securely support the motorcycle on level ground. Block the front wheel so the motorcycle will not roll in either direction.

2. To protect the taillight/brake light finish, remove the assembly (A, **Figure 109**) as described in this chapter.

3. Disconnect the two license plate bullet connectors under the rear fender.

4. Remove the bolts securing the rear turn signal mounting bracket assembly (B, **Figure 109**) to the rear fender and remove the assembly.

5. Pull the license plate socket assembly from the license plate assembly.

6. Remove the bulb from the socket assembly and install a new bulb.

7. If necessary, remove the bolts and washers securing the license plate assembly to the mounting bracket. Do not lose the collar in the rubber grommets.

8. Installation is the reverse of removal. Note the following:
   a. Make sure all connections are free of corrosion.

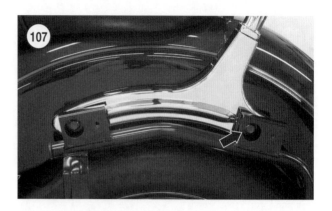

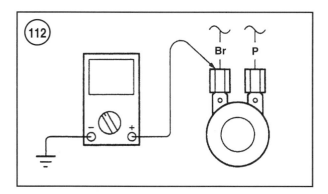

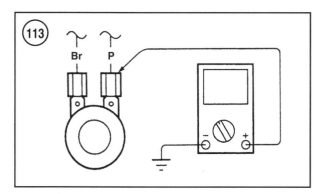

b. Apply a dielectric compound to the electrical connectors before reconnecting them.

c. Make sure the connectors are tight.

SIGNAL SYSTEM

The signal system includes the horn, turn signal lights, brake light and indicator lights (except the high beam indicator, which is part of the lighting system). In the event of trouble with any of these lights, check the affected bulb/component first. Bulb specifications are in **Table 2**. If the bulb is good, follow the signal system troubleshooting procedures in Chapter Two.

HORN

Removal/Installation

Both horns are mounted on the left side of the frame.

1. To remove the front horn, perform the following:
   a. Remove the horn mounting bolts (**Figure 110**).
   b. Disconnect the connectors from the two spade terminals on the back of the horn and remove the horn.
2. To remove the front horn, perform the following:
   a. Remove the horn mounting bolts (**Figure 111**).
   b. Disconnect the connectors from the two spade terminals on the back of the horn and remove the horn.
3. Installation is the reverse of removal. Make sure all spade connections are free of corrosion and are tight.

Circuit Test

Perform the following test if either or both of the horns do not sound.

1. Check the continuity of the horn switch as described in this chapter. Replace the left handlebar switch if the horn switch is faulty.
2. Check the voltage on the battery side of the horn circuit as follows:
   a. Set a voltmeter to the 20 DC volt range.
   b. Back probe the connector. Connect the voltmeter positive test lead to the brown horn terminal and connect the negative test lead to a good frame ground (**Figure 112**).
   c. Turn the ignition switch on and check the voltage on the meter. It should read battery voltage.
   d. If the reading is less than battery voltage, the wiring between the ignition switch and the horn is faulty.
3. Check the voltage on the ground side of the horn circuit as follows:
   a. Set a voltmeter to the DC 20 volt range.
   b. Back probe the connector. Connect the voltmeter positive test lead to the pink horn terminal and connect the negative test lead to a good frame ground (**Figure 113**).
   c. Turn the ignition switch on and check the voltage on the meter. It should read battery voltage.
   d. If the voltage is less than battery voltage, replace the horn.
4. Repeat Steps 1-3 for the remaining horn.

TURN SIGNALS

Refer to **Figure 114** and **Figure 115**.

10

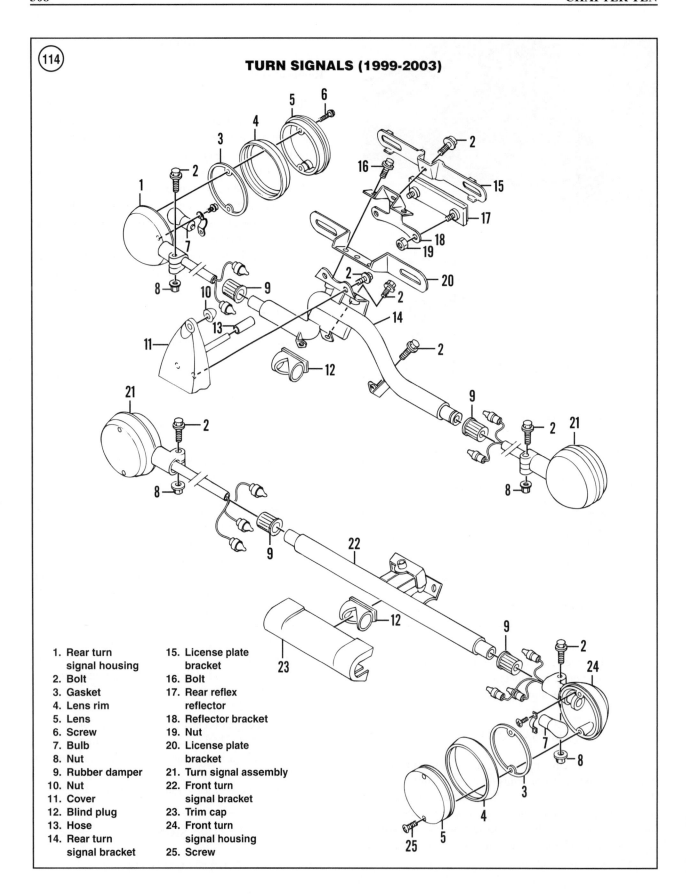

TURN SIGNALS (1999-2003)

1. Rear turn
   signal housing
2. Bolt
3. Gasket
4. Lens rim
5. Lens
6. Screw
7. Bulb
8. Nut
9. Rubber damper
10. Nut
11. Cover
12. Blind plug
13. Hose
14. Rear turn
    signal bracket
15. License plate
    bracket
16. Bolt
17. Rear reflex
    reflector
18. Reflector bracket
19. Nut
20. License plate
    bracket
21. Turn signal assembly
22. Front turn
    signal bracket
23. Trim cap
24. Front turn
    signal housing
25. Screw

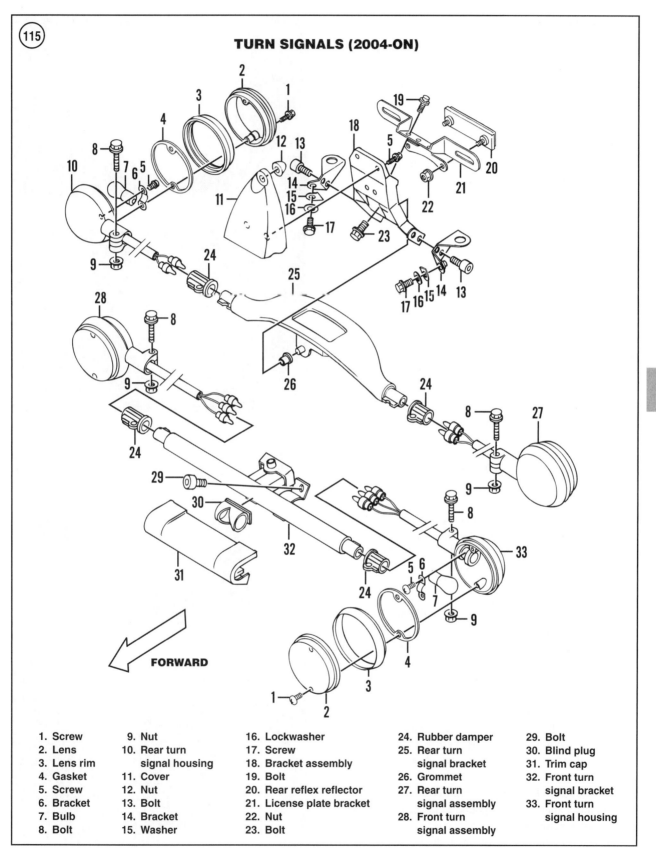

TURN SIGNALS (2004-ON)

FORWARD

10

1. Screw	9. Nut	16. Lockwasher	24. Rubber damper	29. Bolt
2. Lens	10. Rear turn	17. Screw	25. Rear turn	30. Blind plug
3. Lens rim	signal housing	18. Bracket assembly	signal bracket	31. Trim cap
4. Gasket	11. Cover	19. Bolt	26. Grommet	32. Front turn
5. Screw	12. Nut	20. Rear reflex reflector	27. Rear turn	signal bracket
6. Bracket	13. Bolt	21. License plate bracket	signal assembly	33. Front turn
7. Bulb	14. Bracket	22. Nut	28. Front turn	signal housing
8. Bolt	15. Washer	23. Bolt	signal assembly	

Turn Signal Bulb Replacement

1. Remove the screws and remove the lens (**Figure 116**) and rim from the housing.

2. Wash the inside and outside of the lens with a mild detergent.

3. Turn the bulb (A, **Figure 117**) counterclockwise and remove it. Install the new bulb and turn it clockwise to lock it in place.

4. Make sure the gasket (B, **Figure 117**) is in place on the housing. Replace if it is hard or deteriorated.

5. Install the lens ring and lens. Do not over tighten the lens screws as this will crack the lens.

Turn Signal Assembly Removal/Installation

Front turn signal

1. Securely support the motorcycle on level ground. Block the rear wheel so the motorcycle will not roll in either direction.

2. Remove the mounting screw (**Figure 118**) on each side of the headlight housing and lower the lens assembly from the housing.

3. Disconnect the headlight connector (**Figure 119**) from the bulb and remove the lens assembly.

4. Disconnect the front turn signal bullet connectors (**Figure 120**) for either or both turn signal(s).

5. Feed the turn signal wires out through the hole in the headlight housing.

6. Remove the screws (A, **Figure 121**, typical) and remove the lens (B) and rim from the housing.

7. Remove the nut from the clamp bolt (C, **Figure 121**), and pull the turn signal assembly and its wires from the mounting bracket. Do not lose the rubber damper on the end of the mounting bracket.

8. To remove the turn signals and the mounting bracket assembly, perform the following:

    a. Remove the headlight case assembly as described in this chapter.

    b. Remove both windshield mounting brackets (A, **Figure 122**) as described in Chapter Fifteen, models so equipped.

    c. Remove the mounting bolts and remove the turn signal mounting bracket (B, **Figure 122**).

9. Installation is the reverse of removal. Note the following.

    a. Make sure all connections are free of corrosion.

    b. Apply a dielectric compound to the electrical connectors before reconnecting them.

    c. Make sure the connectors are tight.

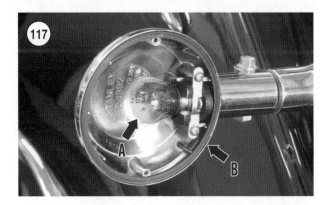

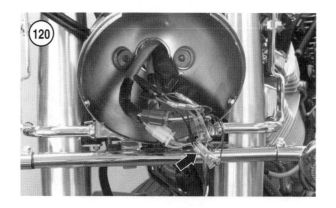

Rear turn signal (1999-2003 models)

1. Securely support the motorcycle on level ground. Block the front wheel so the motorcycle will not roll in either direction.

2. Remove the cover from the license plate bracket.

3. Disconnect the rear turn signal bullet connectors for either or both turn signal(s) inside the housing on the license plate bracket (**Figure 104**).

4. Remove the screws and remove the lens (**Figure 116**) from the housing.

5. Remove the nut from the clamp bolt (**Figure 123**, typical), and pull the turn signal assembly and its wires from the mounting bracket. Do not lose the rubber damper on the end of the mounting bracket.

6. To remove the both turn signals and the mounting bracket assembly, proceed as follows:

    a. Remove the bolt (**Figure 124**) on each side securing the mounting bracket to the rear fender.

    b. Slowly remove the bracket assembly while carefully pulling the electrical harness through the opening in the rear fender.

7. Installation is the reverse of removal. Note the following.

    a. Make sure all connections are free of corrosion.

    b. Apply a dielectric compound to the electrical connectors before reconnecting them.

    c. Make sure the connectors are tight.

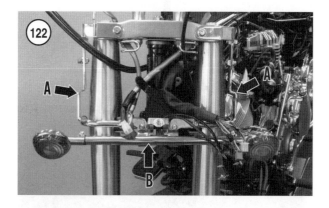

Rear turn signal (2004-on models)

1. Securely support the motorcycle on level ground. Block the front wheel so the motorcycle will not roll in either direction.

2. Remove the cover from the license plate bracket.

3. Disconnect the rear turn signal bullet connectors for either or both turn signal(s) inside the housing on the license plate bracket.

10

4. Remove the screws and remove the lens (**Figure 116**) from the housing.

5. Remove the nut from the clamp bolt (**Figure 123**, typical), and pull the turn signal assembly and its wires from the mounting bracket. Do not lose the rubber damper on the end of the mounting bracket.

6. To remove the turn signals and the mounting bracket assembly, proceed as follows:

    a. To protect the taillight/brake light finish, remove the assembly (A, **Figure 109**) as described in this section.

    b. Disconnect the two license plate bullet connectors and the four turn signal bullet connectors under the rear fender.

    c. Remove the bolts securing the rear turn signal mounting bracket assembly (B, **Figure 109**) to the rear fender.

    d. Slowly remove the bracket assembly while carefully pulling the electrical harness through the opening in the rear fender and remove the assembly.

7. Installation is the reverse of removal. Note the following.

    a. Make sure all connections are free of corrosion.

    b. Apply a dielectric compound to the electrical connectors prior to reconnecting them.

    c. Make sure the connectors are tight.

Turn Signal Flash Test

Perform the following check if a turn signal light or the turn signal indicator light does not flash.

1. Securely support the motorcycle on level ground. Block the front wheel so the motorcycle will not roll in either direction.

2. Turn the ignition switch off.

3. Remove both seats as described in Chapter Fifteen.

4. Remove both side covers as described in Chapter Fifteen.

5. Remove the relay unit (**Figure 125**) from the mounting tang on the frame. Disconnect the 6-pin from the relay.

6. Check the voltage into the relay side of the relay circuit as follows:

    a. Set a voltmeter to the 20 DC volt range.

    b. Connect the voltmeter positive test lead to the brown terminal in the harness side of the connector (A, **Figure 126**). Connect the voltmeter negative test lead to a good ground.

    c. Turn the ignition switch on and check the voltage on the meter. It should read battery voltage.

7. Check the output voltage from the relay as follows:

    a. Set a voltmeter to the 20 DV volt range.

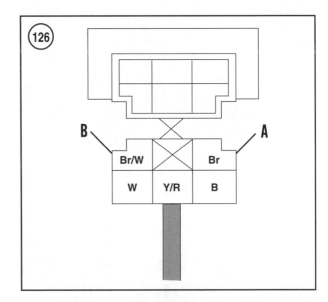

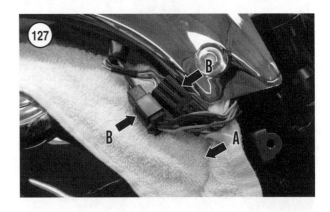

    b. Backprobe the flasher relay and connect the voltmeter positive test lead to the brown/white terminal (B, **Figure 126**). Connect the voltmeter negative test lead to a good ground.

    c. Turn the ignition switch on, and turn the flasher switch on (either left or right).

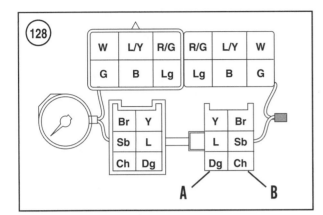

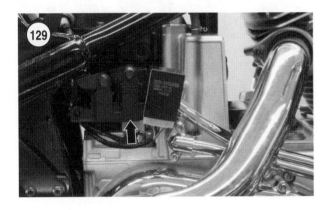

d. Check the voltage on the meter. It should read battery voltage.

e. Replace the relay if output voltage is less than battery voltage.

8. If the turn signal indicator lamp is not flashing, check the indicator lamp wiring as follows:

a. Cover the fuel tank with a towel (A, **Figure 127**) to protect the finish.

b. Remove the front screw on each side and the rear screw and washer securing the meter assembly to the fuel tank.

c. Partially remove the meter assembly and disconnect the two meter assembly six-pin electrical connectors (B, **Figure 127**).

d. Set the voltmeter to the 20 DC volt range.

e. Connect the voltmeter positive test lead to the affected terminal in the harness side of the connector: chocolate for the left side (A, **Figure 128**) and dark green for the right side (B). Connect the voltmeter negative test lead to a good frame ground.

f. Turn the ignition switch on, turn on the turn signal switch for that side, and check the voltage on the meter. It should read battery voltage.

g. If the reading is less than battery voltage, the wiring between the turn signal switch and the connector is faulty.

9. Install all components removed.

Flasher Relay Removal/Installation

The flasher relay is located on the mounting bracket next to the relay unit.

1. Securely support the motorcycle on level ground. Block the front wheel so the motorcycle will not roll in either direction.

2. Remove the rider seat as described in Chapter Fifteen.

3. Remove the frame side covers as described in Chapter Fifteen.

4. Remove the bolts securing the relay mounting bracket (**Figure 129**). Move the bracket away from the frame and carefully turn it around.

5. Disconnect the connector from the flasher relay.

6. Installation is the reverse of removal. Note the following:

a. Make sure all connections are free of corrosion.

b. Apply a dielectric compound to the electrical connectors prior to reconnecting them.

c. Make sure the connectors are tight.

PASSING LIGHT RELAY

A passing light relay and harness is provided on some later models, for use with passing lights. Use the following procedure to test the relay after it has been removed from the motorcycle.

Passing Light Relay Test

The following test requires a 12-volt battery, jumper leads and an ohmmeter.

1. Note and record the harness wire colors and their respective terminals on the relay.

2. Set the ohmmeter to read continuity.

3. Connect the ohmmeter and battery to the following terminals on the relay.

a. Connect the positive ohmmeter lead to the red/yellow terminal.

b. Connect the negative ohmmeter lead to the blue/black terminal.

c. Connect the positive battery jumper lead to the white/black terminal.

d. Connect the negative battery jumper lead to the red/black terminal.

4. Check for continuity on the ohmmeter.

a. If there is continuity, the relay is in good condition.

10

b. If there is no continuity, the relay is faulty.

5. Disconnect the battery and ohmmeter from the relay.

NEUTRAL INDICATOR LIGHT

Circuit Test

1. Securely support the motorcycle on level ground. Block the front wheel so the motorcycle will not roll in either direction.

2. Remove the rider seat as described in Chapter Fifteen.

3. Remove the front screw on each side and the rear screw and washer securing the meter assembly to the fuel tank.

4. Partially remove the meter assembly and disconnect the two meter assembly 6-pin electrical connectors (B, **Figure 127**).

5. Check the voltage in the circuit as follows:

a. Set a voltmeter to the 20 DC volt range.

b. Connect the voltmeter positive test lead to the brown terminal in the harness side of the meter assembly connector (A, **Figure 130**). Connect the voltmeter negative test lead to the sky blue terminal (B, **Figure 130**).

c. Shift the transmission into neutral, turn the ignition switch on, and check the voltage on the meter. It should read battery voltage.

d. If the reading is less than battery voltage, the wiring between the ignition switch and the meter connector is faulty.

SPEED SENSOR

NOTE
The manufacturer does not provide a test procedure for the speed sensor.

Removal/Installation

1. Securely support the motorcycle on level ground. Block the front wheel so the motorcycle will not roll in either direction.

2. Remove the rider seat as described in Chapter Fifteen.

3. Remove both frame side covers as described in Chapter Fifteen.

NOTE
Figure 131 is shown with the rear cylinder and cylinder head removed to better illustrate the steps.

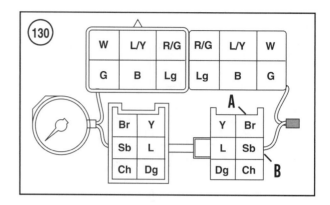

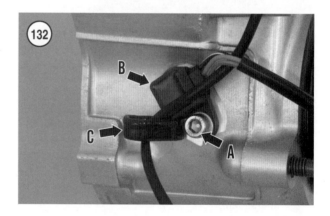

4. Disconnect the 3-pin speed sensor connector (**Figure 131**) (one blue/yellow, one white, one black/blue wire).

5. Release any cable ties or holders that secure the speed sensor wire to the frame. Note the location of these ties and note how the speed sensor wire is routed along the motorcycle.

NOTE
Figure 132 is shown with the engine removed from the frame and the crankcase disassembled to better illustrate the steps.

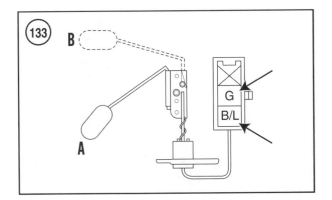

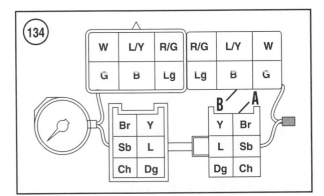

6. If the resistance is not within specification, replace the sender assembly.

7. Installation is the reverse of removal.

Circuit Test

1. Securely support the motorcycle on level ground. Block the front wheel so the motorcycle will not roll in either direction.

2. Remove the rider seat as described in Chapter Fifteen.

3. Cover the fuel tank with a towel (A, **Figure 127**) to protect the finish.

4. Remove the front screw on each side and the rear screw and washer securing the meter assembly to the fuel tank.

5. Partially remove the meter assembly and disconnect the two meter assembly 6-pin electrical connectors (B, **Figure 127**).

6. Check the voltage in the circuit as follows:

    a. Set a voltmeter to the 20 DC volt range.

    b. Connect the voltmeter positive test lead to the brown terminal in the harness side of the meter assembly connector (A, **Figure 134**). Connect the voltmeter negative test lead to the connector's blue terminal (B, **Figure 134**).

    c. If the reading is less than battery voltage, the wiring between the ignition switch and the meter connector is faulty.

6. Remove the Allen bolt (A, **Figure 132**) securing the speed sensor to the speed sensor. Withdraw the speed sensor (B, **Figure 132**) from the crankcase. Note the location of the cable guide (C, **Figure 132**).

7. Installation is the reverse of removal. Note the following:

    a. Tighten the speed sensor bolt securely.

    b. Make sure all connections are clean and tight.

DECOMPRESSION SOLENOID

NOTE
The manufacturer does not provide a test procedure for the decompression solenoid.

Removal/Installation

1. Securely support the motorcycle on level ground. Block the front wheel so the motorcycle will not roll in either direction.

2. Remove the rider seat as described in Chapter Fifteen.

3. Remove both side covers as described in Chapter Fifteen.

4. Remove the screws securing the solenoid cover (**Figure 135**) and remove the cover.

5. Disconnect the solenoid from the actuator (A, **Figure 136**) in the camshaft cover.

6. Remove the mounting bolts (B, **Figure 136**) and remove the solenoid from the crankcase.

FUEL LEVEL SENDER

Resistance Test

1. Remove the fuel level sender from the base of the fuel tank as described in Chapter Nine.

2. Connect the ohmmeter test probe to the green terminal and the other test probe to the black/blue terminal.

3. Hold the fuel level sensor in its normal operating position in the fuel tank.

4. Position the float in the normal empty position (A, **Figure 133**). There should be 140-143 ohms in this position.

5. Position the float in the normal full position (B, **Figure 133**). There should be 11-13 ohms in this position.

10

7. Follow the electrical harness from the decompression solenoid (and alternator stator) (**Figure 137**) behind the transfer gearcase assembly and up behind the fuse panel.

8. Disconnect the 3-pin white stator connector (**Figure 138**) (three white wires) from the wiring harness.

9. Disconnect the two decompression solenoid electrical connectors as follows:

   a. 2-pin brown connector (green/red and black/ blue wires).

   b. 2-pin brown connector (red/white and yellow/ black wires).

> *NOTE*
> **Figure 139** *is shown with the transfer gear-case removed to better illustrate the step.*

10. Carefully remove the two sets of wires, contained within the plastic conduit (**Figure 139**) from behind the transfer gearcase assembly and behind the fuse panel.

11. Withdraw the solenoid wire and connectors from the plastic conduit.

12. Installation is the reverse of removal. Note the following:

   a. Make sure all connections are free of corrosion.

   b. Apply a dielectric compound to the electrical connectors before reconnecting them.

   c. Make sure the connectors are tight.

SWITCHES

Testing

Test the switches for continuity with an ohmmeter or a test light (see Chapter One). The continuity diagrams for various switches are in the wiring diagrams at the back of this manual.

For example, **Figure 140** shows a continuity diagram for the horn switch. It shows which terminals should have continuity when the horn switch is in a given position.

HORN SWITCH

Button position	Wire color	
	P	B
Push	•————————•	
Off		

The line on the continuity diagram indicates that there should be continuity between the black and pink terminals when the horn switch is pressed. When the horn switch is pressed, an ohmmeter connected to the black and pink terminals should indicate little or no resistance (a test lamp should light).

The horn switch diagram also indicates there should be no continuity between these terminals when the switch is free. When the horn switch is released, the ohmmeter should indicate infinite resistance (a test lamp should not light) between the black and pink terminals.

When testing switches, note the following:
1. First check the fuses in the relevant circuit as described in this chapter.
2. Check the battery as described in Chapter Three. Charge the battery to the correct state of charge, if required.
3. Disconnect the negative battery cable if the switch connectors are not disconnected from the circuit.

CAUTION
Do not attempt to start the engine with the battery negative cable disconnected. This will damage the wiring harness.

4. When separating two connectors, pull the connector housings and not the wires.
5. After locating a defective circuit, check the connectors to make sure they are clean and properly connected. Check all wires going into a connector housing to make sure each wire is properly positioned and secure.
6. Push connectors together until they click into place.
7. When replacing a handlebar switch assembly, route the cables correctly so they will not be crimped when the handlebar is turned from side to side.

Left Handlebar Switch Replacement

1. Remove the fuel tank as described in Chapter Nine.
2. Remove the mounting screw (**Figure 141**) on both sides of the headlight housing and lower the lens assembly from the housing.

3. Disconnect the headlight connector (**Figure 142**) from the bulb and remove the lens assembly.
4. Disconnect the 6-pin blue and 6-pin white electrical connectors within the headlight case.
5. Carefully feed the left turn signal leads and connectors through the opening in the headlight housing (**Figure 143**).
6. Disconnect the two spade connectors from the clutch switch.
7. Remove the screws and separate the switch housing halves (A, **Figure 144**) from the handlebar.
8. Unhook the cables from the plastic clips on the handlebar.

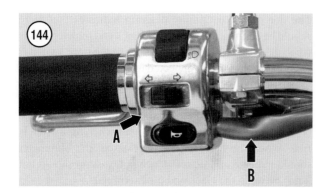

9. Remove the switch housing and wiring cable (B, **Figure 144**).

10. Installation is the reverse of these steps. Note the following:

    a. Position the switch assembly so the edge of the switch half mating surface aligns with the index mark on the handlebar.

    b. Make sure all connections are free of corrosion.

    c. Apply a dielectric compound to the electrical connectors before reconnecting them.

    d. Make sure the connectors are tight.

Right Handlebar Switch Replacement

1. Remove the fuel tank as described in Chapter Nine.

2. Remove the mounting screw (**Figure 141**) on both sides of the headlight housing and lower the lens assembly from the housing.

3. Disconnect the headlight connector (**Figure 142**) from the bulb and remove the lens assembly.

4. Disconnect the 4-pin black electrical connector within the headlight case.

5. Carefully feed the right turn signal leads and connector through the opening in the headlight housing (**Figure 143**).

6. Disconnect the two spade connectors from the front brake switch.

7. Remove the screws and separate the switch housing halves (A, **Figure 145**) from the handlebar.

8. Disconnect the throttle cables from the switch housing as described under *Throttle Cable Replacement* in Chapter Nine.

9. Hook the cables onto the plastic clips on the handlebar.

10. Remove the switch housing and wiring cable (B, **Figure 145**).

11. Installation is the reverse of removal. Note the following:

    a. Engage the pin on the switch housing with the hole in the handlebar.

    b. Make sure all connections are free of corrosion.

    c. Apply a dielectric compound to the electrical connectors before reconnecting them.

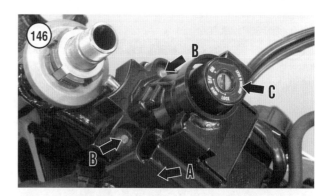

    d. Make sure the connectors are tight.

    e. Adjust the throttle cable free play as described in Chapter Three.

Ignition Switch Replacement

1. Remove the fuel tank as described in Chapter Nine.

2. Remove the handlebar and upper fork bridge as described in Chapter Twelve.

3. Disconnect the black 4-pin connector on the right side of the switch from the wiring harness.

4. Remove the bolts on each side securing the ignition switch bracket (A, **Figure 146**) and remove the bracket.

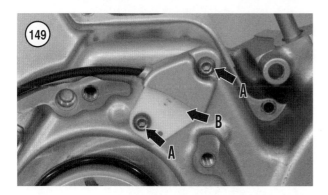

5. Remove the small screws on each side of the ignition switch.

6. Drill out and remove the shear bolts (B, **Figure 146**) securing the ignition switch to the mount on the frame back bone.

7. Remove the ignition switch (C, **Figure 146**) and harness from the frame.

8. Installation is the reverse of these steps. Note the following:

    a. Install *new* shear bolts to secure the ignition switch. Tighten the bolts until the heads shear off.

    b. Make sure all connections are free of corrosion.

    c. Apply a dielectric compound to the electrical connectors before reconnecting them.

    d. Make sure the connectors are tight.

    e. Install all items removed.

Neutral Switch Replacement

The neutral switch (**Figure 147**) is located on the right side of the crankcase behind the transfer case oil lines and inner cover.

1. Remove the rider seat as described in Chapter Fifteen.

2. Remove both frame side covers as described in Chapter Fifteen.

3. Remove the transfer gearcase oil lines, outer cover and inner cover as described in Chapter Six.

4. Disconnect the sky blue bullet connector (**Figure 148**) from the harness.

5. Follow the electrical wire from the neutral switch, behind the transfer gearcase assembly and behind the fuse panel.

NOTE
Figure 149 is shown with the engine removed and disassembled to better illustrate this step.

6. Remove the screws (A, **Figure 149**) securing the neutral switch (B) and cover. Remove the neutral switch from the crankcase.

7. Installation is the reverse of removal. Note the following:

    a. Install a *new* O-ring onto the neutral switch and apply a light coat of oil to it.

    b. Install the neutral switch and tighten the screws securely.

    c. Make sure the electrical bullet connector is free of corrosion and is tight.

Sidestand Switch Replacement

1. Remove the rider seat as described in Chapter Fifteen.

2. Remove both frame side covers as described in Chapter Fifteen.

3. Partially remove the left side footrest assembly to gain access to the sidestand switch. Refer to Chapter Fifteen.

4. Remove the mounting screw (A, **Figure 150**) and remove the sidestand switch (B) from the frame mounting bracket.

5. Follow the electrical wire from the sidestand switch, under the clutch cover and up behind the fuse panel. Remove any tie wraps and clips securing the wire to the frame.

NOTE
Figure 151 is shown with the rear cylinder and cylinder head removed to better illustrate the steps.

6. Disconnect the blue 2-pin sidestand switch connector (**Figure 151**) from its harness.

10

7. Installation is the reverse of these steps. Note the following:

   a. Make sure all connections are free of corrosion.

   b. Apply a dielectric compound to the electrical connectors before reconnecting them.

   c. Make sure the connectors are tight.

   d. Make sure the sidestand switch electrical wire is routed along the same path noted during removal.

   e. Secure the switch wire to the same points noted during removal.

Clutch Switch Replacement

1. Disconnect the two spade connectors from the clutch lever switch.

2. Remove the switch screw and remove the switch from beneath the clutch lever.

3. Installation is the reverse of removal.

Front Brake Switch Replacement

   The front brake light switch is located beneath the front brake master cylinder, which has been removed for clarity in these photos.

1. Disconnect the spade connectors from the front brake switch.

2. Remove the switch mounting screw (A, **Figure 152**) and remove the switch (B) from the base of the master cylinder.

3. Installation is the reverse of removal. Check the switch operation. The rear brake light should come on when the front brake lever is applied.

Rear Brake Switch Replacement

   The rear brake switch is mounted on the brake pedal/ footrest bracket.

1. Securely support the motorcycle on level ground. Block the front wheel so the motorcycle will not roll in either direction.

2. Remove the fuel tank as described in Chapter Nine.

3. Partially remove the right side footrest assembly to gain access to the rear brake light switch. Refer to Chapter Fifteen.

4. Follow the electrical wire from the rear brake pedal switch, in front of the engine and up to the rollover valve. Disconnect the 2-pin black connector (**Figure 153**) from the harness.

5. Disconnect the spring (A, **Figure 154**) from the boss on the brake pedal and remove the switch (B) from the bracket mount.

6. Installation is the reverse of these steps. Note the following:

   a. Apply dielectric grease to the electrical connector before reconnecting it.

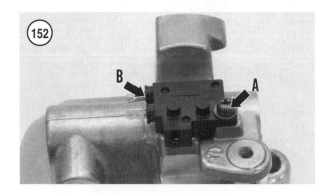

   b. Make sure the electrical connector is free of corrosion and completely coupled.

   c. Make sure the rear brake light switch electrical wire is routed along the same path noted during removal.

   d. Adjust the rear brake switch as described in Chapter Three.

SELF-DIAGNOSTIC SYSTEM

   All models are equipped with a self-diagnostic system that checks the throttle position sensor, speed sensor, decompression solenoid and fuel level sender. When the ignition switch is turned on, the engine indicator light on the meter assembly turns on. If these sensors are operating

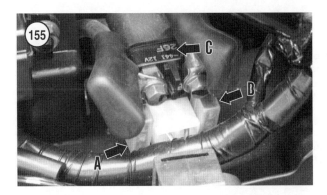

Three flashes (code 3) indicates a throttle position sensor fault. Test the throttle position sensor as described in Chapter Nine.

Four flashes (code 4) indicates a speed sensor fault.

Six flashes (code 6) indicates a decompression solenoid fault.

Eight flashes (code 8) indicates a fuel level sender meter fault. Test the fuel level sender as described in this chapter.

FUSES

Whenever a fuse blows, determine the reason for the failure before replacing the fuse. Usually, the trouble is a short in the wiring. This may be caused by worn through insulation or a disconnected wire shorting to ground.

CAUTION
Never substitute foil or wire for a fuse. Never use a higher amperage fuse than specified. An overload could result in fire and complete loss of the motorcycle.

Main Fuse Replacement

The 30-amp main fuse (A, **Figure 155**) and a spare (B) are located on the starter relay.

1. Remove the rider seat as described in Chapter Fifteen.
2. Remove the left side frame side panel as described in Chapter Fifteen.
3. Remove the relay (C, **Figure 155**) from the rubber mount.
4. Remove the fuse cover from the main fuse.
5. Use needlenose pliers and remove the fuse from the holder.
6. Replace the fuse if it has blown.
7. The replacement fuse must have the same amperage rating as the original.
8. Install a *new* fuse and push it in until it bottoms.
9. Install all items removed.

Fuse Replacement

Fuses other than the main fuse are located in the fuse box, located under the left side frame cover. The five fuses, and their amperage ratings, are listed in **Table 3**.

1. Remove the rider seat as described in Chapter Fifteen.
2. Remove the left side frame side panel as described in Chapter Fifteen.
3. Hinge open the fuse box cover (A, **Figure 156**).
4. Use needle nose pliers and remove the suspected fuse (B, **Figure 156**) from the box.
5. Inspect the fuse and replace if it has blown.
6. The replacement fuse must have the same amperage rating as the original.
7. Install a *new* fuse and push it in until it bottoms.
8. Install all items removed.

10

properly, the engine indicator light goes out after approximately 1.4 seconds or when the engine is started.

If the self-diagnostic system detects an error in a component, the engine indicator light flashes an error code after the initial 1.4-second period. The engine indicator light flashes the error code, turns off for three seconds, then repeats the error code. The light flashes the error code until the engine is started.

If an error is detected, the engine indicator light illuminates once the engine is running. To determine the code at this point, turn the engine off, then turn the ignition switch on. Watch the engine indicator light and count the number of flashes.

Table 1 ELECTRICAL SYSTEM SPECIFICATIONS

Battery	
Type	Maintenance free (sealed) YTX20L-BS
Capacity	12 V 18 AH
Open circuit voltage @ 20° C (68° F)	
Charging voltage (output voltage)	
1999-2005	14 volts/21 amps @ 5000 rpm
2006-on	14 volts/28 amps @ 5000 rpm
Cylinder numbering	Rear cylinder No. 1, front cylinder No. 2
Fuel level sender resistance	
Empty position	140-143 ohms
Full position	11-13 ohms
Ignition minimum spark gap (air gap)	6 mm (0.24 in.)
Ignition coil	
1999-2003	
Primary coil resistance	1.53-2.07 ohms @ 20° C (68° F)
Secondary coil resistance	12-18 k ohms @ 20° C (68° F)
2004-on	
Primary coil resistance	1.32-1.78 ohms @ 20° C (68° F)
Secondary coil resistance	12-18 k ohms @ 20° C (68° F)
Ignition timing	
1999-2003	10° BTDC @ 1000 rpm
2004-2005	10° BTDC @ 900 rpm
2006-on	5° BTDC @ 900 rpm
Ignition system	TCI
Pickup coil resistance	248-372 ohms @ 20° C (68° F)
Recommended spark plugs	NGK DPR7EA-9, Denso X22EPR-U9
Rectifier capacity	
1999-2005	18 amps
2006-on	22 amps
Withstand voltage (all years)	200 volts
Spark plug gap	0.8-0.9 mm (0.031-0.035 in.)
Spark plug cap resistance	10 k ohms
Starter	
Output	0.8 kW
Armature coil resistance	25-35 meg ohms @ 20° C (68° F)
Brush length	
1999-2005	10 mm (0.39 in.)
2006-on	12.5 mm (0.49 in.)
Brush length service limit	5 mm (0.20 in.)
Brush spring pressure	7.65-10.01 N (27.0-35.3 oz.)
Commutator outer diameter	28 mm (1.10 in.)
Commutator diameter service limit	27 mm (1.06 in.)
Starter relay amperage rating	
1999-2005	100 amps
2006-on	180 amps
Starter relay coil resistance	4.18-4.62 ohms @ 20° C (68° F)
Stator coil resistance	
1999-2005	0.45-0.55 ohm @ 20° C (68° F)
2006-on	0.225-0.275 ohm @ 20° C (68° F)
Turn signal flasher relay	
Frequency	75-95 cycles/min
Wattage	
1999-2003	27 watts
2004-on	23 watts
Voltage regulator no-load output	14.1-14.9 volts

Table 2 BULB SPECIFICATIONS

Item	Voltage/wattage
Headlight (high/low beam)	12 V 60/55 W

(continued)

Table 2 BULB SPECIFICATIONS (continued)

Item	Voltage/wattage
Taillight/brake light (USA, California, Canada models)	
1999-2003	12 V 8/27 W
2004-on	LED
Front turn signal/position light (USA, California, Canada models)	
1999-2003	12 V 27/8 W
2004-on	12 V 23/8 W
Rear turn signal (USA, California, Canada models)	
1999-2003	12 V 27 W
2004-on	12 V 213 W
Turn signals (Europe and Australia models)	12 V 21 W
License light (2004 only)	12 V 5 W
Meter light	
1999-2003	14 V 1.7 W
2004-on	14 V 0.56 W
Neutral indicator light	
1999-2003	12 V 1.7 W
2004-on	14 V 1.12 W
Turn signal indicator light	
1999-2003	12 V 1.7 W
2004-on	14 V 1.12 W
High beam indicator light	
1999-2003	12 V 1.7 W
2004-on	14 V 1.12 W
Fuel level indicator light	LED
Engine trouble indicator light	LED

Table 3 FUSES

Main fuse	30 A
Headlight fuse	
2006-2007 Road Star Midnight, All Road Star Silverado models	20 A
1999-2007 All other models	15 A
Ignition	15 A
Odometer fuse	
2006-2007 Road Star Midnight, All Road Star Silverado models	10 A
1999-2007 All other models	5 A
Carburetor heater	10 A
Signal	10 A

Table 4 ELECTRICAL SYSTEM TORQUE SPECIFICATIONS

Item	N•m	in.-lb.	ft.-lb.
Alternator			
Cover bolts	10	88	–
Flywheel bolt			
1999-2003	160	–	118
2004-on	80	–	59
Stator bolts[1]	7	62	–
Clutch cover screws	10	88	–
Footrest bolts	48	–	35
Ignition coil bolts	7	62	–
Meter cover-to-fuel tank	7	62	–
Pickup coil bolts[2]	7	62	–
Pickup coil cable guide bolts	7	62	–
Primary drive gear and pickup coil rotor bolt[1]	115	–	85
Neutral switch			
1999-2003	7	62	–
2004-on	4	35	–
Starter clutch Allen bolts	24	–	18
Starter mounting bolts	7	62	–
Starter relay nuts	7	62	–

1. Apply a medium-strength thread locking compound
2. Apply a low-strength thread locking compound

CHAPTER ELEVEN

WHEELS AND TIRES

This chapter describes repair and maintenance procedures for the wheels and tires. When inspecting any of the components described in this chapter, compare all measurements to the tire and wheel service specifications in the tables at the end of this chapter. Replace any component that is worn, damaged or out of specification. During assembly, tighten fasteners to the specified torque.

MOTORCYCLE STAND

Many procedures in this chapter require that the motorcycle be supported with a wheel off the ground. A quality motorcycle front end stand (**Figure 1**) does this safely and effectively. Before purchasing or using a stand, check the manufacturer's instructions to make sure the stand will work on the motorcycle. If the stand requires any modifications or adjustment, perform the required service before lifting the motorcycle. Due to the unique contour of the lower section of the rear swing arm, a swing arm safety stand should not be used.

A center jack (**Figure 2**, K&L MC450 Center Jack) works well for this motorcycle. When using a jack, have an assistant hold the motorcycle in an upright position. Place a piece of wood across the jack and position the jack underneath the front, or rear, of the frame under the en-

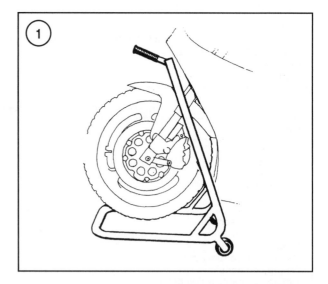

gine. Operate the jack and lift the motorcycle until the front or rear wheel just clears the ground.

When using a motorcycle stand, have an assistant standing by. Some means to tie down one end of the motorcycle is also needed. Regardless of the method used, make sure the motorcycle is properly supported before walking away from it.

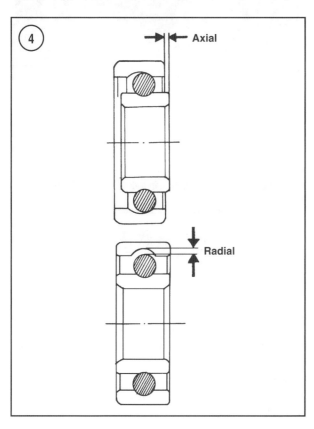

BRAKE ROTOR PROTECTION

Be careful when removing, handling or installing a wheel with a disc brake rotor. Brake rotors are thin in order to dissipate heat and to minimize un-sprung weight. A rotor is designed to withstand tremendous rotational loads, but it can be damaged by a side impact.

Protect the rotor when servicing a wheel. Never set a wheel down on the brake rotor. It may be bent or scratched. When a wheel must be placed on its side, support the wheel on wooden blocks. Position the blocks along the outer circumference of the wheel so the rotor lies between the blocks and does not rest on them.

Also protect the rotor when transporting a wheel to a dealership or tire specialist. Do not place a wheel in a car trunk or truck bed without protecting the rotor from side impact.

If the rotor is knocked out of true by a side impact, a pulsation will be felt in the brake lever or pedal when braking. Damaged rotors must be replaced.

WHEEL INSPECTION

During inspection, compare all measurements to the specifications in **Table 1**. Replace any part that is damaged, out of specification or worn to the service limit.

1. Remove the wheel as described in this chapter.

2. Inspect the seals (A, **Figure 3**) for excessive wear, hardness, cracks or other damage. If necessary, replace the seals as described in this chapter.

3. Inspect the bearings as follows:

    a. Turn each bearing inner race (B, **Figure 3**) by hand. Each bearing must turn smoothly with no trace of roughness, binding or excessive noise. Some axial play (side-to-side) is normal, but radial play (up and down) must be negligible. See **Figure 4**. If either wheel bearing is damaged, replace them both as described in this chapter.

    b. Check the bearing outer seal (**Figure 5**) for buckling or other damage that would allow dirt to enter the bearing.

    c. Check the bearing fit in the hub by trying to move the bearing with your hand. The bearing should be tight in the bore. Loose bearings allow the wheel to wobble. If a bearing is loose, the bearing bore in the hub is probably worn or damaged.

4. Remove any corrosion from the axle and collars with a piece of fine emery cloth.

WARNING
Do not attempt to straighten a bent axle.

11

5. Check axle runout by rolling the axle along a surface plate or a piece of glass. If the axle is not straight, replace it.

6. Install the wheel on a truing stand. Check wheel runout as follows:

    a. Measure the radial (up and down) runout of the wheel rim with a dial indicator as shown in **Figure 6**.

    b. Measure the axial (side to side) runout of the wheel rim with a dial indicator as shown in **Figure 6**.

7. If the wheel runout is out of specification (**Table 1**), inspect the wheel bearings as described in Step 3.

    a. If the wheel bearings are good, the wheel must be replaced.

    b. If either wheel bearing is worn, disassemble the hub and replace both bearings as a set.

8. Check the tightness of the brake disc bolts (**Figure 7**). If a bolt is loose, remove and reinstall the bolts with medium-strength threadlocking compound. Clean any old threadlocking compound from the threads and tighten the bolts to 23 N•m (17 ft.-lb.).

9. Visually inspect the brake discs and measure the brake disc deflection as described in Chapter Fourteen. If deflection is excessive, measure the wheel runout. If wheel runout is within specification, replace the brake disc.

10. Inspect the wheel rim for dents, bending or cracks. Check the rim and rim sealing surface (alloy wheels) for scratches that are deeper than 0.5 mm (0.01 in.). If any of these conditions are present, replace the wheel.

11. On laced wheels, check the spoke tension as described in this chapter.

WHEEL BEARINGS

Removal

The Motion Pro bearing removal tool in **Figure 8** can be ordered through most motorcycle dealerships. The

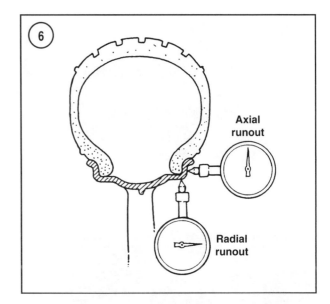

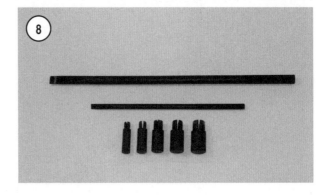

Motion Pro tool can be purchased as a set, or as individual pieces. Similar tools are also available from Kowa Seiki.

1. If still in place, remove the collar from the hub.

2. Pry the oil seal out of the hub (**Figure 9**). Support the tool with a rag to avoid damage to the hub and/or brake disc. Discard the oil seal.

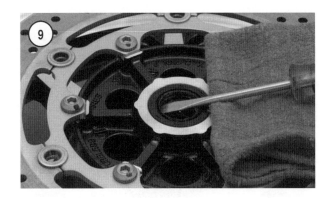

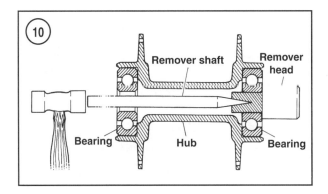

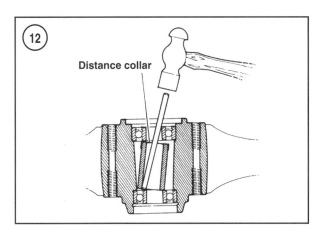

Distance collar

3. On alloy rear wheels, remove the snap ring on the right side securing the bearing.

4. Select the correct size remover head and insert it into the inner race of one bearing (**Figure 10**).

5. From the opposite side of the hub, insert the remover shaft through the hub bore and into the slot in the backside of the remover head. Position the hub with the remover head resting against a solid surface. Strike the remover shaft to force it into the slot in the remover head. This tightens the remover head against the bearing inner race.

6. Reposition the wheel. Strike the end of the remover shaft with a hammer and drive the bearing out of the hub (**Figure 11**). Slide the bearing and tool assembly out of the hub.

7. Tap the remover head to release it from the bearing.

8. Remove the distance collar, and collar (rear alloy wheel). Note how the distance collar is positioned in the hub. It must be reinstalled with the same orientation during assembly.

9A. On front hubs, repeat this procedure and remove the bearing from the other side.

9B. On laced rear wheels, the left side of the rear hub is equipped with two ball bearings. Drive out each bearing as described in this procedure.

9C. On alloy rear wheels, the left side of the rear hub is equipped with a ball bearing and needle bearing. Drive out the bearings as follows:

    a. Use a long drift and hammer (**Figure 12**) and drive the ball bearing out of the right side of the hub.

    b. Use a long drift and hammer and drive the ball bearing out of the left side of the hub.

    c. Remove the snap ring, and drive the needle bearing out of the left side of the hub.

10. Clean the hub and distance collar with solvent. Dry them with compressed air.

11. Install new bearings as described in this section.

Installation

NOTE
The left and right bearings are not identical in the rear hub. Install each bearing into its proper location in the hub.

1. Place the bearings in a freezer overnight. This will ease installation.

2. Blow any dirt or debris out of the hub before installing the bearing.

3. Pack the open side of each bearing with grease.

4A. Install bearings in the front hub as follows:

    a. Position the bearing so the manufacturer marks face out and place the bearing squarely on the bore open-

11

ing on the left side of the hub. Select a bearing driver or socket (**Figure 13**) with an outside diameter that matches the outside diameter of the bearing. Drive the bearing into the bore until it bottoms.

b. Turn the hub over. Install the distance collar and center it against the left bearing's inner race.

c. Position the right bearing so the manufacturer marks face out squarely against the bore opening. Using the same socket (**Figure 13**) or bearing driver, drive the bearing partway into the bore. Stop and check the distance collar. If it is still centered within the bearing, install the axle partway through the hub and center the spacer. Remove the axle and continue installing the bearing until it bottoms.

4B. On laced rear wheel models, install rear hub bearings as follows:

a. Position the left inner bearing so the manufacturer marks face out and place the bearing squarely on the bore opening on the left side of the hub. Select a bearing driver or socket with an outside diameter that matches (or is slightly smaller than) the outside diameter of the bearing. Drive the bearing into the bore until it bottoms.

b. Repeat sub-step a and install the left outer bearing.

c. Turn the hub over. Install the distance collar and center it against the left bearing's inner race.

d. Place the right bearing so the manufacturer marks face squarely against the bore opening. Select a bearing driver or socket (**Figure 14**) with an outside diameter that matches the outside diameter of the bearing and drive the bearing partway into the bore. Stop and check the distance collar. It must still be centered within the bearing. If it is not, install the axle partway through the hub and center the spacer. Remove the axle and continue installing the bearing until it bottoms.

4C. On cast rear wheel models, install the rear hub bearings as follows:

a. Position the left bearing so the manufacturer marks face out and place the bearing squarely on the bore opening on the left side of the hub. Select a bearing driver or socket with an outside diameter that matches (or is slightly smaller than) the outside diameter of the bearing. Drive the needle bearing into the bore until it bottoms.

b. Install the snap ring. Repeat Sub-step a and install the ball bearing into the left side of the hub.

c. Turn the hub over. Install the collar and the distance collar and center it against the left bearing inner race.

d. Place the right bearing so the manufacturer marks face out squarely against the bore opening. Select a

bearing driver or socket (**Figure 14**) with an outside diameter that matches the outside diameter of the bearing and drive the bearing partway into the bore. Stop and check the distance collar. It must still be centered within the bearing. If it is not, install the axle partway through the hub and center the spacer. Remove the axle and continue installing the bearing until it bottoms.

5. Reassemble the hub as described in this chapter.

FRONT WHEEL

Removal

1. Securely support the motorcycle with the front wheel off the ground. Block the rear wheel so the motorcycle will not roll in either direction.

2. Inspect the wheel bearings as follows:

a. Hold the wheel along its side, and try to rock it back and forth. If there is any play at the axle, the wheel bearings are worn or damaged.

b. Have an assistant apply the brake. Rock the wheel again. On wheels with severely worn bearings, there will be play even though the wheel is locked in position.

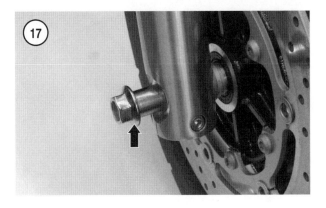

a. Remove the brake hose lower holder bolt and release the brake hose lower holder and the reflector bracket (A, **Figure 15**).

b. Remove the caliper mounting bolts from the caliper (B, **Figure 15**).

c. Rotate the caliper off the brake disc. Use a stiff wire or bungee cord to suspend the caliper from the motorcycle.

d. Wrap a shop rag around the caliper so the front fender will not be scratched. Secure the rag with a tie wrap or rubber band.

5. Repeat Step 4 for the other front brake caliper.

CAUTION
The full-size front fender wraps low over the front wheel. The motorcycle must be raised very high to remove the wheel with the fender installed. Therefore, remove the front fender before removing the front wheel.

6. Remove the front fender as described in Chapter Fifteen.

7. Loosen the clamp bolt (**Figure 16**) in the right fork slider.

8. Loosen the front axle (**Figure 17**) and remove the axle from the right side.

9. Roll the wheel from between the fork legs. Remove the collar from each side of the hub.

CAUTION
Do not lay a wheel on the brake disc. The disc could be scratched or bent.

10. Set the tire and wheel on two wooden blocks.

11. Inspect the front wheel as described in *Wheel Inspection* in this chapter.

Installation

1. Inspect the axle and the axle bearing surfaces of the fork sliders for burrs and nicks.

2. Lubricate the axle with lithium grease.

3. Apply a light coat of lithium grease to the lips of the seal in one side of the hub and install the collar.

4. Repeat Step 3 on the other side and install the other collar.

5. Roll the wheel into place between the fork legs. Make sure the arrow on the tire points in the direction of forward rotation.

6. Insert the front axle (**Figure 17**) through the right fork slider and the hub, and thread the axle into the left fork slider. Do not tighten it to the final torque at this time.

c. Spin the wheel and listen for excessive wheel bearing noise. Grinding or catching noises indicate worn bearings.

d. If either bearing is worn or damaged, replace both wheel bearings as a set. Refer to the hub disassembly procedures in this chapter.

3. Insert a wooden block between the brake lever and the handlebar grip. Use a rubber band to hold the block in place.

4. Remove a brake caliper as follows:

7. Ensure the front axle collar is in place on the right side (**Figure 18**) and left side (**Figure 19**).

8. Install the front fender as described in Chapter Fifteen.

9. Install a brake caliper as follows:

    a. Remove the shop rag from the caliper and route the brake hose along the path noted during removal.

    b. Lower the caliper (B, **Figure 15**) onto the brake disc. Be careful not to damage the leading edge of each brake pad during installation.

    c. Install the caliper mounting bolts (**Figure 20**, typical). Apply medium-strength thread locking compound to the bolt threads and tighten to 40 N•m (30 ft.-lb.).

    d. Install the brake hose lower holder bolt and release the brake hose lower holder and the reflector bracket (A, **Figure 15**). Tighten the bolt securely.

10. Repeat Step 9 and install the other brake caliper.

11. After the wheel is completely installed, rotate it several times to make sure it turns freely. Apply the front brake as many times as necessary to ensure the brake pads properly engage the brake disc.

12. Pump the fork several times to ensure the fork legs slide in smoothly and that the front axle is centered with the fork.

13. Tighten the front axle to 78 N•m (58 ft.-lb.), then tighten the clamp bolt to 20 N•m (15 ft-lb.).

FRONT HUB

Disassembly/Inspection/Assembly

Refer to **Figure 21** or **Figure 22**.

1. Remove the front wheel as described in this chapter.

2. If still in place, remove the collar from each side of the hub.

> *CAUTION*
> *Do not lay a wheel on the brake disc. The disc could be scratched or bent.*

3. Use wooden blocks to support the wheel. Place the tire on the blocks so the brake disc will not be damaged.

> *CAUTION*
> *The hub can be serviced with the brake disc and hub plate in place. Nonetheless, consider removing the brake disc so it will not be damaged.*

4A. On laced wheel models, perform the following:

    a. Remove the bolts (A, **Figure 23**) securing the brake disc cover and brake disc.

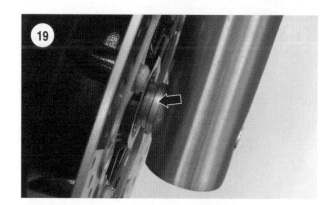

    b. Remove the disc cover (B, **Figure 23**) and the brake disc (**Figure 24**).

4B. On cast wheel models, perform the following:

    a. Remove the brake disc bolts (A, **Figure 25**) and remove the brake disc from the hub. Repeat on the opposite side.

    b. Pry the seal (B, **Figure 25**) from each side of the hub. Place a shop rag beneath the pry tool so the hub will not be damaged.

4. Inspect the bearings as described in *Wheel Inspection* in this chapter. If necessary, remove and replace the bearings as described in this chapter.

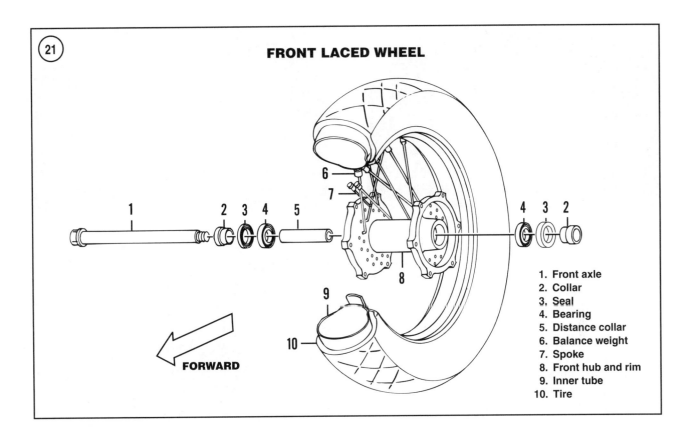

FRONT LACED WHEEL

1. Front axle
2. Collar
3. Seal
4. Bearing
5. Distance collar
6. Balance weight
7. Spoke
8. Front hub and rim
9. Inner tube
10. Tire

FORWARD

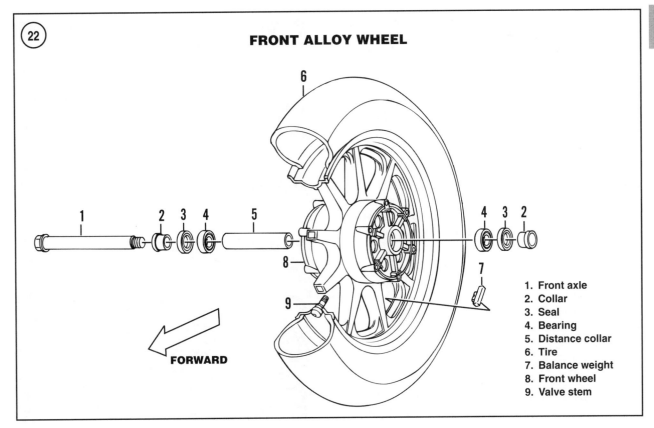

FRONT ALLOY WHEEL

1. Front axle
2. Collar
3. Seal
4. Bearing
5. Distance collar
6. Tire
7. Balance weight
8. Front wheel
9. Valve stem

FORWARD

11

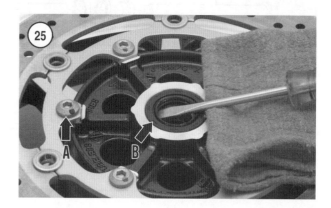

6. Pack the lips of a new seal with lithium soap grease. Drive the seal in squarely with a seal driver or large diameter socket (**Figure 26**) seated on the outer portion of the seal. Drive the seal until it seats against the bearing or when the outer surface is flush with the hub.

7. Repeat for the seal on the opposite side of the hub.

8. Install the brake disc, if it was removed, as follows:

   a. Set the brake disc in place so its arrow points in the direction of forward rotation.

   b. On laced wheel models, make sure the insulator pad (**Figure 27**) is in place and set the brake disc cover on the hub (B, **Figure 23**).

   c. The brake disc bolts are specifically designed for this application. If replacing the bolts, always use original equipment Yamaha brake disc bolts.

   d. Use a small amount of medium-strength thread locking compound on the brake disc bolts prior to installation.

   e. Evenly tighten the brake disc bolts in a crisscross pattern. Tighten the bolts to 23 N•m (17 ft.-lb.).

REAR WHEEL

Removal

1. Securely support the motorcycle on level ground. Block the front wheel so the motorcycle will not roll in either direction.

2. Remove both seats as described in Chapter Fifteen.

3. On models so equipped, remove both saddlebags as described in Chapter Fifteen.

4. Remove the muffler assembly as described in Chapter Nine.

5. Remove the screws securing the drive belt upper cover and remove the cover.

6. Loosen the rear axle nut (**Figure 28**).

7. Have an assistant hold the motorcycle in an upright position. Place a piece of wood across a jack and position the

jack underneath the rear of the frame under the engine. Operate the jack and lift the motorcycle until the rear wheel just clears the ground.

8. Loosen the rear brake caliper mounting bracket bolt (**Figure 29**).

9. Loosen the rear axle adjuster locknut (A, **Figure 30**) on both sides.

10. Loosen the adjusting bolts (B, **Figure 30**) in equal amounts on both sides to achieve the maximum amount of drive belt slack.

11. Remove the rear caliper mounting bolts (**Figure 31**). Leave the caliper on the brake disc at this time.

> *CAUTION*
> *The full-size rear fender wraps down low over the rear wheel, the motorcycle must be raised very high to remove the wheel with the fender installed. Therefore, partially remove the rear fender before removing the front wheel.*

12. Partially remove the rear fender as follows:
    a. Remove the two bolts (**Figure 32**) securing the front edge of the fender to the frame.
    b. Remove the bolts (**Figure 33**) securing the rear fender to the saddlebag mounting bracket.

11

c. Loosen, but do not remove, the front mounting throughbolt and nut (**Figure 34**).

d. Have an assistant raise the rear of the fender sufficiently to clear the rear wheel.

e. Reinstall the bolts (**Figure 35**) securing the back rest to the rear fender.

13. Remove the axle nut (A, **Figure 36**), washer (B) and adjusting plate (C) from the right side.

14. Withdraw the axle (A, **Figure 37**) from the left side.

15. Push the rear wheel forward and derail the drive belt from the driven sprocket.

16. Roll the rear wheel toward the rear and remove it. Do not lose the collar on each side of the rear hub.

17. Lower the rear fender, install the two bolts (**Figure 32**) and tighten securely.

18. Insert vinyl tubing or a piece of wood between the brake pads in the caliper.

19. Inspect the rear wheel as described in *Wheel Inspection* in this chapter.

20. If necessary, disassemble the driven sprocket clutch hub as described later in this chapter.

Installation

1. If removed, install the driven sprocket clutch hub onto the rear hub. Make sure the long collar (**Figure 38**) is in place.

2. Apply a coat of lithium grease to the rear axle, bearings, seals and stepped collar.

3. Remove the two bolts (**Figure 32**) securing the front edge of the fender to the frame.

4. Have an assistant raise the rear of the fender enough to clear the rear wheel.

5. Remove the vinyl tubing or wood from between the brake pads in the caliper.

6. If removed, install the collar onto each side of the hub.

7. Position the rear wheel with the driven sprocket on the left side.

8. Push the rear wheel forward and guide the brake disc into the caliper being careful not to damage the leading edge of the brake pads.

9. Install the drive belt onto the driven sprocket, and make sure the drive belt is properly seated within the sprocket grooves.

10. Pull the wheel toward the rear and align the rear axle holes to the swing arm.

11. Install the left side adjusting plate (B, **Figure 37**) onto the rear axle and install the axle from the left side.

12. Push the rear axle (A, **Figure 37**) through the swing arm, rear hub, rear caliper mounting bracket and swing arm.

b. Tighten the front mounting throughbolt and nut (**Figure 34**) securely 88 N•m (65 ft.-lb.).

16. Do not tighten the rear brake caliper mounting bracket bolt (**Figure 29**). It will be tightened when the drive belt is adjusted.

17. Install the drive belt upper cover and tighten the screws securely.

18. Install the muffler assembly as described in Chapter Nine.

19. On models so equipped, install both saddlebags as described in Chapter Fifteen.

20. Install both seats as described in Chapter Fifteen.

21. Adjust the drive belt tension as described in Chapter Three.

REAR HUB

Preliminary Inspection

> *CAUTION*
> *Do not remove the wheel bearings for inspection. The bearings are damaged during removal and cannot be reused. Remove wheel bearings only if they must be replaced.*

1. Remove the rear wheel as described in this chapter.

2. The condition of the rear wheel bearings is critical to the tracking and acceleration performance of the motorcycle. Check the wheel bearings whenever the wheel is removed or as one of the first steps when diagnosing handling or noise problems.

3. Insert the axle through the hub and turn the axle by hand. Each bearing should turn smoothly without noise or excessive play.

4. If the rear wheel was not inspected during removal, inspect it as described in *Wheel Inspection* in this chapter.

Disassembly/Assembly

Refer to **Figure 41** and **Figure 42**.

1. Remove the rear wheel as described in this chapter. Set the wheel on wooden blocks.

2. If still in place, remove the collar (A, **Figure 43**) from the right side of the hub.

3. Pull the driven sprocket assembly straight up and remove it from the hub. Do not lose the long collar (**Figure 38**) within the assembly.

4. Remove the rubber dampers (**Figure 44**) from the driven sprocket assembly.

5. Remove the brake disc bolts (B, **Figure 43**) and remove the brake disc from the hub.

13. Install the right side adjusting plate, (C, **Figure 36**), washer (B), and nut (A) onto the rear axle. Tighten the axle nut finger tight at this time.

14. Make sure the rear axle collar is in place on the right side (**Figure 39**) and left side (**Figure 40**).

15. Lower the rear fender as follows:

  a. Lower the rear fender into position and install the two bolts (**Figure 32**) securing the front edge of the fender to the frame. Tighten the bolts to 48 N•m (35 ft.-lb.).

11

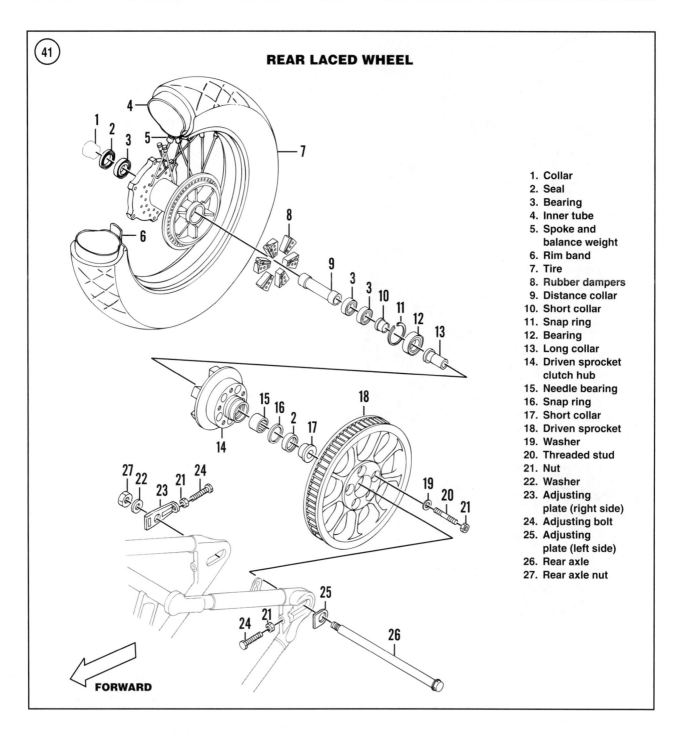

41

REAR LACED WHEEL

1. Collar
2. Seal
3. Bearing
4. Inner tube
5. Spoke and
   balance weight
6. Rim band
7. Tire
8. Rubber dampers
9. Distance collar
10. Short collar
11. Snap ring
12. Bearing
13. Long collar
14. Driven sprocket
    clutch hub
15. Needle bearing
16. Snap ring
17. Short collar
18. Driven sprocket
19. Washer
20. Threaded stud
21. Nut
22. Washer
23. Adjusting
    plate (right side)
24. Adjusting bolt
25. Adjusting
    plate (left side)
26. Rear axle
27. Rear axle nut

FORWARD

6. Pry the seal (**Figure 45**) from the right side of the hub. Place a shop rag beneath the pry tool so the hub will not be damaged.

7. Inspect the bearings as described under *Wheel Inspection* in this chapter. If necessary, remove and replace the bearings as described in this chapter.

8. Inspect the rear hub as described in this section.

9. Pack the lips of a *new* seal with lithium grease. Drive the seal in squarely with a seal driver or a large diameter socket (**Figure 46**) seated on the outer portion of the seal. Drive the seal until it seats against the bearing or when the outer surface is flush with the hub.

10. Install the driven sprocket assembly into the hub. If necessary, lubricate the dampers with soapy water. Push the sprocket in until it bottoms.

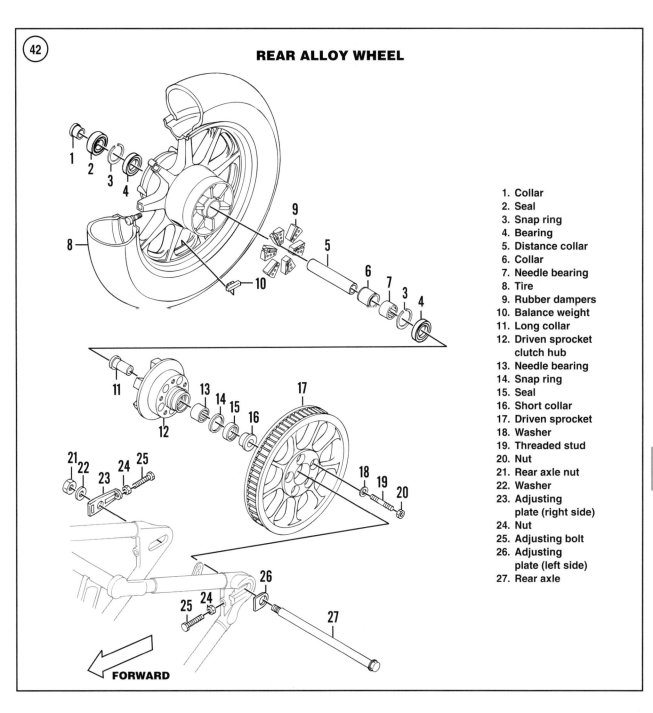

42 **REAR ALLOY WHEEL**

1. Collar
2. Seal
3. Snap ring
4. Bearing
5. Distance collar
6. Collar
7. Needle bearing
8. Tire
9. Rubber dampers
10. Balance weight
11. Long collar
12. Driven sprocket clutch hub
13. Needle bearing
14. Snap ring
15. Seal
16. Short collar
17. Driven sprocket
18. Washer
19. Threaded stud
20. Nut
21. Rear axle nut
22. Washer
23. Adjusting plate (right side)
24. Nut
25. Adjusting bolt
26. Adjusting plate (left side)
27. Rear axle

FORWARD

11

Inspection

1. Inspect the bearings as described in *Wheel Inspection* in this chapter. If necessary, remove and replace the bearings as described in this chapter.

2. Inspect the rubber dampers (**Figure 44**) for cracks, wear or other signs of deterioration. Replace the dampers as a set.

3. Inspect the raised ribs for the rubber dampers in the rear hub (**Figure 47**) and the driven sprocket assembly (**Figure 48**) for cracks or damage.

DRIVEN SPROCKET CLUTCH HUB

Disassembly/Assembly/Inspection

1. Remove the rear wheel as described in this chapter.

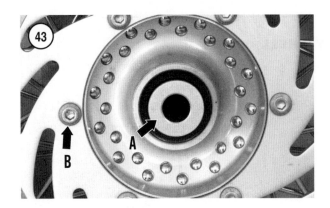

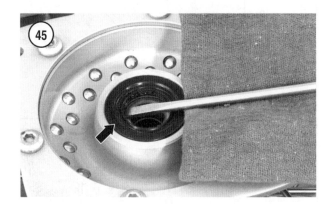

2. Loosen the self-locking nuts. Remove the driven sprocket clutch hub from the rear wheel.

3. Remove the self-locking nuts and washers (**Figure 49**) and remove the hub from the wheel.

4. Inspect the sprocket teeth (**Figure 50**). If the teeth are visibly worn, replace the drive belt and both sprockets.

5. Installation is the reverse of removal. Install *new* self-locking nuts. Tighten the nuts to 95 N•m (70 ft.-lb.).

Bearing Removal

1. Remove the driven sprocket clutch hub from the rear wheel.

2. If still in place, remove the short collar from the left side of the hub.

3. Pry the seal (**Figure 51**) from the left side of the hub. Place a shop rag beneath the pry tool so the hub will not be damaged.

4. Remove the snap ring from the left side of the hub.

5. If still in place, remove the short collar (A, **Figure 52**) from the right side of the hub.

6. Remove the large snap ring (B, **Figure 52**) from the right side of the hub.

7. Place the clutch hub with the right side facing down.

8. Tap the long collar and right side bearing from the clutch hub.

9. Turn the clutch hub over with the right side facing up.

10. If necessary, use a long drift and tap the needle bearing from the left side of the clutch hub.

Bearing Installation

1. Place the bearings in a freezer overnight. This will ease installation.

2. Blow any dirt or debris out of the clutch hub before installing the bearings.

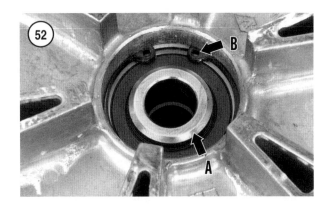

3. If removed, position the needle bearing with the manufacturer marks facing out and place the bearing squarely on the bore opening on the left side of the clutch hub.

4. Select a bearing driver or socket with an outside diameter that matches the outside diameter of the bearing. Drive the needle bearing into the bore until it bottoms.

5. Install a *new* snap ring and make sure it seats correctly in the hub groove.

6. Pack the lips of a *new* oil seal with lithium grease. Drive the seal in squarely with a seal driver or a large diameter socket seated on the outer portion of the seal. Drive the seal until it seats against the bearing or until the outer surface is flush with the hub.

7. Turn the clutch hub over.

8. Position the long collar with the shoulder side going in last and install the long collar.

9. Position the bearing so the manufacturer marks face out and place the bearing squarely on the bore opening on the right side of the clutch hub.

10. Select a bearing driver or socket with an outside diameter that matches the outside diameter of the bearing. Drive the bearing into the bore until it bottoms.

11. Install a *new* snap ring and make sure it seats correctly in the hub groove.

11

DRIVE BELT

CAUTION
When handling a new or used drive belt, never wrap the belt in a loop smaller than 5 in. (127 mm) or bend it sharply. This will weaken or break the belt fibers and cause premature belt failure.

Removal/Installation

CAUTION
If the existing drive belt is being reinstalled, install it so it travels in the same direction. Be-

fore removing the belt, mark an arrow on the top surface of the belt facing forward.

1. Install wooden blocks or a floor jack under the transmission and engine assembly.
2. Remove the drive pulley (A, **Figure 53**) as described in Chapter Six.
3. Remove the rear wheel as described in this chapter.
4. Remove the swing arm as described in Chapter Thirteen.
5. Remove the drive belt (B, **Figure 53**) from the frame.
6. Installation is the reverse of removal. Note the following:
   a. If the existing drive belt is being reinstalled, install it so it travels in the direction noted prior to removal. If a new drive belt is being installed, it can be installed in either direction.
   b. Adjust the drive belt tension as described in Chapter Three.

Inspection

Do not apply any type of lubricant to the drive belt. Inspect the drive belt and teeth (**Figure 54**) for severe wear, damage or oil contamination.

Refer to **Figure 55** for various types of drive belt wear or damage. Replace the drive belt if it is worn or damaged.

LACED WHEEL SERVICE

The laced or wire wheel assembly consists of a rim, spokes, nipples and hub (containing the wheel bearings, distance collars and seals).

Loose or improperly tightened spokes can cause hub damage. Periodically inspect the wheel assembly for loose, broken or missing spokes, rim damage and runout. Wheel bearing service is described in this chapter.

Component Condition

Inspect the wheels regularly for runout, even spoke tension, and visible damage. When a wheel has a noticeable wobble, it is out of true. Loose spokes usually cause this, but it can be caused by impact damage.

Truing a wheel corrects the radial and lateral runout to bring the wheel back into specification. The condition of the individual wheel components will determine success in truing the wheel.

1. Spoke condition—Do not attempt to true a wheel with bent or damaged spokes. Doing so places excessive tension on the spoke and rim. The spoke may break and/or

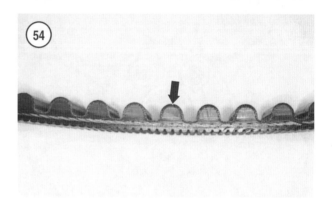

pull through the hole in the rim. Inspect spokes carefully and replace any that are damaged.

2. Nipple condition—When truing a wheel, the nipple should turn freely on the spoke. It is common for the spoke threads to become corroded and make turning the nipple difficult. Spray a penetrating liquid onto the nipple and allow sufficient time for it to penetrate. Use a spoke wrench and work the nipple in both directions and apply additional penetrating liquid. If the spoke wrench rounds off the nipple, remove the tire from the rim and cut the spoke(s) out of the wheel.

3. Rim condition—Minor rim damage can be corrected by truing; however, trying to correct excessive runout caused by impact damage will damage the hub and rim due to over-tightened spokes. Inspect the rims for cracks, flat spots or dents. Check the spoke holes for cracks or enlargement.

Wheel Truing Preliminaries

Before checking runout and truing the wheel, note the following:

1. Make sure the wheel bearings are in good condition.

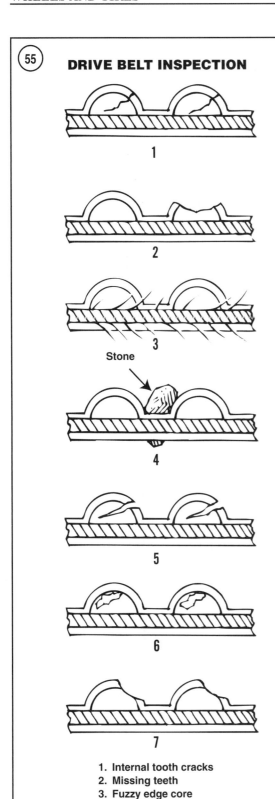

DRIVE BELT INSPECTION

1. Internal tooth cracks
2. Missing teeth
3. Fuzzy edge core
4. Stone damage
5. External tooth cracks
6. Chipping
7. Hook wear

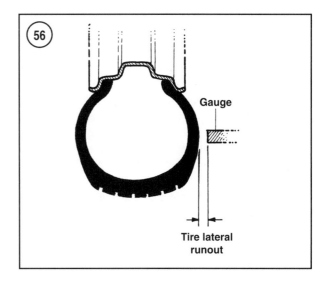

Gauge

Tire lateral runout

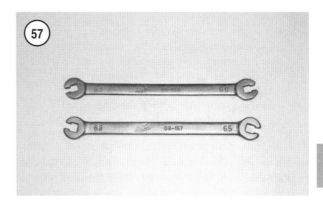

11

2. A small amount of runout is acceptable. Do not attempt to true the wheel to a perfect zero reading. Refer to **Table 1** for specifications.

3. Perform a quick runout check with the wheel on the motorcycle by placing a pointer against the fork or swing arm and slowly rotating the wheel (**Figure 56**).

4. Perform major wheel truing with the tire removed and the wheel mounted in a wheel truing stand.

5. Use a spoke nipple wrench of the correct size. Using the wrong type of tool or one that is the incorrect size will round off the spoke nipples, making adjustment difficult. Quality wrenches (**Figure 57**) grip the nipple on four corners to prevent damage. Tighten spokes to 3 N•m (27 in.-lb.).

Wheel Truing Procedure

1. Set the wheel in a truing stand.

2A. When using a dial indicator, check rim runout as follows:

a. Measure the radial runout with a dial indicator as shown in **Figure 58**. If radial runout exceeds the service limit specified in **Table 1**, replace the rim.

b. Measure the lateral runout with a dial indicator as shown in **Figure 58**. If lateral runout exceeds the service limit specified in **Table 1**, replace the rim.

2B. If a dial indicator is not available, check rim runout as follows:

a. Position a pointer against the rim as shown in **Figure 59**. Spin the wheel slowly and check the lateral runout.

b. Adjust the position of the pointer and check the radial runout.

3. If lateral runout is out of specification, the rim needs to be moved relative to the centerline of the wheel. See **Figure 60**. To move the rim to the left, for example, tighten the spoke(s) on the left of the rim and loosen the opposite spoke(s) on the right.

NOTE
The number of spokes to loosen and tighten will depend on the amount of runout. As a minimum, always adjust two or three spokes in the vicinity of the rim runout. If runout affects a greater area along the rim, adjust a greater number of spokes.

4. If radial runout is excessive, the hub is not centered within the rim. The rim needs to move relative to the centerline of the hub. See **Figure 61**. Draw the high point of the rim toward the centerline of the hub by tightening the spokes in the area of the high point and by loosening spokes on the low side. Tighten and loosen the spokes in equal amounts to prevent distortion.

5. Rotate the wheel and check runout. Continue adjusting the spokes until runout is within the specification in **Table 1**. Be patient and thorough, adjusting the position of the rim a little at a time.

6. After truing the wheel, seat each spoke in the hub by tapping it with a flat nose punch and hammer. Recheck the spoke tension and wheel runout. Readjust if necessary.

7. Check the ends of the spokes on the tube side of the rim. Grind off any spoke that protrudes from the nipple so it will not puncture the tube.

WHEEL BALANCE

An unbalanced wheel is unsafe. Depending on the degree of unbalance and the speed of the motorcycle, a rider may experience anything from a mild vibration to a violent shake that may result in loss of control.

Before balancing a wheel, thoroughly clean the wheel assembly. Make sure the wheel bearings are in good con-

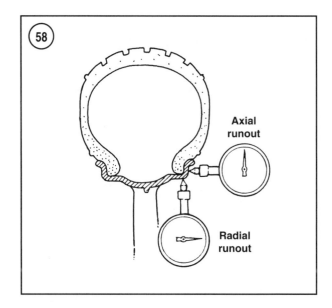

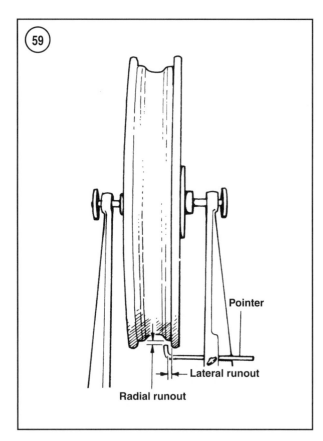

dition and properly lubricated. The wheel must rotate freely. Also make sure the balance mark on the tire aligns with the valve stem. If not, break the tire loose from the rim and align it before balancing the wheel. Refer to *Tire Changing* in this chapter.

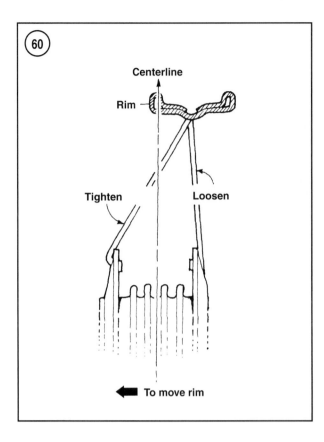

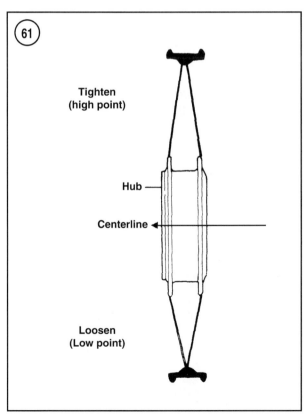

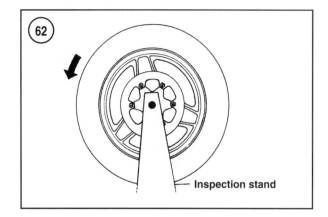

NOTE
Balance the wheels with the brake disc and driven sprocket assembly attached. These components rotate with the wheel and affect the balance.

1. Remove the wheel as described in this chapter.
2. Make sure the valve stem and the valve cap are tight.
3. Mount the wheel on a stand such as the one shown in **Figure 62** so it can rotate freely.
4. Check the wheel runout as described in this chapter. Do not try to balance a wheel with excessive runout.
5. Remove any balance weights mounted on the wheel.
6. Give the wheel a spin and let it coast to a stop. Mark the tire at the highest point (12 o'clock). This is the wheel's lightest point.
7. Spin the wheel several more times. If the wheel keeps coming to rest at the same point, it is out of balance. If the wheel stops at different points each time, the wheel is balanced.

NOTE
Adhesive test weights are available from motorcycle dealerships. These are adhesive-backed weights that can be cut to the desired length and attached directly to the rim.

8. Loosely attach a balance weight (or tape a test weight) at the upper or light side (12 o'clock) of the wheel.
9. Rotate the wheel 1/4 turn (3 o'clock). Release the wheel and observe the following:
   a. If the wheel does not rotate (if it stays at the 3 o'clock position), the correct balance weight was installed. The wheel is balanced.
   b. If the wheel rotates and the weighted portion goes up, replace the weight with the next heavier size.
   c. If the wheel rotates and the weighted portion goes down, replace the weight with the next lighter size.

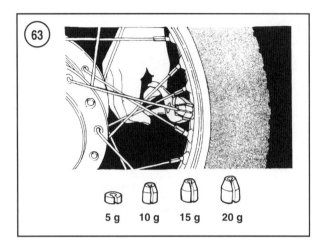

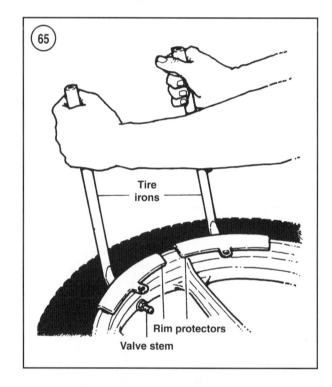

d. Repeat this step until the wheel remains at rest after being rotated 1/4 turn. Rotate the wheel another 1/4 turn, another 1/4 turn, and another to see if the wheel is correctly balanced.

10. Remove the test weight and install the correct weight.
   a. On laced wheels, firmly crimp the balance weight onto the spoke(s) with a pair of pliers (**Figure 63**).
   b. On alloy wheels, crimp the balance weight onto the rim (**Figure 64**).

TIRE CHANGING (LACED WHEELS)

Laced or wire wheels can easily be damaged during tire removal. Special care must be taken with tire irons to avoid scratches and gouges to the outer rim surface. Insert rim protectors (**Figure 65**) or scraps of leather between the tire iron and the rim.

Removal

CAUTION
Support the wheel on two blocks of wood, so the brake disc does not contact the floor.

1. Remove the wheel as described in this chapter.
2. If the tire will be reinstalled, place a balance mark on the tire opposite the valve stem location (**Figure 66**) so the tire can be reinstalled in the same position for easier balancing.
3. Remove the valve core to deflate the tire.
4. Press the entire bead on both sides of the tire away from the rim and into the center of the rim.
5. Lubricate both beads with soapy water.

CAUTION
*Use rim protectors (**Figure 65**) between the tire irons and the rim to protect the rim from*

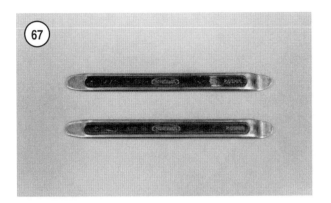

*damage. Also, use only quality tire irons without sharp edges (**Figure 67**). If necessary, file the ends of the tire irons to remove rough edges.*

6. Insert the tire iron under the upper bead next to the valve stem (**Figure 68**). Press the lower bead into the center of the rim and pry the upper bead over the rim with the tire iron.

7. Insert a second tire iron next to the first to hold the bead over the rim (**Figure 69**). Work around the tire, prying the bead over the rim with the first tool. Be careful not to pinch the inner tube with the tire irons.

8. When the upper bead is off the rim, remove the nut from the valve stem. Remove the valve from the hole in the rim and remove the tube from the tire (**Figure 70**).

NOTE
Step 9 is required only if it is necessary to completely remove the tire from the rim.

9. Stand the wheel upright. Force the second bead into the center of the rim. Insert the tire iron between the second bead and the side of the rim that the first bead was pried over. Pry the second bead off the rim (**Figure 71**), working around the wheel with two tire irons as done earlier.

10. Inspect the rim as described in this section.

Installation

NOTE
Before installing the tire, place it in the sun or in a hot, closed car. The heat will soften the rubber and ease installation.

1. Install the rubber rim band. Align the hole in the band with the valve hole in the rim.

2. Liberally sprinkle the inside of the tire with talcum powder to reduce chafing between the tire and tube.

3. Most tires have directional arrows on the sidewall. Install the tire so the arrow points in the direction of forward rotation.

4. If the tire was removed, lubricate the lower bead of the tire with soapy water and place the tire against the rim. Align the valve stem balance mark (**Figure 66**) with the valve stem hole in the rim.

5. Using your hand, push as much of the lower bead past the upper rim surface as possible. Work around the tire in both directions (**Figure 72**).

6. Install the valve core into the valve stem in the inner tube.

7. Put the tube into the tire and insert the valve stem through the hole in the rim. Inflate the tube just enough to round it out. Too much air will make tire installation difficult; too little air increases the chance of pinching the tube with the tire irons.

8. Lubricate the upper tire bead and rim with soapy water.

9. Press the upper bead into the rim opposite the valve stem. Pry the bead into the rim on both sides of this initial point with your hands and work around the rim to the valve stem. If the tire pulls up on one side, either use a tire iron or a knee to hold the tire in place. The last few inches are usually the toughest and also the place where most tubes are pinched. If possible, continue to push the tire into the rim with your hands. Re-lubricate the bead if necessary. If the tire bead pulls out from under the rim, use both of your knees to hold the tire in place. If necessary, use a tire iron and rim protector for the last few inches (**Figure 73**).

> *CAUTION*
> *Make sure the valve stem is not cocked in the rim (**Figure 74**).*

10. Wiggle the valve stem to make sure the tube is not trapped under the bead. Set the valve squarely in its hole.

> *WARNING*
> *In the next step, seat the tire on the rim by inflating the tire to approximately 10 percent above the recommended inflation pressure listed in **Table 3**. Do not exceed 10 percent. Never stand directly over a tire while inflating it. The tire could burst and cause severe injury.*

11. Check the bead on both sides of the tire for an even fit around the rim, then re-lubricate both sides of the tire. Inflate the tube to seat the tire on the rim. Make sure both beads are fully seated and the tire rim lines (**Figure 75**) are the same distance from the rim all the way around the tire. If the beads will not seat, release the air from the tire. Lu-

bricate the rim and beads with soapy water, and re-inflate the tube.

12. Bleed the tire pressure down to the recommended pressure listed in **Table 3**. Install the valve stem nut, and tighten it against the rim, then install the valve stem cap.

13. Balance the wheel as described in this chapter.

Inspection

1. Remove and inspect the rubber rim band. Replace the band if it is deteriorated or broken.

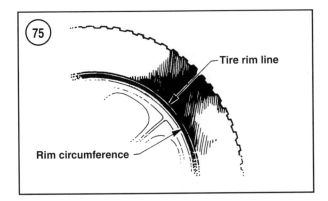

Tire rim line

Rim circumference

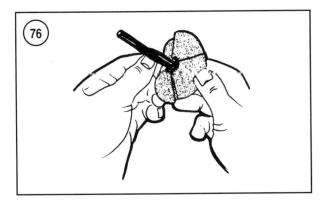

2. Clean the inner and outer rim surfaces of all dirt, rust, corrosion and rubber residue.

3. Inspect the valve stem hole in the rim. Remove any dirt or corrosion from the hole.

4. Inspect the rim profiles for any cracks or other damage.

5. If the tube will be reused, reinstall the valve core, inflate the tube and check it for any leaks.

6. While the tube is inflated, clean it with water.

7. When reusing the tire, carefully check it inside and outside for damage. Replace the tire if there is any damage.

8. Make sure the spoke ends do not protrude from the nipples into the center of the rim.

TIRE CHANGING
(ALLOY WHEELS)

WARNING
Do not install an inner tube inside a tubeless tire. The tube will cause an abnormal heat buildup in the tire.

Tubeless tires have the word TUBELESS molded in the tire sidewall and the rims have TUBELESS on them.

If the tire is punctured, remove it from the rim to inspect the inside of the tire and apply a combination plug/patch

from inside the tire (**Figure 76**). A Plug applied from the outside of the tire should only be used as a temporary roadside repair.

Follow the repair kit manufacturer's instructions as to applicable repairs and any speed limitations. In most cases it is a good idea to replace a patched or plugged tire as soon as possible.

Removal

The wheels can easily be damaged during tire removal. Special care must be taken with tire irons to avoid scratching and gouging the outer rim surface. Protect the rim by using rim protectors or scraps of leather between the tire iron and the rim (**Figure 65**). The alloy wheels are designed for use with tubeless tires.

When removing a tubeless tire, be careful not to damage the tire beads, inner liner of the tire or the wheel rim flange. Use tire levers or flat-handled tire irons (**Figure 67**) with rounded ends.

CAUTION
While removing a tire, support the wheel on two blocks of wood, so the brake disc does not contact the floor.

1. Place a balance mark opposite the valve stem (**Figure 66**) on the tire sidewall so the tire can be reinstalled in the same position for easier balancing.

2. Remove the valve core to deflate the tire.

CAUTION
*Removal of tubeless tires from their rims can be very difficult because of the exceptionally tight bead/rim sealing surface. Breaking the bead seal may require the use of a bead breaker (**Figure 77**). Do not scratch the inside of the rim or damage the tire bead.*

3. Press the entire bead on both sides of the tire into the center of the rim.

4. Lubricate the beads with soapy water.

NOTE
*Use rim protectors (**Figure 65**) or insert scraps of leather between the tire irons and the rim to protect the rim from damage.*

5. Insert the tire iron under the bead next to the valve stem (**Figure 78**). Force the bead on the opposite side of the tire into the center of the rim and pry the bead over the rim with the tire iron.

11

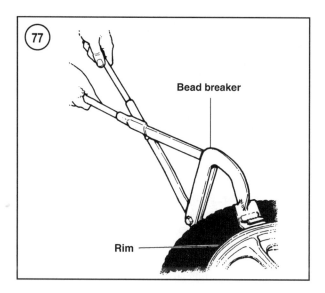

6. Insert a second tire iron next to the first to hold the bead over the rim (**Figure 79**). Then work around the tire with the first tool prying the bead over the rim.

NOTE
Step 7 is required only if it is necessary to completely remove the tire from the rim.

7. Set the wheel on its edge. Insert a tire tool between the second bead and the same side of the rim that the first bead was pried over (**Figure 80**). Force the bead on the opposite side from the tool into the center of the rim. Pry the second bead off the rim, working around the wheel with two tire irons as with the first.

8. Inspect the valve stem seal. Because rubber deteriorates with age, it is advisable to replace the valve stem when replacing a tire.

Installation

1. Carefully inspect the tire for any damage, especially inside.

2. A new tire may have balancing rubbers inside. These are not patches and should not be disturbed.

3. Manufacturers place a colored spot near the bead, indicating a lighter point on the tire. Install the tires so this balance mark (either the manufacturer's or the one made during removal) sits opposite the valve stem (**Figure 66**).

4. Most tires have arrows on the sidewall. Install the tire so the arrow points in the direction of forward rotation.

5. Lubricate both beads of the tire with soapy water.

6. Place the backside of the tire into the center of the rim. The lower bead should go into the center of the rim and

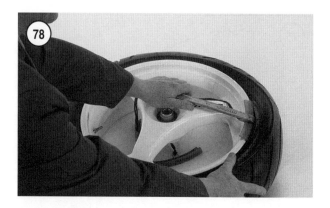

the upper bead outside. Work around the tire in both directions (**Figure 81**).

7. Starting at the side opposite the valve stem, press the upper bead into the rim (**Figure 82**). Pry the bead into the rim on both sides of the initial point with a tire tool, working around the rim to the valve (**Figure 83**).

8. Check the bead on both sides of the tire for an even fit around the rim.

9. Place an inflatable band around the circumference of the tire. Slowly inflate the band until the tire beads are pressed against the rim. Inflate the tire enough to seat it against the rim. Deflate and remove the band.

> *WARNING*
> *Never exceed 56 psi (4.0 k/cm²) inflation pressure as the tire could burst, causing severe injury. Never stand directly over the tire while inflating it.*

10. After inflating the tire, make sure the beads are fully seated and the tire rim lines are the same distance from the rim all the way around the tire (**Figure 75**). If the beads will not seat, deflate the tire, re-lubricate the rim and beads with soapy water and re-inflate the tire.

11. Inflate the tire to the required pressure. Refer to tire inflation pressure specifications in **Table 3**. Screw on the valve stem cap.

12. Balance the wheel assembly as described in this chapter.

Table 1 WHEEL SPECIFICATIONS

Wheel size 1999-2003	
Front	16 × MT3.00
Rear	16 × MT3.50
Maximum runout service limit	
Axial	0.5 mm (0.02 in.)
Radial	1 mm (0.04 in.)
Wheel size 2004-on (laced and alloy wheel)	
Front	16M/C × MT3.00
Rear	16M/C × MT3.50
Maximum runout service limit (laced wheel)	
Axial	2 mm (0.08 in.)
Radial	2 mm (0.08 in.)
Maximum runout service limit (alloy wheel)	
Axial	1 mm (0.04 in.)
Radial	1 mm (0.04 in.)
Brake disc deflection	0.1 mm (0.004 in.)

Table 2 TIRE SPECIFICATIONS

Item	Specification
Tire sizes	
Front	130/90-16 67H
Rear	150/80 B16 71H
Tire series	
1999-2003	
Front	G703 Bridgestone
	D404 Dunlop
Rear	G702 Bridgestone
	D404 Dunlop
2004-2005	
Front	G703 Bridgestone (U.S. and Canada)
	D404 Dunlop (Canada)
Rear	G702 Bridgestone (U.S)
	D404 Dunlop (Canada)
2006-on	
Front	G703 Bridgestone
	D404 Dunlop
Rear	G702 Bridgestone
	D404 Dunlop
Minimum tread depth	
1999-2003	1.6 mm (0.06 in.)
2004-on	1.0 mm (0.04 in.)

Table 3 TIRE INFLATION PRESSURE[1]

1999-2003 models	
0-90 kg (0-198 lb.)	
Front tire	250 kPa (36 psi)
Rear tire	250 kPa (36 psi)
90 kg (198 lb.)-maximum load[2]	
Front tire	250 kPa (36 psi)
Rear tire	280 kPa (40 psi)
2004-on models	
0-90 kg (0-198 lb.)	
Front tire	250 kPa (36 psi)
Rear tire	250 kPa (36 psi)
90 kg (198 lb.)-maximum load[2]	
Front tire	250 kPa (36 psi)
Rear tire	280 kPa (40 psi)

1. Tire inflation pressure applies to original equipment tires. Aftermarket tires may require different inflation pressures; refer to the aftermarket manufacturer's specifications.
2. Maximum load equates to the total weight of the cargo, rider, passenger and accessories.

Table 4 WHEEL TORQUE SPECIFICATIONS

Item	N•m	in.-lb.	ft.-lb.
Brake caliper mounting bolts	40	–	30
Brake disc bolts*	23	–	17
Drive belt adjuster locknut	32	–	24
	(continued)		

Table 4 WHEEL TORQUE SPECIFICATIONS (continued)

Item	N•m	in.-lb.	ft.-lb.
Driven sprocket nuts	95	–	70
Front axle	78	–	58
Front axle clamp bolt	20	–	15
Rear axle nut	150		111
Rear brake caliper bracket bolt	40	–	30
Rear fender			
Front edge of fender bolts	48	–	35
Throughbolt and nut	88	–	65
Wheel spoke nipples	3	27	–

*Apply a medium-strength thread locking compound.

CHAPTER TWELVE

FRONT SUSPENSION AND STEERING

This chapter describes service procedures for the handlebar, front fork and steering components. When inspecting the components, compare any measurements to the specifications tables at the end of this chapter. Replace any component that is worn, damaged or out of specification. During assembly, tighten components to the torque specification in **Table 2**.

FRONT FORK

Before concluding the front fork has problems, drain the fork oil and refill the fork legs with the proper type and quantity of fork oil as described under *Assembly* in this section. If a problem(s) still exists, such as poor damping or a tendency to bottom or top out, follow the service procedures in this section.

To simplify fork service and to prevent the mixing of parts, service each fork leg individually.

Removal (Fork Not To Be Serviced)

Refer to **Figure 1**.

NOTE
This procedure is shown with the headlight and front turn signal assembly removed for photo clarity. It is not necessary to remove either component.

1. Securely support the motorcycle with a front end stand. Block the rear wheel so the motorcycle will not roll in either direction.
2. On models so equipped, remove the windshield and mounting brackets as described in Chapter Fifteen.
3. Remove the fuel tank as described in Chapter Nine.

CAUTION
Cover the frame and engine with plastic to protect them from accidental brake fluid spills. Immediately wash spilled brake fluid off any painted or plated surface. Brake fluid will damage the finish. Use soapy water and rinse the area thoroughly.

4. Remove the front wheel as described in Chapter Eleven.
5. Remove the front fender as described in Chapter Fifteen.
6. Remove the Allen screws (**Figure 2**) securing the brake hose guide to the lower fork bridge. Slide the guide down the brake hose.
7. Remove the front brake caliper and brake hose holder from the slider, as described in Chapter Fourteen. Insert

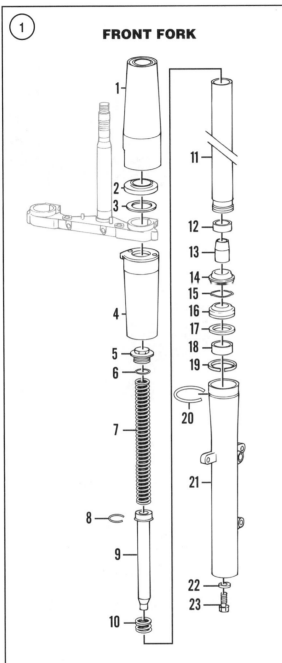

FRONT FORK

1. Upper cover
2. Gasket
3. Washer
4. Lower cover
5. Cap bolt
6. O-ring
7. Spring
8. Piston ring
9. Damper rod
10. Rebound spring
11. Fork tube
12. Fork tube housing
13. Oil lock piece
14. Dust cap
15. Retaining ring
16. Oil seal
17. Spacer
18. Slider bushing
19. Ring
20. Plastic spacer ring
21. Slider
22. Copper washer
23. Allen bolt

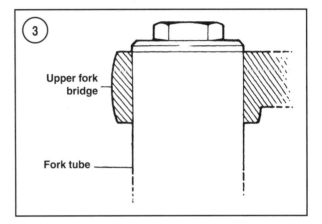

Upper fork bridge

Fork tube

vinyl tubing or a piece of wood between the pads in the caliper.

8. Note that the top edge of the fork tube aligns with the top of the upper fork bridge (**Figure 3**). The fork leg must be reinstalled to the same height during assembly.

NOTE
It is not necessary to completely remove the upper fork bridge and handlebar assembly. Leave all components attached to the handlebar.

9. Remove the upper fork bridge and handlebar assembly as described in this chapter. Rest the assembly with the handlebar attached across the frame and tarp.

CAUTION
The edges of the fork covers are very sharp. Wear gloves and exercise caution to avoid injury.

10. Slide the upper cover (**Figure 4**) up and off the fork tube.

11. Remove the gasket (**Figure 5**) and the washer (**Figure 6**) from the fork tube.

12

12. Remove the Allen screw (**Figure 7**) securing the lower cover. Move the lower cover down on the slider.

13. Loosen the lower clamp bolts (**Figure 8**).

14. Rotate the fork tube and slide it and the lower cover (**Figure 9**) down and out of the lower fork bridge.

Installation (Fork Leg Not Serviced)

1. Install the lower fork cover (**Figure 9**) onto the fork tube if it was removed.

2. Rotate the fork leg and install it through the lower fork bridge. Tighten the lower fork bridge clamp bolts (**Figure 8**) enough to hold the fork leg in place.

NOTE
The upper fork bridge/handlebar assembly must be temporarily installed so the fork leg can be installed at the proper height.

3. Install the upper fork bridge/handlebar assembly (A, **Figure 10**) onto the front fork legs and the steering stem. Install the steering head washer and nut (B). Tighten the steering head nut securely.

4. Loosen the lower fork bridge clamp bolts. Reposition the fork assembly and align the top edge of the fork tube with the top edge of the upper fork bridge as shown in **Figure 3**.

5. Tighten the lower fork bridge clamp bolts (**Figure 8**) to 20 N•m (15 ft.-lb.).

6. Remove the upper fork bridge/handlebar assembly and place it on the frame.

7. Move the lower cover up and into position, install the Allen screw (**Figure 7**) and tighten securely.

8. Install the washer (**Figure 6**) onto the fork tube. Position the gasket with the raised lip facing up and install the gasket (**Figure 5**).

9. Install the upper cover onto the fork tube and position it correctly onto the lower fork bridge (**Figure 4**).

10. Install the upper fork bridge/handlebar assembly as described in this chapter.

11. Install the brake hose through the brake hose guide and install the brake hose guide onto the lower fork bridge. Install the Allen screws (**Figure 2**) and tighten securely.

12. Install the brake hose holder onto the slider.

13. Install the front wheel as described in Chapter Eleven.

14. Install the front fender as described in Chapter Fifteen.

15. Install the front brake caliper(s) as described in Chapter Fourteen.

16. Remove the plastic cover from the engine and frame.

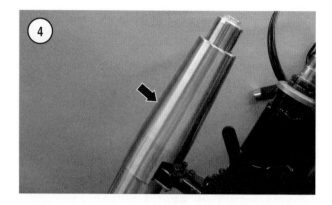

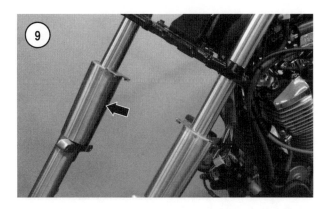

17. On models so equipped, install the windshield and mounting brackets as described in Chapter Fifteen.

18. Install the fuel tank as described in Chapter Nine.

Removal/Disassembly (Fork Leg Requires Service)

1. The following Yamaha special tools, or their equivalents, are needed to service a fork leg.

    a. Damper rod holder: part No. YM-1300-1 (U.S.) or 90890-01426 (U.K.).

    b. T-handle: part No. YM-01326 (U.S.) or 90890-01326 (U.K.).

    c. Fork seal driver: Yamaha part No. YM-33963 (U.S.) or 90809-01367 (U.K.).

    d. Driver adapter: part No. YM-8020 (U.S.) or 90890-01374 (U.K.).

NOTE
The fork leg Allen bolt can be removed without using the damper rod holder and T-handle. However, the Allen bolt cannot be tightened without these tools.

2. Securely support the motorcycle on a level surface.

NOTE
This procedure is shown with the headlight and front turn signal assembly removed for photo clarity. It is not necessary to remove either component.

3. Securely support the motorcycle with a front end stand. Block the rear wheel so the motorcycle will not roll in either direction.

4. On models so equipped, remove the windshield and mounting brackets as described in Chapter Fifteen.

5. Remove the fuel tank as described in Chapter Nine.

CAUTION
Cover the frame and engine with plastic to protect them from accidental brake fluid spills. Immediately wash spilled brake fluid off any painted or plated surface. Brake fluid will damage the finish. Use soapy water and rinse the area thoroughly.

6. Remove the front wheel as described in Chapter Eleven.

7. Remove the front fender as described in Chapter Fifteen.

8. Remove the Allen screws (**Figure 2**) securing the brake hose guide to the lower fork bridge. Slide the guide down the brake hose.

9. Remove the front brake caliper and brake hose holder from the slider, as described in Chapter Fourteen. Insert vinyl tubing or a piece of wood spacer between the pads in the caliper.

10. Loosen the Allen bolt as follows:

    a. Place a drain pan beneath the fork leg.

    b. Use an impact wrench, or socket and wrench, and to loosen the Allen bolt (**Figure 11**) from the bottom of the fork leg. Do not remove the bolt at this time as the fork oil will drain out.

12

11. Note that the top edge of the fork tube aligns with the top of the upper fork bridge (**Figure 3**). The fork leg must be reinstalled to the same height during assembly.

NOTE
Use a 6-point socket on the cap bolt. A 12-point socket will damage the cap bolt.

12. Use a 6-point socket to break loose the cap bolt and slowly loosen the cap bolt (**Figure 12**). Do not remove the cap bolt at this time.

NOTE
It is not necessary to completely remove the upper fork bridge and handlebar assembly. Leave all components attached to the handlebar.

13. Partially remove the upper fork bridge and handlebar assembly as described in this chapter. Rest the assembly with the handlebar attached across the frame and tarp.

CAUTION
The edges of the fork covers are very sharp. Wear gloves and exercise caution to avoid injury.

14. Remove the upper cover (**Figure 4**) from the fork tube.
15. Remove the gasket (**Figure 5**) and the washer (**Figure 6**) from the fork tube.
16. Remove the Allen screw (**Figure 7**) securing the lower cover. Move the lower cover down on the slider.
17. Loosen the lower clamp bolts (**Figure 8**).
18. Rotate the fork tube and slide it along with the lower cover (**Figure 9**) down and out of the lower fork bridge.
19. Remove the lower cover from the fork assembly.
20. Reinstall the fork assembly into the lower fork bridge (**Figure 13**). Tighten the lower fork bridge bolts to 20 N•m (15 ft.-lb.).

NOTE
It may be necessary to slightly heat the area on the slider around the oil seal before removal. Heat the area with a rag soaked in hot water. Do not apply a flame directly to the fork slider.

21. There is an interference fit between the bushing in the fork slider and the bushing on the fork tube. To remove the fork slider from the fork tube, firmly grasp the slider, pull hard on the slider using quick up-and-down strokes (**Figure 14**), and loosen the slider from the fork tube.
22. Keep the fork assembly vertical and take it to the workbench for further disassembly.

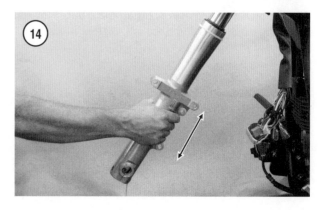

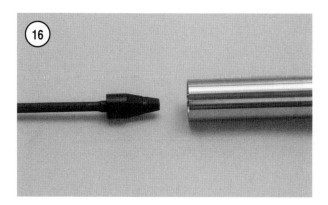

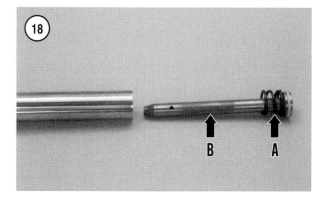

23. Remove the Allen bolt and gasket from the base of the slider and drain the fork oil.

24. Install the fork slider in a vise with soft jaws and tighten securely.

> *WARNING*
> *The cap bolt (**Figure 15**) is under **very heavy** spring pressure. Exercise caution when removing the cap bolt.*

> *NOTE*
> *Use a 6-point socket on the cap bolt. A 12-point socket will damage the cap bolt.*

25. Place a 6-point socket on the cap bolt (**Figure 15**). Slowly loosen the cap bolt while applying pressure on the socket and cap bolt especially during the end of the cap bolt thread engagement. The spring will push the cap bolt off the fork tube and may damage the cap bolt threads.

26. Remove the cap bolt, and pour out the remaining fork oil.

27. Remove the fork spring.

28. If the Allen bolt could not be loosened during Step 10, remove it now as follows:

   a. Install the damper rod holder onto the T-handle.

   b. Insert the T-handle and holder into the fork tube (**Figure 16**) until the holder engages the damper rod. Hold the damper rod, and loosen then remove the Allen bolt along with its copper washer from the base of the slider.

   c. Remove the tools from the slider.

29. Separate the slider from the fork tube.

30. Remove the oil lock piece from the damper rod and withdraw the damper rod and rebound spring from the fork tube.

31. Remove the dust cap, stopper ring, oil seal, spacer and slider bushing from the fork tube.

> *NOTE*
> *Do not remove the fork tube bushing (**Figure 17**) unless it will be replaced. Inspect it as described in this chapter.*

32. Inspect all parts as described in this section.

Assembly
(Fork Leg Was Serviced)

1. Coat all parts with fresh SAE 5W fork oil before installation.

2. If removed, install a *new* slider bushing (**Figure 17**) as described in *Inspection* in this section.

3. Slide the rebound spring (A, **Figure 18**) onto the damper rod (B).

12

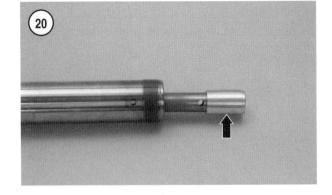

4. Insert the damper rod into the fork tube until the rod emerges from the fork tube end (**Figure 19**). Install the oil lock piece (**Figure 20**) onto the damper rod.

5. Temporarily install the fork spring to hold the damper rod in place.

6. Install the fork tube into the slider (**Figure 21**) and guide the oil lock piece into position. Remove the fork spring.

7. Install the Yamaha damper rod holder onto the T-handle. Insert the tool into the fork tube (**Figure 16**) so the rod holder engages the damper rod.

8. Install a *new* copper washer onto the Allen bolt.

9. Apply a medium-strength thread locking compound to the threads of the Allen bolt. Insert the Allen bolt through the bottom of the slider (**Figure 22**) and thread it into the damper rod.

10. Hold the damper rod with the special tool (**Figure 23**) and tighten the Allen bolt to 20 N•m (15 ft.-lb.). Remove the special tools.

11. Slide a *new* slider bushing (A, **Figure 24**) and washer (B) down the fork tube.

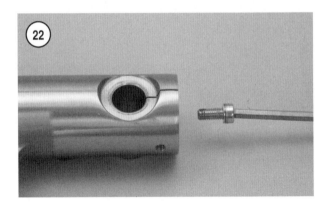

CAUTION
Use the Yamaha fork seal driver and adapter to install the slider bushing and washer in the next step. If these tools are not available, use a universal oil seal driver or a piece of galvanized pipe and a hammer. If both ends of the pipe are threaded, wrap one end with duct tape to prevent the threads from damaging the interior of the slider.

12. Drive the slider bushing and washer into place (**Figure 25**) until the bushing bottoms in the slider.

13. Remove the special tool.

CAUTION
The plastic wrap installed in the next step protects the oil seal so it will not be torn during installation.

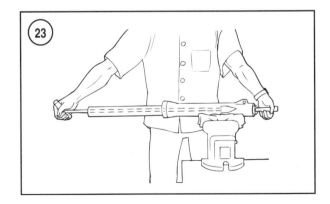

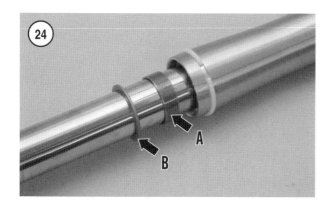

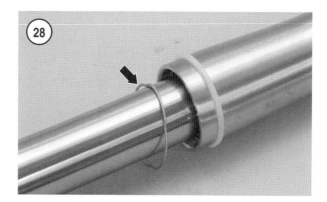

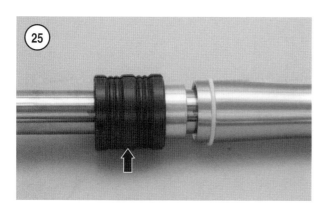

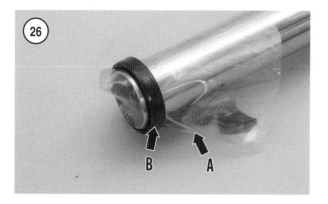

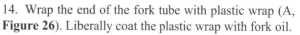

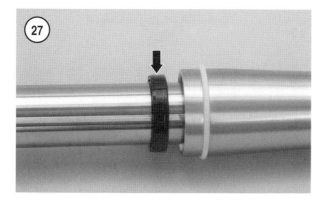

14. Wrap the end of the fork tube with plastic wrap (A, **Figure 26**). Liberally coat the plastic wrap with fork oil.

15. Lubricate the lips of the *new* oil seal with fork oil. Position the oil seal so the manufacturer's marks faces up, away from the fork slider. Install the oil seal onto the fork tube (B, **Figure 26**).

16. Remove the plastic wrap and slide the oil seal (**Figure 27**) down into position.

17. Use the same tool used in Step 12 to drive the oil seal into the slider until the retaining clip groove in the slider can be seen above the top of the oil seal.

18. Install the retaining clip (**Figure 28**) down the fork tube and seat the clip into the groove in the slider. Make sure the clip is completely seated in the slider groove.

19. Lubricate a *new* dust seal with fork oil. Slide the seal down the fork tube and install it into the fork slider.

20. Carefully tap the dust seal (**Figure 29**) into the slider.

21. Secure the fork leg upright in a vise with soft jaws. Fill the fork leg with the correct quantity of SAE 5W fork oil. Refer to **Table 1** for the specified quantity.

22. Slowly pump the fork up and down several times to distribute the fork oil, then let it settle.

23. Compress the fork completely and measure the fluid level after the fork oil settles. Use an oil level gauge to measure the fluid level from the top of the fork

12

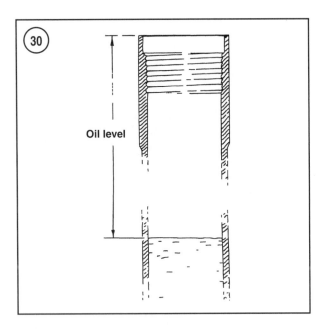

tube (**Figure 30**). If necessary, add or remove oil to set the fluid level to the level in **Table 1**.

24. Slowly pull the fork tube up away from the slider until it is fully extended.

25. Position the fork spring into the fork tube so the slightly tapered end goes in first and install the fork spring (**Figure 31**).

26. Install a *new* O-ring seal (**Figure 32**) onto the cap bolt. Apply molybdenum disulfide grease to the cap bolt threads.

NOTE
The following step requires an assistant to correctly thread the cap bolt onto the fork tube.

27. Place the fork slider on the ground on a piece of wood. Have the assistant hold the fork assembly vertical with the fork tube fully extended and held tightly so it will not rotate while the cap bolt is installed.

28. Place a 6-point socket onto the cap bolt (**Figure 33**) and use a T-handle socket driver (**Figure 34**), or equivalent, that will provide a place to apply downward force onto the cap bolt in Step 27.

WARNING
*The cap bolt (**Figure 15**) is under **very heavy** spring pressure. Exercise caution when removing the cap bolt.*

CAUTION
Proceed very slowly in the next step to avoid damaging the cap bolt threads since it is

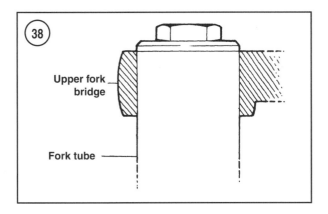

very easy to cross-thread the cap bolt while compressing the fork spring.

29. Pad the top of the T-handle socket driver with several shop cloths. Press down on the socket driver, correctly align the cap bolt to the fork tube and *slowly* thread the cap bolt into the fork tube. If necessary, unscrew the cap bolt and try again until alignment is correct. Tighten the cap bolt securely. The cap bolt will be tightened to specification after the fork is installed on the motorcycle.

30. Install the fork assembly as described earlier in this chapter.

Installation

1. Install the lower fork cover (**Figure 35**) onto the fork tube if it was removed.

2. Rotate the fork leg and install it through the lower fork bridge. Tighten the lower fork bridge clamp bolts (**Figure 36**) enough to hold the fork leg in place.

NOTE
The upper fork bridge/handlebar assembly must be temporarily installed so the fork leg can set to the proper height.

3. Install the upper fork bridge/handlebar assembly (A, **Figure 37**) onto the front fork legs and the steering stem. Install the steering head washer and nut (B, **Figure 37**). Tighten the steering head nut securely.

4. Loosen the lower fork bridge clamp bolts. Reposition the fork assembly and align the top edge of the fork tube with the top edge of the upper fork bridge as shown in **Figure 38**.

5. Tighten the clamp bolts on the lower fork bridge (**Figure 36**) to 20 N•m (15 ft.-lb.).

6. Remove the upper fork bridge/handlebar assembly and place it on the frame.

7. Move the lower cover into position, install the Allen screw (**Figure 39**) and tighten securely.

8. Install the washer (**Figure 40**) onto the fork tube. Position the gasket with the raised lip facing up and install the gasket (**Figure 41**).

9. Install the upper cover onto the fork tube and position it correctly onto the lower fork bridge (**Figure 42**).

10. Install the upper fork bridge/handlebar assembly as described in this chapter.

11. If the fork leg was disassembled, tighten the cap bolt (**Figure 43**) to 23 N•m (17 ft.-lb.).

12. Install the brake hose through the brake hose guide and install the brake hose guide onto the lower fork bridge. Install the Allen screws (**Figure 44**) and tighten securely.

13. Install the brake hose holder onto the slider.

14. Install the front wheel as described in Chapter Eleven.

15. Install the front fender as described in Chapter Fifteen.

16. Install the front brake caliper(s) as described in Chapter Fourteen.

17. Remove the plastic cover from the engine and frame.

18. On models so equipped, install the windshield and mounting brackets as described in Chapter Fifteen.

19. Install the fuel tank as described in Chapter Nine.

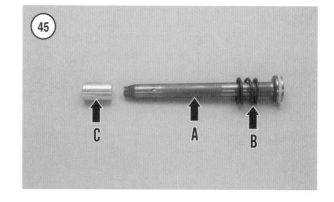

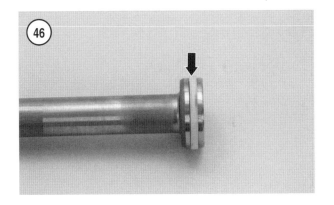

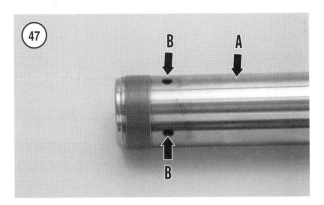

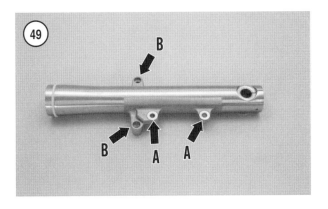

20. If necessary, bleed the front brakes as described in Chapter Fourteen.

Inspection

1. Thoroughly clean all parts in solvent and dry them with compressed air.

2. Clean out the oil holes in the damper rod with compressed air.

3. Check the damper rod assembly for:
   a. Bent, cracked or otherwise damaged damper rod (A, **Figure 45**).
   b. Excessively worn rebound spring (B, **Figure 45**).
   c. Damaged oil lock piece (C, **Figure 45**).
   d. Excessively worn or damaged piston ring (**Figure 46**).

4. Check the fork tube for straightness and for signs of wear or scratches. If it is bent or severely scratched, replace it.

5. Check the fork tube (A, **Figure 47**) for chrome flaking or creasing. This condition will damage the oil seal.

6. Make sure the oil flow holes (B, **Figure 47**) are open. Clean out if necessary.

7. Check the seal area of the slider (**Figure 48**) for dents, scratches or other damage that would allow oil leaks.

8. Check the slider for dents or exterior damage that may cause the upper fork tube to hang up during riding. Replace it if necessary. Check for cracks or damage to the brake caliper (A, **Figure 49**) and fender mounting bosses (B).

9. Inspect the front axle threads (**Figure 50**) in the left side slider for damage. If damage is slight, chase the threads with a metric tap. If damage is excessive, replace the slider.

10. Check the plastic spacer ring (**Figure 51**) for fatigue or deterioration.

12

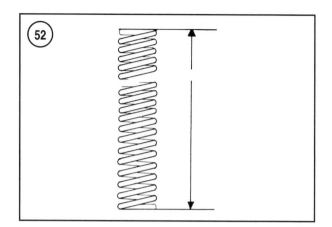

11. Measure the uncompressed length of the fork spring (**Figure 52**). If the spring has sagged to the service limit (**Table 1**), replace it.

12. Inspect the fork tube (A, **Figure 53**) and slider (B) bushings. If either is scratched or scored, replace them. If the Teflon coating is worn off so the copper base material is showing on approximately 3/4 of the total surface, replace the bushing.

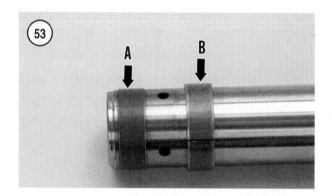

   a. To replace the fork tube bushing, open the bushing slot with a screwdriver and slide the bushing off the fork tube.

   b. Lubricate the new bushing with fork oil, open its slot and slide it onto the fork tube groove.

13. Install a *new* fork cap O-ring (**Figure 54**). Lubricate the O-ring with fork oil before installation.

14. Inspect the upper cover (A, **Figure 55**), gasket (B) and washer (C) for wear or damage.

15. Inspect the lower cover (**Figure 56**) for wear or damage.

16. Replace any parts that are worn or damaged. Simply cleaning and reinstalling unserviceable fork components will not improve performance of the front suspension.

HANDLEBAR

Removal

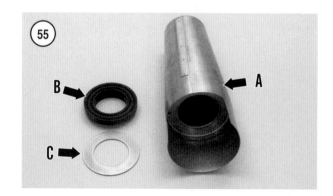

CAUTION
Cover the front fender, frame and fuel tank with plastic to protect them from accidental brake fluid spills. Immediately wash spilled brake fluid off any painted or plated surface. Brake fluid will damage the finish. Use soapy water and rinse the area thoroughly.

1. Securely support the motorcycle on level ground. Block the front wheel so the motorcycle will not roll in either direction.

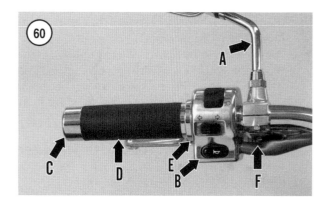

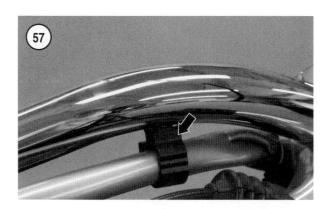

2. On models so equipped, remove the windshield as described in Chapter Fifteen.

3. Unhook the electrical cables from the plastic clips (**Figure 57**) on the handlebar.

4A. On the right side of the handlebar, perform the following:

    a. Loosen the locknut, turn the mirror *clockwise* (A, **Figure 58**), and remove it from the master cylinder.

    b. Remove the two master cylinder clamp bolts (B, **Figure 58**) and remove the master cylinder (C) from the handlebar. Secure the master cylinder to the frame with a bungee cord. Make sure the master cylinder reservoir remains upright. This prevents brake fluid spills and helps keep air out of the brake system. Do not disconnect the hydraulic brake line.

    c. Remove the right handlebar switch assembly (D, **Figure 58**) as described in Chapter Ten.

    d. Disconnect the throttle cable ends (**Figure 59**) from the throttle grip.

    e. Remove the handlebar weight (E, **Figure 58**) and slide the throttle grip assembly (F) from the handlebar.

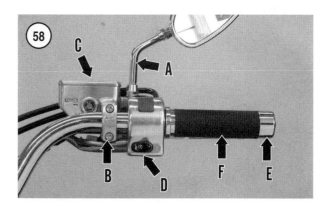

4B. On the left side of the handlebar, perform the following:

    a. Loosen the locknut, turn the mirror *counterclockwise* (A, **Figure 60**), and remove it from the master cylinder.

    b. Pull the rubber boot (**Figure 61**) off the clutch cable adjuster.

    c. Loosen the locknut (A, **Figure 62**) and turn the adjuster (B) to gain the maximum amount of slack in the clutch cable. Disconnect the clutch cable from the clutch lever assembly.

12

    d. Remove the left handlebar switch (B, **Figure 60**) as described in Chapter Ten.

    e. Unscrew the end weight (C, **Figure 60**).

    f. Insert a thin-bladed screwdriver under the hand grip (D, **Figure 60**). Spray electrical contact cleaner under the hand grip, and twist it quickly to break its seal and remove it from the handlebar.

    g. Remove the inner trim ring (E, **Figure 60**).

    h. Loosen the clutch lever clamp nut (F, **Figure 60**), and remove the clutch lever assembly.

5A. On 1999-2003 models, perform the following:

    a. Remove the trim caps, then loosen the clamp bolts (**Figure 63**) on both upper handlebar holders.

    b. Remove both upper handlebar holders from the handlebar and lift the handlebar from the lower handlebar holders.

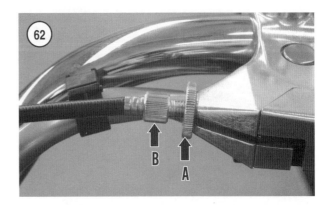

5B. On 2004-on models, perform the following:

    a. Remove the trim caps, then loosen the clamp bolts (**Figure 64**) on the upper handlebar holder.

    b. Remove the upper handlebar holder from the handlebar and lift the handlebar from the lower handlebar holders.

6. If removed, replace the left hand grip as follows:

    a. Apply a thin layer of rubber cement to the end of the handlebar when installing a *new* grip.

    b. Slide the grip onto the handlebar and wipe off excessive cement.

    c. Check the hand grip after 20 minutes to make sure it is tight.

WARNING
Do not ride the motorcycle with a loose hand grip. Loss of control will occur.

Installation

Installation is the reverse of removal. Note the following:

1. Replace the handlebar if it is bent.

2. On 1999-2003 models, position the upper holders with the arrow facing forward.

3. Make sure the punch mark on the handlebar aligns with the top edge of the lower handlebar holder. Refer to A, **Figure 65** and A, **Figure 66**.

4. On 1999-2003 models, tighten the front handlebar holder clamp bolts first, then tighten the rear bolts to 23 N•m (17 ft.-lb.). There should be a gap at the rear of the holders (B, **Figure 65**).

5. On 2004-on models, tighten the front handlebar holder clamp bolts first, then tighten the rear bolts to 28 N•m (21 ft.-lb.). There should be a gap at the rear of the holder (B, **Figure 66**).

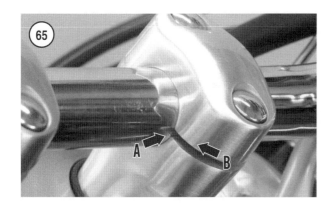

6. Position the clutch lever bracket (A, **Figure 67**) so the gap in the bracket clamp aligns with the index mark (B) on the handlebar.

7. Install the left handlebar switch and the right handlebar switch as described in Chapter Ten.

8. Lubricate the ends of the clutch and throttle cables with lithium grease.

9. Lubricate the throttle grip assembly with lithium grease.

10. Install the front brake master cylinder as follows:

    a. Position the master cylinder so the face of the clamp mating surface aligns with the mark on the handlebar. See A, **Figure 68**.

    b. Install the master cylinder clamp so the ▲UP (B, **Figure 68**) stamped on the clamp faces up.

    c. Tighten the clamp bolts to 10 N•m (88 in.-lb.). Tighten the upper clamp bolt first, then the lower bolt. There should be a gap at the lower part of the clamp after tightening. Do not pinch the electrical wires between the clamps.

11. On 2004-on models, tighten the handlebar weights to 23 N•m (17 in.-lb.).

Inspection

Check the handlebar along the entire mounting area for cracks or damage. Replace a bent or damaged handlebar immediately. If the bike is involved in a crash, examine the handlebar, steering stem and front fork carefully.

STEERING HEAD

Removal

The Yamaha ring nut wrench (part No. YU-33975 [U.S.] or 90890-01443 [U.K.]) or an equivalent tool is required to disassemble and reassemble the steering head.

Refer to **Figure 69**.

1. Securely support the motorcycle with a front end stand. Block the rear wheel so the motorcycle will not roll in either direction.

2. On models so equipped, remove the windshield and mounting brackets as described in Chapter Fifteen.

3. Remove the headlight housing as described in Chapter Ten.

4. Remove the front turn signal assembly as described in Chapter Ten.

5. Remove the fuel tank as described in Chapter Nine.

CAUTION
Cover the frame and engine with plastic to protect them from accidental brake fluid

12

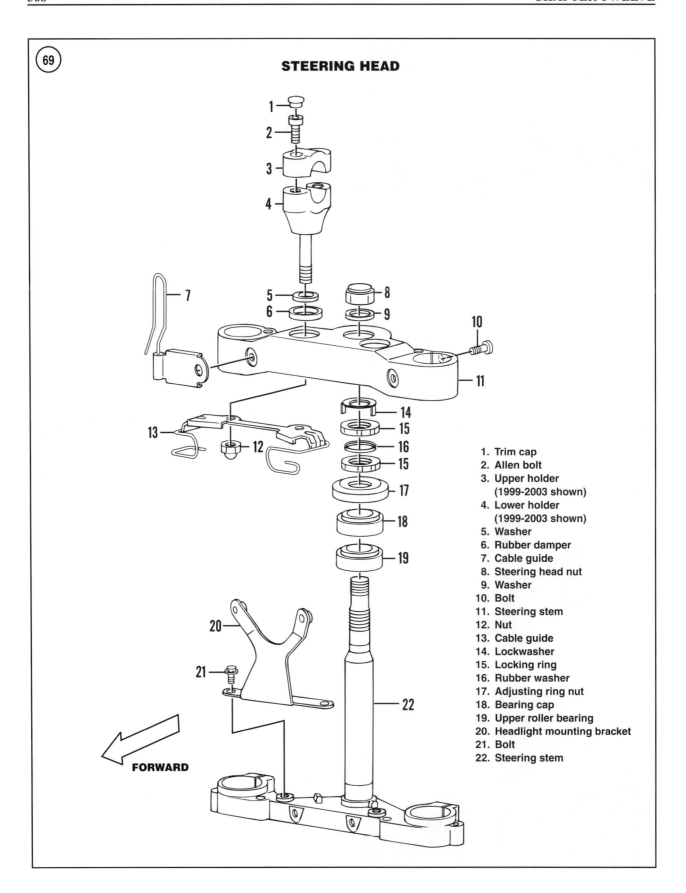

STEERING HEAD

1. Trim cap
2. Allen bolt
3. Upper holder
   (1999-2003 shown)
4. Lower holder
   (1999-2003 shown)
5. Washer
6. Rubber damper
7. Cable guide
8. Steering head nut
9. Washer
10. Bolt
11. Steering stem
12. Nut
13. Cable guide
14. Lockwasher
15. Locking ring
16. Rubber washer
17. Adjusting ring nut
18. Bearing cap
19. Upper roller bearing
20. Headlight mounting bracket
21. Bolt
22. Steering stem

FORWARD

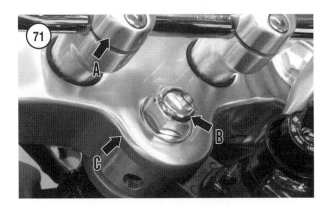

spills. Immediately wash spilled brake fluid off any painted or plated surface. Brake fluid will damage the finish. Use soapy water and rinse the area thoroughly.

6. Remove the front fork as described in this chapter.

7. Remove the front brake hose assembly as described in Chapter Fourteen.

8. Unhook all cables and hoses from the cable guides (**Figure 70**).

9. Remove the handlebar assembly (A, **Figure 71**) as described in this chapter.

10. Remove the steering head nut and washer (B, **Figure 71**).

11. Lift the upper fork bridge off the steering head (C **Figure 71**) straight up and off the steering stem.

12. Remove the lock washer (**Figure 72**) off of the top of the ring nuts.

13. Loosen and remove the locking ring nut (**Figure 73**), then remove the rubber washer (**Figure 74**).

14. Hold onto the lower end of the steering stem assembly.

15. Loosen and remove the adjusting ring nut (**Figure 75**).

16. Remove the bearing cap (**Figure 76**).

12

17. Lower the steering stem assembly down and out of the steering head (**Figure 77**).

18. Remove the upper roller bearing from the steering head. The lower roller bearing will remain on the steering stem.

19. Inspect the steering stem and bearings as described in this section.

Installation

1. Liberally apply lithium grease to the bearings (**Figure 78**) and races (**Figure 79**).

2. Install the lower bearing onto the steering stem, if removed.

3. Install the upper roller bearing (**Figure 80**) into the upper race.

4. Carefully slide the steering stem up (**Figure 77**) through the frame steering head and hold it in place.

5. Install the bearing cap (**Figure 76**) and the adjusting ring nut (**Figure 75**).

6. Adjust the steering head bearings as follows:
    a. Set a torque wrench at a right angle to the ring nut wrench (**Figure 81**).
    b. Seat the bearings within the steering head and tighten the adjusting ring nut to 52 N•m (38 ft.-lb.).
    c. Loosen the adjusting ring nut one turn.
    d. Tighten the adjusting ring nut to 3 N•m (26 in.-lb.).

7. Inspect the steering head as described in Chapter Three. If there is any binding or looseness, inspect the steering head as described in this section.

8. Install a *new* rubber washer (**Figure 74**), and the locking ring nut (**Figure 73**). Tighten the locking ring nut finger-tight. Check the slots on the locking ring. They should align with those on the adjusting ring nut. If they do not, tighten the locking ring nut until alignment is achieved. If necessary, hold the adjusting ring nut so it does not move when the slots are aligned.

9. Install the *new* lock washer (**Figure 72**) so its fingers are seated in the ring nut slots.

10. Install the upper fork bridge (C, **Figure 71**) onto the steering stem shaft. Loosely install the washer and the steering head nut (B).

11. Install the handlebar assembly (A, **Figure 71**) as described in this chapter.

12. Temporarily insert both fork tubes through the lower and upper fork bridges.

13. Tighten the lower bridge pinch bolts (**Figure 82**) to hold the fork tubes in position. Then tighten the steering head nut (B, **Figure 71**) to 130 N•m (96 ft.-lb.).

14. Turn the steering stem by hand to make sure it turns freely and does not bind. If the steering stem is too tight, the bearings can be damaged; if the steering stem is too

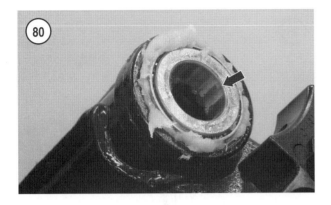

loose, the steering will become unstable. Readjust if necessary.

15. Remove the fork tubes and install them as described in this chapter.

16. Install all cables and hoses into the cable guides (**Figure 70**).

17. Install the front brake hose assembly as described in Chapter Fourteen.

18. Install the fuel tank as described in Chapter Nine.

19. Install the front turn signal assembly as described in Chapter Ten.

20. Install the headlight housing as described in Chapter Ten.

21. On models so equipped, install the windshield and mounting brackets as described in Chapter Fifteen.

Inspection

1. Clean the upper and lower bearings with degreaser. Thoroughly dry both bearings with compressed air. Make sure all solvent is removed from the lower bearing on the steering stem (**Figure 78**).

2. Remove old grease from the outer races in the steering head (**Figure 83**), then clean the outer races with a rag soaked in solvent. Thoroughly dry the races with a lint-free cloth. Check the races for pitting, galling and corrosion. If any of these conditions exist, replace the races as described in this chapter.

3. If any race is worn or damaged, replace the race and bearing as an assembly as described in this chapter.

4. Check the welds around the steering head for cracks and fractures. If there is any damage, have the frame inspected and, if possible, repaired by an experienced frame repair shop.

5. Check the bearings for pitting, scratches or discoloration indicating wear or corrosion. Replace the bearing if any roller is less than perfect.

6. If the bearings are in good condition, pack them thoroughly with grease. To pack the bearings, spread some grease in the palm of your hand and scrape the open side of the bearing cage across your palm until the bearing is completely full of grease.

7. Thoroughly clean all mounting parts in solvent. Dry them completely.

8. Inspect the ring nuts and washer for wear or damage. Inspect the nut threads. If necessary, clean them with an appropriate size metric tap or replace the nut(s). If the threads are damaged, inspect the appropriate steering stem thread(s) for damage. If necessary, clean the threads with an appropriate size metric die.

9. Check the underside of the steering head nut for damage. Replace the nut as necessary.

12

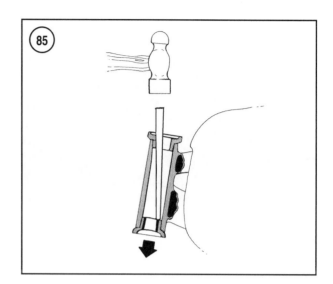

10. Inspect the steering stem and the lower fork bridge (**Figure 84**) for cracks or other damage. Make sure the fork bridge clamping areas are free of burrs and the bolt holes are in good condition.

11. Inspect the upper fork bridge for cracks or other damage. Check both the upper and lower surface of the fork bridge. Make sure the fork bridge clamping areas are free of burrs and the bolt holes are in good condition.

STEERING HEAD BEARING RACES

Do not remove the upper and lower bearing outer races unless they are going to be replaced. These races are pressed into place and will be damaged during removal. If removed, replace the outer races, the inner races, and the bearings as a set. Never reuse an outer race that has been removed. It is no longer true and will damage the bearings if reused.

1. Chill new bearing races in a freezer to shrink the outside diameter.

2. Remove the steering stem as described in this chapter.

3. Insert a brass or aluminum drift into the steering head and carefully tap the lower race out from the steering head (**Figure 85**). Repeat this procedure for the upper race.

4. Clean the race seats in the steering head. Check for cracks or other damage.

5. Apply grease to a new upper race and insert the race into the steering head with the open side facing out. Square the race with the race bore. Tap it slowly and squarely with a block of wood (**Figure 86**).

LOWER BEARING REPLACEMENT

Do not remove the lower bearing unless it will be replaced. The bearing can be difficult to remove. If it cannot be easily removed as described in this procedure, have a Yamaha dealership replace the bearing.

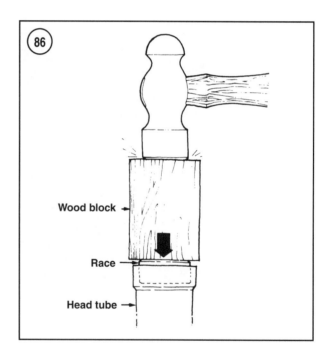

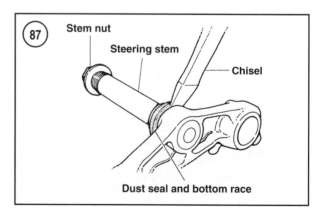

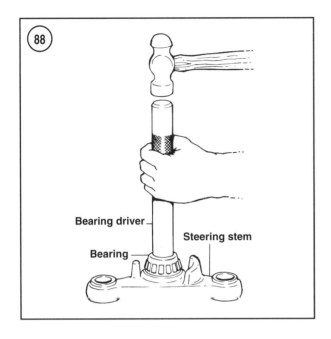

Bearing driver

Steering stem

Bearing

Never reinstall a bearing that has been removed. It is no longer true and will damage the rest of the bearing assembly if reused.

1. Install the steering stem head nut onto the top of the steering stem to protect the threads.

2. Use a chisel to drive the bearing/seal assembly from the steering stem (**Figure 87**). Work around in a circle and slowly drive the assembly from the shoulder on the steering stem. Remove the bearing and seal. Discard them both.

3. Clean the steering stem with solvent and dry it thoroughly.

4. Slide a new dust seal and the lower bearing onto the steering stem.

5. Align the bearing inner race with the machined shoulder on the steering stem.

6. Drive the bearing onto the steering stem shoulder with a piece of pipe that matches the diameter of the inner race (**Figure 88**).

Table 1 FRONT SUSPENSION SPECIFICATIONS

Item	Specification	Service Limit
Fork oil		
Viscosity	Yamaha fork oil 5WT	
Capacity per leg	554 ml (18.7 oz.)	
Oil level*	110 mm (4.33 in.)	–
Front fork travel	140 mm (5.51 in.)	–
Fork spring stroke	0-140 mm (0-5.51 in.)	–
Fork spring free length	571 mm (22.5 in.)	566 mm (22.3 in.)
Fork tube		
Runout	–	0.20 mm (0.008 in.)
Outer diameter	43 mm (1.69 in.)	–
*Measured from top of the fully compressed fork tube with the fork spring removed		

Table 2 FRONT SUSPENSION AND STEERING TORQUE SPECIFICATIONS

Item	N•m	in.-lb.	ft.-lb.
Front brake hose banjo bolt	30	–	22
Fork bridge			
Lower clamp bolt	20	–	15
Upper clamp bolt	10	88	–
Fork			
Cap bolt	23	–	17
Damper rod Allen bolt*	20	–	15
Front axle	78	–	58
Front axle pinch bolt	20	–	15
(continued)			

Table 2 FRONT SUSPENSION AND STEERING TORQUE SPECIFICATIONS (continued)

Item	N•m	in.-lb.	ft.-lb.
Front brake hose			
Clamp bolt	10	88	–
3-way joint bolt	7	62	–
Banjo bolt	30	–	22
Front caliper mounting bolt			
1999-2003	27	–	20
2004-on	40	–	30
Front master cylinder clamp bolt	10	88	–
Handlebar holder bolts			
1999-2003	23	–	17
2004-on	28	–	21
Handlebar weights (2004-on)	23	–	17
Steering stem adjust nut			
Initial	52	–	38
Final	3	26	–
Steering stem head nut	130	–	96

*Apply a medium-strength threadlock to the threads.

CHAPTER THIRTEEN

REAR SUSPENSION

This chapter includes repair procedures for servicing the rear shock absorber, suspension linkage and swing arm.

When inspecting the rear suspension, compare any measurements to the specifications at the end of this chapter. Replace parts that are damaged, worn or out of specification. During assembly, tighten fasteners to the specified torque.

SHOCK ABSORBER AND SUSPENSION LINKAGE

Removal/Installation

Refer to **Figure 1**.

The shock absorber and suspension linkage can be removed with the swing arm in place, as shown in this procedure. Because the working space is limited, the swing arm, shock absorber and suspension linkage may be removed as an assembly, then disassembled after removal.

NOTE
This procedure is shown with the engine removed to better illustrate the steps.

1. Securely support the motorcycle with the rear wheel off the ground so the rear shock absorber is not compressed. Block the front wheel so the motorcycle will not roll in either direction.

2. Remove the muffler assembly as described in Chapter Nine.

3. Remove the lower horn as described in Chapter Ten.

4. On the right side, remove the nut and washer (**Figure 2**) from the shock absorber front mounting bolt. Withdraw the front mounting bolt (**Figure 3**) from the left side.

5. Withdraw the collar (**Figure 4**) from the shock absorber and connecting rods.

6. Remove the bolt and nut (**Figure 5**) securing the shock absorber to the relay arm.

7. Remove the shock absorber.

8. Remove the bolt, nut and washer (**Figure 6**) securing the connecting rods to the relay arm. Remove both connecting rods (**Figure 7**).

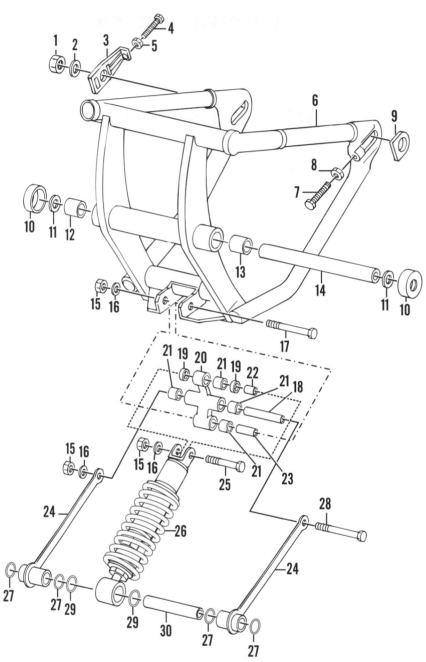

SHOCK ABSORBER, SHOCK LINKAGE AND SWING ARM

1. Rear axle nut
2. Washer
3. Adjusting plate-right side
4. Adjusting bolt
5. Nut
6. Swing arm
7. Adjusting bolt
8. Nut

9. Adjusting plate-left side
10. Thrust cover
11. Washer (1999-2003 only)
12. Needle bearing
13. Needle bearing
14. Collar
15. Nut
16. Washer

17. Bolt
18. Long collar
19. Seal
20. Relay arm
21. Needle bearing
22. Short collar
23. Collar

24. Connecting rod
25. Bolt
26. Shock absorber
27. O-ring
28. Bolt
29. O-ring
30. Collar

13

9. Remove the bolt, nut and washer (A, **Figure 8**) securing the relay arm to the swing arm. Remove the relay arm (B, **Figure 8**).

10. Inspect the shock absorber and suspension linkage as described in this section.

11. Installation is the reverse of removal. Note the following:

    a. Apply molybdenum disulfide grease to all pivot collars.

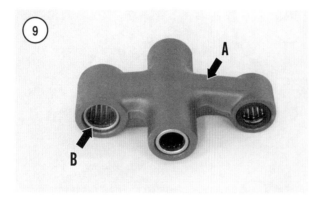

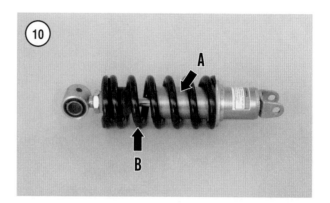

b. Position the relay arm with the curved surface (A, **Figure 9**) facing rearward and with the wider boss (B) installed onto the swing arm.

c. Install all bolts from the left side of the frame.

d. Tighten the relay arm-to-swing arm bolt and nut to 59 N•m (43 ft.-lb.).

e. Tighten the connecting rods-to-relay arm bolt and nut to 59 N•m (43 ft.-lb.).

f. Tighten the shock absorber-to-relay arm bolt and nut to 40 N•m (30 ft.-lb.).

g. Tighten the shock absorber-to-frame bolt and nut to 59 N•m (43 ft.-lb.).

Shock Absorber Inspection

1. Clean the shock absorber mounts and hardware in solvent and dry with compressed air.

2. Inspect the shock absorber. If the damper housing (A, **Figure 10**) is leaking, bent or damaged, replace the shock absorber.

3. Inspect the shock spring (B, **Figure 10**) and the spring retainer for cracks or damage. If damaged, replace the shock absorber.

4. Inspect the upper mount bushing (**Figure 11**) and O-rings (**Figure 12**) for wear or damage.

5. Inspect the lower mount (**Figure 13**) for elongation, cracks or other damage.

6. If any part of the shock absorber is worn or damaged, replace the shock absorber. Replacement parts are unavailable.

7. Replace the mounting hardware as necessary.

Suspension Linkage Inspection

1. Clean the linkage, collars and mounts in solvent and dry with compressed air.

2. Inspect the connecting arms (**Figure 14**) as follows:

a. Check for dents or other damage.

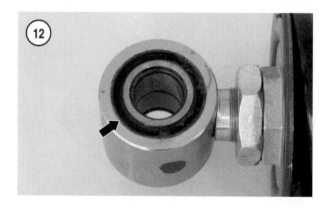

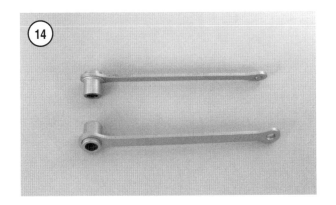

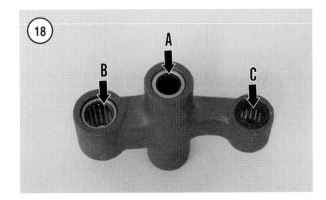

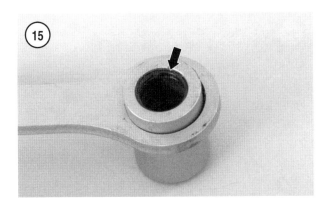

b. Inspect the O-ring (**Figure 15**) on each side of the front mounts for damage and deterioration. Replace as necessary.

c. Check the rear mounting holes for cracks or elongation.

3. Inspect the needle bearings in the relay arm as follows:

NOTE
Three different length collars are used in each mount in the relay arm. Install each collar in the proper mount.

a. Remove the collars (**Figure 16**) from the relay arm mount.

b. Wipe excess grease from the bearings, and visually inspect the needles (**Figure 17**) for pitting, wear or other damage.

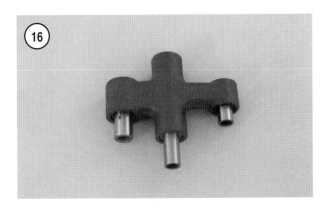

c. Insert the collar into its bearing and turn the collar by hand. The bearing should turn smoothly without binding or excessive noise.

d. If any bearing is worn or damaged, replace it as described in this section.

e. Two bearings are used in the middle relay arm mount (A, **Figure 18**). If either bearing in this mount is worn, replace both bearings as a set. Install each bearing so it is flush with the outside edge of the bearing bore.

f. When installing a needle bearing in a mount that uses just one bearing, center the bearing in the mount.

4. Check the collar(s) for scoring or excessive wear. Replace collars as necessary.

5. Inspect each seal (**Figure 19**). Replace seals that show signs of leakage or damage or are brittle.

6. Replace the mounting hardware as necessary.

13

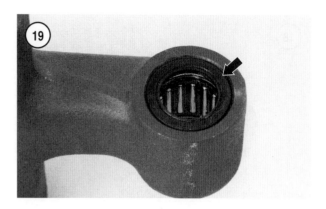

Needle Bearing Replacement

1. Before removing any needle bearing, measure and record the bearing outer surface from the relay arm outer surface. The bearings must be installed in the same location within the relay arm.

2. Use a blind bearing remover to remove each bearing from the middle mount (A, **Figure 18**) on the relay arm. Follow the tool manufacturer's instructions.

3. Remove the seal (**Figure 19**) from each side of the rear mount.

4. Use a hydraulic press and remove a needle bearing from the front (B, **Figure 18**) and rear (C) relay mounts. Support the relay arm in the press and use a driver that matches the outside diameter of the needle bearing.

5. Thoroughly clean the bearing bore with solvent and dry with compressed air.

6. Pack the new bearing with molybdenum disulfide grease.

7. Use a swing arm bearing installer, like the Motion Pro Swing Arm Bearing Tool (part No. 08-0213) and install the new bearing. Follow the manufacturer's instructions.

8. If a tool is not available, fabricate one from a socket, three large washers, a threaded rod and two nuts. Assemble the washers, threaded rod, bearing and nuts. Hold the lower nut with a wrench and turn the upper nut to press the bearing into the bearing bore. Turn the nut slowly and watch the bearing carefully. Make sure it does not turn sideways.

9. Press the *new* needle bearing(s) into the same location within the relay arm as noted in Step 1.

SWING ARM

Refer to **Figure 1**.

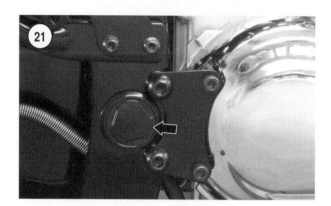

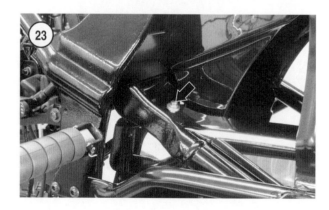

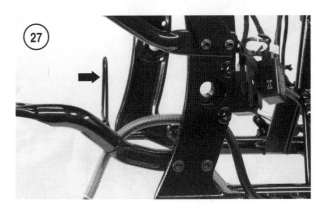

Removal

1. Securely support the motorcycle with the rear wheel off the ground. Block the front wheel so the motorcycle will not roll in either direction.

2. Remove the rear wheel as described in Chapter Eleven.

3. Remove the rear brake caliper and mounting bracket as described in Chapter Fourteen.

4. Remove the pivot shaft trim cap from each side of the frame. Refer to **Figure 20** and **Figure 21**.

5. Place a box under the swing arm to prevent it from moving down in Step 6.

6. Remove the front bolt, washer and nut (**Figure 22**) securing the shock absorber and suspension linkage to the frame.

7. Check the swing arm needle bearing as follows:

    a. Make sure the swing arm pivot shaft nut is tightened to 125 N•m (92 ft.-lb.). Tighten if necessary.

    b. Grasp both ends of the swing arm, and move it up and down. The swing arm should move smoothly with no binding or abnormal noise from the bearings. If there is binding or noise, the bearings are worn and must be replaced.

    c. Try to move the swing arm from side to side in a horizontal arc. There should be no movement. If there is more than a slight amount of movement, the bearings are worn and must be replaced as described in this section.

8. Remove the bolts securing the drive belt upper guard. Refer to **Figure 23** and A, **Figure 24**. Remove the upper belt guard (B, **Figure 24**).

9. Remove the bolts securing the drive belt lower guard (**Figure 25**) and remove the lower belt guard.

10. On the right side, remove the bolt and clamp (**Figure 26**) securing the rear brake hose to the swing arm. Also remove the hose guide (**Figure 27**).

11. Remove the bolts securing the mud guard (**Figure 28**) and remove the mud guard.

13

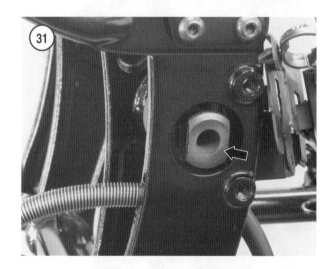

12. On the left side, remove the pivot bolt nut (**Figure 29**) and washer (**Figure 30**).

13. Have an assistant secure the swing arm.

14. On the left side, carefully tap the pivot bolt out toward the right side.

15. On the right side, withdraw the pivot bolt (**Figure 31**) from the frame and swing arm. Move the swing arm toward the rear and remove it from the frame.

16A. On 1999-2003 models, do not lose the thrust cover and washer (**Figure 32**) on each side of the pivot area on the swing arm.

16B. On 2004-on models, do not lose the thrust cover (**Figure 32**) on each side of the pivot area on the swing arm.

17. Inspect the swing arm as described in this section.

Installation

1A. On 1999-2003 models, install the washer and thrust cover (**Figure 32**) onto each side of the pivot area on the swing arm.

1B. On 2004-on models, install the thrust cover (**Figure 32**) onto each side of the pivot area on the swing arm.

2. Lubricate the thrust cover washer with molybdenum disulfide grease and install the washer into the thrust cover.

3. Raise the swing arm into position so its pivot points are opposite the frame pivot points.

4. Insert the pivot bolt (**Figure 31**) from the right side and tap it onto place in the frame. Position the pivot bolt so its flats are located within the frame boss tabs to keep it from rotating.

5. Place a box under the swing arm to hold it in place.

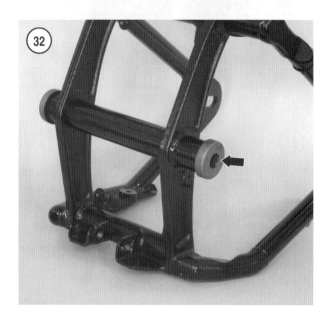

6. On the left side, install the washer (**Figure 30**), and nut (**Figure 29**).

7. Tighten the pivot bolt nut to 125 N•m (92 ft.-lb.).

8. Move the swing arm up and down and check for ease of movement. If there is any binding, correct the problem.

9. On the right side, perform the following:
   a. Insert the rear brake hose though the guide (**Figure 27**) and install the guide onto the swing arm.
   b. Install the bolt and clamp (**Figure 26**) securing the rear brake hose to the swing arm.

10. Install the drive belt lower guard (**Figure 25**) and tighten the bolts securely.

11. Install the drive belt upper guard and tighten the bolts securely. Refer to **Figure 23** and A, **Figure 24**.

12. Move the shock absorber and suspension linkage assembly into position and install the front bolt, washer and nut (**Figure 22**). Tighten the bolt and nut to 59 N•m (43 ft.-lb.).

13. Remove the box under the swing arm.

14. Install the pivot shaft trim cap onto each side of the frame. Refer to **Figure 20** and **Figure 21**.

15. Install the rear brake mounting bracket and caliper as described in Chapter Fourteen.

16. Install the rear wheel as described in Chapter Eleven.

17. Push down on the rear of the motorcycle to ensure the rear suspension operates smoothly with no binding.

Inspection

If any portion of the swing arm is damaged, replace it. Do not try to repair a damaged swing arm.

1. Check the pivot bolt for straightness. A bent bolt will restrict the movement of the swing arm.

2. Inspect the pivot bolt threads for thread damage. Clean and dress the threads as necessary.

3. Check the welds on the swing arm (**Figure 33**) for cracks or fractures.

4. Inspect the shock absorber mounting bosses (**Figure 34**) for cracks and/or elongation.

5. Withdraw the collar (**Figure 35**) from the swing arm needle bearings.

6. Check the swing arm pivot bearings as follows:
   a. Turn each bearing by hand. A bearing should turn smoothly without excessive play or noise.
   b. Use a lint-free cloth to remove surface grease from the bearings.
   c. Check the bearing rollers for evidence of wear, pitting or rust.
   d. If either bearing is damaged, replace both bearings. Refer to *Needle Bearing Replacement* in this chapter.

13

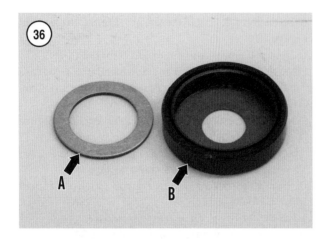

e. Install each swing arm bearing so it is located at the correct depth as noted during removal.

7. Inspect the thrust cover (A, **Figure 36**) and washer (B) (1999-2003 models) from each side of the frame pivot.

8. Inspect the adjusting bolt and locknut (**Figure 37**) on each side for possible thread damage. Replace as necessary.

9. Inspect the swing arm pivot points (**Figure 38**) on the frame for wear or damage.

Table 1 REAR SUSPENSION SPECIFICATIONS

Item	Specification mm (in.)
Rear wheel travel	110 (4.33)
Shock absorber travel	50 (1.97)
Shock absorber spring	
Free length	187 (7.36)
Installed length	
XV16A, XV17A	172 (6.77)
XV16AT, XV17AT	169 (6.65)
Spring stroke	0-50 (0-1.97)
Swing arm free play (maximum)	1 (0.04)

Table 2 REAR SUSPENSION TORQUE SPECIFICATIONS

Item	N•m	in.-lb.	ft.-lb.
Connecting arm-to-relay arm nut	59	–	43
Drive belt lower cover bolts	7	62	–
Mud guard bolts	7	62	–
Relay arm-to-swing arm nut	59	–	43
Shock absorber-to-frame nut	59	–	43
Shock absorber-to-relay arm nut	40	–	30
Swing arm pivot bolt nut	125	–	92

CHAPTER FOURTEEN

BRAKES

The brake system on all models consists of dual front discs and a single disc in the rear. This chapter describes the service procedures for brake system components.

When inspecting the brakes, compare any measurements to the specifications in the table at the end of this chapter. Replace parts that are damaged, worn or out of specification. During assembly, tighten fasteners to the specified torque.

BRAKE SERVICE

When working on hydraulic brakes, all tools and the work area must be absolutely clean. Caliper or master cylinder components can be damaged by tiny particles of grit that enter the brake system. Do not use sharp tools inside the master cylinders, calipers or on the pistons. Sharp tools could damage these components and interfere with brake operation.

If there is any doubt about the ability to service a brake component safely and correctly, take the job to a Yamaha dealership or brake specialist.

Consider the following when servicing the front and rear brake systems:

1. Disc brake components rarely require disassembly. Do not disassemble them unless necessary.

2. When adding brake fluid, only use brake fluid clearly marked DOT 4 from a sealed container. Other grades of brake fluid may vaporize and cause brake failure.

3. Always use the same brand of brake fluid. One manufacturer's brake fluid may not be compatible with another's. Do not mix different brands of brake fluids.

4. Brake fluid absorbs moisture, which greatly reduces its ability to perform correctly. Purchase brake fluid in small containers and properly discard any small leftover quantities. Do not store a container of brake fluid with less than 1/4 of the fluid remaining. This small amount absorbs moisture very rapidly.

WARNING
When working on the brake system, do not inhale brake dust. It may contain asbestos, which can cause lung injury and cancer. Wear a face mask that meets OSHA require-

14

ments for trapping asbestos particles, and wash hands and forearms thoroughly after completing the work.

> ### WARNING
> *Never use compressed air to clean any part of the brake system. This releases harmful brake pad dust. Use an aerosol brake parts cleaner to clean parts when servicing any component still installed on the motorcycle.*

> ### CAUTION
> *Do not use silicone based (DOT 5) brake fluid on the motorcycles covered in this manual. Silicone-based fluid can damage these brake components leading to a brake system failure.*

> ### CAUTION
> *Never reuse brake fluid (like the fluid expelled during brake bleeding). Contaminated brake fluid can cause brake failure.*

5. Always keep the master cylinder reservoir cover installed to keep dust or moisture out of the system.

6. Use only DOT 4 brake fluid or isopropyl alcohol to wash parts. Never use petroleum-based solvents on the brake system's internal components. The seals will swell and distort, and have to be replaced.

7. Whenever any brake banjo bolt or brake line nut is loosened, the system is opened and must be bled to remove air. If the brakes feel spongy, this usually means air has entered the system. For safe operation, refer to *Brake Bleeding* in this chapter.

PREVENTING BRAKE FLUID DAMAGE

Brake fluid will damage most surfaces on a motorcycle. To prevent brake fluid damage, note the following:

1. Protect the motorcycle before beginning any service requiring draining, bleeding or handling of brake fluid. Anticipate which parts are likely to leak brake fluid, and use a large tarp or piece of plastic to cover the areas beneath those parts. Even a few drops of brake fluid can extensively damage painted, plated or plastic surfaces.

2. Keep a bucket of soap and water close to the motorcycle while working on the brake system. If brake fluid spills on any surface, immediately wash the area with soap and water, then rinse it thoroughly.

3. To help control the flow of brake fluid when refilling the reservoirs, punch a small hole into the seal of a new container. Place this hole next to the edge of the pour spout.

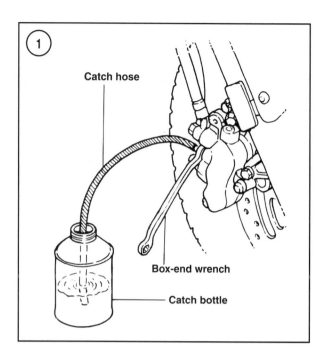

BRAKE BLEEDING

General Bleeding Tips

Bleeding the brakes removes air from the brake system. Air in the brakes increases brake lever or brake pedal travel, and it makes the brakes feel soft or spongy. Under extreme circumstances, it can cause complete loss of brake pressure.

The brakes can be bled manually or with the use of a vacuum pump. Both methods are described here. Only use fresh DOT 4 brake fluid when bleeding the brakes. Do not reuse old brake fluid and do not use DOT 5 (silicone based) brake fluid.

1. Clean the bleed valve and area around the valve before beginning. Make sure the opening in the valve is clear.

2. Use a box-end wrench to open and close the bleed valve. This prevents damage to the valve, especially if the valve is rusted in place.

3. Replace a bleed valve with damaged threads or with a rounded hex head. A damaged valve is difficult to remove and cannot be properly tightened.

> ### NOTE
> *The catch hose (**Figure 1**) is the hose installed between the bleed valve and the catch bottle.*

4. Use a clear catch hose so the fluid can be visually inspected as it leaves the bleed valve. Air bubbles in the

catch hose indicate that air may be trapped in the brake system.

5. Open the bleed valve just enough to allow fluid to pass through the valve and into the catch bottle. If a bleed valve is too loose, air can be drawn into the system through the valve threads.

6. If air is entering through the valve threads, perform one of the following:

   a. Apply silicone brake grease around the valve where it emerges from the caliper. The grease should seal the valve and prevent the entry of air. Wipe away the grease once the brakes have been bled.

   b. Remove the bleed valve and apply Teflon tape to the valve threads. Reinstall the valve and tighten it securely. Make sure the Teflon tape does not cover the passage in the bleed valve.

7. If the system is difficult to bleed, tap the banjo bolt on the master cylinder a few times. This should dislodge air bubbles that may have become trapped at the hose connection. Also tap the banjo bolts at the brake hose union (beneath the lower fork bridge), at the calipers and any other hose connections in the brake line.

Manual Bleeding

1. Make sure all banjo bolts in the system are tight.

2. Remove the dust cap from the bleed valve on the caliper assembly.

3. Connect a length of clear tubing to the bleed valve (**Figure 1**, typical). Place the other end of the tube into a clean container. Fill the container with enough fresh brake fluid to keep the end submerged. The tube should be long enough that its loop is higher than the bleed valve to prevent air from being drawn into the caliper during bleeding.

NOTE
When bleeding the front brakes, turn the handlebars to level the front master cylinder.

4. Clean all debris from the top of the master cylinder reservoir. Remove the top cover, diaphragm plate and the diaphragm from the reservoir.

5. Add brake fluid to the reservoir until the fluid level reaches the reservoir upper limit. Loosely install the diaphragm and the cover. Leave them in place during this procedure to keep dirt out of the system and so brake fluid cannot spray out of the reservoir.

6. Pump the brake lever or brake pedal a few times, then release it.

7. Apply the brake lever or pedal until it stops and hold it in this position.

8. Open the bleed valve with a wrench (**Figure 1**, typical). Let the brake lever or pedal move to the limit of its travel, and then close the bleed valve. Do not release the brake lever or pedal while the bleed valve is open.

NOTE
As break fluid enters the system, the level in the reservoir drops. Add brake fluid as necessary to keep the fluid level 10 mm (3/8 in.) below the reservoir top so air will not be drawn into the system.

9. Repeat Steps 6-8 until the brake fluid flowing from the hose is clear and free of air. If the system is difficult to bleed, tap the master cylinder or caliper with a soft mallet to release trapped air bubbles.

10. Test the feel of the brake lever or pedal. It should feel firm and offer the same resistance each time it is operated. If the lever or pedal feels soft, air is still trapped in the system. Continue bleeding the system.

NOTE
The setting on the front brake lever adjuster affects bleeding. Initially bleed the front brakes with the adjuster turned to the softest setting. Once the brakes feel solid; check the feel with the adjuster in several different settings. If the lever feels soft at any setting or if the lever hits the handlebar, air is still trapped in the system. Continue bleeding the system.

11. When brake system bleeding is complete, disconnect the hose from the bleed valve. Tighten the bleed securely.

12. When bleeding the front brakes, repeat Steps 1-11 on the opposite front caliper.

13. Add brake fluid to the master cylinder to correct the fluid level.

14. Install the diaphragm, diaphragm plate and top cap. Make sure the cap is secure.

NOTE
Do not ride the motorcycle until the front and rear brakes, and the brake light are working properly.

15. Test ride the motorcycle slowly at first to make sure the brakes are operating properly at full hydraulic advantage.

Vacuum Bleeding

1. Make sure all banjo bolts in the system are tight.

14

2. Remove the dust cap from the bleed valve on the caliper assembly.

NOTE
When bleeding the front brakes, turn the handlebars until the front master cylinder is level.

3. Clean all debris from the top of the master cylinder reservoir. Remove the top cover, diaphragm plate and the diaphragm from the reservoir.

4. Add brake fluid to the reservoir until the fluid level reaches the reservoir upper limit. Loosely install the diaphragm and the cover. Leave them in place during this procedure to keep dirt out of the system and so brake fluid cannot spray out of the reservoir.

5. Assemble the vacuum tool following the manufacturer's instructions.

6. Connect the pump's catch hose to the bleed valve on the brake caliper (**Figure 2**).

NOTE
When using a vacuum pump, keep an eye on the brake fluid level in the reservoir. It will drop quite rapidly. This is particularly true for the rear reservoir, which does not hold as much brake fluid as the front. Stop often and check the brake fluid level. Maintain the level at 10 mm (3/8 in.) from the top of the reservoir so air will not be drawn into the system.

7. Operate the vacuum pump to create vacuum in the hose.

8. Use a wrench to open the bleed valve. The vacuum pump should pull fluid from the system. Close the bleed valve before the brake fluid stops flowing from the system or before the master cylinder reservoir runs empty. Add fluid to the reservoir as necessary.

9. Operate the brake lever or brake pedal a few times, and release it.

10. Repeat Steps 7 and 9 until the fluid leaving the bleed valve is clear and free of air bubbles. If the system is difficult to bleed, tap the master cylinder and caliper housing with a soft mallet to release trapped air bubbles.

11. Test the feel of the brake lever or brake pedal. It should feel firm and offer the same resistance each time it is operated. If the lever or pedal feels soft, air is still trapped in the system. Continue bleeding the system.

12. When bleeding is complete, disconnect the hose from the bleed valve and tighten securely.

13. When bleeding the front brakes, repeat Step 1-12 on the opposite front caliper.

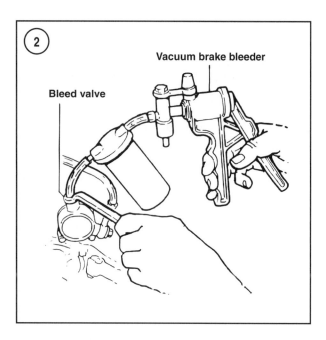

14. Add brake fluid to the master cylinder to correct the fluid level.

15. Install the diaphragm, diaphragm plate and top cap. Make sure the cap is secured in place.

NOTE
Do not ride the motorcycle until both brakes and the brake light are working properly.

16. Test ride the motorcycle slowly at first to make sure the brakes are operating properly.

BRAKE FLUID DRAINING

Before disconnecting a front or rear brake hose, drain the brake fluid to reduce the amount of fluid that can spill out when system components are removed.

This section describes both the manual and vacuum methods for draining the brake system.

Manual Draining

An empty bottle, a length of clear hose and a wrench are required for this procedure.

1. Remove the dust cap from the bleed valve. Remove all dirt from the valve and its outlet port.

2. Connect a length of clear hose to the bleed valve on the caliper. Insert the other end into a container (**Figure 1**, typical).

3. Apply the front brake lever or the rear brake pedal until it stops. Hold the lever or pedal in this position.

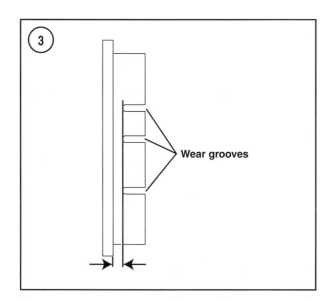

Wear grooves

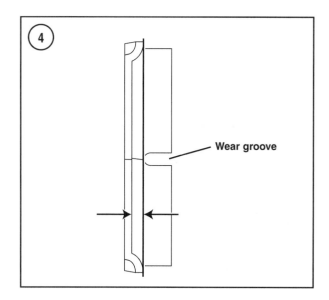

Wear groove

4. Open the bleed valve with a wrench and let the lever or pedal move to the limit of its travel. Close the bleed valve.

5. Release the lever or pedal, and repeat Step 3 and Step 4 until brake fluid stops flowing from the bleed valve.

6. When draining the front brakes, repeat this on the other brake caliper.

7. Discard the brake fluid.

8. When draining is complete, disconnect the hose from the bleed valve and tighten securely.

Vacuum Draining

A hand-operated vacuum pump is required to perform this procedure.

1. Connect the pump's catch hose to the bleed valve on the brake caliper (**Figure 2**, typical).

2. Operate the vacuum pump to create vacuum in the hose.

3. Use a wrench to open the bleed valve. The vacuum pump should pull fluid from the system.

4. When fluid has stopped flowing through the hose, close the bleed valve.

5. Repeat Steps 2-4 until brake fluid no longer flows from the bleed valve.

6. When draining the front brake system, repeat this procedure on the opposite caliper.

7. Discard the brake fluid.

8. When draining is complete, disconnect the hose from the bleed valve and tighten securely.

BRAKE PADS

Brake pad wear depends on riding habits and conditions. Manufacturers typically do not provide a recommended mileage interval for changing the brake pads. Periodically check the brake pads for wear. Look into the caliper assembly and inspect the wear indicators (**Figure 3** or **Figure 4**, typical).

To maintain even brake pressure on the disc, always replace both pads in a caliper at the same time. When replacing the front brake pads, replace both pads in both front calipers at the same time. If any front brake pad is worn to the service limit (**Table 1** or **Table 2**), replace all four pads as a set.

Note that the brake hose does not need to be disconnected from the caliper during brake pad replacement. If the hose is removed, the brakes will have to be bled. Disconnect the hose only when servicing the brake caliper.

WARNING
Use brake fluid clearly marked DOT 4 from a sealed container. Other types may vaporize and cause brake failure. Always use the same brand of brake fluid. Do not intermix brake fluids from different manufacturers. They may not be compatible.

WARNING
Do not ride the motorcycle until the brakes are operating correctly with full hydraulic advantage. If necessary, bleed the brake as described in this chapter.

WARNING
Check the pads more frequently when the wear limit lines approach the disc. On some

14

pads, the wear lines are very close to the metal backing plate. If pad wear happens to be uneven, the backing plate may contact the disc and cause damage.

> *CAUTION*
> *When purchasing new pads, make sure the compound of the new pads is compatible with the disc material. Remove any roughness from the backs of the new pads with a fine-cut file.*

Front Brake Pad Replacement (1999-2003 Models)

1. Securely support the motorcycle on level ground. Block the rear wheel so the motorcycle will not roll in either direction.

2. Remove the mounting bolt and nut and release the brake hose holder (**Figure 5**) and side reflector from the fork leg.

3. Remove the retaining bolts (A, **Figure 6**) and remove the caliper (B) from the caliper bracket. Suspend it from the frame or handlebar with a bungee cord.

4. Remove the outboard brake pad and shim (**Figure 7**) and the inboard pad from the caliper bracket (**Figure 8**).

5. Inspect the brake pads as described later in this section.

6. Remove the pad spring (A, **Figure 9**) from the caliper and check it for wear or fatigue. Replace the pad spring as necessary.

7. When new pads are installed in the caliper, the master cylinder brake fluid level will rise as the caliper pistons are repositioned.

   a. Clean all debris from the top of the master cylinder.

   b. Remove the screws securing the master cylinder reservoir cap. Remove the cap, diaphragm holder and the diaphragm from the master cylinder.

   c. Slowly push the caliper pistons (B, **Figure 9**) into the caliper. Watch the reservoir to make sure brake fluid does not overflow. Remove fluid if necessary.

   d. The pistons should move freely. If they do not move smoothly without sticking, remove the caliper and service it as described in this chapter.

8. Push the caliper pistons until they bottom in the bore to allow room for the new pads.

> *WARNING*
> *Position each brake pad so the friction material faces toward the brake disc.*

9. If removed, install the pad spring (B, **Figure 9**) into the caliper and onto the caliper bracket. If necessary, install *new* pad springs when installing new brake pads.

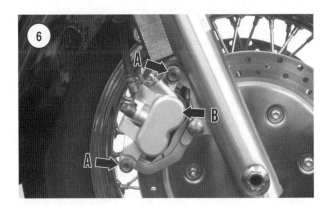

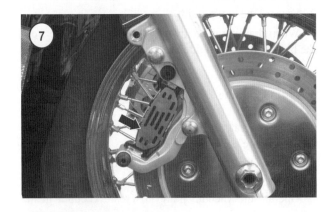

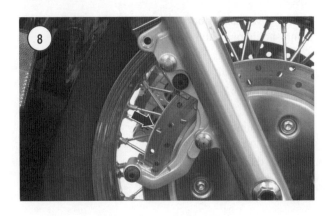

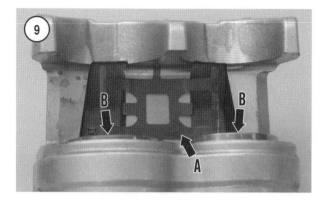

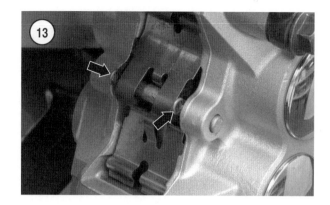

10. Install the inboard pad (**Figure 10**), then outboard pad and shim (**Figure 11**), into the caliper bracket. The ears on each pad must straddle the pad springs in the caliper bracket (**Figure 12**).

11. Lower the caliper (B, **Figure 6**) onto the brake pads and the caliper bracket. Push it down until it bottoms.

WARNING
Use just enough grease to lubricate the caliper mounting bolts in the next step. Excess grease could contaminate the brake pads. Do not allow any grease on the brake pads or on the threads of the bolts.

12. Lubricate the mounting bolts with lithium grease.

13. Install the mounting bolts (A, **Figure 6**) and tighten to 27 N•m (20 ft.-lb.).

14. Install the brake hose holder (**Figure 5**) and side reflector onto the fork leg and tighten the bolt securely.

15. Repeat Steps 2-14 to replace the pads in the opposite front caliper.

16. Support the motorcycle with the front wheel off the ground. Spin the wheel and pump the brake lever until the pads are seated against the disc.

17. Refill the master cylinder reservoir, if necessary, to maintain the correct fluid level. Install the diaphragm, diaphragm holder and top cap. Tighten the cap screws securely.

18. Test ride the motorcycle slowly at first to make sure the brakes are operating properly with full hydraulic advantage.

14

Front Brake Pad Replacement (2004-on Models)

1. Securely support the motorcycle on level ground. Block the rear wheel so the motorcycle will not roll in either direction.

2. Remove both clips (**Figure 13**) from the pad pin.

3. Withdraw the pad pin (**Figure 14**) from the caliper.

4. Remove the pad spring (**Figure 15**) from the caliper.

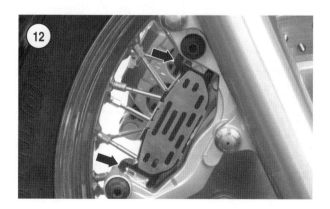

5. Pull straight up and remove the outboard brake pad and shim and the inboard pad and shim from the caliper.

6. Inspect the brake pads as described later in this section.

7. When new pads are installed in the caliper, the master cylinder brake fluid level will rise as the caliper pistons are repositioned.

   a. Clean all debris from the top of the master cylinder.

   b. Remove the screws securing the master cylinder reservoir cap. Remove the cap, diaphragm holder and the diaphragm from the master cylinder.

   c. Slowly push the caliper pistons into the caliper. Constantly check the reservoir to make sure brake fluid does not overflow. Remove fluid if necessary.

   d. The pistons should move freely. If they do not move smoothly without sticking, remove the caliper and service it as described in this chapter.

8. Push all four caliper pistons in (**Figure 16**) until they bottom in the bores to allow room for the new pads.

WARNING
Position each brake pad so the friction material faces toward the brake disc.

9. Install the inboard pad and shim (**Figure 17**), then outboard pad and shim (**Figure 18**), into the caliper.

10. Install the pad spring (**Figure 15**) onto the pads.

11. Push down on the pad spring and insert the pad pin (**Figure 14**) through both pads and the pad spring.

12. Rotate the pad pin so the two clip holes are facing straight out to accept the clips.

13. Install both clips (**Figure 19**) into the pad pin holes. Make sure the clips are correctly seated on the pad pin (**Figure 13**).

14. Repeat Steps 2-13 to replace the pads in the opposite front caliper.

15. Support the motorcycle with the front wheel off the ground. Spin the wheel and pump the brake lever until the pads are seated against the disc.

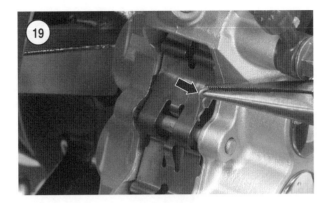

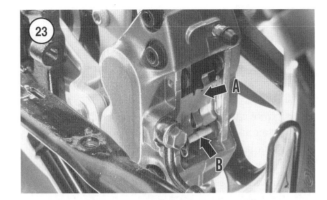

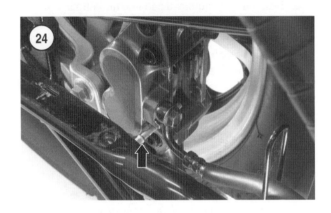

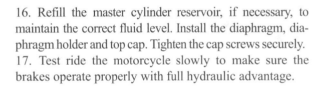

16. Refill the master cylinder reservoir, if necessary, to maintain the correct fluid level. Install the diaphragm, diaphragm holder and top cap. Tighten the cap screws securely.

17. Test ride the motorcycle slowly to make sure the brakes operate properly with full hydraulic advantage.

Rear Brake Pad Replacement

1. Support the motorcycle on a level surface. Block the front wheel so the motorcycle will not roll in either direction.

2. Remove the right side saddlebag as described in Chapter Fifteen, on models so equipped.

3. Remove the muffler assembly as described in Chapter Nine.

4. Remove the caliper pad cover (**Figure 20**).

5. Remove the clip (**Figure 21**) from each pad pin. Note that each clip sits between the caliper and the outboard brake pad. The clips must be reinstalled in this location during assembly.

6. Remove the upper pad pin (**Figure 22**).

7. Unhook the pad spring (A, **Figure 23**) from the lower pad pin (B) and remove it. Note that the arrow mark on the spring is facing down. The spring must be installed with this same orientation during assembly.

8. Remove the lower pad pin (**Figure 24**).

14

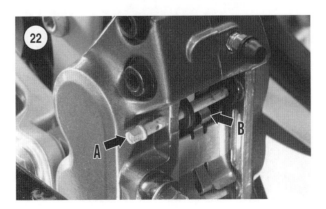

9. Remove the outboard brake pad (**Figure 25**) and the inboard pad (**Figure 26**) from the caliper.

10. Inspect the brake pads as described in this section.

11. When new pads are installed in the caliper, the master cylinder brake fluid level rises as the caliper pistons are repositioned.

    a. Remove the screw (A, **Figure 27**) securing the reservoir and cover to the frame.

    b. Remove the cover (B, **Figure 27**) from the cap.

    c. Clean all debris from the top of the master cylinder.

    d. Unscrew the cap (**Figure 28**), diaphragm plate and the diaphragm.

    e. Install the old outboard pad into the caliper. Use the pad to slowly push the piston into the caliper until the piston bottoms. Constantly check the reservoir to make sure brake fluid does not overflow. Remove brake fluid if necessary.

    f. Remove the outboard pad and repeat Sub-step c with the inboard pad.

    g. The pistons should move freely. If they do not move smoothly without sticking, remove the caliper and service it as described in this chapter.

WARNING
Position each brake pad so the friction material faces in toward the brake disc.

12. Install a new inboard pad (**Figure 26**) into the caliper, and then install the outboard pad (**Figure 25**).

13. Install the lower pad pin (**Figure 24**) and rotate it so the clip hole is facing straight out to accept the clip.

14. Install the clip (**Figure 29**). The clip must sit between the caliper body and the outboard pad.

15. Position the new pad spring so the arrow mark on the spring faces down. Hook the pad spring (A, **Figure 23**) onto the lower pad pin (B).

16. Push the pad spring back into the caliper and install the upper pad pin (A, **Figure 22**). The upper finger of the pad spring must be behind the pad pin (B). Rotate the pad pin so the clip hole is facing straight out to accept the clip.

17. Install a clip (**Figure 30**) through the hole in the retaining pin. The clip must sit between the caliper and the outboard brake pad as shown in **Figure 21**.

18. Install the pad cover (**Figure 20**) onto the caliper. Make sure it snaps into place.

19. Support the motorcycle with the rear wheel off the ground. Spin the wheel and pump the brake pedal until the pads are seated against the disc.

20. Check the fluid level in the master cylinder reservoir. Add brake fluid as necessary to correct the fluid level.

    a. Install diaphragm, diaphragm plate and screw on the cap (**Figure 28**). Tighten the cap securely.

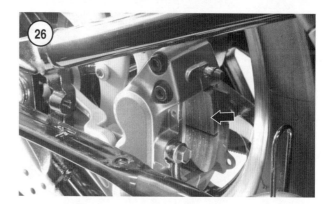

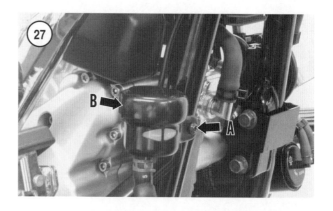

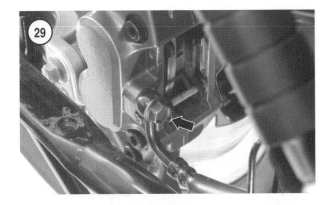

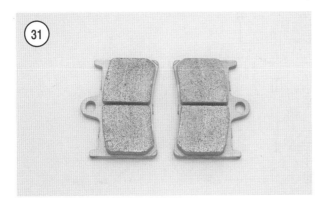

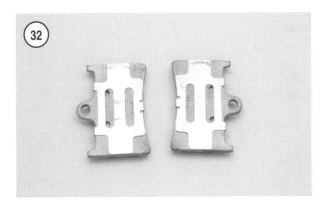

b. Install the reservoir and cover to the frame and tighten the screw (A, **Figure 27**) securely.

21. Install the muffler assembly as described in Chapter Nine.

22. Install the right side saddlebag as described in Chapter Fifteen, on models so equipped.

23. Test ride the motorcycle slowly at first to make sure the brakes are operating properly with full hydraulic advantage.

Brake Pad Inspection

1. Inspect the brake pads (**Figure 31**) as follows:

   a. Inspect the friction material for light surface dirt, grease and oil contamination. Remove light contamination with sandpaper. If contamination has penetrated the surface, replace the brake pads.

   b. Inspect the friction material for uneven wear, damage or contamination. Both pads should show approximately the same amount of wear. If the pads are wearing unevenly, the caliper may not be operating correctly.

   c. Measure the thickness of the friction material with a vernier caliper. Replace both brake pads if the thickness on either pad is equal or less than the service limit listed in **Table 1** or **Table 2**. When servicing the front brakes, replace both pads in both front calipers if any pad is worn to the service limit.

   d. Inspect the metal shim plate (**Figure 32**, typical) on the back of the pad for corrosion and damage.

WARNING
Cleaning the brake disc is especially important if new pads are being installed. Many brake pad compounds are not compatible.

2. Use brake parts cleaner and a fine grade emery cloth to remove all road debris and brake pad residue from the brake disc surface.

3. Inspect the brake disc as described in this chapter.

4. Check the friction surface of the new pads for any debris or manufacturing residue. If necessary, clean the pads with an aerosol brake cleaner.

5. Check the pad springs for wear or fatigue. Replace a pad spring if it shows any sign of damage or excessive wear.

6. Install new pad spring(s) when installing new brake pads.

14

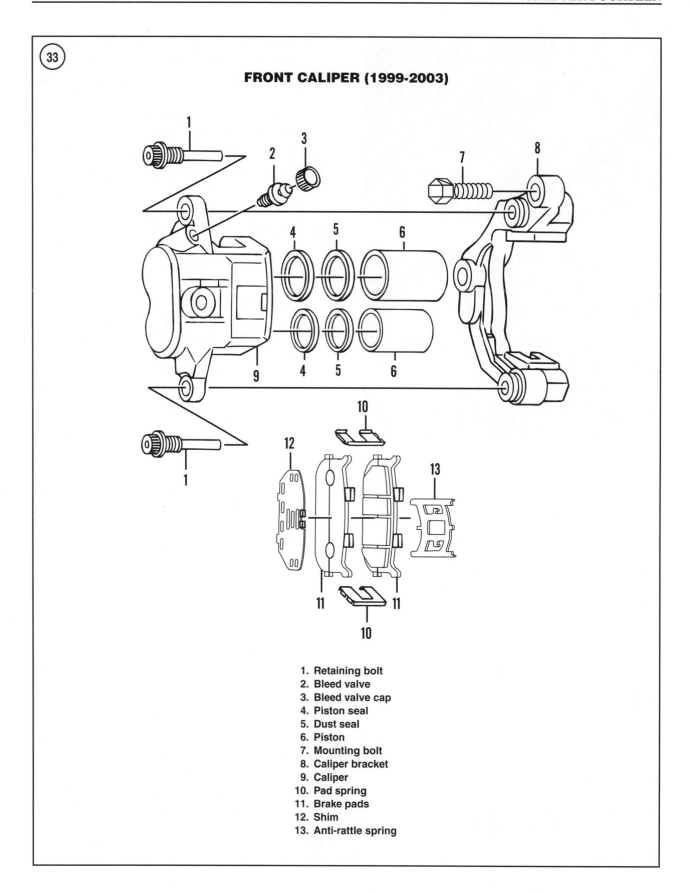

FRONT CALIPER (1999-2003)

1. Retaining bolt
2. Bleed valve
3. Bleed valve cap
4. Piston seal
5. Dust seal
6. Piston
7. Mounting bolt
8. Caliper bracket
9. Caliper
10. Pad spring
11. Brake pads
12. Shim
13. Anti-rattle spring

FRONT CALIPER
(1999-2003 MODELS)

Refer to **Figure 33**.

Removal

1. Securely support the motorcycle on level ground. Block the rear wheel so the motorcycle will not roll in either direction.

2. Remove the mounting bolt and nut and release the brake hose holder (**Figure 34**) and side reflector from the fork slider.

3. Note that the brake hose neck sits against the outboard side of the indexing post on the caliper. The hose must be installed on this side of the post during assembly.

4. Remove the mounting bolts (A, **Figure 35**) and remove the caliper from the caliper bracket.

5. Remove the banjo bolt (B, **Figure 35**) from the caliper. Remove the brake hose and the two copper washers from the caliper.

CAUTION
Brake fluid damages paint and finish. Immediately wash any spilled brake fluid from

the motorcycle. Use soapy water and rinse the area completely.

6. Place the loose end of the brake hose into a resealable plastic bag to keep foreign matter out of the system and to prevent brake fluid from dripping out.

7. Remove the brake pads as described in Steps 1-6 of *Front Brake Pad Replacement (1999-2003 Models)* in this chapter.

8. Remove the caliper bracket mounting bolts (**Figure 36**) and remove the bracket from the fork slider.

9. Disassemble and inspect the caliper as described in this section.

Installation

1. Install the caliper bracket onto the fork slider.

2. Apply a medium-strength threadlocking compound to the threads of the caliper bracket mounting bolts and install the bolts (**Figure 36**). Tighten the bolts to 40 N•m (30 ft.-lb.).

3. Install the brake pads as described in Steps 9-12 of *Front Brake Pad Replacement (1999-2003 Models)* in this chapter.

4. Place the brake hose against the caliper port so the brake hose neck sits on the outboard side of the indexing post. Install a *new* copper washer on each side of the brake hose fitting. Tighten the banjo bolt finger tight.

5. Install the caliper onto the brake pads and caliper bracket.

6. Apply a medium-strength threadlocking compound to the threads of the caliper mounting bolts and install the bolts (A, **Figure 35**). Tighten the bolts to 27 N•m (20 ft.-lb.).

7. Tighten the banjo bolt (B, **Figure 35**) to 30 N•m (22 ft.-lb.).

8. Install the brake hose holder (**Figure 34**) and side reflector onto the fork slider. Install the mounting bolt and nut and tighten securely.

14

9. Add brake fluid to the reservoir and bleed the brakes as described earlier in this chapter.

Disassembly/Assembly

Refer to **Figure 33**.

1. Remove the brake pads and brake caliper as described in this section.

> *WARNING*
> *In the next step, the pistons will come out of the caliper body with considerable force. Keep your hands out of the way. Wear shop gloves and apply air pressure gradually. Do not use high pressure air or place the air hose nozzle directly against the hydraulic line fitting in the caliper body. Hold the air nozzle away from the inlet, allowing some of the air to escape.*

2. Pad the pistons with shop rags or wood blocks. Block the exposed housing fluid port holes on the caliper housing. Apply compressed air through the caliper hose port and blow the pistons out of the caliper. Remove the pistons from the caliper cylinders.

> *CAUTION*
> *In the following step, do not use a sharp tool to remove the dust and piston seals from the caliper cylinder. Sharp tools could damage the cylinder surface. The caliper will have to be replaced if the cylinder surface is damaged.*

3. Use a piece of plastic or wood to carefully remove the dust seal (A, **Figure 37**) and the piston seal (B) from their grooves in each caliper cylinder. Discard all seals.

4. Clean all caliper parts and inspect them as described in this section.

> *WARNING*
> *Never reuse the old dust seals or piston seals. Very minor damage or age deterioration can make the seals ineffective.*

5. Coat the *new* dust seals and piston seals (**Figure 38**) with fresh DOT 4 brake fluid.

6. Carefully install the *new* piston seal (B, **Figure 37**) and dust seal (A) into the grooves in the caliper cylinders. Make sure the seals are properly seated in their respective grooves.

7. Coat the pistons and caliper cylinders with fresh DOT 4 brake fluid.

8. Position each piston with the open end facing toward the brake pads (**Figure 39**) and slide the pistons into the

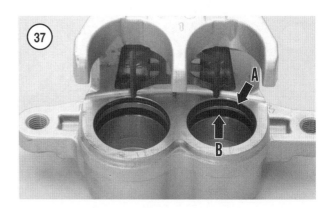

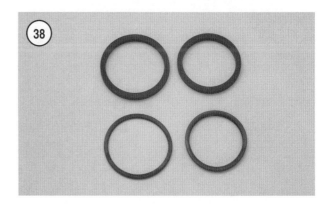

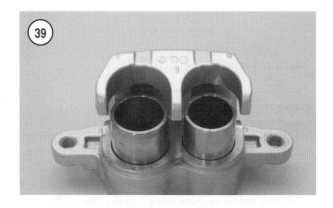

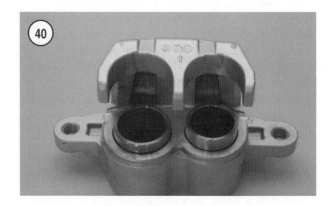

caliper cylinders. Push the pistons in until they almost bottom in the cylinders (**Figure 40**).

9. Install the pad spring. Make sure the spring is completely seated in the bottom of the caliper body (**Figure 41**).

10. Install the brake pads and caliper as described in this section.

Inspection

1. Clean all parts, except brake pads, with clean DOT 4 brake fluid. Place the cleaned parts on a lint-free cloth while performing the following inspection procedures.

2. Inspect both seal grooves (A, **Figure 42**) in each cylinder for damage. If they are damaged or corroded, replace the caliper assembly.

3. Inspect the fluid opening (**Figure 43**) in the base of each cylinder bore. Apply compressed air to the opening and make sure it is clear. Clean out the opening with fresh brake fluid if necessary.

4. Inspect the walls (B, **Figure 42**) in each cylinder for scratches, scoring or other damage. If there is rust or corrosion, replace the caliper assembly.

5. Measure the inside diameter of each cylinder bore with a bore gauge (**Figure 44**). Replace the brake caliper if the inside diameter of either bore exceeds the specification in **Table 1**.

6. Inspect the pistons (**Figure 45**) for scratches, scoring or other damage. If they are rusty or corroded, replace the pistons.

7. Inspect the caliper body for scratches or other damage (**Figure 46**). Replace the caliper assembly if necessary.

8. Inspect the pad spring(s). Replace a spring if it is cracked, worn or shows signs of fatigue.

9. Inspect the caliper bracket as follows:

   a. Remove the pad springs (A, **Figure 47**) from the pad holder if they have not been removed, and in-

14

spect the springs. Replace both pad springs if either one is cracked, worn or shows signs of fatigue.

  b. Inspect the pad holder (B, **Figure 47**) for cracks or other damage. Replace the caliper assembly if necessary.

  c. Inspect the boots (C, **Figure 47**), and replace a boot that is torn or hard.

  d. Inspect the mounting bolt holes (D, **Figure 47**). If they are worn or damaged, replace the caliper assembly and inspect the bolt holes on the fork leg.

10. Remove the bleed valve (A, **Figure 48**) from the caliper body. Apply compressed air to the opening and make sure it is clear. If necessary, clean out the bleed valve with fresh brake fluid. Install the bleed valve finger-tight. It will be tightened to specification during brake bleeding.

11. Inspect the threads (**Figure 49**) for the banjo bolt and the mounting bolt (B, **Figure 48**) for wear or damage. Clean any minor thread damage. Replace the bolts and the caliper assembly if necessary.

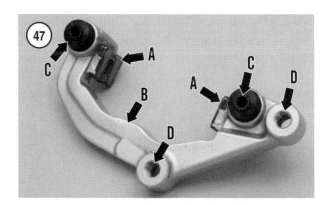

FRONT CALIPER
(2004-ON MODELS)

Removal

Refer to **Figure 50**.

1. Securely support the motorcycle on level ground. Block the rear wheel so the motorcycle will not roll in either direction.

2. Remove the mounting bolt and nut and release the brake hose holder (**Figure 51**) and side reflector from the fork slider.

3. Note that the brake hose neck sits behind the indexing post (A, **Figure 52**) on the caliper. The hose must be installed on this position against the post during assembly.

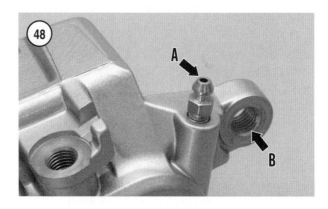

4. Remove the brake pads as described in Steps 2-5 of *Front Brake Pad Replacement (2004-on Models)* in this chapter.

5. Remove the banjo bolt (B, **Figure 52**) from the caliper. Remove the brake hose and the two copper washers from the caliper.

> *CAUTION*
> *Brake fluid damages paint and finish. Immediately wash any spilled brake fluid from the motorcycle. Use soapy water and rinse the area completely.*

6. Place the loose end of the brake hose into a resealable plastic bag (A, **Figure 53**) to keep foreign matter out of the system and to prevent brake fluid from dripping out.

7. Remove the mounting bolts (B, **Figure 53**) and lift the caliper (C) from the caliper bracket.

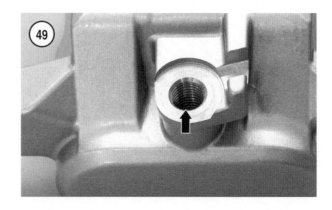

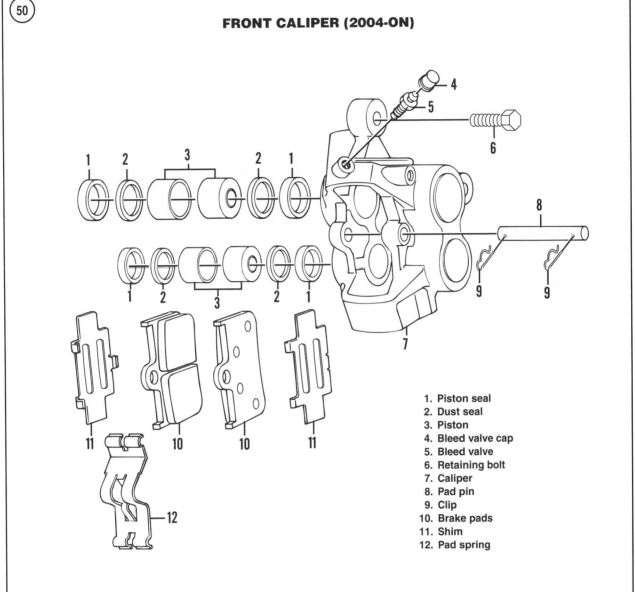

FRONT CALIPER (2004-ON)

1. Piston seal
2. Dust seal
3. Piston
4. Bleed valve cap
5. Bleed valve
6. Retaining bolt
7. Caliper
8. Pad pin
9. Clip
10. Brake pads
11. Shim
12. Pad spring

14

8. Disassemble and inspect the caliper as described in this section.

Installation

1. Install the caliper onto the fork slider.
2. Apply a medium-strength threadlocking compound to the threads of the caliper mounting bolts and install the bolts (B, **Figure 53**). Tighten the bolts to 40 N•m (30 ft.-lb.).
3. Place the brake hose neck behind the indexing post (A, **Figure 52**) on the caliper.
4. Install a *new* copper washer on each side of the brake hose fitting. Install and tighten the banjo bolt (B, **Figure 52**) to 30 N•m (22 ft.-lb.).
5. Install the brake pads as described in Steps 8-13 of *Front Brake Pad Replacement (2004-on Models)* in this chapter.
6. Move the brake hose holder (**Figure 51**) and side re-flector onto the fork slider. Install the mounting bolt and nut and tighten securely.
7. Add brake fluid to the reservoir and bleed the brakes as described earlier in this chapter.

Disassembly/Assembly

Refer to **Figure 50**.
1. Remove the brake pads and brake caliper as described in this section.

> *WARNING*
> *In the next step, the pistons may come out of the caliper body with considerable force. Keep your hands out of the way. Wear shop gloves and apply air pressure gradually. Do not use high pressure air or place the air hose nozzle directly against the hydraulic line fitting in the caliper body. Hold the air nozzle away from the inlet, allowing some of the air to escape.*

2. Insert a piece of wood through the caliper and press the wood down against the inboard piston (**Figure 54**).
3. Block the exposed housing fluid port holes on the cali-per housing. Apply compressed air through the caliper hose port and blow the pistons out of the caliper.
4. Repeat for the outboard set of pistons. Remove all four pistons from the caliper. Clearly label the pistons so they can be reinstalled in their original cylinders in the caliper.

> *CAUTION*
> *In the following step, do not use a sharp tool to remove the dust and piston seals from the*

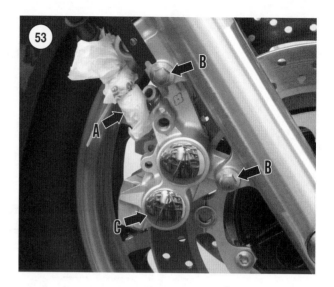

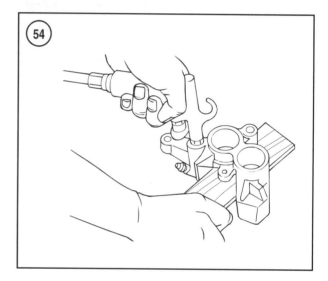

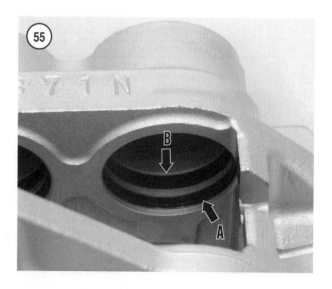

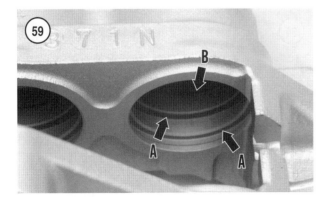

caliper cylinder. Sharp tools could damage the cylinder surface. The caliper will have to be replaced if the cylinder surface is damaged.

5. Use a piece of plastic or wood to carefully remove the dust seal (A, **Figure 55**) and the piston seal (B) from their grooves in each caliper cylinder. Discard both seals.

6. Clean all caliper parts and inspect them as described in this section.

WARNING
Never reuse the dust seals or piston seals. Very minor damage or age deterioration can make the seals ineffective.

7. Coat the new dust seals and piston seals (**Figure 56**) with fresh DOT 4 brake fluid.

8. Carefully install the new piston seal (B, **Figure 55**) and dust seal (A) into the grooves in the caliper cylinders. Make sure the seals are properly seated in their respective grooves.

9. Coat the pistons and caliper cylinders with fresh DOT 4 brake fluid.

10. Position each piston with the open end facing toward the brake pads (**Figure 57**) and slide the pistons into the caliper cylinders. Push the pistons in until they almost bottom in the cylinders (**Figure 58**).

11. Install the brake pads and caliper as described in this section.

Inspection

1. Clean all parts, except brake pads, with clean DOT 4 brake fluid. Place the cleaned parts on a lint-free cloth while performing the following inspection procedures.

2. Inspect both seal grooves (A, **Figure 59**) in each cylinder for damage. If they are damaged or corroded, replace the caliper assembly.

3. Inspect the fluid opening in the base of each cylinder bore. Apply compressed air to the opening and make sure it is clear. Clean out the opening with fresh brake fluid if necessary.

4. Inspect the walls (B, **Figure 59**) in each cylinder for scratches, scoring or other damage. If there is rust or corrosion, replace the caliper assembly.

5. Measure the inside diameter of each cylinder bore with a bore gauge (**Figure 60**). Replace the brake caliper if the inside diameter of either bore exceeds the specification in **Table 1**.

6. Inspect the pistons (**Figure 61**) for scratches, scoring or other damage. If they are rusty or corroded, replace the pistons.

14

7. Inspect the pad spring (**Figure 62**). Replace a spring if it is cracked, worn or shows signs of fatigue.

8. Remove the bleed valve from the caliper body. Apply compressed air to the opening and make sure it is clear. If necessary, clean out the bleed valve with fresh brake fluid. Install the bleed valve finger-tight. It will be tightened to specification during brake bleeding.

9. Inspect the threads (A, **Figure 63**) for the banjo bolt for wear or damage. Clean any minor thread damage. Replace the caliper assembly if necessary.

10. Inspect the mounting bolt holes (B, **Figure 63**) for elongation or damage.

11. Inspect the caliper body for scratches or other signs of damage (C, **Figure 63**). Replace the caliper assembly if necessary.

FRONT MASTER CYLINDER

Removal

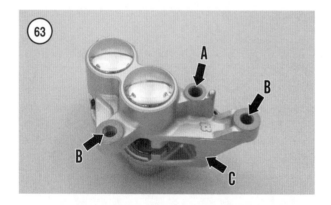

CAUTION
Cover the fuel tank and front fender with a heavy cloth or plastic tarp to protect them from brake fluid spills. Wash spilled brake fluid off any painted or plated surfaces immediately. Brake fluid will damage the finish. Use soapy water and rinse the area completely.

1. Drain the brake fluid from the master cylinder as described earlier in this chapter.

2. Remove the reservoir cap, diaphragm plate and diaphragm.

3. Remove the nut from the lever bolt and remove the bolt (A, **Figure 64**).

4. Place your hand under the brake lever to catch the compression spring when the brake lever is removed.

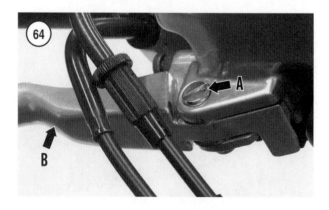

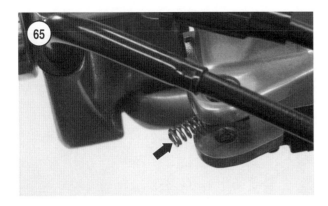

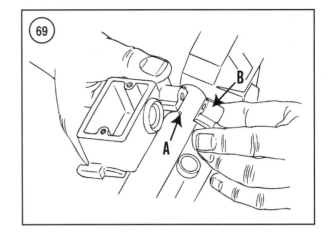

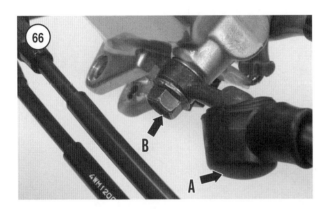

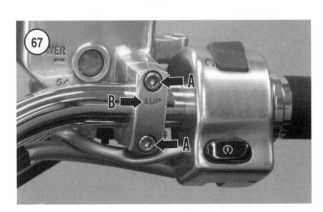

5. Slowly pull the brake lever (B, **Figure 64**) away from the master cylinder. Remove the compression spring (**Figure 65**) from the receptacle in the master cylinder.

6. Pull back the boot (A, **Figure 66**) and remove the banjo bolt (B) securing the brake hose to the master cylinder. Remove the brake hose and both copper washers.

7. Place the loose end of the brake hose into a resealable plastic bag to keep foreign matter from the system and to protect the motorcycle from leaking brake fluid.

8. Remove the two clamp bolts (A, **Figure 67**) and clamps (B). Move the master cylinder away from the handlebar. Pour out and discard any remaining brake fluid. Never reuse brake fluid.

9. Remove the electrical connectors (A, **Figure 68**) from the brake switch on the master cylinder.

10. Remove the master cylinder (B, **Figure 68**) from the handlebar.

Installation

1. Reconnect the brake switch electrical connectors (B, **Figure 68**).

2. Position the master cylinder so the face of the clamp mating surface aligns with the mark on the handlebar (A, **Figure 69**).

3. Install the master cylinder clamp (B, **Figure 69**) so the UP stamp faces up (B, **Figure 67**).

4. Tighten the clamp bolts (A, **Figure 67**) to 10 N•m (88 in.-lb.). Tighten the upper clamp bolt first, then the lower bolt. Make sure there is a gap at the lower part of the clamp after tightening. Do not pinch the electrical cable in the clamps.

5. Install the brake hose on the master cylinder. Place a *new* copper washer on each side of the hose fitting and tighten the banjo bolt to 30 N•m (22 ft.-lb.).

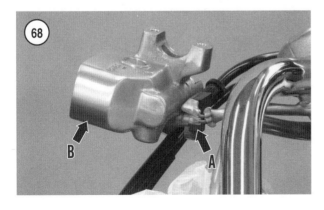

14

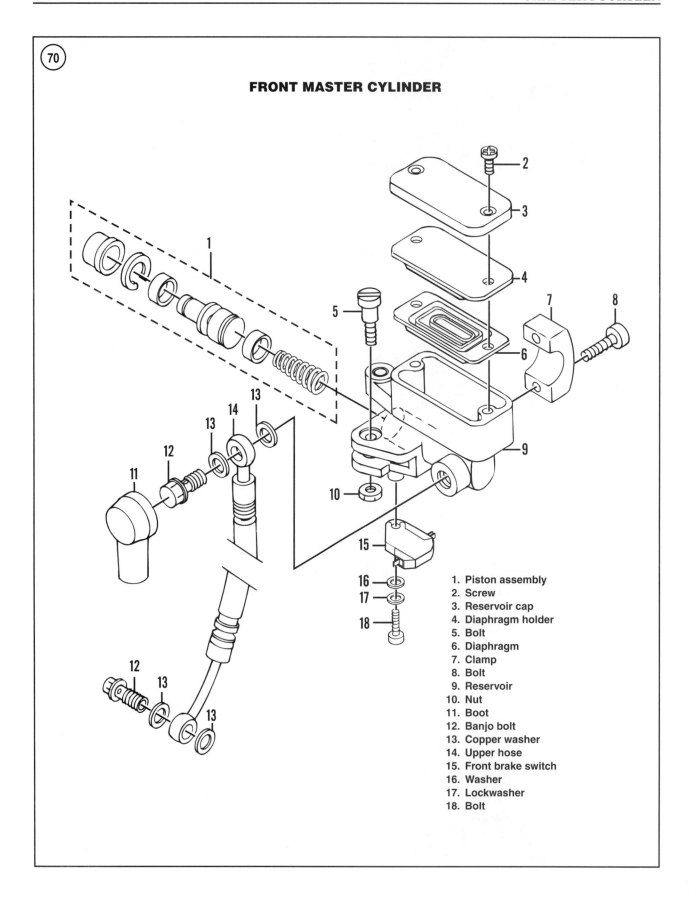

FRONT MASTER CYLINDER

1. Piston assembly
2. Screw
3. Reservoir cap
4. Diaphragm holder
5. Bolt
6. Diaphragm
7. Clamp
8. Bolt
9. Reservoir
10. Nut
11. Boot
12. Banjo bolt
13. Copper washer
14. Upper hose
15. Front brake switch
16. Washer
17. Lockwasher
18. Bolt

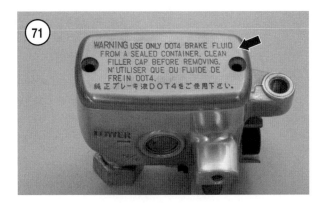

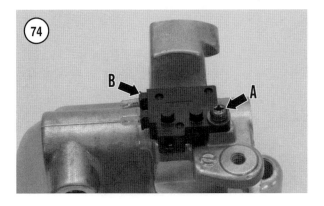

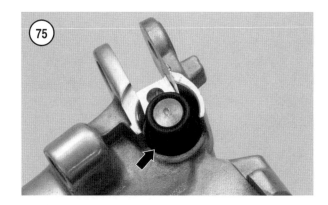

6. If removed, install the compression spring (**Figure 65**) into the receptacle in the master cylinder.

7. Slide the brake lever (B, **Figure 64**) into place on the master cylinder body. Make sure the compression spring engages the boss on the master cylinder body.

8. Lubricate the lever pivot bolt with lithium grease, and secure the brake lever to the body with the pivot bolt (A, **Figure 64**) and nut. Tighten the nuts securely.

9. Add fresh DOT 4 brake fluid to the master cylinder and bleed the brake system as described in this chapter.

10. Install the diaphragm and diaphragm plate into the reservoir. Secure the reservoir cap in place with the two mounting screws and tighten securely.

11. Bleed the rear brake as described in this chapter.

12. Test ride the motorcycle slowly at first to make sure the brakes are operating properly with full hydraulic advantage.

Disassembly

Refer to **Figure 70**.

1. Remove the master cylinder as described in this chapter.

2. If still in place, remove the reservoir cap (**Figure 71**), diaphragm plate (**Figure 72**) and diaphragm (**Figure 73**). Pour out and discard any remaining brake fluid. Never reuse brake fluid.

3. Remove the screw, lock washer and washer (A, **Figure 74**) securing the brake light switch (B). Remove the switch.

4. Remove the boot (**Figure 75**) from the master cylinder bore.

5. Remove the snap ring (A, **Figure 76**) from its groove in the cylinder bore, then remove the piston assembly (B).

6. Inspect the master cylinder as described in this section.

14

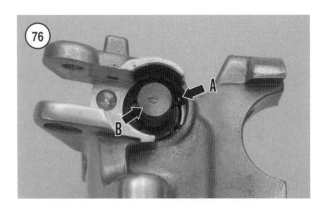

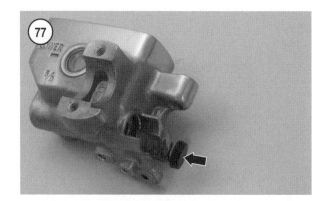

Assembly

Refer to **Figure 70**.

> *CAUTION*
> *When installing the piston assembly, do not*
> *allow the cups to turn inside out. This will*
> *damage the cups and allow brake fluid to*
> *leak into the cylinder bore.*

1. Lubricate the piston assembly and the cylinder bore
with fresh brake fluid.

2. Install the spring assembly into the cylinder bore as
shown in **Figure 77**.

3. Install the piston into the bore (**Figure 78**) and press
the piston into the bore and secure it in place with a *new*
snap ring (**Figure 79**). The snap ring must be seated in the
groove inside the cylinder bore as shown in A, **Figure 76**.

4. Lubricate the boot with fresh brake fluid. Position the
boot so the end with the lip faces into the master cylinder
bore and carefully roll the boot over the piston so the boot
seals the master cylinder bore (**Figure 75**).

5. Install the diaphragm (**Figure 73**), diaphragm plate
(**Figure 72**) and cap (**Figure 71**).

Inspection

1. Clean all parts in fresh DOT 4 brake fluid. Place the
master cylinder components on a clean lint-free cloth.

2. Inspect the cylinder bore and piston contact surfaces
for scratches, wear or other signs of damage. Replace the
master cylinder body if necessary.

3. Inspect the inside of the reservoir for scratches, wear
or other signs of damage. Replace the master cylinder
body if necessary.

4. Make sure the passage in the bottom of the brake fluid
reservoir (**Figure 80**) is clear.

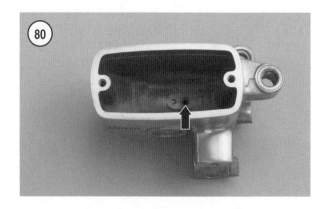

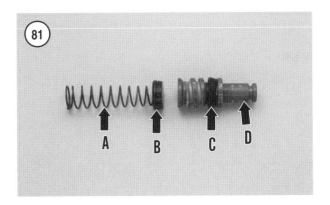

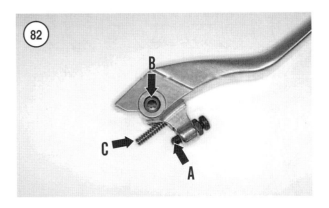

NOTE
*The spring (A, **Figure 81**), primary cup (B), secondary cup (C), piston (D), snap ring and boot are sold as a master cylinder kit. If any part is worn or damaged, replace the master cylinder kit.*

5. Check the end of the piston (D, **Figure 81**) for wear.

6. Check the primary cup (B, **Figure 81**) and secondary cup (C) on the master piston for damage, softness or swelling.

7. Check the hand lever end of the adjuster screw (A, **Figure 82**) for signs of wear. Replace the screw if necessary.

8. Remove and inspect the brake lever bushing (B, **Figure 82**). Replace the bushing if it is worn or elongated.

9. Remove the compression spring (C, **Figure 82**) from the hand lever. Replace the spring if it is worn or shows signs of fatigue.

10. Check the reservoir diaphragm (A, **Figure 83**) and cover (B) for damage and deterioration. Replace if necessary.

11. Inspect the banjo bolt threads in the master cylinder brake port (**Figure 84**). If the threads are damaged or partially stripped, replace the master cylinder body.

12. Measure the inside diameter of the master cylinder bore with a bore gauge (**Figure 85**). Replace the master cylinder if the inside diameter equals or exceeds the specification in **Table 1**.

13. Inspect the master cylinder body for scratches or other damage. Replace the master cylinder assembly if necessary.

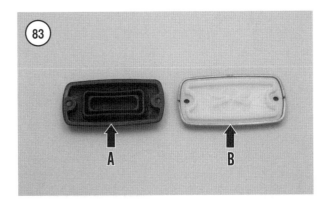

REAR BRAKE CALIPER

Refer to **Figure 86**.

Removal

1. Securely support the motorcycle on level ground.

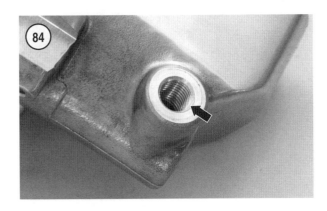

14

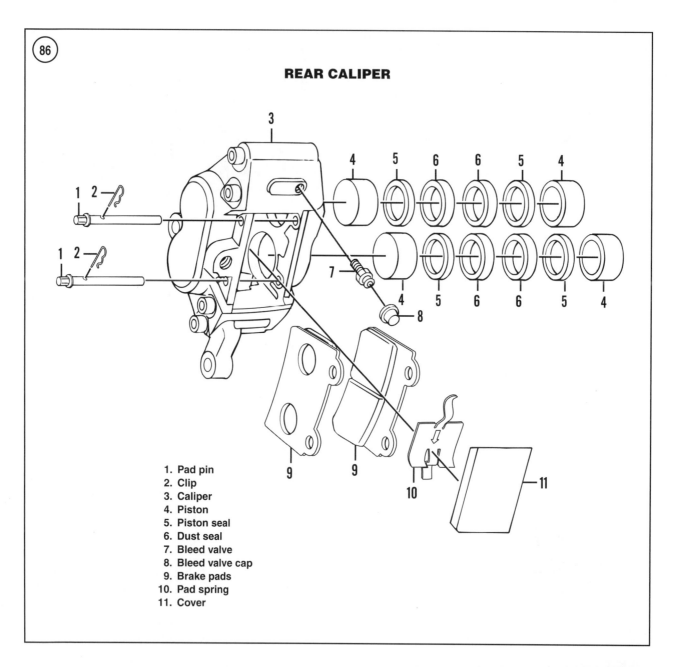

86

REAR CALIPER

1. Pad pin
2. Clip
3. Caliper
4. Piston
5. Piston seal
6. Dust seal
7. Bleed valve
8. Bleed valve cap
9. Brake pads
10. Pad spring
11. Cover

2. Remove the muffler assembly as described in Chapter Nine.

3. On models so equipped, remove the right side saddlebag as described in Chapter Fifteen.

4. Drain the brake fluid from the rear brake as described in this chapter.

5. Note that the brake hose neck sits behind the indexing post (A, **Figure 87**) on the caliper. The hose must be installed on this position against the post during assembly.

6. Remove the banjo bolt (**Figure 88**) from the caliper and separate the brake hose from the caliper. Remove and

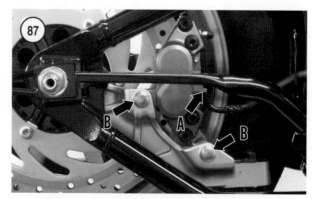

87

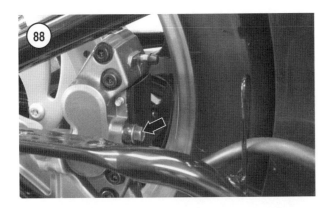

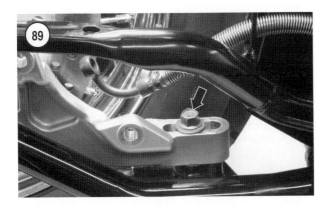

a. Support the engine on a jack to take weight off the rear wheel.

b. Remove the bolt and washer (**Figure 89**) securing the caliper mounting bracket to the swing arm.

c. Remove the rear axle nut (A, **Figure 90**) and withdraw the rear axle sufficiently to clear the caliper mounting bracket.

d. Carefully remove the caliper mounting bracket (B, **Figure 90**). Do not scratch the brake disc.

e. Move the rear axle back into position and install the rear axle nut. Tighten securely.

Installation

1. If removed, install the caliper mounting bracket at follows:

a. Remove the rear axle nut (A, **Figure 90**) and withdraw the rear axle sufficiently to clear the caliper mounting bracket.

b. Carefully install the caliper mounting bracket (B, **Figure 90**). Do not the scratch the brake disc.

c. Align the rear axle hole in the bracket and move the rear axle back into position and install the rear axle nut. Tighten finger-tight at this time.

d. Apply a medium-strength thread locking compound to the mounting bolt threads.

e. Install the bolt and washer (**Figure 89**) securing the caliper mounting bracket to the swing arm.

f. Tighten caliper bracket bolt to 48 N•m (35 ft.-lb.).

g. Tighten the rear axle nut to 150 N•m (111 ft.-lb.).

h. If necessary, adjust the drive belt tension as described in Chapter Three.

i. Remove the jack from under the engine.

2. Lower the caliper over the brake disc and seat it on the caliper bracket.

3. Apply a medium-strength thread locking compound to the mounting bolt threads.

4. Install the caliper mounting bolts (B, **Figure 87**) and tighten to 40 N•m (30 ft.-lb.).

5. Secure the brake hose to the caliper with the banjo bolt (**Figure 88**). Place *new* washers on either side of the brake hose fitting.

6. Position the brake hose so the neck sits behind the indexing post (A, **Figure 87**) on the caliper.

7. Tighten the banjo bolt 30 N•m (22 ft.-lb.).

8. Install the brake pads as described in Steps 11-20 of *Rear Brake Pad Replacement* in this chapter.

9. Install the muffler assembly as described in Chapter Nine.

10. On models so equipped, install the right side saddlebag as described in Chapter Fifteen.

11. Bleed the rear brake as described in this chapter.

discard the two washers. New washers must be used during installation.

7. Insert the end of the brake hose into a plastic bag so brake fluid will not leak onto the motorcycle.

8. Remove the brake pads as described in Steps 4-10 of *Rear Brake Pad Replacement* in this chapter.

9. Remove the caliper mounting bolts (B, **Figure 87**), and lift the caliper from the disc and caliper bracket.

10. If necessary, remove the caliper mounting bracket as follows:

14

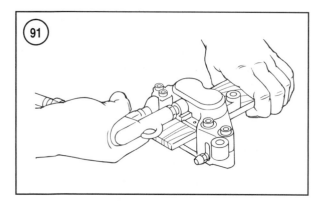

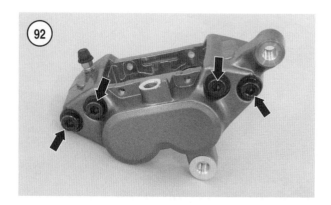

12. Test ride the motorcycle slowly at first to make sure the brakes are operating properly with full hydraulic advantage.

Disassembly

Refer to **Figure 86**.

1. Remove the caliper and the brake pads as described in this section.

2. Set the caliper on a bench with the outboard side facing down.

3. Insert a piece of wood through the caliper and press the wood down against the inboard pistons (**Figure 91**).

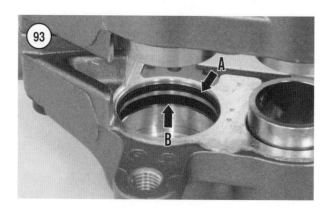

> *WARNING*
> *In the next step, the piston may shoot out of the caliper body with great force. Keep your hands out of the way. Wear shop gloves and apply air pressure gradually.*

4. Apply compressed air through the brake hose fitting and blow the inboard pistons out of the cylinder.

5. Repeat for the outboard set of pistons. Remove all four pistons from the caliper. Clearly label the pistons so they can be reinstalled in their original cylinders in the caliper.

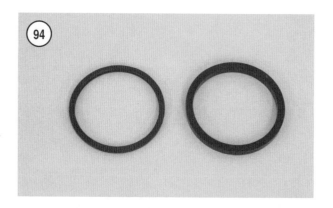

> *CAUTION*
> *In the following step, do not use a sharp tool to remove the dust and piston seals from the caliper cylinder. Sharp tools could damage the cylinder surface. The caliper will have to be replaced if the cylinder surface is damaged.*

> *NOTE*
> *Yamaha recommends servicing the rear caliper without removing the caliper bolts (**Figure 92**). This caliper can be serviced without separating the caliper halves.*

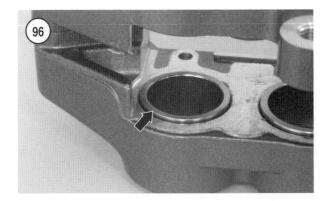

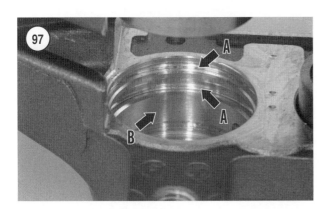

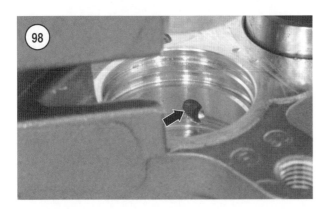

6. Use a piece of plastic or wood to carefully remove the dust seal (A, **Figure 93**) and the piston seal (B) from their grooves in each caliper cylinder. Discard all seals.

7. Clean all caliper parts and inspect them as described in this section.

Assembly

> *WARNING*
> *Never reuse the old dust seals or piston seals. Very minor damage or age deterioration can make the seals ineffective.*

1. Coat the *new* dust seals and piston seals (**Figure 94**) with fresh DOT 4 brake fluid.

2. Carefully install the *new* piston seal (B, **Figure 93**) and dust seal (A) into the grooves in each caliper cylinder. Make sure the seals are properly seated in their respective grooves.

3. Coat the pistons with DOT 4 brake fluid.

> *CAUTION*
> *Install each piston into its original cylinder. The outboard piston must be installed in the outboard side of the caliper and vice versa.*

4. Position the piston with its open end up and insert into the cylinder (**Figure 95**).

5. Press the piston into the cylinder until it bottoms (**Figure 96**).

6. Repeat for the remaining pistons.

7. If removed, install the bleed valve and tighten securely.

8. Install the brake pads and caliper as described in this section.

Inspection

1. Clean all parts, except brake pads, with clean DOT 4 brake fluid. Place the cleaned parts on a lint-free cloth while performing the following inspection procedures.

2. Inspect both seal grooves (A, **Figure 97**) in each cylinder for damage. If they are damaged or corroded, replace the caliper assembly.

3. Inspect the fluid opening in the base of each cylinder bore (**Figure 98**). Apply compressed air to the opening and make sure it is clear. Clean out the opening with fresh brake fluid if necessary.

4. Inspect the walls (B, **Figure 97**) in each cylinder for scratches, scoring or other damage. If there is rust or corrosion, replace the caliper assembly.

5. Measure the inside diameter of each cylinder bore with a bore gauge (**Figure 99**). Replace the brake caliper if the

14

inside diameter of either bore exceeds the specification in **Table 1**.

6. Inspect the pistons (**Figure 100**) for scratches, scoring or other damage. If they are rusty or corroded, replace the pistons.

7. Inspect the pad spring. Replace a spring if it is cracked, worn or shows signs of fatigue.

8. Remove the bleed valve from the caliper body. Apply compressed air to the opening and make sure it is clear. If necessary, clean out the bleed valve with fresh brake fluid. Install the bleed valve finger-tight. It will be tightened to specification during brake bleeding.

9. Inspect the threads (**Figure 101**) for the banjo bolt for wear or damage. Clean any minor thread damage. Replace the caliper assembly if necessary.

10. Inspect the threads (A, **Figure 102**) for the mounting bolts for wear or damage. Clean any minor thread damage. Replace the caliper assembly if necessary.

11. Inspect the caliper body for scratches or other signs of damage (B, **Figure 102**). Replace the caliper assembly if necessary.

12. Inspect the caliper bracket (**Figure 103**) for cracks, scratches or other signs of damage. Replace the caliper bracket if necessary.

REAR BRAKE MASTER CYLINDER

Refer to **Figure 104**.

Removal

1. Drain the brake fluid from the rear brake as described in this chapter.

> *NOTE*
> *The master cylinder can be removed while the brake pedal/footrest assembly is installed on the motorcycle. However, the master cylinder parts are more easily accessible if the brake pedal/footrest is removed first.*

2. Remove the brake pedal/footrest assembly as described in this chapter.

3. Disconnect the reservoir hose (**Figure 105**) from the master cylinder.

4. Remove the cotter pin and washer. Pull the clevis pin from the master cylinder clevis.

5. Separate the master cylinder clevis (A, **Figure 106**) from the brake lever (B).

6. Remove the bolts (C, **Figure 106**) securing the master cylinder to the brake pedal/footrest assembly. Remove the

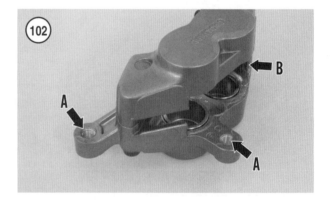

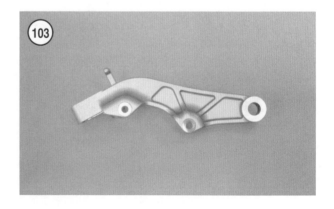

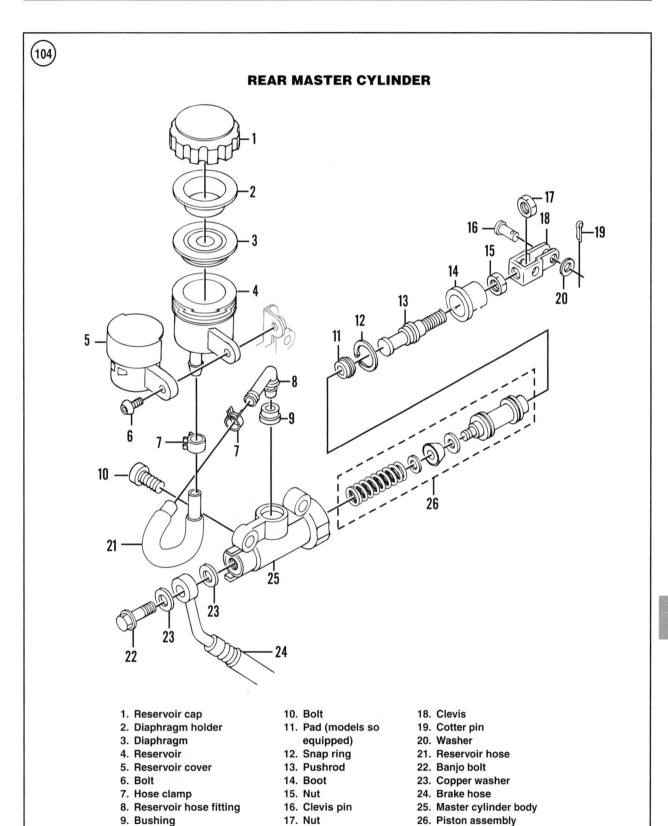

104

REAR MASTER CYLINDER

1. Reservoir cap
2. Diaphragm holder
3. Diaphragm
4. Reservoir
5. Reservoir cover
6. Bolt
7. Hose clamp
8. Reservoir hose fitting
9. Bushing
10. Bolt
11. Pad (models so equipped)
12. Snap ring
13. Pushrod
14. Boot
15. Nut
16. Clevis pin
17. Nut
18. Clevis
19. Cotter pin
20. Washer
21. Reservoir hose
22. Banjo bolt
23. Copper washer
24. Brake hose
25. Master cylinder body
26. Piston assembly

14

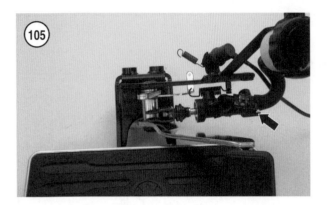

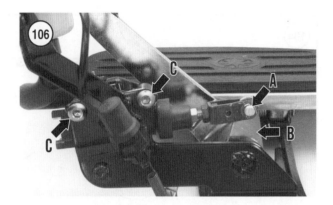

master cylinder assembly from the brake pedal/footrest assembly.

Installation

1. Install the master cylinder onto the brake pedal/footrest assembly and install the mounting bolts (C, **Figure 106**). Tighten the mounting bolts to 23 N•m (17 ft.-lb.).

2. Move the brake pedal (B, **Figure 106**) into position on the master cylinder and install the master cylinder clevis pin (A).

3. Install the washer and a *new* cotter pin. Bend the ends of the cotter pin over completely.

4. Connect the reservoir hose (**Figure 105**) onto the master cylinder and move the hose clamp into position.

5. Install the brake pedal/footrest assembly as described in this chapter.

6. Add brake fluid and bleed the brakes as described in this chapter.

Disassembly

1. Remove the rear brake master cylinder as described in this chapter.

2. Roll back the dust boot (**Figure 107**) and remove the snap ring (**Figure 108**) from its groove in the cylinder bore.

3. Remove the pushrod assembly (**Figure 109**), then the piston assembly and spring (**Figure 110**) from the cylinder bore.

4. If necessary, pull straight up and remove the reservoir hose fitting (**Figure 111**) out of the bushing in the master cylinder port.

5. Inspect the master cylinder and reservoir as described in this section.

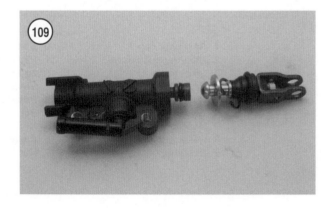

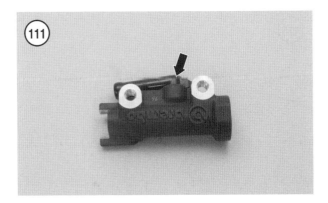

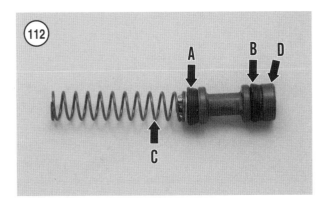

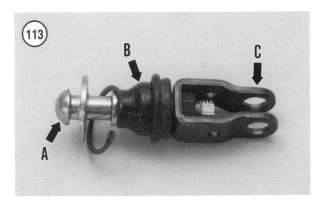

Assembly

1. If removed, install the reservoir hose fitting (**Figure 111**) into the bushing in the master cylinder port.

2A. If reinstall the piston, soak the piston in fresh brake fluid for at least 15 minutes to make the primary (A, **Figure 112**) and secondary cups (B) pliable. Coat the inside of the cylinder with fresh brake fluid before assembling the parts.

2B. If installing a new master cylinder kit, soak the new primary and secondary cups in brake fluid for at least 15 minutes. Roll the primary cup (A, **Figure 112**) onto the inboard end of the piston; roll the secondary cup (B) onto the outboard end.

3. If removed, install the spring (C, **Figure 112**) onto the piston.

CAUTION
When installing the piston assembly, do not allow the cups to turn inside out. This will damage the cups and allow brake fluid to leak within the cylinder bore.

4. Install the piston/spring assembly (**Figure 110**) into the master cylinder.

5. Place a dab of grease on the end of the pushrod, and slowly push the spring and piston into the master cylinder with the pushrod assembly. Make sure the end of the push rod engages the seat in the master piston.

6. Install the snap ring (**Figure 108**) and make sure it is completely seated in its groove in the master cylinder. Pull out on the pushrod to ensure that the snap ring is correct sealed.

7. Slide the dust boot (**Figure 107**) into position. Make sure it is firmly seated against the master cylinder.

8. Install the master cylinder as described in this chapter.

Inspection

The piston, piston seals, spring assembly, pushrod and boot are all replaced as a kit. Individual parts are not available. If any of these parts are faulty, purchase the master cylinder kit.

1. Clean all parts in fresh DOT 4 brake fluid. Place the master cylinder components on a clean lint-free cloth.

2. Check the seat of the piston (D, **Figure 112**) where it contacts the pushrod for wear.

3. Check the primary cup (A, **Figure 112**) and secondary cup (B) for damage, softness or swelling.

4. Inspect the piston body and the spring (C, **Figure 112**) for damage or bending.

5. Inspect the end of the pushrod (A, **Figure 113**) where it contacts the piston for damage.

14

6. Inspect the pushrod dust boot (B, **Figure 113**) for tears or other signs of damage.

7. If any of the parts inspected in Steps 2-6 are worn, damaged or bent, replace all of them with the master cylinder kit.

8. Inspect the clevis (C, **Figure 113**) for cracks, bending or other signs of damage.

9. Inspect the cylinder bore and piston contact surfaces for signs of wear or damage. If either part is less than perfect, replace the master cylinder.

10. Inspect the banjo bolt threads (**Figure 114**). If the threads are damaged or partially stripped, replace the master cylinder assembly.

11. Inspect the threads of the master cylinder mounting bosses (**Figure 115**). If the threads are damaged or partially stripped, replace the master cylinder assembly.

12. Make sure the passages in the inlet port are clear.

13. Measure the master cylinder inside diameter with a bore gauge (**Figure 116**). If the inside diameter is out of specification (**Table 2**), replace the master cylinder body.

14. Inspect the reservoir diaphragm (A, **Figure 117**) and cap (B) for tears, cracks or other signs of damage. Replace as necessary.

15. Inspect the reservoir and hose for cracks, wear or other signs of damage. Replace as necessary.

BRAKE PEDAL/FOOTREST ASSEMBLY

Refer to **Figure 118**.
Removal

The rear brake master cylinder and reservoir are part of the brake pedal/footrest assembly.

1. Drain the brake fluid from the rear brakes as described in this chapter.

2. Note that the brake hose neck sits between the indexing posts (A, **Figure 119**) on the master cylinder. The hose must be installed on this position between the posts during installation.

3. Remove the banjo bolt (B, **Figure 119**) and separate the brake hose from the rear master cylinder. Insert the hose into a resealable plastic bag so brake fluid will not leak onto the motorcycle.

4. Remove the screw (**Figure 120**) securing the reservoir and cover to the frame.

5. Follow the electrical wire from the rear brake pedal switch, around in front of the engine and up next to the rollover valve. Disconnect the 2-pin black connector (**Figure 121**) from the harness.

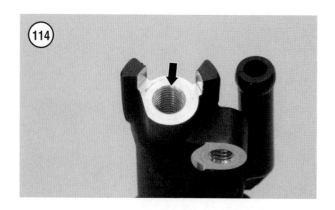

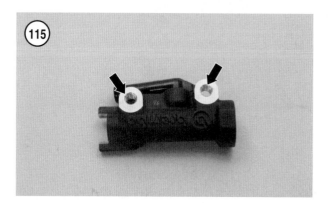

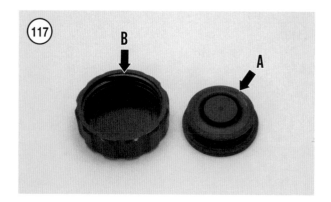

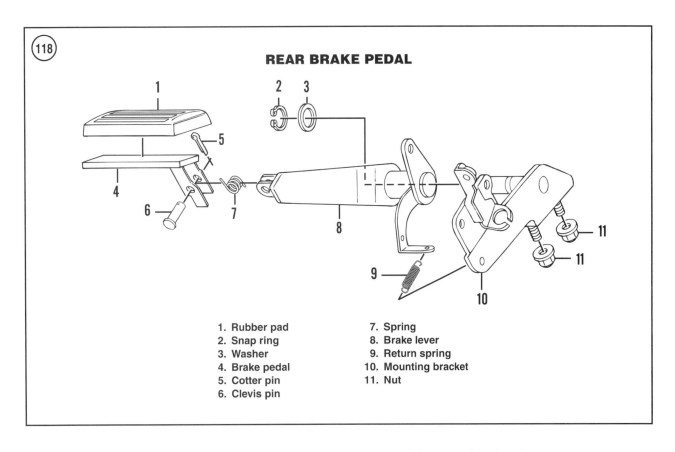

REAR BRAKE PEDAL

1. Rubber pad
2. Snap ring
3. Washer
4. Brake pedal
5. Cotter pin
6. Clevis pin
7. Spring
8. Brake lever
9. Return spring
10. Mounting bracket
11. Nut

6. Remove the bolts (**Figure 122**) securing the brake pedal/footrest assembly to the frame. Hold the reservoir to the assembly and remove the assembly.

7. If necessary, remove the brake pedal as follows:

   a. Disconnect the return spring from the brake lever (**Figure 123**).

   b. Remove the snap ring and washer (A, **Figure 124**) securing the brake pedal/lever to the mounting bracket.

   c. Pull the brake pedal/lever (B, **Figure 124**) from the mounting bracket pivot shaft.

14

8. If necessary, remove the self-locking nuts (**Figure 125**) securing the brake pedal/lever mounting bracket to the footrest mounting bracket. Separate the two assemblies and discard the two nuts.

Installation

1. If removed, install the brake pedal/lever mounting bracket onto the footrest mounting bracket. Install *new* self-locking nuts to 16 N•m (142 in.-lb.).

2. If the brake pedal was removed, perform the following:

    a. Lubricate the brake pedal pivot shaft with lithium soap grease and slide the pedal onto the mounting bracket shaft.

    b. Install the washer (A, **Figure 124**) and the snap ring securing the brake pedal/lever to the mounting bracket. Make sure the snap ring is seated correctly in the groove.

    c. Connect the return spring onto the brake lever (**Figure 123**).

3. Set the brake pedal/footrest assembly in place on the right side of the frame. Install the bolts (**Figure 122**) and tighten to 48 N•m (35 ft.-lb.).

4. Connect the rear brake switch connector.

5. Move the reservoir into position on the frame down tube and install the screw (**Figure 120**). Tighten the screw securely.

6. Install the brake hose onto the port on the rear master cylinder. Position the brake hose neck sits between the indexing posts (A, **Figure 119**) on the master cylinder. Install a new copper washer on each side of the hose fitting and tighten the banjo bolt (B, **Figure 119**) to 30 N•m (22 ft.-lb.).

7. Fill the master cylinder and bleed the system as described in this chapter.

8. Adjust the brake pedal height and rear brake switch as described in Chapter Three.

BRAKE DISC

Inspection

A brake disc can be inspected while it is installed on the wheel.

1. Clean any rust or corrosion from the disc, and wipe it clean with brake parts cleaner. Never use oil-based solvents. They may leave an oil residue on the disc.

2. Measure the thickness of the disc at several locations around the disc with a vernier caliper or a micrometer (**Figure 126**). Replace the disc if the thickness in any area

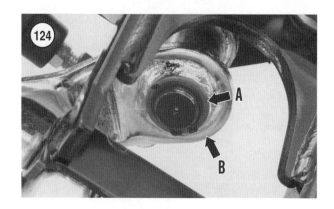

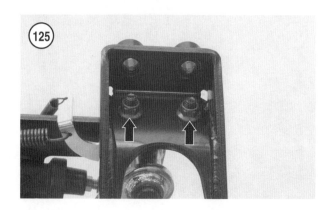

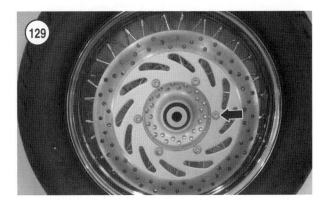

is equal to or less than the service limit specified in **Table 1** or **Table 2**.

3. Check the disc runout as follows:

    a. Make sure the disc mounting bolts are tight prior to running this check.

    b. Mount a dial indicator so its plunger sits 2-3 mm (0.09-0.12 in.) from the outside diameter of the disc.

    c. Slowly rotate the wheel and watch the dial indicator. Replace the disc if runout is out of specification.

4. A used disc will usually have some radial grooves. If these grooves are large, they will reduce brake effectiveness and increase brake pad wear. If large grooves are evident, consider replacing the disc. The discs cannot be machined, as the removal of material will reduce the disc thickness below the specification.

5. If there is evidence of disc overheating due to unequal pad pressure, inspect the following:

    a. The caliper for binding on the caliper pin.

    b. The caliper piston for binding in the caliper.

    c. Make sure the master cylinder relief port is clear.

    d. The master cylinder primary cup for wear or damage.

Removal/Installation

1. Remove the front or rear wheel as described in Chapter Eleven.

> *CAUTION*
> *Set the tire on two wooden blocks. Do not set the wheel down on the brake disc surface. It could be scratched or damaged.*

2. Insert a piece of wood or vinyl tube between the pads in the caliper(s).

3. Remove the brake disc bolts as follows:

    a. Front laced wheel: A, **Figure 127** and the hub cover (B).

    b. Front alloy wheel: **Figure 128**.

    c. Rear wheel: **Figure 129**.

4. Lift the brake disc (**Figure 130**, typical) from the hub.

5. Clean the threaded holes in the hub.

6. Clean the brake disc mounting surface on the hub.

7. On front alloy wheels, check the front brake disc floating fasteners (**Figure 131**) for damage or looseness. If any are damaged, replace the brake disc.

8. Installation is the reverse of removal while noting the following:

    a. The brake disc bolts are specifically designed for the application. If replacing the bolts, always use Yamaha brake disc bolts.

14

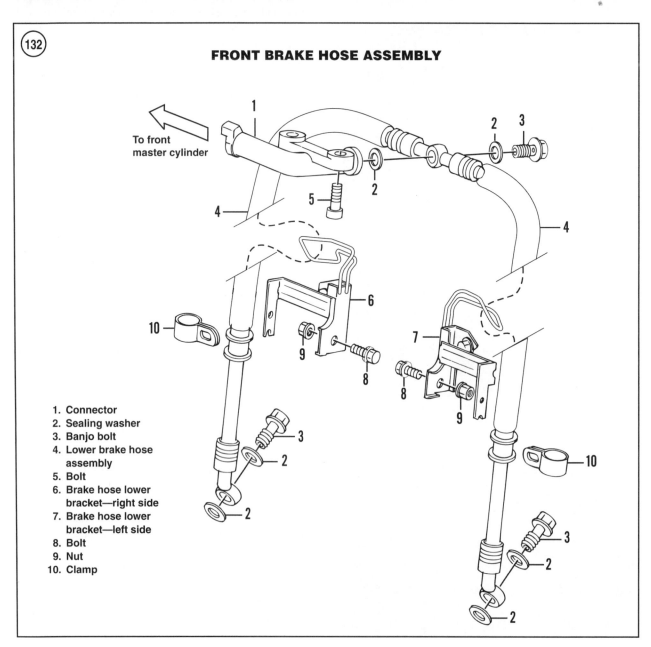

FRONT BRAKE HOSE ASSEMBLY

To front
master cylinder

1. Connector
2. Sealing washer
3. Banjo bolt
4. Lower brake hose assembly
5. Bolt
6. Brake hose lower bracket—right side
7. Brake hose lower bracket—left side
8. Bolt
9. Nut
10. Clamp

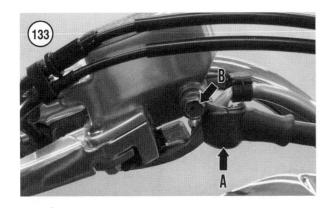

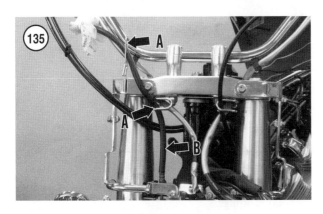

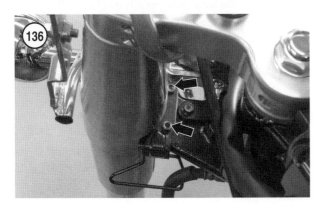

b. Install a disc so its arrow points in the direction of forward wheel rotation.

c. Apply a small amount of a medium-strength threadlocking compound to the bolt threads.

d. Evenly tighten the brake disc bolts in a crisscross pattern to 23 N•m (17 ft.-lb.).

BRAKE HOSE REPLACEMENT

Front Brake Hose Assembly

Check the brake hose assembly (**Figure 132**) at the brake system inspection intervals listed in Chapter Three. Replace the hose assembly if any portion is cracked, bulging or shows signs of chafing, wear or other damage.

1. Use plastic to cover areas of the motorcycle where brake fluid could spill.

2. Note how the brake hose assembly is routed through the frame and steering stem. Make a drawing so the new assembly can be routed along the same path as the original hose assembly.

3. Drain the brake fluid from the front brake system as described in this chapter.

4. To replace the upper master cylinder hose, perform the following:

    a. Slide the rubber boot (A, **Figure 133**) off the banjo bolt.

    b. Remove the banjo bolt (B, **Figure 133**) and sealing washers from the front master cylinder.

    c. Remove the banjo bolt (A, **Figure 134**) and sealing washers from the lower brake hose assembly connector.

NOTE
On models with a windshield, the upper hose guide is located on the windshield mounting bracket.

    d. Remove the upper hose from the hose guide(s) (A, **Figure 135**) and remove the hose (B).

5. Remove both front caliper assemblies as described in this chapter.

6. Remove the front fender as described in Chapter Fifteen.

7. Remove the front wheel as described in Chapter Eleven.

8. If still in place, remove the hose clamp securing the brake hose to the lower bracket on the fork slider.

9. Remove the Allen bolts (**Figure 136**) securing the brake hose guides and remove both guides. Refer to **Figure 137** and **Figure 138**.

10. Remove the bolts (B, **Figure 134**) securing the lower brake hose assembly connector to the lower fork bridge.

14

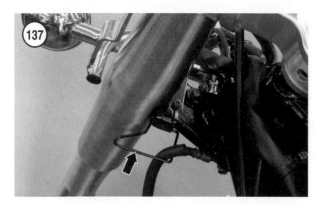

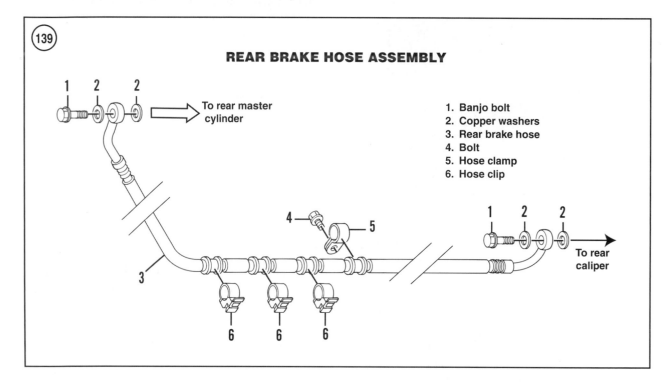

REAR BRAKE HOSE ASSEMBLY

To rear master cylinder

1. Banjo bolt
2. Copper washers
3. Rear brake hose
4. Bolt
5. Hose clamp
6. Hose clip

To rear caliper

11. Slowly lower the lower brake hose assembly down and remove it from the frame.

12. Installation is the reverse of removal. Note the following:

   a. Compare the new and old hoses. Make sure they are the same.

   b. Clean the banjo bolts and hose ends to remove any contamination.

   c. Refer to the notes made during removal and route the new hose along the same path as the original hose. Secure the hose to the motorcycle at the same locations noted during removal.

   d. Replace any banjo bolt with a damaged head or threads.

   e. Install a *new* copper washer on each side of a brake hose fitting.

   f. Tighten the banjo bolts to 30 N•m (22 ft.-lb.).

   g. After replacing the lower brake hose assembly, turn handlebars from side to side to make sure the hose does not rub against any part or pull away from its brake component.

   h. Refill the master cylinder and bleed the brakes as described in this chapter.

WARNING
Before riding the motorcycle, confirm that the brake lights work and that the front and rear brakes operate properly with full hydraulic advantage.

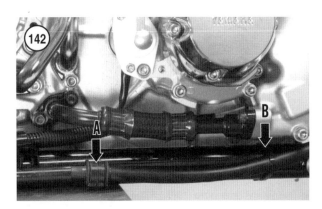

i. Slowly test ride the motorcycle to confirm that the brakes are operating properly.

Rear Brake Hose Assembly

Refer to **Figure 139**.

1. Remove the exhaust system as described in Chapter Nine.

2. Use plastic to cover areas of the motorcycle where brake fluid could spill.

3. Drain the brake fluid from the rear brake system as described in this chapter.

4. Note how the brake hose is routed along the frame and swing arm. Make a drawing so the new hose can be routed along the same path as the original hose.

5. Note that the brake hose neck sits between the indexing posts (A, **Figure 119**) on the master cylinder. The hose must be installed on this position between the posts during installation.

6. Remove the banjo bolt (B, **Figure 119**) and separate the brake hose from the rear master cylinder. Insert the hose into a resealable plastic bag so brake fluid will not leak onto the motorcycle.

7. Remove the *Brake Pedal/Footrest Assembly* as described in Chapter Fifteen.

8. Remove the banjo bolt (A, **Figure 140**) from the rear caliper.

NOTE
Figure 141 is shown with the rear wheel removed to better illustrate the step.

9. Remove the screw and clamp (**Figure 141**) securing the brake hose to the inside surface of the frame.

10. Withdraw the brake hose from the guide (B, **Figure 140**) on the swing arm.

11. Release the brake hose from the clips (A, **Figure 142**) and tie wraps (B) on the lower frame rail.

12. Installation is the reverse of removal. Note the following:

    a. Compare the new and old hose. Make sure they are the same.

    b. Clean the banjo bolts and hose ends to remove any contamination.

    c. Refer to the notes made during removal and route the new hose along the same path as the original hose. Secure the hose to the motorcycle at the same locations noted during removal to keep the hose away from the exhaust system.

    d. Replace any banjo bolt with a damaged head or threads.

    e. Install a *new* copper washer on each side of a brake hose fitting.

    f. Tighten the banjo bolt to 30 N•m (22 ft.-lb.).

    g. Refill the master cylinder and bleed the brakes as described in this chapter.

WARNING
Before riding the motorcycle, confirm that the brake lights work and that the front and rear brakes operate properly with full hydraulic advantage.

    h. Slowly test ride the motorcycle to confirm that the brakes are operating properly.

14

Table 1 FRONT BRAKE SPECIFICATIONS

Item	Standard mm (in.)	Service limit mm (in.)
Brake fluid	DOT 4	
Brake pad thickness		
1999-2003	6.0 (0.24)	0.5 (0.02)
2004-on	5.5 (0.22)	0.5 (0.02)
Brake disc runout		
1999-2003	–	0.10 (0.004)
2004-on Canada models	–	0.15 (0.006)
2004-on U.S., California	–	0.10 (0.004)
Brake disc thickness	5.0 (0.20)	–
Brake lever free play (at hand lever)	2-5 (0.08-0.20)	–
Caliper cylinder bore (1999-2003)		
Leading bore	30.1 (1.19)	–
Trailing bore	33.3 (1.31)	–
Caliper cylinder bore (2004-on)		
Leading bore	27.0 (1.06)	–
Trailing bore	30.2 (1.19)	–
Master cylinder bore	15.8 (0.62)	–

Table 2 REAR BRAKE SPECIFICATIONS

Item	Standard mm (in.)	Service limit mm (in.)
Brake fluid	DOT 4	
Brake pad thickness		
1999-2003	7.5 (0.30)	0.5 (0.02)
2004-on	7.0 (0.28)	0.5 (0.02)
Brake disc runout		
1999-2003	–	0.10 (0.004)
2004-on	–	0.15 (0.006)
Brake disc thickness	7.0 (0.28)	–
Brake pedal height (top of brake pedal above top of footrest board)	100 (3.9)	
Caliper cylinder bore		
Leading bore	30.23 (1.19)	–
Trailing bore	33.96 (1.34)	–
Master cylinder bore	12.7 (0.50)	–
Brake pedal height	Rider preference	

Table 3 FRONT BRAKE TORQUE SPECIFICATIONS

Item	N•m	in.-lb.	ft.-lb.
Brake disc bolt*	23	–	17
Brake hose banjo bolt	30	–	22
Caliper bleed valve	6	53	–
Front caliper			
Bracket mounting bolts*	40	–	30
Caliper-to-bracket bolts*	27	–	20
Front master cylinder			
Clamp bolt	10	88	–
Cover screw	2	18	–
*Apply a medium-strength threadlock to the threads.			

Table 4 REAR BRAKE TORQUE SPECIFICATIONS

Item	N•m	in.-lb.	ft.-lb.
Brake pedal lever bracket-to-footrest			
mounting nuts	16	142	–
Brake disc bolt*	23	–	17
Brake hose banjo bolt	30	–	22
Caliper bleed valve	6	53	–
Footrest mounting bolts	48	–	35
Rear axle nut	150	–	111
Rear caliper			
Mounting bolt*	40	–	30
Bracket mounting bolt*	48	–	35
Rear master cylinder			
mounting bolt	23	–	17
*Apply a medium-strength threadlock to the threads.			

14

CHAPTER FIFTEEN

BODY AND FRAME

SEATS

Removal/Installation

Refer to **Figure 1**.

1. To remove the rider seat, proceed as follows:
   a. Turn the ignition switch *counterclockwise* to the OPEN position. Do not push down on the ignition key when turning it.
   b. Pull straight up on the seat (**Figure 2**) and remove it.
2. To remove the passenger seat, proceed as follows:
   a. Remove the bolt securing the rear of the seat. Refer to **Figure 3** or **Figure 4**.
   b. Pull the seat (**Figure 5**) toward the rear until the seat tang disengages from the seat bracket on the rear fender. Remove the seat.
3. To install the rider seat, insert the rear projection (**Figure 6**) on the rear into the holder on the frame, then push down on the seat until the hook (**Figure 7**) locks into place.

SIDE COVERS

Removal/Installation

Refer to **Figure 8**.

CAUTION
The left side cover must be removed first.

1. Securely support the motorcycle on level ground. Block the front wheel so the motorcycle will not roll in either direction.
2. Remove the rider seat as described in this chapter.
3. Remove the screw and washer (A, **Figure 9**) securing the left side cover (B) to the frame.
4. Pull the left side cover straight out and disconnect it from the locating posts on the right side cover. Remove the cover and do not lose the two inner rubber grommets.
5. Remove the bolt (**Figure 10**) securing the right side cover to the inner frame bracket.

① SEATS

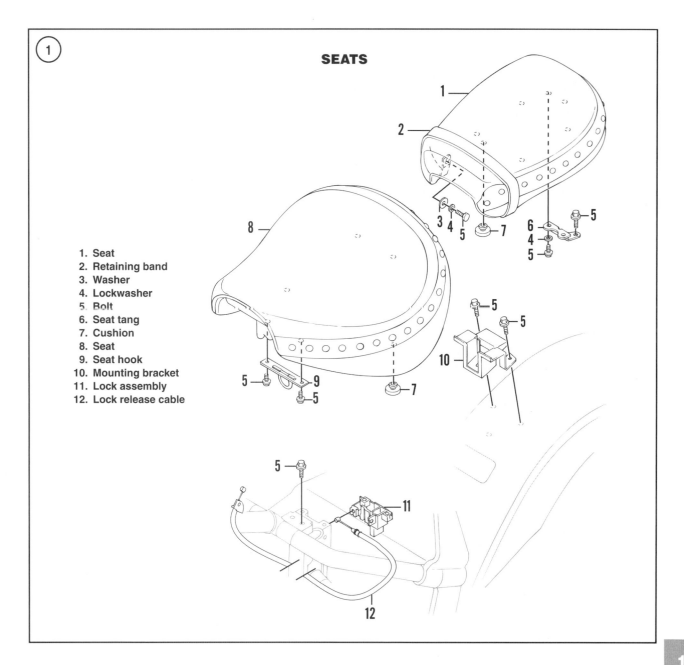

1. Seat
2. Retaining band
3. Washer
4. Lockwasher
5. Bolt
6. Seat tang
7. Cushion
8. Seat
9. Seat hook
10. Mounting bracket
11. Lock assembly
12. Lock release cable

15

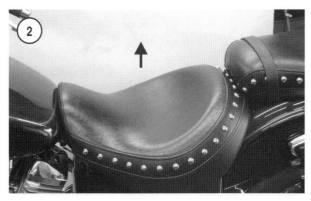

②

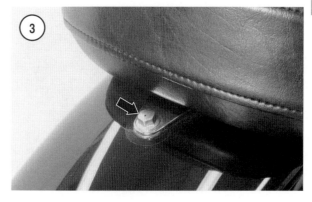

③

FRAME SIDE COVERS

1. Bolt
2. Collar
3. Side cover mounting bracket
4. Nut
5. Pad
6. Battery box
7. Pad
8. Relay unit bracket
9. Label
10. Name plate
11. Bolt
12. Washer
13. Side cover-right side
14. Grommet
15. Nut
16. Intermediate cover-right side
17. Nut
18. Intermediate cover-left side
19. Pad
20. Side cover-left side

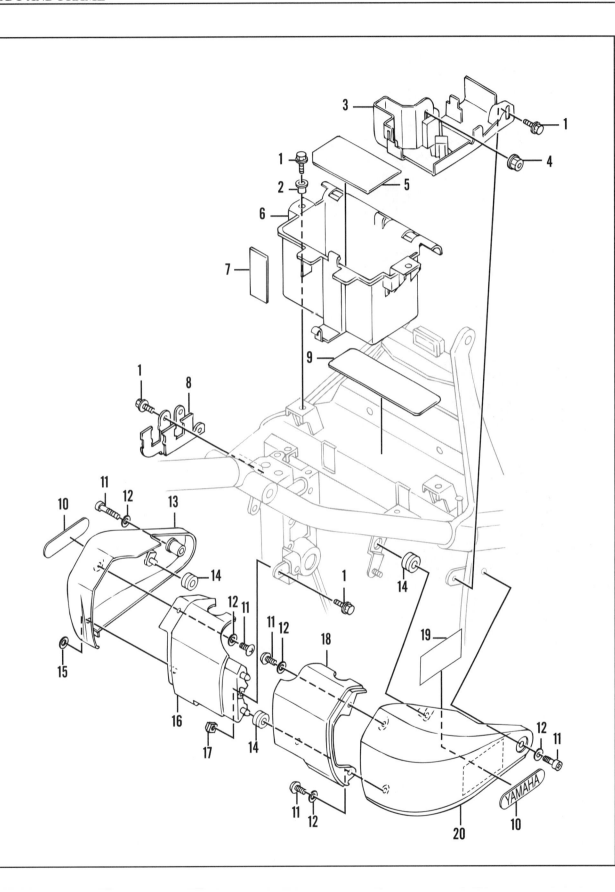

15

FOOTREST AND SIDE STAND

1. Footrest pad
2. Screw
3. Cotter pin
4. Clevis pin
5. Footpeg
6. Footpeg cover
7. Washer
8. Footpeg bracket
9. Bolt
10. Plate
11. Footrest
12. Grommet
13. Washer
14. Nut
15. Pivot pin
16. Return springs
17. Snap ring
18. Spring
19. Footrest bracket
20. Nut
21. Shift lever bracket
22. Collar
23. Bolt
24. Sidestand
25. Nut-self locking
26. Return spring

6. Remove the screw and washer (A, **Figure 11**) securing the right side cover (B) to the frame.

7. Pull the right side cover straight out and remove it.

8. Installation is the reverse of removal. Note the following:

    a. Install the right side cover first and tighten the inner bolt securely.

    b. Apply moisture to the rubber grommets, and install the left side cover. Push it on until it seats correctly on the right side cover posts.

RIDER FOOTREST

Removal/Installation

Refer to **Figure 12**.

1. Securely support the motorcycle on level ground. Block the rear wheel so the motorcycle will not roll in either direction.

2A. On the right side, perform the following:

    a. Remove the bolts (A, **Figure 13**) securing the footrest assembly to the frame.

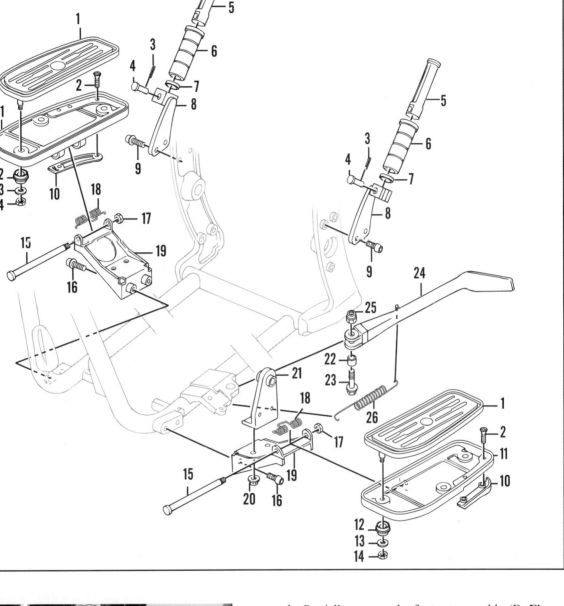

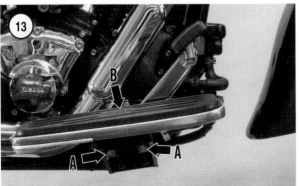

b. Partially remove the footrest assembly (B, **Figure 13**) from the frame.

c. Remove the rear brake pedal and master cylinder assembly as described in Chapter Fourteen, if necessary.

2B. On the left side, perform the following:

a. Loosen the clamp bolt (A, **Figure 14**) and remove the shift shaft lever (B) off the shift shaft.

b. On California models, disconnect the hoses (**Figure 15**) from the charcoal canister.

15

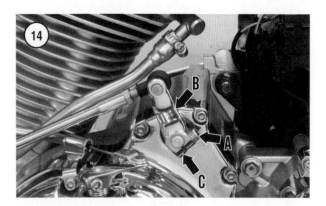

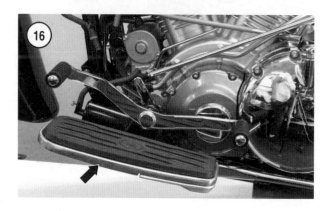

c. Remove the bolts securing the footrest/gearshift assembly (**Figure 16**) to the frame.

b. Remove the footrest/gearshift assembly.

3. Remove the snap ring from the pivot pin.

4. Remove the pivot pin from the footrest and separate the footrest from the bracket. Do not lose the return spring.

5. Installation is the reverse of removal. Note the following:

a. Install the pivot pin through the return spring.

b. Tighten the mounting bolts to 48 N•m (35 ft.-lb.).

c. On the left side, align the slot on the shaft lever (C, **Figure 14**) with the index mark on the shift shaft. Tighten the clamp bolt securely.

PASSENGER FOOTPEGS

Removal/Installation

Refer to **Figure 12**.

1. Securely support the motorcycle on level ground. Block the rear wheel so the motorcycle will not roll in either direction.

2. On the right side, remove the muffler assembly as described in Chapter Nine.

3. Remove the bolts securing the passenger footpeg and bracket to the frame.

4. Remove the footpeg and bracket assembly.

5. If necessary, remove the footpeg from the bracket as follows:

a. Straighten the cotter pin and remove it from the pivot pin.

b. Remove the pivot pin and separate the footpeg from the mounting bracket. Do not lose the washer.

6. Installation is the reverse of removal. Note the following:

a. Install a *new* cotter pin and bend the ends over completely.

b. Tighten the mounting bolts to 48 N•m (35 ft.-lb.).

FRONT FENDER

Removal/Installation

Refer to **Figure 17**.

1. Securely support the motorcycle on level ground. Block the rear wheel so the motorcycle will not roll in either direction.

2. Remove the side reflector (A, **Figure 18**) from the brake hose bracket.

3. Remove the bolts (B, **Figure 18**) securing the front fender to the front forks.

4. Carefully move the front fender forward and off the front wheel and front forks.

5. Installation is the reverse of removal. Tighten the bolts securely.

REAR FENDER

Removal/Installation

Refer to **Figure 17**.

FRONT AND REAR FENDERS

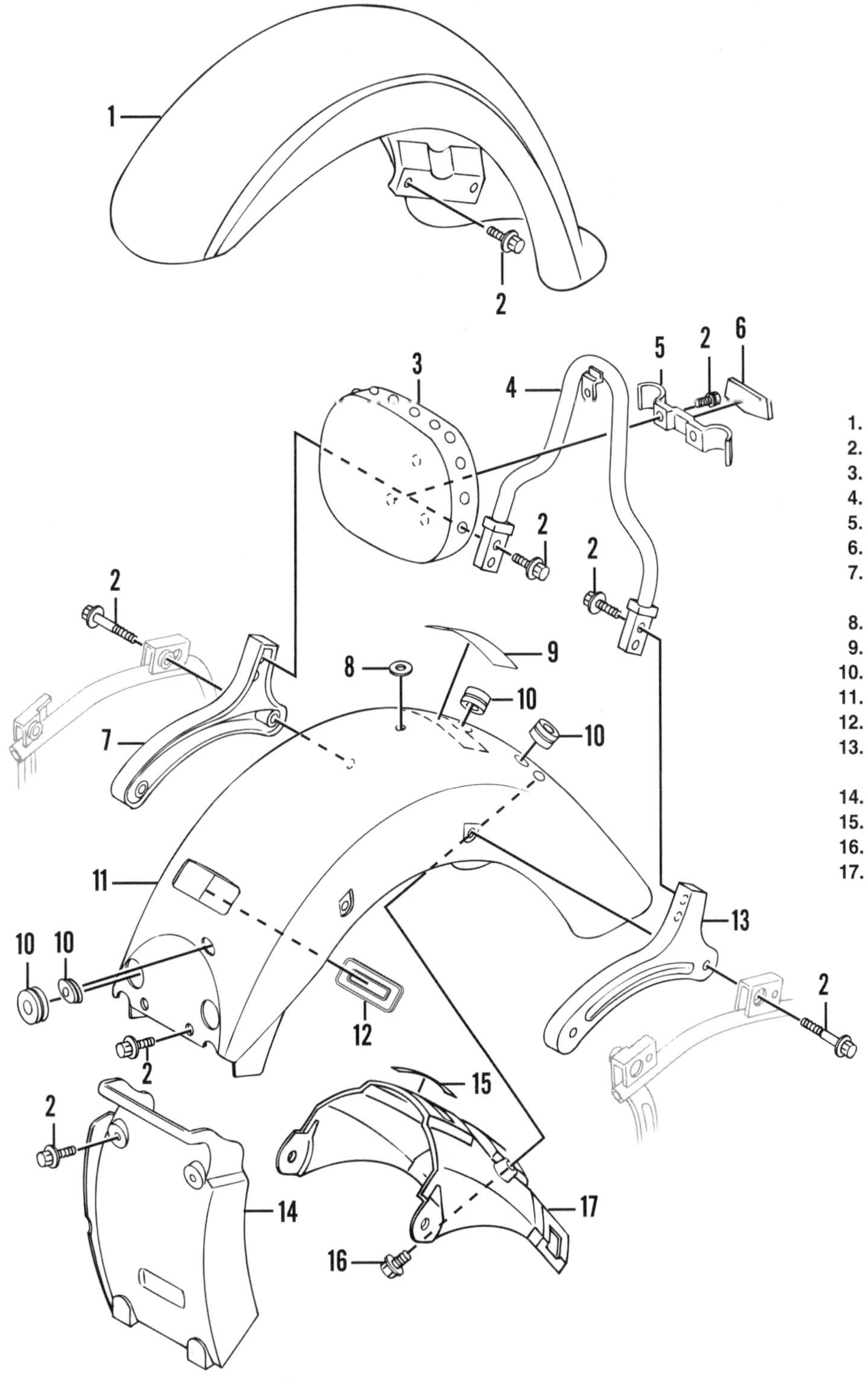

1. Front fender
2. Bolt
3. Backrest
4. Backrest stay
5. Bracket
6. Emblem
7. Mounting bracket (right side)
8. Rubber plug
9. Emblem
10. Rubber grommet
11. Rear fender
12. Rubber cushion
13. Mounting bracket (left side)
14. Mud guard
15. Damper (2004-on)
16. Bolt (2004-on)
17. Rear under panel (2004-on)

15

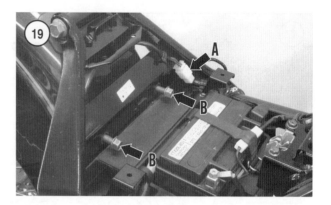

1. Securely support the motorcycle on level ground. Block the front wheel so the motorcycle will not roll in either direction.

2. Remove the rider and passenger seats as described in this chapter.

3. Remove the saddlebags as described in this chapter, on models so equipped.

4. Disconnect the taillight and rear turn signal assembly electrical connector (A, **Figure 19**).

5. Remove the two bolts (B, **Figure 19**) securing the front edge of the fender to the frame.

6. Remove the bolts (**Figure 20**) securing the rear fender to the frame bracket or saddlebag mounting bracket, on models so equipped.

7. Loosen, but do not remove the front mounting throughbolt and nut (**Figure 21**).

8. Have an assistant raise the rear of the fender enough to clear the rear wheel.

9. Reinstall the bolts (**Figure 22**) securing the back rest to the rear fender, on models so equipped.

10. Remove the front mounting throughbolt and nut loosened in Step 6.

11. Remove the rear fender and backrest (models so equipped) from the frame and backrest.

12. Installation is the reverse of removal. Note the following:

    a. Tighten the front mounting throughbolt and nut to 88 N•m (65 ft.-lb.).

    b. Tighten the front bolts to 48 N•m (35 ft.-lb.).

SADDLEBAGS AND MOUNTING BRACKETS

Saddlebag Removal/Installation

Refer to **Figure 23**.

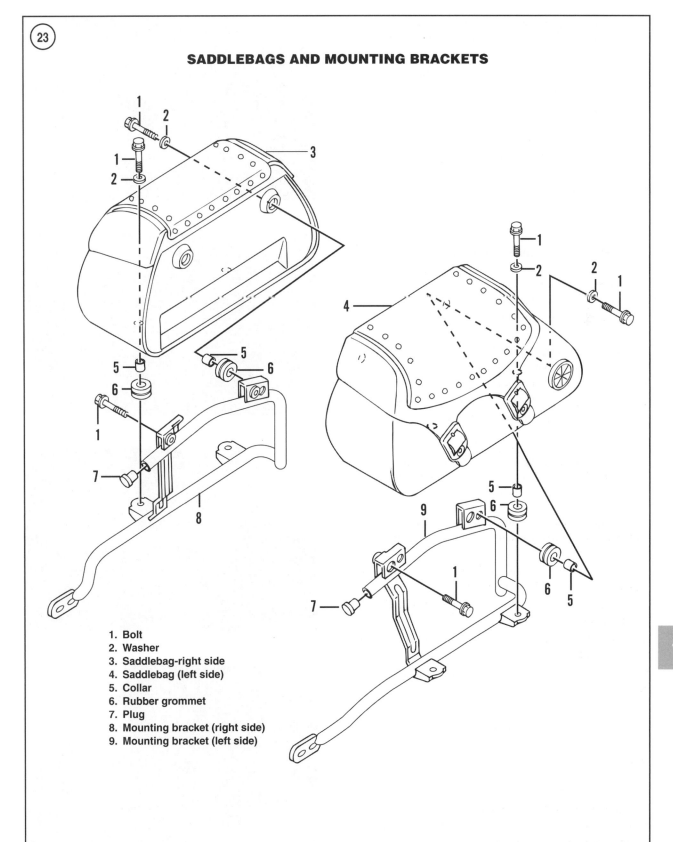

SADDLEBAGS AND MOUNTING BRACKETS

1. Bolt
2. Washer
3. Saddlebag-right side
4. Saddlebag (left side)
5. Collar
6. Rubber grommet
7. Plug
8. Mounting bracket (right side)
9. Mounting bracket (left side)

15

1. Securely support the motorcycle on level ground. Block the front wheel so the motorcycle will not roll in either direction.

2. Open the top cover and secure it in this position.

3. Remove the long bolts and washers at the base of the saddlebag.

4. Remove the shorter bolts and washers (**Figure 24**) at the side of the saddlebag.

5. Remove the saddlebag from the mounting bracket. Do not lose the collar.

6. Repeat for the other side.

7. Tighten the bolts securely.

Mounting Bracket Removal/Installation

Refer to **Figure 23**.

1. Securely support the motorcycle on level ground. Block the front wheel so the motorcycle will not roll in either direction.

2. On the right side, remove the muffler assembly as described in Chapter Nine.

3. Remove the saddlebag as described in this section.

4. Remove the front bolts (A, **Figure 25**) securing the passenger footpeg and the mounting bracket.

CAUTION
*The back rest support assembly (A, **Figure 26**) is also held in place with the saddlebag mounting bracket upper bolts (B).*

5. On models equipped with the back rest, have an assistant secure the backrest assembly while the upper bolts are removed.

6. Remove the upper bolts (B, **Figure 25**) securing the mounting bracket to the rear fender.

7. Carefully remove the mounting bracket (C, **Figure 25**). Do not scratch the rear fender.

8. Reinstall the upper mounting bolts to secure the backrest in place.

9. Installation is the reverse of removal. Tighten the bolts securely.

BACKREST

Removal/Installation

Refer to **Figure 17**.

1. Remove both saddlebags as described in this chapter.

2. Apply duct tape to the fender above where the bolts secure the mounting bracket to the fender.

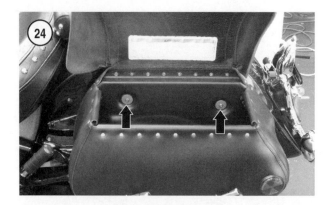

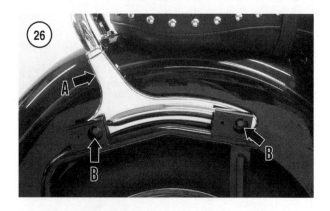

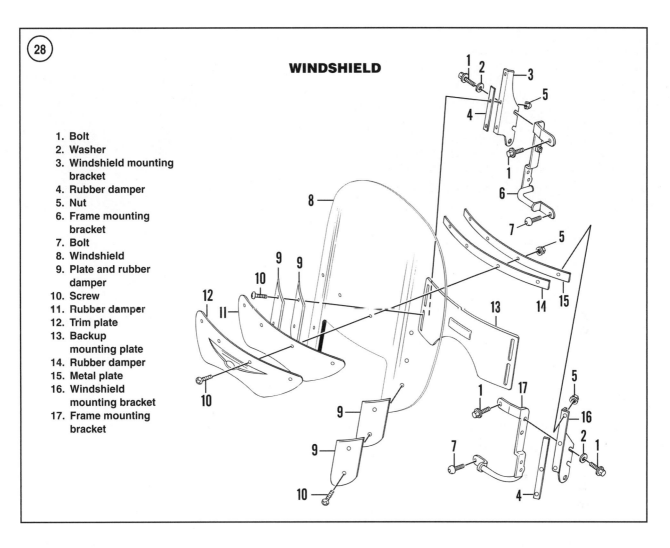

28

WINDSHIELD

1. Bolt
2. Washer
3. Windshield mounting bracket
4. Rubber damper
5. Nut
6. Frame mounting bracket
7. Bolt
8. Windshield
9. Plate and rubber damper
10. Screw
11. Rubber damper
12. Trim plate
13. Backup mounting plate
14. Rubber damper
15. Metal plate
16. Windshield mounting bracket
17. Frame mounting bracket

3. Remove the upper bolts (B, **Figure 26**) securing the saddlebag and backrest mounting brackets to the rear fender.

4. Carefully spread and remove the mounting bracket (A, **Figure 26**). Do not scratch the rear fender.

5. Reinstall the bolts to secure the saddlebag bracket.

6. Installation is the reverse of removal. Tighten the bolts securely.

SIDESTAND

Removal/Installation

Refer to **Figure 12**.

1. Securely support the motorcycle on level ground. Block the rear wheel so the motorcycle will not roll in either direction.

2. Raise the sidestand. Use locking pliers and disconnect the return spring from the sidestand or frame.

3. Hold the self-locking nut (A, **Figure 27**) and remove the pivot bolt.

4. Remove the sidestand (B, **Figure 27**) from the frame mount. Do not lose the collar from the frame boss.

5. Installation is the reverse of removal. Note the following:

    a. Apply lithium grease to the pivot surfaces of the frame boss and sidestand.

    b. Install a *new* self-locking nut and tighten to 48 N•m (35 ft.-lb.).

WINDSHIELD

Removal/Installation

Refer to **Figure 28**.

1. Securely support the motorcycle on level ground. Block the rear wheel so the motorcycle will not roll in either direction.

15

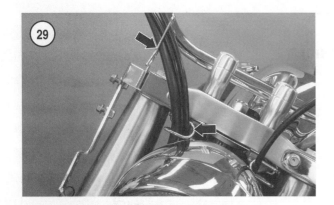

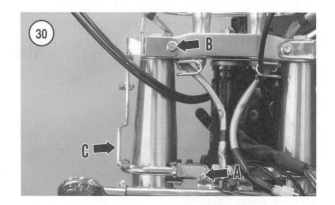

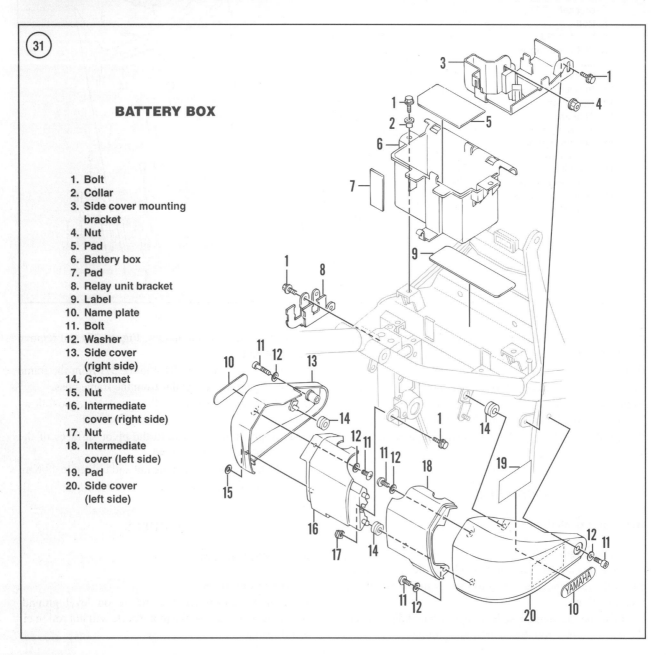

BATTERY BOX

1. Bolt
2. Collar
3. Side cover mounting
   bracket
4. Nut
5. Pad
6. Battery box
7. Pad
8. Relay unit bracket
9. Label
10. Name plate
11. Bolt
12. Washer
13. Side cover
    (right side)
14. Grommet
15. Nut
16. Intermediate
    cover (right side)
17. Nut
18. Intermediate
    cover (left side)
19. Pad
20. Side cover
    (left side)

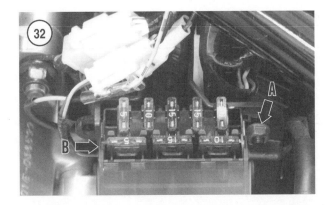

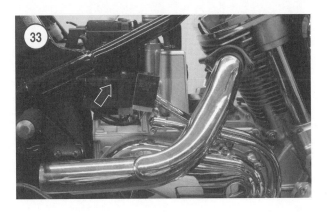

2. Loosen, but do not remove, the two bolts on each side securing the windshield assembly to the frame mounting brackets.

3. Carefully lift the windshield straight up and off the mounting brackets.

4. Place the windshield on several large towels or a blanket to protect the finish.

5. To remove the frame mounting brackets, proceed as follows:

   a. Note the routing of the throttle cables and front brake hose (**Figure 29**) through both bracket guides.

   b. Cover the front fender with a towel or blanket.

   c. Remove the headlight assembly as described in Chapter Ten.

CAUTION
*The front turn signal assembly is also held in place with the frame mounting bracket lower bolts (A, **Figure 30**).*

   d. Remove the lower (A, **Figure 30**) and upper (B) bolts securing the frame mounting bracket (C) to the upper and lower fork bridge.

   e. Remove the frame mounting bracket.

   f. Reinstall the lower bolt (A, **Figure 30**) to secure the front turn signal assembly.

   g. Repeat for the bracket on the other side.

6. Installation is the reverse of removal. Note the following:

   a. Route the throttle cables and front brake hose (**Figure 29**) correctly through both guides.

   b. Tighten the mounting bolts securely.

BATTERY BOX

Removal/Installation

Refer to **Figure 31**.

1. Securely support the motorcycle on level ground. Block the front wheel so the motorcycle will not roll in either direction.

2. Remove both seats as described in this chapter.

3. Remove the frame side covers as described in this chapter.

4. Remove the battery as described in Chapter Three.

5. Remove the nuts (A, **Figure 32**) securing the fuse panel (B) and move the fuse panel away from the plastic bracket.

6. Remove the starter relay unit as described in Chapter Ten.

7. Remove the ignitor unit as described in Chapter Ten.

8. Remove the relay unit (**Figure 33**) from the mounting tang and disconnect the 12-pin electrical connector from the relay. For later models equipped with a passing light relay, disconnect and remove the relay.

9. Remove the bolt securing the relay unit mounting bracket and remove the bracket.

10. Remove the bolts securing the battery box to the frame.

11. Make sure all wiring and hoses are moved out of the way, and pull the battery box straight up and remove it from the frame.

12. Installation is the reverse of removal.

Table 1 is on the following page.

Table 1 BODY AND FRAME TORQUE SPECIFICATIONS

Item	N•m	in.-lb.	ft.-lb.
Footrest mounting bolts	48	–	35
Rear fender			
Front edge of fender bolts	48	–	35
Throughbolt and nut	88	–	65
Side stand nut	48	–	35

INDEX

WIRING
DIAGRAMS

1999-2003 ALL USA, CALIFORNIA AND CANADA XV1600 MODELS

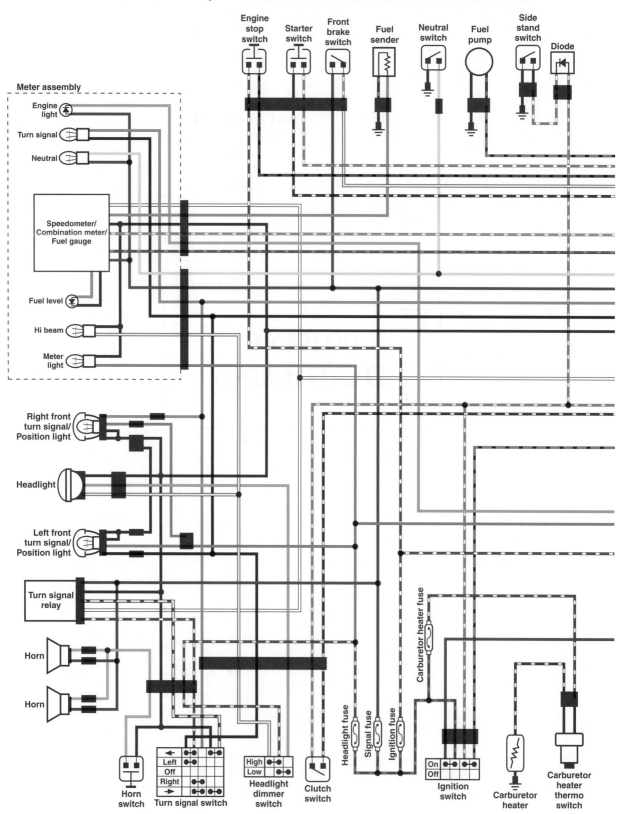

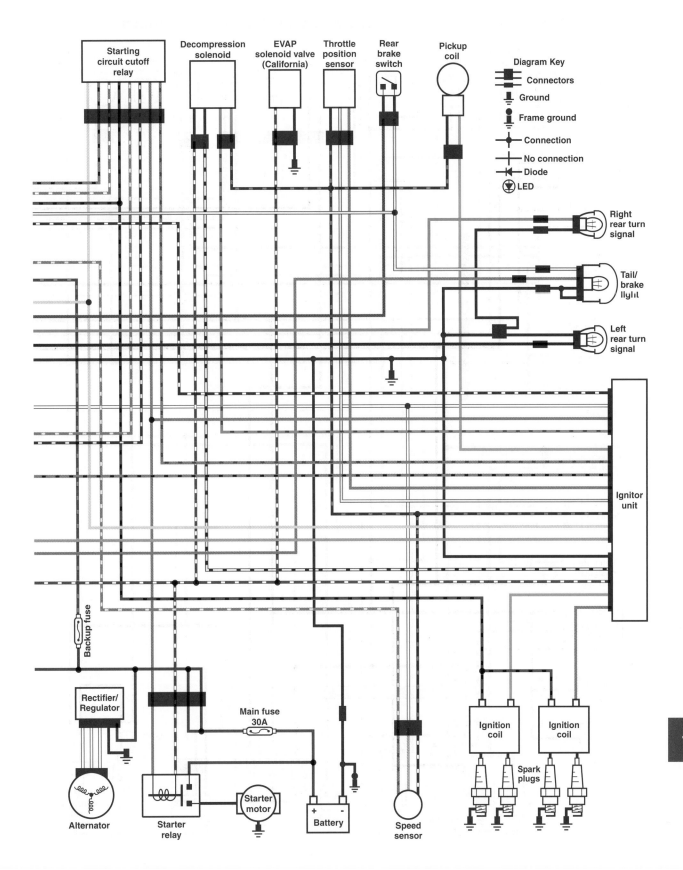

2004-ON ALL USA, CALIFORNIA AND CANADA XV1700 MODELS

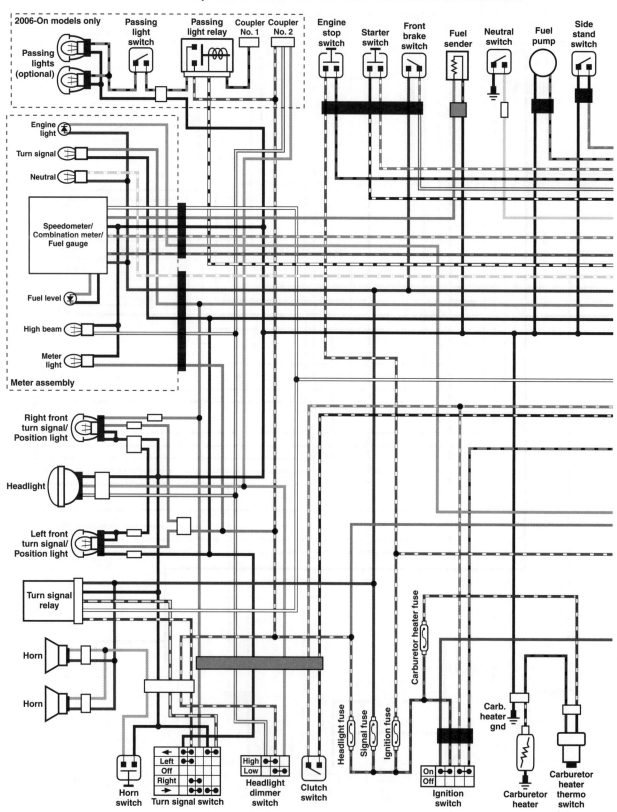

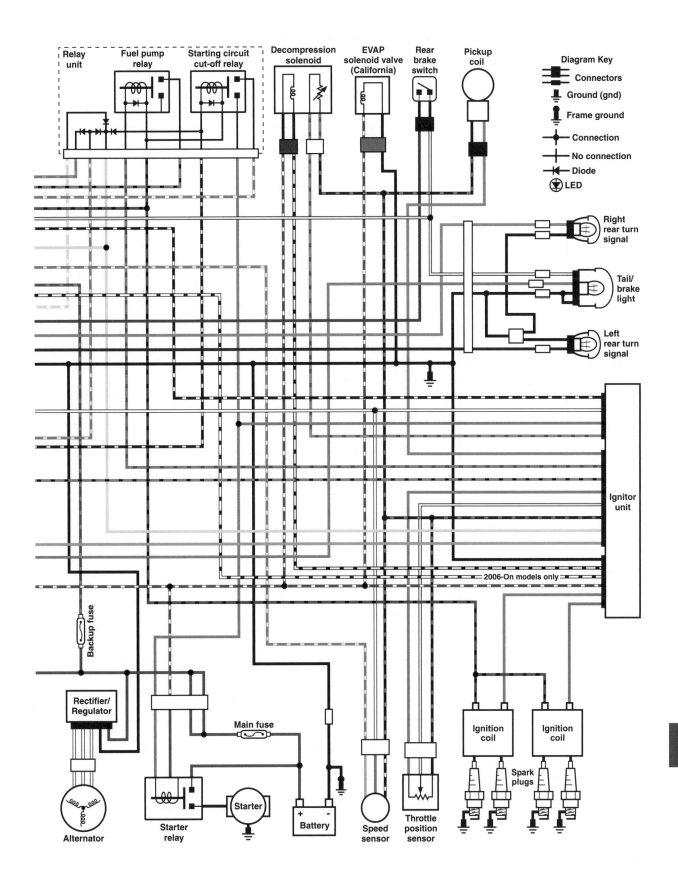

MAINTENANCE LOG

Date	Miles	Type of Service